TILLAMOOK BAY
COMMUNITY COLLEGE

·THE·

International
ENCYCLOPEDIA
OF SEXUALITY

Edited by

ROBERT T. FRANCOEUR

———➤•◄———

Preface by

TIMOTHY PERPER

———➤•◄———

Introduction by

IRA L. REISS

·THE·

International

ENCYCLOPEDIA

OF SEXUALITY

VOLUME III

Spain to the United States

CONTINUUM · NEW YORK

1998

The Continuum Publishing Company
370 Lexington Avenue
New York, NY 10017

Typography, Design Coordination, and Computer Graphics by
Ray Noonan, ParaGraphic Artists, NYC

Printed in the United States of America

Library of Congress Cataloging-in-Publication Data

The international encyclopedia of sexuality / edited by Robert T.
  Francoeur ; foreword by Timothy Perper ; preface by Ira L. Reiss.
    v.   cm.
  Includes bibliographical references and index.
  ISBN 0-8264-0838-9 (v. 1 : alk. paper)
    1. Sex—Encyclopedias.   2. Sex customs—Encyclopedias.
I. Francoeur, Robert T.
HQ21.I68   1997
306.7'03—dc20   95-16481
                                                 CIP

3-Volume Set ISBN 0-8264-0841-9

Vol. 3 ISBN 0-8264-0840-0

CONTENTS

Spain
(*Reino de España*)

Jose Antonio Nieto, Ph.D., with Jose Antonio Carrobles, Ph.D.,
Manuel Delgado Ruiz, Ph.D., Felix Lopez Sanchez, Ph.D.,
Virginia Maquieira D'Angelo, Ph.L.D., Josep-Vicent Marques, Ph.D.,
Bernardo Moreno Jimenez, Ph.D., Raquel Osborne Verdugo, Ph.D.,
Carmela Sanz Rueda, Ph.D., and Carmelo Vazquez Valverde, Ph.D.*

Contents

Demographics and a Historical Perspective

A. Demographics

Spain, with Portugal to its west, occupies the Iberian peninsula in the southwest corner of Europe, south of France. With a land mass of 194,896 square miles, it is the size of the states of Arizona and Utah combined.

---

*This chapter was coordinated by Jose Antonio Nieto, Ph.D.; it was translated by Laura Berman, M.A., Ph.D. (cand.) and Jose Nanin, M.A.

Spain has a high, arid central plateau broken by mountain ranges and river valleys. The northwest is heavily watered, while the south has lowlands and a Mediterranean climate.

The 1995 population of 39.4 million is 72.8 percent Spanish, 6.4 percent Catalan, 8.2 percent Galician, and 2.3 percent Basque. Three quarters of the population live in the cities. The 1995 age distribution was 14 years and younger, 17 percent, and 15 to 64, 68 percent, with 15 percent over age 65. Life expectancy at birth in 1995 was 75 for males and 82 for females. The birthrate was 11 per 1,000 and the death rate 9 per 1,000, for an annual natural increase of 0.2 percent. Infant mortality was 7 per 1,000 live births. The literacy rate is 97 percent, with compulsory schooling to age 16. Spain has one hospital bed per 234 persons, and one physician per 257 persons. The per capita domestic product in 1995 was $12,700 U.S.

B. A Brief Historical Perspective

Spain was settled by Iberians, Basques, and Celts, partly overrun by the Carthagenians from North Africa, and conquered by Rome about 200 B.C.E., In the fifth century of the Common Era, the Visigoths, who were then in power, adopted Christianity. By 711, an Islamic invasion from North Africa had displaced the Visigoths. Christian forces started a reconquest from the north that promoted a Spanish nationalism. The marriage of Ferdinand II of Aragon and Isabella I of Castile in 1491 led to the final expulsion of the Moors with the fall of Granada. The Spanish Inquisition, established in the thirteenth century, was infamous for its persecution and forced conversion of Jews and Moslems. The discovery of the New World by Columbus in 1492, the conquest of Mexico by Cortes, and of Peru by Pizarro marked the start of Spain's Colonial Empire. The Spanish Empire also included, at one time, The Netherlands, parts of Italy and Germany, the Philippines, Florida, and much of Central and South America. Cuba, Puerto Rico, and the Philippines were ceded in the Spanish-American War of 1898.

Spain's king was replaced by a dictatorship between 1923 and 1930, when the monarchy returned. A republic, declared in 1931, ended with a devastating three-year civil war (1936-1939) between the republicans and the military under General Francisco Franco. During World War II, Spain remained neutral, although favoring relations with the fascist countries. Franco set the stage for Prince Juan Carlos to return as Spain's king after his death in 1975. Catalonia and the Basque country were granted self-rule and autonomy in 1980.

1. Basic Sexological Premises

A. Character of Gender Roles

Stereotypes of masculinity and femininity have changed. Male heterosexism is still present in society, but it has not the strength it used to have. By the same token, women express their sexuality more openly. The extreme form of masculinity, *machismo*, no longer has societal approval. On the other hand, sexual purity of women no longer depends on the claim of virginity and chastity before marriage (see Section 5A/B). Men and women are sexualized human beings. There is no longer room for the radical expressions of patriarchal heterosexism that used to depict women as desexualized persons without sexual needs. "Women must stay at home with a broken leg" is the English translation of the proverb, *La mujer en casa con la pata quabradaa*, that Spanish men traditionally cited to assign sexual passivity to the feminine gender role. Nowadays, this is a memory.

B. Sociolegal Status of Males and Females

Politically speaking, adolescents are considered adults at age 18, when they can exercise the right to vote. However, responsibility for penal (criminal) acts is reached two years earlier, at age 16. Political and penal age are the same for males and females.

C. General Concepts of Sexuality and Love

The Republic of 1931 recognized women's right to vote, their right to divorce, and, to a certain degree, the right to sexual liberty. With the triumph of Franco in 1939, affectionate and sexual relationships returned to the traditional model tied to the Catholic Church. Sex was considered wrong, love was eternal and only within marriage, and the moral double standard between the sexes reigned. Couples engaged in long courtships, men maintained extramarital relationships, and husbands claimed that they were defending their honor by nearly killing their wives who were presumed to have been adulterous. A very popular song expresses this love ideology: *Solamente Una Vez se Ama en la Vida* (One Only Loves Once in Life).

In the 1960s, tourism, the labor emigration to other European nations, and economic development introduced more-liberal customs to society. The automobile and student apartments facilitated sexual encounters without commitment. The contraceptive hormonal pill became available, despite the opposition of Franco's government. By the end of the 1960s, paternal authoritarianism had decreased, and women's presence in the labor and educational segments of society had become stronger.

The decade of the 1970s was a period of significant change. The feminist movement appeared, and couples began living together before marriage. Social pressure for sexual education appeared. A democratic free press was established. Legalized divorce recognized the right to love more than once in a lifetime.

The 1980s introduced changes of a different sort. Evidence of liberal sexual attitudes was widespread among intellectual and political activists, as expressed in the increase in premarital relationships, family planning, and voluntary interruption of pregnancy (abortion having been legalized, although with certain limits as described in Section 9C. On the other hand, an economic recession, coupled with fatigue among the avant-garde minority, created more-conservative attitudes. These forces caused older children to delay leaving their homes of origin, and to reevaluate the institution of marriage.

This panorama of attitudes is pluralistic. It encompasses a measurable degree of sexual revolution, along with a rebirth of sensitive interaction (*Reivinicación de la ternura* [recognition of emotions, affections, and tenderness]). In recent years, it has become obvious that among many young couples, there is an unstable truce between women, who have changed a great deal after having become aware of the double standard, and men, who had changed little and still avoid home and child care tasks. A theoretical rather than real egalitarianism of the sexes has prevailed and still dominates Spanish culture.

2. Religious and Ethnic Factors Affecting Sexuality

A. Source and Character of Religious Values

Although most of Spain's people are nominally Roman Catholic, the liturgical and moral orthodoxy of the Catholic Church are very weakly obeyed, except for some regions in the north. The majority of Spaniards do not accept or follow the Church's precepts regarding sexuality. Despite strict Catholic sexual expectations and the preaching on sexuality from pulpits and confessional boxes, popular and influential rituals and festivals have sexuality at their center. These celebrations are evidence of the paradoxical attitude of Spanish society to sexuality, especially that of the young. In other words, sexuality is celebrated. May Poles, pigs, Christs, donkeys, bulls, Judas, the Carnival Kings, and similar allegories of hyper-genitality and virility are keystones in Spanish Fiestas. In Spain, sexuality is an essential element and center of the festival domain.

However, in a typical paradox, the ritual reign of sexuality irreversibly leads to ceremonial destruction. Those same rituals that are centered on the metaphors of masculinity also recognize the fundamental role to which women must conform. Women are the *concitadoras* (who stir up emotions and feelings in men, stimulate them to action, and excite jealousy or hatred, interest or curiosity), as well as the watchful guardians (*vigilantes*) of their male opponents. This process of absorption is completed by converting the inappropriate sexual drives of male youth into social energy.

One has to consider the possibility that religion's cultural obsession for stimulating/repressing virility determines the expression of Spanish sexuality today. One consequence of this cultural conception of manliness as something basically extremely vulnerable, is the ambivalent tolerance of males who violate the sexual mores, as long as their noncompliance remains a private matter.

B. Source and Character of Ethnic Values

The ethnic and religious values that serve as guidelines for the sexual behavior of the Spanish should not be perceived of as being homogeneous throughout this country. Different ethnic cultures and different social strata create contrasts, some, like the distinction between urban and rural, being more obvious than others. Keeping in mind this high level of variability, one can still identify a substratum base that determines sexual conduct and attitudes among the Spanish. This sexual ethos is characterized by a stress on (preference for) controlling the sexual conduct of the young, especially males, and mainly with the aim of guaranteeing the family procreation.

The cause of the anxiety the community associates with the sexual conduct of male youths has to deal with the strategy of socialization that they undergo. In traditional Spain, boys abandoned their childhood status to incorporate the life of an active young man as soon as they were considered mature enough, usually around age 16. In this phase, they were expected to gain sexual experience, generally by means of masturbation, visits to brothels, and sporadic contacts with relatives, especially with female members such as female cousins and younger aunts. These traditional avenues for sexual initiation of adolescents have been recently replaced by the growing social acceptance of premarital relations.

The culture valued the sexual exploits of male youth and provided an abundance of opportunities, including community celebrations and public dances, which generally encouraged erotic relationships.

The social education of women in traditional Spanish society encouraged them to play their appropriate role in the social order. Women had the responsibility of taking advantage of the continual erotic stimulation and the hypervalue of masculinity that drives young men in order to attract them into the courting game that ends in marriage. Young women were expected to develop strategies that produced maximum enticement and minimal satisfaction, creating for the young male a desire that was never completely in accordance with the social mores. The woman embodied a game of approach-avoidance until just before or within marriage. A young woman's ability to employ her virginity as a bargaining tool makes the impatience and lack of sexual discipline of the male socially productive and profitable. The young male is caught in an extensive web of engagements associated with courtship that resolves itself by fully assimilating him into the institution of the family.

3. Sexual Knowledge and Education

A. Government Policies and Programs for Sex Education

The Spanish government has not adopted or implemented any general plan to improve the knowledge and attitudes of Spanish people toward sexuality. Indirectly, one could support sexual education in provisions of the Spanish Constitution, under the educators' "liberty of class" (Article 20.1); children's rights according to the international agreement laws (Article 39); the rights of humans in general (Article 10.2); and the right to understand the full development of personality and the liberty of teaching (Article 27). In the *Official Bulletin of the State* (January 21, March 6, 1981), the government proposed addressing some minimal sexual issues in school, from preschool through secondary school, within the areas of "affectionate and social behavior" and/or the natural sciences.

In explaining Article 27 of the Constitution, *The Organic Law of the Right to Education* (1985) insisted on the freedom of teachers and the autonomy of school centers. This autonomy provides a margin of freedom that permits schools to introduce sexual education. The most ambitious proposal from the educational point of view was created by the Minister of Education in *LOGSE, The General Organic Law of the Educational System*, approved in 1991. This law explicitly defends and reiterates the necessity of sexual education within school at different grade levels.

This law appears positive because it formulates concrete objectives and supports a place in the curricula for education in sexual topics, because it promotes attitudes of gender equality and discourages discrimination between the sexes, and because it opts for an open curriculum that permits schools and professors to include sexual topics within the context of concrete programs. However, the authors also view this law as insufficient, because it does not clearly and systematically spell out the objectives and information contents for the different school levels.

In reality, the law contains only partial proposals. These programs treat sexuality horizontally, across all course content areas, instead of contextually and longitudinally within a concrete area of health or quality of life. Thus, sexual education is only provided in the basic course content areas and in schools with well-coordinated teams of professors who can adequately provide sexual education. However, adequate sexual education is impossible with this approach. If all teachers in the different disciplines are expected to include sexual education in their courses, they can appropriately address these issues only if they, meaning all teachers in the nation, are adequately educated in this area in addition to their main professional area. And this is impossible without massive funding for teacher education.

Although it seems progressive and favors renovation and freedom of teaching, the option of an open curriculum has limitations. Ideological premises, attitudes of fear, and simple lack of time or training prompts numerous educators to "forget" or avoid addressing sexual issues. In practice, sporadic "forgetfulness" is converted into habitual avoidance.

In summary, current Spanish legislation addresses sexual issues, provides some orientations on specific objectives, but does not guarantee that the education will be delivered. In practice, at least for the moment, there are only a few schools that provide systematic sexual education. It is only unique and isolated educators and groups based in innovative pedagogy that deal with this topic in a systematic fashion.

The most representative exception is in the Community of the Canary Islands, where the autonomous government has freed various educators of Harimaguada to form a group of sexuality educators who provide education in classrooms and systematically plan the delivery of sex education.

B. Informal Sources of Sexual Knowledge

Recent publications on sexuality have been translated into Spanish and are currently available to the general public. There are also numerous publications by Spanish authors. Theater, television, and general communications frequently address the topic of sexuality and sexual issues.

From this point of view, freedom of speech and expression is high. Among the more outstanding examples of informal sexuality education is the state television chain TVE1, which offers a series of thirty programs on sexuality, *We Speak of Sex*, for an adult audience. This series has had a strong social resonance.

The Ministry of Health has carried out a campaign for prevention of unwanted pregnancy geared toward adolescents, stressing the slogan *Pontelo Ponselo*, or "Put it on. Put it on him"—referring to a condom. This campaign has had widespread acceptance. The same Ministry of Health has also published slides and pamphlets on sexuality that are of a reasonably good quality. Therefore, the Spanish society's informal sources of knowledge are equivalent to most European countries. But from the formal point of view, education is not widespread, and seems unlikely to become widespread in the foreseeable future.

4. Autoerotic Behaviors and Patterns

A. Children and Adolescents

A national study on masturbation in children and young people found that 76.7 percent stated that they began masturbating between the ages of 10 to 15 years. Knowledge about masturbation came from conversations and readings (74.8 percent for males and 57.2 percent for women).

Studies carried out with 12- to 13-year-old elementary school students in *Education General Basica* (EGB) indicated that 87.74 percent of the girls and 38.42 percent of the boys had never masturbated. The numbers lessened when groups of 14- to 17-year-old high school students were studied from *Baccalaureate Unified Polyvalent* (BUP). In this study, 70.51 percent of the girls and 12.16 percent of the boys stated that they had never masturbated. All the data seem to indicate that the age of first masturbation differs notably between males and females. Almost three quarters of the boys, 71.4 percent, began masturbating between the ages of 10 and 12 years, while only 10 percent of the girls stated they have masturbated at that age. The percentages of adolescents masturbating clearly increases between 15 and 17 years.

The most-consistent masturbation frequency in children is once a month, with 25.7 percent of adolescents masturbating once a day. At this age, masturbation is commonly accompanied by feelings of blame, more in females (47.3 percent) than in males (44.3 percent), while the level of derived satisfaction is greater in males (60.3 percent) than in females (26.2 percent).

In university students, 19.1 percent of the males and 12.6 percent of the females report frequent masturbation. In a survey of university students, 90.8 percent of the males and 60.6 percent of the females reported that they have engaged in masturbatory behavior on some occasion.

B. Adults

A national survey reported that 54.8 percent of adult men and 33.0 percent of adult women reported masturbation on some occasion. In a study of stable couples, it appeared that 50.1 percent of the men and 23.5 percent of the women masturbated. Frequent masturbation is greater in men than in women: 7.14 percent of men masturbated almost daily and only 3.8 percent of the women masturbated that frequently.

While 100 percent of men masturbate in the final years of puberty (14 to 19 years) and in early adulthood (20 to 25 years), this percentage begins to diminish starting about age 25. In general, men indicated that the practice of masturbation diminished after having established a stable relationship. On the contrary, the percentage of women who masturbate begins to increase starting at 25 years and is greater during the ages of 30 to 39 years. The majority abandon this practice about age 50.

The principal factors affecting masturbatory practice are religion and level in school: 67.5 percent of the nonbelieving subjects reported masturbation, while 24 percent of Catholics engaged in the behavior. The higher the level of schooling, the greater the rate of practice and frequency of masturbation. Less clear is the association of political orientation as associated with attitudes toward masturbation, although voters with a resolved conservative position tend to have a more-negative attitude on masturbation.

The content of sexual fantasies that accompany masturbation is varied. Among students, images of sexual relations with the opposite sex are predominant (84 percent of males and 49.0 percent of females). Fantasies containing homosexual behavior occur in 6.3 percent of men and in 5.3 percent of women. The factors or motives that commonly inspire masturbation include: thinking about opposite-sex people (66.4 percent), erotic stories about the opposite sex (56 percent), fantasies about a sexual act and modifications of a sexual relation or pornographic movies (42.3 percent).

Masturbation may be preceded by feelings of frustration or depression: 15.9 percent of women and 8.3 percent of men reported depression or irritation; 8.2 percent of women and 13.1 percent of men reported situations of anxiety. The predominant feeling after masturbation is peaceful-ness (58.2 percent), while 10.1 percent experience feelings of blame and remorse. Masturbation continues to have negative connotations, with 12.2 percent considering it a symptom of sexual immaturity and 45.8 percent considering it an indication of sexual dissatisfaction. Only 8 percent con-sidered it an egotistic act; 4.6 percent considered it sinful.

The masturbatory technique most commonly used is manual stimula-tion. Among men, 91.7 percent masturbate with manual stimulation of the penis; among women, 31.7 percent masturbate by stimulating the clitoris, 17.8 percent the vagina, and 4.3 percent the breasts.

5. Interpersonal Heterosexual Behaviors

A/B. Children and Adolescents

Premarital Sexual Activities and Relationships

Heterosexual conduct in Spanish children and adolescents has greatly increased in recent years. Current data indicate that more than 54 percent of the women and 52.7 percent of the men have already had their first date at 13 years. During the period of adolescence, 55 percent of the girls and 66 percent of the boys have maintained affectionate relationships.

Clear differences are observed between boys and girls in sexual behavior. Among EGB (Basic General Education) students, 12 to 13 years, 55 percent of the males have kissed girls, in contrast to 24 percent of the girls who have kissed boys. Kisses involving the tongue is practiced less: 15 percent of the girls and 27 percent of the boys.

More-pronounced gender differences are reported with breast and genital stimulation. Breast stimulation through clothes was practiced by 14 percent of the girls and 39 percent of the boys. The difference in genital stimulation is even greater: 3.5 percent of girls and 33 percent of the boys. Data also indicate that males would rather stimulate their partner's genitals than allow themselves to be genitally stimulated; the opposite is true for girls. Genital contact without penetration is reported by 20 percent of the girls and 31 percent of the boys. In general, sexual behavior of the Spanish children and adolescents intensifies starting at 15 years in all sexual behaviors analyzed.

Attitudes regarding heterosexual relationships have changed most clearly since 1975, the year in which the *FOESSA Report* recognized the national level of intolerant attitudes among adolescents and young women (*a nivel nacional actitudes intolerantes frecuentmente asentadas entre los adolescen-tes y mujeres jóvenes*). Current data indicate that 46 percent of the girls and the 39 percent of the boys continue to consider virginity important, while 13 percent and 23 percent respectively report having engaged in coitus on some occasion. The national mean age for first genital intercourse is between 17 and 19 years, but this differs geographically, with the mean age dropping to 15 to 16 in the coastal regions. On the national level, 52 percent of young males and 37 percent of young females have maintained sexual relationships before 15 years.

Among those who have not had sexual relationships, the most important motives for maintaining virginity for women have been the fear of pregnancy (25 percent), the desire to remain virgins (17 percent), the lack of an opportunity (15 percent), and religious beliefs (13 percent). Among men, the most important motive is the lack of opportunity (56 percent). The data indicate that girls become sexually active within a couple (80 percent), while the boys engage in intercourse more within the frame of a friendship (48 percent). Among the motives mentioned for first sexual relations, the boys mention sexual desire (72 percent) and women mention love (52 percent). A majority of sexually active youths, 70 percent, experience some type of worry during sexual relationships. (See Note by the Translators at the end of this chapter.)

C. Adults

Premarital Courtship, Dating, and Relationships

For comments on the never-married, see Section 5A/B above.

In comparison to other European countries, the occurrence of cohabitation is low. Two percent of Spaniards are involved in a relationship in which time and space is shared but a marriage contract does not exist. On the whole, consensual unions of couples living together form an experimental and symbolic framework that breaks traditional boundaries of the Spanish family structure and forces the creation of different rules for cohabitation and interpersonal relationships.

Marriage and the Family

The age at which adults marry has become clearly delayed in recent years. Various factors, including inflation in the cost of living, especially housing, the increased numbers of women in the work world and their greater sense of independence, the rise in juvenile unemployment and longer periods of education, and cultural indicators not easily quantified in percentages such as the incidence of European patterns, all help to explain the delay of nuptials.

In 1986, the mean age for men's first marriage was 27.3 years; for women, it is 24.8. The decline in the number of births has been very important; the index of fecundity has decreased from 2.0 in 1970 to 1.4 in 1988. In 1991, 1.3 children were born per woman, well below the replacement level of 2.1.

The composition of the family structure has also suffered changes. The *familia troncal* (with several generations of the same family sharing the same dwelling), which was traditional in the rural environment, shows clear signs of retrogression. In the urban areas, the familiar typology of the nuclear family structure reflects changes including the delay of the age of marriage and an increase in marital breakups.

There has been a considerable increase in the number of women and men "singles," that is celibates and divorced, who live alone without pair bonding. Reliable data do not exist to support conclusions around the forms of sexual expression and the satisfaction derived from sexuality for single individuals.

Between 1981 when divorce was legalized and 1988, the number of divorces continued to increase, except for slight decreases in 1983 and 1984. The 1986 rate of divorce was five for every 10,000 Spanish citizens.

Extramarital sexual relationships have been socially condemned, but with a distinct difference in treatment of men and women. A kind of tolerance (*pseudotolera-das*) existed for men who engaged in extramarital sex, while unfaithful women were socially ostracized. In traditional Spain, it was not infrequent in families of high economic standing to find a husband who, along with his wife, shared and maintained a separate living space with a *querida* (mistress). On the contrary, it was unthinkable for the wife to have a lover. Spanish culture clearly contains a sexism that favors sexual expression for men but not for women. As the autonomy and independence of the woman increases in Spanish society, inequalities in sexual extramarital relationships have been decreasing. Yet infidelity—a questionable term that needs to be reformed—is still more frequent in men than in women.

Incidence of Oral and Anal Sex

No legal restriction exists for specific practices like fellatio and cunnilingus. Men perform cunnilingus more than women perform fellatio. The practice is recognized as less frequent in older men and women. It seems that fellatio and cunnilingus are more common in sporadic sexual relationships than in established long-term sexual relationships. There are also no legal restrictions on anal intercourse. However, it is exercised less than the above-mentioned practices.

Sexuality of the Disabled

The sexuality of the mentally deficient and of the physically challenged until recently was generally considered marginal and was ignored. At the present time, it is addressed by public institutions. The Functional Unit of Sexual Rehabilitation and Assisted Reproduction at the National Hospital of Paraplegics of Toledo, specializing in spinal cord injuries, is a pioneer center where the sexuality of the physically challenged is central and considered a positive part of life. Private organizations also exist that are devoted to assisting and aiding the physically challenged in attaining open, expressive, and dignified sexual expression without taboos.

6. Homoerotic, Homosexual, and Ambisexual Behaviors

A. Male Homosexuality

Male homosexuality was not tolerated during the reign of Franco (1936-1975). Under the Franco's *Ley de Peligrosidad Social,* The Law of Social Danger, "homosexuals," including lesbians (although these constitute a separate terra ignota camp) were considered a clear social danger. The political doctrine of this era was based on religious philosophy. In fact, national *catolicismo* was the political doctrine. Consequently, all attitudes and behaviors that were not in accordance with Catholic doctrines were not accepted. All kinds of stigmas were attached to homosexuals, including *grandes pecadores* (those who transgress religious principles) and *rojos* ("reds" [i.e., communists], citizens not in tune with the political ideals and, therefore, anti-Franquists). When homosexuals were recognized, it was not uncommon that they became the subjects of abuse, pejorative phrases, and physical attacks.

June 23, 1977, two years after Franco's death, was celebrated as "gay pride" day, an event with clear political connotations and denotations (*connotaciones y denotaciones políticas*). The public demonstration gave public recognition to homosexuality. Homosexuals ceased to be clandestine and began to call themselves, and be recognized as, gays. In 1978, coinciding with an epoch of transition from authoritarian to democratic rules, the Law of Social Danger was repealed. Homosexuality ceased to be legally persecuted. Socially, however, homophobia continues to exist.

More or less solid homosexual support groups soon appeared all over Spain with the clear and decided intention of defending the rights of homosexuals. With different degrees of activism, they have reached out to the public with manifestos8, conferences, institutes, publicity, debates, a presence in the media, and other practices that have allowed them to impart knowledge and refuse any type of social discrimination.

The vindication of these groups and movements have customarily centered on gaining social rights of homosexual couples who live together, destruction of political files where homosexuality was an element of a suspicion, fighting against employment discrimination, rejecting the relevance of sexual orientation in cases of child custody, and promoting a sane public discourse that does not believe that heterosexuality is the only normal sexual expression.

There is no one homosexual model. As with heterosexual lifestyles, plural expression includes many different patterns of expression. Next to "effeminate" roles are those who express manifestations of "virility," whose ultimate end is to highlight in exaggerated form the dress, attitudes, and conducts that sustains the image of the "male." As for the places for homosexual encounters, these are typical of that found in other Western countries: train and bus stations, parks, specific streets and squares, discos and bars, saunas, and more.

B. Lesbianism

Like other organized phenomena, the appearance of lesbianism in Spain is tied to feminism, which exploded in 1975 after the disappearance of Franquismo and the social effervescence (*efervescencia social*) that followed. After the initial push of the gay movement, which was more visible and organized, the first collective group of lesbians appeared in 1981, surging to almost twenty lesbian organizations all over Spain in 1990.

This surge, however, can be misleading. In reality, lesbian individuals and groups have had to fight a society in denial for the very limited time and visibility they have managed to gain in general. They have also great difficulty in creating organizations with enough weight to be heard.

Some lesbians have created their own collective spaces in order to meet and defend their identity and their rights. Some lesbian bars and discos exist in some cities, and magazines sporadically appear in an attempt to create a forum for education and support. As for sexual roles, this question is debated in interested circles, although no concrete posture has been accepted as respecting the values of all the groups and collectives. In this sense, one could say that a model does not exist for those who are living a lesbian lifestyle or are in a same-sex couple, where they are left to create their own pattern dictated by their own circumstances. This absence of social visibility has its logical consequence in the legal domain.

The period of repression of homosexuality as *conducta de peligrosidad social,* socially dangerous behavior, is now in the past. However, the Spanish legal system has avoided dealing with the topic of the regulation of established gay and lesbian couples. This lack of regulation of the rights generated by living together is creating a significant form of discrimination vis-à-vis married heterosexual couples as well as cohabiting couples. This results in multiple forms of discrimination. For instance, the fear of loss of the custody of children can be traced to the invisibility of the lesbian's right to have a family. Not recognizing marriage or cohabitation creates a negative aftermath involving loss of pensions, inheritance rights, continuity in the lease of housing in case of death of one of the couple, and the exclusion of partners in Social Security. In all these difficulties, there is one exception: *Ley de Reproducción Asistada* (The Law of Assisted Reproduction), approved some years ago, "permits" the utilization of these techniques by women with no heterosexual partner. There have already been some cases publicized in the press.

Despite this one legal right, it can be affirmed that there is a legal void when it comes to defining the rights and respective responsibilities of homosexuals that can only be due to the exclusive legal attention to heterosexual relationships.

7. Gender Conflicted Persons

A clear term does not exist in Spanish that is equivalent of "transgenderism" in English. The conversion of gender identity and gender roles are included within the terms transsexuality, homosexuality, and transvestism. The differences that American sexologists pick up between the style of life of the transgenderist, who chronically cross-codes for gender behaviors and roles, and the transvestite, who only circumstantially and episodically dresses like the opposite sex, are nonexistent in Spain. For us, a transvestite is a person who reverses roles, dresses himself in clothing that does not correspond to his sex, regardless of whether this is permanent, chronic, episodic, or entertainment-related. The typical Spanish heterosexual confuses the transvestite with the homosexual, and the homophobic attitudes and responses that occur with regard to homosexuals are thus applicable in a gross mode to the transvestite.

From a political perspective, at the end of the 1970s, the transvestites worked together with homosexuals and contributed to the ascent and recognition of gay groups. Subsequently, their politics are changing to allow an image that is in alliance with the world of entertainment, transformation, and prostitution. The figure of the female impersonator is commercially marketed.

The first legal change of sex, endorsed by the Supreme Tribunal, occurred in 1979. In 1983, a modification of the Spanish Criminal Code decriminalized sex change by surgical intervention. At present, this surgery occurs in Madrid, Barcelona, and Zaragoza. Male-female sex change is more frequent than the reverse. However, some confusion, contradiction, and lack of uniformity exists, as evidenced by a variety of criteria and different decisions in the legal system.

Surgically effected change of sex is recognized by changing the birth name in the Civil Register. Sex-change surgery, even when registered, brings certain restrictions. They cannot, for instance, legally marry. Transsexuals are typically portrayed as having an "erratic," "exotic," "ambiguous" character, and by their "gender indetermination" in the media.

In 1987, the transsexuals organized, creating an organization to defend their rights. This association is recognized by the Ministry of the Interior.

8. Significant Unconventional Sexual Behaviors

A. Coercive Sex

Sexual Abuse of Children and Incest

Since 1988, matters involving the sexual abuse of children in our country have been handled by the Ministry of Social Matters under the Direction of Legal Protection of the Minor (*Dirección de Protección Jurídica del Menor*);

previously, this was done under the Ministry of Justice. The Royal Ordinance 791/1988 (July 20) created the Centro de Estudios del Menor (Center of Studies of the Minor).

The scientific treatment of this problem makes clear that frequent cases of sexual abuse with children exist, but few are documented. Those cases that become known usually coincide with some other criminal act that has come to the attention of the center. The center, in turn, registers the abuse with the police and security bodies of the state for criminal investigation. In the *Boletín Estadístico de Datos Técnicos* (Statistical Bulletin of Technical Data) of the Ministry of Social Matters, 1992, some relatives of 16-year-old minors were included with youngsters' antisocial behaviors (such as runaways, drug use, robberies, etc.). These biographies were on many occasions marked by child abuse, including sexual abuses. But, as already stated, documentation of these cases is difficult.

In 1991, 113 cases of "criminal" accusations of sexual abuse or rape were reported. In these and other cases of rape, incest, sexual aggression, or exhibitionism, the age of the victims is not specified in the Ministry of Interior data.

As with criminal reporting, the legal system has given most of its attention to child-abuse cases that involve protection of children, their education, and safe placement within the family environment. The effective criminal code, last reformed in 1983, includes various sections on child sexual abuse.

The legal classification of sexual crimes involves the age of the victim and the level of kinship or authority that exists between those implicated in the crime. At this writing, the initial draft of the Penal Code of 1992 is being debated. The draft is designed to provide treatment that is more in accord with the social reality, and picks up the circumstances that aggravate or attenuate criminal responsibility. Chapter V, Article 22, "of the circumstance of relationship/kinship," recognizes that if the wronged person is the spouse or a person tied to a permanent relationship, he or she can attenuate or aggravate the responsibility, according to the nature of the crime.

In describing "crimes against individual or personal freedom/integrity" (*delitos contra la libertad sexual*), Title VII highlights several levels of crime in terms of the age of the person against whom the crime is committed and the level of kinship, relationship, or superiority exercised in their relationship. When parliament approves this new Penal Code, the state will be clearly responsible for minors, the helpless, and unprotected, who suffer the exploitation and sexual oppression from parents, family members, teachers, or strangers. Spanish public opinion is very sensitive about the sexual abuse of minors, because more and more publicity is given to such cases in the mass media, sociological studies, and the research of the Centro de Investigaciones Sociológicas (Center of Sociological Studies, or CIS).

The most recent survey on "Attitudes and Opinions of the Spanish Regarding Childhood" (1991) shows that 46 percent of the responding men and women over age 18 support changing the penal age, presently 16 years, to 18 years. Younger respondents, ages 18 to 25 years, and those who have voted to the political left clearly defend this posture. Over half of those surveyed, 52 percent, believe that the laws protecting children from parents or adults who exploit, abandon, or prostitute their children should be stricter. Spanish society is increasingly open to measures of support and care for children, including intervention by the public administrations to facilitate adoption and foster-home placement.

Sexual Harassment (Acoso Sexual)

In our usage, sexual harassment refers to a "behavior of a sexual character, not desired by the person to which it is directed at." This includes not only aggression and rape but also other behaviors, like verbal offenses, expressions, grimaces, unnecessary touching, etc.

In spite of the many forms sexual harassment can take, central in this definition is the fact that the harassment is deliberate, the perpetrator is conscious of his or her actions and searches for trouble, and the fact that the harassment is imposed on an unwilling person.

While both men and women can be the object of sexual harassment, national and international data indicate that women suffer it most and, in this sense, it is an expression of the patriarchal society rooted in the inequality in gender relationships in both the labor world and in society in general. The first data on sexual harassment in the Spanish work force came out of research on women from diverse labor sectors in the city of Madrid, carried out with the support of the Department of the Woman of a socialist union: Unión General de Trabajadores de Madrid (General Union of Workers of Madrid or U.G.T.).

In this study, sexual abuse and harassment is described in terms of a continuum, with five levels of intimidation and the negative aftermath in the psychological, physical, labor, and social order. In this research, 84 percent of the women had suffered some type of sexual harassment from companions as well as superiors through jokes, flattering remarks, and conversations containing sexual content (level 1); 55 percent had been objects of sexual harassment through nonverbal communication, without physical contact (level 2); 27 percent had suffered through strong verbal conduct and physical contact with sexual intention (levels 3 and 4) and 4 percent had suffered violent behavior to the point of coitus (level 5).

Older women are less subject to sexual harassment than younger women, with women ages 26 to 30 most at risk. In addition, women separated from their spouses, divorced women, and widows also suffer harassment with a greater frequency in all five types of harassment. According to this research and the women themselves, the civil status of women—divorced, widowed, or separated—allows the harasser to perceive them as "easy targets," because the male husband is legally invisible or nonexistent.

The strongest correlate for sexual aggression is the degree of vulnerability the woman has in her work position: the more insecure or vulnerable a woman is, the greater are her chances of being sexually harassed. Since harassment increases in relation to the power of males over females in any situation, the patriarchal hierarchy has been recognized as a central problem in the structural conditions of the Spanish workplace.

A sophisticated report by the (Communist) Union Labor Commissions shows that in a high percentage of the reported cases, the victims are women who are seeking employment, are pending contract renewal, or work in a masculine labor atmosphere. It is impossible to foresee a promising future if women continue to be discriminated against and insecure in their employment, and their work conditions remain inferior to those of males.

Until 1989, the legal system had no instruments that would allow reporting and remedying these practices. The 1989 Statute for Workers deals with the personal rights and dignity of workers and civil servants and the protection from verbal or physical offenses of a sexual nature.

Progressive lawyers have proposed expanding the Penal Code to include an article referring to sexual harassment under the heading of "crimes against individual or personal freedom/integrity" (*delitos contra la libertad sexual*). Nevertheless, in the first draft of the Penal Code of 1992, sexual harassment is not included as a distinct and separate crime. Joining forces, feminist and progressive judges have concluded that the current legal system framework is not sufficient to protect people who attempt to report situations of harassment, either within or outside of the work place.

Rape

In 1989, an important legislative reform was enacted in Spain as a result of a widespread opinion championed by feminist groups, progressive lawyers, the Institute of the Woman, and diverse sectors of the society. The 1989 Organic Law of the Proceedings of the Penal Code replaced the previous headings of "crimes against decency" (*delitos contra la honestidad*) with "crimes against individual or personal freedom/integrity" (*delitos contra la libertad sexual*). This eliminated from the Penal Code a nineteenth-century sexist conceptualization of sexuality and provided strong protection for the personal freedom and integrity of women.

Under the heading of sexual crimes are included rape (*violación*), sexual aggression and statutory rape (*estupro*), and abduction (*rapto*). According to this new gender-free code, rape is not limited to a man who sexually violates a woman through carnal access, vaginally, anally, or orally. It is to have carnal access with a person using strength or intimidation, or when the person is unconscious or deprived of mental capacity. Statutory rape involves carnal access with a person between 12 and 18 years of age. Abduction against the will of the person is considered more severe when the person is under the age of 12.

In the new Spanish legislation, one speaks of "people," not just "women," as victims of rape. This breaks the association between rape and a woman's virginity that was implied in the previous laws that dealt only with vaginal penetration.

However, court procedure still requires that the accusation should be made by the victim, or in cases of a minor or handicapped person, by the parent, legal guardian, or representative, or a member of the Fiscal Ministry. Although the victim may withdraw the accusation, the Fiscal Ministry continues with the official prosecution based on the victim's testimony.

In spite of certain advances in the reformed criminal code, diverse parties have pointed out that rape remains one of the less-reported crimes in spite of its graveness and high incidence. One fundamental reason behind this is the deeply embedded societal belief "that blames the victim for the crime committed against her and for the wide repercussions she will have subsequently in life" (*que tienden a acusar a la victima del propio delito que ha sido cometido contra ella y que tan amplias repercusiones tendra' posteriormente en su vida*).

Efforts in the legal system have been made to denounce this idea of victim precipitation, and the fact that stigmatization of women intensifies when the victims know their aggressor, since it is thought that there are other motives for their accusation. This is a particularly serious charge given that data provided by the *Asociación de Asistencia a Mujeres Violadas* in its 1990 annual report noted that 55 percent of the victims knew their aggressor. This association was created at the state level in 1986 to provide free legal and psychological services to women, to promote public campaigns in favor of reporting such crimes, and to protect the rights of the victim under the law. However, much remains to be done in order to guarantee the utmost assistance to violated women and improve the legal protection of the victim during all prosecution. Without these changes, rape will continue to be a frequent, but rarely prosecuted crime.

B. Prostitution

Prostitution is spread throughout the country in very diverse forms, involving street prostitution, housewives, students, junkies, illegal immigrants, and others. Sex workers also frequent bars, pubs, and clubs of all types, from the more sleazy to the most elegant. Escort services or agencies offer "company" for executives and business men. Massage services are also advertised in the press. In fact, all types of sexual services are offered by individuals or by organizations with many "employees" and a wide range of supplies.

Spain has had an abolitionist legislation since 1956 that supports the reformation of the prostitutes, the persecution of the pimps and go-betweens, and the deterrence of the clients. Prostitution is not monitored, per se, but the law criminalizes those who get some economical benefit from it.

In practice, sex workers have been harassed when caught in raids and/or when accused of other crimes not directly related to prostitution. The go-betweens, clients and others, on the other hand, have been and are tolerated and only arrested when there is a scandal or someone is interested in revenge.

Nevertheless, in social debate of the first draft of the Penal Code, prostitution is completely depenalized, except in cases of minors and when coercion exists. If approved, procuring, pimping, and other activities associated with prostitution would no longer be crimes, and all forms of prostitution, including the bordellos, now forbidden, would be permitted.

Prostitution is tolerated because it is considered a necessary evil. That does not necessarily grant any freedom and the prostitute is supposed to remain in an opaque area in which the activity is not seen or recognized, operating in the world of a hidden economy.

C. Pornography and Erotica

During Franco's regime, pornography was completely prohibited. In recent years, sexually explicit magazines and films have appeared. After an early and short explosion of pornographic materials, prompted by the common belief that the masses were going to consume it voraciously, the situation soon settled down.

Pornographic magazines are sold at newspaper stands and in sex shops. X-rated films are shown in theaters with erotic publicity provided at the doors to entice customers inside. Sex shops increased in number, often near to areas of prostitution, where they display all types of erotic toys and devices. Some sex shops offer video booths and even live sex shows.

The onslaught of the video industry has seriously affected the market of porno theaters, many of which have closed because consumers prefer to rent a videotape and see it in their home. The many couples who now share this activity has shifted the market from the traditional consumer, the single male. Also, some regular television channels, not cable television, offer erotic movies at certain hours, not too late at night, which has also drawn customers away from the porno theaters.

Pornography no longer provokes major controversies in Spain; its "moderate" consumption passes through channels that are clearly defined and accepted.

9. Contraception, Abortion, and Population Planning

A. Contraception

The data that exist on the use of contraceptives and abortion among Spanish youth is scarce, fragmentary, and rarely reliable. Nevertheless, what little data there are allow one to appreciate the fact that the use of contraceptives is very low, although it has been increasing in the last few years due to the problems of STDs and AIDS.

Current data show a linear increase in the use of contraceptives. Between ages 18 and 19, 10.9 percent regularly use some kind of contraceptive, 8.3 percent utilize effective contraceptives, and 2.6 percent ineffective methods. The percentage of regular contraceptive use increases to 54.3 percent for ages 25 to 29 years. Among 15-year-olds, 60 percent maintain or have been sexually active without using any method. In 1977, only 25 percent had utilized some effective method; in 1985 (the last year for which data are available), this percentage increased to 65.5 percent.

In 1985, 98.6 percent of the total number of women between ages 18 and 49 knew of at least one effective method of contraception. This reflects a clear improvement in comparison with 1975 when 10 percent of married women were not acquainted with any effective method. Today, the most utilized methods by women at risk for pregnancy, according to data of the National Survey of Fecundity are: the pill, 14 percent; IUD, 4.8 percent; condoms, 11 percent; rhythm method, 3.8 percent; and coitus interruptus, 13 percent. The best known method is the pill (97.6 percent) and the least known, the diaphragm (56.7 percent).

B. Teenage Unmarried Pregnancies

The annual number of undesired pregnancies among 18- to 19-year-olds is 30,966; for those between ages 20 and 24, 190,839, of which 7.6 percent occurred in spite of contraceptive use.

In 1985, the last year for which official statistics exist, 29,586 children were born to adolescents under age 20; only 207 girls under age 15 gave birth, 0.04 percent of total births of that year.

In 1988, 14,124 women under age 24 years had IVE (*interrupción voluntaria de embarazo*, [voluntary interruption of pregnancy]), 54.17 percent of the total number of abortions. What little data there are indicate an increase in minors giving birth, although, since 1985, that frequency seems to have stabilized. The high number of clandestine abortions among youths, because they cannot opt for IVE without the knowledge of their parents, results in unnecessary uterine perforations, hemorrhages, and infections. So, while maternal and neonatal morbidity and mortality may have diminished in Spain in recent years, adolescents are disproportionately represented in these statistics.

C. Abortion

The law legalizing abortions was proclaimed on July 5, 1985, authorizing three types of abortions: eugenic abortion when the fetus is diagnosed with grave mental and/or physical problems; therapeutic abortion when the pregnancy is a threat to the mother's life or mental health; and ethical abortion in cases of rape or incest. An estimated total of 100,000 IVEs are performed annually in Spain, although the number of legal and recognized abortions is clearly much less. In 1990, 36,095 IVEs were performed and officially recorded in eighty-six different centers. This figure has been relatively stable for several years.

For a variety of reasons—religious, ethical, professional, and economic— the law legalizing abortion met great resistance in a medical profession that welcomed the right of conscience to refuse to perform abortions in official centers. The resistance is obvious in the data documenting that few legal abortions are practiced in public hospitals. Of these, 4.17 percent are performed to prevent physical harm to the mother; almost 100 percent of the abortions performed in private centers are performed for the mental health of the mother. Another pattern is that high-risk IVEs are usually performed in public facilities, while the private centers perform lower-risk IVEs.

At present, the government is studying the possibility of expanding the conditions for legal abortions, adding economic conditions as an acceptable cause for abortion, and allowing first trimester abortions on request. The latter option is advocated by the majority of Family Planning Centers and by progressive women's movements, despite strong legal difficulties.

D. Population Control Efforts

Long-standing religious and political factors in Spain have hindered any attempt to justify the control of fecundity/fertility. The political changes that started in 1975 and the 1978 democratic constitution are changing the "old rules."

The new constitution partially legalized information about and sale of contraceptives. This same year, modification of the Penal Code enabled the government to create the Centers of Family Planning. At first, these centers were exclusively dependent on the state government. However, as such centers proliferated, more and more of them were funded by municipal governments and by private, nongovernmental associations.

In 1984, the National Plan of Centers of Family Planning was developed and linked with the Ministry of Health to facilitate programs dealing with contraceptive methods, STDs, and general material on sexual education, sterility, and fertility. At present, Spain has about seven hundred Centers of Family Planning, actively creating an awareness of the importance of fertility control by distributing sexual information and contraceptives.

10. Sexually Transmitted Diseases

The most reliable estimates on the epidemiology of sexually transmitted disease (STD) in Spain come from the obligatory registrations of the diseases. This registration (*Sistema de Información Sanitaria de las Enfermedades de Declaración Obligada*, or SISEDO, the System of Sanitary Information on the Obligatory Declaration of the Illnesses) is based on the weekly reports primary care physicians make on a series of illnesses. However, as in other countries, only three diseases are reported: gonorrhea, syphilis, and HIV infection. Unfortunately, even with this limited requirement, an estimated 50 percent to 90 percent of actual cases go unreported. Since 1982, a laboratory in the Service of Bacteriology of the National Center of Viral Microbiology and Sanitary Immunology (CNMVVIS) has been analyzing the existence and specific characteristics of gonorrhea strains.

The number of gonorrhea and syphilis cases declined annually from 1985 to 1990, with 1,685 cases of syphilis and 13,702 of gonorrhea, 4.1 and 33.1 cases per 100,000 inhabitants respectively in 1990. The impact of AIDS and safer-sex practices is likely the main factor in this decline. Although a decline in STD cases has also been seen in other European countries, this tendency to decrease is not uniform. In Spain, the data document a decline for only six years, too brief a time to draw any conclusions other than that young people are more at risk, and both men and women are at risk. Among 16- to 25-year-olds, one finds more females than males infected. With syphilis and other STDs transmittable during childbirth, there is an increased risk of congenital STDs and possible serious repercussions for fertility in both sexes.

A few local or regional studies of STDs not reported to SISEDO are available, but nothing on a national level. With no uniform definitions and no standardized diagnostic methods, estimates on these STDs vary from study to study. Nevertheless it is possible to say that chlamydia is a minor problem in Spain as compared to other European countries. But these figures should be considered with caution.

Spain does not have a significant tradition of clinics for STD treatment; patients usually seek treatment from general practitioners. In other countries such as Italy, the situation is very similar, and efforts are being made to improve and structure national epidemiologic surveillance services for the cases of "second generation" STDs, e.g., chlamydia, genital herpes, and genital warts, among others.

11. HIV/AIDS

Clinical criteria for AIDS cases in Spain follow those established by the Centers for Disease Control in the United States. According to the data available from the National AIDS Registry to the end of 1991, Spain's total of 11,555 cases, 288 cases per million inhabitants, puts the nation among the top in number of cases among countries in Europe. The largest increase in cases was produced between 1986 and 1988. At present, the effectiveness of initial preventive campaigns from public organizations seems to have produced a decrease in the number of new cases reported in recent years. The initial exponential pattern seems to be giving way to a linear pattern.

Nevertheless, although the tendency for growth has slowed, the number of new cases continues to grow every year (Hart 1995).

In Spain, intravenous drug users (IVDUs) account for two out of three cases, 64 percent. A much smaller percentage, 16 percent, are homosexual or bisexual. Heterosexuals account for about 5 percent and their linear growth pattern is still not alarming. As of mid-1993, 341 cases of pediatric AIDS have been recorded, 80 percent of these children born to mothers at high risk. This pattern of etiology and distribution contrasts with the predominance of homosexual/bisexual transmission in North America, Western Europe, Australia, and New Zealand, and with the predominantly heterosexual transmission in parts of the Caribbean and sub-Saharan Africa.

Finally, at the end of 1991, 39 percent or 4,454 of the adolescent and adult HIV-positive persons had died, and 42 percent of the pediatric AIDS. The most frequent causes of death are opportunistic infections, 67 percent, and frequent bouts of extrapulmonary tuberculosis, 18 percent. Several prevention programs from the central government are focusing on how to avoid infection, and indirectly, STDs, through safer-sexual practices, use of condoms, use of clean syringes, etc. (Hart 1995).

12. Sexual Dysfunctions, Counseling, and Therapies

A. Concepts of Sexual Dysfunction

Sexual dysfunctions are mainly associated with problems in heterosexual relationships: mainly erectile dysfunction, early ejaculation, and loss of sexual desire in men, and inhibited sexual arousal and orgasm, painful intercourse, and loss of sexual desire in women. The primary characteristic that allows one to consider these dysfunctions as problems is the suffering and malaise they can cause for the people experiencing them.

In general, men and women with a sexual dysfunction are viewed with a certain condescension and tolerance, as patients or sick persons requiring medical assistance or sexological treatment. On the other hand, many Spanish people continue to view sexual dysfunctions in terms of pathological dysfunctions, such as rape, incest, pedophilia, child sexual abuse, exhibitionism, sadomasochism, fetishism, etc.

B. Availability of Diagnosis and Treatment

At the present time, Spain has a considerable and growing number and variety of centers and specialists who diagnose and treat sexual dysfunctions. Treatment can be sought at both public and private facilities, although, in general, private clinics continue to provide the best environment and treatment.

As for the specialists who treat these dysfunctions, they are, in order of importance, psychologists, psychiatrists, and urologists and gynecologists.

A reasonable variety of technology and instruments are available for diagnostic use, mainly adapted from those developed in European countries, although Spain is beginning to develop technology, evaluation instruments, and treatment modalities specially adapted to the Spanish people.

As for the training of therapists, a variety of possibilities currently exist. Most training is available in seminars and courses of specialization, normally lasting some months, offered by graduate programs in psychology and medicine. These courses are usually sponsored and staffed by institutes, clinical centers, and sexological associations all over the country, although they tend to be more common in the provincial capitals, like Madrid or Barcelona.

At the university level, master's and doctoral level programs are available at the University of Salamanca and at the Universidad Nacional de Educacio a Distancia (UNED) in Madrid. These programs include instruction of the many aspects of sexological knowledge, as well as training in diagnostic evaluation, counseling, and the treatment of sexual dysfunctions.

13. Sexual Research and Advanced Education

A. Institutes and Programs for Research and Education

Sexuality research in the academic environment has been marginal and received little support. From the political transition of the late 1970s to the present, the academic gaps in this type of research have been paralleled by the proliferation of news of sexual attitudes and specific sexual practices in magazines and the daily press that is fragmentary, sensationalist, and endowed with little rigor.

The first survey of Spanish sexual behavior, *Encuesta Sobre el Sexo Masculino* (Survey on the Masculine Sex), was carried out in 1966 with a hundred males. In 1972, Serrano Vicens published *La Sexualidad Femenina* (Feminine Sexuality), based on his clinical interviews of 1417 women begun in the 1930s.

There are very few probing interviews, surveys, and empirical studies based on a quantitative methodology. Even surveys and empirical studies based on adolescents and university students are not representative due to the small size of the sample. However, studies have been conducted in Madrid, Valencia, Barcelona, Salamanca, León, Zaragoza, Pamplona, Oviedo, and other cities. Worth noting are the surveys conducted by Jose L. Zárraga (1987) and Malo de Molina, Valls Blanco, and Perez Gomez (1988). At the national level, under the auspices of the Master's in Human Sexuality Program of the Universidad Nacional de Educacio a Distancia (UNED), a study of the sexuality of older males and females, is now under way.

Despite a glaring need, studies in sexuality are only recently appearing in Spanish universities. Specific courses in sexuality are being considered for inclusion in some programs at some universities. In 1991, a course in the psychology of sexuality was an elective in the undergraduate, Licenciatura (B.A.) program in psychology at the University of Salamanca. A Catedra in evolutionary psychology of sexuality was also introduced at the highest academic level. In the same year, the course in sexology at the School of Social Work of the University of Navarra was eliminated. A course in Sexual Anthropology was an elective in one of the UNED programs.

Various universities are currently planning to incorporate diverse viewpoints on sexuality into their Licenciatura programs. The Department of Psychology at the University of Salamanca offers a doctorate in sexology with an obvious psychological orientation. Since 1990, the Universidad Nacional de Educacio a Distancia (UNED) has offered a two-year multidisciplinary master's degree program with a clear sociocultural inclination leading to the diploma, Master in Human Sexuality. This is the first master's degree program in sexuality granted by a Spanish university. This program is sponsored and exists within the Department of Sociology.

Some private institutions, schools, associations, and clinical centers with diverse orientations outside of the university domain also offer programs in sexology: Espill Institute, Incisex, the Lambda Institute (now named Casa Lambda), and the Speculum Institute.

B. Sexological Organizations

The offices of the Federacion Espagnola de Sociedades de Sexología are at: c. Valencians 6 Principla, Valencia 46002 Spain. Local or regional Sociedades de Sexología exist in many cities and provinces in Andalucia, Castilla y Leon, Cataluna, Galicia, Madrid, Malaga, Sevilla, and Valencia. Two regional organizations are:

Societat Catalan de Sexologia, Tren de Baix, 51 2o, 2o 08223 Teraessa, Barcelona, Spain. Phone: 34-3/788-0277.

Sociedad Sexologica de Madrid, C/Barbieri, 3.3 dcha, Madrid 28004 Spain. Phone: 24-1/522-25-10; Fax: 24-1/532-96-19.

About two dozen bulletins and small magazines dealing with sexual issues are published by local psychiatric and psychological organizations, educators, sexological societies, and feminist, lesbian, and gay-male support groups, in such cities as Barcelona, Bilbao, Madrid, Murcia, Pampolona, Rioja, and Salamanca.

There are well over fifty gay, lesbian, feminist, and HIV-positive/AIDS collectives and support groups in Spain. Among the cities with at least one such group are Albacete, Barcelona, Bilbao y Pamplona, Cordoba y Granada, Madrid, Murcia, Malaga, Palma de Mallorca, Salamanca, Santiago de Compostela, Sevilla, Valencia, and Zaragoza. The number of such groups fluctuates, as these local support groups appear and disappear quite often. Catholic or Christian gay groups are functioning in Barcelona, Madrid, and Malaga.

A Note by the Translators
LAURA BERMAN, M.A., PH.D. (CAND.)
AND JOSE NANIN, M.A.

Educators and researchers agree that one crucial informal source of knowledge about sexual issues for children is their parents. The authors of this chapter have discussed the importance and enormity of the changes that occurred with regard to social attitudes toward sexuality in Spain after Franco's death.

While the rapid and radical shift in sexual norms impacted many facets of Spanish life, one of the most important was that of parent-child communications. Young people and their parents are suffering from a significant and atypical generation gap triggered by the political changes that occurred in Spain following Franco's death. The world in which the majority of young Spanish people are living today is tremendously different from that in which their parents grew into adults. Even those children who were born the year Franco died were only 18 in 1994. While the world around them promotes a newfound sexual freedom and liberal expression, the families in which they are being raised are based on the values of the ultratraditional model from Franco's dictatorship.

How then must this affect the ability of parents and children to communicate about sexuality? The traditional value systems and gender-role expectations that governed the consciences of their parents' youth are in direct contrast with present-day powerful social and peer norms that encourage the sexual freedom of their children. The difference between the two sets of norms is clear when one imagines a parent who experienced adolescent dating with a mandatory chaperone or *duenna* confronting an adolescent son or daughter in a social climate in which peers are now likely to lose their virginity before the age of 18. In order for children to benefit from the wisdom and experience of their parents in Spain today, they must not only overcome a generation gap, but a generation crevice that began with the end of the Franco era and the weakening of Catholic-based social controls.

Young people in Spain today have many choices to make about their sexuality. The next generation will not have it as difficult, because the distance between the social and sexual norms of this new generation of parents and the children they have will be much narrower than the current crevice.

References and Suggested Readings

Boletín Epidemiológico Semanal. Instituto de Salud Carlos III. Centro Nacional de Epidemiología. Ministerio de Sanidad y Consumo.
Boletín Estadistico de Datos Tecnicos (Statistical Bulletin of Technical Data). 1992. Madrid: Ministry of Social Matters.

Bosch, S., H. Vanaclocha, S. Guiral, C. Moya, I. Hernandez, and C. Alvarez Dardet. 1988. "Programa de Mejora de la Calidad de la Información Epidemiológica en Enfermedades de Transmisión Sexual." *Medicina Clínica,* 90:229-32.

Calle, M., C. Gonzalez and J. Nuñez. 1988. *Discriminación y Acoso Sexual a la Mujer en el Trabajo.* Madrid: Largo Caballero.

Carrobles, J. A. 1990. *Biologia y Psicofisiologia de la Conducta Sexual.* Madrid: Fundación Universidad-Empresa.

Carrobles, J. A., and A. Sanz Yaque. 1991. *Terapia Sexual.* Madrid: Fundación Universidad-Empresa.

Delgado Perez, (with C. Ureña). May 1992. *La Fecundidad de los Adolescentes en el Conjunto de España y en la Comunidad Autónoma de Madrid.* Madrid: Instituto de Demografía, CSIC.

Delgado y Otros, M., and J. A. Nieto, eds. 1991. *La Sexualidad en la Sociedad Contemporanea Lecturas Antropologicas.* Madrid: Fundación Universidad-Empresa.

del Valle, T., and C. Sanz Rueda. 1991. *Genero y Sexualidad.* Madrid: Fundación Universidad-Empresa.

Hart, Angie. 1995. "Risky Business? Men Who Buy Heterosexual Sex in Spain." In: Han ten Brummelhuis and Gilbert Herdt, ed. *Culture and Sexual Risk: Anthropological Perspectives on AIDS.* Amsterdam: Gordon and Breach Science Publishers.

Lopez Sanchez, F. 1990. *Educación Sexual.* Madrid: Fundación Universidad-Empresa.

Malo de Molina, C., Valls Blanco, Jose Mª, and Perez Gomez, A. 1988. *La Conducta Sexual de los Españoles.* Madrid: Ediciónes B.

Marques, J. V., and R. Osborne. 1991. *Sexualidad y Sexismo.* Madrid: Fundación Universidad-Empresa.

Moreno Jimenez, B. 1990. *La Sexualidad Humana: Estudio y Perspectiva Historica.* Madrid: Fundación Universidad-Empresa.

Nieto, J. A. 1990. *Cultura y Sociedad en las Practicas Sexuales.* Madrid: Fundación Universidad-Empresa.

Sanches, F. L. 1990. *Educación Sexual.* Madrid: Fundación Universidad-Empresa.

Segura Benedicto, A., I. H. Aguado, and C. Alvarez-Dardet Diaz. 1991. *Epidemiologia y Prevención de las Enfermedades de Transmisión Sexual.* Madrid: Fundación Universidad-Empresa.

Usandizaga, J. A. 1990. *Bases Anatomicas y Fisiologicas de la Sexualidad y de la Reproducción Humanas.* Madrid: Fundación Universidad-Empresa.

Zarraga. Jose L. 1987. *La Conducta Sexual de los Jovenes Españoles.* Instituto de la Juventud.

Sweden
(*Konungariket Sverige*)

Jan E. Trost, Ph.D., with Mai-Briht Bergstrom-Walan, Ph.D.

Contents

Demographics and a Historical Perspective

A. Demographics

On the Scandinavian Peninsula in northern Europe, Sweden is bordered by Norway on the west, Denmark on the south, and Finland on the east. One of the oldest democracies in the world, Sweden has lived in peace for two hundred years. As titular head of a constitutional monarchy, the Swedish king has no power except to represent the country symbolically within Sweden and abroad.

Sweden's land mass of 173,731 square miles, larger than the state of California, is mountainous along the northwest border. A quarter of the land is flat or rolling terrain, mainly in the central and southern areas where the largest cities are located.

Of the 8.8 million population in 1995, 90 percent were Swedish, with somewhat more than 2 percent Finnish, a small Lapp population, and a variety of immigrant people (see Section 14). Eighty-five percent of the population live in the cities, mainly Stockholm, Göteburg, and Malmö.

The 1995 age distribution is 19 percent age 14 and younger, 63 percent between ages 15 and 64, and 18 percent over age 65. The population density is 49 per square mile. Life expectancy at birth in 1995 was 76 for males and 81 for females. The 1995 birthrate was 13 per 1,000, total fertility rate (TFR) was 2.1 (1992), and the 1995 death rate was 11 per 1,000, for a stable population. Infant mortality was 6 per 1,000 live births. Sweden had one hospital bed per 177 persons and one physician per 394 persons. The literacy rate was 99 percent, with 100 percent attendance and nine years compulsory schooling—most take another two to three years of schooling. The per capita domestic product in 1995 was $17,600 U.S.

B. A Brief Historical Perspective

The Swedes have lived in present-day Sweden for at least five thousand years, longer than nearly any other European people. Nordic (Gothic) tribes from Sweden played a major role in the disintegration of the Roman Empire and helped create the first Russian state in the nineteenth century. The Swedes accepted Christianity in the eleventh century and soon developed a strong centralized monarchy. In 1435, Sweden became the first European nation to develop a parliament with representatives from all segments of the population. Sweden threw off Danish rule, which began in 1397, in a 1521-1523 revolt led by Gustavus I. The Lutheran Church became the official state religion. For a time in the seventeenth century, Sweden was a major European power, controlling most of the Baltic seacoast. Following the Napoleonic wars, in which Sweden acquired Norway, Sweden maintained an armed neutrality in all later European wars.

1. Basic Sexological Premises

A. Character of Gender Roles

Sweden has the reputation, especially among its own inhabitants, of being the leader in gender equity. Whether this is reality or not, the early strivings for equality—thinking of men and women as equal—started more than a century ago. Women's movements were in the vanguard of these early efforts. In the family and matrimonial law reform of 1920, no differentiation was made between the rights and responsibilities of men and women, husbands and wives. Unfortunately, while the law drew no difference between the genders, the reality of social consciousness and behavior did differentiate. Thus, efforts shifted to achieving gender equity. Today,

Swedes are more prone to think of and work for the process of gender equity, the fair and reasonable treatment of both men and women.

Depending on one's perspective, Sweden has come close to, or is still far from, gender equity. If one takes a public or legal perspective, Sweden has come very far. Officially, women and men are treated equally and have the same rights and responsibilities. From a historical and cultural perspective, when compared with other European countries and those in the Middle East, Sweden is a real pioneer at the cutting edge. However, if we use the ideal of gender equity as the perspective and basis for evaluation, Sweden has a very long way to go. To illustrate: Sweden has led the way for other nations with a gender-neutral parental-leave law that provides almost full salary for up to a year for either parent of a new child. This means that the mother and the father can share this leave any way they want. They can split the paid leave any way they want, or either of them can take all the leave. The reality is far from gender equity. Quite a few new mothers take all the leave of absence from work; fathers never take the full leave. Very few fathers take more than a few weeks off, although their salary is fully paid during this leave. Officially, formally, there is full gender equity; in reality, Sweden is far from gender equity on this, and many other, issues.

B. Sociolegal Status of Males and Females

For both females and males, the age of majority is 18 years. However, it is illegal to have sexual intercourse or engage in sexual (genital) touches with a person under the age of 15 years, regardless of whether the underage person is male or female, whether the couple is same- or opposite-gendered, and whether it is voluntary or involuntary. Sexual intercourse or contact is also prohibited by law under the age of 18 when the younger person is under the custody or supervision of the older person. Otherwise, the legal status and prohibitions, including sexual harassment and rape, are the same for all persons.

C. General Concepts of Sexuality and Love

In general, the Swedes have a liberal and permissive attitude towards sexual relations and intercourse, although, as in all societies, some restrictions are commonly accepted. This is illustrated by a 1992 study on a representative sample of 729 Uppsala University students, aged 19 to 23. About 70 percent of both male and female respondents believed that it is acceptable for a 15-year-old girl to have sexual intercourse with a steady boyfriend; the same percentage approved of a 15-year-old boy having sex with his steady girlfriend. More than 90 percent of both male and female respondents did not approve of a 15-year-old girl having sexual intercourse with a casual partner. Only 40 percent of the males and 50 percent of the female respondents disapproved of a 15-year-old boy having sex with a casual partner. The double standard still colors what is acceptable, "even" in Sweden. It is stronger among males than among females, and this holds true even among the highly educated.

Almost all of those students disapproved of a married or cohabiting person having sexual intercourse with another person other than the spouse or cohabitation partner. In this regard, males and females did not apply a double standard and were equally restrictive in their views of "extra" sexual behavior by both men and women.

Generally speaking, females in this university sample were somewhat more restrictive or less permissive than males, but the differences are generally not significant.

2. Religious and Ethnic Factors Affecting Sexuality

A/B. Source and Character of Religious/Ethnic Values

Almost 90 percent of Swedes are members of the state Lutheran Church. The remaining 10 percent are either atheists or belong to other churches, with slightly over 1 percent Roman Catholic and a scattering of other religious traditions, often stemming from significant immigrations. By international comparison, church attendance is very low. Annually, the 7.6 million members of the Lutheran Church attend less than 20 million services, less than three services per member per year. Stated in another way, less than 3 percent of the population on average attend church on any particular Sunday (*Statistical Yearbook of Sweden* 1993).

At the peak of the Viking culture around the year 1000, people in this part of the world subscribed to the Aesir (Asa) religious belief in a superior race of gods led by Odin. This Nordic religion, with its worship of Odin and Thor, the Aesirs (creators of mankind), and the Vanir (fertility deities linked with land and sea spirits and with dead ancestors), was more concerned with behavior than with doctrines and beliefs.

Around the year 1000 C.E., Christianity was introduced into Scandinavia, often with the threat to either convert to Christianity or to be decapitated. Subsequently, the kings in the various small Nordic kingdoms and their people subscribed to Christianity, at least officially. As occurred elsewhere with the imposition of Christian or other exogenous religions, this conversion did not bring a complete rejection of the early religious practices. In Iceland, for instance, the people accepted the new religion in the year 1000 C.E. only after Pope Sylvester II allowed them to keep their traditional religious customs of eating horse meat and practicing abortion/infanticide (Manniche 1989).

That Christianity's penetration of Scandinavia took centuries is evident in letters various Popes sent from Rome to their bishops, demanding that they make sure the Swedes follow the Christian rules for marrying and not use their traditional "pagan" rituals (Carlson 1965).

In 1527, King Gustavus Vasa decided that Sweden should abandon the Church of Rome and subscribe to the Reformation ideas of Martin Luther. At the time, King Vasa was at war and needed money. Luther maintained that the churches should not be decorated, and that the churches should not own a lot of property. This teaching suited King Vasa quite nicely. It allowed him to confiscate church properties, gold, and other valuables, including copper bells, which he had turned into cannon to support his efforts to break away from the control of the Danish monarchy. Thirty-three years after King Vasa's death, the Swedish Parliament formally accepted his declaration of Lutheranism as the state religion at the "Uppsala Meeting" in 1593.

Today, the Swedish Lutheran Church is very liberal in action, but careful not to take formal stands in most sexual issues, such as premarital sex, cohabitation, and sex education. Like many other churches and congregations, the state church of Sweden is inclined to keep quiet on sexual issues to keep the few members they have.

3. Sexual Knowledge and Education

Carl von Linnaeus (1707-1778), a professor at Uppsala University, is internationally known for his botanical classification of all flowering plants, based on their sexual reproductive systems. A less known, but equally pioneering effort of Linnaeus (as he is more commonly known outside his homeland), was the lectures he gave his students on human sexuality. A few years ago, a manuscript was found, probably written by one of his students, Pehr Dubb, and rewritten by a young relative of Dubb's. In this manuscript, entitled *Om Sättet Att Tilhopa Gå* (On the Way to Be Together), Linnaeus shows a surprisingly great openness and support for sexual intercourse, considering he taught in the mid-eighteenth century. Despite his accuracy in detailing the sexual anatomy of plants, Linnaeus had a somewhat limited, and inaccurate, knowledge of the human female's sexual organs.

A. Government Policies and Programs

School Programs

During the eighteenth and early nineteenth centuries, venereal diseases flourished in Sweden. Starting in 1783, the government ordered its officials to distribute information about these diseases. An almanac published in 1814 provided a lot of information on venereal diseases without a moralistic overtone, and the straightforward message that the earlier the symptoms were taken seriously, the easier it was to treat a disease.

In 1897, the first female physician in Sweden, Karolina Widerstrom (1856-1949), started sex education in some of the schools for girls in

Stockholm. She also published a pamphlet on education and sexual hygiene in 1906. Her perspective was astonishingly far ahead of the times. She claimed, for instance, that for their own health, women should be 20 years old before becoming a mother and the man 24 before becoming a father. She also added that the child had a right to be cared for, and that very young parents would find this hard to provide.

Widerstrom advocated sex education in schools and at home, in a natural environment where children could ask and get proper answers. She maintained that if physicians were the only ones providing sex education, then sex might be perceived as something special and strange, which it should not be.

In 1942, the Swedish Government decided it was preferable for pupils in regular schools to receive education on differences between men and women, and about sexual biology and hygiene. However, this was only a recommendation. Sex education did not become mandatory in all compulsory schools until 1956. Over the years, the content and form of the sexuality education program have been widely discussed. In the beginning, the education was mainly technical and biological in nature. This changed in the 1970s, as the emphasis shifted to education in sexuality, relationships, and living together. The curriculum became "softer" and more human.

Today, no one questions that there should be sexuality education in the compulsory schools. The amount of time devoted to this education and its content is very much up to the individual school, and the individual teacher. As elsewhere, some are good and some are even better.

Swedish sexuality education operates on four levels. In general, at the lowest level, education for pupils age 7 to 10 years deals with menstruation, intercourse, self-pleasuring, contraceptives, fertilization, pregnancy, and childbirth. The same topics are dealt with at higher levels, adjusted to the students' age and maturity. At the middle level, ages 10 to 13, added topics include the physical development at puberty, venereal diseases, homosexuality, exhibitionism, and pedophilia. On the upper level, ages 13 to 16, added topics include: petting, different views of sex roles, premarital relations, marriage and family including the views in some non-Christian cultures, abortion, pornography, prostitution, HIV/AIDS and "safer sex," and where to go for further information and advice. On the college level are included sexual desire, with its variations in the orientation and strength, falling in love, sexual problems and dysfunctions, ethical and religious viewpoints on contraception and abortion, societal support for the family (family law), sexual problems of certain immigrant groups, and the problem of world population.

A severe shortcoming is that teachers and physicians encounter almost no education and training in human sexuality within their professional curriculum. One would assume that they would receive this training, considering that they belong to professions that require education and training to teach and inform others.

Unfortunately, one has to admit that despite many years of effort on the part of some educators, the high-placed and idealistic goals set for sex education in the schools have not been reached, even if Sweden is ahead of most other countries.

Youth Clinics

In addition to sex education in the schools, Sweden has about 150 youth clinics. The first opened in the late 1960s mainly because of the many teenage abortions. Following a 1975 law allowing free abortions, the number of youth clinics increased significantly with a focus on preventing abortion by promoting contraceptive use. Other important tasks were to inform young people about STD, HIV, and AIDS prevention.

Youth clinics, headed by a midwife assisted by a gynecologist, psychologist, and social worker, deal with men and women under age 25, with most of the clients being female. The clinics provide one-on-one consultation. A great number of clients obtain contraceptive pills through these clinics. Clinic staff also participate in sex-education programs in the schools.

Some of the female clients are children of immigrant parents who have a more conservative attitude about the equality of the sexes and oppose premarital intercourse. These situations pose new problems for the sex counselors. Resolving clashes between free Swedish sexual morality and other more-restrictive cultural codes is often difficult.

In some circles, both in Sweden and other countries, there was a fear that Sweden's liberal teenage sexuality and free abortion would increase teenage abortion. However, this did not happen. On the contrary, abortions decreased in the decade following enactment of the new law in 1975. This brought about international attention and was interpreted as a result of the Swedish school programs in sex education and the youth clinics. Many other countries then introduced sex education programs modeled on the Swedish approach.

B. Informal Sources of Sexual Knowledge

As in other Western societies, mass media, print, broadcast, and videotape, are important sources of information for Swedes of all ages. Friends seem to be very important for nonadults. Child pornography is the only pornography prohibited by law, but it is still available. In general, pornography seems to be an important educational resource for quite a few Swedes.

4. Autoerotic Behaviors and Patterns

In the Uppsala University study mentioned in Section 2C, about 15 percent of the males and the females said that to engage in self-pleasuring daily is abnormal. To me this indicates that very few find self-pleasuring abnormal unless it is done daily. As with much else in the field of sexuality, people do not talk about self-pleasuring, so little is really known about what they do and what they think.

In the Uppsala study, the median age for first self-pleasuring was about 13 for males and 14 for women. Almost none of the men had not engaged in self-pleasuring during the past year, while as many as 24 percent of the women had not self-pleasured in a year. Almost 70 percent of the men and about 25 percent of the women engaged in autoeroticism at least once a week.

5. Interpersonal Hetereosexual Behaviors

A. Children

No Swedish studies, either attitudinal nor behavioral, have been done on sexual exploration and sex-rehearsal play among children. These natural behaviors are probably more permitted today that half a century ago. But no one talked about this at that time, and very few talk about it now.

B. Adolescents

There are no puberty rituals and never have been to my knowledge. One could argue that Christian confirmation is a sort of passage rite from childhood to adulthood, but given the current lack of church attendance, that seems fully irrelevant now. Quite a few adolescents have a number of periods of going steady and no one waits until marriage for first sexual intercourse. The median age for first sexual intercourse is around 15 years for both boys and girls (Lewin and Helmius 1983).

C. Adults

Premarital Courtship, Dating, and Relationships

To begin, I want to emphasize the inadequacy and prejudicial tone of the term "premarital." The term presupposes the norm or model that everyone should marry, or at least that almost everyone should. And also that not to marry is deviant behavior, or to be more specific, deviant nonbehavior. As will be shown, that concept has not really been an issue in Sweden. Today, with all couples starting with nonmarital cohabitation, their behavior is not "premarital," but just something they do.

Eilert Sundt, a Norwegian minister and one of the first sociologists, studied people's behavior and norms in the mid-nineteenth century. Among other phenomena, he found the system of night courting (*nattfrieri*). In the rural areas, with often long distances between homes, the young man courting a woman would stay overnight in the same bed with her, but he was not allowed to undress or be under the blankets. This way, young persons could get to know quite a few young persons of the other gender (Sundt 1855/1975). Another important system has been, and still is, the dance places, especially during summertime, where one can invite for a dance even a complete stranger.

I would say that in more-modern times, there is no courtship or dating system. People meet at dancing places, not as commonly as previously, and at bars, schools, college, work, or through friends. There is no Swedish term for what in America is labeled dating. It is even hard to find a similar concept in Swedish for what is denoted by the term, dating.

The term "premarital" is somewhat odd. There is really no corresponding Swedish concept. Prior to the mid-1960s, the term was understandable, but no big issue. True, there were norms against premarital sex, but these were mainly ideal rather than behavioral norms, especially during the period of engagement.

During the 1950s and first half of the 1960s, the marriage rate in Sweden was historically at its peak. Suddenly, this rate started dropping rapidly. "Rapidly," in this context, means a decrease of about 50 percent in less than ten years. No other country has experienced such a rapid demographic change. The marriage rate continued its decline until the beginning of the 1980s (Figure 1). This same tendency appears in remarriage statistics for men (Trost 1993a).

Figure 1

Marriage Rates, Sweden, 1959-1991, First Marriages per 1,000 Not Married

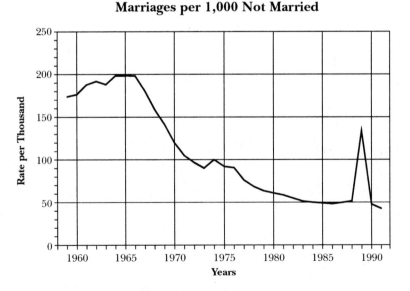

Sources: *Befolkningsförändringar*, different years

What happened in the mid-1960s? Nonmarital cohabitation "under marriage-like conditions" suddenly increased (Figure 2). Cohabitation existed previously, but it was only a very marginal phenomenon (Trost 1979). The data shown in Figure 2 are probably understated, with the actual cohabitation rate more like 25 percent than 20 percent. Cohabitation quickly became a social institution, alongside the old social institution of marriage. One could argue that this change was superficial, and that the relationships are the same, independent of the formal marital status or its absence.

Figure 2

Cohabiting Women in Percentages of All Couples (Married or Not), 1990

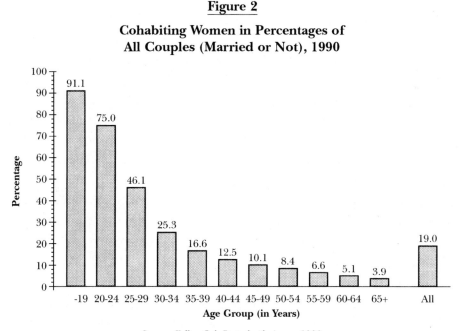

Source: Folk—Och Bostadsräkningen, 1990

When arguing that there is no real change, only a demographic one, I would say that with the Swedish laws and traditions, the dyad constituting the marriage is the same as the dyad constituting the cohabiting couple. The emotional relationships are the same, the quarrels the same, the affection or lack of affection, housing subsidies, child allowance from society, just to mention a few elements, are all the same. The sole difference is the financial arrangements in case of separation/divorce and death of one of the spouses/cohabitants.

However, I would claim that the change here is in some of the norms surrounding marriage and cohabitation. Traditionally in Sweden, as else-where, four elements have been closely connected timewise: (1) the marriage ceremony, (2) moving in together, (3) having sexual intercourse together, and (4) having a first child about a year later.

As mentioned above, the norm against premarital sexual intercourse has never been more than an ideal norm in Sweden. Everyone has always known that Swedish couples had sex together before marriage, only usually no one talked about it. The social change that has occurred since the 1960s is that the four elements are now fully separated. Couples move in together without any ceremony, they have sex independent of the other three elements, and quite a few have children without being married. About half of all Swedish children are born to not-married mothers who are cohabiting with the fathers of the children.

This, in turn, means more than might be imagined at first sight. The social institution of the marriage ceremony has changed. Quite a few couples still marry, but the marriage does not move the couple from one situation to another; they are already living together. Today, Swedish couples do not marry and move in together at the same time; couples who marry have already cohabited as a couple. Some couples believe that a marriage ceremony will change their situation, but it changes nothing for them. For most couples, the marriage ceremony is a true ceremony, and still a sort of rite, not a passage rite but a confirmation rite. The marrying couple do not pass over to a different situation or stage, but rather confirm their relationship and its stability for themselves and for the surrounding social community.

Traditionally, prior to marriage, the couple would become engaged to be married. In Sweden, the engagement event was also a passage rite. The couple showed themselves and others that they were a serious couple. Engagement did not mean that they had decided when to marry, but just that they would marry some time in the future. Often relatives and friends would celebrate the engagement by attending a dinner party and giving the couple gifts for their future home.

Nowadays, quite a few cohabiting couples announce their engagement. However, I have never heard of any couple announcing their engagement before they started cohabiting. The Swedish term for engagement, *förlovning*, literally means a prepromise; the couple promise to marry each other. Today, for most Swedish couples, the term has no connection with marriage. For most couples, what happens is that when they mutually fall in love, they just move in together. After some time, months or years, if they are still cohabiting, they might announce their engagement, their intention to continue as a couple. Eventually, they might also marry, in which case, the marriage means about the same as the engagement, but is a little more serious.

Obviously, more studies are needed of these terms and concepts and their various meanings for people, both for those personally involved, and for the social community.

Sexual Behavior and Single Adults

To my knowledge, no studies of single adults and their sexual behavior can be found in Sweden. What should be remembered, however, is that quite a few of those who are officially classified as singles, and even as living in a one-person household, very often are, one way or another, living in a dyadic relationship. Here I refer to those who are nonmaritally cohabiting, but who are classified, for a number of reasons, as living alone. I also refer to what is nowadays called LAT (living alone together), couples living apart in separate households, but still together as a couple. These dyadic relationships seem to be increasing gradually (Trost 1993b).

Marriage and the Family

The marriage and family structure in Sweden has, as far as is known, always consisted of the nuclear family as an ideal base. Heterosexual couples have married, or the equivalent, and had children. Divorce was almost nonexistent by law, as well as in reality. The number of children averaged around 4.5 per couple. The extended family has never been a Swedish social institution. In rural areas, the son took over the farm after buying out his parents with a contract that gave them a small cottage and paid them in kind until they died. The fertility rate decreased during the last part of the nineteenth century and the first decades of the twentieth century. For a long time, the ideal number of children in Sweden has been between two and three children. The real fertility rate has, for a couple of decades, fluctuated between a total fertility rate (TFR) of 1.6 and 2.1.

The new matrimonial law in effect since 1921 made divorce easier. The divorce rates started increasing during the first decade of this century, and went on increasing until 1950, when they leveled off, till 1966, when the rate again started to rise. The divorce rate has continued increasing, if analyzed carefully, until the last couple of years.

Extradyadic Sex

Nothing is known about the prevalence or incidence of extradyadic sex among Swedes. The sole study where there is some relatively reliable data is from 1967 (*Om Sexuallivet i Sverige* 1969). In this study, about 4 percent of the married persons surveyed had had at least two sexual partners in the previous year, one of which had to be extradyadic. What changes have occurred in the past quarter century is not known. However, the attitudes toward extradyadic sex have not changed as far as we can see, with about 95 percent still negative toward it.

Divorce and Remarriage

Most of those who separate or divorce from a cohabiting relationship soon start a new relationship, a remarriage, a recohabitation, or however one might label it. In 1800 and 1990, the proportion of marriages that were not first marriages was approximately 25 percent. The important difference is that two centuries ago, all remarriages involved a widow or widower. Today, almost all remarriages follow a divorce, meaning that both former spouses are still alive to remarry. Between 1800 and 1990, there was a definite decrease in mortality rates and longer life expectancy, leaving fewer widowed seeking new mates. Heavy emigration at the end of the last century and the beginning of this century also reduced the number of adults remarrying. At the same time, a rise in the divorce rate increased the number of second and subsequent marriages. In the end, the result has been a relatively stable 25 percent of all marriages involving second or subsequent remarriages (Figure 3).

Figure 3

Marriages Where Both Partners Were Never Married, Sweden, in Percentages

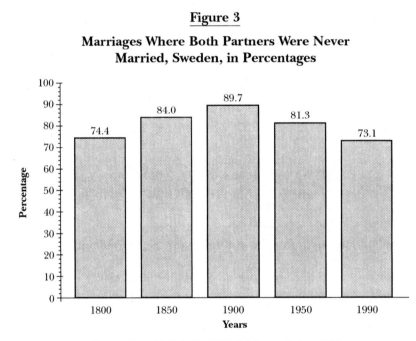

Sources: Historisk Statistik, 1967, Befolkningsrörelsen, 1990

Plural marriages (polygamy) are not legally recognized by law or in reality.

Sexuality and the Physically Disabled and Aged

Sweden has pioneered in sex education for physically handicapped youth, and in training personnel working with them in institutions.

The first Nordic conference on sex and the handicapped was hosted by The Swedish Central Committee for Rehabilitation in Stockholm in 1969. An elected committee of five experts subsequently planned and provided both training for professionals in sexology and education for the disabled. This commission worked for the next ten years, arranging several seminars and courses, carrying on research, and publishing many reports and books about their work.

Students with physical handicaps get the same sex education as others in the Swedish schools. To help handicapped youths visualize love and sex between two disabled persons and between a handicapped and able-bodied person, an educational film/video, *Sex and the Handicapped*, was produced. It has been shown all over the world.

Between 1992 and 1994, a new project, Sexology and the Handicapped, was funded by the Swedish government to do research in the field and provide further training in sexology for personnel working with handicapped persons.

There are no studies on frequencies, occurrences, or varieties of sexual behaviors among the disabled or elderly. While the sexual needs of the disabled and older persons have received more attention in Sweden than in other countries, these phenomena are more often not talked about. There still is a prevailing public attitude that old people have left sex behind and that the disabled should be glad they are alive. Very ambitious attempts at changing this situation are being made by the Swedish association for the disabled, which is raising the issues for both medical personnel and the disabled themselves.

Incidence of Oral and Anal Sex

In the Uppsala study mentioned earlier, 10 percent of the 19- to 23-year-old male students, and almost 20 percent of the women, have had anal sex. In most cases, this appears to be an incidental or occasional experimentation rather than a reoccurring experience.

As for fellatio, about 20 percent of the young women and a third of the men have never experienced it. About 40 percent of the women and 30 percent of the men have practiced fellatio more often than monthly during the past year. The occurrence of cunnilingus shows a very similar picture.

As far as I know, there are no studies about Swedish attitudes about anal sex, fellatio, and cunnilingus—people just don't talk about these behaviors. There are no legal restrictions on what sexual outlets couples or individuals practice, as long as they are mutually voluntary and harmless.

6. Homoerotic, Homosexual, and Ambisexual Behaviors

The state Lutheran Church keeps a low profile on homosexuality, as do most of the other churches and congregations. They are not in favor of varieties other than heterosexuality, and could be interpreted as being negative at least to homosexual behavior, if not to the homosexual inclination—to be homosexual does not mean to behave accordingly.

Almost no Swede would dare to say anything negative about homosexuality or same-gender couples in the mass media or otherwise more or less openly. But all homosexuals easily and often experience hidden and/or open discrimination. The law discriminated between same- and opposite-gender sexuality until the mid-1970s. It was, for instance, illegal for an adult man to have sex with a woman younger than 15 and with another man younger than 18. There was an unspoken presumption that adult women would not have sex with a boy younger than 15. Today, the law is clear in treating males and females equally, and not discriminating by age and gender between same- and opposite-gender relationships.

In Denmark, since October 1, 1989, same-gender couples can register their partnerships. This means that the laws applicable to married couples automatically apply also to these registered couples. Two differences remain. Same-gender couples cannot adopt a child jointly, and if one has a child, the partner cannot adopt the child and become its legal parent along with the natural parent. And there is no official, legal ceremony, or ritual attached to civil registration of same-gender relationships as there is in the marriage of opposite-gender couples. Norway adopted the same law on August 1, 1993. At the time of this writing, it appears that Sweden will follow, enacting the same law during the United Nations Year of the Family in 1994.

The experience in Denmark is that relatively few same-gender couples have registered, a few hundred in all, the majority of whom being male couples. The law has not apparently changed the social attitudes in the general population.

However, in Sweden, since the mid-1960s, many homosexuals and their organizations have been arguing for the right to marry. Sweden was first in taking a step in that direction by putting cohabitation of same-gender couples on a par with cohabiting opposite-gender couples. The 1987 law provides that in the case of separating same- or opposite-gender couples, the partner most in need of the apartment or house has the right to remain in it, even if the lease, deed, or title is written in the other cohabitant's name. The law also states that what the couple have accumulated for common usage in their household should be divided equally in case of death or separation, independent of which cohabitant actually paid for the item.

Riksförbundet för Sexuelit Likaberättigande (RFSL), founded in 1950, is a non-profit organization working for gay and lesbian rights. A special HIV department in RFSL receives economic support from the government for their preventative measures.

7. Gender Conflicted Persons

Transvestites have no special legal status, but since neither they nor society looks on them as deviant or sick, there is and should be no treatment. Many transvestites are members of a chapter of Full Personality Expression (FPE), an international organization for cross-gendered persons. FPE holds monthly meetings and maintains an open house for members, as well as for other interested persons in Stockholm.

By law, transsexuals can and also, in practice, do change their sex, after following a standard course of long observation and treatment by psychiatrists. Following gender reassignment, all legal documents are changed to match the new sex. Estimates suggest that about half of those who sincerely want to change their sex follow through and are allowed to have the operation. Less than a dozen operations are performed annually in Sweden.

8. Significant Unconventional Sexual Behaviors

A. Coercive Sex

Sexual Abuse and Incest

No one knows how frequent child sexual abuse or incest is. It occurs, and a certain number of cases are made known to the police. Of course, there are many more cases than those reported. However, in 1992, only 100 persons were sentenced for incest or for sexual activities with a minor. In the same year, 105 persons were sentenced for child sexual abuse and another 251 for having touched minors sexually.

The sentences for these crimes vary, with a maximum of four years imprisonment for incestuous abuse. Conviction for sexual touching of a minor can bring a sentence of up to one year's imprisonment. If these crimes are severe, the penalty can be up to eight years. These sentences are applied only if physical force or psychological coercion has not been used. If force has been used, the laws for rape are applied.

Sexual Harassment

In Sweden, as in so many other countries, sexual harassment is a new concept, even though the phenomenon is old. Studies made at universities indicate that between 10 percent and 25 percent of female students say they have been sexually harassed. Very few cases are reported. Businesses and schools have not developed any official policies to define and set policies for reporting sexual harassment. However, there is a growing awareness of sexual harassment issues among the people.

Rape

In Sweden, as elsewhere, most cases of rape are never reported and no one knows how frequent they are. It is known that among those rapes reported, most are perpetrated by a person known and trusted by the victim. In 1965, 1,565 cases of rape were reported to the police, and 203 perpetrators were sentenced to imprisonment.

The law differentiates between four types or degrees of rape or sexual assault. The most severe is what could be called flagrant rape or *grov våldtäki*, involving violence and dangerous use of physical force; conviction can bring four to ten years imprisonment. A second type of sexual assault is simple rape (*våldta-ki*), with the penalty ranging from two to six years imprisonment. Sexual force, or *sexuellt tvång*, is not defined as rape, although it involves forced sexual intercourse without the use of violence or threat of violence; the penalty can be up to four years in prison. Finally, there is sexual abuse, or *sexuellt utnyttjande,* in which the perpetrator abuses his or her position of power, authority, or guardianship.

B. Prostitution

Prostitution is prevalent in the centers of the three largest Swedish cities: Stockholm, Gothenburg, and Malmo. Contacts with prostitutes can be made at bars all over the country, but these places are not directly linked with prostitution. Pimping is forbidden and conviction can result in up to four years imprisonment, up to six years, if the case is severe. Very seldom is anyone reported for pimping, and almost never is anyone sentenced.

The police seldom ever take action against prostitutes and their customers, as so often occurs in some other countries. Sweden does not have as many influential moralists with double standards as are found in some other countries.

C. Pornography and Erotica

The production, display, and sale of pornography are permitted unless children are involved in one way or another. Distasteful displays of pornography are not permitted, and involvement of a minor can bring a fine and maximum sentence of six months imprisonment. Very few cases are reported to the police for prosecution. Pornography and erotica are readily available at tobacconists, video stores, and many other places.

9. Contraception, Abortion, and Population Planning

A. Contraception

Sex education, as mentioned above, has a long history in the compulsory schools. This is matched by the availability of, advertisement of, and information on condoms and other contraceptives. Vending machines for condoms can be found in hotels, bars, restaurants, and elsewhere, even at some bus stops on the street. All gas stations, groceries, supermarkets, and tobacconists openly sell condoms and often display them at the counter. Midwives and physicians prescribe contraceptive pills and fit IUDs. Male and female sterilization is free of charge upon request if the person is over age 25.

B. Teenage Unmarried Pregnancies

It should be clear from the discussion of marriage and cohabitation rates above that almost no Swedish teenagers are married. This means that almost all pregnant teenage women are not married. Quite a few of them are cohabiting; how many is not known. About 3 percent of all children born in 1991 were born to mothers younger than 20. As is usually the case, it is not known how old the fathers were. Only about 15 percent of these mothers were married, thus less than a half percent of all children were born to a married teenage mother. The total fertility rate (TFR) for girls 15 to 19 years of age was 13.1, compared with a TFR of 154.1 for women 25 to 29 years of age.

In 1991, there were 3,564 children born to teenage mothers and 6,152 abortions performed on teenagers. Thus, about two thirds of the teenage pregnancies end with an induced abortion.

C. Abortion

Prior to 1939, abortion was illegal in Sweden. In 1939, the law was changed to allow abortion under certain conditions and for specific reasons. Grounds for legal abortion were connected to the eugenic ideas popular in the Western world at that time. In Sweden, as elsewhere, there was an effort to keep the national stock pure and good. Gradually, the perspective changed, more grounds were added, and the law became more liberal. A 1975 law reform gives the woman the right to a legal abortion upon request until the end of the eighteenth week of gestation, without any costs to her.

Prior to the early 1970s, Sweden had an unknown number of illegal abortions and relatively few legal abortions. Estimates of illegally induced abortions during the 1950s range from 10,000 to 100,000 per year; about 5,000 legal abortion were done annually in this era. Now, illegal abortions are nonexistent because the cost of an abortion is covered by national health insurance, and no one other than the pregnant woman has to be involved in the decision, even if the pregnant woman is a minor.

In 1991, the total abortion rate (TAR) was 615.3 (see Figure 4). The specific age rates vary, although the younger the age group, the higher is the abortion rate for women older than 19 years. Since 1975, the TAR has been fairly stable. Since coital activities vary more among teenagers than among older women, the abortion data for teens needs to be considered separately. For 15- to 17-year-olds, the abortion rate has decreased; for older teens, it has remained fairly stable over the years since 1975. The 1975 rates were approximately 16 per 1,000 girls age 15, 29 for girls age 16, and 33 for girls age 17; in 1991, these figures were 9, 17, and 21, respectively, with lows in all groups in 1983-85 of about 7, 12, and 18, and highs in 1988-90 of about 10, 19, and 25, respectively. For older teens, the 1975 rates were approximately 33 per 1,000 girls age 18 and 31 for girls age 19; in 1991, the rates were 28 and 33, respectively, with lows in 1983-85 of about 23 and 26, and highs in 1988-90 of about 31 and 34, respectively.

D. Population Control Efforts

At the end of the nineteenth century, the fertility rate started on a decline that went on until the mid-1930s. By the mid-1930s, the birthrate was below

Figure 4

Abortion Rates in Sweden, 1939-1992, per 1,000 Women Aged 15-44

Sources: Aborter, various volumes

replacement level, and some politicians and others were concerned about the risks of immigration overwhelming ethnic Swedes. During the 1940s, Sweden provided housing subsidies to poor households with minor children, government allowances for all mothers with a child under age 16, and other pronatal incentives. But even before these measures were enacted, the postwar baby boom came with its peak in 1946-47.

When the fertility rate again came to a historic low in the 1960s and especially the 1970s, some politicians and demographers became emotionally concerned and involved. Discussions about new ways to make society more "child friendly" became popular. But the political decisions were hidden behind the mask of social welfare. Since the Nazis were defeated in 1945, very few Swedes have dared to admit being pronatalists.

In modern times, there have been no attempts to reduce the population, unless one counts the discussions about immigration policy as an issue in population growth.

10. Sexually Transmitted Diseases

A. Incidence and Trends

The previously most feared STD, syphilis, is now comparatively rare, dropping from 153 new cases in 1985 to 121 new cases reported in 1991.

Gonorrhea has also decreased, from 5,389 new cases in 1985 to only 617 cases in 1991. Two thirds of these STDs occur in men.

In Sweden, chlamydia was not recognized until recently as an STD. After apparently peaking in 1990 at over 21,000 new cases, a decreasing trend seems to have arrived. Most cases of chlamydia occur in persons under age 30, with two thirds of reported cases detected in females.

Trichomonas, herpes, candida, condyloma, and other diseases are not classified as STDs, and reporting by treating physicians is not required. Thus, no data are available for these infections.

B. Treatment and Prevention Efforts

Treatment for all sexual infections are available free of charge or with only a nominal fee. Propaganda for condom use has traditionally been based on preventing unwanted pregnancies, contrary to the connection made in continental Europe and North America, where condom use has been promoted for prophylactic disease prevention. Swedish propaganda now includes prophylactic use.

Changes in the frequencies of the various STDs suggest a variety of factors. Decreases in gonorrhea and syphilis are connected both with more efficient treatment and increased education about condom use and about the risks of these diseases. The rise in chlamydia in the late 1980s is explained in part by the increased use of the contraceptive pill as an efficient protection against pregnancy and its lack of protection against STDs. The recent decrease in chlamydia is due to increased education and STD prevention.

11. HIV/AIDS

A. Incidence, Patterns, and Trends

According to mid-1993 estimates, Sweden has between 3,000 and 4,000 persons with HIV infection. Each year 300 to 400 new cases have been reported. About 150 persons with HIV convert to full-blown AIDS, according to estimates from 1990 to the present. About 60 percent of the HIV-positive persons are between ages 25 and 39.

B. Treatment, Prevention Programs, and Government Policies

Distribution of free syringes and condoms, more rigorous blood tests for blood donors and transfusions, and increased information and education on safer sex are being used to limit the spread of HIV and other sexually transmitted diseases. Local and national governments strongly support prevention, research, and treatment efforts, both to prevent further spread and to find a cure.

12. *Sexual Dysfunctions, Counseling, and Therapies*

A/B. Concepts of Sexual Dysfunction and Availability of Therapy

Swedish sex therapists, of which there are not many, work with both couples and individuals, using the techniques of the American pioneers William Masters and Virginia Johnson. Some therapists supplement this approach with the psychodynamic methods of Helen Singer Kaplan. The therapists are mostly licensed medical doctors or psychologists with postgraduate training in sex therapy in Sweden, Denmark, or the U.S.A.

Most couples seeking sex therapy are in their 30s and 40s and have had their problems even before they married. Sex therapy is generally short-term therapy, lasting between ten and twenty hours. In many cases, a combination of sex therapy and psychotherapy is needed, because the sexual problem often has its roots in a deeper and broader personality dysfunction that goes back to childhood. Such cases require more intensive, long-term individual therapy.

Treatment is generally not covered by insurance, and most patients have to cover all costs themselves.

13. *Research and Advanced Education*

A/B. Sexological Research and Postgraduate Education

The best known sexological research units can be found at various departments at Swedish universities: University of Gothenburg, Department of Psychology; Umeå University, Department of Rehabilitation; and Uppsala University, the Neurology and Sociology Departments.

Postcollege, graduate-level programs for the advanced study of human sexuality do not exist as programs. At the above-mentioned university departments, regular doctoral degrees are offered within the speciality of sexology.

C. Important Sexological Organizations

The Swedish Sexological Association was established in 1980 with Jan Trost as its first president. At that time the intention was to have an association consisting of members actively working in the scientific field of sexology in various disciplines. Subsequently, the association has changed to a professional organization whose members work clinically with matters related to sexuality, including physicians, psychologists, and contraception counselors.

The address for the Swedish Sexological Association is: c/o Lars-Gösta Dahlström, Gothenburg University, Department of Psychology, P. O. Box 14158, S-400 20 Gothenburg, Sweden.

The Swedish Institute for Sexual Research is based in Stockholm. Director: Mai-Briht Bergstrom-Walan. Address: Tystbergavagen 41, S-111 44 Stockholm, Sweden.

Riksförbundet för Sexuell Upplysning (RFSU), founded in 1933, is a not-for-profit organization working for safe and liberal sex, safe in terms of preventing STDs, unwanted pregnancies, and sexual assaults of all kinds. The address for RFSU is: Rosenlundsgatan 13, S-104 62 Stockholm, Sweden. Or: P. O. Box 17006, S-104 62 Stockholm, Sweden.

Riksförbundet för Sexuelit Likaberäattigande (RFSL), a gay and lesbian education and rights advocacy group, is based at: Stockholms Gay-hus. Sveavägen 57, S-104 30 Stockhom, Sweden. Or: P.O. Box 350, S-101 24 Stockholm, Sweden.

In 1967, a government commission conducted a probability sample survey of about 2,000 men and women aged 18 to 60 years. The interviews, with 90 percent response, dealt with perception of sexual norms, attitudes, and behavior. Details were published by *Statens Offentliga Utredningar (SOU)* (Stockholm), 1969:2.

Nordic Sexology (Nordisk Sexologi) is published quarterly. Publisher's address: Soren Buss Jensen, M.D., Aalborg Psykiatriske Sygehus, Postboks 210, DK-9100 Aalborg, Denmark. Or: Dansk Psykologisk Forlag, Hans Knudsens Plads 1 a. DK-2100 Copenhagen, Denmark.

References and Suggested Readings

Carlson, Lizzie. 1965. *Jag Giver Dig Min Dotter.* Stockholm: Nerenius & Santerus.

Lewin, Bo. 1991. *Att Omplantera Sexualieten.* Uppsala: Uppsala Universitet.

Lewin, Bo. 1987. *Att se Sexualiteten: Om Sexuell Socialisation, Förhållnigssätt och Sexuella Erfarenheter Bland Människor med Medfödda Funktionshinder.* Uppsala: Uppsala Universitet.

Lewin Bo, and Gisela Helmius. 1983. *Ungdom och Sexualitet.* Uppsala: Uppsala Universitet.

Manniche, Erik. 1989. *The Family in Denmark.* Uppsala: Uppsala Universitet.

Månsson, S.-A. 1993. *Cultural Conflict and the Swedish Sexual Myth: The Male Immigrant's Encounter with Swedish Sexual and Cohabitation Culture.* Westport, CT: Greenwood Publishers.

Nordqvist, I., ed. 1972. *Life Together: The Situation of the Handicapped.* Stockholm: Swedish Central Committee for Rehabilitation.

Nordqvist, I., ed. 1984. *Sexualitet, Handikapp, Terapi.* Stockholm: Handikappinstitutet.

Om Sexuallivet i Sverige. 1969. Stockholm: Statens Offentliga Utredningar (SOU).

Rodman, Hyman, and Jan Trost. 1986. *The Adolescent Dilemma.* New York: Praeger.

Statistical Yearbook of Sweden. 1993.

Sundt, Eilert. 1855/1975. *Om Giftermaal i Norge.* Oslo: Gyldendal Norsk Förlag.

Trost, Anne-Christine. 1982. *Abort och Psykiska Besvär.* Västerås: International Library.

Trost, Jan. 1979. *Unmarried Cohabitation.* Västerås: International Library.

Trost, Jan. 1988. *Sexologisk Ordbok.* Uppsala: Uppsala Universitet.

Trost, Jan. 1993a. *Familjen i Sverige.* Family Systems in Sweden. Stockholm: Liber. In press.

Trost, Jan. 1993b. "Family from a Dyadic Perspective." *Journal of Family Issues,* 14:92-104.

Thailand
(*Muang Thai*)

Kittiwut Jod Taywaditep, M.D., M.A., Eli Coleman, Ph.D.,
and Pacharin Dumronggittigule, M.Sc.

Contents

Demographics and a Historical Perspective

A. Demographics

Thailand, formerly known as Siam, is a kingdom with a population of approximately 60 million located in southeast Asia. The total area of Thailand is 512,997 square kilometers. The capital, Bangkok, situated in the central region, is also the largest city, with a population of 7.8 million. Thailand is bordered on the north and west by Myanmar (formerly Burma), on the north and east across the Mekong River by Laos, on the southeast by Kampuchea (Cambodia), and on the south by Malaysia.

Thailand has a very young population with 45 percent of its people under age 14, 49 percent between age 15 and 59, and 6 percent over 60 years old.

Approximately 70 percent live in rural areas and small villages. Life expectancy at birth in 1995 was 66 for men and 71 for women. In 1991, the birthrate was 20 per 1,000, while the death rate was 7 per 1,000, with a 1.3 percent natural annual increase. By 1995, the population growth rate had further slowed to 1.1 percent with a birthrate of 19 per 1,000 and a death rate of 6 per 1,000. Infant mortality is 36 per 1,000 live births. The rate of literacy is 96 percent for men and 90 percent for women, with 96 percent attending six years of compulsory education. Ethnically, 75 percent of the population is Thai, 14 percent Chinese, and 11 percent other. Thailand has one hospital bed per 604 persons, and one physician per 4,327 persons. The per capita domestic product in 1995 was $5,500 U.S.

The chief language of Thailand is Thai, one of the 40 or so languages in the Tai family found in Thailand, Laos, North Vietnam, and parts of China (Crystal 1987). Among a number of languages previously spoken in this region, the Thai language, or Siamese Tai, became the language of administration and prestige in the late twelfth century, with its script invented in 1283 (Wyatt 1984). Today, the regional dialects are also spoken in Thailand, as well as Lao, Chinese, and Malay. English is taught in schools and colleges and is also used in academia, commerce, and government.

B. A Brief Historical Perspective

Historians have hypothesized that Thai (or "Tai") people began migrating from southern China to the central portion of the Indochinese peninsula in the sixth century. Over the centuries, the Thai identity has emerged from the interaction between these Tai people, later immigrants, and the indigenous inhabitants of this region, namely the Mon and Khmer (Wyatt 1984). Following the Burmese destruction of their previous Ayudhya kingdom in 1767, Thai people rose from the ruins with an astonishing vigor. The kingdom of Siam was reconstituted within a few years by combining other principalities and kingdoms (e.g., Chiangmai and Khorat), thereby expanding its territories to include a number of distinct civilizations and peoples in the Indochinese region. The new capital, Bangkok, was established on the bank of the Chaophraya River in 1782, with walls and buildings built from thousands of boatloads of bricks taken from the ruins of Ayudhya. In the new city of shining monasteries and a new royal palace, with bustling canals crisscrossing the city instead of roads, the intermingling of classes, cultures, and ethnicities in the early Bangkok Empire has been vividly depicted by David Wyatt:

> [The] princes and officials constructed homes along the network of canals radiating eastward from the palace and Chinese and Indian merchants built their shops and warehouses along the river to the south. . . . [Outside the main walls of the city,] . . . the Chams attached to the army; there are a group of Malays who manned naval vessels, clustered

around an Islamic house of worship; north of the city, [there was] a settlement of Roman Catholics descended from Portuguese and Japanese Christians. (1984, p. 146)

Thailand has been independent during most of its history, except for a few relatively brief periods of occupation by Burma or the Japanese military. This long-term independence has allowed for a very distinct blend of cultures to thrive over many centuries. Thailand is also the only country in Southeast Asia never taken over by a European power, thanks in part to King Chulalongkorn and his son, King Mongkut, who modernized the country and signed trade agreements with both Britain and France in the late nineteenth century and early twentieth century. The kingdom's name was changed from Siam to Thailand in 1939 during a politically tumultuous time. Reflecting the nationalistic attempt to revise the country's ethnic identity, the new name had a linguistic kinship with Thai-speaking peoples in the periphery of the kingdom, therefore downplaying the powers of the central Siamese people and the Chinese who began to gain economic significance (Wyatt 1984).

The absolute monarchy transferred power to the politicians and the military in a bloodless revolution in 1932, although the monarchy is still held in very high regard in the present Thai society. Thailand considers itself a democratic nation; however, corruption, multiple coups, and the tremendous influence of the military in politics have led journalists to ridicule the nation's democratic system as "half-democracy." After the mid-1992 bloody uprising against the military's longstanding influence in the House of Representatives, the role of the military in politics has been under scrutiny more than ever.

C. Thai Language, Sex Research, and Resources

The Thai Language

In this chapter, romanization of Thai words is adapted from the Thai Royal Academy's system, with the goal of approximating the original pronunciation (without the intonation) while maintaining the readability of the text for readers unfamiliar with the transliteration system. In general, the spelling of Sanskrit-, Pali-, or English-derived vocabulary prefers the reflection of its Thai pronunciation over the etymological origin. Aspirated consonants *p*, *t*, and *k* are represented by *ph*, *th*, and *kh*. For example, *phii* is pronounced "pee," not "fee," and the *th*, as in *kathoey*, is pronounced as the *t* in the words "to" or "ten," not as the *th* in "than" or "think." Proper nouns are represented in romanization with an initial capital letter. Romanization of personal names follows the individual's preference or the spelling in English-language print, and ranks or degrees are, with few exceptions, omitted. In order to facilitate literature searches on an international level, papers and quotations by Thai authors are referred to by their last names, not first names as is common in Thailand.

Gender/Sexuality Studies

Systematic studies of gender and sexuality in Thailand are relatively new. Mostly spurred by the HIV epidemic, the majority of data on sexual behavior was collected in the early 1990s in response to the public health demands. Although considerable data have been generated, critics have pointed out that synthesis on a conceptual level is still needed. Also missing is the documentation of the ancient sexuality in this region, which would have provided a historiographic insight into the dynamics of the Thai sexuality over time. Exchange of findings and discourse among researchers are also hindered to a certain degree by the less-established avenues for publication and presentation. Many papers appear only in local academic bulletins or conferences, whereas others are published in international journals.

Resources

In writing this chapter, we relied primarily on two sources: the published papers and presentations, which provided most of the reviewed empirical data, and the analysis and interpretation of the cultural phenomena in Thailand. Although our analysis of some Thai social constructions and themes (e.g., gender roles and sexual norms) may not represent a consensus, we nevertheless try to present the converged opinions among researchers and observers whom we have worked with over the years. Finally, it is important to bear in mind that what is known about gender and sexuality in Thailand is changing rapidly, and this review summarizes formal and informal observations in Thai society up until early 1997.

1. Basic Sexological Premises

A. The Ideal Gender Images: *Kulasatrii* and *Chaai Chaatrii*

The Ideal Thai Woman

There is not much question that Thailand is a male-dominated, patriarchal society, as political and corporate leadership has always been in the hands of men. On the other hand, the power of Thai women, especially in rural societies, lies in their domestic role as the mother-nurturer (see Keyes 1985; and the discussion in Section 2A). Women in Thailand look up to the role of motherhood as an ideal. A woman's status changes to adulthood at the point of her childbirth, after which she is recognized semi-formally as *mae* or "mother" (Keyes 1984; Pyne 1994). In fact, the preparation for this "mother" title takes place informally much earlier, as young girls or unmarried women are often titled *mae* with an endearing or humorous tone. Thai men refer to the female gender with a sense of reverence as "the gender of mothers" (*phayt mae*), acknowledging women's burden in childbearing and parenting responsibilities. The ultimate insult for Thai men is *yet mae*, which literally translates to "motherfucker" in English, indicating the utmost respect that mothers have in Thai culture.

Regarding the nurturer role, women's specialization in economic-type occupations illustrates their powerful role in providing for the well-being of their families. Women's dedication to nurturance is evident in the expression that a good woman "wakes up earlier and goes to sleep later than her husband." The variety and extent of women's nurturing responsibilities are superbly illustrated in two studies in two vastly different contexts: Penny Van Esterik (1982) depicts the household and religious responsibilities of well-to-do women in western central Thailand; Susanne Thorbek (1988) details the endless household duties of the slum-dwelling women in Khlong Toey, Bangkok. Since the economic climate changed in the 1960s and 1970s, women have accounted for almost half, and sometimes more than half, of the large number of rural Thais who migrate to the cities in order to augment the family income (Keyes 1984). Today, women account for 80 percent of total employment in the ten largest export industries, and 45 percent of the manufacturing work force (data cited in Pyne 1994). Over the years, Thai women have made significant contributions in the arts, education, and commerce. With higher education, women have also risen to leadership positions in the middle class. The "glass ceiling" exists for women in the academic and corporate settings, as evident in the fact that, although there are many women in high positions, the topmost position of an organization still belongs to a man. Nevertheless, aside from the obvious underrepresentation in areas such as the military, law enforcement, and religion, the status of women in Thailand is perhaps higher than other countries in Asia with the exception of Singapore. For more-extensive discussions on the gender division of labor, as well as the impact of the rapid socioeconomic changes in recent decades, the reader is referred to the work by Kirsch (1982) and Hnin Hnin Pyne (1994).

The mother-nurturer role is also idealized in the female code of social and sexual conduct. Historically, the Thai tradition has defined a *kulasatrii* ("virtuous woman") as proficient and sophisticated in household duties; graceful, pleasant, yet unassuming in her appearance and social manners; and conservative in her sexuality. These features bear striking similarities to the traditional "feminine mystique" in other cultures which has come under the criticism of the Western feminist movement. However, the concept of *kulasatrii* has not been overtly discussed in terms of gender inequality or subordination in Thailand. There has been little dialogue devoted to whether the *kulasatrii* role has been restrictive or unjust to Thai women. On the contrary, most contemporary Thai women wholeheartedly endorse the *kulasatrii* notion without resentment, regarding it as a sign of dignity and honor, a sense of cultural identity in which they can take pride. In school, girls are taught what it means to be a *kulasatrii*, while celebrity figures constantly praise its value in the media. As more and more contemporary women work outside of their homes, the ideal image of a *kulasatrii* remains a goal for which a woman must strive, while simultaneously attempting to fulfill new responsibilities necessitated by the changing society.

The Ideal Thai Man

There are two ideal male images available for Thai men. Corresponding to the Buddha's biography, Thai men face the recluse/householder or monastic/secular dichotomy (P. Van Esterik 1982). The monastic-recluse image, personified by the Buddha's life, is the *Sangha*. Through monastic discipline and practice of the *dharma*, monks not only eschew worldly attachments, but also their sexuality and male gender characteristics. On the other hand, the secular male image is represented by the notion of *chaai chaatrii*, which is an embodiment of the typical masculine features also found in other cultures: authority, courage, self-assurance, physical and emotional strengths, and sexual prowess. Various expressions for manhood and manliness reflect an image of a vigorous and muscular warrior: *chaai chaat tha-haan* (referring to the soldier), *chaai ok saam sok* (the muscular chest), *chaai chaat acha-nai* (the stallion's stamina and perhaps muscularity), and *chaai cha-kan* (strength and vigor). In older men, these youth-typical physical features are de-emphasized as other characteristics become more salient, such as bravery, wisdom, and power (in either political, social, or metaphysical spheres). Nurturance is another ideal dimension in men, as exemplified in the image of a prestigious older man, *pho liang*, who earns respect from his community from his resourcefulness and generous contributions. Traditionally, powerful men and politicians in Thai society have always been expected to exhibit this nurturing trait, perhaps modeled after the paternalism of the Siamese kings since the beginning of the kingdom (Kirsch 1985).

The masculine attributes in the *chaai chaatrii* image have found behavioral expression in the image of a *nug layng*. Translated to a midway between "playboy" and "gangster" in English, the term portrays a powerful man of action who works hard and plays equally hard, is supportive of his friends, fierce to his foes, and also a great womanizer (Thorbek 1988). Although popularized and personified by the Prime Minister, Sarit Thanarat, in the late 1950s and early 1960s, the image was hardly a new social construction of the male image. Like Sarit's political ideology, which "exaggerated traditional values and institutions, buttressing social and political hierarchy at the expense of egalitarianism and even human rights" (Wyatt 1984, p. 285), his *nug layng* image was simply a paragon of the traditional Thai male role. Sarit excelled in this role in both politics and private life. While known for his emphasis on cleanliness and orderliness and his harsh measures against crimes, Sarit was also notorious for the number of mistresses he kept, which was somewhere between fifty and two hundred

(Thorbek 1984). Certainly Sarit was not alone in this interpretation of manliness. Over the years, the secular image of Thai men had drifted even further away into the realm of worldly activities and became the antithesis of the *Sangha*. Manliness has become associated with almost every behavior considered by the Thai culture as vices: smoking, drinking, gambling, womanizing, commercial sex, minor wives, public brawls, petty crimes, and corruption, and the list goes on.

Despite such undesirable associations, the code of masculinity has maintained its prestige in Thai society for a long time. Its prestige has only recently has been challenged after one of the male vices—commercial sex—was implicated for the spread of HIV. In part, the Theravada view that ordination is always an option for men (see Section 2 below) could probably account for the longstanding tolerance toward male vices. Further, the ultimate financial control in the households has usually been in the men's hands, therefore, allowing them to foot the expenses from these vices. Another mechanism also helps prevent any violation of the male role prescriptions: secular men who do not participate in these male vices are often labeled by other men with a number of emasculating terms, such as "not a genuine man," a *kathoey* (see Section 7), or *naa tua mia* ("the female face"). The male image's drift away from the religious ideal is best illustrated in the use of the term *tid*. Abbreviated from the Pali term *pandit* and once granted to a layman who had passed through the monkhood and held knowledge of the Buddhist teachings, *tid* has become a term of derision for "a clumsy [man] who is a tyro in the ways of worldly life" (Sathian Kosed, in Rajadhon 1961, p. 69).

Despite the rigidity of Thai gender-role manifestations, it is interesting to note that Thai people perceive transience in gender identity. In Buddhist philosophy, the notion of individual "personality" is false, because a being differs upon each incarnation (Kirsch 1982). Gender differs in every life, with social position, fortune or misfortune, mental and physical dispositions, life events, and even the species (human, animal, ghost, or deity) and location of rebirth (strata of heavens or hells), all of which depend on the being's fund of merit accumulated through committing good deeds in past lives. In the Thai interpretation, women are commonly seen as lower on the hierarchy of merit because they cannot be ordained. Khin Thitsa (1980, cited in Thorbek 1988, p. 84) observed that according to the Theravada view, "a being is born as a woman because of bad *karma* or lack of sufficient good merit."

In Susanne Thorbek's study (1988, p. 97), a woman illustrates her frustration with being a woman: In a minor domestic crisis, she shouts, "Oh, it's my evil fate to have been born a woman!" Somewhat more reservedly, a pious young woman in Penny Van Esterik's study (1982), also admitted her desire to be reborn as a male in order to become a monk. Yet another more "worldly" woman, seemingly satisfied with her female gender and hoping to be reborn as a deity of the sensuous heavens, argued that those who desired a specific gender upon rebirth would be born of indeterminate sex. Even within a lifespan, men's transitions between the *Sangha* and the laity demonstrates the transient nature of gender as the two masculine gender roles are abruptly switched. As serious as they are in observing the gender codes, Thai men and women accept gender identities as important yet temporary. Even those in frustration learn to think life will be "better off the next time around," especially as long as they do not question the inequity of their sometimes arduous, yet transient, states.

B. Romance, Love, and Marriage

Most cultures glorify and idolize romance between men and women, and Thai people are no exception. Themes of quests for eternal love and the consequences of passion—ecstasy, aspirations, heartbreaks, jealously, elopements, and deaths—abound in the Thai folklore, literature, and music. Borrowed from the *karma* concept, people explain an unexpected, overwhelming infatuation in metaphysical terms: They were meant for each other because of destiny (*bu-phay vassana*) or they had made merit together in previous lives.

In the Thai vocabulary, there are specific words for "love," "lust," "infatuation," "love at first sight," "sexual desire," and so on. In particular, the words *khuaam ruk* (love) and *khuaam khrai* (lust) are distinct, although they are sometimes used together as *ruk-khrai* to connote affectionate relationships. As will be evident later in the chapter, premarital sex outside the commercial-sex context is forbidden, and the distinction between love and lust are inculcated in young people to deter them from premarital sex within a romantic relationship. In such warnings, love is usually idealized as pure, noble, and epitomized by patience, responsibility, and maturity, whereas lust embodies the qualities opposite to these virtues. The Third Buddhist Precept—to refrain from sexual misconduct, mostly understood to refer to adultery, rape, sexual abuse of children, and careless sexual activities that result in the sorrow of others—is often used as a reference for the danger and demerit of lust. It is noteworthy that in the Buddhist philosophy, both love and lust are worldly attachments, leading to suffering. Lust, however, is deemed more harmful because it violates the Third Precept. In the Thai society, where people make distinctions between "ideal Buddhism" (i.e., as in the supreme Buddhist philosophy) and "practical Buddhism" (i.e., for the laity, guided by the Five Precepts), it is easy to see why love is socially accepted and lust is not.

Because of the social acceptance of love, various expressions of romance are found in everyday life and art forms. The English-derived term "romantic" has been widely used in Thai to connote an intimate and private ambience for a couple, often without a sexual undertone, such as "romantic" restaurant, music, or sentiment. Women, prohibited from sexual expression unless married (see below), account for a majority of the consumers of popular literature and television drama in which young women's love lives are portrayed. These contemporary romantic tales are enormously popular as is evident in their multiple republications and repeated television and film adaptations. Embedded in these love tales are the cultural scripts on love, romance, and marriage; these scripts reflect the corresponding constructions in the Thai culture at large, as well as provide models for the newer generations of audiences. A certain Western ethos is abundant in these novels, many of which are adaptations from the classics by Jane Austen, and Charlotte and Emily Bronte, for example. However, the ethos, particularly the Victorian values for women and the chivalrous demeanor for men, seems congruent with the Thai conceptualizations of gender and heterosexual relationships, and therefore is not seen by contemporary Thais as foreign. Emphasis on women's virtues, such as the *kulasatrii* code, chastity, patience, and honesty, can be found across a variety of backgrounds and scenarios. The barriers the heroines face symbolize the obstructions Thai women encounter in fulfilling their love, for example, jealous and manipulative women in villain roles (the "bad girl" stereotype, see Section 5A), parental objections, and men's exploitation and sexual discrimination. Cultural and class differences are also significant challenges, ranging from the relationship between a northern woman and a military officer from Bangkok in *Sao Khruea Faa* (which resembles *M. Butterfly*), to the interracial love between a Thai woman and a Japanese soldier during World War II in *Khuu Kam*, to the intergenerational love between a young woman and a rich and handsome "playboy" many years older in *Salakjit*.

In urban areas, shopping malls, coffee shops, school activities, and, to a lesser extent, nightclubs and discotheques provide places for young people to meet. In rural Thailand, Buddhist temples (*wat*) are instrumental in bringing men and women together during the services, temple fairs, and fund-raising ceremonies, where the atmosphere of *sanuk* (fun and enjoyment) predominates (Thorbek, 1988). Young women often appear at the *wat* in their best outfits and hairstyles, and the idiomatic expression that a young woman is attractive enough "to go to the *wat*" highlights the social function of temples in rural Thailand (Sathian Kosed, in Rajadhon, 1961). Young women also take a keen interest in the young monks who, at the end of the Lenten retreat, will leave the monkhood to become "ripe" laymen, ready for marriage and settling down (P. Van Esterik 1982). Flirtation between men and women is allowed, and although women are somewhat restricted by the *kulasatrii* notion, in numerous age-old courting songs, women are quite bold in making allusions to sex or outright marriage propositions (Keyes 1984). However, women's candor about romance and sex is still minimal compared to that of men, and it is even more disapproved for middle- and upper-class women. Kirsch (1984) has speculated that young women in the villages may appear to be deeply concerned with love, marriage, and family because they are striving to fulfill the traditional images of women as "mother-nurturer" in rural environments in which alternative options are severely limited.

In contrast with the passionate nature of courting, the ethos of marriage and parenting emphasizes more the practical and grounded values, such as mutual support, trust, and emotional commitment. In the contemporary Thai image of an ideal marriage, the husband and wife live together in a harmonious, mutually respectful relationship, with the expectation on provision and security weighed towards the man, and the domestic responsibilities towards the woman. A traditional Thai expression compares a married couple to an elephant, with the husband as the two front legs and the wife as the hind ones. In an ideal couple, decision making is the man's responsibility and the woman's role is to be supportive and cooperative. A traditional *kulasatrii* shows deference to her husband as he is the master of the household. In a hierarchical society such as Thailand, where people diligently make obeisance to persons of a higher status, this meant that some women in ancient times showed their husbands an extreme courtesy which today would be reserved for the elders, teachers, or monks.

In the past few decades, lower- and middle-class women have increasingly worked outside of the homes while continuing to be in charge of the household chores and child care. Men, however, have not been expected much to adopt the household responsibilities; it is still quite uncommon to expect married men to take on the same extent of responsibilities as their wives in cooking, cleaning, and parenting. In middle-class families, the women's double responsibility is usually helped by live-in parent(s) or, if they can afford it, maids. In families with lesser means and no live-in parents, the burden on the women can be significant and often becomes a commonly cited cause of sexual disinterest and marital discord (Dumronggittigule, Sombathmai, Taywaditep, and Mandel 1995).

In fact, the divorce rate in Thailand has been growing steadily, paralleling an increase in economic autonomy for women. Divorce and remarrying are not uncommon, although there is a small but palpable degree of stigma, especially among the urban middle-class Thais. We will present further discussions about the tradition of marriage, family settlement, and the dynamics within a married couple in Section 5B.

C. A Double Standard for Sexuality and Gender Stereotypes

One of the most consistent findings from sex research in Thailand is that minor wives and commercial sex are common sexual outlets for men of all ages, social standings, and marital statuses. This tolerance of married men's extramarital sex is merely a part of the larger double standard regarding sexual practices, which mandates different rules for men and for women. As confirmed by studies on child-rearing practices, Thai parents train girls more strictly than boys in the behaviors that are part of the gender roles (Archavanitkul and Havanon 1990). Girls are taught that a good woman remains a virgin until marriage and continues to be emotionally and sexually faithful to her husband afterwards. As adolescents, Thai fathers are known for being particularly protective and possessive of their daughters, exercising great control over their friendships with other teenage boys (Thorbek 1988). For boys, however, sexual abandon is accepted or even encouraged. As Sukanya Hantrakul (1983, quoted in Kaime-Atterhog, Ard-Am, and Sethaput 1994) notes: "Culturally, Thai society flatters men for their promiscuity. . . . Women's magazines always advise women to tolerate the situation and accommodate themselves to it."

This double standard in sexual practices may have culminated into an undercurrent of tension between the genders which, although not readily observable, has been felt and noted by many (e.g., Jackson 1989). Some mistrust and suspicion between the genders can be seen in the negative stereotypes men hold for women, and vice versa. For example, women are stereotyped as emotionally volatile and needy, and they are often manipulative; a Thai proverb notes that the typical Thai woman, while maintaining the *kulasatrii* appearance, possesses "one hundred wagons full of stratagems." Conversely, many women believe that men are often unreliable, unable to have an emotional commitment, inefficient in household management and parenting, and constantly driven by their sexual urges. Many women believe that while men get emotional support and recreation from their male peers, relationships with women exist mostly to fulfill the men's sexual desires, as well as the societal expectations on the men to have a family. However, the men's sexual desires are often perceived as insatiable, with an immature, uncontrollable character like a child's craving—yet "naturally" and "instinctually" driven in a way that can hardly be limited to their spouses. As men continue to search for sexual gratification from commercial sex and minor wives, women unwillingly come to terms with the men's extramarital escapades.

The myth that men's sexual desires are boundless and immutable is quite pervasive (see more discussion in Section 8A). It is common to hear Thai women voice their concern about being raped. When activists demanded that commercial sex be eradicated, respectable men and women have publicly expressed the concern that "good women" would be endangered. Similarly, before HIV became a widespread concern in the Thai society, married women sometimes encouraged their husbands to visit sex workers, in part so they could be relieved of the obligation to serve their husband's sexual demands, and possibly to prevent the husband's worse crime of having a stable, emotionally committed relationship with a minor wife. These examples may reflect Thai women's helplessness regarding the men's presumably uncontrollable sexual drive, and consequently, their strategies to protect themselves and preserve their marriages. More recent surveys (see Section 5B) have found that married women in the HIV epidemic face an even more difficult dilemma as they realize that they are at risk for HIV infection from their husbands' use of commercial sex. Encouraging the husband to have a minor wife as an alternative is still a painful decision for a woman to make.

D. Gender in Everyday Life: Social Manners, the Touch Taboo, Female Pollution, and Gender Segregation

In general, Thai people are noted for their tender, friendly, and graceful ways of social and public behavior. Despite the clear masculine code of conduct, Thai men display less of the overt "masculine" behavior than men in many other cultures. Since the 1940s, urban middle- and upper-class men have adopted the Western chivalrous and "gentlemanly" social manners of "honoring" women, such as opening doors for women, and the "ladies first" etiquette. In addition, nurturance, as stated above, is a quality expected in Thai men, even among those in the position of power (see Kirsch 1985). Therefore, Thai men are often known for their polite, sweet, and caring gestures, as well as their respect for others. Women are expected to be all of these and more: the code of *kulasatrii* contains numerous guidance and taboos for the "proper woman." Thus, the Thai gender-coded rules of conduct seem to place more demands on women than on men, as reflected in an oft-quoted phrase from a poem that "It is hard to be born a woman." The famous male poet who immortalized this phrase, Soonthon Phuu, in fact wrote "but being a man is actually many times more difficult" as a retort to this phrase, but somehow the complete quote never became as popular.

Although urban Thais have adopted Western clothing styles since the early 1940s, formal social situations, such as the workplace, school, and university, still demand that trousers are strictly for men, and skirts or dresses are for women. Because motorcycles are one of the most popular means of transportation in urban Thailand, women who work in offices and female students struggle every day in their dresses while commuting to and from work. As a passenger, women must sit facing the side of the motorcycle to avoid an unseemly sitting position, compromising their balance and safety in so doing. Perhaps it is small, everyday things like this that best illustrates how the life of a *kulasatrii* is not any easier today than it was in Soonthon Phuu's time two hundred years ago.

In ancient Thailand, acquiring an expertise in certain exclusive areas, such as occultism or martial arts, was seen metaphorically as endowing the apprentice with the mentor spirits, known as *mii khruu*, or "under mentorship." Among the numerous rules of conduct for the learned men, some suggest a belief that men are superior to women, and others indicate some anxiety and animosity surrounding sex and the female anatomy. For example, some learned men must refrain from having sex with a woman. Many men were also prohibited from socializing with women (occasionally including the sister or mother) or their mentor spirits might be weakened by the "weaker sex." Certain parts of the female body, such as genitalia, buttocks, or menstrual blood, and anything that contacts these body parts, such as sarongs, were considered sacrilegious and harmful to the learned men. Folklore anecdotes portray a vicious sabotage done by a piece of fabric from a woman's sarong, and a learned man who lost his powers because he had unwittingly walked underneath an elevated house where a woman was physically above him.

Over the years, despite the decline of occultism and superstition, these folk beliefs remain even in those who are not learned men themselves. Tied into the still-popular fatalism (*duang*), many men today believe their destiny can be jeopardized (*choak suay* or "bad luck") by circumstances such as walking under a row of laundry containing women's skirts or underwear, or engaging in cunnilingus. Men are also told not to have sex with a menstruating woman or they might become seriously ill (Fuller, Edwards, Sermsri, and Vorakitphokatorn 1993). Even men who are not superstitious keep away from these situations to protect the integrity of their "manhood" or to avoid social disgrace. Even women themselves observe the behavioral restrictions which flow from this idea of symbolic female pollution. A woman who wears a Buddhist amulet is advised to step out of her sarong instead of pulling it over her head, and sarongs are often separated from men's wear or upper garments in laundry (Manderson 1992).

Examples of gender segregation abound in Thai society. One of the 227 monastic rules of the monks dictates that in addition to being celibate, monks are not to have any physical contact with women. Women, including the monks' family members, are precluded from certain activities in religious ceremonies to prevent any possibility of ritual purity violation, even accidental contact such as a slight brush of hands. Interestingly, this practice can also be seen in the way modern, urbane gentlemen act toward women: a proper gentleman does not touch a woman in casual circumstances. If he transgresses this social etiquette, an apology is in order. To Thai people, this decorum is impelled by two remarkably different, yet compatible cultural imperatives: firstly, the chivalrous, gentlemanly manners of "honoring" women adopted from the West, and secondly, the animistic belief which prohibits men from touching an unmarried woman to prevent an offense to her guardian spirits (*phii puu yaa*). However, one can also discern the prevailing myth of men's boundless sexual desires behind this touch taboo. A man's touching of a woman is assumed to have a sexual intention unless otherwise explained. Gender segregation can also be seen on a more formal, institutionalized level. Thai people are socialized to mingle mostly with members of the same gender from a young age. Single-sex schools are very common. In colleges, all dormitories are men- or women-only, with strict rules prohibiting visitations from the other gender, even the students' family members.

Given the foregoing discussion about the touch taboo and gender segregation, it should come as no surprise that open physical expression of affection between men and women is deemed socially inappropriate in the

Thai society. Until very recently, a (presumably unmarried) young couple would be frowned upon if they walked hand-in-hand affectionately in public. Conservatives openly condemn the influence of Western culture and the media on younger Thais' public behavior toward the other gender. In contrast, public expressions of affection among members of the same gender are quite common. As pointed out by Jackson (1989), Westerners often misinterpret such displays of same-gender affection as an expression of homoeroticism, or misconstrue it as a lack of homophobia among the Thai people. In fact, this same-gender physical intimacy is not viewed in any sexual way by Thai men or women. It is something similar to the sports camaraderie among Western men or casual affection among Western women, and not associated with either homosexuality or an absence of homophobia. Contrary to the Westerners' misperceptions, anti-homosexual attitudes exist in Thai society as they do elsewhere in the world (see Section 6).

In summary, we have outlined a number of key belief systems that underlie the gender construction in Thai society: the Theravada gender roles, folk myths and animistic beliefs, and traditional class-relevant ideals, among others. Although diversified in origins, these belief systems share common elements which enable their assembly into a coherent cultural structure. To illustrate, men in general are allowed greater latitude in their sexual and moral conduct, perhaps because religious salvation awaits them as a viable option; the myth of masculinity which associates maleness with vices and sexual freedom, therefore, finds a corresponding solution in the Theravada role for men. Similarly, a consistent dictum about women can be found across these diverse belief systems. A woman's virtue is based on the degree to which she excels in promoting the well-being of religion and family, and it also depends upon her sexual conduct with men. A woman's moral status, therefore, is always relational and conditional. She is either higher or lower than men because of what she does (and does not do) with men. This idea is consistent with the Theravada role for women, the *kulasatrii* code of the female ideal, and a number of practices couched as ways to protect women from men's exploits.

It is noteworthy that the cultural construction determines whether or not a new practice or idea from another cultural origin will "fit" into the prevailing coherent structure. The relatively Western chivalrous manners, for example, have been assimilated into the Thai culture because they correspond to the indigenous notion that women are "noble" yet "weaker," thus needing honoring treatment and protection. The relatively recent rise of commercial sex in Thailand may be an adoption of capitalism, but Thai people have always been familiar in Buddhist tales with prototype women who commoditize sex in dire straits (Keyes 1984). The popularity of female meditation teachers in the 1970s in Bangkok was a unique phenomenon (J. Van Esterik 1982), but the acceptance seemed to rest upon the perception that these lay teachers, like *mae chii*, would never pursue political or monastic goals. Some Thais did not even see the female meditation teachers as women, because these women did not fit conventional female images. Western feminism has been met with objection as being too radical, unrealistic, or culturally inappropriate, probably because the feminist manifestos do not find much corresponding agenda in the Thai gender construction. While the Thai society is undergoing rapid changes, the fundamental gender construction remains, and it determines which new influences will be selected and which will be discarded. Whatever the result of the transformation may be, the key in predicting the future of gender relations in Thailand lies in unraveling the gender constructions of the past and the present.

2. Religious and Ethnic Factors Affecting Sexuality

A. Religious Factors

Buddhism, the Dominant Religious Factor

The main and official religion of Thailand is Theravada Buddhism, with more than 90 percent of the population following this tradition. The profound influences of Buddhism on gender and sexuality in Thailand are intertwined with Hinduist practice, local animistic beliefs, and popular demonology from ancient times. The predominant animistic belief system involves *phii*, or the spirits, either of ancestral origin or those residing in natural objects. The spirits can inflict illnesses and misfortune upon individuals for deviant conduct, or, on the contrary, they can provide protection, healing, and bring about fortune for those who follow ethics and placate the spirits. In addition, about 4 percent of the population are Moslem, mostly living in the southern part of Thailand. Christianity has become steadily more popular, and over a century of work by the missionaries can be seen in many schools which offer good education to Thai children without seeking to convert them.

The tolerant philosophy of Buddhism and the constitutional guarantees of religious freedom have provided a fertile ground for adoption and admixing new religious beliefs with traditional beliefs. In the Thai eyes, the superstition and metaphysics in animism, demonology, and Hinduist cosmology are not at odds with the Buddhist cosmology depicted in the Buddhist canon and religious folk tales. These strands of belief systems maintain peaceful coexistence, and many Thais follow some of these practices to a certain degree during different parts of their lives.

Although the guidelines to achieve *nirvana* are offered, Buddhism emphasizes to the laity "the middle way" and the importance of avoiding extremism. This pragmatic approach is also seen in the domain of sexuality. Despite the deprecation of sexuality in the ideal Buddhism, celibacy is likely to be pertinent only to the monastic lifestyle, while diverse sexual expression has been tolerated among the lay followers, especially the men for whom sexual, military, and social prowess has always been extolled (Cabezón 1993). The Five Precepts are guidelines for lay Buddhists "for a socially-just life, free of exploitation of oneself and others." Again, pragmatism prevails: All of the Precepts are not rigidly expected in most lay Buddhists in Thailand (as well as in other Buddhist cultures) except for the elderly or extraordinarily pious lay persons (Cabezón 1993).

The Third Buddhist Precept specifically addresses human sexuality: refrain from sexual misconduct or "wrong doing in sexual matters." Although being open to various interpretations, depending on the different contexts, malfeasance is usually considered by Thai people to mean adultery, rape, sexual abuse of children, and careless sexual activities that result in the sorrow of others (Allyn 1991). Premarital sex, prostitution, masturbation, cross-gendered behavior, and homosexuality, on the other hand, are not explicitly mentioned. Any objection to some of these sexual phenomena is perhaps grounded in other non-Buddhist beliefs, such as classism, animism, or Western medical theories. In subsequent sections, we will present further discussions on the Buddhist attitudes toward homosexuality (Section 6) and commercial sex (Section 8B).

Gender Roles in Theravada Buddhism and Their Implications

Many ideal images for men and women are found in religious folk tales, which the monks read or retell during sermons (*thetsana*). These sermons, although rarely translated from the Buddhist canon (*Tripitaka* or *Phra Trai-pidok* in Thai), are taken by most Thais as the authentic teachings of the Buddha (Keyes 1984). Similarly, other ritual traditions, folk operas, and local legends contain gender-relevant images in the depiction of men and women's lives, both sovereign and common, showing their sins and merits through their actions and relationships, all of which purportedly convey Buddhist messages. Thereby, the Theravada world view, both authentic and interpreted through the Thai eyes, has exerted enormous influences on the gender construction in Thailand.

With a firm belief in *karma* and reincarnation, Thai people are concerned with accumulating merit in everyday life in order to attain an enhanced status in rebirth rather than striving for *nirvana* (Kirsch, 1982). Earning merit and an enhanced rebirth status are depicted in the story of Prince Vessantara (or *Phra Vessandon* in Thai pronunciation), who is reborn in his next life as the historic Buddha because of his unconditional generosity expressed by giving away his valuables, including his wealth, children, and wife. In real life, men and women "make merit," and the Theravada culture prescribes different ways for this quest. The ideal "merit making" for men is through ordination in the *Sangha* (order of monks, or in Thai, *Phra Song*). Women, on the other hand, are not allowed to be ordained. Although the order of *Bhikkhuni* (the female equivalent to the *Sangha* monks) was established by the Buddha with some reluctance, the practice disappeared from Sri Lanka and India after several centuries and never existed in Southeast Asia (Keyes 1984; P. Van Esterik 1982). Today, lay women can intensify their Buddhist practice by becoming *mae chii*, (often erroneously translated to "nun"). These are lay female ascetics who shave their heads and wear white robes. Although *mae chii* abstain from worldly pleasures and sexuality, the laity consider giving alms to *mae chii* a lesser merit-making activity than alms given to the monks. Hence, these women usually depend on themselves and/or on their relatives for the necessities of life. Obviously, *mae chii* are not as highly regarded as monks, and indeed many *mae chii* are even perceived negatively (P. Van Esterik 1982).

The fact that the Buddhist religious roles for women are underdeveloped has led Kirsch (1985) to comment that women in Theravada societies are "religiously disadvantaged." Conventionally, the exclusion of women from monastic roles has been rationalized by the view that women are less ready than men to attain the Buddhist salvation because of their deeper enmeshment in worldly matters. Instead, women's greatest contribution to Buddhism lies in their secular role through enabling the religious pursuit for the men in their lives. Hence, the role for women in religion is characterized by the mother-nurturer image: Women support and provide for Buddhism by way of "giving" young men to the *Sangha*, and "nurturing" the religion by alms giving (Keyes 1984). The ways in which Thai women constantly support Buddhist institutions and contribute to various spiritual functions in their communities have been well illustrated in Penny Van Esterik's work (1982).

This mother-nurturer image is also prominent in the Thai women's secular pursuits. Women are expected to provide for the well-being of their husbands, children, and parents. As pointed out by Kirsch (1985), this historical mother-nurturer role has had a self-perpetuating effect on the exclusion of women from monastic roles. Because women are barred from the monastic position, and because the weight of filial and family obligations falls more on women than on men, women are doubly locked in the same secular mother-nurturer role with no other options. They, therefore, are indeed enmeshed in worldly matters, and their redemption lies in the actions of the men in their lives.

Two important religious texts illustrate this condition. In the tale of Prince Vessantara, his wife, Queen Maddi, is praised because of her unconditional support of his generosity. In *Anisong Buat* ("Blessings of Ordination"), a woman with no merit is saved from hell because she had allowed her son to be ordained as a monk (Keyes 1984). In reality, the mother-nurturer image entails a certain life path for women, as noted by Kirsch (1985, p. 319): "Under typical circumstances young women could expect to remain rooted in village life, eventually snaring a husband, having children, and 'replacing' their mothers."

Men, as seen in the depiction of Prince Vessantara and the young son with religious aspirations in the "Blessings of Ordination," are afforded autonomy, as well as geographic and social mobility, to pursue both religious and secular goals, therefore "affirming" the conventional wisdom that men are more ready than women to give up attachments.

Undoubtedly, these differential role prescriptions for men and women have led to a clear division of labor along gender lines. Thai women's role of mother and their routine merit-making activities necessitate their specialization in economic-entrepreneurial activities, such as small-scale trading, productive activities in the field, and craft work at home. Thai men, encouraged by the logistic freedom, prefer political-bureaucratic activities, particularly those in government service (Kirsch 1982). The connection between monastic institutions and polity has always been salient to Thai people (see Kirsch 1982; J. Van Esterik 1982), therefore, positions in bureaucracy and politics represent a man's ideal pursuit should he choose to excel in the secular role. In the nineteenth century, more Thai men began to strive for secular success when the Buddhist reformation in Thailand demanded more intensified discipline in monks; this coincided with an expansion of government occupations that resulted from a bureaucratic system reorganization in the 1890s (Kirsch 1982).

Becoming a temporary member of the monkhood has long been seen in Thailand as a rite of passage which demarcates Thai men's transformation from "raw" to "ripe," or from immature men to scholars or wise men (*bundit*, from Pali *pandit*). In Sathian Kosed's *Popular Buddhism in Thailand* (published in Rajadhon, 1961), young Buddhist men, upon turning 20 years old, are expected to become a monk for the period of about three months during the Buddhist Lenten period. Because the merit from ordination of a married man will be transferred to his wife (and because she must consent to his ordination), parents are understandably anxious to see that their sons are ordained before they get married. Traditionally, a "raw" unordained adult man would be seen as uneducated and, therefore, not a suitable man to be a husband or son-in-law. The man's girlfriend or fiancée, therefore, delights in his temporary monkhood as it should enhance her parents' approval of him. She often sees this as a sign of relationship commitment, and promises to wait patiently for the day he leaves his monkhood at the end of the Lenten period. In Thai society today, this practice of ordination has changed and is less significant, as men are more involved in secular education or occupied by their employment. Statistics show that today, members of the *Sangha* account for a smaller percent of the male population than in earlier times (Keyes 1984). As early as the late 1940s, when Sathian Kosed wrote *Popular Buddhism in Thailand*, there were already some signs of weakening customs around the Buddhist ordination.

Many other phenomena related to gender and sexuality in Thailand today can be traced to the Theravada world view. As will be more evident in subsequent discussions, the Thai culture exhibits a double standard, which gives men a greater latitude to express their sexuality and other "deviant" behaviors (e.g., drinking, gambling, and extramarital sex). Keyes

(1984) has pointed out that whereas women are seen as inherently close to the Buddha's teachings about sufferings, men require the discipline of ordination in order to achieve this insight, for they tend to digress from the Buddhist Precepts. With Keyes' notion in mind, we can speculate that Thai men perceive that demeritorious behaviors can be amended through their eventual ordination. Up to 70 percent of all men in central Thailand become monks on a temporary basis (J. Van Esterik 1982). Other adult males renounce "worldly" living to be ordained to the *Sangha*, living a midlife or old age "robed in yellow" as is commonly said in Thai. With such redemptive options, Thai men may feel little need to suppress their passions and vices. These attachments are, after all, easy to give up and are insubstantial compared to the salvation available to them in their twilight years.

On the contrary, women's lack of access to direct religious salvation makes them work harder to maintain virtuous lives, which means refraining from and disapproving of sexual indulgences, in order to keep their demerit to a minimum. With no access to formal Buddhist scholastic activities, it is unlikely that women would be able to discern which virtues and sins were defined by the Theravada values and which by the local gender construction (see discussion of *kulasatrii* in Section 1A). Further, because women believe that their strongest merit is to be a mother of a son who is ordained, the pressure on women to marry and have a family is heightened. They must do everything to enhance their likelihood of marriage, perhaps including adherence to the ideal female images no matter how difficult. Viewed this way, both men and women in Thai society strongly endorse a double standard regarding gender and sexuality, albeit for different reasons.

Key Beliefs in the Thai Constructions of Gender and Sexuality

Before we proceed to other topics, it may be helpful to summarize the key strands of world views which will be apparent in subsequent discussions of gender and sexuality in Thailand. The most important influences are religious belief systems. Not only do the Five Buddhist Precepts constitute the ethical guidelines for lay people, the Theravada gender images have been passed on to the society through sermons, folk tales and operas, and rituals. Animistic and Hinduist beliefs are embedded in the Thai consciousness through these folk tales, as is evident in metaphysical cosmology and entities, angels and ghosts, heavens and hells.

Other influences can also be identified in contemporary Thai society. For example, the consumerist and capitalist ideology is evident in commercial sex and pornography industries. More recently added to the mix is the newer generation's perception of sexuality in contemporary Europe, North America, and Japan, often interpreted as "modern," liberal, or hedonistic. Another school of thought present in the educated, urban middle class is the Western medical models of diseases and deviance, as well as psychological theories of sexuality; the Thai translations for "the subconscious," "latent," or "ego" are not uncommon in the conversation among the educated. Among other members of the same social strata, one can also discern the rise of contemporaneous Western ideological and political movements, such as feminism, women's studies, and the gay/lesbian identity. In a similar vein, the humanistic approach to understanding sexuality has become more visible in recent years, although it is often mislabeled as "modern," "Western," or "radical." Unfortunately, the humanistic movement may suffer from such misrepresentations in the present cultural climate in which Thai tradition is seen as threatened by Western influences, and many Thai intellectuals are paying lip service to the conservation of traditional Thai identity.

B. Ethnic Differences and Social Structure

Today, there are four regions of Thailand with distinct cultures: the north, the northeast, the central area, and the south. Although regional and cultural differences exist, there is a strong national identity, and the central Thai language is taught and understood throughout the country. This is enhanced by a well-developed mass media and communications system, a good telephone service, and a reliable transportation system servicing all parts of the country. The only exception to this is the hill tribe people in the mountainous regions that surround northern Thailand. The hill tribe people migrated south from China and have remained relatively separate and distinct. However, as the government cracks down on the growing of poppies (for opium and heroin production) and deforestation, the hill tribe people have been moving into the lowlands of Thailand or, through better roads and transportation, commute regularly into the lowland cities for work. Hill tribe people have maintained their own languages, cultures, and customs in the past several centuries. More details on the lives of hill tribe populations can be found in the books edited by Nancy Eberhardt (1988) and McKinnon and Bhruksasri (1983).

Other cultural differences also exist. The stratification of upper, middle, and lower classes is mostly based on the past social hierarchy (*sakdi na*) and the family's financial powers. This social stratification is no longer enforced by contemporary law, but its presence is recognized by most Thais. There is also a distinction between urban and rural Thais. Constituting a majority of the Thai population, people in the rural villages of Thailand have led more-simple lives rooted in rich traditions, with less interference from international cultures or capitalism. Urban Thailand, on the other hand, has gained its cultural richness from the diverse social classes, ethnicities, and international cultures. The rural/urban division is still highly salient to most Thais, even though the differences have become gradually smaller due to the media, improved communication and transportation, and the migration of rural Thais to find work in big cities. Among other changes, gender and sexuality in rural villagers today have been greatly adulterated by the urban cultural images through the ubiquitous popular media (Keyes 1984).

In addition, there is also an ethnic division between the Thais and the 10 percent of the population who are of Chinese descent. Mostly excluded from the upper echelons of nobility, Sino-Thai people have gained power and status through commerce. The ethnic Chinese in Thailand have managed to blend well into the urban middle-class communities with particularly great contributions in commerce and, more recently, the sciences, while still maintaining their traditional heritage through customs and Confucian family values. Despite the longstanding tradition of classes, social mobility is common, and the ethnic Chinese stand as examples of "rags-to-riches" possibilities (Kirsch 1982). Racial prejudice exists on a subtle level, but has never resulted in overt segregation or violence, even during the anti-Chinese nationalistic government in 1939. Readers who are interested in the lives of Chinese and Sino-Thai peoples in Thailand are referred to the work of Anne Maxwell Hill (1988) and William Skinner (1957).

It is important to bear in mind these cultural, regional, and ethnic differences, because they significantly limit generalizations about the sexual attitudes and values in Thailand. In this chapter, a majority of the research data on sexual attitudes and behavior has been derived from samples of lower- and middle-class ethnic Thais. Most empirical studies have been conducted in urban cities, such as Bangkok and Chiangmai, although data from the rural villages of the north and the northeast account for a considerable portion of our review. In addition, Thailand's rapid economic progress in recent decades has had a dramatic impact on every level of sociocultural structures. Likewise, the nature of gender and sexuality in Thai society is undergoing rapid transformations. As a result, the great degree of flux and heterogeneity in Thai society demands that we pay great attention to the contexts in our attempt to understand gender and sexuality in Thailand.

3. Sexual Knowledge and Education

Like parents in many other cultures, most Thai parents do not educate their children about sexuality, and when children ask about sex, they are likely to avoid answering or they provide incorrect information. Since parents are unlikely to display affection in front of their children, role-modeling of affection between the genders is usually derived not from parents, but from literature or the media. Men are more likely to discuss sex with other men, especially when they are socializing and drinking with each other. Women also prefer to discuss sex and their marital issues with their same-gender peers (Thorbek 1988). Sexual communication between a married couple has received much attention among Thai sex and AIDS researchers recently, but data are still scarce (see Section 5B).

Sexual matters are not typically discussed in a serious fashion in the Thai society. When sex is mentioned, it is often in the context of playful banter or humor. Playful joking about sex with striking curiosity and candor is not uncommon. For example, a newlywed couple would be teased lightheart-edly and openly: "Did you have fun last night? Was last night happy? How many times?" (Allyn 1991). As in many cultures, Thai people have an extensive sexual vocabulary (see Allyn 1991). For every colloquialism that Thai people find offensive or obscene, there are a number of euphemistic equivalents. Euphemistic substitutes are made by way of symbolic animals or objects (e.g., "dragon" or "dove" for penis, "oyster" for vagina, and "eggs" for testicles); children's language (e.g., "little kid" or "Mr. That" for penis); extreme obscurity (e.g., "said activity" for having sex, "using mouth" for oral sex, and "Miss Body" for prostitute); literary references (e.g., "Lord of the world" for penis); or medical terms (e.g., "birth canal" for vagina).

With such a variety of alternative terms, Thai people feel that sexual matters in everyday conversation should be tastefully alluded to in moderate amounts, with an artful choice of words, timing, and comic sensibility. Thai people do have a strict sense of social appropriateness surrounding such humor, especially in the presence of elders or women. Discussions about sex are uncomfortable when they are excessively crude or straightforward, overly solemn or intellectual, and socially inappropriate. Such discomfort is reflected in the Thai words which are equivalent to "one-track mind," "dirty mind," "lewd," "sex-obsessed," "sex-crazed," or "nympho" in English, with a variety of nuances ranging from playful to pathologizing to disap-proving. Such attitudes have been one of the barriers for sexuality educa-tion; rather than objecting to content of sexuality education per se, adults and educators feel embarrassed by discussions about sex that seem too intellectual and straightforward.

Sexuality education was introduced in Thai schools in 1978. Although the curriculum has been revised over the years, it has been limited to reproductive issues and sexually transmitted diseases (STDs). As in many other countries, sexuality education in Thailand has been rarely taught in a comprehensive manner. Embedded in the contexts of health education and biology, attention to sociocultural contexts was more an exception than a rule. Although family planning and population control is practiced by most Thais, contraception is not emphasized in school. Instead, a typical Thai gains this knowledge from family planning media campaigns, clinics, and physicians.

Dusitsin (1995) has expressed concerns that Thai people can no longer rely on learning about sex from sexual humor, which contains alarming amounts of sexual myths and misinformation. Dusitsin's proposal of a Program for the Promotion of Sexual Health (see Sections 12 and 13) gives a priority to developing curricula for sexuality education for both students and non-student populations. Other Thai researchers and experts have voiced the same philosophy and have called for more comprehensive curricula, with greater coverage of psychosocial issues such as a discourse on gender, homophobia, and sexual commercialism. They have also urged that sexuality education must have its own identity and objectives clearly distinguished from the highly visible AIDS-prevention campaigns in order to avoid the constricted scope and sex-negative attitudes. Others have also enthusiastically supported the idea of covering non-student populations, who usually have limited access to services and education.

4. Autoerotic Behaviors and Patterns

Very few of the sex surveys conducted in the wake of the HIV epidemic have reported any data about the incidence of masturbation, let alone discussed the attitudes and behaviors surrounding this behavior. This may be due to the fact that masturbation, like most other sexual matters, is somewhat a taboo subject in Thailand, and has been ignored perhaps because it does not have a direct bearing on the public-health agenda.

One study did examine adolescent autoerotic attitudes and behaviors (Chompootaweep, Yamarat, Poomsuwan, and Dusitsin 1991). Many more male students (42 percent) than female students (6 percent) reported having masturbated. The modal age of first masturbatory experience was 13 years. Adolescents were likely to maintain negative attitudes about masturbation, viewing it as "unnatural," or citing myths about masturbation, such as a belief that it causes sexually transmitted diseases. The gender difference found in the rates of reported masturbation is striking, although it is also typical of other domains in sexual surveys in Thailand. Within the same socioeconomic stratum, Thai men always report having much more sexual interest and experience than Thai women. Young women, in particular, might be uncomfortable with the idea of masturbation because it is an acknowledgment of sexual curiosity, which is deemed inappropriate and shameful for women (Ford and Kittisuksathit 1994).

Data on the masturbatory experiences of adults are also scarce. In one study of army conscripts in northern Thailand, 89 percent of the men (age 21) reported having masturbated (Nopkesorn, Sungkarom, and Sornlum 1991). There is little or no formal information on adults' attitudes about masturbation, but the myths held by adults are likely to be different from those of adolescents. One common myth among male adults is that men are endowed with a finite number of orgasms, thus it is advisable to indulge in masturbation in moderation.

Perhaps the general attitudes of Thai people regarding masturbation can be inferred from the terms used to describe the act. The formal Thai terminology for masturbation *sumrej khuam khrai duay tua eng*, which simply means "to consummate sexual desire by yourself," has replaced a former technical term *atta-kaam-kiriya*, which means "sexual act with oneself." The tone of these rather clinical and inconvenient terms is neutral, strictly free of judgment or implications about health consequences. There is really no clear discussion about masturbation, either positive or negative, in the Third Buddhist Precept or in animistic practice. Therefore, any disapproval of masturbation in the Thai society is likely to be a result of the general anxiety surrounding sexual indulgences, or perhaps from the Western anachronism introduced to the Thai thinking by way of past medical education.

Most Thais, however, prefer the playful vernacular *chak wow*, meaning to "fly a kite." The term compares male masturbation to the hand action of flying a kite, a popular Thai pastime. An even more euphemistic term for male masturbation is *pai sa-naam luang*, which means "to go to the grand field," referring to the very popular park area near the royal palace in Bangkok where people fly kites. For women, the slang term *tok bed* is used, meaning "to use a fishing pole." These playful and euphemistic expressions reflect the acknowledgment that masturbation occurs for both men and women, and yet some discomfort prevents a straightforward verbal expression.

5. Interpersonal Heterosexual Behaviors

A. Adolescent Sexual Behavior

Numerous studies up to the mid-1990s have shown that about half of Thai men have sexual intercourse before they are 18 years old, and that most of them have their first experience with a commercial sex worker (e.g., Sittitrai, Phanuphak, Barry, and Brown 1992; Udomratn and Tungphaisal 1990). Justified as a way of preserving the virtue of "good women," Thai adolescents seek premarital sexual experience from commercial sex workers. Prior to the HIV epidemic, there was virtually no stigma attached to this practice. Sex with a sex worker has often been considered a rite of passage and an accepted manner of learning about sex for young men. Some Thai fathers were known to pay sex workers to have sex with their sons as a way of giving their youngsters some sex education or acknowledging their adulthood. In primarily male colleges, senior students welcomed freshmen, most of whom had no prior sexual experience, by accompanying them to the local brothel or bars/cafes which offer commercial sex. In the contemporary Thai society where increasingly fewer men are interested in the *Sangha*, the young men's use of sexual intercourse as a rite of passage seems like a symbolic commentary on how the male image has drifted further away from the monastic role in the direction of worldliness.

Thai male adolescents eagerly look forward to their first intercourse and, as its slang term (*khuen khruu*) roughly implies, a learning process with someone sexually experienced. For many young Thai men, this practice continues beyond their first sexual experience, and commercial sex becomes a bachelor's recreation. In fact, the phrase *pai thiow*, meaning "to go out for fun," is a euphemism for a visit to the brothel. Going to a brothel with friends is a social as well as a sexual experience, often occurring after an evening of drinking or social gathering. Young men who do not seem interested in joining their peers at a brothel are sometimes teased for being homosexual (Ford and Kittisuksathit 1994). This pattern of sexual behavior in young Thai men will be confirmed by more findings reviewed in the section on the premarital sex of adults (see Section 5B).

On the other hand, young women are supposed to be virgins until they are married. Sex is thus not a recreational option for unmarried women as it is for men. Violation of this rule occurs in the cases of prostitutes and "carefree women." A "carefree woman," or an unmarried woman who seeks sexual pleasure from casual partners, is stereotyped as shallow, emotionally disturbed, and self-destructive. She presumably has lost her virginity because she was amoral, careless, gullible, or blindly following the Western code of sexual behavior. Needless to say, sex before marriage for women is the key criterion that distinguishes a "bad woman" from a "good woman." Female sex workers are subject to the same stereotype, but perhaps to a lesser degree, possibly because they are perceived to be forced into commercial sex by poverty. In addition, the *kulasatrii* notion mostly pertains to the upper and middle classes (Pyne 1994), and thus has less to do with the lower-class origin of most sex workers. Despite such class difference, the *kulasatrii* status is much like the Buddhist concept of merit in that it is based on the person's conduct, not on the social standing per se, and it is subject to decline for any transgression. Inasmuch as social mobility and merit accumulation are afforded everyone in Thailand (although perhaps not with equal ease), every woman, every *kulasatrii* can fall from grace if her conduct is compromised. Therefore, gender segregation, the stringent rules of *kulasatrii*, and strict parental supervision all are useful mechanisms for maintaining the virtue of "good" women.

In keeping with the value on women's virginity, the Thai culture prescribes that romantic relationships between young men and women must be without sex. In general, young people in Thailand today choose their own romantic partner, although parents exercise sanctions on their choice and limit their premarital sexual interaction (Ford and Kittisuksathit 1994). As a man and a woman enter a purely romantic premarital relationship, they are known as being each other's *fan*, an originally English term used in Thai with a different connotation. When in a relationship, many young women start to act as if they are practicing the traditional gender script of husband and wife (without the sex) by adopting a more submissive and deferential role with their *fan*. Even under such a non-sexual premise, many young Thai lovers are still very reluctant to reveal that they have a *fan* to parents or adults for fear of disapproval. In the conservative middle-class ethics, romantic interest is inappropriate for adolescents because they cannot support themselves. Many young lovers simply refer to their *fan* as a male or a female friend. This reluctance to disclose romantic relationships remains in many married adults, who refer to a spouse as a *fan* even after years of marriage.

In an exceptional study of adolescence, Chompootaweep et al. (1991) randomly surveyed secondary-level schools in Bangkok and collected questionnaires from 4,337 students (mean age = 14.7) and 454 teachers. Both male and female students reported that the best age to develop a romantic relationship was 18 to 20 years of age, in contrast to the ages 21 to 25, which their teachers thought was the appropriate age to start romantic relationships. This demonstrates the intergenerational difference in attitude toward adolescent romantic relationships; Thai teachers, like Thai parents, see romance between adolescents as precocious and inappropriate. Fifty-five percent of the male students subscribed to the idea that men should have some sexual experience before getting married, while only 24 percent of the female students thought this was appropriate for men. Among the teachers, 74 percent of the male teachers and 58 percent of the female teachers endorsed men's premarital sexual experience. A double standard was clearly illustrated, as only 15 percent of both male and female participants endorsed premarital sex for women. In terms of sexual behavior, 12 percent of the male students and only 1 percent of the female students reported having had intercourse.

These observations have been further confirmed in another excellent study (Ford and Kittisuksathit 1994) which we have cited throughout this chapter. In this study, qualitative data were obtained from focus groups with young factory workers (ages 15 to 24) whose socioeconomic status was more representative of the general Thai youth populations than high-school or college samples. Sexual desire was perceived by both young men and women to be a male attribute. The young men openly expressed their sexual feelings and experiences; the young women felt ashamed of their sexual curiosity and thought women should wait until they were older and married before they found out about sex. In the minds of the young men, sexual intercourse seemed like an adventure, a gain, a forceful act, or an act of satisfying one's greed. Some slang terms used by the young men for sexual intercourse can be roughly translated to "taking," "earning," "playing," "grinding," "gobbling," and "poking the yolk." On the contrary, sexual intercourse was seen by the young women as a loss of their body/self (*sia tua*), and women who have lost their virginity were seen as "impure," "soiled," or "tarnished." In addition, there is a belief that a forbidden sexual experience can predispose a young woman to becoming sexually out of control, (*jai taek*), especially if the liaison ends with the man deserting her. Such a woman might turn into a "carefree woman" or even a prostitute (Thorbek 1988).

In addition to demonstrating a double standard among Thai adolescents, Chompootaweep et al. (1991) also found that the gender and sexual attitudes of Thais in the same urban environment differed as a function of their ages. The young factory workers in Ford and Kittisuksathit's study (1994) pointedly articulated this sense of being in the midst of social transformation. Repeatedly referring to "[things are] different today," these adolescents were acutely aware of their living in a period in which sexual constructions were rapidly changing from the clear prescriptions of the "traditional" norms to the more amorphous and perplexing "modern" ways.

B. Adult Sexual Behavior

Premarital and Adult Sexual Experience

The *Survey of Partner Relations and HIV Infection* (Sittitrai et al., 1992; referred to hereafter as "the *Partner Relations Survey*") is a large population-based study, which examined sexual attitudes and behaviors among 2,801 men and women. Currently married men reported an average of 30.2 premarital sexual partners. Never-married men reported an average of 14.3 premarital sexual partners. The picture was completely different for women, who reported little or no premarital sexual experiences, with means of 0.03 and 0.01 premarital sexual partners for married women and never-married women, respectively. This gender difference again reflects a double standard on premarital sex for men and women. Although the extent of reporting biases could not be determined, as in most sex surveys, the social-desirability biases could have influenced men to over-report and/or women to under-report their premarital sexual experiences. The biases, if there were any, did indeed reflect the double standard that promotes premarital sex in men and discourages it in women.

Many researchers have studied Thai military conscripts in order to describe the sexual behaviors of the general populations of young Thai men. Thai men ages 20 to 22, who are not in higher education, are inducted to the Royal Thai Army by lottery; randomly selected samples therefore provide an excellent representation of men in the lower socioeconomic strata of Thai society (Beyrer, Eiumtrakul, Celentano, Nelson, Ruckphaopunt, and Khamboonruang 1995). In a study of conscripts from northern Thailand in 1990 and 1991 (Nopkesorn et al. 1991), 97 percent of these 21-year-old men reported having had sexual intercourse, with about 54 percent reporting having the first intercourse before the age of 16. The first sexual intercourse for 74 percent of the men was with a female sex worker, compared to 12 percent with a lover, and 8 percent with a girlfriend. A majority of men, 90 percent, had had sex with a female sex worker, mostly starting between the ages of 15 to 18. By the age of 16, about half of the sample had had their first visit to a female sex worker.

Until AIDS became a widespread anxiety in the mid-1990s, commercial sex had been the primary sexual outlet for Thai bachelors, justified as a means of protecting virtuous Thai women from premarital sex. For Thai male adults, the use of commercial sex continues in the same way as it began in adolescence (see Section 5A on adolescent sexual behavior), only with less economic restriction. Taking care of men's sexual needs by offering services from a sex worker is considered part of hospitality in many business dealings. Upon arrival in a new city, traveling men or male tourists often make a point of visiting local brothels or erotic massage parlors as local attractions.

This picture may, however, be changing with a new generation of Thais due to several factors. Young women have been found to be more likely to engage in premarital sexual activity than the previous generations. Western culture, as perceived and interpreted through the Thai eyes, has been implicated in this change over the last few decades. More recently, it has also been attributed to the men's heightened fear of HIV. As prevention campaigns have publicized high rates of HIV infection among female sex workers, Thai men have become more wary of visiting professional sex workers. For example, a decrease in the use of commercial sex workers among the northern Thai conscripts, for example, has been documented over the few years prior to 1996 (Nelson et al. 1996).

In response to the worries about AIDS and commercial sex, Thai men have turned to a number of other ways of fulfilling their sexual desires. While many Thai men have become less sexually active, others, especially those in the urban middle-class settings, have been paying for sex with non-professional sex workers who are not in the sex establishments. Others turn to the big-city singles or nightlife scenes for casual sex with pick-up partners. Finally, there is a growing number of men who have sex with their girlfriends in the context of a committed romantic relationship. Helped by the anonymity of big cities and the widely available contraceptive methods, there are increasing number of cohabiting couples, much to the chagrin of conservatives who are concerned with the virtue of Thai women. Although this phenomenon has been consistently observed in recent studies (e.g., Nelson et al. 1996), many researchers feel that there is much resistance from the Thai public, who are not quite ready to formally approve of these unmarried sexual couples.

Thai women, not unlike those in many other cultures, take risks in having sexual experience. In addition to concerns about pregnancy and health, they face the risks of stigmatization for losing their virginity outside a marriage. As many sex workers have reported, because an unmarried woman's virtue is eminently tied to her virginity, a woman who has lost her virginity has nothing to lose in choosing the path of commercial sex (Thorbek 1988). Other women keep their premarital sexual experience a secret, although the psychological repercussions may continue. A small number of women who are neither secretive nor disturbed by their premarital sex are suspected to have had a "bad influence" from Western culture, or are pathologized as sensation-seeking, promiscuous, or morally corrupt (see the "bad girl" stereotype in Section 5A). The expressions which characterize women who seek sexual gratification with little restraint are *jai ngaai* ("feeble mind/heart"), and *jai taek* ("broken mind/heart"), suggesting that the women are morally corrupt or out of control. Together, the non-professional women who exchange sex for money and the "care-free" single women in the urban nightlife and singles scenes are categorized as *ying ruk sanuk,* or "fun-loving women," or the slang *kai long,* or "stray chicken." These "depraved" women are seen as "only good for sex but not suitable for being the mother of your children."

In spite of the blame on Western influence, the image of "bad" women who seek sexual pleasures is not new. Kirsch (1985) has observed that in the nineteenth century, King Mongkut characterized "spinsters and divor-cees" as "artful women" who viewed monks as "fattened hogs" (i.e., potential husbands); monks exposed to such women's seduction "are likely to be driven crazy by their new found love" (p. 311). Similarly, Penny Van Esterik (1982) has found that some lay villagers were suspicious of *mae chii* (female ascetics) who lived near the temples in which monks resided. She further cites a story recorded by Attagara about a woman who dressed up as a *mae chii* and seduced a local abbot who was so ashamed of his weakness that he held his breath and died. A line in the *Jataka* tales (tales about the Buddha's past lives) says that "Women desire rich lovers like cows seeking new pastures" (p. 76). These illustrations suggest that women who did not fit the model of motherhood, like unmarried women, divorcées, or *mae chii,* might have always been viewed with suspicion, with a projection of the male-typical boundless and uncontrollable sexual desires on to them.

In addition to the well-known "bad woman" stereotype and the *kulasatrii* ideal, there is yet another type of women in the Thai consciousness, namely the widows. (Although this word in Thai can also refer to divorced women, this discussion pertains only to women whose husbands are deceased). Mostly of middle- and lower-class social strata, many widows seem to be less bound by the conservatism of a *kulasatrii,* yet they are not stigmatized as depraved. Because a widow presumably has had sexual experience in her prior marriage, virginity no longer is an issue of virtue for her. Therefore, she can seek sexual pleasure without severe social stigma, given that, of course, scandals such as affairs with married men or pregnancy out of wedlock are avoided. With the exception of female sex workers, widows seem to be the only women in Thai society "allowed" to have sex outside of marriage. In literature, jokes, and popular song lyrics, widows are por-trayed as temptresses: straightforward about their sexual interest—often toward younger men—witty and flirtatious, exuberantly sensual and seduc-tive, and well versed in their sexual practices. To many heterosexual male adolescents, an idealized fantasy of their first sexual experience is an encounter with such a woman who is sexually disinhibited, yet not a sex worker. The Thai culture seems to have an alternative for a woman to be sexually active with less reservations, but she needs to have lost a husband who had introduced her to the joy of sex.

Marriage and Family Dynamics

Choice of a marriage mate is usually based on the individual's preference. Thai women have greater power in their spouse selection than do Chinese-

Thai women in Thailand (Pyne 1994). Elopements are also, however, well known, indicating the power of parental objection (Kirsch 1982). A married couple may reside for a time with the wife's family, but their ideal residence is an independent nuclear household. In extended families, the strong matrilineal ties generally entail men's moving into the woman's family. Well-known exceptions to this custom exist, especially among the ethnic Chinese in Thailand as exemplified in the work with Yunnanese families by Hill (1988). With the couple establishing an independent household in the wife's family compound, both usually continue to work the land owned by the wife's parents, with the son-in-law's labor construed as a form of brideprice. Despite such a matrilocal pattern of postnuptial residence, authority is passed down through the men in the family, and the son-in-law eventually becomes the head of the household (Pyne 1994).

Women maintain strong connections with their mothers, even when migration and poverty make contacts difficult (Thorbek 1982). Women working in cities often send money to their families upcountry, visit them annually, and most return to the villages when their target income is achieved (Pyne 1994) or when their employment or marriage ends.

A traditional Thai marriage is symbolized by tying the bride and groom's wrists with holy string during a ceremony at which the family and community are present (Pyne 1994). A women changes her surname to her husband's upon marriage and her title changes from *naangsao* ("Miss") to *naang* ("Missus"). In addition to the informal gender-neutral *fan*, a variety of terms for husband and wife exist for use in different contexts, ranging from the playful and frank (*phua* for husband, and *mia* for wife) to the formal and polite (*saamii* for husband, and *phan-ya* for wife). There is a slight discomfort with the frank terms for husband and wife, and most Thai people see the formal, legal, slightly detached terms as more civilized and polite. The importance of the couple's image as parents can be seen in the endearing terms for husband and wife, *pho baan* and *mae baan* (father and mother of the home). In fact, the birth of the first child is a critical event for a traditional Thai couple, as it denotes the union and symbolizes a stable relationship (Pyne 1994). Although a preference for having sons has been documented elsewhere (e.g., P. Van Esterik 1982) and it is particularly strong in the Chinese-Thai families, both sons and daughters are valued for different reasons. While the son's potential ordination in the *Sangha* can accumulate merit for the parents (Rajadhon 1961), a daughter is viewed as being reliable and dependable, especially for the care of parents in old age (Pyne 1994). Data from the *Demographic and Health Survey* (cited in Pyne 1994) indicate that half of all married women (ages 15 to 49) intend to have two children, and 80 percent want two or three.

The nurturing responsibilities of contemporary Thai women are undeniable in the statistics of women who work outside of their homes, as well as the proportions of women among migrants and the work force (see Pyne 1994). Employers consider female workers to be hard-working, enthusiastic, loyal, patient, and attentive to detail. Interestingly, centuries ago, the same qualities in Thai women did not escape the eyes of foreign observers. In the seventeenth century, Simon La Loubère (1693, quoted in Kirsch 1982, p. 16) noted on his visit to Siam: "how lazy the ordinary life of the Siamese [commoner] is . . . he does almost nothing but continue sitting or lying, playing, smoking, and sleeping." In contrast, he observed that the Siamese women "plow the land, they sell and buy in the cities"; and "The women . . . are always busy . . . trafficking in the bazaars, doing the light work in the fields and marketing." Similarly, a Chinese visitor to Siam during the Ming dynasty observed that "when there are affairs to be settled [in Siam] they are settled by women. In determination and judgment the women really surpass the men" (Kirsch 1988, p. 27).

In Thai households today, men are typically the main source of income in a married couple. Major decisions of allocating resources thus remain in the hands of the men, whereas the women often manage the finances on a day-to-day basis (Pyne 1994; Thorbek 1988). In general, women are often more organized and economical than their husbands. Many women spend much energy trying to keep their husbands' vices in check with varying degrees of success. Thai women also engage in small homegrown businesses, such as vegetable gardening, market-vendor trading, and fabric weaving, if the family earning from the men is not adequate. Nevertheless, these earning women seem to spend most of their own incomes on the necessities of the family and often give sums of money to their mothers (Thorbek 1988). Similarly, a majority of women in commercial sex businesses send their income to parents, siblings, and other relatives in their native villages (Wawer, Podhisita, Kanungsukkasem, Pramualratana, and McNamara 1996). Thai women take their "nurturer" role seriously and few things can deter them from their mission.

Incidence of Vaginal, Oral, and Anal Sex

Data on the incidence of vaginal, oral, and anal sex among Thai people has been provided by the large-scale *Partner Relations Survey* (Sittitrai et al. 1992). Among sexually experienced participants, vaginal intercourse was by far the most frequent sexual behavior, reported by 99.9 percent of the male and 99.8 percent of the female participants. Other sexual behaviors, however, are much more rare: performing oral intercourse (presumably on the other gender) was reported by only 0.7 percent of the male and 13 percent of the female participants. Receiving oral sex was reported by 21 percent of the male participants and no data were available for the female participants' experience of receiving oral sex. Receptive anal intercourse was experienced by 0.9 percent of the male and 2 percent of the female participants. Insertive anal intercourse was experienced by 4 percent of the male participants.

The striking rarity of the non-genitogenital sexual acts, especially cunnilingus, among Thai people illustrates some sociocultural constructions that play important roles in the Thai sexuality. Even if reporting biases were operating in these findings, the reluctance toward having or reporting oral sex may suggest some aversion to certain body parts, especially the vagina or anus. As previously mentioned, Thai men's anxiety about losing dignity or masculinity from performing oral sex on a woman might have been a cultural residue from occultism and superstition of the past (see previous discussion on *mii khruu* in Section 1D). In addition to this superstitious reasoning, Thais also apply the concepts of social hierarchy and dignity to body parts: certain parts of the body, such as the head or the face, are associated with personal honor or integrity, whereas other "inferior" parts, such as the legs, feet, anus, and the female reproductive organs, are associated with impurity and baseness. This belief is still extremely common in Thai society, even among those who are not particularly superstitious. In the updated belief of body hierarchy, the impurity of inferior body parts is associated with germs or crudeness, while violation is framed as poor hygiene or lack of social etiquette.

In social interactions, the body hierarchy prohibits some behaviors, such as raising one's lower extremities high in the presence of others or touching an older person's head with one's hand (or even worse, with one's foot). In sexual situations, this belief also prevents certain sexual acts. Viewed in this cultural context, one can understand Thai people's repulsion toward oral or anal sex, as well as other sexual acts, such as oral-anal sex or foot fetishism. In these acts, "lowering" a highly guarded body part (e.g., a man's face or head) to contact an organ of a much lower order (e.g., feet or a woman's genitals) can cause damage to the man's personal integrity and dignity. Many Thais today openly disapprove of these sexual acts as deviant, unnatural, or unsanitary, while others are excited by the lack of inhibition they find in Western erotica.

Perhaps due to the lack of direct public health implications, very few studies have generated data on the sexual behavior within married couples. In a 1981 study, a majority of married Thai women (ages 17 to 65) randomly sampled in Bangkok reported low sexual desire or enjoyment after the birth of their children (Bussaratid, Na Ranong, Boonyaprakob, and Sitasuwan 1981). Frequency of sexual intercourse was once a week or less in 49 percent of the women. Only 24 percent reported having orgasm with every intercourse; women 35 years or older reported fewer experiences of orgasm. In another study of female outpatients in 1975, the mean frequency of intercourse was 2.3 per week (Pongthai, Sakornratanakul, and Chaturachinda 1980). Another study examined the sexual behavior in pregnant women ages 17 to 44 in Bangkok and found that sexual abstention increased as pregnancy progressed, ranging from 4 percent of the women in the first trimester to 56 percent of the women in the third trimester (Aribarg, Aribarg, Rakiti, and Harnroongroj 1982). The most common reasons for abstinence and decreased frequency of sex were fear of fetal injury (reported by 30 percent of the women), and somatic symptoms of pregnancy (22 percent). A number of the pregnant women also abstained from sex to protect their fetuses from STD, as 13 percent of the women knew that their husbands had had extramarital sex.

Unfortunately, most of the available data on the sexual behavior within Thai couples are from research conducted prior to 1982. The paucity of more-recent findings points to the need for more research. Information in this area will afford us a better understanding of extramarital sex, sexual dysfunctions, heterosexual transmission of HIV and sexually transmitted diseases, and marital satisfaction and discord.

Extramarital Sex

Perhaps extramarital sexual practices in Thailand are best illustrated by the findings from the *Partner Relations Survey* by Werasit Sittitrai and his colleagues (1992). They found that 31 percent of urban male participants and 12 percent of rural male participants—17 percent overall—reported having had sex outside their relationship in the previous twelve months. The data from women were quite different: only 1 percent of the urban female participants and 0.7 percent of the rural female participants—0.9 percent overall—reported sex outside their relationship in the previous twelve months. The remarkable gender difference in extramarital sex in these findings will be more extensively discussed below.

Despite the historical acceptance, male polygamy is no longer legally or socially acceptable in the contemporary Thai society. However, the tradition continues in modern days in a more secretive fashion. Whereas a "virtuous woman" or *kulasatrii* (see traditional female gender role in Section 1) must remain faithful to her husband, there were no equivalent rules in history mandating fidelity in the "virtuous man." In fact, upper-class Thai men were historically known to maintain mansions with a co-residence of multiple wives and their children. Among the royalty and courtiers in the past, wives were classified as principal, secondary, and slave (Pyne 1994). Today, the tradition of "minor wives" still remains, but the practice is different from that of the past. Also, due to the expense involved, minor wives are mostly limited to the wealthy men, although Thorbek (1988) has also documented the practice in men of lower socioeconomic strata.

Euphemistically called having a "little home," the practice of keeping a minor wife usually occurs today in secrecy from the "primary wife," and minor wives rarely share the home with the man and his family as in the old days. While almost all married women today object to this practice, and indeed for many it has been grounds for divorce, other women learn to cope with their anger and emotional betrayal. Minor wives are viewed with contempt by the Thai society along the lines of being amoral women or home breakers. They do not achieve social or legal recognition as a spouse. A Thai phrase "drinking water from underneath someone else's elbow" illustrates the humiliation and powerlessness of a minor wife, often used to deter young women from considering a relationship with a married male suitor.

Frustrated with the husband's infidelity, potential or real, some married women have been taught by older women and sex journalists to break out of the conservative sexual norms of a *kulasatrii* by adopting the dual role of "a *kulasatrii* outside the bedroom, and a prostitute inside." Extramarital sex for a married woman is, however, not a viable option. In a seminar with participants from rural villages in northern Thailand, men told Pacharin Dumronggittigule and her colleagues (personal communication 1995) that if a woman had more sexual desire than her husband could satisfy, she should "hit her feet with a hammer," indicating their belief that the use of drastic means was needed to suppress women's sexual desires. In a folk-tale epic, *Khun Chaang, Khun Phaen,* the heroine, Wanthong, was persecuted for being torn between her relationships with the two male protagonists. Although women today are not persecuted as was Wanthong, her tragic fate reflects the society's clear prohibitive rule against women's emotional and sexual infidelity.

Whereas minor wives are the secret sexual indulgence for wealthy men, sex with commercial sex workers is widely accepted by almost all male adults, regardless of age, socioeconomic class, or marital status. After marriage, Thai men seem be monogamous with their wives for a period of time, although the duration of this monogamy has not been investigated. A great number, however, resume their use of commercial sex, often in the context of all-male, "husbands' night out" socialization with their peers.

Dumronggittigule and her colleagues (1995) examined the married men's use of commercial sex by conducting focus groups with married villagers in northern Thailand. They found that the cultural processes behind this phenomenon were different from the processes for the Thai bachelors. Thai men visit commercial sex workers after socializing with male friends, a pattern established since the start of their experience with commercial sex. For married men's gatherings, women are not necessarily precluded from the social gatherings, as the meals are often prepared by women, but excessive alcohol consumption and gambling repel women from further participation. Married men reported that their sexual desires are enhanced due to the alcohol and the sex talk among the men. Married women, on the contrary, reported that after a long day of work outside and inside the home, they were not sexually thrilled by their husbands' drunken manners and alcohol smells, and many refused to have sex. Other couples reportedly avoided this conflict by having an a priori agreement that the husbands could take their sexual desire elsewhere.

Moreover, the villagers reported other common causes of diminished sexual attraction within the couple. Women reported that the strenuous work inside and outside the home caused them to be exhausted, irritable, and uninterested in sex, and their husband's drinking and gambling with male friends did not help. Men, on the other hand, commented on their wife's homely appearance, angry temperament, and sexual unresponsiveness, all of which made them turn to drinking, gambling, and commercial sex as recreation. As this spiral of blame and self-defense continued, conflicts and resentment grew. Following what they had seen in other couples, many women decided that consenting to their husband's use of commercial sex could relieve this dilemma. Thus, the use of commercial sex by married men is often consented to or known by their wives. For both men and women, the husband's extramarital sex is not a cause of marital conflicts, but an attempted solution designed to preserve their marriage.

Married women, therefore, do not simply consent to their husband's use of commercial sex because "Thai people have permissive attitudes men's extramarital sex," as is often quoted. In the same study cited above, Dumronggittigule and colleagues (1995) used anonymous questionnaires to collect data from 170 married couples in the villages. They found feelings of frustration, worry, and helplessness among the women who believed their husbands had regular sex with sex workers. Almost all the married women objected to their husband visiting sex workers. Ninety-one percent of these women had asked their husband to refrain from such behavior, but 47 percent of the women believed their husbands would visit or had visited sex workers. Although they felt vulnerable to HIV infection, these married women still did not think that their husband would respond to their fears. Instead, these women would rather protect themselves from HIV by having protected sex with their husbands; 83 percent reported they would be willing to have their husbands use condoms with them. The women's interest in self-protection, however, might not lead to an actual prevention; most couples had never used condoms with each other and were unlikely to change upon the women's requests.

Alcohol Use and Sexual Behavior

The use of alcohol is a regular part of Thai culture and tradition despite the prohibition in the Buddhist Fifth Precept. Many male adolescents in northern Thailand begin drinking commercially produced whiskey or village-prepared liquor at the age of 14 or 15. They will often drink alcohol with a few friends and go as a small group to have sex with sex workers (van Landingham et al. 1993). Adolescent girls will often start drinking at the age of 17 or 18. They are more likely to drink when there are parties as part of a celebration. Drinking and sex in combination is a common way for adolescents to be sexual with one another (Nopkesorn, Sweat, Kaensing, and Teppa 1993). Thai men often report that alcohol makes them "horny," although using condoms is usually more difficult in an intoxicated state. Data confirm that alcohol use does interfere with the use of condoms in the commercial sex settings (Mastro and Limpakarnjanarat 1995).

6. Homoerotic, Homosexual, and Ambisexual Behaviors

A. Attitudes Toward Homosexuality in Buddhism and Thai Society

Although homosexual behavior in Thailand is assumed to be quite common, little formal research has been done. Most of the available data pertain to men, and there is a paucity of information regarding women. There has been a general reluctance, as with other Asian cultures, to openly discuss or scientifically study homosexual behaviors. In a large 1990 population-based survey (Sittitrai et al. 1992), extremely low rates of male homosexual behavior were reported; the authors cautioned that, due to societal attitudes, these estimates were probably too low and reflected the research participants' underreporting of homoerotic and homosexual experiences (the prevalence of same-gender sexual behavior will be further reviewed below).

The attitudes toward homosexuality are quite complex: On the one hand, the behavior is clearly stigmatized, and on the other, tolerated. Probably the manner in which it is expressed is a more critical variable for social acceptance. In the culture in which men's sexual desires are exaggerated, it is understandable that men might, from time to time, hypothetically engage in sexual behavior with other men for pragmatic purposes (e.g., when women are not available or when they need money). Women may face stronger negative sanction than men. Again, a double standard regarding general sexuality may be at play here. Homosexual behavior for women is less tolerated, probably because virtuous women express their sexuality only with their husbands.

Overall, most contemporary Thais view heterosexuality as the norm; homosexuality is seen as a deviance or an unnatural act, often resulting from one's bad *karma* or the lack of merit in past lives. To the more superstitious Thais, homosexual acts, which are an aberration from "how nature intends," are punishable by animistic powers. Contemporary Thais still express their disapproval of homosexuality by saying, often blithely, that "lightning will strike" those who engage in sex with a person of the same gender. The educated Thais understand homosexuality in terms of mental problems or illness. Many think homosexuality is caused by problems in upbringing or parental characteristics (e.g., a domineering mother and a passive father), while others also attribute it to the child's oversocialization with the opposite gender, e.g., a boy spending too much time with his aunts, sisters, or female peers, or not having a father around as a male role model. This pathology model of homosexuality most likely originated in the Western psychiatric theories of sexuality which dominated Western medicine and psychology until the 1960s and 1970s. Many Thai physicians and psychologists still subscribe to these antiquated theories and remain impervious to new research findings or the American Psychiatric Association's declassification of homosexuality as a mental illness in 1974.

Buddhism is mostly silent on the topic of homosexuality. Despite some ambivalence toward homosexuality in many Buddhist cultures, Cabezón (1993) notes Buddhism only condemns homosexuality more for being an instance of sexuality rather than its same-gender sex. "The principal question for Buddhism has not been one of heterosexuality versus homosexuality, but one of sexuality versus celibacy" (p. 82). Cabezón further notes that, as far as the laity are concerned, homosexuality is rarely mentioned as a transgression of the Third Precept in Buddhist texts and oral commentaries.

References to homosexuality have been found in the Buddhist canon and the *Jataka*, the stories of the Buddha's previous lives. Leonard Zwilling has noted that only in the *Vinaya*, the monastic discipline which forms one of the three sections of the Buddhist canon, is there mention of same-gender attraction and effeminacy in men. These instances were, according to Zwilling, "derogated much to the same degree as comparable heterosexual acts" (quoted in Cabezón 1993, p. 88). As for other sections of the Buddhist canon, John Garret Jones (cited in Cabezón 1993) has concluded that there is an implicit affirmation from the silence regarding homosexuality, and the silence is certainly not due to the lack of material.

Whereas the canon is silent about homosexuality, the *Jataka* literature, in which the previously mentioned tale of Prince Vessantara is embedded, is replete with sentiments about same-gender affection. One example can be found in the eloquent past-life stories of the Buddha and his disciple and attendant, Ananda. In one scenario, the Buddha and Ananda are depicted as two deer who "always went about together . . . ruminating and cuddling together, very happy, head to head, nozzle to nozzle, horn to horn." In another story, a serpent king who falls in love with Ananda "encircled the ascetic with snakes folds, and embraced him, with his great hood upon his head; and there he lay a little, till his affection was satisfied" (Jones 1979, quoted in Cabezón 1993, p. 89). These examples are but a few of many instances which articulate same-gender affection in the context of friendships between men in the *Jatakas*. Considering the enormous number of warnings about the dangers of heterosexual relationships, Cabezón argues that the absence of warning about same-gender relationship is remarkable. It suggests that the attitude toward homosexuality in the Indian *Jataka* texts is one of acceptance, and occasionally even a eulogy, of these feelings.

Allyn (1991) cites yet another Buddhist story, possibly a folk version, told on Thai radio about a male disciple who had fallen in love with the Buddha. The disciple expresses admiration for the Buddha's beauty. The Buddha responded to these acts of admiration by a gentle reminder of the body's impermanence, a likely response for a female admirer as well. Taken together with the analysis of the canon and the *Jataka* tales, this story illustrates Buddhism's neutral position on the issue of homosexuality. Nevertheless, it should be noted that some negative attitudes can be found in the Buddhist practice today. For example, some Thai people have heard that a man who acknowledges his homosexuality will be denied Buddhist ordination, although such instances may have been very rare or never enforced.

In contrast to the neutral position of Buddhism, anti-homosexual attitudes are quite common among Thai people. Chompootaweep and colleagues (1991) found that 75 percent of both male and female adolescents reported negative attitudes toward homosexuality. In addition to these disapproving attitudes, Thai people who have sex with the same gender also have other important considerations when they make sexual and relationship decisions. Thais are concerned about matters which would cause an individual or family to lose face, and maintaining relationships with their family is of an extreme importance. To reveal one's homosexual orientation to one's parents would, in a sense, violate the Third Precept of Buddhism, and this has caused many Thai gays and lesbians to hide their homosexuality from their parents for fear of causing them sorrow (Allyn 1991). On the other hand, what an individual does in privacy is less of a concern. Thus, a person's homosexual sex, per se, may be easier for his or her family than other more visible features, such as long-term same-gender relationships (Jackson 1989) or coming out as an openly gay or lesbian person.

The fact that same-gender sex is less stigmatized than the public disclosure of this behavior deserves some discussion. Same-gender sexual experience does not necessarily carry the assumption of homosexuality or a homosexual identity in Thailand (Sittitrai, Brown, and Virulak 1991). There are no laws prohibiting homosexual behavior (Jackson 1989). On the other hand, the social pressure to be in conformity with the expectations of family and culture is extremely intense. Indeed, these sanctions may have a stronger effect than religious or legal sanctions. A public statement of homosexual identity would violate two important values of Thai culture: harmony—not to confront disagreements or conflicts—and the great value placed upon preservation of family units and preserving lineage through marriage and procreation. Allyn (1991) also contends that the anti-homosexual attitudes in the Thai society are primarily the discrimination against the feminine *kathoey* (see Section 7) who, according to stereotype, display overt and loud gender-atypical social manners.

B. Social Constructions of Sexual Orientation in Thailand

The labels homosexual, bisexual, and heterosexual are Western constructs and do not exactly fit the traditional social constructions in Thailand. Assuming a gay or bisexual identity is also a new, if not foreign, concept; for example, there is no translation or the equivalent Thai word for "gay," and as of 1996, the construct "sexual orientation" had not been translated even for academic use. In the past few decades, Thai people have increasingly used the English words "gay" and "lesbian" in both the mainstream and academic contexts. The terms "homo" and "homosexual" are also used. Conventionally, the most widely used term for "homosexual" was an extremely obscure euphemism *len phuean*, roughly translated as "playing with friends." Another popular usage employs a literary analogy, *mai paa deow kan*, meaning "trees in the same forest" (Allyn 1991). The now-rare term *lakka-phayt*, roughly translated to "sexual perversion" in English, was sometimes used to describe homosexuality within the medical context, therefore illustrating the past influence of Western psychiatry.

The technical terms "heterosexual" and "homosexual" were transliterated into Thai twenty or thirty years ago for academic purposes. The term for "heterosexual" was *rug taang phayt*, meaning "loving the different gender" and the term for "homosexual" was *rug ruam phayt*, meaning "loving the same gender." This might indicate that the Thai construct of loving another is inseparable from eroticizing another. By the same logic, bisexuality was subsequently translated to *rug song phayt*, meaning "loving two genders." However, the directly borrowed term "bisexual" and its shortened derivative, *bai*, are more popular and have been part of the Thai sexual vocabulary of late.

More recently, with influences from Western cultures, the concepts of homosexuality and sexual orientation have infiltrated the Thai thinking. These concepts quickly became popularized and transformed to fit the indigenous constructs (see also Section 7 for the discussion of the indigenous concept of *kathoey*). In the following discussions, the Thai social constructions of homosexuality in men and women will be examined separately to maximize clarity. We realize that this approach has its own shortcomings, as male and female homosexualities in most cultures are, conceptually and politically speaking, not discrete entities. However, much more has been written about male homosexuality in Thailand, and a discourse to conceptually bridge the parallel phenomena in men and women has yet to be made. There is still little evidence that the discussion about this construct in one gender can be generalized to the other.

C. Homosexuality in Men

A small number of studies have attempted to find the prevalence of homosexual behavior in men. In a population-based study (Sittitrai et al. 1992), only 3.1 percent of the men reported having had sex with men and women, and 0.2 percent reported it with men exclusively. The authors of the study speculated that these statistics were an underestimation due to underreporting. Cohorts of military conscripts, comprised of men mostly age 21 from lower socioeconomic populations, have also shown varying rates of male-male sexual experience. Among the 1990 conscripts from northern Thailand (Nopkesorn et al. 1991), 26 percent reported having had sex with a man, 15 percent reported past anal intercourse with a man, and 12 percent reported sexual arousal in response to male nudes. In the 1992 conscripts from northern Thailand (Nopkesorn, Sweat et al. 1993), 14 percent reported having had at least one instance of insertive anal sex with a *kathoey* in their lifetimes, 3 percent with non-*kathoey* men, and 3 percent reported having had receptive anal sex. In another study of 2,047 military conscripts from northern Thailand (Beyrer, et al. 1995), 134 men (7 percent) reported having had sex with men; most of these men were also more likely to have higher numbers of female sexual partners than other men who had sex with women exclusively.

In Thai society today, men who have sex with men are either *gay king* or *gay queen*: A *gay king* is a man who plays the insertive role in sex, whereas a *gay queen* takes a passive and receptive role in sex (Allyn 1991). Versatility in sexual behavior is obviously not a traditional construct, and the gender dichotomy pervades the Thai conceptualization of sex between men. Gender dimorphism also necessitates that the society views homosexuality in reference to the fundamental genders of male and female. Also, cross-gendered manners and behavior are seen as indicating the essence of homosexuality in a person (other terms for male homosexuality related to cross-gendered behaviors will be discussed in Section 7). *Gay queens* are assumed to have feminine characteristics, and are therefore, "true homosexuals." On the other hand, *gay kings*, stereotyped as male-acting and male-appearing, are seen as less likely to be "permanently" homosexual. Thai people think that *gay kings* are simply heterosexual men going through a phrase of sexual experimentation with other men. *Gay kings* are also variously referred to as "one-hundred percent male" (*phuu-chaai roi poe-sen*) and "a complete man" (*phuu-chaai tem tua*) (Jackson 1989), which reflects the belief that the insertive homosexual sex act does not jeopardize one's masculinity. The idea that *gay kings* are confused or adventurous heterosexuals can be seen in many Thai movies and fiction about gay relationships with a tragic ending, when the *gay king* hero leaves a devastated *gay queen* to marry a woman. Moreover, the Thai myth of men's boundless sexuality states that "a real man" (i.e., real heterosexual) can derive sexual pleasure from anyone, regardless of gender. The playful term for bisexual men, *suea bai* (meaning "bisexual tiger") connotes this admiration of bisexual men's sexual vigor (Allyn 1991). Bisexual behavior, therefore, is seen as an attribute of *gay kings*, bisexual men, and "indiscriminate" heterosexual men alike.

Actual data on sexual behavior confirm the fluidity of sex between men in Thailand as implied by the classification above. For example, military conscripts who reported same-gender sexual behavior were more likely to be married, have girlfriends, and visit female sex partners more often than their counterparts who have had sex with women exclusively (Beyrer et al. 1995). Northeastern men recruited through the social network of men who had sex with men demonstrated equally complicated behaviors. Their reported sex acts covered a whole gamut of insertive and receptive intercourse, both oral and anal; their sexual partners included both genders of commercial sex workers, casual partners, and lovers (Sittitrai, Brown, and Sakondhavat 1993).

Primary affectional and sexual relationships between men are quite common, although these relationships are not akin to the Western concept of the gay couple. These relationships may be of very short duration, without much long-term commitment, and without much social or familial recognition. There are distinct problems maintaining homosexual relationships. First, because long-term relationships by nature end up being more public, they invite more public scrutiny and negative sanction. Second, the same-sex relationships would interfere with what the heterosexist norm expects of a man: to get married to a woman and have children. Finally, there are no models for same-sex relationships within Thai culture. The only role models would come from *farang* (Westerners), but their codes of conduct would not necessarily work in the Thai culture. This lack of role models and solutions for the Thai male couples has caused much jealousy and conflicts around infidelity, creating many heartaches and failed relationships (Jackson 1989). For many other couples, however, male romantic and sexual relationships adhere closely to the heterosexual model of sex roles: in fact, a *gay king* almost always pairs with a *gay queen*, and Thais find it difficult to comprehend if two *gay kings* or two *gay queens* would settle down together. Following the traditional Thai heterosexual relationship which prescribes monogamy in the women and sexual freedom in the men, *gay kings* also have a tendency to seek out sexual pleasures outside their relationship with a *gay queen*.

In reaching "gay men," *gay kings, gay queens,* and *kathoey* for HIV prevention, there is an effort in Thai society to organize and empower these individuals. This attempt follows HIV-prevention strategies from Western cultures. Local activists and international agencies in Thailand are fostering an adoption of the gay-identity concept to identify, reach, and empower men who have sex with men, in an effort to prevent the spread of HIV among them and their partners, both male and female. There remains an ethical question regarding the cultural imperialism of the West, which is imposing Western-constructed identities on a culture which has maintained different constructs of sexual orientation and sexual behavior. Examination of Thai and other cultures which have diverse constructs of sexual orientation has challenged the universality of categories of sexual orientation adopted by the West. This has forced HIV-prevention campaigns in the West to employ strategies which take into account the fact that not all segments of society identify themselves as gay, straight, or bisexual. One example of such attempts is to identify the population of interest based on their sexual behavior (e.g., "men who have sex with men" or "men who have sex with both men and women"), instead of selecting them by their "risk group" or "gay" or "bisexual" self-identity. Hopefully, the cultural exchange will lead to greater understanding of homosexuality and the promotion of sexual health among those individuals who engage in same-gender sex in any society (Coleman 1996).

Regarding the gay identity in Thailand, there has been a rapid development since the mid-1980s of a gay identity with a Thai twist. Meanwhile, gay enterprising and political activities began to thrive in Bangkok and other big cities. Until the late 1980s, the only regular media coverage on homosexuality was an advice column in the widely popular tabloid *Plaek* ("Strange") titled *Chiiwit Sao Chao Gay* ("The Sad Lives of Gays") in which

Go Paaknaam, a straight-identified columnist, published letters about sexual and relationship problems from men who have sex with men (Allyn 1991). In contrast to the previous coverage which tended to be rare and eccentric, in recent years Thailand has seen a proliferation of magazines in the format of erotica for gay men. In addition to erotica, these publications also provide an avenue for men to meet through personal advertisements, as well as the new forum for exchanging social and political views. More social networks have been formed, often composed of previously isolated gay men, many of whom do not have access to or participate in the thriving gay-bar scenes in big cities. A more solidified yet multifaceted gay identity has slowly evolved as Thai men participate in the discourse on their sexuality through these publications. In the meantime, Thai mainstream media, especially newspaper and magazines, have increased accurate representations of gay life, as well as progressive treatises on homosexuality, although sensationalistic coverage is still common.

In addition, entertainment businesses for gay men have flourished in big cities. A variety of gay restaurants and pubs have been opened, with and without *deg off* ("off-boys," or male sex workers), providing places for leisure, sex, and socialization. Bangkok sports one of the world's most famous gay saunas (bathhouses). Men in these surroundings are motivated not only by a bit of the Thai *sanuk* (fun, pleasure, and enjoyment), but also the camaraderie and the search for a relationship partner (Allyn 1991). These new developments represent a remarkable difference in how men who have sex with men meet one another today; in the past, these encounters were non-public, secretive and often involved commercial sex workers. Instead, the thriving of Bangkok gay scenes allows men who have sex with men to have more continuity between their sexual activities, their social life, and their sexual identity. As Allyn notes: "Love stories were being made here, most of them bittersweet ones. Gay Thai men have perhaps added the key ingredient to the development of a gay identity: love" (p. 157). Allyn further notes that, "Over the past two decades, superficial aspects of Western, particularly American gay culture, have been imported to a certain degree but, as the kingdom traditionally has done, by adaptation, not adoption" (p.158).

One example of such an adaptation is the recent concept of *kulagay* invented by the Thai gay media, although it is still not widely in use. As in *kulasatrii, kula* being "virtuous" or "decent," a *kulagay* is a virtuous Thai gay man who adheres to traditional Thai values, contributes to society, and rejects the Thai stereotypes of the *kathoey* and promiscuity (Allyn 1991). The invention of the *kulagay* identity reflects the movement's attempt to assimilate homosexuality into the social fabric of Thai society by way of deference to the traditional values.

In 1981, a "gay rights" organization called *Chaai Chawb Chaai* (men liking men) was established, but was disbanded shortly thereafter because there was no evidence of discrimination (Allyn 1991). In 1989, two organizations were formed in response to the HIV epidemic: Fraternity for AIDS Cessation in Thailand (FACT), and Gay Entrepreneurs Association of Thailand (GEAT). GEAT is made up of Bangkok bar owners and is concerned with issues of business. After great success from their educational theater group, the White Line, FACT also developed a subsidiary group called FACT Friends which began weekly support groups for the many Thai gay men who were tired of the commercial gay scene. By 1991, FACT was awarded international grants and transformed from a grassroots volunteer organization to a foundation with a formal structure (Allyn 1991).

Despite the many developments of a gay identity in Thailand, the average Thai gay man lives his gay life separately from the other parts of his life. Allyn (1991) speculates that this way of life is sufficient for many, as many Thai gay men have expressed satisfaction. Allyn further suggests that Thai people are trained since childhood to accept their lot in life. Similar to the way the perceived transience of gender helps many Thai women to accept their role (see Section 1), Thai gay men perhaps think that their sexual orientation is only one of the many sufferings a being faces in different incarnations. Therefore, a private sex life and the constraint of being a "model Thai" may not be fraught with as much psychological pain as his Western counterparts might experience. To date, there is no evidence that gay men in Thailand are more psychologically distressed than heterosexual men.

D. Homosexuality in Women

There is an extreme paucity of information on women who have sex with women. Adopted several decades ago, the term "lesbian" is now recognized by most Thai people as describing love or sex between women, along with its derivatives *ael bii* (Thai acronym for "L.B.") and *bian*, which could be used pejoratively or euphemistically. Also, a rather vulgar slang *tii ching*, or "playing [small, paired] cymbals," compares two vaginas in lesbian sex with a pair of opposing, identical concave musical instruments. In the past decade, other terms for lesbianism have come into vogue. Paralleling the *gay king-gay queen* dichotomy in male homosexuality, lesbians are categorized into *thom* (derived from "tomboy") and *dii* (short for "lady"), mostly based on their social manners and appearances. The *thom* women, with the masculine appearance, are assumed to have a dominant role in the relationship. Women who are *dii*, on the other hand, are feminine looking and passive in gender role. Because of the extreme popularity of these terms, most Thais now refer to lesbianism (female homosexuality) as "women being *thom-dii*."

Thai people are quite confused by the feminine *dii* women because they are indistinguishable from the typical Thai women in their social manners. Most Thais speculate that *dii* women will eventually grow out of their phase of experimentation or confusion, and commit to a relationship with a man (much as they think of the *gay king* men). On the other hand, the masculine *thom* women are seen by Thais as women who want to be a man, much as feminine homosexual men are assumed to want to be a woman. Androgynous behavior in women, although not traditionally praised, has been relatively tolerated in adolescents. Popular fiction has portrayed a number of female protagonists who have "tomboy" demeanor: bold, assertive, and boyishly naughty, while nonchalant and unaware of their feminine attractiveness hidden inside. Nevertheless, these characters are unmistakenly heterosexual, as there is never any depiction of homoeroticism or lesbian character in the lives of these tomboys. As a rule, these young heroines always outgrow their tomboy phase as they are transformed into a "fully grown woman" by their first love with a man with whom they marry at the end of the story.

Prior to the late 1980s, Thai people in general seemed to show little awareness of the existence of love and sex between women. In the 1980s, a tabloid ran an advice column for lesbians, *Go Sa Yaang*, by a straight man, Go Paaknaam, following the popularity of his column for gay men (Allyn 1991). Yet, lesbian women never had erotic publications or enterprises as these businesses began to flourish for gay men. However, sex and love between women started to come into public attention in the late 1980s and early 1990s. As more and more young women have shown up in public looking like pairs of a *thom* and a *dii*, displaying public intimacy slightly beyond the usual confines of peer manners, the media have called it an epidemic of *thom-dii-ism*. Much anxiety and concerns have been expressed by parents and the media regarding this increased visibility of lesbianism. Many conservatives search for a cause of lesbianism in the modern or Western values, claiming that women today are taught to strive for power and autonomy. For these conservatives, women are attracted to other women because they have become more like men. Others have blamed androgynous women in the Thai pop culture for modeling gender-atypical behavior and, in turn, inducing lesbian interests among the adoring young fans.

Sensationalistic media and conservatives aside, women who love (and have sex with) women have recently emerged in Thai society with an agenda to forge ahead with a Thai lesbian identity in their own right. Anjaree is a new organization for Thai lesbian women which came into public attention in 1992. The name of the organization comes from merging two words, *anya* and *jaree*, to denote "a different path" (Otaganonta 1995). Aside from publishing a newsletter, *Anjaree Sarn*, the organization also played a key role in setting up the Asian Lesbian Network, which hosted its first meeting in 1990 in Bangkok. This initiative earned Anjaree the Filipa de Sausa Award, presented by the International Gay and Lesbian Rights Commission based in New York, which is given to individuals and groups that take initiatives to promote the rights of sexual minorities. One of the group's founders states in a *Bangkok Post* interview:

> I don't think people need to identify themselves as heterosexuals or homosexuals. American society places much importance on defining oneself as this or that, but in Thailand, sexual orientation has never been a major part of self identity. But we are aware of the obstacles that Thai lesbians face. That's why we have to assert ourselves in this way. Still there is no need for us to identify ourselves only as lesbians. (Otaganonta 1995, p. 36)

As evident in the discussions about homosexuality in men and women above, Western constructions of homosexuality have had inevitable influences in the ways contemporary Thais understand sex and love between people of the same gender. The Thai vocabulary for homosexuality, lesbian, gay, *gay king, gay queen, thom, dii*, all had their origin in the English language. Alternative to the simplistic notion that Thai people are emulating Western sexuality, we argue that Thai people might have found that their indigenous constructions could no longer explain or fit their observations of sexual phenomena. In an attempt to find satisfactory explanations, Thai people have found plausible frameworks in the Western paradigm of sexual orientation and homosexuality which complements their indigenous construction. In the following section, we turn to a review of the *kathoey*, which was possibly the only indigenous social construction of non-heterosexuality in Thailand before the arrival of the Western paradigm.

7. Gender Conflicted Persons

As noted in the previous section, traditional Thai sexuality did not reflect clear distinctions between homosexuality, bisexuality, and heterosexuality as explicitly drawn by Western cultures. Rather, the most salient of all sexual distinctions is the bipolarity of gender: A person is either a man or a woman. Based on these two fundamental male and female genders, the *kathoey* exists as another gender identity in the Thai society. Roughly equivalent to the English term "hermaphrodite," *kathoey* (pronounced "ka-thoey") has been defined as a "person or animal of which the sex is indeterminate" in the Thai-English dictionary (McFarland 1982). Despite such a medical connotation, *kathoey* has been used, at least in the last several decades, to describe a biologically male person who has sex with men, therefore covering a gamut of male homosexualities.

The use of the term *kathoey* to describe male homosexualities, however, has slowly given way to the more contemporary *gay* and its derivatives. Today, *kathoey* mostly refers to men who have feminine social behaviors, without much specific reference to their biological gender or sexual behavior. Being associated with feminine characters and other stereotypes (see below), the term is considered derogatory by Thai gay men today, many of whom adamantly distinguish themselves from *kathoey*. Other derogatory slang words, applied to both gay men and *kathoey*, are *tut* and *tutsii* (the latter from the title of an American movie, *Tootsie*, starring cross-dressed Dustin Hoffman), which, because their pronunciations are close to the derogatory Thai word for "ass," suggest anal intercourse.

As implied in the usage today, a *kathoey* is a man who sees himself more as a woman and often dresses, to varying degrees, as a women, and is likely to have sex with men. Some take estrogens and progesterone to facilitate breast development and other body transformations. A few will undergo surgical sex-reassignment surgery. This surgery is well known and available in Thailand, although it is extremely expensive by Thai standards. In Western conceptualization, the *kathoey* may be considered either effeminate homosexual men, transvestites, or pre- or post-operative transsexuals, none of which is readily applicable to the traditional construction of sexuality in Thailand. Thai people mainly see the *kathoey* as either the "third gender," or a combination of the male and female genders. Alternatively, they are also seen as a female gender, but of the "other" variety, as reflected in a synonym *ying pra-phayt song*, meaning "women of the second kind."

These understandings of the *kathoey* suggest that Thai people have traditionally tried to make sense of this phenomenon in fundamental male-female terms. As a result, the Thai interpretations of the *kathoey* have been within the confines of the gender bipolarity. Nevertheless, the *kathoey* have been a well-known category in the sexual and gender typology of the Thai culture. Children and adults can often identify at least one *kathoey* in every village or school. Despite their subtle "outcast" status, the village *kathoey* are often given duties in local festivities and ceremonies, mostly in female-typical roles such as floral arrangements or food preparation. The *kathoey* seem to have adopted the "nurturer" role prescribed to Theravada women, and ideas of female pollution (e.g., the touch taboo and fear of menstruation) are extended to the *kathoey* as well. Social discrimination varies in degrees, ranging from hostile animosity to stereotypic assumptions. Some of the assumptions are based on the idea that the *kathoey* are unnatural, a result of poor *karma* from past lives; other assumptions are typical of generalizations about women as a whole.

To illustrate the stereotype, the Thai cinema and contemporary literature usually dramatize the *kathoey* as highly histrionic in gestures, emotionally unstable, subject to men's abandonment, and thus leading lives of bitterness, loneliness, suicides, or promiscuity. Although there are plenty of *kathoey* who hold other professions, stereotype predicates that many *kathoey* become street sex workers or small-time criminals, and others become beauticians, fashion designers, hair-dressers, florists, artists, or entertainers (Allyn 1991). A few comedians and media personalities have been publicly known for their *kathoey* sensibilities and camp humor, while other *kathoey* celebrities have caused public sensations by their flamboyance or eccentricities. Many *kathoey* have healthy long-term relationships with men, although Jackson (1989) has noted the stereotype of *kathoey* providing financial support to young men with whom they are in a romantic relation-ship. This "kept boy" tradition is an interesting reverse of the minor wife tradition in straight men. Stereotype notwithstanding, the image of *kathoey* as a resourceful member of the community and a benefactor of young men is remarkably more positive than the Western images that most cross-gen-dered individuals are street transsexuals who live marginalized lives in the underworld of drugs and prostitution. In Thailand, *kathoey* find each other or married women for social support and, despite a degree of discrimina-tion from the new gay-identified men, they are well accepted into the contemporary gay scenes.

Because for most Thais, the concepts of gay and *kathoey* are not clearly distinguished from one another, the stereotypic features of the *kathoey* are thought to be also attributes of gay men, particular *gay queens*. Some Thai men who have sex with men alternately refer to themselves as gay for political reasons, and *kathoey* for self-deprecating humor. These images of the *kathoey* (and to a lesser degree, "gay men") in the Thai society bare striking similarities to the stereotyped lives of gay men and drag queens in Western societies before the gay liberation movement in the late 1960s and early 1970s. Interestingly, the American play, *The Boys in the Band* by Mart Crowley, was translated to the Thai context in the late 1980s and became an immensely popular show. The appreciation that the mainstream audi-ence had for the images of *kathoey* and gay men—as individuals struggling with societal pressure and self-hatred—sums up the overall social climate toward homosexuality today: characterized by sympathy, fascination, and curiosity, yet riddled with ambivalence and stereotyping.

Another cross-gendered phenomenon is found primarily in women in the cults of the ancestral spirits (*phii*) in northern Thailand (see also Manderson 1992). Members of the *phii* cults believe that ancestral guardian spirits are passed on matrilineally to young women in order to maintain health, harmony, and well-being in the family. Certain women, by becoming "possessed" by the *phii*, serve as medium for the spirits, and they are called *maa khii*. In their annual ritual, these women, and sometimes children, are possessed by their ancestral spirits and perform dances, which include displays of wild and rude behaviors (e.g., drinking, smoking Thai cigars, and shouting expletives and insults) as well as stereotypically masculine behaviors (e.g., wearing men's clothes and flirting and dancing with young women). However, because of their revered role as *maa khii*, many of these women are held in high esteem. Outside these rituals and performances, these women, most of whom are married to a man and hold respectable roles (e.g., healers and midwives) in their village community, return to their everyday behavior typical of the female gender. Although most of these women do not remember the specific events during the trance, they are well aware of the male characters they take on during the dances. In an inter-esting twist of role, these women hold positions of power, in contrast to the general patriarchal Thai society and the male domination in Buddhism.

While most *maa khii* are women, a noticeable minority are male, and many are also *kathoey*. We have observed that the *maa khii* who are *kathoey* also enjoy a more-revered place in the community, overcoming some of the ordinary stigma they would otherwise experience. During the spiritual dance (*fawn phii*), the mediums who are *kathoey*, like their female counterparts, exhibit male-stereotypical behavior remarkably different from their own manners during ordinary circumstances.

8. Significant Unconventional Sexual Behaviors

A. Coercive Sex

As discussed earlier in Section 1B, the Third Precept of Buddhism professes to refrain from sexual misconduct, mostly understood to refer to adultery, rape, sexual abuse of children, and careless sexual activities that result in the harm to others. Rape is a criminal offense but the law is rarely enforced. However, rape crime reports are abundant in mainstream and tabloid journalism, often written in a sensational and graphic style which seems designed to titillate the reader. No data exist regarding the extent of the problem. In a study of northern Thai men conscripted to the army in 1990 (Nopkesorn et al. 1991), 5 percent of the 21-year-old men reported having forced or coerced a woman for sex. The incidence of incest is not known. These matters are rarely discussed or reported.

Young men in Ford and Kittisuksathit's focus groups (1994) made references to the use of violence in order to force women to acquiesce to intercourse. They rationalized that coercion occurred when their sexual desire was provoked by women beyond self-control, and it was mostly directed to women in casual encounters not their *fans*. Numerous folk music and literature provide a cultural script for courtship and sexual persuasion as apparent in this study. Men see that intercourse involves prior steps of cunning moves, social pressuring, and physical advances, whereas women see intercourse in terms of "submission" or "surrender." Aside from the cultural script, men perhaps generalize from their own experiences of erotic stimulation and ejaculation to the larger patterns of male sexuality. They, therefore, perceive that sexual arousal in men, once initiated, takes its own course and is not subject to control, as characterized by the term *naa meued* or a state of "black-out" from lust.

Social support for women who have been raped or victimized by incest is not widely available. Consistent with the men's rationalization that they are provoked beyond control, a woman is sometimes viewed as provoking rape because of her appearances (e.g., wearing a provocative dress) or her social behavior (e.g., drinking or frequenting potentially unsafe places). Consequently, Thai parents teach their girls not to dress improperly, and not to go alone to unfamiliar places in order to avoid being raped, as if rape is a price one pays for violating the code of *kulasatrii*. Others, following the cultural script of courtship and sex, see rape as an obscure area where men's coercion and women's surrendering cannot be clearly differentiated. Women who have been raped or experienced incest in Thailand are socially stigmatized based on these attitudes, in addition to the perception that the woman is flawed because she has been "violated." Understandably, women or their families rarely report these incidents.

B. Prostitution—Commercial Sex

Although the topic of commercial sex appears under the general section of unconventional behaviors, it should be noted that this phenomenon is not considered unconventional in Thailand. However, the topic deserves a focus separate from the general patterns of sexuality as already covered in the sections on adolescent and adult sexual behaviors (Sections 5A and 5B). In our discussion of this topic, we use the more value-neutral terms, such as "sex worker" and "commercial sex," while reserving the terms "prostitute" and "prostitution" for the contexts which require expression of sociocultural values.

History and Current Situations of Commercial Sex in Thailand

Among Thai people, there is a general attitude that prostitution has always been, and will always be, a part of the social fabric of Thailand. This attitude is primarily rationalized by the prevailing myth that men have a greater sexual desire than women. The endorsement of prostitution does not come from men only; a majority of Thai women, especially of the upper and middle classes, readily agree with this logic. In college-level sexuality education courses, female students openly say that prostitution exists to protect "good women" from being raped. Married women from northern Thai rural villages talk in focus groups about their preference for the husbands to seek out sex workers (given a condom is used) rather than taking on a minor wife. Reflecting the general societal attitudes, the married women believe that prostitution is a practical solution for married men whose greater sexual demand cannot be met by their wives (Dumronggittigule et al. 1995).

Thailand is well known throughout the world for its highly organized and diverse commercial sex businesses. Many tourists visit Thailand for this special interest, although many others are obviously drawn by the culture and nature of Thailand as well as the charming hospitality of Thai people. Tourism caters to men seeking sex in Thailand, and this aspect, which most Thais are not proud of, has been openly acknowledged and advertised. Through the assistance of tour guides or hotel services, commercial sex is available to any male tourist as it is for Thai men. Even outside of Thailand, a large number of Thai sex workers have been working in European countries and Japan since the 1980s; an estimate of 70,000 Thai women are working in commercial sex in Japan alone (Hornblower 1993).

Since the abolition of slavery in 1905, brothels have proliferated steadily and eventually became commonplace throughout the country. The sex industry proliferated during the Vietnam War in the 1960s and 1970s. As military bases of the United States of America were built up in Thailand, many women were induced into the entertainment and sex businesses for American servicemen. When the war ended in 1976, tourism began to grow and has become the largest source of foreign income. Meanwhile, commercial sex became an inevitable part of the tourist attraction (Limanonda 1993).

Prostitution became technically illegal in 1960 from the United Nations' pressure (Brinkmann 1992). In 1966, the Entertainment Places Act led to a plethora of new businesses which served as fronts for commercial sex, such as erotic massage parlors, bars, nightclubs, coffee shops, and barber shops (Manderson 1992). Ironically, although prostitution is illegal, these sex businesses often have government or police officials among their owners. In other cases, these officials are paid by the establishment owners to avoid enforcing the law (Brinkmann 1992). Subsequent attempts from the Thai government to eradicate prostitution have occurred over the years, most notably in 1981 and 1982, but all have been quickly abandoned (Rojanapithayakorn and Hanenberg 1996). Instead, the Thai government has focused on controlling sexually transmitted diseases (STDs) among sex workers using the police authorities and the structure of public-health services (see below).

The number of commercial sex workers in Thailand was estimated to be around 500,000 to 700,000 in 1980 (Thepanom Muangman, Public Health Faculty, Mahidol University; cited in Keyes 1984). The clientele of these sex workers have been estimated to be about 80 percent Thai (data cited in Manderson 1992). Most sex workers in rural and urban areas work in establishments such as brothels, restaurants, bars, or erotic massage parlors, all of which are under the management by men. "Direct" sex workers, or those who have sex with their clients on the premises, such as in brothels or erotic cafes, usually charge lower fees and, therefore, are popular among working-class and younger men. "Indirect" sex workers work under the premise of selling other services, such as massage or dancing, with the option to have sex with clients who offer to *off* them (or take them out) for an additional sum or fee. The fee for "direct" sex workers varies from 50 baht (U.S. $2.00) to 500 baht (U.S. $20.00), while that of "indirect" sex workers varies from 500 baht (U.S. $20.00) to several thousands of baht (Weniger et al. 1991)

The demographic and socioeconomic characteristics of female sex workers have been reported in a study of 800 female sex workers from two provinces, one in the north and another in the south (van Griensven, Limanonda, et al. 1995). Only 1 percent of the women reported that they were younger than 16 years of age, and 11 percent reported starting working in commercial sex before the age of 16. The national origin was Thai for

85 percent of the women, with 8 percent Burmese and 1 percent Chinese, and 6 percent from a northern hill tribe. Most of the women, 80 percent, were from rural areas, while 89 percent had moved directly from their village of origin to an urban area primarily to work as sex workers. Most had low levels of education: 87 percent completed less than seven grades of school and 25 percent could not read or write.

Government Surveillance of Commercial Sex Workers

A system of monitoring sex workers has been in place because the government has long implicated them for the spread of STDs (Rojanapithayakorn and Hanenberg 1996). Most "direct" sex workers in Thailand are under the STD monitoring system, which the Department of Communicable Disease Control (DCDC) has adapted over a period of forty years. There are hundreds of government STD/AIDS clinics all over Thailand, each keeping a logbook of its local commercial sex establishments. The logbook contains location of the businesses, and it is frequently updated with the help of STD patients who show up for services. The officers semiannually visit these establishments to assess the numbers of sex workers and other changes; their enumeration of establishments has been reported regularly since 1971.

In 1990, the Sentinel Surveillance reported that each sex worker had an average of two customers per night, with the mean of 2.6 for direct sex workers, and 1.4 for indirect sex workers (unpublished data, cited in Rojanapithayakorn and Hanenberg 1996). In 1994, the compiled lists of commercial sex establishments showed thirty-seven different kinds of sex businesses, mostly concentrated in Bangkok and provincial towns. The report also showed there were on average sixty-seven commercial sex establishments in most provinces, with an average of 663 female sex workers per province. The total number of sex workers who worked in listed establishments was approximately 67,000 in 1994. These numbers reflect sex workers who are under the surveillance system by the government.

Vithayasai and Vithayasai (1990) provided the first evidence that by 1988 HIV was already spreading among female sex workers and their customers in northern Thailand. Many other studies have consistently shown that female sex workers in the north have disproportionately higher rates of HIV infection than those in other parts of Thailand; brothel-based female sex workers were found to have an HIV incidence of 20 seroconversions per 100 person-years of follow-up (cited in Mastro and Limpakarnjanarat 1995). In 1994, the national median prevalence of HIV infection was 27 percent among brothel-based commercial sex workers (Division of Epidemiology, Thai Ministry of Public Health; data cited in Mastro and Limpakarnjanarat 1995).

Female sex workers have many barriers to having protected sex with their clients, for example, clients' insistence on not using condoms (Pramualratana, Podhisita, et al. 1993), lack of negotiation strategies (Brinkmann 1992), clients' healthy and attractive appearance and the sex workers' trust in "regular" acquainted clients (Wawer et al. 1996), and alcohol use by either the client or the sex workers (Mastro and Limpakarnjanarat 1995). However, this picture has changed dramatically by the mid-1990s as the government's nationwide 100 Percent Condom Program came into effect. Whereas the 1989 survey of sex workers found that 14 percent of their sex acts were with a condom, the rate increased to over 90 percent in December 1994 (Rojanapithayakorn and Hanenberg 1996; see more discussion in Section 11).

Male Commercial Sex Workers

The number of male sex workers in Thailand has been estimated to be approximately 5,000 to 8,000 (Brinkmann 1992), a number much smaller than the estimates of female sex workers. Although there are very few studies on male sex workers, a study has provided a glimpse of the demographics and sexual behavior of men who work in gay bars with commercial sex (Sittitrai, Phanuphak, et al. 1989). Many of these men, referred to in Thai as "business boys," stated that their primary sexual attraction was for women. They reported that their sexual behavior outside of the bars was predominately heterosexual and many had sex with female sex workers for sexual pleasure. Similar findings were found in the study of male commercial sex workers in northern Thailand: 58 percent of them described themselves as preferring female partners outside of work, and 14 percent of all men were married (Kunawararak et al. 1995).

At the beginning of the 1990s, male sex workers' HIV seroprevalence remained comparatively low compared to the alarmingly high rates in female sex workers, and this was hypothesized to be due to the male sex workers' use of condoms from early on in the HIV epidemic. However, recent findings can no longer sustain this optimism. In a recent study (Kunawararak et al. 1995) in which male sex workers were followed prospectively from 1989 to 1994, their HIV prevalence increased from 1.4 percent to 20 percent, with an overall incidence of 11.9 per 100 person-years, a rate considerably higher than those found in any other groups of Thai men.

Most sex workers in Thailand enter the commercial sex business in their late teens or early 20s, and many others in their early teens. The phenomenon of children in commercial sex will be the focus of the following section. However, it is important to note that much of the discussion about the sociocultural factors that lead young women and men into the sex industry will be applicable to both child, adolescent, and adult sex workers as well.

Child Sex Workers

Much to the embarrassment of the Thai officials and activists alike, commercial sex involving children has become a tourist draw to Thailand. The

HIV pandemic has fueled the demand of a great number of customers for younger sex workers because of their perceived likelihood of being free of HIV infection and other STDs. In many brothels, children as young as 10 and 11 are promoted by managers as "fresh" and "healthy," and the price is prorated accordingly. In contrast to this myth, child sex workers are reported to have very high HIV seroprevalence, above 50 percent according to Hiew (1992). New evidence suggests that women who start as sex workers at a young age might be more susceptible to HIV infection than those who start later, even after controlling for the effects from the work duration (van Griensven et al. 1995).

Children proven to be virgins are especially sought after by Chinese and Middle Eastern clients. There is an ancient Chinese myth that "deflowering" a virgin girl will revitalize the sexual potency of an old man and make him prosper in business (O'Grady 1992). Others are sexually attracted to children and adolescents because of their youthful qualities. Because child sex workers are accessible in Thailand, the country has become a tourist destination for those who believe in these myths, as well as pedophiles and ephebophiles around the world. In their own countries, they could be imprisoned, castrated, or killed for being caught having sex with a child. In Thailand, however, their sexual behaviors go unnoticed and only cost them some money.

In theory, sex with children is illegal in Thailand, but the law has rarely been enforced. More recent external and internal pressures on the exploitation of children in commercial sex have led to some changes, but to what extent is unknown (see below). These pressures also have made it difficult to estimate the number of child sex workers in Thailand, as they are "going underground" (Boonchalaksi and Guest 1994). The estimates have ranged from 30,000 to 40,000 proposed by the Thai Red Cross and Sittitrai and Brown (1991), to 800,000 suggested by the Center for the Protection of Children's Rights. Estimates have been calculated based upon the ratio of child to adult sex workers, with children making up 20 to 40 percent of all the sex workers in Thailand. The most scientific report available to us has estimated the prevalence of child sex workers to be 36,000 (Guest 1994). This number comprises 1.7 percent of the female population who are below the age of 18.

The buying and selling of child sex workers in Thailand is a lucrative business, as it is elsewhere in Asia (*End Child Prostitution in Asian Tourism*, ECPAT, 1992, cited in Kaime-Atterhog, Ard-Am, and Sethaput, 1994). Girls and boys (albeit mostly girls) are brought into Thailand from the hill tribe areas, Myanmar (Burma), China, Kampuchea (Cambodia), and Laos (Friends of Women Foundation 1992). In addition, they are also bought from rural Thailand for as high as U.S. $8,000 (Serrill 1993) and brought to the cities and larger tourist locations. Farmers under greater economic pressures have been forced to make many sacrifices, including sending their children to work in the cities in order to send money home (Srisang

1990). These farmer parents are not always aware that their children are to become sex workers. In other cases, the entry into the sex industry does not happen until after an initial period of working in other low-paying jobs.

The business of finding job placements in the cities for rural children is not a new phenomenon. However, the growth of this business, and its connection to the sex industry, have been boosted by the socioeconomic shift in decent decades, and now it can be found in most parts of the country. As Thailand is moving toward the status of a newly industrialized country (NIC), most of the rapid economic development is concentrated in urbanization and industrialization. Although all socioeconomic strata have enjoyed their share of the country's economic boom, income inequalities have widened and poverty persists (Pyne 1994). Wealth is concentrated in the cities, while the rural poor are becoming more and more landless, and profits from their domestic businesses in rural areas are diminishing. Poverty, combined with the women's obligation to provide for their parents, and the lack of job opportunities for unskilled laborers, create an enormous pressure that has forced many Thai women to consider the sex industry as an occupation.

While many children and young women have been bought, most available data suggest that the process is not involuntary or forced. Hantrakul (1988, quoted in Manderson 1992) has pointed out that, "More and more prostitutes . . . have shown their strong determination in stepping in the profession. Sex is harnessed to an economic end. Men are seen as targets, a source of income" (p. 467). Data from van Griensven et al. (1995) support this notion: When asked how they entered commercial sex, 58 percent of the female sex workers said it was their own decision, and 37 percent said a friend or relative had advised them. Only 3 percent reported that they were either sold by their parents or recruited by an agent or employer. A number of the women, 14 percent, also had one or more sisters in commercial sex. Poverty was the most common reason for entering the profession, reported by 58 percent of the women.

After years of living through the sociocultural changes which have put more strains on rural women, being a sex worker to support one's family has become an acceptable value in several communities in the north. Some children go into this business without reservation and with full parental permission and support. Many of these girls return home with honor, marry, and repeat the cycle by sending their own daughters into the sex business when they come of age (Phongpaichit 1982; Limanonda 1993). This phenomenon is also true of some of the hill tribe villagers. Almost all sex workers are clear about their desire to quit working in the sex industry once their goals of income are met, and many would return to their native villages to marry and take care of their parents. Upon reintegration into the village, women who have worked as sex workers may be subject to condemnation, but it is usually based not on their prostitution, but on their having sex outside of marriage (Manderson 1992). This offense, however, can be amended by their active accumulation of merit, such as caretaking of parents and helping local charities. In any case, many women have already been recognized by family and the community for their previous remittances during the years of work in the city, as their financial contributions are already evident in the family's house, motorcycle, and even donations to the local temple. Although the cults of ancestral spirits (*phii puu yaa*) frown upon women's premarital sex, the act of kinship loyalty and filial piety is considered adequate to propitiate the spirits. In fact, when commercial sex agents recruit women from the villages, they frequently offer some "customary payments" to the family and the ancestral spirits much like a brideprice. With an income up to twenty-five times the median income of women in factories and clerical jobs (Phongpaichit 1982), sex workers can easily redress their sexual misdemeanors by their generous support of kinship.

Nonetheless, other evidence suggests that many children and families are deceived by the brokers, and that the children are led to believe they will go to the cities to work as domestic servants or waiters/waitresses, only to find themselves forced into commercial sex. Sometimes, coercion takes the form of financial threats rather than physical confinement of the women. Many women must continue working to earn the sum of money for which their families are indebted to the commercial sex agents. For example, 31 percent of the female sex workers in van Griensven's study (1995) reported they were in debt to their employer. Worse cases are seen in women in commercial sex businesses in foreign countries. In a 1993 article in *Time* magazine, Hornblower (1993) reported that numerous Thai women are working in Japan as "virtual indentured sex slaves" in bars controlled by Japanese gangsters. These women, mostly from rural villages of Thailand, are usually sold by Thai brokers for an average of U.S. $14,000 each, and then resold to the clubs by Japanese brokers for about U.S. $30,000. The women are obligated and threatened to work under hostile circumstances to earn this sum of money, but very few can.

The recent concern about child sex workers in Thailand seems to have been fueled by the awareness of the HIV pandemic and the growing anguish about child victimization around the world. Initially, the pressure for a governmental policy towards child sex workers came from foreign sources, with the pressure more recently internalized. When the government of Prime Minister Chuan Leekpai took office in 1992, he promised to eliminate child sex workers during his term of office. Impressive work has been done by the Task Force to End Child Exploitation in Thailand, a coalition of twenty-four government and private agencies dedicated to exposing European links of child sex trade in Thailand (Serrill 1993). Brothels in Thailand known to employ children were raided and closed, and the events were highly publicized in Thai newspapers (Kaime-Atterhog et al. 1994). However, data are still lacking regarding the extent of success in reducing child sex trade. Although some reports have mentioned the age restriction that sex workers must be at least 18 years old (e.g., Kunawararak et al. 1995), statistics still show a small number of female sex workers under 15 years old in brothels (e.g., van Griensven et al. 1995).

Sociocultural Factors Behind the Entry to Commercial Sex

One consistent finding across many studies of female and child sex workers is that a large number come from the northern provinces of Thailand (Redd Barna 1989; Archavanitkul and Havanon 1990; van Griensven et al. 1995; Wawer et al. 1996). It has been theorized that these young women are especially in demand because of the long-held admiration for their lighter skin compared to their counterparts in the northeast or the south of the country. Others have theorized that working in the sex business is a tradition long present in the north. Formerly part of the kingdom of Lanna, this part of the country was more often at war with other kingdoms and had a history of being colonized. It was the custom to use women from the area to placate the occupying forces through the offering of sex services (Skrobanek 1988).

In addition to these perspectives, others have offered hypotheses that take into account sociocultural factors that are not unique to northern Thailand and are thus applicable to the general Thai culture as well. Lenore Manderson (1992), for example, eloquently argues that commercial sex, much like Buddhist monasteries, provides alternatives for both men and women to step out of their ordinary cultural roles. For men, the alternative is in the sexual realm; commercial sex provides a sexual outlet for the unmarried men and a way for married men to step temporarily outside their marriage while avoiding a divorce. For young women, she argues, the process of leaving behind (temporarily) their kinship as well as their "normal sexuality" (i.e., sex with affectional ties) gives women an alternative option to become self-sufficient. By supporting themselves and their family through the commoditization of sex, these young women achieve a degree of autonomy without having to enter the role of "mother" or marriage. Traditionally, *mae chii* undergo a similar process of abandoning attachments (in their case, worldly and sexual pleasures) in order to achieve autonomy in the spiritual realm. In a society in which women are expected to be mother or wife, female sex workers and *mae chii* reject both roles in the way they use (or do not use) their bodies and sexuality.

Other scholars, such as Khin Thitsa, Thomas Kirsch, and Charles Keyes, have looked even deeper into the Theravada gender construction for the cultural explanation of commercial sex. Keyes (1984) acknowledges that prostitutes have never been stigmatized in Buddhist societies because the women still have the opportunity to alter their behavior at some time; prostitutes and courtesans were indeed among the alms of women in early Buddhist society. Despite such tolerance in the Buddhist society, he suggests that the rise of commercial sex in contemporary Thailand has more to do with the emergence the new images of men and women which are associated with sex without any tempering moral irony found in traditional popular Buddhism. According to Keyes, the decision to enter commercial sex in

Thailand today is the women's "participation in the increasingly material-istic culture of Thailand" (p. 236), probably driven by the "secularized image of woman as sex object" (p. 236). A number of scholars and activists have made similar comments. The growth of commercial sex in Thai society cannot be explained by the traditional gender roles in Buddhism; quite the opposite, it thrives on the increasingly consumerist and materialistic nature of the contemporary Thai culture.

On the other hand, Kirsch (1985) argues that women's choice of enter-ing commercial sex is not necessarily at odds with the range of "ideal" female images in Buddhism. In particular, the Buddhist-sanctioned mother-nurturer image of women has found a new expression in the new sociocul-tural context, where young rural women have expanded their means of providing for the family to a new arena, "in towns, cities, the nation, and beyond" (p. 313).

C. Pornography and Erotica

The popularity of pornography and erotica in contemporary Thailand cannot be denied, although we were not able to identify formal data on its extent and variety. Erotic magazines and videotapes, most of which are designed for the male customer, are available in street markets, newsstands, and video stores. Imports and unauthorized copies of foreign (mostly American, European, and Japanese) erotica are easily available and popu-lar. Thai-produced erotica tends to be more suggestive and less explicit than the XXX-rated erotica produced in the West. Heterosexual erotica has a greater market, but same-sex erotica is also available.

By exploring the production and consumption of pornographic and erotic materials in Thailand, we can better understand Thai people's attitudes toward this topic, as well as the underlying social constructions of gender and sexuality. While there is no equivalent of the term "pornogra-phy," the nonjudgmental colloquialism is the suffix *po*, ("nude") added to the format of the medium (e.g., books, magazines, pictures, movies, and dances); hence *phaap po* is a nude picture. The more judgmental suffix *laa-mok* ("obscene") is also used, especially by the press to convey journalistic technicality or even an air of morality. Sex videos are also called *nang ek*, or "X movies," although censorship in Thailand does not use the nominal rating system used in the United States. There is also a tongue-in-cheek distinction of *po tae mai plueay*, or "nude but not naked," implying the more discreet depiction of the unclothed bodies.

Although none of these terms indicates the gender of the customers or users, Thai people generally see that pornography is chiefly men's indul-gence, consistent with the idea that vices and sex are men's recreation.

Depiction of nude female bodies or women in swimsuits on calendars are not an uncommon sight in male-dominated settings, such as bars, construction sites, warehouses, and auto shops. Caucasian and Japanese models are also as popular as Thai models. In fact, until a few decades ago when domestic production of pornography was prohibited by poor technology and strict laws, Thai men relied on pirated copies of Western porn and imported magazines, such as *Playboy*. Hence, the last few generations of Thai men have been exposed to Western sexuality primarily through pornography from Europe and North America. Because these materials portray sexual practices with the variety and explicitness unprecedented in the Thai media, Thai people who are acquainted with Western pornography have come to associate Westerners with sexual disinhibition and hedonism.

Prior to the popularity of videotapes, imported and pirated, Western erotica was available in the underground market in the formats of print, 8-millimeter film, and photographic slides. Illegal prints of Western hardcore pornography, known as *nangsue pok khao*, or "white-cover publication" were produced by small, obscure publishers, and surreptitiously sold in bookstores, by mail order, or by solicitors in public areas. Nationally distributed magazines on display at newsstands and bookstores have burgeoned since the late 1970s. Following the format of American publications such as *Playboy*, these magazines, such as *Man*—among the earliest of its genre—print glossy photographs of Thai female models, and feature regular as well as erotic columns. The proliferation of gay men's erotic magazines followed in the mid-1980s.

The legal status of these magazines, straight and gay, is somewhat ambiguous. While sometimes up to twenty or thirty different publications compete on the newsstands for years, the police have also made numerous raids on publishers and bookstores that carry these so-called "obscene" magazines. Such raids often follow a moral surge in politics or an administrative reform in the police department. Similar arrests have been made with the video rental stores that carry pornographic films. Interestingly, grounds for objection to these pornographic materials have never been based on the material's unauthorized status or even the exploitation of women. As known by all the customers and providers of pornography in Thailand, the disapproval is due to the "sex and obscenities" involved. In news coverage of these raids, officials commonly espouse Buddhist moral messages about sexual stoicism and, less often, the degradation of the *kulasatrii* image. Thai censorship of films has also been more strict on sexual matters than on violence, even when the sex or body exposure appears in nonexploitative contexts. In formality and the law, the Thai society is more sex-negative than what its sex industry has led most outsiders to believe.

The depiction of the Thai female models in Thai erotic magazines for heterosexual men is perhaps an embodiment of the modern, urban "bad girl" image. Although many of them are indeed recruited from the commercial sex scenes in Bangkok, the glossy images and the accompanying biographies suggest that the models are single, educated, and middle-class adventurous women who do these poses on a one-time-only basis. To the reader, these women might as well be *kulasatrii* elsewhere, but here they let their hair down in front of the camera and become modern, beautiful, and sensual women who are in touch with their sexuality. Neither are these models the ordinary "carefree" women available in the one-night-stand scenes; their model-quality appearance is more than what the reader could expect in those environments. Hence, these models represent a high-end variant of carefree women, characterized by their overwhelming sexual magnetism, an excellent match indeed for men and their boundless sexual desires. A few famous models in the erotica industry have gone on to fashion, music, and acting in television or film with great success.

The image of these celebrity erotica models can be juxtaposed, like the other side of the coin, with that of the beauty-pageant winners, such as Miss Thailand, who also frequently become media celebrities. Both images are of Thai women who achieve success and fame because of their appearance. Pageant contestants and winners always take great pains to extol the virtues of Thai women in their public statements, and many openly object to the pageant's swimsuit display requirement. Pageant winners invariably stress their "nurturer" ideology by speaking of helping children, the elderly, and the disabled. In contrast, erotica models send off an air of iconoclastic indifference in their seductive, hedonistic, and "I don't care" statements. Interestingly, women's indifferent and autonomous attitudes, along the lines of "I am who I am" or "I don't give a damn," have become fashionable and used in numerous poetry and song lyrics by female pop stars. This image, however, is not a new image for women in Thai society, because the "bad women" image has always been around. Nevertheless, the tough "I-am-who-I-am" statements are urban women's announcement of their moral independence, setting them in contrast with the conventional perceptions that women in the sex industry and "carefree" women are fooled into their positions, and that women in general are helpless abiders of societal values. As more and more contemporary women are becoming dissatisfied with the traditional role or the victim stereotype, these iconoclastic sentiments seem refreshing: Adopting the role opposite to a *kulasatrii* by choice is an act of liberation.

Thailand is also famous for its sex shows in the go-go nightclubs (*baa a-go-go*), most notoriously in the red-light districts of Patpong, Pattaya, and Chiangmai. Approaching these performances of dances, sexual tricks, and intercourse as cultural texts, Lenore Manderson (1992) has examined the continuity which links these public sex shows with the disempowerment of women, prostitution, and the Thai social constructions of sex and gender. Although the extreme explicitness and violent themes in these shows undeniably reflect misogyny and subordination of women, she also notices that the themes reflect what Thai people understand about the sexuality of Thai men and of the Westerners in the audience. These acts are what the sex industry thinks will captivate the (mostly) male clientele. The themes thus represent not the everyday sexuality but the erotic possibilities on the edge of male libidinal fantasy, their "wildest dreams."

Salient in the imageries designed to excite, thrill, or even shock the male customers is the ruleless, "anything goes" atmosphere. Disinhibition pervades the bars in which customers have quick access to sex on the premises. The unpredictable, even improbable, performances, including genital manipulation of objects or snakes, and sex between women, all affirm a polysexual theme. Another theme designed to excite is the extreme objectification of women as sex objects for sale. Sex workers are numbered for customers' selection, and their nakedness (or uniform bar costume) enhances their anonymity. Finally, there is a theme of satire in which men are insulted and parodied for their fear of the female genitalia, the widespread touch taboo and gender segregation are overturned, and the Thai gender-power hierarchy toppled. Naked women dance on a raised platform, literally placing men under the female genitalia (Manderson 1992).

9. Contraception, Abortion, and Population Planning

A. Contraception and Population Control

Thailand is extremely proud of its relatively high rates of contraceptive use and successful population control. Birthrates have been declining over the years. In 1995, the Institute for Population and Social Research at Mahidol University reported that the natural growth rate was about 1 percent. The fertility rates have also decreased significantly in the last few decades, from six births per woman in the 1960s to two births per woman in the late 1980s (cited in Pyne 1994).

The contraceptive prevalence rates have increased dramatically in the last two decades, from 15 percent to 68 percent among married women (cited in Pyne 1994). Contraceptive methods are readily available and utilized (Sittitrai et al. 1992). Common methods of contraception in Thailand include hormone pills and injections, intrauterine devices (IUDs), vaginal inserts, rhythm, condoms, withdrawal, vasectomy, and female tubal ligation. For women, the contraceptive hormonal pill is by far the more-preferred method. However, the most-prevalent method today is female sterilization, followed by the pill, while the least-popular method is the condom (cited in Pyne 1994).

The success of contraception in Thailand has been invariably linked to Mechai Viravaidya, the man *Time* magazine called "a champion of condoms, a pusher of the Pill, a voice for vasectomies." ("The Good News," *Time* 1989). Launched by Viravaidya in 1974, the private nonprofit organization, Population and Community Development Association (PDA), has tackled overpopulation by promoting family planning and distributing birth control devices. The PDA proactively places temporary birth control clinics where people gather, in bus terminals, village fairs, and buffalo markets. At these unconventional sites, they dispense condoms and the pill; free IUDs and vasectomies are even offered on special occasions. Playful but persuasive jingles promoting family planning punctuate music and soap operas on the radio, reaching every household in Thailand. Helped by his humor, creativity, and charisma, the success of the PDA and Viravaidya can be seen in the growing financial support from the government. Moreover, Thai people now use the term *mechai* as a slang term for condoms.

In the *Partner Relations Survey* (Sittitrai et al. 1992), the research participants reported that condoms were readily available. Considerable proportions of the participants reported having used them some time in their lifetimes: 52 percent of the men, 22 percent of the women, or 35 percent overall. Attitudes toward condoms were not especially surprising. Most men feared a lack of pleasure or diminished sexual performance with the use of the condom, and couples found using condoms threatening to the trust in their relationship.

Recently, the heightened HIV awareness and the government-sanctioned 100 Percent Condom Program have significantly increased the use of condoms, especially in the context of commercial sex (see also Sections 8B and 11). Although the government received condoms from foreign donors before 1990, all condoms provided to sex workers since 1990 have been bought by the country's own funds (Rojanapithayakorn and Hanenberg 1996). In 1990, the government distributed about 6.5 million condoms; in 1992, they spent U.S. $2.2 million to buy and distribute 55.9 million condoms. Commercial sex workers receive as many free condoms as they require from government STD clinics and outreach workers. On the national level, the recent increase in condom use has been documented to relate in time and magnitude with the overall decline of STDs and HIV incidence.

B. Abortion

Abortion is illegal in Thailand except when performed for medical reasons. Most Thais are strongly anti-abortion, mainly because of the First Precept of Buddhism which prohibits killing of living beings. In general, "living beings" are interpreted as people, animals, and sometimes small creatures, but most Thais also see this Precept as pertaining to the aborting of a fetus as well. Again, premarital or extramarital sex is frowned upon and there is little sympathy for the woman who becomes pregnant out of wedlock. She is most likely to be viewed as at fault for becoming pregnant, because only women (not men) can control their sexual desire. Thus, abortion has often been associated with a lack of morals and virtue on the woman's part.

In Ford and Kittisuksathit's study (1994), the young women who worked in factories were well aware of the dilemma of premarital pregnancy in the lives of their friends or siblings. Most expressed great concerns about unwanted, premarital pregnancy, which is a clear indicator of "sinful behavior" they have committed. In discussing the consequences of sex, women mostly talked about the feared premarital pregnancy, with allusions to "baby dumping," infanticide, and abortion, whereas young men focused on issues of STD and HIV. Most women expressed the hope that their partner would care for and marry them, and the child could be kept. Other young women clearly insisted that they would seek an abortion because they were emotionally and financially not ready for having a child. The blame for unwanted pregnancy, as expressed by both the young men and women, was placed on the woman for "allowing" intercourse to occur.

Apart from the social stigma, there are other important reasons behind Thai women's decision to have abortion. Pregnancy presents a grave problem for women in low-paying jobs in which employers have little tolerance of absenteeism (Pyne 1994). Having a child in urban environments is expensive, and, because few companies offer support for maternal and child care, a woman risks losing her employment due to the additional task of parenting. For rural women who migrate to work in the cities, losing their jobs means jeopardizing their only source of income on which they and their family upcountry depend.

In curious contrast to the prevailing anti-abortion attitudes, abortion is not rare in practice. Illegal abortion clinics, many of which are run by non-professional women, offer traditional but unsafe techniques of abortion, such as forceful massage or injecting chemicals into the uterus. Thorbek (1988) has documented experiences of women who had undergone such traumatic procedures and the adverse health consequences. A more-pragmatic approach has been developed in recent years, thereby allowing women to have safe, confidential abortion operations in many urban clinics. In these clinics, medically trained professionals use standard medical procedures, such as suction, to remove the fetus. Never advertising openly, these urban clinics rely on word of mouth to draw clients, and fairly large fees are charged. To date, there has not been a Thai-equivalent of the Western movement that has gained recognition of a women's right to choose to have an abortion.

10. Sexually Transmitted Diseases

Thailand reports high rates of sexually transmitted diseases (STDs). In the *Partner Relations Survey* (Sittitrai et al. 1992), the lifetime prevalence rates of STDs were 49 percent among urban men and 33 percent among rural men, or 38 percent overall. Much lower proportions of women reported a history of STDs: 11 percent in urban women and 9 percent in rural women, or 10 percent overall. Gonorrhea and non-gonococcal urethritis (NGU) were the most common STDs in male participants, whereas chlamydia and urethritis were the most common in female participants. Knowledge about STD prevention and treatment was inadequate, especially in the face of the HIV pandemic. Data from military conscripts have confirmed the linkage between STDs and HIV infection. In these young men from lower socioeconomic backgrounds, HIV infection was strongly associated with a history of STDs (Nelson et al. 1996), particularly a positive serology for syphilis, a history of gonorrhea, syphilis, genital herpes, genital warts, and genital ulcers (Beyrer et al. 1995).

Almost all STD cases in Thailand could be traced to commercial sex. In a 1989 report, 96 percent of male clients at government STD clinics attributed their infection to having had sex with a sex worker (cited in Rojanapithayakorn and Hanenberg 1996). The government STD clinics carry out the Ministry of Public Health's sentinel surveillance (previously described in Section 8B) and have notably provided STD-related services to the general population and medical examinations to sex workers for at least twenty years. Although sex workers are encouraged to have a weekly examination, records show that they visited government STD clinics only once every seven weeks in 1994. Male sex workers have been also included in sentinel surveillance since 1989 (Kunawararak et al. 1995). In addition, these clinics trace the partners of individuals with STD. The male clients are asked to name the establishments from which they might have contracted STD, and outreach workers are then dispatched for further tests or scheduling treatment for the sex workers. The government STD clinics also have good collaboration with the police offices, allowing enforcement against uncooperative establishments.

11. HIV/AIDS

HIV was first detected in Thailand in 1984 (Limsuwan, Kanapa and Siristonapun 1986). The government was slow to respond to the pandemic and its entry into Thailand. Economic pressures created by the need for tourist dollars and the early low numbers of actual AIDS cases slowed the government's response to the pandemic (Sricharatchanya 1987).

This slow response caught Thai governmental officials and health care providers unprepared for the rapid explosion of new cases of HIV infection and AIDS. Infection rates remained quite low through 1987, mostly affecting men who had sex with men. Then, there was a rapid increase in seroprevalence among injecting drug users (IDUs). In 1988, 86 percent of known seropositive cases were among IDUs, 4 percent were men who had sex with men, and 2 percent were heterosexual women. By 1990, another shift had occurred and shortly thereafter female sex workers showed extremely high seroprevalence rates. This phase of the pandemic was first detected in northern Thailand in 1989 (Limanonda, Tirasawat, and Chongvatana 1993; Vithayasai and Vithayasai 1990). As injecting drug use was shown to be very rare among sex workers, heterosexual intercourse was then identified as a potentially effective mode of HIV transmission in Thailand. In 1991, the HIV seroprevalence among urban brothel sex workers in a northern province rose to 49 percent (Ministry of Public

Health, 1991). Because many Thai men have unprotected sex inside and outside of their marriage, high rates of HIV infection were soon detected not only in sex workers, but also in their clients, pregnant women, and newborns. The 1994 national median prevalence rates of HIV infection were 8.5 percent among men attending STD clinics, and 1.8 percent among women attending prenatal clinics (Division of Epidemiology, Thai Ministry of Public Health; data cited in Mastro and Limpakarnjanarat 1995).

A series of studies have focused on the men newly conscripted to the military in order to infer the extent of HIV infection among Thai men at large. Prior to 1993, the HIV-seroprevalence rates in these northern conscripts ranged between 10 percent and 13 percent (Beyrer et al. 1995; Nelson et al. 1996), considerably higher than the rates among conscripts from other parts of the country. Some unique sexual patterns of the young men in northern Thailand have been linked to their greater risk of HIV infection. When compared to men from other provinces, upper-northern young men were more likely to have initiated sexual activity at a younger age—before age of 16—to have had their first experience with a female sex worker, to have had more frequent sexual contacts with sex workers, and to have reported a history of STDs (Nopkesorn, Mastro et al. 1993; Nopkesorn, Sweat et al. 1993).

Estimates have indicated that the number of persons living with HIV totals several hundreds of thousands (Division of Epidemiology, MOPH. 1984-1993). The forecast is grim in terms of further HIV infection and its socioeconomic impact on the entire country (Sittitrai et al. 1992). However, by the mid-1990s, there has been some good news of behavioral change and decreasing new cases of HIV infection. Paralleling the success of the mass advertising campaign and the 100 Percent Condom Program, condom use in commercial sex increased from 14 percent of the sex acts in 1989 to 90 percent of the sex acts in 1994 (Rojanapithayakorn and Hanenberg 1996). As the government distributed massive amounts of condoms to commercial sex establishments all over the country, the incidence of STDs correspondingly decreased by over 85 percent. Meanwhile, the HIV seroprevalence among the military conscripts from northern Thailand declined from 10.4 percent in 1991 to 6.7 percent in 1995 (Nelson et al. 1996). New conscripts have greater proportions of men who never had sex with sex workers, and greater proportions of men who never had STDs.

Initiated in 1989 on a small-scale basis, the widely successful 100 Percent Condom Program was later adopted nationwide, with participation from every province in Thailand by April 1992 (Rojanapithayakorn and Hanenberg 1996). The program promotes condom use by sex workers and their clients without exception. Sex workers are instructed to withhold service and refund the fee upon the client's refusal to use a condom. The program utilizes the preexisting structures of the police and the Ministry of Public Health's STD surveillance system to enforce compliance from commercial sex establishments. STDs, monitored by the hundreds of government STD clinics around the country, are used as a marker of non-compliance with the program. When the source of STD is traced to a non-compliant establishment, temporary or indefinite closure of the business by the police is warranted. With the cooperation from every sex establishment, customers quickly learn that they cannot go elsewhere to find a sex worker who would allow unprotected sex, and the commercial sex establishments understand that they are not losing clients to competitors.

12. Sexual Dysfunctions, Counseling, and Therapies

Within Thai psychiatry and psychology, there has not been much focus on the treatment of sexual dysfunctions or disorders. There is recognition of some sexual dysfunctions, but it is mostly limited to male erectile or ejaculatory problems. Vernacular expressions exist for these male sexual dysfunctions, suggesting Thai people's familiarity with these phenomena. For example, *kaam tai daan* means "sexual unresponsiveness" in men or women. There are a few terms for male erectile dysfunction: the playful *nokkhao mai khan* ("the dove doesn't coo") and the more cruel *ma-khuea phao* ("roasted eggplant"; Allyn 1991). Another slang, *mai soo* ("not up for a fight"), suggests an injury on the man's male pride for not being able to enter a "battle" with prowess. Premature ejaculation is referred to with a playful yet humiliating analogy *nokkra-jok mai than kin naam*, or "faster than a sparrow can sip water."

The incidence of various sexual dysfunctions have not yet been investigated. However, in the past two or three decades, many sex columns have appeared in the mainstream newspapers and magazines, offering advice and counsel in rather sexually explicit, but technical, detail. These are most often written by physicians who claim expertise in treating sexual problems and disorders. Other columnists in women's fashion and housekeeping magazines present themselves as older, experienced women who offer sage advice to younger ones about sex and relationships. The concepts of "squeeze technique" or "start-stop" techniques have been introduced to the typical middle-class Thai through these extremely popular advice columns.

A more systematic and academic effort to establish therapeutic services for sexual dysfunctions is underway. In the proposal for a multi-component interdisciplinary Program for the Promotion of Sexual Health (to be housed within the Chulalongkorn University in Bangkok), Nikorn Dusitsin (1995) included a counseling clinic and hotline counseling as one of the program's main components. Responding to the need for more sex counselors and educators, the program also contains workshops and courses aimed at training intermediate-level educators, including social workers, teachers, and military personnel, in order to provide sexuality counseling and education. Dusitin proposed a problem-based, participatory format for the curricula of these intensive workshops. The content of the curriculum was proposed to combine physiology, psychology, and sociocultural contexts.

13. Research and Advanced Education

In a review of the history of sex research in Thailand, Chanya Sethaput `(1995) noted the remarkable changes in methodologies and scope of sex research before and after the HIV epidemic in Thailand. These differences lent themselves to a pragmatic classification of pre- and post-AIDS eras of Thai sex research. She noted that only a handful of sex surveys were conducted before the HIV epidemic started in Thailand in 1984. In the pre-AIDS era, she identified the earliest study in 1962 in which the focus was on attitudes towards dating and marriage. In fact, most of the pre-AIDS research was concerned with the attitudes and knowledge in premarital sex, extramarital sex, cohabitation of unmarried couple, sexually transmitted diseases, and abortion. Sampled mostly from the educated, urban populations, such as college or high-school students, these early studies found gender differences in the attitudes of men and women, confirming the existence of a double standard in the sexual domain. Assessment of sexual behaviors was more of an exception than a rule. Early findings on sexual knowledge among Thai people had been used in the design of a curriculum for sexuality education which was later enforced by the Ministry of Education in schools across the country.

An abundance of studies have emerged after the first cases of AIDS were identified in Thailand about 1984. Driven by a public-health agenda, the post-AIDS sex research expanded its objectives to include more diverse questions (Sethaput 1995). Initially focused on "high-risk groups" such as sex workers and "gay" men, the populations of interest subsequently expanded to the customers of commercial sex (college students, soldiers, fishermen, truck drivers, and construction and factory workers), spouses and partners of men who visited sex workers, and other "vulnerable" groups, such as adolescents, and pregnant women. Present samples are no longer limited to convenience samples in urban cities or colleges, but include also rural villages, housing projects for the poor, and work sites, for example. Face-to-face interviews, which previously would have been difficult or unacceptable, have become a more-common assessment method, along with focus-group discussions and other qualitative techniques. Sexual behaviors have become more prominent in the researchers' inquiry, as questionnaires and interview schedules have become increasingly candid and explicit, with a newfound assumption that respondents are more open about sexuality. Previously ignored topics have become main research questions, for example, AIDS knowledge, attitudes toward condoms, masturbation, and same-gender attraction and homosexuality. New research questions have also attempted to identify vulnerability factors to HIV-risk behavior. Guided by the theory of reasoned behavior and the health-belief model, this entails the assessments of psychological variables and individual differences.

Sethaput (1995) briefly reviewed findings, which have formed the basis of the current understanding of sexuality in Thailand. The following findings are now widely known and accepted:

- most populations have a saturation of knowledge regarding HIV transmission,
- extramarital and premarital sexual practices are common in men,
- married women are often well aware of their husbands' use of commercial sex,
- there is a double standard regarding gender and sexual expressions for men and women, and
- the discovery of new, evolving sexual patterns, such as the formation of a sexual network among unmarried men and women in urban settings.

This accrued fund of knowledge from cumulative research has also formed the foundation of our review in this chapter.

A recent publication on *General Sex Education* by Wasikasin, Aimpradit, et al. (1994) represents a renewed and integrative energy in sexology and research in Thailand (1994). This work, published by the Thammasat University, Bangkok, was written by two social workers, two physicians, and a lawyer. As a textbook, it offers an unprecedented integration of disciplines, and its attention to psychosocial contexts is far from the sole emphasis on reproductive biology common in earlier publications.

To date, there is no training in sexological research per se. Most researchers in the area of HIV/AIDS have received training from Western institutions, or have applied their basic training in other areas of research to sexual topics. There are a few notable sexologists, for example, Dr. Suwattana Aribarg at the Chulalongkorn University in Bangkok. Dr. Aribarg and her husband give lectures in human sexuality to medical students and she provides counseling through the Chulalongkorn Psychiatric Clinic. Other sex researchers in various institutes and universities in Thailand have also put forth their efforts to the academic and public attention, and many have gradually received greater national and international recognition over the years.

In late 1995, the Mahidol University Institute for Population and Social Research organized an important seminar on sex research. Charged with enthusiasm, the event brought together key sex researchers in Thailand and their body of knowledge, symbolizing a renaissance of sex research in Thailand. Fongkaew (1995), for example, delineated basic paradigms and constructs commonly used in sex research, and cautioned Thai sex researchers to be aware of their own assumptions and values. Some researchers challenged fellow researchers to theorize and problematize data on sexuality and gender, pushing toward the formation of a theoretical model that could capture the sexual complexities in Thailand. Other researchers urged that investigations must be led by pragmatic implications; much data is still needed for the advancement of social issues, for example, the improvement of the status of women and increasing social acceptance of gays and lesbians. Key ingredients for effective interventions are yet to be identified, especially the often overlooked "positive factors" which might protect individuals from behavioral or attitudinal problems. Finally, there was a consensus that researchers should take a more-assertive role in making specific recommendations based on the findings from their research.

As of 1995, advanced education in human sexuality was not available in Thailand, and most Thai scholars still needed to study abroad. In the aforementioned seminar on sex research in Thailand, Dusitsin (1995) stated that the training of new sexological researchers was one of the priorities of his proposed Program for the Promotion of Sexual Health. Through the efforts of the Asian Federation of Sexology and the World Association for Sexology, increasing numbers of Thai sexologists have been identified. The first sexological organization in Thailand, the Sexology Society, was formed in May, 1995. The organization, chaired by Dr. Nikorn Dusitsin, is located at the Institute of Health Research, Chulalongkorn University, in Bangkok.

Summary

Sexuality in Thailand, like the country's peaceful yet interesting coexistence of peoples and cultures, is a convergence of values and practices resulting from admixing of cultures over the centuries. In recent years, these sexual attitudes and behaviors have undergone enormous changes influenced by the rapid economic growth, urbanization, exposure to Western cultures, and, most recently, the HIV epidemic. While economic growth has afforded the country more effective population control and improved public health services, certain strata of the society have suffered from socioeconomic pressures. The growth of tourism, combined with the indigenous attitudes toward sexuality, commercial sex, and homosexuality, have provided fertile grounds for the commercial sex industry to flourish in Thailand despite its illegal status. Exploitation of children for commercial sex purposes, and the high rates of HIV infection among sex workers and the population at large, are some of the many problems that have followed. The rise of HIV infection has caused Thai people to question and challenge many sexual norms and practices, most notably the men's rite-of-passage practice of having the first sexual intercourse with a female sex worker.

Although well known for their general tolerance and harmony, the lack of conflicts or hostility in the Thai society does not necessarily indicate that Thai people always maintain embracing attitudes about gender inequality, homosexuality, abortion, or sexuality in general. The Third Buddhist Precept clearly prohibits sex which causes sorrow in others, such as irresponsible and exploitative sex, adultery, sexual coercion, and abuse. Other phenomena, such as masturbation, prostitution, subordination of women, and homosexuality, remain uncertain. Most of the current attitudes about these practices can be traced to non-Buddhist sources. Today, these non-Buddhist beliefs are primarily a blend between indigenous concepts (e.g., class structures, animism, and gender codes) and Western ideologies (e.g., capitalism and medical and psychological theories of sexuality).

Thailand is noted for being a male-dominated patriarchal society, and the gender roles and expectations for Thai men and women differ accordingly. Despite the fact that many Thai men in the past had households with many wives, polygamy is no longer socially or legally acceptable. Mutual monogamy as well as emotional commitment constitute today's ideal marriage. Traditionally, men and women in Thai society depend on each other for the fulfillment of both religious and secular goals, as well as their needs for love and passion. Despite such reciprocal need, the existence of power differential is clear, and it may have been affirmed by the gender hierarchy sanctioned by Theravada Buddhism. Passion, courtship, romance, and love between men and women are glorified, and the love-inspired sentiments in Thai literature and music can rival the jubilance and pathos in any other culture.

Nonetheless, an uneasy tension between the genders is evident in the way Thai men and women view one another, especially in the areas of intimacy, trust, and sexuality. A double standard for men and women still exists in the practices of premarital and extramarital sex. Manliness, or *chaai chaatrii*, has become increasingly associated with various vices, especially the search for sexual gratification. A man is encouraged to seek sexual pleasure as recreation, and sex with commercial sex workers represents an acceptable and "responsible" behavior to fulfill the sexual desires of single and married men. On the other hand, the dichotomous stereotype of the good-woman/bad-woman exists: a "good" woman, personified in the image of a *kulasatrii*, is expected to be a virgin when she marries and to remain monogamous with her husband; otherwise she is categorized as "bad." Men and women are socialized to maintain distance from the opposite gender. Newer generations of Thai people are finding that the clear-cut traditional gender constructions can no longer explain their evolving, amorphous forms of gender relations.

In the traditional household, Thai women have always excelled at their mother-nurturer role. Outside the household context, women have made tremendous contributions, especially in the areas of the arts, business, and academia. Women are still a long way from achieving equal recognition in the political and religious hierarchies. Today, Thai women struggle with modern realities in the work force while simultaneously striving toward the positive, if difficult, ideal of a *kulasatrii*.

Another area that has received recent attention is male and female homosexual behaviors. Same-gender sexual behavior was traditionally recognized as associated with the gender-nonconformity among the *kathoey*, who were seen as a "third gender." Indigenously, the *kathoey* were relatively tolerated and often held some special social roles in the community. Previously an undiscussed topic, the Thai vocabulary managed without a word for homosexuality by using a euphemism such as "trees in the same forest" until the past few decades. More recently, the words "gay" and "lesbian" have been adopted from English, illustrating the search for vocabularies to represent types of homosexualities, which had existed without labels. Homophobia, stereotypes, and misconceptions about homosexuality are common, especially among the middle class who have learned antiquated Western psychiatric theories. On the other hand, gay businesses and sex industry have grown to significant visibility. Meanwhile, a few advocate groups have emerged to advance their agenda and formulate new social identities for gays and lesbians in Thailand.

Sexological research in Thailand is at an exciting stage. Prompted by the HIV/AIDS epidemic and the controversies regarding the commercial sex industry, large amounts of data have been collected on sexual behaviors and attitudes. Descriptive studies on sexual practices and norms have offered valuable insights into the sexuality of Thai people, although much more data are needed, especially in certain areas not directly associated with public health (e.g., abortion, rape, and incest). Still in its infancy stage, sex therapies and counseling in Thailand are starting to adopt Western psychology, and the providers could learn much more from further research to help customize their services to fit the unique features of the Thai sexuality. Care must be taken when Western models or assumptions are applied to Thai sexual phenomena. Characterized by interwoven traditions over centuries, the people of Thailand defy such simplification, as their constructions of gender and sexuality continue on an evolving course which is as mystifying as it is enlightening.

References and Suggested Readings

Allyn, E. 1991. *Trees in the Same Forest: The Men of Thailand Revisited.* San Francisco: Bua Luang Publishing.

Archavanitkul, K. and N. Havanon. 1990. "Situation, Opportunities and Problems Encountered by Young Girls in Thai Society." Research report funded by Terre des Hommes, Bangkok, Thailand.

Aribarg, A., S. Aribarg, W. Rakiti, and S. Harnroongroj. 1982. "Sexual Behavior During Pregnancy." *Journal of Psychiatric Association Thailand,* 27:147-160.

Boonchalaksi, W. and P. Guest. 1994. *Prostitution in Thailand.* Salaya, Phutthamonthon Nakhon Pathom, Thailand: The Institute for Population and Social Research, Mahidol University.

Brinkman, U. K. 1992. *Features of the AIDS Epidemic in Thailand.* Department of Population and International Health: Working Paper Series, No. 3.

Beyrer, C., S. Eiumtrakul, D. D. Celentano, K. E. Nelson, S. Ruckphaopunt, and C. Khamboonruang. 1995. "Same-Sex Behavior, Sexually Transmitted Diseases and HIV Risks Among Young Northern Thai Men." *AIDS,* 9:171-176.

Bussaratid, S., S. Na Ranong, V. Boonyaprakob, and C. Sitasuwan. 1981. "Sexual Behavior in Married Thai Females." *Siriraj Hospital Gazette,* 33:84-90.

Cabezón, J. E. 1993. "Homosexuality and Buddhism." In A. Swidler, ed., *Homosexuality and World Religions.* Valley Forge, PA: Trinity Press International.

Chompootaweep, S., K. Yamarat, P. Poomsuwan, and N. Dusitsin. 1991. "A Study of Reproductive Health in Adolescence of Secondary School Students and Teachers in Bangkok." *Thai Journal of Health Research,* 5(2).

Coleman, E. 1996. "Importing and Exporting Constructs of Homosexuality." *Sexuality and Human Bonding: Proceedings of the XII World Congress of Sexology.* Amsterdam: Elsevier.

Crystal, D. 1987. *The Cambridge Encyclopedia of Language.* New York: Cambridge University Press.

Dusitsin, N. 1995. "Program for the Promotion of Sexual Health." In A. Chamratrithirong, chairperson, *Directions in Research on Sexual Behavior in Thailand.* Seminar conducted at the meeting of the Mahidol University Institute for Population and Social Research, Bangkok, Thailand.

Division of Epidemiology. 1984-1993. *Statistics on Reported Cases of AIDS, ARC and HIV Seropositives.* Thailand: Office of the Permanent Secretary of Ministry of Public Health.

Dumronggittigule, P., S. Sombathmai, K. Taywaditep, and J. Mandel. 1995. *"HIV Prevention Strategies Among Northern Thai Married Couples: A Study from the Village."* Paper presented at the Third Conference on AIDS in Asia and the Pacific, September, 1995, Chiangmai, Thailand.

Eberhardt, N., ed. 1988. *Gender, Power, and the Construction of the Moral Order: Studies from the Thai Periphery.* Monograph 4. University of Wisconsin-Madison, Center for Southeast Asian Studies.

Fongkaew, W. 1995. "Gender Roles and Sexuality in Thai Sex Research." In A. Chamratrithirong, chairperson, *"Directions in Research on Sexual Behavior in Thailand."* Seminar conducted at the meeting of the Mahidol University Institute for Population and Social Research, Bangkok, Thailand.

Ford, N. J. and S. Kittisuksathit. 1994. "Destinations Unknown: The Gender Construction and Changing Nature of the Sexual Expressions of Thai Youth." *AIDS Care,* 6:517-531.

Friends of Women Foundation. 1992 (June). *Newsletter,* 3:1.

Fuller, T. D., J. N. Edwards, S. Sermsri, and S. Vorakitphokatorn. 1993. "Gender and Health: Some Asian Evidence." *Journal of Health and Social Behavior,* 34:252-271.

Guest, P. 1994. "Guesstimating the Unestimateable: The Number of Child Prostitutes in Thailand." In O. Ard-am and C. Sethaput, eds. *Child Prostitution in Thailand: A Documentary Analysis and Estimation on the Number of Child Prostitutes* (pp. 73-98). Bangkok, Thailand: Institute for Population and Social Research, Mahidol University.

Havanon, N., A. Bennett, and J. Knodel. 1992 (June). *Sexual Networking in a Provincial Thai Setting.* AIDS Prevention Monograph Series Paper No. 1. Bangkok: G. M Press Printing Service Co, Ltd.

Hiew, C. 1992. *Child Prostitutes as Victims of Tourism in Children in Prostitution: Victims of Tourism in Asia.* Bangkok, Thailand: ECPAT.

Hill, A. M. 1988. "Women Without Talents Are Virtuous." In N. Eberhardt, ed. *Gender, Power, and the Construction of the Moral Order: Studies from the Thai Periphery.* Monograph 4. University of Wisconsin-Madison, Center for Southeast Asian Studies.

Hornblower, M. 1993 (June 21). "The Skin Trade." *Time*, pp. 44-52.

Jackson, P. A. 1989. *Male Homosexuality in Thailand: An Interpretation of Contemporary Thai Sources.* Elmhurst, NY: Global Academic Publishers.

Kaime-Atterhog, W., O. Ard-Am, and C. Sethaput. 1994. "Child Prostitution in Thailand: A Documentary Assessment." In O. Ard-am and C. Sethaput, eds. *Child Prostitution in Thailand: A Documentary Analysis and Estimation on the Number of Child Prostitutes* (pp. 37-71). Bangkok, Thailand: Institute for Population and Social Research, Mahidol University.

Keyes, C. F. 1984. "Mother or Mistress But Never a Monk: Buddhist Notions of Female Gender in Rural Thailand." *American Ethnologist*, 11:223-241.

Kirsch, T. 1982. "Buddhism, Sex-Roles, and the Thai Economy." In P. Van Esterik, ed. *Women of Southeast Asia.* Occasional Paper No. 9. DeKalb: Northern Illinois University, Center for Southeast Asian Studies.

Kirsch, A. T. 1985. "Text and Context: Buddhist Sex Roles/Culture of Gender Revisited." *American Ethnologist*, 12:302-320.

Kunawararak, P.,C. Beyrer, C. Natpratan, W. Feng, D. D. Celentano, M. de Boer, K.E. Nelson, and C. Khamboonruang. 1995. "The Epidemiology of HIV and Syphilis Among Male Commercial Sex Workers in Northern Thailand." *AIDS*, 9.

Limanonda, B. 1993. "Female Commercial Sex Workers and AIDS: Perspectives from Thai Rural Communities." Paper presented at the 5th International Conference on Thai Studies—SOAS at Centre of South East Asian Studies, School of Oriental and African Studies (SOAS), University of London, London, England, July 5-10.

Limanonda, B., P. Tirasawat, and N. Chongvatana. 1993. *The Demographic and Behavioral Study of Female Commercial Sex Workers in Thailand.* Publication No. 207/36. Bangkok: Institute of Population Studies, Chulalongkorn University.

Limsuwan, A., S. Kanapa, and Y. Siristonapun. 1986. "Acquired Immune Deficiency Syndrome in Thailand: A Report of Two Cases." *Journal of the Medical Association of Thailand*, 69:164-169.

Manderson, L. 1992. "Public Sex Performances in Patpong and Explorations of the Edges of Imagination." *Journal of Sex Research*, 29:451-475.

McFarland, G. B. 1982. *Thai-English Dictionary.* Stanford, CA: Stanford University Press.

McKinnon, J., and W. Bhruksasri, eds. 1983. *Highlanders of Thailand.* Kuala Lumper: Oxford University Press.

Ministry of Public Health. 1991. *Sentinel Surveillance of HIV Infection.* Bangkok, Thailand: Ministry of Public Health.

Nelson, K. E., D. D. Celentano, S. Eiumtrakul, D. R. Hoover, C. Beyrer, S. Suprasert, S. Kuntolbutra, and C. Khamboonruang. 1996. "Changes in Sexual Behavior and a Decline in HIV Infection Among Young Men in Thailand." *New England Journal of Medicine*, 335:297-303.

Nopkesorn, T., T. D. Mastro, S. Sangkharomya, M. Sweat, P. Singharaj, K. Limpakarn-janarat, H. Gayle, and B. Weniger. 1993. "HIV-1 Infection in Young Men in Northern Thailand." *AIDS*, 7:1233-1239.

Nopkesorn, T., S. Sungkarom, and R. Sornlum. 1991. *"HIV Prevalence and Sexual Behaviors Among Thai Men Aged 21 in Northern Thailand."* Research Report No. 3. Program on AIDS. Bangkok: The Thai Red Cross Society.

Nopkesorn, T., M. D. Sweat, S. Kaensing, and T. Teppa. 1993. *Sexual Behavior for HIV-Infection in Young Men in Payao.* Research Report No. 6. Program on AIDS. Bangkok: The Thai Red Cross Society.

O'Grady, R. 1992. *The Child and the Tourist: The Story Behind the Escalation of Child Prostitution in Asia.* Bangkok, Thailand: The Campaign to End Child Prostitution in Asian Tourism.

Otaganonta, W. 1995 (June 21). "Women Who Love Women." *Bangkok Post*, pp. 29; 36.

Phongpaichit, P. 1982. *From Peasant Girls to Bangkok Masseuses.* Geneva, Switzerland: International Labour Office.

Pongthai, S., P. Sakornratanakul, and K. Chaturachinda. 1980. "Marriage and Sexual Activity." *Journal of Medical Association Thailand*, 63:11-14.

Pramualratana, A., Podhisita, C., Kanungsukkasem, U., Wawer, M. J., and McNamara, R. 1993. "The Social Context of Condom Use in Low-Priced Brothels in Thailand: A Qualitative Analysis." Paper presented at the 3rd National AIDS Seminar, Bangkok, Thailand.

Pyne, H. H. 1994. "Reproductive Experiences and Needs of Thai Women: Where Has Development Taken Us?" In G. Sen and R. C. Snow, eds. *Power and Decision: The Social Control of Reproduction.* Boston: Harvard University Press.

Rajadhon, A. 1961. "Popular Buddhism in Thailand." In W. J. Gedney, ed./trans. *Life and Ritual in Old Siam: Three Studies of Thai Life and Customs.* New Haven, CT: Human Relations Area Files Press. (Original work published 1948, 1949).

Redd Barna. 1989. *The Sexual Exploitation of Children in Developing Countries.* Redd Barna, Norway.

Rojanapithayakorn, W., and R. Hanenberg, R. 1996. "The 100 Percent Condom Program in Thailand." *AIDS*, 10:1-7.

Serrill, M. S. 1993 (June 21). "Defiling the Children." *Time*, p. 52.

Sethaput, C. 1995. "A Historical Review of Research on Sexuality in Thailand." In A. Chamratrithirong, chairperson, *Directions in Research on Sexual Behavior in Thailand.* Seminar conducted at the meeting of the Mahidol University Institute for Population and Social Research, Bangkok, Thailand.

Sittitrai, W., T. Brown, and C. Sakondhavat. 1993. "Levels of HIV Risk Behaviour and AIDS Knowledge in Thai Men Having Sex with Men." *AIDS Care*, 5:261-271.

Sittitrai, W., T. Brown, and S. Virulak. 1991. "Patterns of Bisexuality in Thailand." In R. Tielman, M. Carballo, and A. Hendriks, eds. *Bisexuality and HIV/AIDS.* Buffalo, NY: Prometheus Books.

Sittitrai, W., P. Phanuphak, J. Barry, and T. Brown. 1992. *Thai Sexual Behavior and Risk of HIV Infection: A Report of the 1990 Survey of Partner Relations and Risk of HIV Infection in Thailand.* Bangkok, Thailand: Program on AIDS. Thai Red Cross Society and Institute of Population Studies, Chulalongkorn University.

Sittitrai, W., P. Phanuphak, N. Satirakorn, E. E. Wee, and R. E. Roddy. 1989. "Demographics and Sexual Practices of Male Bar Workers in Bangkok." Fifth International Conference on AIDS, June 4-9, Abstract no. M.D.P. 19).

Skinner, W. G. 1957. *Chinese Society in Thailand: An Analytical History.* Ithaca, NY: Cornell University Press.

Skrobanek, S. undated. *Strategies Against Prostitution: The Case of Thailand.* Bangkok, Thailand: Foundation for Women.

Sricharatchanya, P. 1987 (November 5). "Scare Stories Spur Thailand into Action." *Far Eastern Economic Review*, p. 52.

Srisang, S. S. 1990. "Tourism and Child Prostitution in Thailand." In *Caught in Modern Slavery: Tourism and Child Prostitution in Asia* (pp. 37-46). Bangkok, Thailand: The Ecumenical Coalition on Third World Tourism.

Time. 1989 (January 2). "The Good News: Thailand Controls a Baby Boom," p. 50.

Thorbek, S. 1987. *Voices from the City: Women of Bangkok.* London: Zed Books.

Udomratn, P., and S. Tungphaisal. 1990. "Sexual Behavior in Thai Society." *Journal of Psychiatric Association Thailand*, 35:115-127.

Van Esterik, J. 1982. "Women Meditation Teachers in Thailand." In P. Van Esterik, ed. *Women of Southeast Asia.* Occasional Paper No. 9. DeKalb: Northern Illinois University, Center for Southeast Asian Studies.

van Griensven, G. J. P., B. Limanonda, N. Chongwatana, P. Tirasawat, and R. A. Coutinho. 1995. "Socioeconomic and Demographic Characteristics and HIV-1 Infection Among Female Commercial Sex Workers in Thailand." *AIDS Care*, 7:557-565.

van Landingham, M., S. Suprasert, W. Sittitrai, and C. Vaddhanaphuti. 1993. "Sexual Activity Among Never-Married Men in Northern Thailand." *Demography*, 30(3).

Vithayasai, V., and P. Vithayasai. 1990. "An Analysis of HIV Infection Rates in Northern Thailand." *Thai AIDS Journal*, 2:99-108.

Wasikasin, W., N. Aimpradit, S. Kiatinan, P. Likhitlersuang, and S. Boonchalearmwipat. 1994. *General Sex Education.* Bangkok, Thailand: Thammasat University.

Wawer, M. J., C. Podhisita, U. Kanungsukkasem, A. Pramualratana, and R. McNamara. 1996. "Origins and Working Conditions of Female Sex Workers in Urban Thailand: Consequences of Social Context for HIV Transmission." *Social Sciences and Medicine*, 42:453-462.

Weniger, B. G., K. Limpakarnjanarat, K. Ungchusak, S. Thanprasertsuk, K. Choopanya, S. Vanichseni, T. Uneklabh, P. Thongcharoen, and C. Wasi. 1991. "The Epidemiology of HIV Infection and AIDS in Thailand." *AIDS*, 5 (Suppl. 2), s71-s85.

Wyatt, D. K. 1984. *Thailand: A Short History.* New Haven, CT: Yale University Press.

Ukraine
(*Ukrayina*)

Tamara Govorun, Ph.D., and Borys M. Vornyk, Ph.D.

Contents

Demographics and a Historical Perspective

A. Demographics

Located in southeastern Europe, Ukraine is bordered on the north by Belarus, by the Russian Federation on the northeast and east, Moldovia and Romania on the southwest, and by Hungary, Poland, and the Slovak Republic on the west. It shares a Black Sea border with Turkey. The estimated population in 1991 was 52.2 million—56 percent female and 46 percent male, with an age distribution of 25 percent below age 19, 62 percent ages 20 to 59, and 13 percent over age 60. (The *1996 World Almanac* gives the 1995 population as 51.9 million). Sixty-eight percent of the people live in cities, with the capital of Kyiv or Kiev having a population over 2.6 million. Average life expectancy at birth in 1995 was 66 for males and 75 for females. The 1995 annual birthrate was 12 per thousand, the death rate was 13 per thousand, and the infant mortality rate was 20 per thousand births, for a natural increase of 0 percent. Literacy is 99 percent. Ukraine has one hospital bed per 75 persons and one physician per 228 persons. The 1995 per capita domestic product was $3,960 U.S.

Ukraine's territory is as large as France and Denmark combined. Ukraine has a homogeneous society—73 percent of its 52 million people are ethnic Ukrainians, 22 percent Russian, and 5 percent Jews, Poles, Moldovians, Bulgarians, and others.

B. A Brief Historical Perspective

For most people, Ukraine was unknown as a country until recent times, although it has a very ancient and rich history and a highly developed national identity and culture. Its relative obscurity is due to the fact that Ukraine has been an independent free nation for only eight years in this century. Although the Ukrainians gave the world the first example of a democratic constitution and republic under the Cossacks in the 1500s and 1600s and never waged war against any other country, they continually had to resist numerous invasions by neighboring nations. For almost three hundred years prior to 1917, part or all of Ukraine was a colonial part of Czarist Russia. At the turn of the last century, Austria-Hungary controlled part of Ukraine within its empire. Ukraine was an independent nation for three years from the end of World War I in 1918 until it was taken over by the Russian Communists in 1921. Seventy years as part of the Soviet Union under Moscow followed, with independence and freedom regained with the collapse of the Soviet Union in 1991. The national flag of Ukraine has the most peaceful colors: the upper half is blue as a symbol of a cloudless sky or birth-giving water, and the lower half is yellow as a symbol of ripe wheat or the sun. Its modern state insignia, the Triad (*Tryzub*) can be traced back to Kyiv Rus. It symbolizes the unity of spirit, wisdom, and will as the source of individual and national development. (For additional historical and ethnic perspectives, see Section 2A below.)

1. Basic Sexological Premises

A. The Character of Gender Roles

In order to draw connections between contemporary problems and histori-cal setting, attention must be paid to the main feature in gender relation-ships that distinguishes Ukraine from Russia and from the other former Soviet states. This is the high status of Ukrainian women as mother, sister, and wife. Throughout history, Ukraine had not been characterized by the traditional patriarchal family structure that existed, for example, in Russia; gender roles in Ukraine contrast sharply with female dependency and submissiveness. There were no male-dominated marriage relationships, and Ukrainian women held high positions in both family and community settings. This was due in part to sociocultural circumstances. Throughout the several different periods of sexual-culture development in Ukraine, sex and gender behavior grew from beliefs in ancient pagan cultures that valued the feelings, sensations, desires, and pleasures of sexual intercourse. Intimacy was considered to be harmonious with nature and male-female relationships.

The origin of Ukraine, the Kyiv Rus, was governed by a highly educated woman, Queen Olga (reign 946-966), who began the country's conversion to Christianity. There are also many historical witnesses of the gender-equality norms in later times, particularly during the rule of the grand dukes of Kyiv in the eleventh century. The marital agreement, for example, was based on mutual desires of both the male and the female to establish a family. Mutual respect for male and female was the norm, as well as respect for responsibilities in housekeeping and child rearing. In Ukrainian customs, tradition, and especially folklore, it is hard to find accounts of either physical or mental abuse of women, or inequalities in family relationships between husband and wife.

In many Ukrainian regions, the woman selected her spouse and often initiated the marriage relationships. Later, especially during the period of the Cossack Republic during the sixteenth and seventeenth centuries, the women educated the children, organized the communities, and maintained their own organizations of social activity while men were away on military service. According to the numerous historical evidences, there was no wide gap between the observed behavior patterns of men and women. The roles of Ukrainian women and men in the family and the social continuum were mutually inclusive. Sadly, three hundred years of Russian governance, and especially seventy years of Soviet oppression, have greatly affected family and gender development in Ukraine.

The idea of gender equality has had a major impact on Ukrainian social life, even though it was interpreted as a complete similarity in jobs, education, and culture for males and females. For seventy years of Soviet rule, women were tractor drivers, builders, fabric workers, and collective farmers whose emotional life and female identification were less connected with family and children and more with job success and Communist party activities. In Ukraine, women continue to be the main labor force for heavy and dangerous jobs that jeopardize their reproductive health.

In many ways, the Soviet society remained sexist because gender differences were emphasized in many spheres. It imposed separateness between women and men in traditional responsibilities for child and family care. Even in the secondary school curriculum, a course in "home servicing" was only for girls and assumed different experiences for boys and girls with wide-ranging consequences. It supported women's attachment to the family and their concern with cooking, caring, and nurturing, while autonomy and public involvement was expected of men.

The complexity of the Russian totalitarian society contributed to the existence of numerous gender subcultures and created a lot of confusion in gender self-identity. Thus, the educational system was and is still oriented to raising girls as self- and task-oriented, knowledgeable, ambitious, and independent persons. On the other hand, the social system as a whole was oriented toward dependency, obedience to authority, and passivity, traits typically identified with femininity in a patriarchal culture. Thus, the communist society created particular behavior patterns manifested by women because the social environment left almost nothing for personal self-actualization in social and family life. In addition to supporting the husband and family, Ukrainian women are still expected to hold a full-time job outside the home; in fact, they have no choice other than to work outside the home. Women remained socially dependent because society maintains a lot of prejudice against women occupying high positions, especially in the social structure. Only a small percentage of women obtain academic grants, prestigious positions, or social recognition as politicians. Instead of the state developing support industries to lighten the burden of women in housekeeping, men and women engaged in an endless and fruitless discussion of which gender was the stronger.

The demasculinization of Ukrainian culture was intensified by the feminization of most institutions involved in socialization. Education, medicine, and even engineering remained extremely sexist, with the assumption that women by nature possessed the necessary abilities to be engaged in these activities. Social, economic, and political inefficiency—we are still discussing whether Ukrainian society should recognize private property—left almost no opportunities for effective problem solving, training in management skills, persistence, and competitiveness for men. Lack of autonomy, self-sufficiency, pursuit of self-interest, and competence had contributed very much toward the demasculinization of the male population in Ukraine.

Finally, in the society where there was lack of responsibility and respect for personality, both genders were losing such human characteristics as being cooperative, warm, sympathetic, loving, creative, and altruistic in relationships, sensitive to others, and intelligent in communications. Thus, Ukrainian society could not provide adequate training for children to develop competent and responsible gender and sexual behavior.

B. General Concepts and Constructions of Sexuality and Love

During the Soviet period in Ukraine, sex was a taboo subject as far as the mass media, scientific investigation, and education were concerned. After the 1920s, the only legitimate function of sexuality was reproduction. The emphasis on sex education for adults was exclusively focused on information about the reproductive systems and on social and moral control of sexual behavior. The communist society selected the information that was communicated in sex education, focusing on physiology and romantic love, while avoiding discussion of values, trust, intimacy, self-awareness, and concern for others.

Society is always a kind of external support for personal development, and self-conception provides values and orientation for sexual behavior. The communist image of sexual behavior was always negative. Sex was considered a "bad" part of one's personality that was in disharmony with the "good" part that involved strict conscious control and abstinence. This viewpoint grew out of the prevailing negative attitude toward personal freedom and intimacy, self-respect, and personal responsibility. It is apparent that the totalitarian society could not help children understand the changes of their bodies and emotions, or teach them responsible decision making. Even in the mid-1980s, when schools recognized the necessity of sex education and faced the task of informing teenagers about love and intimacy, the compulsory course in family and family relationships did not include any information about sex. It was a sexless course about sexless behavior. The same situation existed in society in general.

A humorous episode from the Gorbachev era of the Soviet Union, much quoted among sexologists, illustrates well the prevailing situation. At the time, as Soviets were discovering Western culture, a meeting of American and Soviet women was being carried on by satellite television. The groups discussed common interest issues, such as housekeeping, child rearing, etc. At one point, an American woman asked, "And what about sex in your country?" There was a prolonged pause, when most of the Soviet women in the audience responded, "There is no sex at all in our country!"

Although Ukrainian society has become more permissive sexually in recent years, it still does not provide adequate values for human sexual activity. With the breakdown of the Soviet regime, sexuality became one of the most important symbols of social and cultural liberation. Widespread public silence and ignorance about sex in former years has been replaced by everyday representations in commerce and movies. Television programs and filmmakers exploit sex, but still present it as a part of personality that is hardly related to the self-ideal and is quite dissonant with accepted family gender roles. Public display of the bodies of young women as available sexual objects for men, and sexual intercourse as something far from personal relationships in advertising and mass media, perpetuate the distances between men and women as social beings and between sex and the family.

Ethnicity, culture, national customs, and traditions help create models of gender behavior, develop respect for values, and develop some interpersonal skills. Sexual competence involves many personality qualities and activities that should be taught to children as they develop. Family-oriented customs and traditions that help gender socialization processes, such as marriage, housekeeping, and parenthood, have almost been destroyed in most regions of Ukraine because of the Soviet ideal of creating a new society without ethnicity and religion. The incidence of divorce and child abuse and neglect documented in Ukraine reflects this influence. The incidence of divorce and abuse in the eastern part of Ukraine where traditions were lost is two and a half times higher than in the western regions that retained many of their traditions after they were joined to Ukraine during the 1940s. In the west, teenage girls know an enormous number of things about housekeeping, bringing up children, and proper treatment of relatives, because they are involved in sophisticated and living traditions that are maintained by their families. In the east, family life is extremely narrow and still centered on Soviet holidays. A comparison of family holidays in the U.S.A. and the Soviet Union reveals some significant differences. The personal, individual expression of Mother's Day in the U.S.A. contrasts strongly with the celebration of "The Day of International Solidarity of Women" imposed on Ukrainians by the Soviet system. While Americans honor their individual mothers, Ukrainians for seventy years celebrated the progress of women in the work force.

For three generations, the Ukrainians have grown up in this system, which neglected personal dignity and expressions of respect. The social system as well as family communications were mostly oriented to punishment rather than to the encouragement of self-worth. Another evidence of this distortion can be found in the language people use to address each other in public places. In Ukraine, there are proper words for addressing a person as a sexual human being, as there are in America or other countries, such as miss, missus, lady, sir, mister, gentleman, etc. As a result of the Soviet imposition of the word "comrade," referring to persons who share political ideas in common, the salutations *panni* and *pan*, "respectful woman or man," were almost totally eliminated from usage. Today, Ukrainians address a person mostly by their gender identity "woman" or "girl" for females, and "man," "young man," or "guy" for males. So, the social and sexual identity of the individual oppose each other. Such greetings are mutual and cause no offense or embarrassment to anyone. The fact that most Ukrainians consider these sexual definitions of the self as a normal social greeting does not mean that it is unimportant to the sexual culture. Those Ukrainians who allow themselves to be defined as belonging to a particular sex are those who were raised with a lack of respect for individual personality.

2. Religious and Ethnic Factors Affecting Sexuality

A. Character of Ethnic Values

Ukrainians have developed as an ethnic group over a period of at least three to four thousand years. Scientists distinguish several periods in the development of Ukrainian religious values. At the beginning of the twentieth century, scientists found the first archaeological evidence of an ancient settlement and culture on the territory of Ukraine. These have been dated back to 4500 to 2000 before the Common Era and the birth of Christ. The culture was named Trypil'ska, after the name of village Trypillja near Kyiv (Kiev) where the first signs of this ancient culture were discovered. Similarities in gender roles and behaviors between this ancient culture and elements of the modern Ukrainian culture make this discovery particularly significant. The people of the Trypil'ska culture were agricultural, living in small and large families in separate houses usually situated in circles near rivers. The most wonderful of the remains of this civilization unearthed were ceramic figures of different women and the special places or shrines in houses where these were placed. All of the figures showed obvious evidence of a connection with religious beliefs, specifically a Mother cult and worship of the female. These figures have pronounced sexual signs and even such details as fatness and hairdos. The principal role of a woman in Trypil'ska culture was connected with a highly developed agricultural cult in which the female symbolized fertility and the Goddess Earth. It all gave a woman the right to be a priestess and a head of the family.

From the seventh to the third centuries B.C.E., Indo-European Scythian tribes controlled the Ukrainian steppes.

The period from 500 to 900 C.E. is the time of the Slavic tribes and Slavic community development as a separate ethnic population. Slavic tribes began migrating from the northwest into what is now Russia in the fifth century. The division of the ancient Slavs into various tribes began in the second to fourth centuries when the Goth and Huns forced them to split. In the south, they eventually formed the tribes of the Polianians, Siverianians, Derelianians, etc. Some of these tribes were united in Kyivan Rus by the spread of Christianity from Byzantium (Constantinople) in the tenth and eleventh centuries; Volodymyr the Saint was converted in 988.

Western historians give greater importance than do Ukranian historians to the role of Scandinavian chieftains, Norsemen or Vikings, in the ninth century. A common Western view claims that the Viking Rurik founded the first Russian dynasty in 862 in Novgorod—hence the distinction between Novgorod and Kyivan Rus, and the possible origin of the term Russian. Ukranians scholars trace the origin of the term Rus to the common root of many Ukrainian rivers, Ros', Rosavitsa, Rosava, etc., where Slavic tribes settled. Hence, the Slavs were called Rusychi or Rusyny, and Rus is the synonym of Ukraine but not Russia. Ukrainian historians note that Rus existed long before the arrival of the Norsemen, and that the word Russia, referring to a nation, does not occur until Peter the Great.

The Moguls overran the country in the thirteenth century, destroying Kyiv in 1240. Kyiv was freed from Mogul conquest after 80 years in 1320, when Lithuanian Duke Gedimin (ca. 1275-ca. 1340), together with Rus dukes and their military troops, fought the Moguls in three battles, the last and largest of which was held by the river Irpin' near Kyiv. After that victory, the Lithuanians ruled the country with the help of Rus dukes. In 1386, when the Lithuanian Kingdom united with Poland, Rus, according to the convention, received a separate government which was called Het'man. As time passed, Poland extended its power over Ukraine. In addition, while the eleventh-century grand dukes of Kyian Rus held such centralized power as existed, most of the sons of the Kyivan Rurikovechi Dynasty ruled in Novgorod.

From the thirteenth to the sixteenth centuries, Kyiv was under the influence of Poland and western Europe, with the 1500s and 1600s being the time of the Cossack Republic. In 1547, Ivan the Terrible formally proclaimed himself the first czar of the Rus, and Russia the true successor of the fallen Roman and Byzantine Empires. In 1654, Ukraine asked the czar of Muscovy for protection against Poland and signed the Treaty of Pereyasav, which recognized the sovereignty of Moscow. The Cossacks under Chemelnytsky may have wanted a full defensive partnership, such as now exists between the Canada and the United States. Moscow, however, interpreted the treaty as an invitation to take over Kyiv. Peter the Great (1682-1725) extended Moscow's domain, and in 1721 founded the Russian Empire, which included Ukraine.

As described by Veles (Rehbinder 1993), the Slavic culture was pagan, based on the worship to the numerous gods of the Great Mother Nature. The unity of female and male substances was considered a kind of magical activity for enriching the fertility of the Earth. Even today, the Ukrainians sing some seasonal songs (*koljadky* and *tsedrivky*), which are a kind of communication and dialogue of the individual with nature—animals, plants, sun, moon, and wind. A summer holiday of love, Kupala, has persisted from ancient times down to the present. In this ancient context, sexual intercourse is viewed as a relationship, the attachment feeling to the partner.

Nestor the Chronicler (ca. 1056-1114) supplemented and continued the primary Rus chronicles in *Povist Vremennykh Lit* (*A Tale of Bygone Years*) (1990). A monk in the Kyivan Cave Monastery and the most educated man of his time, Nestor described the differences in sex and gender behavior between the tribes: "Polyany—Slavs who lived in the central regions of what is now modern Ukraine—maintain their parents' traditions, peaceful and obedient, and their marriage customs." The neighboring Derevljany "lived like animals, killed each other . . . and there was no marriage customs other than kidnapping the young women." Nestor the Chronicler also condemned another neighboring culture where the people "had vulgar, disgraceful words and used them in the presence of parents and women." They also "did not know about marriage, but cavorted between villages. The men traveled around, playing, dancing, and singing all kinds of devil songs, stealing wives for themselves—women they found agreeable—and having two or three wives." His view was certainly colored by his perspective as a Kyivan monk. The Derevljany had killed Ihor, the husband of Queen Olga (c. 890-969), who in turn wiped out several of their towns.

The prominent feature of the ancient Slavic psychology was love-living, life-loving, and a tenderness and joyful mood. When Nestor the Chronicler wrote about Ihor's campaign, he described the feelings of attachment, and emotional evolvement of the ancient Slavs. Later on, when Kyivan (Kievan) Rus reached its heyday in the reign of Grand Prince Jaroslav the Wise

(1019-1054), the Church, which represented Christianity, could not eliminate this sensitive character of pagan culture. Christianity, with its cult of emotionless asceticism and abstinence, could not overcome the cheerful character of folk traditions and either tried to adopt and incorporate some of them into religious holidays or to prohibit them altogether. Thus, the Christian tradition began its long coexistence with ancient ethnic values. (See Section 1 in the chapter on Russia for further elaboration on this coexistence.)

B. Sources and Character of Religious Values

Three quarters of the Ukrainian people are Eastern Orthodox, 13.5 percent Ukrainian Catholic or Uniate, 2.3 percent Jewish, and 8.2 percent Baptist, Mennonite, Protestant, and Moslem.

From the eighth century, Ukraine was also known as Rus. In 988, the rulers and people of Kyiv adopted Christianity. During the reign of Prince Oleg, Kyiv was referred to as the "mother of Rus cities," which explains the particular importance given to the development of Christianity in this region. As a result of a jurisdictional division between Church and secular power, matrimonial and family cases fell within the Church's competence and domain. Legislation of the norms of matrimonial law dates from the second half of the eleventh century. As recorded in the legislative code of Prince Jaroslav the Wise, and later in other books, the new legal code incorporated the centuries-old experience of eastern Slavic social life.

The Church assumed an exclusive right to register marriages and insisted on rooting out pagan traditions. For example, marriage without a religious ceremony was considered to be void. In its views of marriage and family life, the Church was guided by the norms of Christian morality. The Church sought to incorporate into the mass consciousness ideas of the sanctity and inviolability of marriage and conjugal fidelity.

Men and women who were related up to the sixth generation were forbidden to marry. In addition, children from one family could not marry the brothers or sisters in another unrelated family. These restrictions were obviously adopted from Byzantine law, but were less strictly enforced. In Kyivan Rus, men married when they were 15 years old, while women married between ages 13 and 14. The Church forbade marriage of Christians with non-Christians. Engagement usually involved mutual consent and was followed by a festive dinner. Cheese was an obligatory dish shared by the bride and groom; the ritual of cutting cheese and bread meant that agreement had been reached. A lack of virginity in either partner was not an obstacle to marriage. There was a law that proclaimed the woman-slave free if she was tempted into intercourse and gave birth to a child. In case an unmarried woman gave birth to a child, she had to live in some church facility and was socially culpable. It was forbidden to have two spouses. Divorce was allowed only in exceptional cases and only after a court trial. A wife's adultery could be a serious reason for divorce; not so with a husband's adultery. After divorce, a husband had to pay his former wife a large financial compensation.

The Church in Kyivan Rus controlled norms of sexual behavior. First of all, it was forbidden to have any sexual relations between relatives and even relatives-in-law. Any intercourse outside the marital union was considered sinful, even when totally secret. Considerable attention was paid to any sexually deviant behavior. Thus, punishment for zoophilia was recorded in the statutes of Kyivan Rus. Childbearing was protected, and the Church took care for pregnant women and helped them. Anyone associated with an abortion or attempted abortion was guilty of a serious crime.

Within a marriage, and in society in general, there was a moral responsibility to respect all persons, regardless of gender, in Kyivan Rus. Thus in the *Edification to Children* by Volodymyr Monomach (1052-1125) one finds a great appreciation of the individual: "Protect widows, do not let the powerful ruin anyone. . . . Let your eyes look down but your soul aspire to height. . . . Love your wife, but don't let her control you" (1991).

The ancient and cheerful ethnic culture, coupled with moral Christian demands, helped to produce gender behavior patterns based on mutual respect of men and women, feelings of connection and attachment to each other, and the capacity to appreciate the romantic love as well as erotic sensations (Chubyns'kyj 1994). For the Ukrainian couple, intimacy was characterized by affection, consent, and long-lasting commitment. The psychology of love is widely described in Ukrainian songs, which are considered the best in the world and expressive of the national character (Shlemkevych 1992). The respect for women was so appreciated among the Ukrainians that Mirza-Avakjants wrote in 1920 that "the modern woman of every country could envy the position of Ukrainian woman in the sixteenth and seventeenth." More than a century and a half of the Cossack republic strengthened the independent-woman position in family life and made this a national characteristic.

3. Sexual Knowledge and Education

Sex-education problems in Ukraine are closely connected with recovery from the long period during which sexual culture was monitored by the Communist party. In the last four years, as a result of common efforts by Ukrainian scientists, especially physicians, psychologists, and teachers, the National Program Planning for the Family has been developed. An important direction in this program is sex education. The basic idea is to unite the efforts of educational institutions for children, parents, and the mass media in the process of socialization about sexuality. The main idea is to supply all children from preschool to college with a compulsory sex-education program that provides adequate knowledge of the emotional, psychological, and physical aspects of gender and sexual behavior. In addition, this program includes discussions of self-understanding, intimacy, family life, values, attitudes, orientations, and skills concerning the behavior and relationships of both genders.

Teachers, psychologists, and sexologists have created such a program to provide information about human sexuality, including discussion of human reproduction, pregnancy, childbirth, sexual responses, contraception. abortion, and sexually transmitted diseases. Developers of the program were conscious that the most important value for children of postcommunist society is to develop the ability to understand and respect the individual person. That is the reason the context of this program leads children to question, "Where did I come from?" "What do I want to be?" and "Who am I?" The development of self-reflecting capacity with regard to gender and sexual behavior is emphasized at every age level.

To a large degree, sex and gender behavior begins in the home. At various stages, children should receive knowledge about sex and reproduction from their parents. Thus, the new program initiated efforts to encourage family-based sexuality education. A substantial gap, however, exists between the knowledge provided by the family and the average child's curiosity needs. This gap makes clear the need for child- and parent-oriented knowledge that revives national family customs and traditions.

The authors of the program are interested in exploring the social influences, especially television, which create the sexual environments in which our children are growing up. Ukrainian mass media, however, are preoccupied with non-family-oriented commerce and movies. Still, many scientists have begun to collaborate with mass media, especially television, to prepare sexually oriented programs for adolescents, teenagers, and their parents. (See Section 5A for more details on the sexual knowledge of children and their sources of such information.)

4. Autoerotic Behaviors and Patterns

Ukrainian folk beliefs, proverbs, parables, and humorous refrains condemn autoerotic behavior and ridicule it as unnatural and abusive for the potential marital partner. This widespread opinion contributes very much to the contemporary Ukrainian negative attitude towards autoerotic behaviors.

A. Children and Adolescents

There is a lot of misunderstanding and fear among adults concerning children's autoeroticism. As the young child starts to explore his or her genitals, a strong punishment usually follows when adults detect this natural curiosity. Thus, from early childhood, the deliberate manipulation of genitals is mostly prohibited by the family and social environment. Most children do not receive any information about their genitals as the source of pleasure and good feelings. Parents usually worry so intensely about the occurrence of masturbation that this initial sexual experience is immediately suppressed whenever discovered. Still, what surveys are available suggest that by 6 years of age, between 2 and 10 percent of children have engaged in self-pleasuring.

Normally, the second period of interest in exploration of one's own body appears at puberty. The practice of masturbation considerably increases during these years and occurs alone or with other children in pairs or small groups. There are a lot of myths among the people about the harmful results of masturbation. Some boys believe it will impair or make intercourse impossible in the future, or result in mental retardation. Similarly, many physicians commonly consider adolescent masturbation to be harmful when it becomes a dominant concern, the focus for leisure activity, or a source of strong feelings of guilt. There is, however, some shift among health care professionals to accept adolescent masturbation as a normal activity. Still, most parents try to restrict teenage masturbation. In comparison to the Western experience in sex education, autosexuality during childhood is considered by most Ukrainians not as a pleasurable kind of sexual expression but as a hindrance to sexual pleasure. This may be partly connected with the former imposition of the Soviet ideas about sex as shameful, and not a useful human activity for the socialist society.

For children who are being raised in orphanages, outside a family, the opening of the sexual sensations generated in the genital areas usually becomes a habit. Thus, masturbation provides an easy way for self-soothing, reducing tension, and calming down for many boys and girls. Children raised in an emotionally deprived environment frequently seek consolation in their own bodies.

B. Adults

Autoerotic satisfaction among adults is widespread. It often occurs as a part of intercourse for sexual stimulation. Adults who are not in some sexual relationships are very often engaged in self-stimulation. Masturbation is also engaged in, despite moral and social prohibitions, as a way for releasing sexual excitement and tension.

Modern sexological clinics and sex shops sell devices for genital massage to stimulate an orgasm. The most usable by women, and rather popular for sexual self-pleasuring, are vibrators and dildoes for clitoral and vaginal stimulation. Among men, the most enjoyable are active devices that substitute for intercourse. Male masturbation is often connected with the increased sexual excitement of men observing their own nude body or its parts. Some elements of narcissism may occur during adolescence, when sexual excitement affects some parts of their own body, especially the erect penis. This may be only a temporary period in sexual development, but some boys stay on this self-loving stage for a longer period. Cases of narcissism among adult women are very rare.

5. Interpersonal Heterosexual Behaviors

The complexity of interactions between the former Soviet system and indigenous Ukrainian traditions has resulted in many areas of tension and confusion in sexual behavior and gender identity.

A. Children

Sexual Knowledge and Attitudes

Juvenile sexual behavior is a kind of a mirror of the social problems and its influence on the development of gender consciousness. The traditional role expectations that determine the activity of boys and girls are assimilated by children by their fifth or sixth year of age.

Recent studies conducted in Ukraine by sexologists Iryna Vovk, Ihor Gorpinchenko, Zoreslava Shkiriak-Nyzhnik, and Borys Vornyk; and psychologists Myrosluv Borishevskyj, Oksana Shurgan, Tamara Govorun, and Svitlana Kyrylenko investigated the attitudes of elementary school children, adolescents, and teenagers toward family gender roles. They also examined their knowledge of sexual reproduction. In conversation with 6- and 8-year-old boys and girls, we asked such questions as: Where do you hear the word sex? Do you know what this word means? Can you explain it in your own words? When people have sex, do they have sex to give life for a new baby? Is sex always connected with childbirth? What are the names of the male sexual organs? Can you name female sexual organs? What are their proper names? Why are people ashamed of sexual organs? Can you explain where babies come from? Where did you receive this information? What did your mom tell you about sex and childbirth? What did your dad tell you about sex and childbirth? Did anyone else ever tell you about intimate settings? If so, who were those people? We asked the children about desirable and undesirable feelings and attitudes toward family relationships, and asked them to explain their own desires and wishes for themselves regarding their appearance, skills, traits, friends, etc. We also asked them similar questions about the opposite sex.

We asked the children to draw something pleasant and desirable for them. Most pictures were strongly family- and gender-oriented. Mom, dad, and child together, sitting in a flat or walking. Most children who lived in single-parent families usually expressed their strong wish for mom and dad to live together. We asked the children to choose from pictures which home task was better for mother and father. Gender expectations for both sexes were traditional: mother's role was always connected with some service, tutoring, or guardian activity, and especially with housekeeping. Father's role was connected with machinery, military, or driving activity and oriented to passive roles in the home.

Gender Images

The ideal man for most Ukrainian boys is Superman from the American movies. The ideal appearance for girls is usually connected with the American Barbi doll. In assessing the personal features of the opposite or the same sex, children esteem modern clothing much more often than some skills, habits, or moral qualities. Findings indicated that more than 80 percent of children ages 6 to 8 could not identify the words for the sexual parts of the body for either the same or opposite sex. Those who could give some kind of explanation used many crude words and felt embarrassed and shy. More than 75 percent of the children did not understand the meaning of "birth control" and "sexual intercourse." Less than 20 percent knew from where a baby comes, and only 30 percent of those who did know received this knowledge from parents or another adult relative. Only 15 percent of the children could explain the intimate behavior in connection with human feelings of love, friendship, and the desire to have a baby.

Children's awareness of their own body was extremely narrow. About half of the children considered the sexual parts of the body as places of the most bad feelings and experienced shame in being naked or seeing an adult naked. The shame of body exposure is even greater in children from small towns and villages. The rather prudish approach to nudity and bodily functions has greatly affected the sexual behavior of children. In observing some paintings with nude bodies, most elementary school children express their confusion by laughing, chattering, and showing some kind of ignorance.

B. Adolescents

Attitudes Toward Nudity and Body Functions

The ambivalence toward nudity, bodily functions, personal hygiene, and patterns of sexual behavior, combined with the lack of proper sexual education, increases during adolescence and impacts sexual and gender self-perception. We asked 12- to 13-year-old boys and girls questions concerning their knowledge of the main physiological changes in body functions during adolescence. More than 70 percent of the boys demonstrated poor understanding of the indicators of growing up as a man or a woman. Although many adolescents have seen many movies with sexual themes, only a third of them had ever discussed sexual topics with a relative or teacher. Most boys were extremely shy when explaining the function of a condom or the origin of a baby. More than 65 percent used the pronoun "it" rather than the terms penis, vagina, breast, and uterus. (See Igor Kon's comments on similar issues in Section 1B of the chapter on Russia.)

In comparison to boys, 70 percent of the girls interviewed had discussed the topic of male and female body maturation at puberty with their mothers, grandmothers, or elder sisters. The topic of bodily functions, however, remained uncomfortable for girls to discuss. More than 60 percent of the girls replied to the questions "Are you glad to be growing up as a woman?" and "What feelings do you experience during your period?" that it would be better without the menstruation cycle, pubic hair, or breast development; that it made them feel dirty, sick, or bad. These responses may be connected in part with the poor availability of feminine hygiene products.

Their reaction might be more positive if they did not have difficulties and anxiety connected with school toilet facilities. Is it partly connected with pain or feeling unwell? The interviews revealed that menstrual periods make them more serious (heavy) because of hygiene problems and the embarrassment before classmates, boys, and teachers of physical education. Many Ukrainians continue to experience emotional problems as they get older because of the social taboos surrounding menstruation and the social embarrassment of talking about the subject.

Ukrainian adolescent boys experienced the same discomfort answering the questions "What do you know about menstruation?" and "What do you know about erections and pollution." Only 25 percent of the boys received proper sex explanations from their mothers, about 10 percent from fathers, and the rest from peer groups.

Was the sexual knowledge expanded substantially throughout the adolescent years? Most of the children obtained good information about the reproductive system from school lessons on biology. But most adolescents of both sexes still showed a poor understanding of the questions concerning sexual behavior and sexual feelings. Such questions as "What is AIDS?" "How does one protect him/herself from contracting AIDS?" "Can a condom prevent pregnancy or transmitted diseases?" "Is masturbation harmful to ones health?" "Can a child in adolescent age become a father or a mother?" and "What do you know about using birth control?" embarrassed the adolescents. In talking about sexual subjects, most adolescents could not find appropriate words for the sexual organs.

These findings suggested that children viewed these topics regarding body functions, intercourse, and relationships to be shameful aspects of their personality. The adolescent sex vocabulary of most boys and girls was full of vulgar ("dirty") words. Most Ukrainian adolescents consider clothing as an important expression of masculine or feminine behavior, and regard it as an important factor in their personality and physical beauty.

When assessing the problems of gender self-consciousness in teenagers in Ukraine, we see a growing gap between the lack of sexual knowledge and sexual experience, the practice of gender behavior, and moral/psychological maturity.

Satisfaction with Parental Lifestyles

Observing the wealth of the West, combined with the poverty of the native country, has impacted gender self-consciousness and sex orientations of youth. Ukraine is rearing a third generation of children who are strongly dissatisfied with their parent's family and social life. Fathers, and especially mothers with double duties, are rarely viewed as role models. Investigations concerning values and orientations of teenagers reveal that prostitution is considered to be a normal occupation among 40 percent of students. More than 50 percent of teenagers value money and good leisure time over having a nice family and happy parenthood in the future.

Sexarche and Teenage Pregnancy

There is a growing tendency for Ukrainian youth to become involved in sexual intercourse at an earlier age. According to studies conducted in large industrial cities among the students at professional high schools, more than 50 percent of the women and 80 percent of the men have engaged in sexual activity before age 17.5. In 1980, the average age of first sexual experience was 19 years for men and 20 for women. Currently, nearly half of the sexually active females become pregnant at least once during their teenage years. Teenage pregnancy continues to increase every year and early motherhood has become a reality for thousands of teenager girls. According to survey data, more than 50 percent of teenagers are sexually active at least with 3 partners before the age of 20. For most teenagers, sex exists as a curiosity that may involve a kind of commitment but not love and passionate feelings. Most sexually active teenagers do not protect themselves from an unwanted pregnancy, because sexual knowledge, including information about contraceptives, remains low and comes mainly through interaction with peers.

Ukrainian teenagers usually plan their nearest future with creation of their own families, as the median age for marriage is now 19 to 21 years for female and 21 to 23 for males. Ukrainian teenagers usually do not consider economic and psychological maturity as necessary conditions for getting married. More than 80 percent of teenagers who get married consider themselves very dependent on their parents and family for financial support, for help with housing, and assistance in taking care of their children. A lack of privacy and opportunity for experiencing premarital sexual relationships leads teenagers to consider their sexual (physical) maturity sufficient basis for marriage. That is why about 45 percent of young couples are divorced within the first year of their marriage.

As evidence of the separateness between the sexual sphere and personality itself in mass consciousness, we might consider the content of the sex vocabulary of Ukrainians. The Ukrainian youth have adopted a lot of abusive words from the Russian sexual vocabulary that express bondage of women, rape, and humiliation of the people engaging in sexual intercourse. This is partly a result of the authoritarian society that encouraged cruel attitudes toward women and a misconception of male behavior.

C. Adults

Premarital Sexual Relationships, Dating, and Courtship

In the late 1960s, premarital sex was a taboo for both the fiancé and fiancée, as the bride should be a virgin until marriage. The ethic of premarital virginity during dating was a major theme in sex education and mass media. To abstain from sex meant to escape from being betrayed by the groom or from potential pregnancy. The statistics of those years reveal the increasing quantity of unmarried mothers and the forced weddings. In recent decades, the situation has changed considerably. Today, most teenagers and adults consider sex before marriage rather acceptable, and thus premarital sex relations are widespread.

The initial selection of a potential mate usually occurs among a reference group—college mates, colleagues at work, or a common-interest community that brings together people with similar values, education, or cultural levels. The length of courtship for young couples is usually about twelve to eighteen months between meeting and marriage, with dating two to three times a week. In various strata of people, dating activity takes different forms. Dating is mostly oriented toward dancing, visiting friends, parties, cinemas, bars, and cafeterias.

The discovery of one other person in a romantic relationship is followed by the wedding arrangements initiated mostly by the man. The choice of a mate is determined by the young people themselves, as it was in ancient Ukraine, although the parents usually have to confirm the engagement. The final ceremony of marriage depends on religious, ethnic, and cultural level and social group.

In Soviet times, a lot of Communist symbols were included in the wedding process—a ritual of laying flowers at the local Lenin monument, special greetings, and promises. Wedding ceremonies in a church were prohibited and couples who had religious weddings were often prosecuted by the authorities. Nowadays, the wedding ceremony has become more relaxed, but it is still formalized. In the countryside, people keep traditions of a large wedding celebration with almost all villagers invited as guests. A lot of fun, music, singing of celebration songs, dancing, treating, and role playing characterize such family holiday. Usually, any large wedding celebration is very expensive for parents, who have to carry the burden of wedding debts sometimes after the young have divorced.

A few years ago, some registry offices started to propose that couples use a relationship contract to define some problems of their future family life. These contracts usually do not include any legal documentation and are used as a moral obligation that helps the bride to clear up some unexpected areas of marital interaction.

Sexual Behavior and Relationships of Single Adults

The number of single Ukrainians is increasing significantly, especially among highly educated people—teachers, physicians, engineers, and business owners. Psychologists trace this phenomena to increasing levels of personal aspiration and expectations of potential partners of the opposite sex. The single trend is occurring in every age group and for both sexes.

It is difficult to tell with any accuracy how many persons remain single because of unrealistic expectations of a significant other, immaturity in emotional responses and communications, or egocentrism. Singles include adults who have never been married and divorced women with children. Most of them are lonely and have many problems in maintaining a relationship with a person of the opposite sex. Most places of entertainment cater to teenagers for meetings with mates. Because of the lack of privacy in their own flat or available rooms in hotels it becomes embarrassing and hard for a single person to get together and be intimate with a partner.

During the last two decades some marriage bureaus, consultation family centers, and radio programs have started providing matrimonial services, advertising in order to introduce the partners and help with dating. There are obvious proposals in some newspapers for dating that serve sexual purposes.

The frequency of intercourse for couples under age 20 is ten to fifteen times a week; among couples 20 to 30, five to seven times a week; for couples 30 to 40, four times a week; among couples 40 to 50, two or three times a week; one to two times for couples 50 to 60 years; and once or twice a month for couples over age 60.

Marriage and Family

Despite an increasing number of singles, most Ukrainians live in families. In Ukraine, the minimum age for marriage is 17 years for women and 18 for men. The marriage can be dissolved by mutual consent of the spouses. The divorce is equally available to both men and women. The husband is required to provide the maintenance of children until they are 18 years old. Custody of children, maintenance, and property must be decided before the couple divorce.

The typical family in Ukraine is a nuclear family. This kind of family started to increase from the 1930s after the dissolution of the extended family pattern. Shifts in family structure were mostly triggered by increasing urbanization. Millions of young people were induced to migrate to urban industrial regions in search for employment, education, and occupational mobility. In 1920, 20 percent of Ukrainians lived in cities areas; by 1980, this percent had more than tripled. This process has increased labor participation rates for women and decreased the size of the nuclear family. More than half of all Ukrainian families are one-child families.

The nuclear family has increased the demands for equal sharing of responsibilities and household roles between the spouses, as well as raised the intrafamily factors like emotional support, shared values, sexual satisfaction, common income distribution, attention and expression, mutual assistance, and moral protection.

Divorce and Remarriage

The increasing divorce rates are a reflection of the diminished dependence of spouses on each other and the desire of obtaining a legal marital dissolution rather than remaining an harmful relationship.

The incidence of divorce has increased rapidly since the 1960s. A recent study conducted by Zubov Chujko (1994) showed the number of divorces per thousand nationwide was 3.9 in 1991 and 4.4 in 1993. There is a great difference in the divorce rates for urban and rural citizens, 5.5 per thousand compared with 1.9 per thousand in rural areas. Surveys indicate that about 75 percent of divorced men remarry within five years and only half of divorced women within ten to fifteen years after their divorce. In the case of remarriage, the rights of all children of every spouse are protected as stepchildren.

Cohabitation

In the past twenty-five years, as the marriage rate slowly declined, the number of unmarried cohabiting couples quadrupled. In Ukraine, there is no special law regulating cohabitation, but legislation does offer some protection for the rights and responsibilities of cohabiting partners, and their children who are protected as though the couple was married. While the legal system provides some rights for persons who cohabit for some period of time, these rights are much less than those of married couples.

D. Persons with Physical Disabilities, and Older Persons

Unfortunately, most individuals with disabilities are cut off from the active contacts with the social environment. The services for any social assistance, education, welfare, and transportation facilities are almost totally absent, as they were in former Soviet times when the needs of this population were mostly ignored by society and treated as a family concern. Privacy and independence are vital for the physically handicapped. Even in large cities, it is hard to find the convenient access and passages across the streets, as well as a lot of other facilities for the disabled. These necessities affect the development of sexuality very much because of the personal isolation. Only specialized sanatoriums offer places for temporary relationships of individuals with special needs. In Ukraine today, there are about 60 disabled persons per thousand under 60 years of age.

Only recently has the Ukrainian society begun to recognize the abused fate of the physically handicapped, and to break their isolation by improving the conditions of their existence by providing for common interests—sports, education, hobbies, and therapy—and by slowly increasing their access to social allowances.

The Ukrainian society also needs to overcome a rather strict and condemnatory attitude toward any sexual activity by older people or public acknowledgment of same. In comparison to Western contemporaries, Ukrainian women over 40 years old usually consider themselves too old for any sexual intimacy, and thus stop taking care of their own appearance and sexual attractiveness.

E. Incidence of Oral and Anal Sex

Traditionally, in Ukraine, sex was an extremely personal and very private matter. Moral, emotional, gender, and age factors influence attitudes toward anal sex and its enjoyment. While anal sex holds a great attraction for male homosexuals, and heterosexual couples may engage in anal sex for the enjoyment of one or both partners, there are no special studies undertaken to discover the frequency of anal sex. What data are available usually come from sexological clinics. According to this data, more than 30 percent of males have had an experience with anal sex in their teenage years. In jails, anal sex is usually engaged in as a temporary substitute for heterosexuality, or for maintenance of power.

Oral sex is rather popular for both heterosexual and homosexual couples. It is also very often practiced by adolescents. Cunnilingus is mostly a part of couple foreplay during lovemaking in order to stimulate female orgasm. It is used in a many cases by men with sexual dysfunctions. Fellatio is much more widespread as a kind of foreplay for intercourse, or as a separate sexual activity. Fellatio technique involving partial penis penetration into the woman's mouth, or penis licking, sucking, or kissing, are very popular among the lovers of all ages, but mostly among teenagers and persons under age 30.

6. Homoerotic, Homosexual, and Ambisexual Behaviors

Historically, gender and sexual behavior in Ukraine were strongly influenced by the Christian tradition, which restricted any manifestation of sexuality and considered homosexual orientation as a great sin. Ukraine, as well as the other states of the former Soviet Union, was and still remains a very heterosexist society with strict gender stereotyping. All social institutions and social opinion place considerable pressure on gay men and lesbian women. Most individuals with a same-sex orientation kept their sexual drives and orientation deeply hidden.

The democratic processes in the newly independent Ukraine gave the opportunity for the people with gender dysphoria to share the discovery of their sexual orientation and gender-identity problems within sympathetic communities and support groups, in the mass media, and with specialists—physicians, sexologists, and psychologists. However, most Ukrainians still consider homosexual behavior as abnormal and socially unacceptable and reject both male and female homosexuality.

A. Children

Because information on sexology and psychology of gender was prohibited in former Soviet Ukraine, little is known about the early experiences of those who today identity themselves as gay or lesbian. No national research on the developmental sexuality in childhood was conducted.

In an ideological system that denies any nonheterosexual form of behavior, children with a same-sex orientation encounter a lot of discrimination and even violence. Atypical gender behavior during childhood is usually ridiculed within the society and results in being rejected by parents, relatives, or teachers as not adjusted to the male or female social role. In early childhood, the measurement of gender-role behavior includes easily observable facts, such as preference for same play interests, toys, sex peers, dressings, etc.

The behavior markers of gender identity emerge in Ukrainian children typically between ages 2 and 5 years. At puberty, a child's sexual interests and desires normally emerge. In many features, lesbian, gay, and bisexual youths are similar to other children. However, a pervasive heterosexism of the social environment at home and school causes young gay men or lesbians to experience their cross-gender feelings and behavior in isolation from the significant others. Because of the inner conflict stirred by social and family rejection, they must hide their sexual attraction from others at the very time they are becoming aware of it. Growing up with forbidden and unacceptable sexual attractions influences personality development, often resulting in a negative image of the self as a homosexual female or male.

The initial recognition of same-sex attraction usually becomes evident at puberty and adolescence. Discovery of one's orientation often leads to some sexual activity involving persons of the same sex, starting with simple touching, kissing, petting, stroking the genitals, oral-genital contact, and, more rarely, anal intercourse.

Although attendance at a professional high school or summer camp provides wide opportunity for teenage sexual experimentation, and many adolescents have even more homosexual than heterosexual encounters, they are not considered as really gay or lesbian behavior. The capacity to respond sexually to a person of the same gender in teenage years is considered being bisexual rather than homosexual. Many teenagers who identity themselves as homosexual in fact are bisexual. Many such Ukrainian youths try to change their sexual orientation by different kinds of therapies. These usually are not successful in reaching the desired goal. A predominant sexual attraction to persons of the same gender, with a constitutional lack of attraction to members of the opposite gender in late teenage years, signals the development of a homosexual orientation.

B. Adults

Gender Roles, Courtship, and Relationship Patterns

In the Ukrainian society where intimacy and relationships have been focused primarily on heterosexual patterns of behavior, the sexual minority groups try to develop their own language for communicating with similarly minded peers, courtship, and discovering sexual roles for future inter- course. The image of the self as a homosexual female or male is mostly dependent on the success of lifelong intimacy with a partner, and on the opportunity for the self-extension in experiencing the feelings of sexual attractiveness, physical fitness, and good looks. In a traditionally hostile society, coming out as a homosexual poses great problems. The inability to define one's self in terms of social and private activities thus becomes a common characteristic of adults with gender dysphoria.

Many lesbian women and gay men are modeling their relationships on heterosexual behavior forms and communication. A lifelong monogamous commitment is often a desirable model of homosexual relationship. The partners share household and home labor in accordance with active (mas- culine) and passive (feminine) roles in a sexual intercourse. There are a lot of jealous feelings in the attitudes towards each other, passionate love, and sympathy. Many homosexual adults develop their sexual and romantic relationships much as heterosexual couples do, but with the significant difference of fear for manifesting that love and attachment in a hostile environment. In contrast to gay men, many lesbian couples have made parenting an important part of their life. But because homosexual rela- tionships are usually hidden, long-term monogamous homosexual couples are rare in Ukraine.

Despite the hostile social environment, homosexual adults elaborate some elements in dressing, gestures, and behavior that signal a homosexual orientation to knowledgeable observers. Still, even in metropolitan Kyiv, homosexual persons meet each other in covert ways and endure some period for tentative exploration before overtly connecting. Usually there are some places in cities and towns where homosexual individuals can meet each other. In such public places, including sections of certain parks, certain bars, and steam baths, homosexual persons can safely meet, interact, and relate to each other.

In former Soviet times, disclosure or discovery of homosexual orienta- tion meant destruction, ostracism in the workplace and family, forced hospital treatment, and even prison. Lesbians and gays today are as diverse as the society to which they belong. They differ widely in both educational level and economic status. Depending on their social status, they may either conceal their sexual orientation or be open about it. They may have multiple partners, or prefer one. Feelings of unhappiness due to the lack of a mate, feelings of alienation, a minimum of understanding regarding their situation, stressful life experiences, anxiety, depression, and substance abuse are common difficulties in the private lives of homosexual persons in Ukraine.

Social Status

The social attitude regarding homosexual persons in the former Soviet Ukraine was determined by statute N121 in the criminal code, which supported penalties for male homosexuality, as well as for the homosexual seduction of children, teenagers, and adults, and punishment for homosexual rape. Female homosexuality was not noted as criminal in that law.

In postliberation Ukraine, researchers and clinicians studying the patterns and quantity of homosexual, lesbian, and bisexual behavior have rejected the Soviet diagnosis of homosexuality as deviant and a mental illness, and now make use of the Western paradigms, statistics, and assessment measures, particularly those of the American Alfred Kinsey and his colleagues.

This dramatic shift, coupled with the beginning of the democratic process in Ukraine, has given impetus for homosexuals to "come out from the closet." Today, Ukrainians can openly visit a consulting center to meet a sexologist or psychologist to discuss some private problems concerning lesbian or gay orientation or activity. Today, lesbian women and gay men are becoming more open about their sexual identities and social processes in which developmental changes affect their life. One can easily find many advertisements in the erotic newspapers placed by homosexuals of both sexes seeking a partner. There has also been some recent efforts to organize a gay liberation movement. In May 1995, the First Ukrainian International Congress of Homosexuals and Lesbians, which called itself "Two Colors," was held in Kyiv. An initiative group was organized to serve the social, political, and cultural needs of the gay and lesbian population, by promoting a positive image for the homosexual status in society. In comparison to Western gay liberation movements, Ukrainian lesbians and gays are not separate in their social needs; they are one in their efforts to promote common ideas.

Although homosexuals in postsocialist Ukraine are not relegated to a deviant status, there is still a lot of prejudice against gay and lesbian persons, and many individuals oriented toward the same-sex sexuality keep their attitudes hidden. This is partly due to the rigid manifestation of cultural heterosexism, as well to a reminiscence of Soviet mass psychology of nonreconciliation and nontolerance of anyone who does not fit the majority model. Homophobic tendencies among Ukrainians were and are mostly connected with gay men but not lesbians. This is due in part to a fear for the younger generation being molested, seduced, or infected by HIV. But another factor is an ancient blame for men's abstinence from heterosexual intercourse causing a decrease in childbirth, threatening the future of the nation.

The Ukrainian Homosexual Culture

The basic demographic characteristics and size of the homosexual population in Ukraine remains a subject of debate. Some scientists estimate the size of exclusively homosexual at 2 percent for females and 2 to 4 percent for men, with predominantly gay or lesbian bisexuals approximately 10 percent of the population, about 5.2 million people. Some scientists believe the figures should be much larger for the former Soviet state. Little is yet known about the relationships of homosexual couples, as well as about the functioning and life course of families with lesbian and gay adults.

As mentioned, most homosexual women and men try to remain invisible. The dominance of exclusively heterosexual orientations in Ukrainian society presses homosexuals to hide their drives and attitudes. One result of this hostile environment is the number of men and women who pose as transsexuals to obtain sex-change surgery in order to change their sex on their passports, and thus obtain the opportunity for a legal relationship with a partner of the desired sex. In Ukraine, there are many more such individuals with female-to-male orientation than in western Europe. Ukrainian scientists have suggested the significant importance of social factors in the origin of such orientation because of the high valuation by the Soviet system for manifestation of masculine features and of masculine traits expressed by women. Thus, lesbian women are more independent, dominant, unconventional, and self-sufficient than most Ukrainian heterosexual women.

Among gay men, who are known as "blues," there is usually a division for a passive partner who receives his partner's penis anally, and an active partner who plays the inserter role in anal or oral sex. The predominant forms of genital sex by gay men are fellatio and mutual masturbation.

The patterns of a sexual partnership among gays and lesbians are significantly influenced by the former Soviet sexist society with strict polarization of gender roles in housekeeping, raising the children, and in the social sphere. What limited statistics are available suggest that only about 1.5 percent of gay male couples achieve a stable, long-lasting relationship of more than five years; 2.7 percent have relationships that last three years, while about 7 percent have relationships that last a year or so. Lesbians and gays have occasional sexual encounters for anonymous short-time enjoyment; some have sex in pairs or in groups. Some homosexual couples emphasize social needs rather than purely sexual contacts.

Homosexual as well as bisexual relationships satisfy many social, sexual, and emotional needs—many homosexual couples enjoy common professional interests, shared lifestyle, cognitive satisfaction, and cooperation, although their welfare in Ukrainian society is generally not so high. Although there are many different challenges in gay and lesbian experiences, including communications and intimacy, the main widespread problems involve a special need for a positive self-redefinition, coming out as a part of personality development and interpersonal growth, and social activity and well-being as an affirmation of the personality. Ukrainian society needs to provide a social environment in which gay and lesbian persons can feel that their sexual orientation is not pathological or immoral.

7. Gender Conflicted Persons

The beginning of the democratic processes in Ukraine allowed the problems of people with gender conflicts to surface. Because of this, Ukrainian society faces some new questions about the status of such individuals in a postsocialist society and the ways in which they interact with the public, family, and friends.

Ukrainian scientists consider that the cases of gender dysphoria, in which a person rejects his or her biological sex and requests surgery and the gender identity of the opposite sex, occurs in about 1 out of every 30,000 to 50,000 persons.

During the Soviet rule, the only center that provided medical treatment and sex-change surgery for transsexuals was in Moscow. In the late 1980s, when legal and medical procedures for altering sex were for the first time performed in Kyiv, female-to-male transsexuals outnumbered male-to-female transsexuals seven to one. In Western countries, the proportion is about equal or favors male-to-female by about three to one. The reasons for this sharp difference might be social-learning experience and the prevailing status of men in Soviet society.

A government commission for transsexualism has recently been organized in Kyiv to deal with the individuals with gender dysphoria. The chairman is Professor Borys Vornyk (Address: 8 Smolenska vul., Kyiv 252057). Its members include qualified transgendered "alienist" persons, surgeons, sexologists, psychologists, and lawyers. The clinical and psychological strategy for managing sex change and identity cases is based on the best of foreign experience and practice. The procedure of personality evaluation before undergoing sex reassignment are based on preliminary criteria: originally over age 21, but since 1995 over age 25; having no children under age 18; no criminal offenses; a consistent gender disorder not connected with psychosis—absence of mental diseases or psychosis, a long-standing (from early childhood age) irreversible cross-gender identification with positive self-conception, physical appearance and demeanor as a member of the opposite sex, and a strong identity with the opposite sex; and referral to "nuclear" transsexual by a psychiatrist and psychologist based on at least one year of psychotherapy—a stable ego conception, and economic and residence stability—minimum problems in self-support, sexual satisfaction of self and the partner if involved, a positive relationship with family, adequate psychological support, and an adequate understanding of the hazards of the operation.

The commission considers the importance of family diagnosis in an evaluation of gender identity, as the transsexuals will meet a lot of psychological problems involving military registration and alienation from and nonacceptance by society.

Many people react negatively to the phenomena of transsexualism and transvestism, because these contradict the traditional gender behavior and assumptions.

A transvestite's social and family situation is usually very difficult, because the lack of privacy in everyday life does not allow him to have the opportunity to dress even partially as a member of the opposite sex. The cases of male-to-female cross-dressing are usually connected with a hyperfeminine expression. The lack of community and the nonavailability of public places for mixing with others as a woman restrict the options for cross-dressing.

Cases of berdachism and other atypical sexual identities are extremely rare in Ukraine and exist mostly as rumors rather than as clinical or scientific studies.

8. Significant Unconventional Sexual Behaviors

The incidence of socially unaccepted kinds of sexual behaviors are increasing rapidly as the process of political and economic reconstruction affects the whole culture and everyone in it.

A. Coercive Sexual Behavior

Child Sexual Abuse, Incest, and Pedophilia

Any kind of child molestation has always been condemned in Ukrainian society and Ukrainian folk traditions consider any sexual abuse of children as the most heinous of crimes.

Known cases of sexual abuse are mostly connected with girls assaulted between 3 and 7 or 8 years old. More than half of the offenders are close friends or neighbors of the parents. More than half the victims have been killed by the seducers after the pedophilic acts because of the fear for criminal responsibility and punishment. The penalty for sex molestation is the same as for the rape of a minor or incest; Statute 117 of the criminal code mentions the penalty from three to fifteen years in jail, and even death. Most of the perpetrators of this crime are men 20 to 30 years old.

More often than not, cases of pedophilia are not connected with penetration, only with genital fondling or handling. The children involved in such sex games with adults are about equally male or female.

The frequency of pedophilia in our country is sometimes connected with homeless girls and boys who run away from home to escape from parents, and are, in turn, victimized by adult male strangers in return for some food, money, reward, and temporary shelter. Usually, they do not report their offenders and keep the sexual experience secret from parents and others. Cases of incest are a rather rarely reported form of child sexual abuse. Thus, in 1994, Ukrainian courts registered about 1 case of incest in 15,000 cases of sexual assault. Accounts of sex between a parent and child are more frequent than are officially reported. Sexual relations between a mother and son or a father/stepfather and daughter are seldom discovered or reported. Very few scientific statistics and little information are available about sexual relations between brothers and sisters. The recent development of sexual consultation centers with psychoanalytic services will help in obtaining data on the incestuous involvement of children in Ukraine.

Sexual Harassment

[*Note*: In this section, the Ukrainian authors adopt a broader and less specific definition of sexual harassment than is common in Western usage. (Editor)] Violations of personal boundaries, a basic element in the administrative-commanding system of the former Soviet Ukraine, made sexual harassment an everyday normative behavior in official and informal relations. Fear of the authority that was taught by the Soviets fostered a tolerant attitude towards sexual harassment as a usual and expected behavior of authorities and subordinate persons. Although Statute 119 in the Ukrainian criminal code deals with a penalty for forcing a woman to engage in sex, no incidents of such violations were ever reported or registered.

Incidents of sexual harassment between the children of a different age mostly take place in the orphanage houses, and in summer or winter youth camps. The most common cases are connected with masturbation and fellatio. Sexual intercourse usually occurs among older children. As this aspect of child relations is most sensitive and vulnerable for youngsters, the teachers who discover such incidents prefer to keep them hidden from the community.

Sexual harassment behavior is widespread, especially among youths. Sexual remarks, jokes, explicit conversation about having sex, as well as such behavior as following, staring, leering, and taunting are regarded by both men and women as inoffensive and even just larking. Such behavior is mostly considered to be an acceptable way of getting acquainted in public places, and as normal masculine communication in mixed-gender interactions.

Sexual Assault and Rape

The incidence of rape is growing very quickly. Stranger rape accounts for about 94 percent of all reported rape cases; 67 percent involve group or gang rape; 13 percent result in serious physical harm. According to the criminal statistics for the Kyiv region, most of the reported perpetrators were under age 20. Most of the victims were under the age of 18. Most of the rapists did not have a previous criminal record and used alcohol.

B. Prostitution

The danger of prosecution does not limit the offers of sexual services in return for financial gain. Prostitution is not legal in Ukraine, but is also not forbidden by legislation. After the colonization of Ukraine, especially from the eighteenth century, prostitution started to spread, especially in urban areas, although between 1843 and the October 1917 Revolution, it was somewhat restricted by special edict. Today, there is no law in the criminal code of Ukraine on prostitution, except the remark regarding a penalty of not less than five years in prison for compelling anybody to engage in prostitution for profit.

There are several grades of prostitutes according to their financial status and education. The higher-class prostitutes are known as "hard currency." They have sufficient means to rent a room at a hotel and to share information about potential clients. These women are educated and sophisticated, skilled in both conversation and sexual activity; their clients are mostly foreigners. The middle class of prostitutes, call girls, deal with regular rich businessmen and tourists, and rich customers at bars and restaurants. The lowest class of prostitutes work the streets and railway stations; they service all comers and may trade sex for drugs or alcohol. The average age of prostitutes is about 30. Most had their first intercourse before age 17 with a stranger rather than in a loving relationship with someone they knew. Most do not have a permanent job and their sex business is a financial necessity for supporting themselves, family, and children. Eighty percent of the men availing themselves of commercial sex are 30 years or older.

Historically in the Ukrainian community, there was always a negative attitude toward women who had sexual relations with men outside marriage. But today from at least the early 1970s, the attitude towards prostitution, especially among the youth and middle-aged adults, is very permissive. What is more, prostitution is considered by teenagers to be among the most-prestigious professions, just as desirable as being a fashion model. stewardess, or interpreter. The main reason for this is the impossibility within the socialist economic system of earning sufficient salary in any highly qualified occupation. Prostitution makes a decent, even comfortable, life possible. The economic turmoil that has prevailed since the 1991 collapse of the Soviet system has only accelerated this trend toward acceptance of prostitution. Only the older generation is confused by the view of prostitution as a business matter.

C. Pornography and Erotica

A Project of Law prohibiting the production and distribution of pornography, and the formation of the Presidential commission on obscenity, were still being discussed in the Ukrainian Parliament as of mid-1995.

Although Ukrainian society has become more permissive sexually, it does not provide adequate values of human sexual activity. With the breakdown of the Soviet regime, sexuality became one of the most important symbols of social and cultural liberation. Widespread public ignorance about sex in former years has been replaced by everyday representation in commerce and movies. Television programs and filmmakers have exploited sex; the display of the bodies of young women as available sexual objects are not only on cinema screens, but in advertising, on posters, photographs, and drawings. After seventy years of repression, Ukraine has a large market for pornographic products. Television programs portray and revel in various types of sexual experience, and frank expressions of nudity with erotic excitement are displayed in public places for everybody.

The public discussion of the harmful role of pornography for grownup sexual expectations and values makes it clear that under the slogans of democracy, new businessmen are exploiting sex roles, promoting the image of a happy life associated with sexual pleasure, drinking, smoking, and male control of the opposite sex.

Newly opened sex shops and the appearance of such newspapers as *Pan Plus Pani* and the sex magazine *Lel* have broken all previous taboos on sexual subjects, recognizing the sexual culture and providing sexual education for different age groups. Artistic eroticism has started to recover from years of repression, producing pictures, stories, and theater plays in the best national traditions, based on gender equality in relationships, personal freedom and dignity, Ukrainian humor, and the pursuit of a full-blooded life.

9. Contraception, Abortion, and Population Planning

A. Attitudes, Education, Availability, and Usage of Contraceptives

The maintenance of an appropriate population level is vital to the survival of any society, but especially for Ukraine after the Soviet takeover. During the famines deliberately created by Soviet policy in 1920 and especially

1933, six million Ukrainian peasants from the central, east, and south regions died from hunger or were removed from their native land to Siberia and the Far East. The devastation of World War II also reduced Ukraine's population significantly.

From the middle of 1979, the Ukrainian birthrate started to drop rapidly; since the end of 1980, the birthrate has remained below the replacement rate. Although the former Soviet authorities tried to encourage families to have more children in order to get a larger labor force, their efforts did not reverse the trend. By the end of 1960, most Ukrainian women had to combine parenthood with professional work because of economic needs and the necessity of guaranteeing family income.

As a consequence, Ukraine is characterized by the rapidly increasing proportion of older persons. In 1960, there was one person of pension age for every 11.5 nonpension persons. Today, the ratio is one in every six. And the birthrate continues to decline. Under such circumstances, the social and economic situation has had a great impact on the family: We have an increase of single persons of marriageable age, and a high proportion of divorce (51 to 52 divorces per 1,000 families) and one-parent families (the number of one-parent families in 1995 constituted 10.8 percent of all families in the country and 14.8 percent in towns and cities).

Historically, most Ukrainian families did not limit the number of their children, nor did religious doctrine permit use of contraception. However, sexual intercourse was forbidden during major religious festivals. And most women knew about medicinal herbs that could be used to prevent pregnancy or induce a miscarriage. In the eleventh century, the daughter of King Jaroslav Mudryj Jevpraksija wrote the first book on the medical use of herbs, describing their use in preventing or terminating pregnancy. The average Ukrainian family was large, with the women sometimes having more than ten childbirths and five to nine surviving children.

The involvement of Ukrainian women in the labor force in 1930 and in 1950 reduced the number of childbirths and increased the number of induced abortions, even though from 1936 to 1955 abortion was forbidden by Soviet law. In the end, economic factors enabled the government to give impetus to a family planning policy and promote the development of contraception. Nevertheless, from the late 1960s to the present, Ukraine remains at the head of countries where abortion is the main form of birth control. In 1993, there were 104.2 abortions for every 1,000 women between ages 18 and 34. In 1994, there were between 110 and 115 abortions for every hundred childbirths.

There are several factors behind the reliance on abortion for family planning. Because of the lack of sex education in the former Soviet Union, the main form of family planning was natural, either withdrawal (coitus interruptus) or the "rhythm," basal metabolism/calendar methods. Because these natural methods are not effective for pregnancy prevention and the abortion rate was increasing dramatically, the Ministry of Public

Heath was able to start teaching sexually active adults about contraception. The methods promoted included condoms, diaphragms, cervical caps, intrauterine devices, and spermicides.

Since sex-education programs were focused on adults, the sexual behavior of youths was not regarded as important for family planning. In the context of such policies, the incidence of teenage pregnancy started to rise. A second reason for the failure of the government program to promote contraception was the fact that the sex-education programs were focused mostly on women in gynecological clinics, and not on all women of childbearing age. This policy ignored the family as a unit of a man and a woman and the male's responsibility in family planning. With this policy, husbands simply assumed that the wife would take responsibility for contraception, which they sometimes, but not always, did.

But the major factor was that the most effective birth-control methods, such as oral contraceptives and hormonal implants, were not recommended by the physicians and remained unpopular among both adults and teenagers. In addition to the strong prejudice against the hormonal contraceptive pills, another factor in their nonuse is their high cost in Ukraine.

From 1994 on, tubal ligation for the female and male vasectomy have been increasingly chosen by Ukrainian couples who do not want any more children or who prefer to remain childless.

In general, Ukraine needs a greater availability of contraception and improved sex information in order to reduce the increasing numbers of unwanted pregnancies.

B. Teenage Pregnancies

Although the main sex-education policy in Ukraine remains as it was in former Soviet times, with abstinence for youth declared the best birth-control method, every year the average age of the first intercourse for teenagers becomes lower. In 1995, sexarche occurred at about the age of 17 for both females and males. The number of teenage pregnancies is growing rapidly, with an estimated 15 percent to 18 percent of all pregnancies being to women under the age of 18 years of age (Bogdushkin and Andreev 1995). In the three years, 1992 to 1994, the number of abortions among the teenagers has increased 9.3 percent (according to hospital reports) and the number of illegal abortions by 23 percent (Ryzhko 1995).

Teenage pregnancy is often a motivation for establishing a marriage relationship. According to one survey, unmarried pregnancy occurred among 83 percent of young couples under 20 years old; 71 percent of them considered the childbirth undesirable. The decision to have an abortion or to keep a child is made by the young woman, with additional agreement of parents or relatives when the girl is under 16 or 17 years old. There are no special schools or classes for pregnant teenagers. Usually the relatives take the responsibility for a newborn baby. The destiny of such babies is often unhappy when a young mother gives her child up for the adoption or to an orphanage. During recent decades, the population of the rejected babies in an orphanage has increased many times in comparison to the number of the orphaned children in Ukraine after World War II. The high rate of adolescent pregnancy demonstrates that Ukraine needs to improve its school and community sex-education programs and to provide free, low-cost contraceptive services to all teenagers who need them.

C. Abortion

Abortions have been legal in Ukraine since 1955. They are available to any woman after the age of 18 years and are mostly free of charge—the state pays the medical expenses of low-income women. The abortion is usually done at a special clinic or gynecology department up to twelve weeks after the last menstrual period. Although abortions usually are medically safe, many factors affect the women after an operation: anxiety, depression, and complications in reproductive function. For 7.7 percent of Ukrainian women who are considered at risk for subsequent fertility and pregnancy, the first pregnancy is interrupted by abortion. (See also Section 9A above.)

The average Ukrainian women in her early 40s has experienced two or more abortions. Most women do not use any contraceptive method because of cost or unavailability. Recently, there has been a growing antiabortion movement in Ukraine, especially among some religious denominations, scientists, teachers, and some social organizations. These groups emphasize that a woman should take responsibility either for preventing pregnancy or giving the life for a new baby because of the right to life of the unborn fetus.

D. Efforts to Regulate Population Growth

With a regard to the demographic situation, the Ukrainian government considers the improvement of living standards for all women, but especially for young couples, as a measure of fertility, womanhood, and parenthood. For this purpose, the Committee of Women's Affairs, the Children and the Population was organized in April 1995 by the cabinet of the ministers of Ukraine. The committee started to develop family-planning policy and different social programs to permit the women and the families to promote their well-being, their health, and parenthood. The emphasis is on the improvement of women's status, maternal and child-health care, and family welfare. A family planning education strategy, the use of contraceptives, hygiene, and nutrition, are the basis of the committee's program. Family planning medical and psychological counseling services are becoming available in a number of towns of Ukraine.

10. Sexually Transmitted Diseases

The history of the medical treatment of sexually related diseases in the nineteenth century was connected with such scientists as J. Zelenev. J. Popov, B. Zadoroznij, and J. Mavrov. In Czarist Ukraine around 1850, 10 percent of all reported illnesses involved venereal diseases. Syphilis and gonorrhea were found mostly in the large industrial centers like Kyiv, Kharkiv, Odesa, and Mykolajiv. In 1901, *The Journal of Skin and Venereal Diseases* was founded in Charkiv; it carried articles describing the symptoms of common sexually transmitted diseases and their complications.

World War I and the October 1917 Revolution led to widespread sexual promiscuity and increasing cases of venereal diseases. In 1920 in Ukraine, the special dispensaries for treating STDs were organized in all large cities. This helped to slow the spread of these infections. World War II created a huge new public health problem, which lasted until 1950. In comparison to other former Soviet republics, Ukraine was characterized by the lowest level of STDs, due to the sanitary preventive measures.

A. Incidence, Patterns, and Trends

After the dissolution of the U.S.S.R., social factors such as large-scale migrations, the ease of reproducing erotic and pornographic videos and their availability, changes in the economic situation, and the double moral standard have influenced the recent outburst of venereal diseases. In Ukraine, as in other countries, the teenaged population appears hardest hit by the STD epidemic. Venereal diseases are increasing in epidemic proportions among teenagers because of lack of knowledge, early sexual experience, multiple sexual partners, and a high level of sexual activity.

In the past five years, syphilis cases among 14-year-old boys has increased about 400 percent, for 15- to 17-year-olds by about 800 percent. Among teenage girls, syphilis has increased by about 500 percent. Venereal diseases affect about 15,000 reported cases among teenagers. Females and males between the the ages of 17 and 27 are most at risk of infection, and they account for the majority of all STD cases reported. In the past five years, the common infections like syphilis, gonorrhea, herpes, and chlamydia have increased about 300 percent in adult females and by 400 percent in adult males. This continuing increase in the incidence of STDs is creating urgent social problems.

B. Availability of Treatment and Prevention Efforts

In Ukraine today, there is a system of STD control, and appropriate health care is available throughout the country for people of all ages, in the rural areas as well as in the cities and large metropolitan areas. Everyone can obtain free and confidential routine medical testing and care. It is obligatory for all the personnel of medicine, nutrition, and provision services to be tested periodically for STDs and HIV, since the best way to fight the epidemic process is to block it. Some clinics provide resident treatment, some dispensaries provide out-patient care with pre- and post-test counseling. All services are free, with the patient paying only for medication when they can afford it. Besides medical service, these clinics provide free printed contraception and HIV/AIDS information.

The program for high-risk youth includes testing and follow-up care. Special venereal departments provide a wide range of medical services, all free and confidential. The only requirement for the patient is to identify all the partners so they can be tested and referred to medical services in case treatment is needed. Some venereal clinics offer extensive treatment for individuals addicted to drugs or alcohol, or to a person whose behavior put him or her at risk for being infected.

Ukrainian physicians prepare special information for adolescents aged 14 to 18 in order to give them the facts they need to protect themselves from STDs. But this work is insufficient in the area of mass media, especially television and in educational programs in the schools, where some are still embarrassed when speaking of "sexually transmissible." A sexually enlightened society is not afraid to influence the consciousness and attitudes of the masses with an honest voice.

11. HIV/AIDS

The epidemiology of HIV and AIDS infection in Ukraine demonstrates worrisome trends. The epidemic reached all but three of the twenty-one regions of the state, Volyn', Khmelnyts'kyj, and Rivne.

A. Incidence, Patterns, and Trends

By April 1, 1995, there were 429 persons infected with HIV, 210 of them being citizens of Ukraine and 219 foreigners. Sixty percent were male and 40 percent female. Of this total, thirty-six cases were full-blown AIDS, of which seventeen are already dead, including four children. Every year the number of HIV-positive men and women increases by about 35 percent. The rate of infection is growing more rapidly among those who engage in intravenous (IV) drug use or are sexual partners of such users. Thus, in the Mykolajiv region, most of the HIV cases are spread by IV drug users. There are now in Ukraine more than 40,000 registered drug users, 75 percent of them sharing needles as a regular practice.

Most of the current victims, 66.2 percent, were infected during sexual intercourse, mostly heterosexual, often with IV drug user partners. Twenty infants, 4.7 percent of the cases, contracted HIV during delivery. The policy of routinely offering HIV testing to all pregnant women can play a vital role in preventing the spread of this disease.

B. Availability of Treatment and Prevention Programs

The first national project for HIV/AIDS prevention was adopted in February 1992 and ran through 1994. A second program was planned to run until 1997. Both plans were developed by a national committee against AIDS and are supported by a number of organizations: the Ministry of Public Health, the Ministry of Economics, Social Defense Ministry, and the Agency for Youth and Sports. The general lines of the programs include promotion of condom use, an educational project, mass-media action, and providing health care clinics.

The general goal is to slow down the epidemic of HIV and save thousands of lives. Medical aspects of the program are designed to reduce or eliminate the risk of getting HIV. The health workers have set themselves an ambitious goal: mass awareness and understanding of how sexual intercourse can be made safer to reduce the risk of getting HIV. Another effort is to supply the population with condoms; approximately 150 million condoms will be provided annually for the needs of the Ukrainian population. The medical campaign against AIDS also requires testing donated blood and blood products by checking two million blood samples annually.

Special attention will be given to laboratory testing for HIV-infection. More then 170 institutions will make four million tests a year, using clinical tests produced by the American firm Abbott and French Sanofi Diagnostic Pasteur. The state will also promote development of a national industry for transfusion blood screening. The program also contains measures for health care of the laboratory and hospital personnel in order to reduce the risk of their becoming infected.

The development of AIDS service organizations requires special training programs for responding without fear to the needs of all HIV-infected people who require medical or psychological help. Already, clinics in regional centers serve people with HIV or AIDS. Usually they offer confidential medical services, pre- and post-test counseling, meals, housing and rental assistance, and complete medical evaluations. Again, all such services are free and confidential. The national program includes research studies of the viral causes of AIDS, the development of new diagnostic and treatment methods of diagnosis, and the search for an AIDS vaccine.

The main program direction is on promoting AIDS awareness among the population. A mass-media effort on radio and television and in the newspapers should be effective in raising the knowledge about AIDS, especially how everyone can gain some protection. The information-educational work is focused on separating the scientific facts from the myths, and providing information about the connection between sexual intercourse, oral and anal sex, and HIV transmission. High-risk groups will receive special attention. The financial cost for the National Program is 1,481,823 million rubles plus $12,248,600 American dollars.

In 1991, the Ukrainian Parliament adopted a bill about the prevention against AIDS infection and protection of the population. A national committee supported by the Ukrainian president has been organized as the main center for creative central and regional area programs for the fight against AIDS. This committee provides a wide range of educational, economic, and social policy concerning AIDS-related work. The chairperson of the National Committee is Professor Matsuka Hennadiy (Address: 3 Mechnikova vul., Kyiv, 252023; fax 380-44-244-3811).

12. Sexual Dysfunctions, Counseling, and Therapies

A. Concepts of Sexual Dysfunction

Until the mid-1970s, the concept of sexual dysfunction in the Soviet Ukraine was limited to disorders in the reproductive functioning. This view was widespread in an authoritarian society where the individual was considered only a small screw in a large mechanical machinery. Yet, even without knowledge about social and personality psychology, many urologists and gynecologists tried to treat their patients' sexual problems by dealing with their individual psychological difficulties.

A network of sexological consultation centers began to appear in Ukrainian cities in 1964. The inspiration for this development came from Ivan Unda (1924-1994), a professor of sexology, who emphasized the connection between physiological and psychological factors in human sexual functioning. He taught that sexual problems, such as lack of sexual desire, inhibited sexual arousal and orgasm, premature ejaculation, and other dysfunctions, stem from a combination of sociocultural, individual, and interpersonal factors.

While sexual problems vary from individual to individual, today's Ukrainian scientists consider sexual problems as stemming from three sources: (1) personal subjective feelings, emotions, attitudes, and values; (2) socially acquired attitudes and expectations, as well as the partner's reactions; and (3) physiological disorders mostly associated with stress, depression, and illness. In recent years, one must add to the usual etiologies of sexual dysfunction the individual's response to the economic difficulties and political situation in postsocialist Ukraine, which increasingly can be related to sexual problems.

One particular consequence of seventy years of Soviet authoritarianism is evident in the psychology of the Ukrainian female and male. While other aspects of this influence are gender-related, one effect pertains equally to both females and males. This has resulted in problems in the ability to listen, to understand, to forgive, and to resolve conflict on the basis of respect for the individual person.

B. The Availability of Diagnosis and Treatment

Since 1989, every large city in Ukraine has had its family or sexology consultation centers where sexologists and psychologists have begun to work together. Medical examination of the individual or couple is accompanied by psychological testing.

Many women and men are seeking help at these centers, be it guidance, information, or reassurance. The number of sexological problems are considerable, but most are connected with the individual psychological culture. The diagnostic services of the consultation centers focus on the communications abilities and relationships between wife and husband or lovers and the psychology of human sexual response. The latter is not limited to coitus, but extends to all the pleasurable and negative sensations associated with any sexuoerotic contact.

The treatment part of the counseling deals with couple guidance and relationship problems, and on teaching interpersonal skills that can be applied in their everyday interactions as a couple. The program, usually a combination of traditional psychotherapy with behavioral-oriented therapy, is aimed at personal growth of the patient(s) and sexual healing, using dialogue, role playing, and group therapy. Constant efforts are made to help the patient(s) develop a warm and well-functioning relationship.

Most counseling services are free of charge and confidential. There are some nongovernmental family consultation services, available for those who can afford them.

C. Therapist Training and Certification

Sexological or family consultation centers are staffed primarily by physician-sexologists, and by clinical psychologists and psychiatrists. Medical sexology as a specialty for physicians is taught by gynecologists, by psychiatrists in graduate courses at the medical universities in Kyiv, Odesa, Dnipropetrovs'k, and other cities, and in postgraduate courses at the Ukrainian Physicians' Improvement Institute in Charkiv. Psychological problems in sexology are studied at the Teachers Training Universities in postgraduate courses, and in the doctoral program at the Institute of Psychology. The Ministry of Public Health of Ukraine, the Ministry of Education, the State Universities and their scientific boards establish the criteria for programs, course work, and requirements for licensing and certification in fields involved in diagnosis and treatment of sexual dysfunctions.

13. Research and Advanced Education

A. Institutes and Programs for Sexological Research

Several government agencies are involved in and support sexological research. These include seven divisions of the Ministry of Public Health of Ukraine. Other organizations are:

Kyiv Research Institute of Urology and Nephrology, Professor Olexandr Vozianov, Director; Department of Sexopathology, Androgyny, and Sexology Clinic, Professor Ihor Gorpinchenko, Chairperson. Address: 9 a In. Kotsubinskyj vul., Kyiv 252053. Telehone: 38-044-216-5054; fax 38-044-244-6862. Research includes: the sexology and andrology of aging; the Chernobil catastrophe and changes in the reproductive function; development of objective diagnostic method for sexual dysfunctions; and investigation of the pathospermia factors in infertility couples.

Kyiv Research Institute of Clinical and Experimental Surgery, Professor Valerej Saenko, Director. Address: 30 Herojiv Sevastopolia vul., Kyiv 252180. Telephone: 38-044-483-1374; fax 38-044-483-5219. Research includes: improvement and development of body surgery corrections of transsexual persons; diagnosis and treatment of the vascular impotence; and endo-orthopedic prosthetic appliances.

Kyiv Central Institute for the Physicians Improvement—Medical and Social Problems of the Family Division, Professor Zoreslava Shkiriak-Nyzhnyk, Chairperson. Address: 8 Manujil'skoho vul., Kyiv 252054. Telephone: 380-44-213-6271; fax 380-44-213-6271. Research includes: family and female health at all ages.

Common Ukrainian-Holland Center for Human Reproduction, Iryna Vovk, President. Address: 8 Manujil'skoho vul., Kyiv 252054. Telephone: 38-044-213-1446; fax 38-044-213-7125. Research includes sex information for children and teenagers.

Kyiv Research Sexology and Andrology Center, Professor Borys Vornyk, Chairperson. Address: 8 Smolenska vul., Kyiv 252057. Telephone: 380-044-228-0103; fax 380-44-543-8421. Research includes: adult sexual dysfunction; male and female infertility; personal disharmonies in sexual relationships; social and biological factors in transsexuality and homosexuality; hospital investigation and the treatment of sexual diseases (prostatitis, urethrities, epidermities, etc.); and treatment of gender-identity disorders and conditions.

Institute of Gerontology, The Academy of Medical Sciences, Department of Genetics and Mathematical Modeling, Professor Volodymyr Vojtenko, Chairperson. Address: 67 Vyzhhorods'ka vul., Kyiv 252114. Telephone: 380-44-431-0524; fax 380-44-432-9956. Research includes the development of human sexuality in the later years.

Ukrainian Institute for the Physicians Improvement, The Chair of Sexology and Medical Psychology, Professor Valentyn Kryshtal', Chairperson. Address: 81/85 Myronositska vul., Charkiv 310023. Telephone: 38-057-245-1056. Research includes: matrimonial disharmonies, causes as well as medical and psychological methods for the evaluation of dysfunctional couples; marital therapy and treatment programs.

Other major institutes with programs for sexology-related research include three whose main focus is education, the first two below being in the Ukrainian Ministry of Education:

State Ukrainian Pedagogical University, Ofter M. Drahomanov, Chair of Psychology and Pedagogy, Dr. Tamara Govorun, Research Program Manager. Address: 9 Pyrohova vul., Kyiv 252030. Telephone: 380-044-216-3007; fax 380-44-224-2251. Research includes: techniques for teaching human sexuality courses; childhood sexual development and behavior; and comparisons of gender behavior in cross-cultural investigations.

Institute for the System Researchers Studies in Education, The Department of Child Upbringing, Dr. Svitlana Kyrylenko, Research Programs Manager. Address: 37 Petra Sahajdachnoho vul., Kyiv 252070. Telephone: 380-44-416-0441; fax 380-44-417-8336. Research includes: conception of childhood sexuality and models for sexual education; sexual behavior and parent-teenager communications; and sexual knowledge in secondary and high schools.

Ukrainian Academy of Pedagogical Sciences, Institute of Psychology, The Laboratory of the Psychology of Nurturing: Professor Myroslav Boryshevskiy, Chairperson. Address: 2 Pan'kivs'ka vul., Kyiv 252030. Telephone: 380-44-244-3320; fax 380-44-244-1963. Research includes: development of gender self-consciousness in childhood and adolescence; parental roles in developing child sexuality; and development of sex-education programs for children and teenagers.

B. Graduate Programs and the Advanced Study of Human Sexuality

Most specialists who deal with human sexuality in Ukraine fit into three categories: sexologists, physician/sexologists, and psychologists. According to the basic college education, there are a variety of postgraduate advanced courses of study available in Ukraine. Some of these are listed here with their focus, sponsoring agency, and address.

Master's degree programs in human sexuality. Ministry of Public Health of Ukraine, Ukrainian Institute for the Physicians Improvement, The Chair of Sexology and Medical Psychology, Professor Valentyn Kryshtal', Chairperson. Address: 81/85 Myronositska vul., Kharkiv 310023. Telephone: 380-57-245-1056.

Graduate courses in sexology for the physicians' advanced training; doctorate programs in sexuality and family studies. Ministry of Public Health of Ukraine. Address: Kyiv Research Institute of Urology and Nephrology, 9 a In. Kotsubinskiy vul., Kyiv 252053. Fax: 380-44-244-6862.

Postgraduate courses on sexology for an academic degree in medicine. Ministry of Public Health of Ukraine. Address: Ukrainian Institute of the Physicians Improvement, Mykola Chjesjuk, Director. 17 Korchahintsiv vul., Charkiv 310000. Telephone: 380-57-211-3556; fax 380-57-211-3556.

Postgraduate courses on sexology for an academic degree in medicine. Ministry of Public Health of Ukraine, Ukrainian State Medical University. Address: Department of Psychiatry, Professor Olexandr Naprijenko, Chairperson, 13 Shevchenka bulv., Kyiv 252004. Telephone: 380-44-435-3554.

Graduate courses on sexology for the physicians' advanced training courses. The Academy of Pedagogical Sciences, Institute of Psychology. Address: 2 Pan'kivs'ka vul., Kyiv 252033. Telephone: 380-44-244-1963.

Postgraduate courses on sexual behavior for an academic degree in psychology. The Ukrainian Ministry of Education, The State Ukrainian Pedagogical University, by M. Dragomanov. Address: 9 Pyrohova, Kyiv 252030. Fax: 380-44-224-2251.

There are also postgraduate courses on sexual behavior for an academic degree in psychology or in pedagogy.

C. Ukrainian Sexological Journals

Two sexological journals are published in Ukraine:

The Journal of Sexology and Andrology. Address: Editor, 9 a Kotsubynskoho vul., Kyiv 252053. Fax: 380-44-244-6862.

The Journal of Sexopathology and Andrology. Address: Borys Vornyk, Ph.D., Editor, 8 Smolenska vul., Kyiv 252057. Fax: 380-44-228-0103 (a semi-annual publication).

There are three popular mass-media publications in Ukraine dealing with sexuality:

Pan Plus Pani. Address: a/ja. 71. Ternopol 282001. Telephone: 380-35-225-0724 (a weekly newspaper).

Interesnaja Gazeta. Address: 50 Peremohy bulv., Kyiv 252047. Telephone: 380-44-441-8257; fax 380-44-446-9101 (a newspaper).

Lel. Address: Editor, Chyrkovsrly, 38/44 Dehtjarivs'ka vul., Kyiv 252103. Telephone: 380-44-211-0268 (a quarterly Ukrainian erotic magazine).

D. Major Sexological Organizations

The Ukrainian Society of Sexologists. Address: 9 a In. Kotsubinskiy vul., Kyiv 252053. Telephone: 380-044-216-5054; fax 380-44-244-6862. This national professional organization includes physicians, psychologists, and teachers in secondary high schools, colleges, and graduate schools who unite their efforts in scientific research and applied work on human sexuality.

The European-Asian Association of Sexologists. Address: 8 Smolenska vul., Kyiv 252057. Telephone: 380-44-446-1346; fax 380-44-228-0103. This is an international organization of sexologists from former Soviet republics and of professionals from abroad. Its annual meetings in sexual science are usually held in September in Kyiv, the capital of Ukraine.

The Institute of Reproductive Medicine, Professor Phedir Dachno, Director. Address: 2b Herojiv Kosmosu vul., Kyiv 252148. Telephone: 380-44-478-3068; Fax 380-44-478-3068.

14. Ethnic Minorities

Ukraine is motherland to many ethnic groups. Bulgarians, Serbs, and Poles have been settled in Ukrainian territory since the eighteenth century,

Moldavians since the sixteenth century, Gypsies since the fifteenth century, and Jews since the fourteenth century. Most of these ethnic minorities identify themselves with some nation in the world, but some of them, like the Budjak Gaguasers and Tavrida Tartars, have developed as an ethnic group within Ukraine, and thus consider themselves a native minority population.

A. The Tartars

In the 1940s, all Tartars, descendants of various Mogul and Turkish tribes, were forced to leave their homes in Ukraine. Today, those who survived Stalin's genocide policies are trying to return to the Crimea and Tavrida steppes.

The Tartar family, as any family, is a system for social control and inculcating cultural behavior patterns for all its members. Before their forced eviction, the Tartars lived mostly in extended families. These family communities included two or more brothers with their wives, married children, and grandchildren. Such kin constituted an independent economic and social group which remained a primary vehicle for preserving and transferring customs and traditions.

Most Tartar families today are nuclear, although the authority of males, especially older males, is maintained as a tradition. In all family settings, the superiority of males is considered normal and natural. Marriage is prohibited within seven generations of blood kinship. Tartar sexual culture is more permissive for men, whether young or old; women are held to much stricter standards. The wife's devotion to her husband is very much appreciated and expected, as well as the obedience of all women to their father, brothers, and male relatives by marriage. The family is viewed as a social, religious, and moral unity, based on the wife's efforts to support her husband and maintain a positive psychological climate among the relatives. That is why developing honesty and innocence is the main focus in raising girls. The Tartars have different rituals to protect virginity, and its public manifestation indicates the important role virginity plays in the appreciation of marital intimacy. It is taboo for bridegrooms to admit sexual competence before their wedding.

In modern Tartar wedding celebrations, a lot of ethnic prescriptions are maintained. The women's and men's communities are located in different rooms. Newlyweds are expected to show the groom's relatives the signs of the bride's virginity by the time of marriage. The young wife puts a red kerchief on her head, while her husband wears a red ribbon-belt around his waist as a symbol of sexual innocence. Red strings link the generations, as well as brothers, sisters, and relatives by marriage. All play special roles during the wedding ceremony and try to help the young couple as they settle into married and family life. According to ethnic beliefs, sexual feelings and private matters should be subject to human reason and the stability of marital relationships. Some traditional presents for newlyweds symbolize the support of the family: a wedding candle to make life light and clear and a round meat pie (*kobete*) to symbolize good health and children.

B. Koreans

Koreans as an ethnic minority came to Ukraine mostly after World War II. In families where one spouse is Korean and the other non-Korean, national customs are much more carefully maintained when the wife is Korean than when the husband is Korean and his wife non-Korean. Korean gender behavior is determined by the commandments of Conphutsy ideals of great respect for ancestors, harmony within the marital unit and society, strict subordination of the younger to their elders, and the high authority of the father and male relatives.

Korean marriage is considered not only the unity of husband and wife, but of two families or kins. Although the dominant position of the male is preserved in all family matters, the Korean woman does not change her last name after marriage. Thus, many Korean families in Ukraine have doubled names with two surnames. The Korean minority has adjusted to Ukrainian holidays but try to preserve their national festivals. One of the more important of these is the commemorative feast in which every person celebrates in him- or herself the past, the present, and the future of parentage.

An appreciation of the growing personality and the older generation is at the core of most Korean family holidays. Among these are the celebration of a hundred days after the baby's birth. The belief is that if a hundred guests share in the banquet that day, the child will live a happy and long life. When a baby is 1 year old, he or she may foretell his or her future destiny. For that purpose, the parents place some different toys before the child. If the baby chooses the money, it will be successful in business in the future; if a book is chosen, the future adult will be lucky in science and intellectual pursuits; and so on.

Since Korean marriage is considered to be a union of two kins, special gender behavior patterns are honored during the wedding ceremony. The bride and groom stand face to face, bow to each other, ritually clean the hands, exchange goblets of wine, and drink from the cup. Usually, Korean families remember and commemorate four times a year at least four generations of their ancestors who are known by name and profession.

The sexual attitudes and customs of Tartar and Korean ethnic minorities in Ukraine, like any ethnic minority in any coutry, are continually undergoing change and adapting, being influenced by the majority culture and, at the same time, more or less influencing and changing that majority culture.

References and Suggested Readings

Bogdushkin N., and M. Andreev. 1995. "The Problem of the Young Pregnancy and Childbirth." *Kharkov Medical Journal*, 1.

Boryshevskyj, Myroslav. 1990. *Psychologichni Pytannia Statevoho Vyhovannia Uchniv (The Psychological Questions of Sex Nurturing the Pupils)*. Kyiv: Edition Radjanska Shkola (in Ukrainian).

Boryshevskyj, Myroslav. 1992. *Stateve Vychovannya (The Sex Nurturing)*. Kyiv: Encyclopedia of the Mother and Child. Edition Ukrainian encyclopedia after Bazhana (in Ukrainian).

Chubyns'kiy, P. 1994. "Shameless Songs." *Lel*, 6(17).

Chujko, L. 1994. "The Tendencies of Family Development." *Economical Reforms in Ukraine*. SINTO.

Gorpinchenko, Ihor. 1991. *Herontologicheskaya Seksopatologija (Herontology Sexopatology)*. Kyiv: Edition Zdorovja (in Russian).

Gorpinchenko, Ihor. 1991. *Otkrovenno o Sokrovennom (Sincerely about Innermost)*. Kyiv: Edition Zdorovja (in Russian).

Govorun, Tamara, and Oksana Shargana. 1990. *Bat'kam pro Stateve Vychovannya Ditej (For Parents about Sexual Education of the Children)*. Kyiv: Edition Radjanska Shkola (in Ukrainian).

Jul'ko Alexander. 1994. *Spravochnik po Seksologiji (Reference Book on Sexology, Sexopathology, and Andrology)*. Kyiv: Edition Zdorovja (in Russian).

Kryshtal, Valentyn, et al. 1990. *Seksualnaja Garmonija Supruzeskoj Pary (Sexual Harmony in Marital Couples)*. Charkov: Edition Interbook (in Russian).

Kyrylenko, Svitlana, Tamara Govorun, et al. 1995. *Problemy Simejnoho ta Statevoho Vychovannya. (The Problems of the Family and Sexual Upbringings)*. Kyiv: Vydavnytstvo Vyschych Uchbovych Zakladiv (in Ukrainian).

Mirza Avakjants, N. 1920. *Ukrainian Woman in XVI-XVIIc*. Poltava: Private printing.

Monomach, Volodymyr. 1991. "The Edification of Children." In V. Rychka, ed. *Behind the Chronicler Lines*. Kyiv: Soviet School.

Nestor the Chronicler. 1998. "The Song of Ihor's Compaign." In *A Tale of Bygone Years*. Kyiv: Soviet Writer.

Paraschuk, Jurij. 1994. *Besplodije v Supruzestve (Infertility in Conjugality)*. Charkov: Edition Zdorovja (in Russian).

Rehbinder, B. 1993. *Veles Book: The Life and Religion of Ancient Slavonic*. Kyiv: Photovideoservis.

Ryzhko, P. 1995. "Venereal Diseases." *Charkov Medical Journal*, 1.

Shkirjak-Nyznyk, Zoreslava, and Emilia Nepochatova-Kurashkevich. 1990. *Seksualna Kultura Simejnych Vidnosyn (The Sexual Culture of a Family Relationship)*. Kyiv: Edition Znannya (in Ukrainian).

Ukrainian Soul. 1992. Kyiv: Pheniks.

Unda, Ivan, and Ludmila Imshenetskaya. 1990. *Besplodie v Supruzestve (Infertility in Conjugality)*. Kyiv: Edition Zdorovja (in Russian).

Unda, Ivan, and Leonid Unda. 1990. *Sotsial'no-Psichologicheskije e Medico-Biologicheskije Osnovy Simejnoj Zhyzni (Social-Psychological and Medical-Biological Basis of the Marital Life)*. Kyiv: Edition Vyscha Shkola (in Russian).

Vornyk, Borys. 1995. *Sexologia dlja Vsech (Sexology for All)*. Kyiv: Edition "ABK-Press" (in Russian).

Vozianov, Olexandr, Igor Gorpinchenko, et al. 1995. *Clinichna Seksologija e Andrologija (Clinical Sexology and Andrology)*. Kyiv: Edition Zdorovja (in Ukrainian).

Zhyla, Vladimir, and Jurij Kushniruk. 1990. *Garmonija e Discharmonija Intimnoj Zhyzni (Harmony and Disharmony of the Intimacy Life)*. Kyiv: Edition Zdorovja (in Russian).

The United Kingdom of Great Britain and Northern Ireland

Kevan R. Wylie, M.B., Ch.B., M.Med.Sc., M.R.C.Psych., D.S.M.,
with Anthony Bains, B.A., Tina Ball, Ph.D.,
Patricia Barnes, M.A., CQSW, BASMT (Accred.),
Rohan Collier, Ph.D., Jane Craig, M.B., MRCP (UK),
Linda Delaney, L.L.B., M.Jur., Julia Field, B.A.,
Danya Glaser, MBBS, D.Ch., FRCPsych.,
Peter Greenhouse, M.A., MRCOG, MFFP,
Mary Griffin, M.B., M.Sc., MFFP,
Margot Huish, B.A., BASMT (Accred.),
Anne M. Johnson, M.A., M.Sc., M.D., MRCGP, FFPAM,
George Kinghorn, M.D., FRCP, Helen Mott, B.A.(Hons.),
Paula Nicolson, Ph.D., Jane Read, B.A.Hons., UKCP,
Fran Reader, FRCOG, MFFP, BASMT (Accred.),
Gwyneth Sampson, DPM, MRCPsych.,
Peter Selman, DPSA, Ph.D., José von Bühler, R.M.N., Dip.H.S.,
Jane Wadsworth, B.Sc., M.Sc., Kaye Wellings, M.A., M.Sc.,
and Stephen Whittle, Ph.D.
Consulting Editors for this chapter were
Maria Bakaroudis, M.A., and James Shortridge, M.A.

Contents

*This chapter was coordinated by Kevan R. Wylie, M.B., Ch.B., M.Med.Sc., M.R.C.Psych., D.S.M.

Demographics and a Historical Perspective

KEVAN R. WYLIE

A. Demographics

The United Kingdom, composed of England, Wales, Scotland, and Northern Ireland, faces the northwestern edge of Europe. The British Isles, with 94,226 square miles (about the size of New York State), are separated by the English Channel from France on the south, Belgium, the Netherlands, Denmark, and the southern tip of Norway to the east. To the west, across the Irish Sea, is the Republic of Ireland. In 1920, the British Parliament divided Northern Ireland from Southern Ireland and gave each its own parliament and government. A few years later, when Ireland became a dominion and then an independent republic, six of the nine counties of Ulster in the northeast corner of the country chose to remain a part of the United Kingdom.

Geographically and culturally, the main island of the British Isles has three regional entities, England, Scotland, and Wales. The Principality of Wales in western Britain has an area of 8,019 square miles and a population of about three million. After early Anglo-Saxon invaders drove the Celtic people into the mountains of Wales, these people, who became known as Welsh ("foreign"), developed their own distinct nationality. English is the dominant language, with less than 20 percent of the people of Wales speaking both English and Welsh; some 32,000 speak only Welsh. The former kingdom of Scotland occupies the northern third of the main British island. The central lowlands, a belt approximately sixty miles wide stretching from the Firth of Clyde to the Firth of Forth, divides the farming region of the Southern Uplands from the granite Highlands in the north. About three quarters of Scotland's five million people live in the Lowlands, concentrating in the industrial center of Glasgow (population three quarters of a million) and the capital Edinburgh (population half a million). The Hebrides, Orkney, and Shetland Islands are also part of Scotland. England, the heart of the United Kingdom, has a population of close to fifty million people. London, the capital, has a population of about seven million; Birmingham, the second largest city, has a population of about a million.

The United Kingdom of Great Britain also includes the Channel Islands, the Isle of Man, Gibraltar (between Spain and Africa), the British West Indies and Bermuda in the Caribbean, the Falkland Islands and dependencies in the South Atlantic, the Crown Colony of Hong Kong in Asia, and Pitcairn Island in the Pacific Ocean.

According to the 1991 census, the population of the United Kingdom was 55,486,800. Wales had an estimated 1994 population of 2.9 million; Scotland, 5.1 million, and Northern Ireland, 281,000. The 1995 age distribution in the United Kingdom was: below age 14, 19.2 percent; ages 15 to 59, 60.1 percent; and over age 60, 20.7 percent. Ninety-two percent of the population lives in the cities. Ethnically, 81.5 percent are English, 9.6 percent Scottish, 2.4 percent Irish, 1.9 percent Welsh, and 1.8 percent Ulstermen. West Indians, Indians, and Pakistanis constitute about 2 percent of the population. The main religions are Anglican (Church of England) and Roman Catholic.

Life expectancy at birth in 1995 was 74 for males and 80 for females. The birthrate was 13 per 1,000 population and the death rate 11 per 1,000, for a natural increase of 0.3 percent per year. Literacy is 99 percent with twelve years of compulsory schooling and 99 percent attendance. The United Kingdom has one hospital bed per 146 persons and one physician per 611 persons. The per capita domestic product was $16,900 U.S.

B. A Brief Historical Perspective

Until about ten thousand years ago, Britain was connected to the European continent by a land bridge that made it convenient for peoples to migrate back and forth. With the end of the last great Ice Age, and the slow but inevitable melting of the ice masses that covered Europe and North America, the sea level gradually rose, separating the continent from the British Isles with the English Channel. Despite the new obstacle, people continued migrating, as the Celts did to the isles some 2,500 to 3,000 years ago. This Celtic influence can still be found in the language and culture of the Welsh and Gaelic (Irish) enclaves. England became part of the Roman Empire in 43 of the Common Era. The Roman legions withdrew in 410. In subsequent centuries, particularly the eighth through eleventh centuries, waves of Germanic Jutes, Angles, and Saxons competed with Danish invaders for control of the island. In 1066, Duke William led the Norman conquest of Britain, bringing continental feudalism and the French language, essential elements in later English culture.

In 1215, the nobles forced King John to sign the Magna Carta, guaranteeing the rights of the people and the rule of law, and setting the stage for the development of a parliamentary system of government. Defeat in the Hundred Years War with France (1338-1453) was followed by a long civil war, the War of the Roses (1455-1485). While European countries were racked by wars, English culture and a strong economy flourished under the powerful Tudor monarchy and a long period of domestic peace. Establishment of the Church of England in 1534 under the monarch separated England's religious institutions from the authority of Rome. Under Queen Elizabeth I, England became a major naval power, with colonies in the Americas. Britain's trade throughout Europe and the Orient also expanded. Scotland became part of England in 1603 when James VI of Scotland became James I of England. A struggle between Parliament and the Stuart kings, a bloody civil war (1642-1649), and establishment of a republic under the Puritans, ended with the restoration of the monarchy in 1688. The sovereignty of Parliament was confirmed in the "Glorious Revolution" of 1688 and a Bill of Rights in 1689.

The eighteenth century in England was distinguished by a strengthening of the parliamentary system and technical and entrepreneurial innovations that produced the Industrial Revolution. England lost its colonies in the American Revolution, expanded its empire with growing colonies in Canada and India, and strengthened its position as a leading world power. The nineteenth century was marked by extension of the vote in 1832 and 1867, formation of trade unions, development of universal public education, the spread of industrialization and urbanization, and, under Queen Victoria (1837-1901), the addition of large parts of Africa and Asia to the empire.

Britain suffered huge casualties and economic dislocations as a result of World Wars I and II, Although industrial growth returned after the wars, Britain lost its leadership role to other nations. Ireland became an independent republic in 1921, but the Irish question has persisted. In recent years, the socialized medicine, social security support systems have posed increasing questions for the government and people.

1. Basic Sexological Premises

PAULA NICOLSON

A. Character of Gender Roles

Gender roles in the United Kingdom have been influenced both by social class, which has ensured the maintenance of gender segregation, particularly among the upper and working classes, and by fluctuating demographic, political, and cultural changes over the past eighty years that have stimulated shifts in traditional gender-role patterns. For example, during World War II, women were employed in manufacturing, commerce, and agriculture, aided by good state provision of day care for children. Following the demobilization of the male population in the 1950s, however, there was a political emphasis on "pronatalism" in order to replenish the population and to free up employment possibilities for men. In this context, women's responsibility for the mental and physical health of their families was encouraged with a return to traditional gender lifestyles.

Although since the mid 1980s there has been a clear political commitment to seeing men and women as equal, a division of labor remains in the home that spills over into the workplace. This distinguishes men's and women's behavior and expectations along traditional stereotypical lines: Men are seen as powerful, rational, and "naturally" the breadwinners, and women are seen as dependent, emotional, and "naturally" suited to the domestic sphere. Nevertheless, feminist influence, coupled with high levels of male unemployment since the early 1980s among all social classes, has forced many men to take greater responsibility and interest in child care than previously. The resulting image of the "new man," in touch with his emotions and with nurturing skills, remains, however, a contestable image. Finally, increased educational opportunities have enabled women to enter professional life, a process that has increased since the 1970s, although few women rise above middle-management level.

B. Sociolegal Status of Males and Females

Males and females officially have equal status in the United Kingdom in terms of human rights, but there remain certain sociopolitical distinctions. For instance, many women receive reduced unemployment benefits and pensions because they have not had to pay full contributions during their working lives and have had career breaks. However, women are entitled to a retirement pension at the age of 60, while the retirement age for men remains 65. This is currently the subject of political debate and proposed statutory changes.

The legal age of consent for heterosexual women and men is 16. Only recently was the age of consent for homosexual men reduced from 21 to 18. Further indication of inequality based on sexual orientation is the judgment upholding the ban on both homosexual men and lesbians in the armed services.

The age of heterosexual consent means that it is not legal for doctors to prescribe contraceptives to women and men under the age of 16 without parental consent, a contentious issue that remains unresolved.

Certain legal judgments have demonstrated inequalities in attitudes towards women and men. Some adolescent and older men found guilty of rape, for instance, have received relatively light punishments; in some rape cases, women have been portrayed as guilty of "contributory negligence"; and men who have killed their female partners because they "nagged" or were unfaithful were given light sentences or had the murder charge changed to manslaughter. Conversely, women who killed male partners after years of violent physical and sexual abuse have been found guilty of murder and given long-term prison sentences. This is indicative of the underlying ideology that remains in favor of male domestic authority and the traditional view of the male sex drive as dominant.

Finally, unmarried mothers are frequently portrayed by politicians as being irresponsible, and their entitlement to state benefits has been questioned. However, this has been counterbalanced to some extent by the creation of the controversial Child Support Agency, which has pursued absent fathers for child maintenance.

C. General Concepts of Sexuality and Love

The majority of the population in the United Kingdom are able to choose their sexual partners on the basis of attraction and love. This, however, does not apply among some minority ethnic groups, nor to social class groups where a socially suitable marriage is encouraged.

Since the late 1960s, there has been an increased liberalization of attitudes towards sexuality. The age of first heterosexual intercourse for women has declined from a median age of 21 for those born in the 1930s and 1940s to 17 years for those born between 1966 and 1975. The gap between the age of first intercourse for women and men has narrowed over the past fifty years, and for the current generation of young people, it is virtually the same for both sexes. A sizable minority of both sexes are sexually active before the age of 16. A high proportion of sexually active 16-year-olds do not use contraception (Wellings et al. 1994).

With more people changing sexual orientation over the course of their life, the category "homosexual" is no longer seen as discrete and exclusive (Dance 1994). However, it remains the case that heterosexuality is taken as the norm, and sexual satisfaction is understood to be orgasm for both partners during vaginal intercourse (Nicolson 1993). There has been an increase in availability of health practitioners specializing in sexual problems, and in the willingness of couples and individuals to seek psychosexual counseling when they fail to achieve sexual satisfaction.

Serial monogamy rather than life-time marriage is now the norm in the United Kingdom as in the U.S.A., with fewer people getting married and as many as one in two marriages ending in divorce.

2. Religious and Ethnic Factors Affecting Sexuality
JOSÉ VON BÜHLER

A. Sources and Character of Religious Values

Since the 1950s, Britain has become increasingly a pluralistic country in terms of cultures, ethnicity, and religion. Hinduism mixes with Roman Catholicism, Islam with Judaism, and Methodism with Buddhism. Some of these religions are almost inseparable from their social fabric, culture, and ethnic grouping. Others offer a moral and spiritual framework separate from ethnic practices. The common denominator in the existence of this pluralism is that, apart from the establishment franchise of Anglicanism, which in reality makes it the "state religion," all religious bodies in the United Kingdom are equal under the law of the land. This equality confers certain rights and privileges in respect of education, worship, social welfare, and democratic political rights.

However, the multifaceted character implied in interdenominationality in many instances is generally not understood by the public at large, or even the members of the various groups. Philosophically and socially, there is frequently a disconnection that does not allow for cross-fertilization of ideas. Nor does it allow for comparative analysis of the positive approach to sexual concepts and even sexual activities in many religions when their scriptures are properly understood! In this climate, it is easy for fundamentalists of every denomination to represent human sexuality in the religious/spiritual content as negative and somehow taboo. This tension was noted in a 1992 report from the Sex Education Forum, an umbrella body for several religious and secular organizations concerned with providing and supporting sex education for young people. The report, *An Enquiry into Sex Education: Report of a Survey of LEA Support and Monitoring of School Sex Education* (Thompson and Scott 1992), clearly identified: "anxieties concerning ethnicity and religious issues to be a significant barrier to the effective provision of sex education." Indirectly, the report confirmed that the distance between religious legal equality and ethnic, social, and moral framework patterns and concepts is rather unequal among the various religious and ethnic groups in the United Kingdom.

Prior to the 1950s, the religious influences forming sexual constructs came almost exclusively from "the official church" of England, and "unofficially" from the other Christian denominations. In recent decades, the picture has become more complex. Since midcentury, the Church of England's approach to social morality and sexuality has fluctuated between two poles, the traditionalists and the modernists, or the "permission givers" and the "orthodox moral directors." With the national religious scene resembling the circular approach of the politicians to sexual knowledge and attitudes, the sociosexual control and influence appears to bounce back and forth between church and state according to a mutually cooperative formula. In many cases, however, liberal attitudes have triumphed, as evidenced by the Church's acceptance of divorce, homosexuality, and contraception. In other cases, the traditionalists have retained a firm moral control. This doctrinal "pendulum" is confusing for the majority of the population who are not experts at moral and theological niceties and subtleties. The people themselves are part of the system of confusion: While expecting clear and definite moral messages from both establishment and Church, they reserve the right to judge the validity of those messages, even when they are biblically based.

With quiet, behind-the-curtains efficiency, the Roman Catholic Church has been influential in shaping national morality and sexuality. Its most authoritarian pronouncements about homosexuality and abortion have been tempered by professions of love for the individual while condemning same-gender sexual activity. To the democratic soul of the British people, Roman Catholic moral doctrine appears autocratic and dictatorial, even while it provides a secure, unchangeable frame of reference that is not answerable to cultural and ethnic differences, a characteristic attractive to the orderly British. Other Christian denominations, such as Methodism and the evangelical Protestant churches, swing between permission and condemnation. Methodists, for instance, accept that sexual learning should present the biologically functional principles and, at the same time, should be equally aware of human relationships and their influence in the happiness of the individual.

Whatever the sexual-moral code of the many Christian traditions in Britain, the individual appears to have the final word in moral choices, as long as these choices are based on "fairness" and "not hurting other people." Nonetheless, it appears that religious beliefs are still a major influence on sexual attitudes and values. In this regard, for instance, the findings of the research study *Sexual Attitudes and Life Styles* (Johnson, Wadsworth, Wellings, and Field 1994), regarding first sexual intercourse are rather revealing:

> Respondents belonging to the Church of England or other Christian Churches (excluding the Roman Catholic Church) were less likely to experience sexual intercourse before the age of 16, and those from non-Christian religions even less likely to do so. More surprisingly perhaps, given the position of the Roman Catholic Church on sexual behavior, those reporting Roman Catholic affiliation are no less likely than those reporting other affiliations to report intercourse before the age of 16, and if anything slightly more so.

Notice that this applies exclusively to first sexual intercourse and not to other sexual intimacies.

In the ever-swinging pendulum of action and counteraction, an example of final choice control is that of the decision made recently by members of the Church of England regarding homosexuality. Whereas the moral traditionalists within the hierarchy of the Church have tried to reverse the acceptance of gay priests, priest advocates of homosexual rights have topped the polls in the Southward and London dioceses in elections for the Church of England's General Synod, the "church's parliament."

Nonetheless, Christianity no longer has total influencing control over the sexual morality of the British people. The pluralistic and interdenominational society in existence in Britain has seen to that. The influence of Islam, for instance, is evident in national moral pronouncements because of the increasing number of adherents to the faith and its sexual moral code. In common with Catholicism, Islamic sexual and moral teachings transcend ethnicity and culture. Human sexuality is not a taboo subject but must be dealt with in the context of the family with an open mind and in a way enriching to the individual's developmental and religious perspectives.

The influence of Hinduism and its sexual-moral code on the general population has not been as public. Hinduism is a pragmatic religion, and perhaps because of this pragmatism, issues of sex and sexual activities and practices are rarely discussed. Traditionally, there is an association between religion, erotica, and the highly culturally priced art of love, but in modern culture, one suspects that this connection is the domain of the "literati" and quite foreign to the contemporary Hindu family. Judaism teaches that sexual pleasure is an integral part of the marital/sexual relationship. In its positive view of sexual relations, the principle of pleasure and sharing mutual happiness by a physical relationship is validated.

B. Character of Ethnic Values

As suggested above, ethnicity plays an important part in the development of sexual and moral values, sometimes in connection with and sometimes apart from its religious connections. Four major cultural and ethnic components constitute the United Kingdom, the Irish, Scottish, Welsh, and the English themselves. Even within these groups, geographical position and class are influential. It is interesting to see that, although the various Christian denominations have adherents in every area of the British Isles, the ethnic groupings are numerically visible in the denomination of choice geographically. The Scottish have a tradition of Calvinism and Presbyterianism, the Northern Irish of Orange Protestantism, the Welsh of Chapel Christianity and Methodism, and the English as loyal but convenient subjects of Anglicanism in the tenets of the Church of England. This is, of course, a simplification of the religious/ethnic distribution, but it gives an idea of the association between ethnic values, religious tradition, and the influence of moral-theological principles on sexual values, and the acceptance or denial of sexual behavior. In this mixing pot of cultures, colors, religions, and nationalities, the views are almost infinite, and the British public has an almost inexhaustible amount of choices, although the majority of them are still of the prohibitive (sex-negative) kind. Yet, despite the many ethnic and religious prohibitions of sex, the British show an almost universal acceptance of sex before marriage, teenage sexuality, and the public discussion of topics such as homosexuality that were avoided not too long ago.

The British, according to Johnson, et al. (1994), view sex outside a regular relationship as wrong, monogamy is upheld more by women than men, women show a greater tolerance of homosexuality than men, and, in general, there appears to be an attitudinal trait for permissiveness. In the United Kingdom today, moral, religious, and ethnic influences on sexual attitudes, values, and behavior are no longer a case of *Roma locuta est, causa finita est* ("Rome has spoken, the argument is closed"), but more one of *Vox Populi* ("the voice of the people") with spiritual insurances.

3. Sexual Knowledge and Education
JOSÉ VON BÜHLER AND PATRICIA BARNES

A. Government Policies and Programs

Historically, there has been a reluctance to legislate in the area of sex education in England and Wales. The government has taken formal responsibility for this only in recent years, prior to that issuing general "guidelines" on the general content and moral code. The actual responsibility for the delivery of sex education was undertaken by independent voluntary agencies. Prior to World War II, the focus was on social hygiene, public health, and personal morality, addressing predominantly issues of sexually transmitted disease and unplanned pregnancy.

In the postwar years, educational philosophy and research adopted a sociological perspective and centered on the family. A partnership developed between educational and health establishments, and slowly the form and content of sex education became more concerned with the general well-being of the individual.

In 1968, the government provided funding to the newly formed Health Education Authority and the voluntary agencies, particularly the Family Planning Association (F.P.A.) and National Marriage Guidance Council (N.M.G.C.), to train teachers and provide resources for sex education. Although the political agenda was predominantly preventative in terms of public health, developments in sociological and psychological thinking were woven into educational efforts. These Personal and Social Educational Programs (P.S.E.) inevitably had a heterosexual and reproductive orientation. The medical and nursing professions began to teach from a "humanistic" platform, but it would be some time before a clear definition of humanistic principles in the discussion and delivery of sex education existed. The union of social trends and public policy brought about the beginning of social awareness of a sexuality in which the individual's personal growth mattered and sexual concepts started moving away from the purely biological.

The late 1970s and early 1980s saw the public face of feminism, antiracism, and gay liberation. The impact on local government and education was in the form of legislation on equal opportunities and antiracist policies. Despite a growing social need and awareness, a formal educational curriculum in sexuality for secondary, higher, and professional education did not exist. Some medical schools experimented, not without problems, with seminars and study days. They were influenced by a growing number of professional counselors and sex therapists, pioneers in the principles of particularity and personal entitlements in the field of sexual development. The Local Education Authorities, for example, were responsible for providing sexual curriculum guidance to schools, but the government did not involve itself in the growing revisionist consensus developing between education, health, and voluntary agencies, which put the person at the center of this consensus.

The political ethos of the 1980s concentrated on a dramatic return to a "new moral framework," which in essence represented a return to Victorian values. The role and function of the local education authorities and F.P.A. was inherently discredited. The responsibility for sex education in secondary schools (11- to 18-year-olds) suddenly transferred to the individual school governing bodies (H.M.S.O. 1987). The requirement was that sex education should be delivered within a moral framework, and that parents had to be consulted about the curricular nature. In 1987, the Department for Education issued guidelines and specific directives to school governors on the teaching of so-called controversial subjects, such as HIV, AIDS, and homosexuality. The guidelines and directives conveyed a clear public message that sex education was viewed by the government as inherently controversial. This message caused a fundamental dilemma between the needs of pupils and the requirements of the system. This dilemma was also present between the health needs in an age in which sexual awareness became part of a larger social picture and the apparent reluctance of responsible government bodies to accept sex education in its wider context of human sexuality.

At this time, there was politically little to be done regarding sex education in colleges, universities, and medical and nursing education. The academic input in these areas was neither of an official nature nor sufficiently effective to present a case for socially individualistic approaches. In many ways, this was supportive of the political status quo. The legislative disinterest in the activities of higher and professional education in the field of human sexuality and the dedicated work of individuals allowed universities and medical schools to design and deliver functional and integrative programs in human sexuality. Thankfully, these educational programs provided the United Kingdom with practitioners, teachers, and researchers in the field of sexuality since the mid-1980s. At the same time, voluntary agencies became repositories of the considerable body of knowledge and skills in the education and therapeutic interventions in human sexuality. It is difficult to understand today how such dichotomies could exist hand in hand with the World Health Organization's definition of sexual health. That definition clearly affirms the primacy of a "social and personal ethic." It also affirms the need for "freedom from fear, shame, guilt, false beliefs and other psychological factors inhibiting sexual response and impairing sexual relationships." University, medical, and professional education and the therapeutic professions tried to synthesize the issues of education and health, particularity by establishing working and investigative groups. The advantage of these groups was that many of their members were experts in the field of human sexuality.

In 1988, Section 28 of the Local Government Act was enacted to prohibit the Local Education Authorities from "promoting homosexuality." Much confusion ensued. In reality, this clause only applied to the Local Education Authorities' activities and not to educational processes in the classroom. However, this act firmly reestablished the religious/moral influence on sex education.

Also in 1988, a National Curriculum in education was introduced. This differentiated between the "core" or mandatory subjects of mathematics, English, and science that had specific curricula to cover at different key stages and the "noncore" subjects. Sex education was a "noncore" item. In the interest of public health, however, the reproductive and disease components were included in the core science curriculum, and therefore were obligatory to teach.

In 1990, the National Curriculum Council published *Curriculum Guidance 5: Health Education*, which recommended that the nine health education themes (of which sex education was one) should be coordinated across the curriculum. Four key stages representing age bands were identified to assist delivery of appropriate information in a developmental manner. However, many revisions in both guidance and legislation occurred subsequently with particular reference to the sex education component.

Advised by counselors and sexual and marital psychotherapists, the medical and nursing professions perceived sex education as important in their own clinical effectiveness in the treatment of sexual dysfunction. Some medical schools and nursing colleges established their own sexual health curriculum, but once more the teaching input focused primarily on the organic and health content of sexuality. The integrative delivery of the subject, supposedly suited to increase knowledge and change attitudes both in higher and professional education (von Bühler and Tamblin 1995), depended on the clinical and scientific expertise of a few professionals, who, in many cases, had to fight against long-held concepts and prejudices. This situation led to an educational lottery with little academic cohesion and, of course, the unavoidable controversy between the purely medical and the more-eclectic approach.

Health economics and a realistic awareness of social needs obliged the government to produce the *Health of the Nation* document in 1992, identifying key areas for intervention. Among the goals listed were the reduction of pregnancies of girls aged 13 to 15 by 50 percent, from 9.5 per 1,000 girls in 1989 to no more than 4.8 per 1,000 girls by the year 2000. England has the highest rate of teenage pregnancies among western European countries. In the document, school sex education was seen as a central means by which the pregnancy targets might be achieved.

Meanwhile an amendment to the Education Act of 1993 was passed without debate in Parliament (effective from September 1994). This required:

1. all secondary schools to have a sex education policy that includes teaching on HIV/AIDS and sexually transmitted disease,
2. biological aspects of sexual behavior to be taught in the science curriculum, and
3. a parental right to withdraw children from all or part of the non-science sex education.

The implications of these amendments are daunting, both in terms of the individual and society. There is much evidence to suggest that the majority of parents do not have the skills or desire to be responsible for the sex education of their children (Allen 1987). More often than not, the needs of girls are understood and addressed more effectively than those of the boys or groups of people with special needs.

The recent authoritative study by Wellings, Field, Johnson, and Wadsworth (1994), *Sexual Behaviour in Britain: The National Survey of Attitudes and Lifestyles,* examined trends in age at first sexual intercourse, and these trends show that during the past four decades, the median age at first heterosexual intercourse has fallen from 21 years to 17 years for women and from 20 to 17 for men. The proportion of respondents reporting sexual intercourse before the age of 16 has increased from fewer than 1 percent in women aged 55 and over, to nearly one in five of those in their teens. (*Note:* This study has also been published as Johnson, et al. 1994, *Sexual Attitudes and Lifestyles.*)

The people of the United Kingdom need to ask what are the real risks for sexually active children and young people? What are the implications for children who receive either none or fragmented and perhaps unreliable sex education? Human sexual activity is associated with increasing levels of risk and disease, unplanned pregnancy, and marital relationship breakdown. The health and sex education of the British government are far too vulnerable to the swings of political and moral pressures. Adolescent sexuality and sexual activity are realities. Effective sex education should offer adequate information, enable the development of communication and social skills, and provide opportunities to explore attitudes, values, and beliefs in a pluralistic society. The balance of these three elements is crucial if sexual issues for the individual and the nation are to be tackled realistically.

B. Informal Sources of Sexual Knowledge

In common with most western European countries, the media plays an important and increasingly more acceptable role in popular sex education.

British television frequently uses specialists in human sexuality and human relationships in research and program presentation. Sex programs are scientifically based in some instances, and in others positive learning occurs through humor and candid discussion of issues. These programs are pluralist. Likewise, radio has increased its importance and credible influence in sex education. Magazines for all ages are available, usually with literary articles of sexual relevance. In 1993, a new educational resource emerged: that of the Sex Education Video in which sexually explicit images are used to teach, for instance, the nature of orgasm and the importance of masturbation. Accustomed to total censorship of more explicit material, the British public still has to pass judgment on these "educational videos."

Professional and voluntary agencies independent of the government frequently publish books or guides on sexuality covering all aspects of sexual function and meaning, from infertility to menopause, from the realities of being gay to the psychodynamics of marriage. Of course, the newspapers are a good fountain of information reporting on sexual matters, particularly after these have been debated in Parliament. Unfortunately, not all newspapers are married to the truth scientifically or philosophically. The theater, cinema, music, and advertising images are also part of the informal sex education movement. Finally, the United Kingdom is rich in voluntary and professional organizations dealing with sexual and relationship issues whose members are active in teaching and bringing to the notice of the general public the importance of sexual knowledge in ownership of their sexuality.

4. Autoerotic Behaviors and Patterns

MARGOT HUISH

The *Shorter Oxford Dictionary* cites the derivation of the word masturbate from the Latin root *manus* (hand) and *stuprare* (to defile) and defines "to masturbate" as "to practice self abuse," with the added definition of "abuse or revilement of oneself, self-pollution." Colloquial and slang forms of the word continue to be used as terms of abuse and derision. However, there are many rich colloquial words and phrases for masturbation, such as "the five knuckle shuffle," "playing the one-eyed piccolo," and "tossing the caber," which graphically describe male rather than female activity. Sex therapists often find that clients express discomfort with the word masturbation and all that it implies. The impression is that clients will use masturbate to describe autoerotic behavior, but will frequently use other forms of expression to describe similar mutual activity in their relationship. This perhaps reinforces the notion that sole masturbation is considered undesirable, whereas mutual or shared masturbation is more acceptable.

Historically, attitudes regarding masturbation have been negative and condemnatory. Masturbation has been seen both as a sin and as a sickness in the teachings of Judaism and Christianity. Not until the end of the nineteenth century was there a shift from the belief that masturbation was the cause of insanity to the suggestion that it was the cause of neurosis and neurasthenia. David S. G. Kay (1992) comments that:

> Following World War I, the major focus shifted from the purely medical to the psychological and to psychiatric analysis of masturbation. . . . Between the two world wars, medical professionals began to perceive masturbation as a harmless sexual behaviour. . . . The Psychoanalytic Society reinforced a conviction that masturbation was not the cause of medical or psychiatric disorders. Recidivistically, various preachers and educators continued to reinforce the Judeo-Christian sex ethic with their condemnation of masturbation . . . [while] psychologists and psychiatrists began to research the relationship between anxiety, guilt and masturbation, since the guilt and anxiety related to masturbation were considered emotionally damaging when transmitted by the family, religion, medicine, law and education.

The impression gathered informally from seven United Kingdom sex therapists is that a high percentage of clients and their partners regard self-masturbation as embarrassing, while others view it as an undesirable practice, cloaked in secrecy and creating feelings of shame and guilt. These negative views appear to have been replicated by respondents involved in the question design work for the survey of *Sexual Attitudes and Lifestyles in the United Kingdom* (1990/1991) (Wellings 1994). Questions on masturbation were reluctantly excluded because the discussion on masturbatory practice had met with distaste and embarrassment. The view of masturbation as a sexually separate, secret, and dark activity may be reinforced in some people's minds when they read national newspaper reports of occasional accidental deaths resulting from unusual autoerotic practices, such as autoasphyxiation and various extreme forms of bondage.

Despite, or perhaps because of, the Victorian legacy of repression and negative attitudes towards masturbation, the activity is frequently mentioned in some comedy programs on United Kingdom television and radio. However, the subject has also been presented with a refreshingly positive image in television and video sex education programs. This reflects the therapeutic value of masturbation as held by professionals within the psychosexual counseling and therapy practices, which reinforces its "normality" and status as a pleasurable sexual expression in its own right. It is perhaps also reflective of the need to encourage safer sex in the age of HIV and AIDS. Therapists have noticed how clients have responded to the "permission giving" aspects of the recent programs when they discuss masturbation. However, within the multicultural mix in the United Kingdom, there are many who associate masturbation, and especially ejaculation, with illness, fatigue, anxiety, mental illness, and loss of power. The more "open" attitude towards masturbation is reflected in radio phone-in programs and in magazines, especially those geared towards the young.

In a recent sex survey in *More!* magazine, completed by over 3,000 females aged between 16 and 25 years, 33 percent said they never masturbated, 33 percent did so rarely, 15 percent masturbated once a week, and 14 percent did so more than once weekly. Forty-four percent of the respondents used fantasies during masturbation, but surprisingly, only 11 percent reported masturbation as the best way to reach orgasm—oral sex and penetrative sex scored higher at 41 percent and 28 percent, respectively.

In an unpublished study, Sevda Zeki reported that out of twenty women aged 65 to 74 years, and twenty aged 75 to 91 years, more-permissive attitudes towards sex had significant statistical relationships with higher reported amounts of masturbation and orgasms in masturbation. A higher level of composite knowledge had a significant relationship with higher reported amounts of masturbation, while women who knew the role of the clitoris in achieving orgasm were more likely to masturbate than those who did not understand clitoral function. Women who had the most permissive attitudes towards women masturbating in their later years were more likely to report that they themselves masturbated.

Sex therapists confirm that sexual knowledge, education, and permissiveness are significant in all age groups when considering views, attitudes, and experience of sex in general and masturbation in particular. The impression given by sex therapy clients during history taking is that a small number of male clients report self-masturbation between ages 4 and 10, but the highest percentage recall starting masturbation between 10 and 14 years. Female clients report starting to masturbate anywhere between 10 and 25 years, but far greater numbers are concentrated at 15 years and upwards, with an impression that a significant number of women have never chosen self-masturbation as a way of expressing their sexuality. It is also the impression that male partners are less likely to expect their female partners to self-masturbate, while these same female partners expect that their husbands/boyfriends do masturbate in secret, especially when there is a sexual dysfunction that precludes or limits the opportunity for penetrative sex. Clients, especially female clients, in individual therapy sessions often admit to self-masturbation, but do not wish their partners to know this information. Therapists report a greater acceptance of masturbation among single clients, and point out that there are many people with physical and learning disabilities for whom masturbation may be the only outlet for the expression of sexual feelings.

Project SIGMA, the first British in-depth study of sex, gay men, and AIDS, surveyed 1,083 gay and bisexual men over a four-year period between 1987 and 1991. Self-masturbation was reported during their lifetime by 99.5 percent of men, while 90 percent reported doing so within the previous month (average seventeen times). The percentages by age group of those engaging in self-masturbation during the previous month were: under age

21, 86 percent; 21 to 30, 92 percent; 31 to 40, 94 percent; and 40 plus, 81 percent. As David S. G. Kay (1992) states:

> Although the high incidence of masturbation is useful information for encouraging its acceptance by clients, the ability of masturbation to produce orgasm has more therapeutic importance. Masturbation has been used in the treatment of erectile failure, premature and retarded ejaculation, general sexual dysfunction, and primary and secondary orgasmic dysfunction. . . . There appear to be no rational arguments for regarding masturbation as undesirable as a private form of sexual activity.

5. Interpersonal Heterosexual Behaviors

A/B. Children and Adolescents   DANYA GLASER

Little research has been conducted on the sexual behavior of children and adolescents in the United Kingdom. Findings from one study of children in different preschool settings show that many children are curious about each others' genitalia, expressing this curiosity by looking at and touching each other. The extent to which such exploratory behavior has mature sexual meaning is unclear. A smaller proportion of pre-school children enact sexual intercourse, usually by lying on top one another while fully dressed. It is likely that such behavior is imitative of adult behavior based on prior observation. These behaviors do not generally give rise to adult concerns unless the children appear preoccupied by genitally oriented activity or the behavior is coercive towards other children.

Oral-genital contact appears to be very rare, as are attempts to insert fingers or objects into another child's vagina or anus. Coercive, preoccupied or very explicitly imitative behavior is associated with previous significant and inappropriate exposure to adult sexual activity, or sexual abuse of the child.

C. Adults   JANE WADSWORTH, ANNE M. JOHNSON,
                                          KAYE WELLINGS, AND JULIA FIELD

The National Survey of Sexual Attitudes and Lifestyles

In 1990 and 1991, Wadsworth, Johnson, Wellings, and Field undertook a large population survey in Great Britain, *The National Survey of Sexual Attitudes and Lifestyles* (Johnson et al. 1992, 1994; Wellings et al. 1994). A key aim of this survey was to provide information for models to predict the epidemic of HIV using data on partnerships and activity, but in addition, this study provided valuable information about sexual behavior in the United Kingdom as well as specific information of practical use in the planning of sexual health services—genitourinary medicine clinics, family planning, and sex education—and health promotion strategy.

The national study involved interviews of a random sample of 18,876 men and women aged 16 to 59. The responses were obtained partly through a face-to-face interview and partly from a booklet which was completed by the respondent and sealed in an envelope out of sight of the interviewer to ensure complete confidentiality. Questions were asked about first sexual experiences, sex education, contraception, fertility, numbers and sex of partners, frequency of sexual intercourse, prevalence of different sexual practices, and, for men, contact with prostitutes. Other topics included attitudes towards sexual behavior and AIDS, family of origin and current family circumstances, educational achievements, and employment. The full methodology has been published (Johnson et al. 1994; Wadsworth et al. 1993). Among the more important findings were the following:

1. *Age at First Heterosexual Intercourse (Sexarche).* The median age at first intercourse for men and women now in their 50s was 20, while for those under 20 it was 17, a decline of three years over three decades. An increase among young people in intercourse under the age of 16—in Britain the age of legal consent for women—is closely associated with this change. Seven percent of men and 1 percent of women now in their 50s first had intercourse before they became 16, while 28 percent of the men and 19 percent of the women aged 16 to 19 had done so.

2. *Number of Partners of the Opposite Sex.* The numbers of heterosexual partners reported in different time intervals are shown in Table 1. Very similar proportions of both men and women had no partners in the previous year, in the last five years, or ever. Three quarters of men and women had only one partner in the previous year, while half the men and two thirds of the women had one partner in the previous five years. However, men were more likely to report large numbers of partners than women.

The number of partners was strongly related to age and marital status. Twenty percent of young people, aged 16 to 24, reported no partners in the previous five years, but they were twice as likely as those aged 25 to 34 to report ten or more partners. In contrast, over 80 percent of those aged 45 to 59 had one partner in the previous five years. Married people were less likely to have had more than one partner in the previous year (5 percent of men and 2 percent of women) than single people (28 percent of men and 18 percent of women).

Those who were cohabiting (by their own description as living with a partner of the opposite sex to whom they were not married) were less likely to have had only one partner than those who were married (15 percent of men and 8 percent of women had more than one partner in the last year). Multivariate analysis showed that age and marital status were most strongly

Table 1

Number of Partners of the Opposite Sex in Different Time Intervals (in Percentages)

Time Interval	Number of Partners	Male (*n* = 8,047)	Female (*n* = 10,059)
Ever	0	6.8	5.9
	1	20.9	39.1
	2	10.7	17.0
	3-4	18.6	18.4
	5-9	19.5	13.2
	10+	24.5	6.8
In the past 5 years	0	8.9	9.3
	1	56.4	67.1
	2	10.1	11.3
	3-4	12.2	8.2
	5-9	8.1	3.7
	10+	4.8	0.2
In the past year	0	13.3	14.2
	1	72.5	78.6
	2	8.4	4.9
	3-4	4.1	1.8
	5+	1.8	0.1

Percentages approximated by the General Editor from a bar graph provided by the authors and adapted from Johnson, Wadsworth, Wellings, and Fields, 1994, p. 115.

associated with numbers of partners, but first intercourse before age 16 was also positively associated with numbers of partners.

3. Frequency of Sexual Intercourse. The median frequency of intercourse was three times during the preceding four weeks. But this varied with age as well as with the length and status of the current relationship. Among married or cohabiting people aged 16 to 24, the median frequency was seven times in the previous four weeks. Multivariate analysis showed that in addition to age and marital status, frequency of intercourse was inversely related to the duration of the current relationship, but positively associated with numbers of partners in the last five years.

4. Sexual Practices. For the majority of respondents, sexual intercourse involved vaginal intercourse. Oral sex (fellatio and/or cunnilingus), anal sex, and nonpenetrative sex were less commonly practiced (Table 2). Younger people were more likely to report sexual practices other than vaginal intercourse, as were those in long-term relationships.

Table 2

Prevalence of Different Sexual Practices in the Previous Year (in Percentages)

	Men (n =7,870)	Women (n = 9,786)
Vaginal Intercourse	85.6	84.7
Cunnilingus/Fellatio	62.6	56.6
Nonpenetrative Sex	65.6	60.5
Anal Sex	6.9	6.1

Percentages approximated by the General Editor from a bar graph provided by the authors and adapted from Johnson, Wadsworth, Wellings, and Fields, 1994, p. 164.

Those who had more than one partner in the previous year were also more likely to report oral, anal, and nonpenetrative sex than those who had one partner. Oral sex and nonpenetrative sex have become more commonly practiced among respondents who became sexually active in recent decades compared with those who became sexually active in the 1950s and 1960s, but no such trend is shown for anal sex.

5. *Sexual Diversity.* Sexual experience with a partner of the same sex at some time in their lives was reported by 3.6 percent of the men and 1.8 percent of women. These proportions appear not to have changed with successive generations, but there are pronounced geographical variations, particularly among men. In the previous five years, 1.4 percent of the men had had a male partner in Great Britain as a whole. In greater London, however, this proportion was 4.6 percent, just over three times as many.

Considering only those who have ever had a homosexual partnership (Figure 1), only 9 percent of men and 5 percent of women have been exclusively homosexual throughout their life. In the last year, 19 percent of the men had male partners, 62 percent had female partners, and 10 percent had both male and female partners. Similar patterns were found for women respondents, but a slightly higher proportion had exclusively male partners.

6. *Attitudes to Sexual Behavior.* Data on attitudes towards sexuality showed that people in Great Britain have a strong commitment to monogamy, together with marked toleration of premarital sex. Fewer than 10 percent of respondents believed that sex before marriage is wrong, but 80 percent of respondents felt that sex outside marriage is wrong.

Commitment to a regular ("steady") relationship was valued almost as highly as marriage, particularly among women. Homosexual relationships were considered to be wrong by almost 60 percent of women and 70 percent of men. Attitudes towards sexuality varied considerably with experience. For example, fewer than 50 percent of the men who have experienced sex

Figure 1

Sex of the Partners of Respondents Who Ever Had a Homosexual Relationship

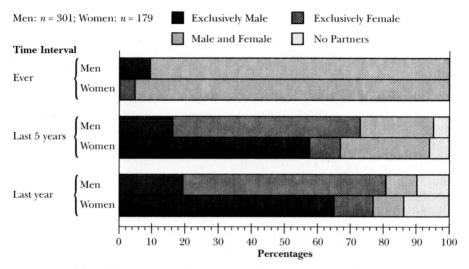

Adapted from Johnson, Wadsworth, Wellings, and Fields, 1994, p. 210.

outside marriage considered adultery to be wrong, compared with 80 percent of the men who had not had this experience.

These data show considerable diversity of sexual behavior in the general population of the United Kingdom. The majority have faithful relationships with one partner ("serial monogamy"), even if during their lifetime the majority of British men and women have had more than one partner.

Frequency of sexual intercourse is strongly related to the duration of the relationship, as well as to the respondent's age. Vaginal intercourse is the most popular form of having sex, and experience of anal intercourse is reported by only about one in twenty respondents, slightly more by men than women. Greater diversity in sexual practices is more likely among those who report more partners.

Patterns of homosexual behavior show geographical variations with a markedly increased prevalence in central London. More than half of those of either sex who have ever had a partner of the same sex have had one or more partners of the opposite sex also. There have been changes in heterosexual behavior across the generations, particularly in the age of first sexual intercourse and the increase in those who have experienced sexual intercourse before the age of 16.

The pattern of partnerships clearly shows that people in Great Britain have larger numbers of partners when they are young and if they have not settled into a committed relationship. Men have more partners than women and nearly a quarter of men reported ten or more partners. There are, however, some differences between couples who are married and those who are living together without being married. In particular, the data suggest that extra relationships are more likely among those who are cohabiting than among married couples.

D. Sex and Persons with Disabilities   TINA BALL

Historically, the whole area of sexuality for people with disabilities has been seen as problematic and negative within the United Kingdom. Fears of "moral degeneracy" and eugenic theories led to the mass segregation of people with learning disabilities in institutions throughout most of the twentieth century (Burns 1993). People with physical disabilities have often been seen as asexual (Williams 1993). The sexual and relationship difficulties of people with acquired cognitive impairments (and their partners) have been particularly unmentionable and even unthinkable.

At present, there are several strands contributing to changes in this picture. Some people continue to believe that sexuality should not be considered for those with disabilities. Some parents of young people with congenital disabilities often express fears and anxieties as their children begin to express sexual interests and wish they could stay as "holy innocents." However, the growing self-advocacy movements and the political movements of people with disabilities have ensured that disabled people's own voices have been heard asserting their sexual natures and needs. An example of this would be the way in which the leadership of the Association to Aid the Sexual and Personal Relationships of People with a Disability (formerly SPOD) has been taken over by people with disabilities.

Professionals have developed a range of sex education approaches and packages for persons with disabilities. Typical of these materials are those designed for people with learning disabilities (Craft 1991; McCarthy and Thompson 1992). Involving parents in these educational initiatives has been shown to be very valuable (Craft and Crosby 1991). Another example is the sex education materials created by people with learning disabilities for their own use (People First 1993).

The incidence of sexual problems is probably higher among people with all kinds of disabilities than it is in the general population. Negative attitudes towards people with disabilities lead to restricted opportunities for the development of sexual relationships; at the same time, an impaired or negative self-image can inhibit healthy sexual functioning. Some kinds of physical disabilities directly cause sexual problems, e.g., spinal cord injuries and multiple sclerosis. The growth in importance of physical treatments for erectile dysfunction, in particular, appears to be leading to a much more active approach to the assessment and treatment of such difficulties in specialist services, with many employing nurses and other health-care professionals to work with persons who have sexual problems linked with or resulting from their disabilities. There remains much room for improvement in this area. The awareness and understanding of the impact of particular disabling conditions on women's sexual functioning and relationships remains less well understood and has certainly received less attention in the literature (Williams 1993).

Sexual dysfunction in people with learning disabilities has also received little attention. Studies have indicated a high level of negative experiences of sex, including dyspareunia in women with learning disabilities (e.g., McCarthy 1993). There is undoubtedly a higher than average incidence of sexual abuse of both women and men with learning disabilities (Turk and Brown 1993). The law recognizes this vulnerability and there are specific laws designed to protect people with learning disabilities from sexual exploitation (Gunn 1991). The complexity of the legal situation at times deters staff members who are working with people with learning disabilities from offering appropriate support and education, especially if they are already uneasy with sexual issues. Several local authorities, health authorities, and voluntary agencies have designed policy statements on sexuality in an attempt to provide clear guidelines for care staff and other professionals (e.g., East Sussex 1992; Hertfordshire County Council 1989). There are also increasing moves to work to prevent and treat sexual abuse in people with learning disabilities (Craft 1993).

E. Incidence of Oral Sex and Anal Sex   KEVAN R. WYLIE

The *National Survey of Sexual Attitudes and Lifestyles* (1994) revealed that oral sex was a common experience, although less so than vaginal intercourse and nonpenetrative sex. Experience of cunnilingus was slightly greater for both men (72.9 percent) and women (66.2 percent) than fellatio (69.4 percent of men and 64.0 percent of women). Overall experience of oral sex was reported by 75.2 percent of men and 69.2 percent of women. More than 80 percent reported practicing both forms of oral sex in the previous year, and it was usually practiced alongside vaginal intercourse.

Anal intercourse was practiced by less than 7 percent of all men and women, although a higher percentage of men had experience with it (13.9 percent of men and 12.9 percent of women). It was rarely practiced in isolation from other sexual activities. At the time of the survey legal restrictions made such a practice an offense, which has subsequently been changed. (See also Section 8 on rape.)

6. Homoerotic, Homosexual, and Ambisexual Behaviors
ANTHONY BAINS

Heterosexism, the assumption that everyone is heterosexual and the subsequent discrimination against same-sex desire and attraction in men and women, is a significant cultural ideology in the United Kingdom. Sexual diversity in all its manifestations is not encouraged legally, socially, or politically.

The legal situation for lesbians and gay men in the United Kingdom is not a positive one. There are no laws to protect lesbians and gay men from discrimination. Male homosexuality was only partially decriminalized in 1967, for those men over the age of 21, with the stipulation that it would occur in private and with no more than two persons present. The age of consent for sex between men has since been reduced to age 18 (The Criminal Justice and Public Order Act 1994), but this is still two years above that for heterosexuals. Significantly, legislation has never stipulated an age of consent for lesbians, due to the invisibility of, and public refusal to accept lesbian sexuality.

Other examples of discrimination against lesbians and gay men include their being banned from the Armed Forces and being ineligible for marriage under British law. A piece of legislation in the late 1980s also legitimized prejudice and discrimination against homosexuals. Section 28 added a new Section 2A to the Local Government Act of 1986, which states that a local authority shall not "intentionally promote homosexuality or publish material with the intention of promoting homosexuality." It would appear that such legislation is supported to a significant extent by social attitudes. Wellings et al. (1994) reported that 70.2 percent of men and 57.9 percent of the women surveyed believe that sex between two men is always or mostly wrong.

The experience of institutionalized or personal homophobia and heterosexism can affect the self-esteem of lesbians, gay men, and bisexuals, with implications for their emotional and mental well-being. In the face of such marginalization and stigmatization, the process of "coming out"—informing people of one's homosexuality or bisexuality and thus challenging preconceptions of heterosexuality—can be incredibly empowering. Acknowledging one's own sexual identity, informing those who share one's surroundings, and meeting people who share one's sexual identity to gain support and solidarity can be a major step on the road to healthy self-acceptance for many lesbians, gay men, and bisexuals.

In spite of the oppressive culture towards lesbians, gay men, and bisexuals, or perhaps because of this, strong, diverse lesbian, gay, and bisexual communities have developed, predominantly in the larger cities of the United Kingdom, such as London, Manchester, and Edinburgh. There are networks across the United Kingdom, reaching into the more rural areas, to provide a range of services to lesbians, gay men, and bisexuals, including telephone helplines, counseling, and social groups. There are also numerous lobbying groups from all shades of the political spectrum, working for lesbian, gay, and bisexual rights.

The emergence of HIV and its devastating impact on gay communities has led to a huge community response, with many of the United Kingdom's major national and local voluntary groups being set up by gay men.

Lesbians, gay men, and bisexuals meet each other in a variety of settings, and through various means, at pubs and cafés, saunas, social groups, parties, parks, and other "cruising areas," as well as through personal advertisements in a variety of publications. Most of the United Kingdom's larger cities and towns have a commercial gay scene and some semblance of a visible lesbian, gay, and bisexual community. The media has also been used to exchange information and promote this sense of community. There are national and local lesbian and gay newspapers, magazines, radio programs, and film festivals. The mainstream-quality media also often run stories and features from a lesbian and gay perspective. Lesbian and gay film seasons and programs have also been screened on television.

The growing confidence among lesbian, gay, and bisexual communities has also been illustrated by the increasing number and scale of festivals and parades around the United Kingdom, where lesbians, gay men, and bisexuals have come together, building and promoting a sense of community. In 1995, the annual Lesbian, Gay, and Bisexual Pride Festival in London attracted approximately 200,000 people.

The lesbian, gay, and bisexual communities of the United Kingdom are diverse, with same-sex desire cutting across age, class, ethnicity, religion, culture, ability, and health status. This is illustrated by the plethora of support and interest groups that have emerged to address these concerns.

7. Gender Conflicted Persons
STEPHEN WHITTLE AND GWYNETH A. SAMPSON

Transvestism and transsexualism are moderately visible phenomenon in United Kingdom society in the 1990s. However, this is a fairly recent state of affairs and the reasons for this are manifold, despite the fact that there is little legal recognition of the new gender status of a person who experiences a gender conflict or has undergone sex-reassignment treatment.

Male transvestism has long been a feature of the theater from the late medieval period when cross-dressing males provided the female characters for the stage. Cross-dressing, or drag as it is referred to, remains popular as a stage act, with artists such as Danny la Rue and more recently Lily Savage gaining national popularity. Female cross-dressing has not had such prominence, the writer Radclyffe Hall and the entertainer Vesta Tilly being notable exceptions in the 1920s and 1930s.

However, transvestism has remained a peripheral activity with little social acceptance on a more personal level. Since the Beaumont Society was organized in the late 1960s to provide advice and safe social meeting venues for heterosexual transvestites, there has been a gradual proliferation of similar groupings. There now exists a variety of organizations and venues throughout the country where men may crossdress in discrete venues. The development of "gay village" areas in the late 1980s and 1990s in many major cities has provided other locales, such as public houses and clubs, where heterosexual and homosexual transvestites may meet and socialize. There is also a large underground network of "contact magazines" that allow homosexual and bisexual transvestites to make sexual contacts. It is difficult to estimate the total number of transvestites in the United Kingdom, as there has been little if any attempt to extrapolate figures.

There is little social acknowledgment of female cross-dressing. Female cross-dressing is generally viewed as belonging to a particular subgroup of lesbian culture, radical lesbians and "butch dykes," although 1995 witnessed the opening of the first "drag king" club, Naive, in London.

Transsexuals are a much more visible feature of British society, having gained considerable media interest. Newspapers, women's magazines, and television have regular features concerned with transsexualism. Nonetheless, the individual transsexual may be in fact far more hidden than this media interest otherwise portrays. The first recorded transsexual surgery in Britain was performed in 1944 by Sir Harold Gilles, an eminent plastic surgeon, on Michael Dillon, a female-to-male transsexual. Since then, several thousand transsexuals have gained sex-reassignment surgery in the United Kingdom or abroad. Again, little work has been done to count the total number of transsexuals, but estimates based upon the numbers who have attended recognized Gender Identity Clinics put the figure of those who have joined self-help organizations and those who have gained media attention at around 10,000 to 15,000 transsexuals in the United Kingdom (McMullen and Whittle 1995). Several have published highly regarded autobiographical accounts—most notably racing-car driver Roberta Cowell (1954), the climber and *London Times* journalist Jan Morris (1974), models April Ashley (1982), Caroline Cossey (1991), Tula, and, most recently, journalist Paul Hewitt (1995) and Raymond Thompson (1995).

Some individuals with gender-identity disorder seek medical help and support. In the United Kingdom, this is usually provided by general practitioners and psychiatric services; the number of individuals seeking such help is unknown.

In the United Kingdom, the classification of mental and behavioral disorders is by the *ICD-10 Classification of Mental and Behavioural Disorders.* Diagnostic criteria from *ICD-10* and *DSM-IV* (*Diagnostic and Statistical Manual*) identify that the individual has a strong and persistent cross-gender identification, with persistent discomfort with his or her sex or sense of inappropriateness in the gender role of that sex. There is a preoccupation with getting rid of primary and secondary sex characteristics, e.g., requests for hormones or surgery, or a belief that he or she was born the wrong sex. To make a diagnosis, symptoms must have been present for at least two years and cause clinically significant distress or impairment in social, occupational, or other important areas of functioning. Differential diagnoses include fetishistic transvestism (cross-dressing for sexual excitement), schizophrenia, or temporal lobe epilepsy. The help individuals request includes personal counseling, relationship counseling, education, endocrine therapy, speech therapy, advice on social skills and personal grooming, gender-re-alignment surgery, and follow-up care after gender reassignment.

Historically, several centers established local Gender Identity clinics—e.g., Charing Cross Gender Identity Clinic was established by psychiatrist John Randell in the early 1970s. The separation of the Purchaser and Provider elements of health delivery in the United Kingdom has now altered the provision of National Health Service care to gender-conflicted persons. Purchasing authorities vary in the help they will purchase locally, and many authorities have not yet developed clear guidelines for purchasing or providing a service for gender-conflicted persons. Some do not purchase a service, others will purchase assessment by a professional—usually a psychiatrist but may be a psychologist or nurse—for diagnosis without any further treatment. A limited number will purchase assessment and therapy. In terms of provision, general practitioners may prescribe endocrine therapy, and some psychiatric services provide counseling, specific training, and medical treatment. The provision of gender-realignment surgery within the National Health Service is very limited; the majority of individuals seek this privately.

There is limited research in the United Kingdom to evaluate the benefits of gender-reassignment therapy, but there is a view that medical interventions can lead to an improved quality of life for the individual. There is also a widely accepted view that hastily undertaken medical and surgical interventions, often conducted at the urgent behest of the applicants, can sometimes lead to disastrous results, including suicide. The small number of specialist National Health Services in the United Kingdom all concur with the guidelines for ethical clinical practice drawn up by the Harry Benjamin International Gender Dysphoria Association.

The majority of transvestites (dual-role transvestism) do not seek clinical treatment or help unless their behavior causes secondary relationship or social difficulties. Fetishistic transvestism is commonly reported as an earlier phase by transsexuals and, therefore, in some individuals may represent a stage in the development of transsexualism.

The current legal position for transsexuals was embodied in the common law decision in the case of Corbett vs. Corbett (1970, All ER, 33-48). In this case, the marriage between a male-to-female postsurgical reassignment transsexual and a male partner was declared to be void. It was held that, for the purposes of marriage, transsexuals would always be of their original sex designation at birth. It has also been held that the birth certificate records in the United Kingdom are a record of historical fact, and hence unalterable unless there was a substantial mistake at the time of registration. As a result, although transsexuals on one level seem to be accommodated by the United Kingdom law in that most of their personal documentation can be altered to show their new gender grouping and their new name, their birth certificate records, which are used as a form of identification for many purposes, will still show their old status and name, and they cannot marry a member of the opposite-gender (i.e., same-sex) grouping. This means that for all legal purposes they remain a member of their natal sex grouping. The iniquities that result from this, not only in terms of personal privacy, but also inadequate protection in employment legislation, have meant that transsexuals in the United Kingdom have taken the government to the European Court of Human Rights on several occasions. The case of Rees v. UK (1987, 9 EHRR 56) led to a compromise solution whereby passports may now record the new name and gender status of the transsexual on production of a sworn declaration of name change and a doctor's letter to the effect that the gender change undergone is permanent.

However, transsexuals have not been satisfied with this solution and are continuing to plead their cause to the government through the campaigning group Press for Change, which provides legal advice and encourages parliamentary lobbying. As of 1995, Press for Change was supporting two cases before the European Commission of Human Rights, one before the European Court of Justice, and had several more waiting on the sidelines.

There are several self-help organizations for transsexuals, and many join these, albeit often only in their initial stages of transition. The largest are The Gender Trust, which predominately caters to male-to-female transsexuals, and the FTM Network, which caters to female-to-male transsexuals. At any one time, both of these organizations have over 350 members. Transsexualism is becoming increasingly socially accepted in the United Kingdom with transsexuals retaining or obtaining high-status job positions, including in education, positions in local government, and high-profile positions in the entertainment industry. It must only be a matter of time before transsexuals obtain full legal recognition of their new status alongside their increased social acceptance.

8. Significant Unconventional Sexual Behaviors

KEVAN R. WYLIE

A. Child Sexual Abuse, Incest, and Pedophilia

Any form of sexual contact between adults and children evokes an emotive reaction. Sexual abuse of young children, intrafamilial sexual abuse (usually incestuous), and extrafamilial (usually pedophilia) are all offenses in the United Kingdom. Increasing awareness of child sexual abuse (CSA) has ensured a more-sympathetic approach to dealing with victims. It is accepted that sexual abuse is a traumatic event for most children, and for some, that it is followed by a post-traumatic stress reaction. The advantages and limitations in applying therapy to such a framework in the United Kingdom have been described by Jehu (1991).

There is evidence of an increased number of proceedings against offenders over the last decade, but it remains unclear whether this is a real increase in the number of offenses or improved methods of securing evidence for prosecution. While real or reporting patterns may have changed through the influences of feminism, media attention, academic acceptance, and public sensitization to such crimes, it is probably the case that "old attitudes die hard." There have been cases in the United Kingdom in which public opinion has turned surprisingly against those reporting child sexual abuse (the Cleveland affair, Orkney ritual abuse, and Rochdale Satanic abuse cases).

Police, social services, educational, and health services are now duty-bound to inform each other when cases of alleged abuse occur. Regional units within the United Kingdom have facilities to record interview sessions on video of children being asked open questions about the alleged abuse. Recent changes brought about by the Criminal Justice Act (1994) allow the use of video disclosure of abuse to a social worker for presentation in court. Video links within the court allow questioning of the minor in a room separate from the court to avoid the minor's facing the offender directly. Social workers have a statutory duty to be involved with families when children are placed on the "At Risk" register and must act on the balance of probability. The police, on the other hand, must establish beyond reasonable doubt that an offense has occurred. Offenders are charged with indecent assault. Inappropriate touching and the circumstances of the event are pivotal in deciding to embark with criminal proceedings. Corroborative statements, whenever possible, and medical evidence is often vital. There is however, no time limit for bringing such offenses to court.

There is currently debate in the United Kingdom regarding the reality of "false memory syndrome," with cases of abuse being alleged up to twenty years or later than the alleged offenses took place. There are reports in the United Kingdom of men in their 60s and 70s being given short custodial sentences for offenses of sexual abuse or incest that occurred many years previously.

In 1994, prosecution of around 2,000 cases of indecent assault on females under 16 years of age were initiated and around 65 percent of those charged were found guilty. Only half of these were given custodial sentences. The punishment can be ten years imprisonment. It has been argued by Fisher and Howells (1993) that significant social-skill deficits occur in some sex offenders. Where these exist, the deficit is in the cognitive component of social competence. Sex offenders often have major difficulties in establishing and maintaining longer-term intimate relationships, with factors likely to include empathy deficits and inappropriate culturally induced expectations concerning sexual relationships. A recent article presented opinion as to whether a sexual offender should be allowed castration where there is a history of persistent sexual abuse (Alexander et al. 1993).

In law, incest is the act of intercourse by a man with a woman he knows to be his daughter, granddaughter, sister (or half sister), or mother. Three quarters of the cases reported involve father-daughter incest. Incest implies consent—although this is no defense—and is differentiated from unlawful sexual intercourse with a girl under the age of 13 or 16. All are offenses under the Sexual Offenses Act 1956. The punishment for incest is seven years custodial sentence, unless the girl is under 13. If this is the case (effectively constituting rape), the punishment is life imprisonment. The number of persons proceeded against on the offense of incest are a small proportion of those charged with CSA.

The incidence of pedophilia is unknown in the United Kingdom. A small central unit exists to investigate this area, and while the offense is abhorred, limited resources are available to seek out actively and investigate crimes being committed by pedophiles. Several lobby groups now exist to promote awareness of the existence of this problem and the need for active targeting of police time towards preventing the continuation of such practices. Further, to date no national register exists to identify individuals when changing residence. It is not normally the case that such offenders are offered therapy unless supervised probation is ordered. (See also Section 8E below.)

B. Sexual Harassment   HELEN MOTT AND ROHAN COLLIER

Incidence

Sexual harassment is a widespread problem in British society. What marks it as an "unconventional" behavior, therefore, is not a question of rarity but the fact that it is recognized as wrongful conduct under the law, particularly that relating to the workplace (see below). Its roots in patriarchal society mean that, for the most part, it is women who suffer most from sexual harassment inflicted by men, although the concept has been extended to cover alternative permutations. While sexual harassment, as an exercise in gendered power relations, can be seen to affect women in all walks of life (Wise and Stanley 1987), in general usage, the term is understood to refer primarily to the experience of women in the workplace.

There are as many definitions of sexual harassment as there are theoretical approaches to it, although most contain the common elements of citing conduct based on sex or of a sexual nature that is unwelcome or offensive, and/or detrimental to the interests of the recipient. This emphasis on the recipient creates a tension between objective and subjective standards, so that although the term "sexual harassment" is common currency, people's ideas about what constitutes it can vary widely. Thus, a National Opinion Polls survey in 1991 found that one in six women said they had experienced sexual harassment, but when they were asked whether they had experienced certain kinds of unwanted sexual behavior that offended them, the figure rose to one in three (Collier 1995, 56). The results of this survey, and others like it, suggest that people may be reluctant to label the full range of potentially sexually harassing behaviors as harassment per se.

The likelihood of a formal complaint being made to the authorities in the case of sexual harassment also appears to be low. Davidson and Earnshaw (1991) found that 65 percent of personnel directors in their study believed that between 70 and 100 percent of cases were never reported to them. This supports North American research (e.g., Livingston 1982, who claims that only 2.5 percent of harassment victims took any official action). For reasons such as these, it is therefore very difficult to attempt to quantify the incidence of sexual harassment. Recent surveys in Britain seem to show that, on average, between 30 percent and 50 percent of women claim to have experienced sexual harassment at work (Marks 1991; Industrial Society 1993; London Buses Ltd. 1991; Mott and Condor 1995), although in certain occupations, such as the police force, the figure has been as high as 90 percent (Her Majesty's Inspectorate of Constabulary 1993). The scale of the problem suggests that it is ill-advised to concentrate upon the likely psychological "profile" of the harasser (or, indeed, the recipient). While individual factors may be relevant to individual cases, it is clear that sexual harassment is essentially a social problem.

Legal Penalties

As noted above, it is rare for complaints to reach any level of "authority," and it is, therefore, rarer still for the legal system to become formally involved. Although not a named civil wrong or criminal offense, sexual harassment cases in Britain can be brought within the ambit of several laws. Presently, most cases are dealt with at Industrial Tribunal under the Sex Discrimination Act (1975). This Act, which is applicable to all institutions, makes it unlawful to discriminate by treating a woman less favorably than a man on the grounds of her sex. It also makes it unlawful to victimize a woman who has complained of sexual harassment, to promise or withhold benefits in exchange for sexual favors, or to subject her to any detrimental action. All of these elements of the Sex Discrimination Act can be relevant to sexual harassment in the workplace, and are applicable to men as well as women, although the scarcity of recorded cases brought by men tends to suggest that this application is more theoretical than practical. Generally, both the individual harasser and the relevant organization will be jointly liable, unless the organization can prove that it has taken reasonable steps to prevent sexual harassment. Complainants can expect to receive monetary compensation (for which there is no upper limit) for financial loss, medical expenses, and damages such as injury to feelings. Tribunals may also require that the organization takes steps to prevent harassment happening again, or to transfer the harasser within the organization.

Cases can also be brought to the Industrial Tribunal under the Employment Protection (Consolidation) Act (1978) when a person has been an employee of the relevant organization for at least two years full-time. Victims of harassment might claim constructive dismissal (if they were in effect obliged to resign), or unfair dismissal if, as a direct or indirect consequence of being sexually harassed, they were dismissed from work. The Tribunal can rule for the reinstatement, reengagement, or for compensation of the injured party (subject to certain financial limits).

The number of cases involving sexual harassment brought to the Industrial Tribunal in Britain under the Sex Discrimination Act has been steadily increasing since 1986. There is concern that the requirement under the Act to prove disparate treatment of the sexes prevents some cases from being adequately addressed. The aim of the Tribunal is to uphold the rights of the victim, and thereby to provide a remedy, such as compensation. This can certainly penalize the perpetrator by the award of damages, but there is no power to punish. For these reasons, legal commentators such as Dine and Watt (1995) have recently called for more victims of harassment to take their cases to the civil or criminal courts, a practice that is currently rare.

In the civil courts, victims of harassment can have wider remedies available to them. For example, they can sue the employing organization for breach of contract through having failed in their implied duty of trust and confidence. The harasser can be sued for the tort of trespass to the person. This would certainly cover actual physical touching, and may well include verbal harassment. Where the harasser has physically touched the victim, they may also be prosecuted in the criminal courts for various offenses, such as assault, indecent assault, or false imprisonment, that are recognized under the criminal law.

In 1991, the EC issued a Code of Practice concerning sexual harassment, following a recommendation asking member states to promote awareness of the unacceptable nature of sexual harassment. This code points out that sexual harassment is a form of sex discrimination and is, therefore, unlawful under the Equal Treatment Directive (1976). The code also provides for the inclusion of harassment on the grounds of sexuality, in addition to gender, as "sexual harassment," and makes explicit links between racial and sexual harassment. (British theorists such as Kitzinger [1994] have commented upon the secondary victimization of, for example, lesbians and members of other "minority" groups as a part of sexual harassment.) In addition, the code recommends that organizations provide a clear policy prohibiting sexual harassment in the workplace and guaranteeing prompt and efficient action in the event of harassment. Taken together with the current British laws, this Code of Practice should strengthen the hand of those seeking to challenge the prevalence of sexual harassment in the workplace.

Social Response

The category of behavior that we now call sexual harassment has a very long history, although its naming has come relatively very recently. Sexual harassment as a concept came to Britain from North America in the late 1970s and early-80s with the publication of Farley's (1978) and MacKinnon's (1979) highly influential texts. These texts, however, were academic, and it is only much more recently that "sexual harassment" has passed into the wider domain, so that since the late 1980s, it has been a topic for public discussion and debate. Since that time, there has been coverage in the press of successful Industrial Tribunal cases, and the subject has been addressed as a story line in the two most popular television soap operas. In the year running from May 1993 to May 1994, no less than 90 articles in *The Times* newspaper discussed sexual harassment.

Women are now much more aware of their rights and have higher expectations in terms of how they are treated at work than in the past. However, a recent study (Mott and Condor 1995) revealed that women continue to find it difficult to confront sexual harassment, as dominant workplace ideologies that legitimize unsolicited sexual behavior and mitigate against confrontation remain. It is also clear that the pervasive and everyday nature of much sexual harassment (especially in the form of sexual remarks and "joking") in many workplaces makes it unrealistic to expect an immediate changeover to zero tolerance.

There is also evidence that both women (e.g., Mott and Condor 1995) and men (e.g., Watson 1994) sometimes provide explanations for sexual harassment based on a reductionist view, which Watson has termed a "conceptual red herring": that sexual harassment is primarily a behavior driven by sexual motivation. This approach, which has much in common with early approaches to the phenomenon of rape, can serve to obfuscate the important issues of power, responsibility, and resolution. It is anticipated that, with time, the prevalence of this view will decrease.

Results from many studies have shown that sexual harassment can have a devastating effect for victims, both in terms of their performance at work and their personal well-being. Eighty-six percent of harassment victims in the COHSE (1991) study reported an adverse effect on emotional well-being, while 33 percent said that their quality of work deteriorated. Despite this, and despite the potential risks of litigation, the response of many organizations and trade unions to the problem has not been adequate. In the study mentioned above, over half the employees who complained of harassment felt that their complaints had not been dealt with adequately, and 10 percent found that they, rather than the harasser, had effectively been punished by being transferred to another job or department. An Industrial Society survey (1993) found that 60 percent of British employers had no sexual harassment policy in place.

C. Rape   KEVAN R. WYLIE

In England and Wales, rape is defined as sexual intercourse with a woman without her consent. This must involve penile penetration "to the slightest degree" of the vagina. Emission is not necessary for the act to constitute rape. Penetration of the anus constitutes "buggery," and penetration of the mouth constitutes "gross indecency" or "indecent assault." Attitudes towards rape have changed over the last couple of decades, with women feeling more able to report cases to the police. There was a twofold increase in the proportion of rapes committed by "intimates" (30 percent of all rapes by 1985) and in the number of rapes taking place indoors, particularly in the home of the victim, which had similarly doubled (30 percent of all rapes by 1985).

Police forces now have dedicated nonpolice-station units where persons alleging rape are counseled. These units often resemble living dwellings rather than the institutional nature of the police station. Within the units are video interview rooms and a medical suite. Premises and facilities of victim examination suites are reviewed by Lewington and Rogers (1995). Should the victim be willing to make a formal statement, attempts to trace the offender take place to allow for questioning of the suspect. It remains the case that victims of rape experience anonymity during court proceedings, while the offender is not offered such protection.

Victims are offered support by Rape Crisis and Victim Support units. Cohn (1990) found that the incidence of rape, as well as assault, burglary, collective violence, and domestic violence, increased with ambient temperature, at least up to about 85° Fahrenheit, and concluded that, in general, the most violent crimes against persons occurred linearly with increasing ambient temperature, while property crimes did not strongly relate to temperature changes.

The issue of "date rape" has started to make an impression in the United Kingdom, although it does not constitute a specific offense as such. The issue of stranger rape has been construed by some as "clumsy seduction." Marital rape is now accepted as an offense.

Rape is an offense under the Sexual Offenses Act 1956 and there has been a threefold increase in the number of cases in which proceedings have started in the courts in England and Wales over the last decade. Of the 1,625 cases proceeded against in 1994, just under a quarter were found guilty and sentenced. Almost all of these cases were punished with immediate custodial sentences, which is normally life imprisonment. Sentencing has shown a general trend towards an increased length of custodial sentence passed. In sentencing, judges are less likely to regard prior consensual contact as a valid reason for passing noncustodial sentences on convicted rapists (Lloyd 1991).

A number of male partners of rape victims remain seriously troubled many months after the rape (Bateman and Mendelssohn 1989) and have become profoundly worried about their identity as men, shunning their male friends, avoiding sexual contact with their partner, and withdrawing from regular social interaction. They may require intensive psychoanalytic therapy to begin to understand what it means for them that their partner has been raped.

In a review of sexual offenders, rapists were found more likely to report having a current female partner and to have experienced consenting heterosexual intercourse with an adult, than were nonincest offenders against male children. However, no evidence emerged that rapists and nonincest offenders against female children differed significantly in this respect (Bownes 1993). Using the GRIMS and GRISS questionnaires, the investigation found evidence of marital and relationship difficulties and sexual problems among all offense categories of those sentenced for sexual offenses as being substantially higher than those among the general population. A prevalence of 62 percent for marital/relationship dysfunction among offenders who had a current relationship with an adult female partner, and a prevalence of 57 percent for sexual dysfunction amongst offenders who had experienced heterosexual intercourse with an adult, were reported. Treatment programs need to address these elements.

Until recently, buggery with a male under the age of 21, or with a woman or with an animal, led on conviction to punishment with life imprisonment. However, when Section 143 of the Criminal Justice and Public Order Act 1994 came into force on November 3, 1994, the amended Section 12 of the Sexual Offenses Act 1956 (The Acts of Buggery) in effect legalized anal intercourse for consenting couples over 18 years of age, be they gay or heterosexual. About 10 percent of cases are thought to be heterosexual and, unless force accompanies the act, these cases rarely proceed to court. Where anal intercourse occurred as a result of sexual assault, this amendment would obviously not apply.

While Mezey and King (1989) had difficulty in getting victims to cooperate with an interview for their research project on male rape, their results indicated that failure to report to the police was a problem. Most of the assailants and subjects were homosexual or bisexual, and only a few cases conformed to the stereotype of sudden unprovoked attack by complete strangers in a public place. The assault had considerable impact on the subjects' sexual identity. It was concluded that these findings suggest that male victims' immediate and long-term responses were similar to those described by female rape victims.

A study by Hickson et al. (1994) reported the prevalence of nonconsentual sex amongst homosexually active men as 27.6 percent, of which 3.9 percent involved female assailants. A third of the men had been forced into sexual activity, usually anal intercourse, by men whom they had previously had consensual sexual activity with. These results supported that belief that male rape is not usually committed by men identified as heterosexual.

The majority of those persons found guilty of buggery were given immediate custodial sentences. Around 40 percent were found guilty of the 379 cases in which proceedings took place in 1994.

What is commendable is the high detection rate by the United Kingdom police of sexual offenses that are reported as having been committed, particularly for rape, unlawful sexual intercourse with girls under 16, incest, and buggery. There are less-successful detection rates with indecent assault on females aged 16 years and over, when compared to the offenses of indecent assault on females under 16 years of age, with a similar but less marked pattern seen with indecent assault on a male in both age groups.

The "clear-up" rates for sex crimes are generally considered to be substantially higher than those for other crimes. There are, of course, an unestimatable number of sex crimes never reaching the police.

D. Prostitution   KEVAN R. WYLIE

It has been estimated that in major cities in the United Kingdom outside of London, between 800 and 1,000 women work as prostitutes at any one time. An excess of 10,000 male clients use such services in any one city. Paying for sex remains a stigmatized behavior, although 6.8 percent of men reported paying for sex with a woman at some time and 1.8 percent had done so within the last five years (Wellings et al. 1994). Recent experience was most common in the age group of men aged 25 to 44, although prevalence of ever paying for sex was five times more common in the older age group (10.3 percent vs. 2.1 percent). It was most common in widowed, separated, and divorced men within the last five years, and the men were more likely to be from social classes I and II (possibly away from home on business). A history of a homosexual partner (at any time) was associated with specifically raised odds of commercial sex contact (possibly some bisexual men).

The prostitute population is not stable. Women enter and leave, depending upon life circumstances. The risk of HIV through sexual services is very low, and the risk of contracting HIV is much greater through the use of drug injecting. It has been argued that if a sexual act is consensual and does not harm others, it should be acceptable to repeal the laws prohibiting soliciting. By doing so, it would free street working women from harassment, and reduce police and court time of those who are attempting to uphold a law that does little to abolish the "trade" (Carr 1995). The *National Vice Squad Survey* (Benson and Matthews 1995) found that one third of police vice squads want brothels to be legalized.

Prostitution can constitute one of several offenses. These include "curb crawling" (approaching a prostitute and being a "nuisance") and soliciting under the Sexual Offenses Act 1985, behaving in an indecent manner in a public place under the Vagrancy Act 1824, loitering or soliciting for the purposes of prostitution under the Street Offenses Act 1959, and procurement of persons for immoral purposes under the Sexual Offenses Acts 1956 and 1967. Women offer sexual services to men within several settings. Such services are usually offered within the so-called red light areas of a town or city. Establishments offering saunas and massage parlors are usually a cover for offering such services. These can range from masturbation of the man ("hand relief") and oral sex to intercourse (usually with the insistence of using a condom).

Establishments known as brothels exist, usually a house with several rooms being used by women offering sexual services. Such brothels are usually run by a "madam." The equivalent on the street are girls working for a "pimp." Both the provider and organizer, as well as the user, can be charged with one or more of the above offenses. The policy of many police forces in the United Kingdom would be to caution a prostitute on a couple of occasions and advise her of support services to try and help her move away from using such activity as the route for financial gain. Often such persons need assistance in severing the link with their "pimp," to whom they may be in debt or exploited through addiction to drugs. Many of the punishments carry short custodial sentences as an option, although the vast majority are dealt with by fine. The average fine for curb crawlers in 1995 was £110. The exceptions are conviction of living on the earnings of prostitution or exercising control over a prostitute, where a custodial sentence is much commoner. However, cases cannot be brought on the uncorroborated word of a prostitute or solely on police evidence.

Soliciting by a man is an offense usually dealt with by the courts by a fine, if indicted. There is increasing awareness of male prostitution, particularly in the capital city. Such men are called "call boys" and many offer their services to visiting business men in hotels. This is an area where detection by the police is very low. Low levels of reporting occur and usually the police are only aware as a consequence of robbery or associated assault. Of the 124 cases proceeded against in 1994, 89 were found guilty.

It is generally felt that the tolerance towards prostitution in England and Wales is fairly high, provided that such occurs in private. Much of the action of the police is in an attempt to appease complaining residents. An interesting development in the United Kingdom has been the call by the Inland Revenue for disclosure of such income by prostitutes for payment of Income Tax.

In mid-1996, the Government-controlled telephone company, British Telecom, joined Westminster, London's largest borough, in a crackdown on prostitutes who paste sexually explicit business cards advertising their services on the 700 bright red phone kiosks available to the public on the streets. After using computers to locate the offending prostitutes, telephone inspectors notify them they have one week to cease their postings. If the postings continue, the telephone company blocks their incoming calls. In announcing their effort, authorities said their objection "is not with prostitution as such, but with the people who illegally litter and deface the city's streets with this offensive and often pornographic advertising material." School teachers had complained that schoolchildren have been found collecting and trading the cards, many of which are illustrated.

In early 1996, British Telecom and Westminster sanitation teams, starting as early as 6 A.M. each day, removed 150,000 cards a week, 1.1 million such cards in an eight-week period; an estimated seven million cards are removed in a year. "Vice-carders," mostly young men hired by a half dozen prostitutes to post their cards, follow the sanitation teams, creating a no-win situation.

In 1991, the last time Westminster officials tried a similar scheme, Oftel, the Government telecommunications-regulating authority, said that blocking incoming calls was a violation of advertisers' rights. Before the current campaign, British Telecom changed its contract for all its customers, stipulating that they cannot advertise their telephone number in public phone kiosks. Whatever the success this effort has in controlling this advertising, it will not stop prostitutes from advertising their sexual services. Prostitution is legal in Britain, and so sex workers will continue advertising in other outlets, such as community newspapers. (See the discussion of *pikku bira* in Section 8B of the chapter on Japan.)

E. Pornography and Erotica   KEVAN R. WYLIE

There has been a general relaxation within England and Wales over erotica and nudity when displayed within newspapers and on television. There has been a trend away from the "page 3" bare-breasted girl in the tabloid press, in part fueled by complaints from feminists, but also due to increased availability of such material elsewhere. Hard pornography cannot be shown on British television, nor can scenes of an erect penis or bondage. Among European nations, only Ireland appears stricter than the United Kingdom, with no nudity or pubic hair permitted.

Despite such liberalism, there remains tight enforcement against many forms of pornographic material. Possession of adult pornography does not in itself constitute an offense. However, possessing obscene material for gain, whether that be to lend, publish or display, would constitute an offense under the Obscene Publications Act 1959/1964. The law explicitly forbids pornography involving minors and extends to taking indecent photographs of children (Protection of Children Act 1978). The sentence on conviction is three years imprisonment. Possession of photographs of child pornography carries punishment usually by fine (but six months custodial sentence is possible), and associated investigation may ensue for possible child sexual abuse and of pedophilia. A proactive measure against pedophilia exists whereby photographic developers are requested to inform the police when they notice suspicious photographs of young children. The increasing incidence of transfer of pornographic material using personal computers over the Internet has led to rising concern. However a group, Parents Against Injustice (PAIN), campaigns against overzealous misinterpretation of innocent family photographs of children bathing, running in the garden naked, or being bounced on grandfather's knee. The fact is that photographs can be very subjective.

Many book classics were banned under the Obscene Publications Act, and the infamous 1960 obscenity trial prevented copies of *Lady Chatterley's Lover* and *Queen Mab*, first published in 1829, from home ownership. Daniel Defoe was one of the earliest English authors to include superpermissive parent figures, incestuous relationships, and lower-class characters who were all sexually uninhibited, passionate, and with responsive female characters. The links between poverty and exploitation and between sexual attitudes and cultural practice has been noted many times over. However, pornography has certainly moved more from the "peep shows" and cinemas to the home, with the increasing numbers of videotapes displaying such material.

Pornographic videotapes are now obtainable through mail order, both within the United Kingdom and from Europe. Self-help videos, like *The Lover's Guide* had sold 1.3 million copies by late 1995. Although explicit, they are considered educational and have a license. The importation of obscene pornography, however, constitutes a criminal offense, although it is acknowledged that it occurs in considerable volume, given relaxed cross-country border controls within Europe. Political action was taken in 1993 to prevent satellite programming of pornographic material from Red Hot Dutch into the United Kingdom. This involved making it an offense to sell "smart cards" or advertise and publish information about the service. A similar course of action was taken in 1995 to ban the Swedish channel TV Erotica. The 1990 Broadcasting Act forbids programs that might "seriously impair the physical, mental or moral development of minors."

The United Kingdom now has three subscription-pay-TV adult soft-porn channels, Adult Channel, Television X, and Playboy TV, all of which operate in a scrambled form at nighttime. There are approximately 100,000 subscribers. The Church of England and Methodist Church have sold their shares in the BSkyB company because of this new venture.

9. Contraception, Abortion, and Population Planning

A. Contraception Attitudes and Use   FRAN READER

Contraception is widely accepted although there remains considerable variance between knowledge about and actual use of contraception. There is a constant trend towards a more-open discussion about contraception and sexuality that has been accelerated by the arrival of HIV and AIDS.

The Education Reform Act of 1988 places a statutory responsibility on schools to provide a broad and balanced curriculum that "promotes a spiritual, moral, cultural, mental, and physical development of pupils at the school and in society," and which "prepares pupils for the opportunities, responsibilities, and experiences of adult life." This philosophy forms the basis of Personal and Social Education (PSE), which is a theme running throughout a child's life a school. Sex education is part of the wider topic of health education. Health education is not a mandatory foundation subject, but it is expected to be a theme that is incorporated across the whole curriculum. School governors have the responsibility to decide whether and/or what sex education should be taught. In Scotland, there is no legislation regarding the teaching of sex education in schools. Each Local Authority decides or delegates the decision to the individual school, and the curriculum guidelines define sexuality and relationships as an important area of health education. In Northern Ireland, heath education is given as one of six mandatory cross-curricula themes in the Education Reform Order of 1989. Sex education is not specifically mentioned, but it is widely accepted and expected to form a major component of health education.

The age of consent for sexual activity is 16 in England, Wales, and Scotland, and 17 in Northern Ireland. Doctors may prescribe contraception to under-16-year-olds (17-year-olds in Northern Ireland). The present legislation in England and Wales follows the House of Lords Ruling in the Gillick case of 1985. The Law Lords ruled that "a girl under 16 of sufficient understanding and intelligence may have the legal capacity to give valid consent to contraceptive advice and treatment including necessary medical examination." In Scotland, the Age of Legal Capacity Act came into force in September 1991, bringing Scotland in line with England and Wales. In Northern Ireland, a similar legal situation exists, except the medical age of consent is 17.

In 1993, the Government launched its Health of the Nation Initiative. Sexual Health was one of the key sections, with one of the targets being to halve the rate of unplanned pregnancy in under-16-year-olds by the year 2000. This has given backing to initiatives to improve sex education programs and the provision of contraceptive services.

Since 1974, all contraceptive advice provided by the National Health Services and all prescribed supplies were made available free of charge, irrespective of age and marital status. In the United Kingdom, most contraceptive services are provided by either General Practitioners (GP physicians) or by Community and Hospital Clinics. Community and Hospital Family Planning Clinics have always been able to supply condoms free of charge. This has not been available to GPs, although some practices now offer this service. Government policy supports the dual provision and choice to maximize the uptake of services; however, over the past ten years there has been a marked reduction in the number of Community Family Planning Clinics with a shift to GP provision. Since 1990, new contractual arrangements were introduced for GPs that affected their fees and allowances encouraging a greater emphasis on Health Promotion. This system has continued to shift contraceptive care to General Practice. The Community Family Planning Clinics have therefore looked to complement GP services, and specifically target teenagers and vulnerable groups that may have problems in accessing care from general practitioners.

Community Clinics, backed up by specialist contraceptive clinics in hospitals, also tend to provide a wider range of contraceptive methods than are available through General Practice physicians. Snowdens's research in 1985 showed that only 55 percent of the women using Family Planning Clinics were prescribed the pill as opposed to 84 percent of GP patients. This trend has continued. Community Clinics, therefore, remain a service of choice for those women wishing to use the less-common methods of contraception, and they remain the main source of training for physicians and nurses.

Contraception is now recognized as a part of core training for all GPs and obstetricians and gynecologists. Specialists in the field undergo training through the Faculty of Family Planning and Reproductive Health Care, which is part of the Royal College of Obstetricians and Gynecologists. Since the Health of the Nation Initiative, there has been an increasing shift to integrate the community and hospital contraceptive services with community and hospital services for sexually transmitted diseases. Doctors and nurses initially trained in one or the other discipline are now entering into joint training programs. It is now common practice to be advised to use contraception to prevent unplanned pregnancy backed up by either the male or female condom for the prevention of sexually transmitted disease. This message is particularly stressed for couples at the start of all new relationships.

Contraceptive methods currently available in the United Kingdom are combination oral contraception, progesterone-only pills, long-acting injectable progestogens, five-year levonogestrel implants, intrauterine devices with levonorgestrel (IUS), copper intrauterine devices, male and female condoms, diaphragms and cervical caps, natural family planning, and male and female sterilization. The combined oral contraceptive pill is the most common method of contraception used by women under 30. In total, it is used by 22 percent of women between the ages of 16 and 49. Conversely, sterilization is the most common method used over the age of 30, with male and female sterilization being equally represented. In total, 23 percent of 16- to 49-year-olds use sterilization as their method. Condom usage has increased in recent years, and with this a decrease in the use of oral contraceptives. The use of combined oral contraception always fluctuates, tending to fall after a media-publicized concern about safety. In October 1995, the Committee on Safety of Medicines (CSM) raised concern about pills containing the progestogens, desogestrel and gestodene, and an increased risk of venous thrombosis. As with similar pill scares in the past, this is likely to generate a further fall in the uptake of the combined pill as a method of contraception.

Recently introduced methods of contraception include the female condom, Femidom, introduced in 1992. So far, this method has not caught on, and the male condom maintains dominance as the most popular barrier method. The five-year, six-capsule levonorgestrel implant was introduced in 1993. There was an initial enthusiasm for this method that has now diminished because of problems with erratic bleeding in the early months of use and occasional difficulty in the removal procedure. However, the method has settled to take a valid place in the range of contraceptives provided in the United Kingdom popular for women who consider their family complete, but do not wish to take the step of sterilization. An intrauterine device with levonogestrel (IUS) was introduced into the United Kingdom in 1995 with a three-year license for contraceptive use. It is anticipated this license will be extended to five years in the near future, and also extended to include use for the management of menstrual problems. It is anticipated that this new method will be widely accepted in the United Kingdom, particularly for the management of contraception in older women. The United Kingdom is awaiting with interest the introduction of the Unipath Personal Contraceptive System for the accurate electronic prediction of the fertile phase. Trials have been ongoing in the United Kingdom for the past couple of years.

Emergency contraception with both the hormonal and IUD methods are widely available within the United Kingdom through general practitioners, community clinics, sexually transmitted disease (STD) clinics, and accident and emergency departments. There is still considerable confusion in the population about the use of emergency contraception. This relates to it being marketed initially as the morning-after pill, which has led to misunderstandings regarding the duration between unprotected intercourse and the time for the effective use of emergency contraception. In 1995, there has been a wide campaign to promote the use and understanding of emergency contraception. There is currently a debate in the United Kingdom about making hormonal emergency contraception available through pharmacies without a medical prescription.

B. Teenage (Unmarried) Pregnancy   MARY GRIFFIN

United Kingdom data specifically relating to unmarried teenagers are scarce. Official statistics have been collected by separate organizations in England and Wales, Scotland, and Northern Ireland, but uniform data have not been gathered for the three groupings. The information given in this section is mainly for England and Wales, with a little, where available, on Scotland and Northern Ireland.

The trend in the United Kingdom is increasingly towards teenage mothers not marrying (Family Planning Association 1994). Some prefer to cohabit with their partner, since there is little stigma attached to this, although many maintain a single-parent lifestyle. Indeed, it can be advantageous for teenagers not to marry in terms of welfare benefits and housing, although cohabiting teenage mothers do have the highest rate of reported homelessness (18 percent), according to recent research from the *National Child Development Survey* (Joseph Rowntree Foundation 1995). The trend away from marriage is reflected in the outcome of conceptions in England and Wales for 1992 for all women under 20, the total number being 93,000, of which 8,300 were conceptions inside marriage. Of the 84,700 conceptions outside of marriage, 37 percent were legally aborted, 58 percent led to maternity outside of marriage, and only 5 percent to maternity inside marriage (OPCS 1992). Looking at live births for 16- to 19-year-olds in England and Wales, in 1983, 56.3 percent were registered outside of marriage, but this had increased to 87.8 percent by 1993 (OPCS). In Scotland, for the 15-to-19 age group, the percentages rose from 54.5 in 1984 to 89.3 in 1994 (General Register Office for Scotland). Even in Northern Ireland, which tends to be more conservative and a few years behind social trends on the mainland, single parents are no longer a rarity and are increasingly accepted without social stigma.

While 16 years is legally the lowest age for marriage in the United Kingdom, parental consent is required up to the age of 18 in England, Wales, and Northern Ireland, but not in Scotland. In the first three regions, written consent of both parents is required, even if they are estranged, so that some teenagers wishing to marry may not be able to do so before the birth of the baby if this legal requirement cannot be fulfilled.

Looking at trends over the last two decades, the introduction of free contraception in 1974 led to a decline in teenage pregnancy rates. In 1973, the total conception rate per 1,000 teenagers in England and Wales was 9.2 for 13- to 15-year-olds (and therefore unmarried) and 75.2 for 15- to 19-year-olds (marital status unspecified). Ten years later, the rates were 8.3 and 56.0, respectively, of which just over half were terminated for the 13-to-15 age group and a third for the 15-to-19 age group. Thereafter, rates increased until a peak in 1990 (10.1 for the 13-to-15 group, with half legally terminated, and 69.0 for the 15- to 19-year-olds, with just under a third terminated) (OPCS). The peak came a year later in Scotland, but there was no particular trend in Northern Ireland.

Several factors probably contributed to this phenomenon. Firstly, the Gillick case, which eventually concluded in 1985 in favor of young people's rights, caused a great deal of confusion over teenagers' access to confidential help and advice, and anxieties still persist (Wareham and Drummond 1994), despite the joint statement referred to by Mrs. Gillick in a letter to the *British Medical Journal* (Gillick 1994). Secondly, the onset of economic recession led to a decline in young people's job opportunities. A third contributory factor was cuts in family planning clinics, thereby restricting access to services (Brook Advisory Centres 1995). The Government's concern over the rise in teenage pregnancies led to teenage sexual health being identified as one of the key areas targeted for action in their policy document, *Health of the Nation* (Department of Health, 1992)—a specific aim being to reduce the 1989 conception rate in under-16-year-olds by at least 50 percent by the year 2000. Rates are already falling again and teenagers are far less likely to have a baby today than twenty-five years ago.

In England and Wales, the total conception rate per thousand for 13- to 15-year-olds in 1993 was 8.1 (with 50 percent legally terminated) and for 15- to 19-year-olds, 59.6 with just over one third terminated. In Northern Ireland, the total number of live births to under-15-year-olds for 1990-93 inclusive ranged between 4 to 7, but rose to 11 in 1994. Total live births to 15- to 19-year-olds (marital status unspecified) rose to 1,856 in 1992, but has since fallen to 1,486 in 1994 (General Register Office for Northern Ireland). Since Northern Ireland is not as liberal towards abortion as the other three countries, some pregnant teenagers go to the larger cities on the mainland to obtain abortions. Legally, the situation with regard to abortion in Northern Ireland is a very gray area, and those involved in women's health and welfare agencies are aware that doctors there are increasingly prepared to widen grounds for justifying therapeutic abortion in the interests of a teenager's physical or mental health. This trend may be reflected in the statistics, though official figures for terminations were unavailable due to the legal situation.

With regard to the social background of young parents, longitudinal data from the *National Child Development Survey* show that half the teenage mothers who were single when their babies were born went on to cohabit with or marry the father. The study found no significant differences in childhood factors between young parents whose babies were born within marriage and those who were single or cohabiting when they gave birth. The data also suggested that the predisposition to have a child when young was independent of any thoughts about marriage, cohabitation, or single parenthood. Sixty-seven percent of those married at the time of conception had planned the pregnancy, compared with 26 percent of those cohabiting, 17 percent who married during pregnancy, and 8 percent who had no live-in relationship before birth (summarized by Joseph Rowntree Foundation 1995).

Despite the expansion of services and increased provision of information for teenagers in the United Kingdom since *Health of the Nation*, it seems that risk-taking behavior, failure to anticipate risk, lack of knowledge, and errors in the use of contraception are still major causes of unwanted teenage pregnancies (Lo et al. 1994; Pearson et al. 1995; Wareham and Drummond 1994).

C. Abortion   JANE READ AND LINDA DELANEY

Legal Status and Availability

Until 1967, most pregnancies could not lawfully be terminated by abortion. The Offenses Against the Person Act of 1861 specifically criminalized both successful and unsuccessful abortion attempts by those who assisted women and by pregnant women themselves (curiously, the former, but not the latter, could be convicted, even if there was found to be no pregnancy). However, as prosecutions under the 1861 Act had to establish that the accused acted "unlawfully," it became possible to defend a criminal charge by showing that the abortion was carried out in the honest belief, based on reasonable grounds and adequate knowledge, that the continuance of the pregnancy would turn the woman into "a physical or mental wreck"; this was the outcome of the famous case of R. vs. Bourne (1939-1KB 687), brought after an eminent surgeon performed an abortion on a 14-year-old who had been raped and whose mental well-being was said to have been gravely threatened by the resulting pregnancy.

In 1967, Parliament provided statutory defenses by passing the Abortion Act. Substantially amended by the Human Fertilization and Embryology Act of 1990, the Abortion Act of 1967 permits abortion on liberal therapeutic and eugenic grounds if two registered medical practitioners—one would suffice in an emergency—certify the existence of such a ground, and the abortion is carried out by a registered medical practitioner. In brief, the amended law allows abortion when it is performed to prevent grave permanent injury to the mental or physical health of the woman, or risk to her life, or the birth of a "seriously handicapped" child. For these three situations, there is no time limit; in other cases, the limit is the end of the twenty-fourth week of pregnancy.

An important change in the 1967 Act resulting from enactment of the Human Fertility and Embryology Act 1990 is the severance of the link that applied previously with the Infant Life (Preservation) Act 1929. The effect of this has been, paradoxically, a slight liberalization of the Abortion Act as it was between 1967 and 1990. Prior to 1990, women could not, under any circumstance, have their pregnancy terminated after the twenty-eighth week of pregnancy, since, under the Infant Life (Preservation) Act of 1929, this was considered to be the point at which a fetus became viable. Although Clause (a) (given below) states a limit of twenty-four weeks of pregnancy, there is no mention of a time limit for the other three clauses. In effect, the situation in England and Wales is that abortion is rarely done after twenty-two weeks of pregnancy. Essentially, any woman who is considering a decision to terminate her pregnancy, whether as a result of her social, economic, personal, family, or medical circumstances, must have the consent of two medical practitioners before the abortion may be performed.

The clauses in the Abortion Act 1967, as amended by the HFE Act 1990, under which she can do this and to which the two doctors must conform are as follows:

1. that the pregnancy has not exceeded its twenty-fourth week and that the continuance of the pregnancy would involve risk to the life of the pregnant woman, or of injury to the physical or mental health of the pregnant woman or any existing children of her family, greater than if the pregnancy were terminated; or
2. that the termination is necessary to prevent grave permanent injury to the physical or mental health of the pregnant woman; or
3. that the continuance of the pregnancy would involve risk to the life of the pregnant woman, greater than if the pregnancy were terminated; or
4. that there is a substantial risk that if the child were born it would suffer from such physical or mental abnormalities as to be seriously handicapped. (The Abortion Act 1967 as amended HMSO)

Thus, it is clear that the procedures for a woman to have a legal termination of her pregnancy are grounded not only in the medical aspects, but are based on the need to adhere to the law of abortion. When a woman presents for consideration of an abortion, therefore, she is entering a legal process.

There is no requirement on the part of Health Authorities to provide abortion services, and abortion provision is not consistent across the country. In some areas, the service may be relatively available through the Health Service, and in other areas, there will be little provision, and women will either have to pay for a legal termination in the private sector or nonprofit charity sector, as well as possibly having to travel some distance to get to a private clinic.

Social Attitudes Toward Abortion

There is evidence that attitudes toward abortion and provision of abortion have liberalized over the past ten to fifteen years. In a fact sheet on the legal and ethical issues surrounding abortion, the Family Planning Association quotes the *British Social Attitudes Survey*, in which it was shown that the number of United Kingdom people who felt abortion should be allowed when a woman's health was endangered increased from 87 percent in 1983 to 95 percent in 1989. This trend was consistent when other questions, such as the economic situation of the woman and her family, and the woman's own choice, were considered (FPA *Factsheet 6B*, 1992, p. 4).

This trend is also reflected in the medical profession. "A national survey of consultant gynecologists in 1989 found that 73 percent believed that a woman should have the right to choose abortion" (Paintin 1992, 968). This same survey, carried out by Savage and Francome, also showed that 87 percent of gynecologists at the Royal College of Obstetricians and Gynecologists had been right to oppose one of the more recent changes to the Abortion Act, the Alton Bill. There seems to be a general understanding that people feel that the current system works quite well.

Incidence

The latest available figures (Office of Population Census and Surveys *Monitor*, April 11, 1995) show that during 1993 a total of 168,711 abortions were performed in England and Wales, 2 percent fewer than in 1992 when the total was 172,063. The 1992 total figure included both the resident and nonresident figures, with 160,495 resident women obtaining abortions and the remainder being accounted for mainly by Irish women seeking an abortion abroad since it is not legal in the Republic of Ireland. The 1992 TOP (terminations of pregnancy) rate for residents of the United Kingdom was 12.51 per 1,000 women.

The reason most frequently cited by women seeking an abortion was risk of injury to the physical and mental health of the pregnant woman. The main provider was the National Health Service. Section 4 of the Abortion Act of 1967 affords legal protection to health care workers who refuse to participate in abortion on grounds of conscience. Prospective fathers, on the other hand, were, in Paton vs. Trustees of BPAC (1979—QB 276), denied the right to intervene to prevent an abortion.

There has been little change in the proportion of women seeking abortion since the introduction of the 1967 Abortion Act. In a 1992 article in the *British Medical Journal,* David Paintin, then a Research Fellow at St. Mary's Hospital, London, observed that: "The lack of change in the proportion of pregnancies ending in legal abortion suggests that the behavior factors that lead to unwanted conception and abortion are intrinsic to our society and that easy availability is not a primary factor in the decision concerning abortion" (Paintin 1992, 967). This is an important point, since those who oppose abortion seem to believe that should abortion become more "freely" available, there would be a marked increase in the number of women who choose legal abortion, and that any "loosening" of the restrictions that pertain to abortion in England and Wales should therefore be opposed. In England and Wales, in 1991, the vast majority of legal abortions—88 percent—were performed before the thirteenth week of pregnancy (Family Planning Association *Factsheet 6A,* 1994, Table 6, 7).

D. Population Planning Programs and Policies   PETER SELMAN

"No population policy please, we're British!" (Coleman and Salt 1992).

Despite the fact that birthrates in the United Kingdom have been falling since the late nineteenth century, and the fertility rate has dropped below replacement level (namely, a Net Reproduction Rate below 1.00) between 1927 and 1943 and since 1973, the population of the United Kingdom has grown steadily, with a reduction in size evident only in the late 1970s, when the population fell from 55,922,000 in 1974-1975 to 55,835,000 in 1978-79. Since then, the population has increased steadily to 58 million in 1992. Experts project the population of the United Kingdom will surpass 62 million by the year 2031, after which a steady decline is expected with the population returning to the 1992 level by the year 2061 (OPCS 1994).

The initial fall in the birthrate occurred, as in most countries, without any government pressure and in the face of opposition to birth control. In England and Wales, the period total fertility rate fell from 4.8 in the 1870s to a low point of 1.72 in 1933 (OPCS 1987). It was at this stage that we find the first signs of concern over population decline, as birthrates fell to below replacement level, and differences in fertility became apparent as middle-class groups married late and had few children while lower-working-class people had a substantially higher fertility. This led to concern about the quality of the population and to the development of the eugenics movement. A number of publications warned of the dangers of depopulation (Charles 1936; Glass 1936; Hogben 1938), a national decline (Reddawa 1939), "race suicide" (McCleary 1943), and a rejection of parenthood (Titmuss 1942). Charles (1938) projected the British population for 1995 at 20 million, a little more than a third of the actual population today.

In 1944, a Royal Commission on Population was set up to consider whether Britain was indeed facing a population decline and whether measures should be taken "in the national interest" to influence future trends. The Royal Commission reported in June 1949, soon after the 1947 crude birthrate was announced as 20.5, the highest figure since the end of World War I, and the net reproduction rate (NRR) had risen to 1.21. The commission saw this as a temporary aberration and projected a long-term decline in population. The Commission did not, however, recommend any counter action and no official population policy followed. Others were less sanguine (McCleary 1943; Titmuss 1942); in the same year Eva Hubback (1947) projected the 1999 British population at 34 million.

No one predicted that within a decade the birthrate would be rising sharply to the highest level since the end of World War I (Holmans 1963). Nor was there any expectation that migration would play a role in boosting population growth: "The Royal Commission never dreamt that 2.5 million colored immigrants and their descendants would be living in Britain just thirty years after their report" (Coleman and Salt 1992). Restrictions on Commonwealth immigration were introduced in the early 1960s and have since been maintained by both political parties. However, these policies are due more to racist concerns than to any fear of excess population. Nevertheless, it is important to note that, without such immigration and the consequent births to immigrants and their descendants, Britain's population would by now most certainly be in decline.

By 1964, the crude birthrate had risen to 18.5 and the total fertility rate to 2.93 (0PCS 1987), and in 1965 the General Register Office projected a population for England and Wales in 2001 of over 66 million. This led to new concerns about overpopulation. In 1971, a Population Panel was appointed following the publication in that year of a White Paper responding to a report from the House of Commons Select Committee on Science and Technology on the Population of the United Kingdom, which had concluded that "the government must act to prevent the consequences of population growth becoming intolerable for the every day conditions of life."

The *Report of the Population Panel* was published in March 1973, by which time the birthrate had fallen substantially and the net reproduction rate was once again below 1.00. It concluded that the population of Great Britain would "almost certainly rise from 54 million in 1971 to around 64 million in the course of the first decade of the next century . . . [and to] over 80 million around the middle of the next century." If, however, fertility were to fall rapidly, population could decline to 40 million by 2050, and there would be "profound changes in the age structure" with serious social consequences. Reviewing the implications of anticipated growth, the Panel concluded that "there is no reason to suppose that 64 million (by the beginning of the twentieth century) would be in any way intolerable or disastrous," but that "to absorb a further 20 million by 2051 could be much more intractable" so that "a slower rate of increase . . . is clearly preferable." Less attention was paid to the possibility of a population decline, other than to state that "if there were to be a fall in fertility which led . . . to an excess of deaths over births, this should not be a cause of public concern."

No explicit population policy was recommended, although the Government was advised to extend family planning services and inform people about the fact of the population problem. The panel was less happy about persuading people of the advantages of smaller families and opposed fiscal and other disincentives to having children. By 1977, the crude birthrate had fallen to 11.5 and the total fertility rate to 1.66, the lowest levels since records began, and any further measures to discourage parenthood were viewed as inappropriate.

Since then, the crude birthrate has risen again and has remained steady between 13 and 14 since 1985. In 1990, the total fertility was 1.8, below replacement level, but high in comparison with other European countries such as Italy (1.29) and Spain (1.3). The population is, nevertheless, projected to grow until the second quarter of the next century (OPCS 1994). Concern is expressed over the implications of an aging population (Johnson and Falkingham 1992), but there is no overt policy to increase fertility, and recently more concern has been focused on rising divorce rates, the decline in marriage, and the associated increase in childbearing outside marriage, especially among teenagers (Selman 1996).

Despite two substantial reports on population, the United Kingdom has never developed a population policy, which is probably just as well, given the wrong assumptions each report made about the future. Whether this will continue to be the case in the next century, if a significant population decline occurs alongside a more rapidly aging population, remains to be seen.

10. Sexually Transmitted Diseases
PETER GREENHOUSE

A. Incidence, Patterns, and Trends

The United Kingdom's unique network of specialist clinics (see Section 10B) collect detailed statistics for the Department of Health (HMSO 1995/16), which reflect trends in sexually transmitted diseases (STD) with a high degree of accuracy. These statistics give a better indication of the true incidence of STD in the United Kingdom than those of most other countries, because of the relative low proportion of infections treated outside the National Health Service. It is estimated that over 95 percent of the epidemic STD, namely, syphilis and gonorrhea, are managed at the NHS clinics. The proportion is somewhat less for the more endemic diseases—chlamydia, genital herpes, and genital warts—because of their covert nature, with the proportion for chlamydia being recently reduced by a belated surge of interest among gynecologists, contraceptive care professionals, and general practice physicians. The majority of HIV care is also organized from the NHS clinics (see Section 11).

Control of syphilis and gonorrhea has been particularly successful in the United Kingdom (see Table 3). There are fewer cases of infectious syphilis per year in men in England (194 cases in 1994) than there are clinics in the United Kingdom, 230. The figure for women was roughly half the male figure, 110 cases in 1994. Twenty percent of the male cases were acquired through homosexual contact. The median age for new cases of syphilis is higher than for other STDs, 33 for men and 28 for women. Syphilis has become an imported disease, having been virtually eliminated as a congenital infection, with only one infection reported in 700,000 live births in 1993.

Table 3

Incidence of Gonorrhea and Syphilis, England, 1918 to 1994

Disease	Number of New Cases in Selected Years (in Thousands of Cases)										
	1918	1920	1922	1930	1940	1946	1955	1964	1977	1987	1994
Gonorrhea	17.4	37.9	27.9	40.5	26.3	47.4	17.4	37.9	58.7	24.5	11.6
Syphilis	26.8	42.1	24.2	18.9	11.4	24.2	5.0	3.8	4.2	1.8	1.3

Approximated by the General Editor from a line graph supplied by the authors.

The pattern of gonorrhea cases during the 1900s (Table 3) can act as a surrogate marker for other sexual activity, closely refecting changes caused by demographics, war, travel, contraceptive practice, and sexual mores (Greenhouse 1994). The gonorrhea pattern can also illuminate these social trends. The post-World War II decline in gonorrhea cases was due to the arrival of penicillin and the reactionary morality of the 1950s. This was followed by a tremendous rise in the 1960s, as the baby boomers reached adolescence, sexual behavior gradually changed, and contraception increased. The maximum incidence of gonorrhea occurred in 1976, with 58,725 cases, in conjunction with the all-time peak in prescriptions for the oral contraceptive pill. Starting in 1986, the incidence of gonorrhea dropped by 50 percent in two years following the public HIV-education campaign directed at the heterosexual population. There is now less gonorrhea in the United Kingdom than at any time since record keeping began. The current rate is around one sixth that of twenty years ago. Statistics for 1994 record 11,574 cases, with an overall rate of 37 per 100,000 population aged 15 to 64 (HMSO 1995/16). However, the rate varies considerably with age and sex; the highest incidence occurred in women aged 16 to 19 years, and increased from 95 cases to 123 per 100,000 between 1993 and 1994 (HMSO 1995/16; *Communicable Disease Report* 1995, 62-63). Detailed information on geographic distribution, antibiotic-resistant strains, and location of acquisition is also published (*Communicable Disease Report* 1995, 62-63).

Chlamydia trachomatis, the principal preventable cause of pelvic inflammatory disease, infertility, and ectopic pregnancy, is the commonest curable STD in the United Kingdom. All isolation rates for chlamydia substantially underestimate its true incidence, since screening tests are, at best, 75 to 80 percent sensitive, and most infected men and women show no symptoms. The cases identified at NHS STD clinics represent only the tip of the iceberg. The differential age and sex rates for chlamydia (*Communicable Disease Report* 1995, 122-123) are similar in distribution to those of gonorrhea (*Communicable Disease Report* 1995, 62-63), herpes and warts (*Communicable Disease Report* 1995, 186-187), and representative of all STD combined, with highest rates in adolescent women, and a late lower peak in male cases. The peak incidence of 360 cases per 100,000 women aged 16 to 19 years—four times more than in men of the same age—should be compared with observed rates from 9.5 percent to 23 percent in studies of women of this age who are having an abortion. No significant differences were found in the chlamydial isolation rates (of around 10 percent) in women attending clinics for either contraception, abortion, or STD (Radcliffe 1993), although, even nowadays, most women are not routinely screened in the contraception clinics. Chlamydia and nonspecific genital infection rose steadily until 1986, peaking at 157,792 cases, and has shown a slight decline since then, despite improved diagnostic techniques.

At least 85 percent of all pelvic inflammatory disease (PID) is sexually acquired, a minimum of 75 percent due to chlamydia. Around 10 percent of pelvic inflammatory disease is treated in a hospital. The massive drop in gonorrhea in the United Kingdom in 1986 to 1988 was not matched by a significant drop in hospital cases of acute salpingitis. A similar phenomenon in 1970-77 in Sweden alerted Westrom (1988) to the true etiology of salpingitis, and appropriate diagnosis, treatment, contact tracing, and education was initiated. In both countries, salpingitis incidence had doubled between 1965 and 1974. From 1978 to 1983, salpingitis admissions were halved in Sweden (Westrom 1988), but increased by 50 percent from 1975 to 1984 in Britain, which almost two decades later has yet to introduce a similar salpingitis-prevention campaign. Contact-tracing studies indicate very high infection rates of over 70 percent in male partners of women with salpingitis, the vast majority of whom are asymptomatic.

There has been a continuing long-term upward trend in first-attack incidence of both genital herpes and genital warts, full details of which have been published (*Communicable Disease Report* 1995, 186-187). Herpes is more common in women, increasing from 32 to 98 per 100,000 between 1981 and 1994. Seroepidemiological studies in the United Kingdom show that around 90 percent of men and women aged 25 to 34 have antibodies to both herpes viruses (HSV 1 and 2), of which about one third are HSV 1. Up to 50 percent of oral lesions have been found to harbor HSV 1. Thus, although oral and genital herpes infection is ubiquitous, relatively few individuals suffer overt symptoms, and many will have acquired oral infection in childhood. This information is of considerable value in diffusing the stress of a first-episode attack acquired sexually.

Full details of the minor STDs are also available from published statistics (HMSO 1995/16). Long-term trends in total attendance for all diagnoses shows a continuous increase to a current high of 671,281 in 1993. Records show an increasing proportion of clinic attenders are female, from one seventh in 1950 to one quarter in 1960 and one third in 1970. Now, 51 percent of all attenders are women, with some clinics up two thirds, depending on the extent of contraceptive and other sexual health services provided. These trends are set to continue as the clinical workload comes closer to reflecting the gross disparity in STD morbidity suffered by women.

B. Treatment and Prevention

Thanks to exceptional, far-sighted public-health legislation, the United Kingdom has had specialist clinics offering free and entirely confidential STD advice and treatment in every major town since 1917. Accessible care is available to all regardless of nationality or domicile. Voluntary contact tracing and treatment of partners is facilitated by health advisers, without the intrusion of coercive legislation. The United Kingdom is the only country where Venereology (currently known as Genito-Urinary Medicine) developed as a distinct medical specialty in its own right (Waugh 1990), rather than as a minor adjunct to other fields, such as dermatology in Europe, or infectious diseases and public health in the United States. Consequently, Britain has a well-trained, academically based specialist body, whose numbers have doubled in the last decade as the result of substantial government investment in improved premises, equipment, and expanded support staff. The specialty coordinates clinical care and epidemiologic research, and can implement rapid and consistent responses to changing public-health priorities in the control of STD, having been ideally placed to take the lead in caring for HIV (see Section 11). The advantage of this approach is evidenced by the relatively low prevalence of HIV and other STDs compared to most countries other than Scandinavia (see Section 10A above).

An important disadvantage is that other specialists are poorly trained or are unaware of STD, and are unlikely to be able to broach the subject (Clarke 1995) without either embarrassment or moralism. (This holds the greatest potential for damage in women's heath care.) Not only are most genitourinary physicians untrained in gynecology, most gynecologists and family planning specialists were, until recently, ignorant of the significance of covert STD in their patients. This resulted in considerable morbidity from uterine instrumentation during abortion or IUD insertion, and multiple recurrences of salpingitis due to reinfection from untreated partners, leading to increased chronic dyspareunia, ectopic pregnancy, and infertility.

Despite governmental interference in school sex education policy (see Section 3A), there have been substantial advances in the general level of education on HIV and, to a lesser extent, on contraception, aided by the government's Health of the Nation Initiative on sexual health. Education on conventional STD, however, has been almost entirely neglected. Sexual health education is usually delivered by those without specific knowledge or experience of STD care. Thus the public as a whole, including health professionals, remain largely ignorant in this area. In the recent international survey on STD awareness for the American Social Health Association (Clarke 1995), the United Kingdom compared poorly against five other countries. Only 1 percent of Britons had heard of chlamydia, and 75 percent said that their doctors would not talk about sex or STD. This ignorance, combined with the traditional British attitude of prurience and prudishness about sex, creates the societal taboo of STD. This stigma, causing guilt, shame, and blame, is based on misinformation, fear, and an automatic presumption of infidelity, which is often erroneous due to the very asymptomatic nature of most STD that causes them to be endemic. This major pitfall results in substantial psychosexual trauma that plagues work in all fields of sexology.

A simple solution will be found in the increasing integration of sexual health promotion with clinical service provision. Teaching that most STDs produce no symptoms, can be present for many years, are acquired from partners who are likewise unaware, and may, therefore, have been present before the current relationship, should do much to destigmatize the subject. Furthermore, a national consensus of specialists in public health, family planning, genitourinary medicine, and health education has recently promoted a concise definition of sexual health: "the enjoyment of sexual activity of one's choice without causing or suffering physical or mental harm" (Greenhouse 1994). This same consensus agreed that these specialties should progressively converge to provide services for contraception, abortion, STD/HIV, sexual assault, psychosexual care, and health promotion under the banner of sexual health clinics (Greenhouse 1994). Broadening the scope of these services allows access to more appropriately coordinated care "under one roof." This is essential for the youngest in the most vulnerable situations, and may persuade people to attend a clinic to check that they are healthy rather than waiting until they are ill. With careful education input, this should improve public understanding, reduce stigma, prevent iatrogenic morbidity, and achieve even more-effective control of STD in clinical situations where they would previously have gone undetected.

11. HIV/AIDS

JANE CRAIG AND GEORGE KINGHORN

A cumulative total of 11,302 (1,044 or 9 percent of which are female) cases of AIDS have been reported in the United Kingdom between 1982, when reporting began, and the end of August 1995; 7,782 (69 percent) are known to have died (PHLS AIDS Center: *Communicable Disease Report* 1995). The annual number of new cases of AIDS has continued to rise slowly in a linear fashion. Incidence remains lower than in some other European countries;

for example, in 1994, United Kingdom ranked ninth in Europe for the highest rates of reported AIDS cases (PHLS AIDS Center, June 1995). There have been 24,502 laboratory reports of newly diagnosed HIV infections since reporting began in 1984 to the end of June 1995. Of these, 49 did not record sex, and of the remainder, 3,499 (14 percent) were female. A total of 207 AIDS cases and 604 HIV infections in children aged less than 15 years were reported by the end of April 1995. Most children were infected by maternal transmission.

London and its surrounds, the Thames regions, have reported 70 percent of all AIDS cases and 65 percent of all recorded HIV infections in the United Kingdom to date. Of these, two thirds (i.e., half of all cases in England and Wales) have been reported from three London districts. Scotland accounts for 6 percent of all United Kingdom AIDS cases and 9 percent of HIV infections.

Overall, the proportion of HIV infections due to homosexual exposure has been relatively large. However, this varies considerably between different parts of the country. In England, Wales, and Northern Ireland, 75 percent of AIDS cases are attributed to infection acquired through sex between men and only 4 percent of cases are attributed to injecting drug use, whereas, in Scotland, these groups account for 41 percent and 36 percent respectively.

The proportion of reports from different exposure categories has also changed over time. The proportion of AIDS cases in the United Kingdom attributable to sex between men has fallen from 95 percent in 1985 to 70 percent in 1994. The proportion attributed to injecting drug use has risen from 1 percent to 9 percent over the same period and, likewise, the proportion of AIDS cases attributed to heterosexual exposure has risen from 4 percent to 19 percent. Similar trends are seen for HIV infections reported in England, Wales, and Northern Ireland. However, the trend in Scotland is somewhat different, where the proportion of HIV infections attributed to sex between men has doubled in the last ten years, while those attributable to injecting drug use has halved. This may reflect the efforts of locally targeted prevention programs among drug users. The proportion of HIV infection in Scotland due to heterosexual exposure has risen, and more so than in the rest of the country. In the United Kingdom as a whole, the majority of heterosexually acquired infections are attributed to heterosexual exposure while in Africa or, increasingly, Asia, rather than other exposure categories such as partners of injecting drug users.

Genitourinary medicine clinics offer a voluntary, open-access, confidential HIV-testing service nationwide. All blood donors have been tested since 1985. There are several ongoing, anonymous, unlinked HIV-seroprevalence studies at selected sites involving women attending antenatal clinics and attendees at genitourinary medicine clinics who are having blood tests for syphilis screening. Most people who request HIV testing are of low risk, and such requests have often been in response to publicity events such as the death of a public figure from AIDS rather than to large-scale government-sponsored AIDS-education campaigns (PHLS AIDS Center, June 1995).

For United Kingdom residents, medical care and treatments are provided free of charge under the National Health Service. It is recognized that a small but significant number of patients choose to travel to inner London for specialist health care, which contributes to the continuing large numbers of reported cases from these centers.

The gay community has become well-organized and motivated with self-initiated prevention and education campaigns. There are also numerous patient-interest and support groups. Safer-sex practices have been accepted by many, although there is some evidence that younger men are ignoring this message as their rates of newly acquired HIV infection are increasing (Miller et al. 1995). Initiatives, such as outreach work among targeted groups rather than didactic health care messages, seem to be more successful and resources are now directed towards such schemes.

National needle- and syringe-exchange programs have been operational since 1990 and there has also been discussion about extending this service to closed communities such as prisons. The government has identified sexual health as a key issue nationally. Targets for the control of sexually transmitted diseases and for the reduction of the rates of unplanned teenage pregnancy have been set (Secretary of State for Health 1992). Each health district has an obligation to educate and increase awareness among its health-care workers and to have a designated HIV-prevention officer coordinating local government and voluntary sector initiatives.

School sex education remains a controversial topic. Opponents often claim that such lessons reduce the age of first sexual activity. At present, attendance at sex education classes is voluntary and parents have the right to withdraw their children. However, recent research suggests that sex education programs can be effective in delaying the onset and frequency of sexual activity and may also result in an increased use of contraception, in particular condoms (Kirby 1993). Effective programs seem to be those focusing on reducing specific risk behaviors, combined with opportunities to improve personal development and communication skills. This has obvious implications for the provision of school-based sex education in the future.

Overall, there is a greater awareness of HIV infection, but risk recognition remains a issue for many, as is reflected by the increasing number of heterosexual infections acquired abroad. Prevention programs need to target such groups, as well as continuing their efforts amongst other high-risk communities.

12. Sexual Dysfunctions, Counseling, and Therapies
KEVAN R WYLIE

A. Concepts of Sexual Dysfunction

British society appears to be having a reemergence of sexual awareness. After a very conservative attitude towards sex in the first half of the century there was an awakening in the 1960s alongside the increased use of illicit drugs, the emergence of rock and roll, and a "free" society. The permissive society continued into the 1970s and early 1980s, until, like many other countries, the fear of AIDS changed the sexual behavior of many in the mid1980s. Out of this has grown a more-cautious approach to sexual encounters with others and a reemergence of encouraging more satisfying sexual relationships within a monogamous relationship.

There is wider access to articles and books on sexual fulfillment, and awareness of dysfunction has increased, primarily as a result of articles in the popular press and lifestyle magazines. There is some evidence that there has been a reversal of the age of the first sexual experience of teenagers, and there has been an increase in patients requesting help over the wide spectrum of sexual dysfunction. One area where this has become particularly evident is male erectile disorder, for which a proliferation of treatment centers, both within the health service and in the private sector, has developed. A recent attempt to define sexual dysfunction is "the persistent impairment of the normal patterns of sexual interest or response."

B. The Availability of Diagnosis and Treatment

Within the United Kingdom, all patients are entitled to free consultation under the National Health Service. The planning and availability of sexual dysfunction clinics varies widely from area to area. Traditionally, these have been within family planning clinics and have gradually been extended by interested clinicians within gynecology, psychiatry/psychosexual, and genitourinary clinics. The family planning association service has been traditionally run by doctors, although there has been a gradual introduction of nursing and psychology staff into these and other treatment clinics. Seminars held by Doctors Balint and Main in the 1960s and 1970s developed the concept of psychosexual medicine and emphasized the importance of using the physical (vaginal) examination in the management of female sexual problems. In the 1980s, patients with male erectile disorder started to be seen within the urology, rather than psychosexual, clinics, although in the 1990s, it is becoming generally agreed that, because around half of these cases are of a psychological nature and a proportion have both organic and psychological components, there is a need for either dual clinics or access to either. There is an increasing awareness of the need to consider cultural factors in sexual dysfunction, and this is particularly important for various ethnic groups.

A nonhealth service organization offering treatment for sexual dysfunction is available from Relate (formerly Marriage Guidance). Paul Brown, a psychologist, showed in 1974 that psychodynamically trained counselors were able to focus specifically on sexual dysfunctions using behavioral approaches. This organization has a network of specially trained sex therapists who have a training in relationship work. This service is not provided free, but clients are charged nominal sums according to their income—

typically £20 to £30 per session. Other agencies include the Catholic Marriage Advisory Council and the Jewish Marriage Council. Private facilities for diagnosis and treatment of sexual disorder do exist, but are primarily around major cities or areas where no N.H.S. provision is easily accessible.

Treatment approaches include the traditional medical approach using medication, intracavernous injections, VCDs, etc. Psychotherapeutic treatments are usually based on the behavioral model proposed by William Masters and Virginia Johnson, although increasingly with cognitive and systemic strategies incorporated. Some workers continue to use a dynamic model of working with patients. Increasingly, couple therapy is adopted incorporating both relationship and sexual therapy. Surrogacy services are available from the Birmingham clinic run by Martin Cole.

Specialist services for transsexualism exist, with assessment for reassignment surgery possible at Charing Cross Hospital London and St. James's University Hospital, Leeds.

C. Therapist Training and Certification

There is no central certification body within the United Kingdom. The main association is the British Association for Sexual and Marital Therapists (BASMT), which was formed in 1974. This organization approves certain training courses and provides an accreditation process for individuals to apply for. The majority of new therapists will complete an approved course and a further 200 hours of supervised work, alongside fulfilling other criteria (first detailed in 1992) before accreditation. The approved training courses are listed in Section 13. The address for BASMT is P. O. Box 62, Sheffield, S10 3TL.

Currently, a group of BASMT members (The Committee for European Affairs) meets as an approved task force for the European Federation of Sexology. The goals are to establish a consensus within Europe as to what precisely constitutes a multidisciplinary profession of sexology, and subsequently, to devise European Codes of Ethics and Practice for those defining themselves as sexologists; they also seek to define European standards of training and to draw up a European register of accredited practitioners within given subspecialities of sexology.

Medical practitioners may become members of BASMT. Alternatively, they may follow a training course of seminars run by the Institute of Psychosexual Medicine (IPM) and are subsequently examined to become members of the institute. Members are recognized as competent to receive referrals. A diploma recognizes the skills of those who have been training for two years, but do not wish to make the treatment of sexual problems a specialist field. Contact: IPM, 11 Chandos Street, Cavendish Square, London, W1M 9DE.

The Diploma in Sexual Medicine (DSM) is awarded to doctors who can produce evidence of training and experience, as well as successfully passing written and oral examinations in the fields of sexual medicine. Areas in which the above must be demonstrated are gynecology, sexual medicine, and the physical and psychological aspects of assessing and treating sexual problems. Details are available from the Institute of Obstetrics and Gynaecology, Queen Charlotte's Hospital, Goldhawk Road, London, W6 0XG.

The Royal Medical Colleges do not offer training or accreditation in sexual dysfunction, but membership does reflect postgraduate training and examination to an advanced level within a given speciality. Three relevant colleges are:

Royal College of Obstetrics and Gynaecology, 27 Sussex Place, Regents Park, London, NW1 4RG United Kingdom—The Faculty of Family Planning and Reproductive Health Care (RCOG) have a particular interest in the field of psychosexual medicine.

Royal College of Surgeons of England, 35-43 Lincoln's Inn Fields, London, WC2A 3PN, United Kingdom.

Royal College of Psychiatrists, 17 Belgrave Square, London, SW1X 8PG United Kingdom.

13. Research and Advanced Education

KEVAN R. WYLIE

A. Institutes and Programs for Sexological Research

The support and financial availability for research within the United Kingdom remains limited. Several sexological research units exist, including the MRC unit in Edinburgh, and the Institute of Psychiatry and teams in Oxford, Sheffield, and Southampton. There remain many political pressures to frustrate sexological research, with the government declining to finance the *United Kingdom National Survey of Sexual Attitudes in Lifestyle* in 1989. Political influence is also exerted on education with the Health Education Authority shelving a *Pocket Guide to Sex* after the government attacked its colloquial frankness.

B. Programs for the Advanced Study of Human Sexuality

Sex education is now compulsory in state secondary schools as a result of the 1993 Education Act, although reference to nonbiological behavior has been removed from the national science curriculum. The training in human sexuality in United Kingdom medical schools for medical undergraduates has been reviewed by Reader (1994). Education and training in human sexuality, including postgraduate training, has recently been considered by Griffin (1995).

Postgraduate training exists for various professions. The courses are usually attended by both medical graduates, as well as workers from other health-care disciplines. As courses expand to the master's level, the qualifications required for entry into these courses become more stringent.

These are classified as either an approved course by BASMT or nonapproved. The BASMT approved training courses are:

Diploma in Psychosexual Therapy (Marriage Guidance), Herbert Gray College, Little Church Street, Rugby CV21 3AP United Kingdom..

Master of Science degree in The Theory and Practice of Psychotherapy for Sexual Dysfunction, The Porterbrook Clinic, Whiteley Wood Clinic, Woofindin Road, Sheffield S10 3TL United Kingdom.

Diploma in Psychosexual Health Care, Department of Psychiatry, Withington Hospital, Didsbury, Manchester M20 8LR United Kingdom.

Master of Science degree in Human Sexuality, Human Sexuality Unit, 3rd Floor Lanesborough Wing, St. George's Hospital Medical School, Cranmer Terrace, London SW17 0RE United Kingdom.

Master of Science degree in Therapy with Couples, The Registry, Institute of Psychiatry, De Crespigny Park, Denmark Hill, London SE5 8AF United Kingdom.

Certificate in Psychosexual Counseling and Therapy, South East Hants Health Authority, c/o Myrtle Cottage, Selbourne, Nr Alton, Hants GU34 3LB United Kingdom.

Other training courses may apply for BASMT approval in the future. At the time of this writing, the Diploma Course in Psychosexual Therapy, offered by London Marriage Guidance, has provisional approval. A Master of Science degree in Human Sexuality and Relationship Psychotherapy is offered by East Berkshire College, which has not yet sought approval. (See also Section 12C above on therapist training and certification.)

C. Sexological Journals and Periodicals

The major sexological journals in the United Kingdom are:

Sexual and Marital Therapy. Editor: Patricia d'Ardenne, Department of Psychological Medicine, William Harvey House, 61 St. Bartholomews Close, London EC1A 7BE, United Kingdom (Published four times a year from 1996).

The International Journal for Impotence Research. Editors: William L Furlow and Gorm Wagner, Smith-Gordon and Company Ltd., Number 1, 16 Gunter Grove, London SW10 0UJ, United Kingdom (Published quarterly).

British Journal of Family Planning. Editor: Jeannette Cayley, RGOG, 27 Sussex Place, Regents' Park, London NW1 4RG United Kingdom.

The Institute of Psychosexual Medicine Journal. Editors: Dr. H. Montford and Dr. R. Skrine, c/o 11 Chandos Street, London (Published 3 times a year).

The British Journal of Sexual Medicine. Editor: Paul Woolley, Hayward Medical Communications Ltd., 44 Earlham Street, Covent Garden, London WC2H 9LA, United Kingdom (Published six times a year).

Journal of Sexual Health. Editor: Dr. Alan Riley, MAP Publishing, Sussex Court, 10 Station Road, Chertsey, Surrey KT16 8BE, United Kingdom (Published ten times a year).

Perversions: The International Journal of Gay and Lesbian Studies. Editors: Neil McKenna and Linda Semple, BM Perversions, London WC1N 3XX, United Kingdom (Published three times a year).

The Journal of Gender Studies. Editors: Jenny Wolmark and Jenny Hockey, University of Humberside, Ing Lemine Avenue, Hill HU6 7RX United Kingdom (Published twice a year).

D. Important National and Regional Sexological Organizations

Organizations dealing with sexuality include the following:

British Association of Sexual and Marital Therapists, P. O. Box 62, Sheffield S10 3TL United Kingdom.

British Association for Sex and Marital Therapy, 7 Grange Park Place, Thruston Road, Wimbledon, London SW20 0EE. United Kingdom. Telephone/Fax: 44-181-241-1201.

Family Planning Association, 27-35 Mortimer Street, London W1N 7RJ United Kingdom. Telephone: 44-71-636-7866; Fax: 44-71-436-3288.

Marie Stopes UK, 6 Grafton Mews, London W1P 5LF United Kingdom. Telephone: 44-71-383-2494; Fax: 44-71-388-1885.

Sex Education Forum and National Children's Bureau, 8 Wakley Street, London C1V 7QE United Kingdom. Telephone: 44-71-278-9441; Fax 44-71-278-9512.

Institute of Psychosexual Medicine, 11 Chandos Street, Cavendish Square, London W1M 9DE United Kingdom.

British Society for Psychosomatic Obstetrics, Gynaecology and Andrology, 11 Chelmsford Square, London NW10 3AP United Kingdom.

Marce Society (Mental illness related to childbearing), c/o Dr. T. Friedman, Liaison Psychiatry Service, Leicester General Hospital, Gwendoeln Road, Leicester LE5 4PW United Kingdom.

Tavistock Marital Studies Institute, The Tavistock Centre, 120 Belsize Lane, London NW3 5BN United Kingdom.

Institute for Sex Education & Research, 40 School Road, Moseley Birmingham B13 9SN United Kingdom.

Relate, Herbert Gray College, Little Church Street, Rugby CV21 3AP United Kingdom.

E. Service Agencies Offering Telephone Advice

The following are a list of telephone hotlines available in the United Kingdom:

AIDS Helpline: 0800 567123

Victim Support: 0171 735 9166

Pace (gay & lesbian couples): 0171 700 1323

Spod (people with disabilities): 0171 607 8851

National Association for Premenstrual Syndrome: 0173 274 1709

Rape Crisis Centre: 0133 237 2545
Sex Addicts Anonymous: 0171 472 7278
Survivors (male sex-abuse victims): 0171 833 3737
National Association for the Childless: 0121 359 7359

14. Significant Differences in Sexual Attitudes and Behaviors Among Ethnic Minorities

KEVAN R. WYLIE

It is well-acknowledged that sexual function and behavior is affected by both social and cultural influence. Until recently, there has been a trend towards trying to fit patients into existing services without considering development of new therapist skills to meet a patient's individual cultural needs. Specific skills for counseling clients of different cultures have only recently been developed. The approach proposed by d'Ardenne and Mahtani (1989) has been practiced based on using an essentially client-centered and non-hierarchical model. The use of English language and nonverbal communication, as well as bilingualism and the use of interpreters, are important factors to consider. Within their text, there is a large resource list of organizations in the United Kingdom that may help therapists develop cultural knowledge in a certain field.

Clulow (1993) has considered ethnic and religious differences in couple relationships. The presentation of ethnic minorities to sexual dysfunction clinics pose particular problems to clinicians in addition to the cultural issues mentioned above. There are high expectations that physical remedies will be available (Ghosh et al. 1985). An excellent review of presentation of sexual problems within different cultures, clinical assessment, and their management has recently been presented by Bhugra and De Silva (1993). As newer medications become recognized as having potentially beneficial applications in sexual dysfunction, the clinician may have a further armaturarium towards helping some patients within this group.

The issue of HIV, sexuality, and ethnic minorities, particularly Afro-Caribbeans, is an area where there is increasing interest in the United Kingdom.

References and Suggested Readings

Alexander, M., J. Gunn, P. A. G. Cook, P. J. Taylor, and J. Finch. 1993. "Should a Sexual Offender Be Allowed Castration?" *British Medical Journal*, 307:790-93.

Alfred Marks Bureau. 1991. *Sexual Harassment in the Office: A Quantitative Report on Client Attitudes and Experience.* Richmond-upon-Thames: Adsearch.

Allen, I. 1987. "Education in Sex and Personal Relationships." Reprinted in Special Edition on Sex Education, *Sexual and Marital Therapy*, 9(2), 1994.

American Psychiatric Association. 1994. *Diagnostic and Statistical Manual of Mental Disorders, 4th ed.* Washington, DC: American Psychiatric Association.

Bateman, A., and E. F. Mendelssohn. 1989. "Sexual Offences: Help for the Forgotten Victims." *Sexual and Marital Therapy*, 4:5-10.

Benson, C., and R. Matthews. 1995. *The National Vice Squad Survey*. London: Middlesex University.

Bhugra, D., and P. De Silva. 1993. "Sexual Dysfunction Across Cultures." *International Review of Psychiatry*, 5:243-52.

Bownes, I. T. 1993. "Sexual and Relationship Dysfunction in Sexual Offenders." *Sexual and Marital Therapy*, 8:157-65.

Brook Advisory Centres. August 1995. *Teenage Pregnancy—Key Facts*. London.

Burns, J. 1993. "Sexuality, Sexual Problems, and People with Learning Difficulties." In J. Ussher and C. Baker, eds., *Psychological Perspectives on Sexual Problems*. London: Routledge.

Carr, S. V. 1995. "The Health of Women Working in the Sex Industry—A Moral and Ethical Perspective." *Sexual and Marital Therapy*, 10:201-13.

Central Policy Review Staff. 1973. *Report of the Population Panel. Cmnd. 5258*. London: HMSO.

Charles, E. 1936. *The Menace of Under-Population*. London: Watts & Co.

Charles, E. 1938. "Present Trends of Fertility and Mortality." In L. Hogben, *Political Arithmetic*. London: Allen & Unwym.

Clarke, P. June 1995. "Awareness of Sexually Transmitted Diseases: An International Survey." Presented at 19th International Congress of Chemotherapy, Montreal, Canada.

Clulow, C. 1993. "Marriage Across Frontiers: National Ethnic and Religious Differences in Partnership." *Sexual and Marital Therapy*, 8:81-87.

Coleman, D., and J. Salt. 1992. *The British Population: Patterns, Trends, Processes*. Oxford: Oxford University Press.

Collier, R. 1995. *Combating Sexual Harassment in the Workplace*. Buckingham: Open University Press.

Communicable Disease Report. 1995. *Sexually Transmitted Diseases Quarterly Report: Genital Infection with Chlamydia Trachomatis in England and Wales*. London: HMSO, 5:122-23.

Communicable Disease Report. 1995. *Sexually Transmitted Diseases Quarterly Report: Genital Warts and Genital Herpes Simplex Virus Infections in England and Wales*. London: HMSO, 5:186-87.

Communicable Disease Report. 1995. *Sexually Transmitted Diseases Quarterly Report: Gonorrhea in England and Wales*. London: HMSO, 5:62-63.

Confederation of Health Service Employees (COHSE). 1991. *An Abuse of Power: Sexual Harassment in the National Health Service*. Banstead, Surrey: COHSE.

Cossey, C. 1991. *My Story*. London: Faber and Faber.

Cowell, R. 1954. *Roberta Cowell's Story*. Surrey: Windmill Press.

Craft, A. 1991. *Living Your Life: A Sex Education and Personal Development Programme for Care Workers with People with Learning Disabilities*. Wisbech, Cambs: Learning Development Aids.

Craft, A. 1993. *It Could Never Happen Here! The Prevention and Treatment of Sexual Abuse of Adults with Learning Disabilities in Residential Settings*. Chesterfield and Nottingham: Association for Residential Care, National Association for the Protection from Sexual Abuse of Adults and Children with Learning Disabilities.

Craft, A., and M. Craft. 1988. *Sex and the Mentally Handicapped* (rev. ed.). London: Routledge.

Craft, A., and J. Crosby. 1991. *Parental Involvement in the Sex Education of Students with Severe Learning Difficulties: A Handbook*. Nottingham: Department of Mental Handicap, University of Nottingham Medical School.

d'Ardenne, P., and A. Mahtani. 1989. *Transcultural Counseling in Action.* London: Sage Publications.

Dancey, C. 1994. "Sexual Orientation in Women." In P. Choi and P. Nicolson, eds., *Female Sexuality: Psychology, Biology and Social Context.* Hemel Hempstead: Harvester Wheatsheaf.

Davidson, M. J., and S. Earnshaw. 1991. "Policies, Practices and Attitudes Towards Sexual Harassment in UK Organizations." *Women in Management Review and Abstracts,* 6:15-21.

Davies, P. M., F. C. I. Hickson, P. Weatherburn, and A. J. Hunt. 1993. *Sex, Gay Men and AIDS.* London: The Falmer Press, The Taylor & Francis Group.

Department of Health. 1992. *The Health of the Nation: A Strategy for Health in England.* London: HMSO.

Department of Health. 1995. "Sexually Transmitted Diseases. England 1994." *Statistical Bulletin 16.* London: HMSO.

Dine, J., and B. Watt. 1995. "Sexual Harassment: Moving Away from Discrimination." *The Modern Law Review,* 58:343-63.

East Sussex County Council. 1992. *Personal Relationships and Sexuality: Guidelines for Careers Working with People with Learning Disabilities.* Brighton: East Sussex County Council.

Fallowell, D., and A. Ashley. 1982. *April Ashley's Odyssey.* London: Jonathan Cape Ltd.

Family Planning Association (FBA). 1994 (March). *Abortion: Statistical Trends. Factsheet 6A.* London.

Family Planning Association (FBA). 1994 (May). *Abortion: Legal and Ethical Issues. Factsheet 6B.* London.

Family Planning Association (FBA). 1994 (October). *Factsheet 5A: Teenage Pregnancies.* London.

Farley, L. 1978. *Sexual Shakedown: The Sexual Harassment of Women on the Job.* New York: McGraw-Hill.

Fisher, D., and L. L. K. Howells. 1993. "Social Relationships and Sexual Offenders." *Sexual and Marital Therapy,* 8:123-36.

General Register Office (Northern Ireland). *Annual Reports 1990-1994. (Abstract 12).* Belfast: GRO(NI).

General Register Office (Scotland). *Annual Reports 1984 and 1994.* Edinburgh: GRO(S).

Ghosh, G., M. Dubble, and A. Ingram. 1985. "Treating Patients of Asian Origin Presenting in the United Kingdom with Sexual Dysfunction." Paper presented at the Seventh World Congress of Sexology, New Delhi, India.

Gillick, Victoria. 1994. "Letter. Confidentiality, Contraception and Young People." *British Medical Journal,* 308:342-43.

Glass, D. V. 1963. *The Struggle for Population.* Oxford: Oxford University Press.

Greenhouse, P. 1994. "A Sexual Health Service Under One Roof." In J. Pillaye, ed., *Sexual Health Promotion in Genitourinary Medicine Clinics* (Chapter 3). London: Health Education Authority.

Griffin, M. 1995. "Education and Training in Human Sexuality." *International Review of Psychiatry,* 7:275-84.

Gunn, M. 1991. *Sex and the Law: A Brief Guide for Staff Working with People with Learning Difficulties.* London: Family Planning Association.

H.M.S.O. 1987. *Guidance on Sex Education 11/87.* London: Department of Education and Science.

H.M.S.O. 1988. *Circular 12/88. Local Government Act 1988.* London: Department of the Environment.

H.M.S.O. 1988. *Education Reform Act.* London: Department of Education and Science.

H.M.S.O. 1992. *Health of a Nation: A Strategy for Health in England.* London: Department of Health.

H.M.S.O. 1993. *Education Act.* London: Department of Education and Science.

Her Majesty's Inspectorate of Constabulary. (1993). *Equal Opportunities in the Police Service.* London: Her Majesty's Inspectorate of Constabulary.

Hertfordshire County Council. 1989. *Departmental Policies and Guidelines for Staff on the Sexual and Personal Relationships of People with a Mental Handicap.* Hertford: Hertfordshire County Council Social Services Department.

Hewitt, P., and J. Warren. 1995. *A Self Made Man.* London: Headline Books.

Hicken, I. ed. 1994. *Sexual Health Education and Training.* Milton Keynes, England: The English National Board for Nursing Midwifery and Health Visiting, Learning Materials Design.

Hogben, L., ed. 1938. *Polical Arithmetic.* London: Allen & Unwin.

Hubback, E. M. 1947. *The Population of Britain.* London: Penguin Books.

Holmans, A. E. 1963. "Current Population Trends in Britain." *Scottish Journal of Political Economy,* 1:31-56.

ICD-10. Classification of Mental & Behavioural Disorders. Clinical Descriptions and Diagnostic Guidelines. 1992. World Health Organization.

Industrial Society. 1993. *No Offense? Sexual Harassment, How It Happens and How to Beat It.* London: Industrial Society.

Jehu, D. 1991. "Post Traumatic Stress Reactions Among Adults Molested as Children." *Sexual and Marital Therapy,* 6:227-43.

Johnson, A. M., J. Wadsworth, K. Wellings, S. Bradshaw, and J. Field. 1992. "Sexual Lifestyles and HIV Risks." *Nature,* 306:410-12.

Johnson, Anne M., Jane Wadsworth, Kaye Wellings, and Julia Field. 1994. *Sexual Attitudes and Lifestyles.* Oxford, United Kingdom: Blackwell Scientific Publications Ltd.

Johnson, P., and J. Falkingham. 1992. *Aging and Social Welfare.* London: Sage.

Joseph Rowntree Foundation. 1995 (July). "Findings: Social Backgrounds and Post-Birth Experiences of Young Parents." *Social Policy Research,* 80.

Kay, D. S. G. 1992. "Masturbation and Mental Health—Uses and Abuses." *Sexual and Marital Therapy (Journal of the British Association for Sexual and Marital Therapy),* 7(1).

Kirby, D. 1995. "Sex and HIV/AIDS Education in Schools." *British Medical Journal,* 311:403.

Kitzinger, C. 1994. "Anti-Lesbian Harassment." In C. Brant and Y-L. Too, eds. *Rethinking Sexual Harassment.* London: Pluto Press.

Komonchack, J., M. Collins, and D. A. Lane, eds. 1990. *The New Dictionary of Theology.* Dublin: Gill and Macmillan Ltd.

Lewington, F. R., and D. J. Rogers. 1995. "Forensic Services for Victims of Sexual Abuse and Assault." *Sexual and Marital Therapy,* 10:215-29.

Livingston, J. A. 1982. "Responses to Sexual Harassment on the Job: Legal, Organizational, and Individual Actions." *Journal of Social Issues,* 38:5-22.

Lloyd, C. 1991. "The Offense: Changes in the Pattern and Nature of Sex Offenses." Criminal Behaviour and Mental Health, 1:115-22.

Lo, S. V., S. Kaul, R. Kaul, S. Cooling, and J. P. Calvert. 1994. "Teenage Pregnancy—Contraceptive Use and Non-Use." *British Journal of Family Planning,* 20:79-83.

London Buses Ltd. 1991. *Report on a Sexual Harassment Survey Undertaken at Three LBL Workplaces.* London: London Buses Ltd.

MacKinnon, C. 1979. *Sexual Harassment of Working Women: A Case of Sex Discrimination.* New Haven, CT: Yale University Press.

McCarthy, M. 1993. "Sexual Experiences of Women with Learning Difficulties in Long-Stay Hospitals. *Sexuality and Disability,* 11(4):277-85.

McCarthy, M., and D. Thompson. 1993. *Sex and the 3R's: Rights, Responsibilties, and Risks. A Sex Education Resource Package for People with Learning Difficulties.* Brighton: Pavilion.

McCleary, G. F. 1942. *Race Suicide.* London: Allen & Unwln.

McMullen, M., and S. Whittle. 1995. *Transvestites, Transsexuals and the Law.* Belper: Beaumont Trust.

Mezey, G., and M. King. 1989. "The Effects of Sexual Assault on Men: A Survey of 22 Victims." *Psychological Medicine,* 19:205-09.

Miller, D. 1995. *Some of My Best Friends Are Gay.* Tyneside: MESMAC.

Miller, E., P. A. Waight, R. S. Tedder, et al. 1995. "Incidence of HIV Infection in Homosexual Men in London, 1988-94." *British Medical Journal,* 311:545.

Morris, J. 1974. *Conundrum.* London: Cononet Books.

Mott, H., and S. Condor. 1995. "Putting Us in Our Place: Secretaries and Sexual Harassment." Paper presented to the British Psychological Society Social Section Conference, College of Ripon and York St. John, University of York, September 14.

National Education Curriculum Council. 1990. *Curriculum Guidance 5.* York: National Curriculum Council.

Nicolson, P. 1993. "Why Women Refer Themselves for Sex Therapy." In J. M. Ussher and C. D. Baker, eds. *Psychological Perspectives on Sexual Problems.* London: Routledge.

Office of Population Census and Surveys. 1987. *Birth Statistics: Historical Series of Statistics from Registration of Births in England and Wales 1837-1983.* Series FM1, no. 13. London: HMSO.

Office of Population Census and Surveys (OPCS). *Monitor-FM1 and Birth Statistics Series for 1992 and 1993.* London: HMSO.

Office of Population Census and Surveys. 1994. *1992-Based National Population Prejections.* Series PP2, no. 19. London: HMSO.

Office of Population Census and Surveys. 1994. *Monitor. AB94/1.* London: Government Statistical Service.

P.H.L.S. AIDS Centre. 1995. "Communicable Disease Surveillance Centre and Scottish Centre for Infection and Environmental Health." *Communicable Disease Report,* 5:183.

P.H.L.S. AIDS Centre. 1995 (June). "Communicable Disease Surveillance Centre and Scottish Centre for Infection and Environmental Health." Unpublished AIDS/HIV Quarterly Surveillance Tables, No. 28.

Pearson, V. A. H., M. R. Owen, D. R. Phillips, D. J. Pereira Gray, and M. N. Marshall. 1995. "Family Planning Services in Devon, U.K.: Awareness, Experience and Attitudes of Pregnant Teenagers." *British Journal of Family Planning,* 21:45-49.

People First. 1993. *Everything You Ever Wanted to Know about Safer Sex . . . But Nobody Bothered to Tell You.* London: People First.

Paintin, D. October 24, 1992. *British Medical Journal,* 305:967-968.

Radcliffe, K.W., et al. 1993. "A Comparison of Sexual Behavior and Risk Behavior for HIV Infection Between Women in Three Clinical Settings." *Genitourinary Medicine,* 69:441-45

Read, J. 1995. *Counseling for Fertility Problems.* London: Sage Publications.

Reader, F. C. 1994. "Training in Human Sexuality in United Kingdom Medical Schools." *Sexual and Marital Therapy,* 9:193-200.

Reddaway, W. B. 1939. *The Economics of a Delining Population.* London: Allen & Unwin.

Report of the Population Panel. 1973. Cmnd 5258. London: HMSO.

Royal Commission on Population. *Report.* Cmnd. 7956. London: HMSO.

Savage, W., and C. Francome. 1989. *Lancet,* ii:1323-24.

Secretary of State for Health. 1992. *The Health of the Nation: A Strategy for Health in England.* London: H.M.S.O.

Selman, P. 1996. "Teenage Pregnancy in the 1960s and 1980s." In J. Millar and H. Jones, *The Politics of the Family.* London: Avebury.

Snaith, P., A. Butler, J. Donnelly, and D. Bromham. 1994. "A Regional Gender Reassignment Service." *Psychiatric Bulletin*, 18:753-56

Thompson, R., and K. Sewell. 1995. *What Took You So Long?* Harmondsbury: Penguin.

Thomson, R., and L. Scott. 1992. *An Enquiry into Sex Education: "Report of a Survey of LEA Support and Monitoring of School Sex Education."* London: National Children's Bureau.

Titmuss, R. 1942. *Parents Revolt: A Study of the Declining Birth Rate in Acquisitive Societies.* London: Secker & Warburg.

Turk, V., and H. Brown. 1993. "The Sexual Abuse of Adults with Learning Disabilities: Results of a Two-Year Incidence Survey." *Mental Handicap Research*, 6:193-216.

von Bühler, J., and L. Tamblin. 1995. "Sexual Knowledge and Attitudes of Students Attending an Integrative Human Sexuality and Relationship Psychotherapy Programme." Research paper presented at the XIIth World Congress of Sexology, Yokohama, Japan, 1995.

Wadsworth, J., J. Field, A. M. Johnson, S. Bradshaw, and K. Wellings. 1993. "Methodology of the National Survey of Sexual Attitudes and Lifestyles. *Journal of the Royal Statistics Society* (Series A), 156:407-21.

Walker, P. A., J. C. Berger, R. Green, D. R. Laub, et al. 1985. "Standards of Care, the Hormonal and Surgical Reassignment of Gender Dysphoric Persons." *Archives of Sexual Behaviour*, 14:79-90.

Wareham, V., and N. Drummond. 1994. "Contraception Use Among Teenagers Seeking Abortion—A Survey from Grampian." *British Journal of Family Planning*, 20:76-78.

Watson, H. 1994. "Red Herrings and Mystifications." In C. Brant and Y-H Too, eds. *Rethinking Sexual Harassment.* London: Pluto Press.

Waugh, M. A. 1990. "History of Clinical Developments in Sexually Transmitted Diseases." In K. K. Holmes, et al., eds., *Sexually Transmitted Diseases* (2nd ed., Chapter 1). New York: McGraw-Hill.

Wellings, K., J. Field, A. M. Johnson, and J. Wadsworth. 1994. *Sexual Behaviour in Britain: The National Survey of Attitudes and Lifestyles.* Harmondsworth: Penguin.

Westrom, L. 1988. "Decrease in Incidence of Women Treated in Hospitals for Acute Salpingitis in Sweden." *Genitourinary Medicine*, 64:59-64.

Williams, C. 1993. "Sexuality and Disability." In J. Ussher and C. Baker, eds., *Psychological Perspectives on Sexual Problems.* London: Routledge.

Wise, S., and L. Stanley. 1987. *Georgie Porgie: Sexual Harassment in Everyday Life.* London: Pandora Press.

Zeki, Sevda. 1992. Unpublished dissertation for the Master of Science in Clinical Psychology, University College, London.

The United States of America

David L. Weis, Ph.D., and Patricia Barthalow Koch, Ph.D.,
editors and contributors, with other contributions by
Diane Baker, M.A.; Ph.D. (cand.); Sandy Bargainnier, Ed.D.;
Sarah C. Conklin, Ph.D.; Martha Cornog, M.A., M.S.;
Richard Cross, M.D.; Marilyn Fithian, Ph.D.;
Jeannie Forrest, M.A.; Andrew D. Forsythe, M.S.;
Robert T. Francoeur, Ph.D., A.C.S.; Barbara Garris, M.A.;
Patricia Goodson, Ph.D.; William E. Hartmann, Ph.D.;
Robert O. Hawkins, Jr., Ph.D.; Linda L. Hendrixson, Ph.D.;
Barrie J. Highby, M.A.; Ariadne Kane, M.Ed.;
Sharon King, M.S.Ed.; Robert Morgan Lawrence, D.C.;
Brenda Love; Charlene L. Muehlenhard, Ph.D.;
Raymond J. Noonan, Ph.D. (cand.); Miguel A. Pérez, Ph.D.;
Timothy Perper, Ph.D.; Helda L. Pinzón, Ph.D.;
Carol Queen, Ph.D. (cand.); Herbert P. Samuels, Ph.D.;
Julian Slowinski, Psy.D.; William Stackhouse, Ph.D.;
William R. Stayton, Th.D.; and Mitchell S. Tepper, M.P.H.*

Contents

*In addition to the above sexologists who authored specific sections of this chapter, the authors and general editor are grateful to other colleagues who served as special consultants: Mark O. Bigler, L.C.S.W., Ph.D., Bonnie Bullough, R.N., Ph.D.; Vern L. Bullough, R.N., Ph.D.; Sandra S. Cole, Ph.D.; Carol A. Darling, Ph.D.; J. Kenneth Davidson, Ph.D.; Clive Davis, Ph.D.; Karen Komisky-Brash, M.A.; Barbara Van Oss Marin, Ph.D.; Ted McIlvenna, Th.D, Ph.D.; John Money, Ph.D.; Gina Ogden, Ph.D.; Paul Okami, Ph.D.; Letitia Anne Peplau, Ph.D.; and Stephanie Wadell, M.A. Although these colleagues generously contributed resource materials and their expertise for sections of the chapter, the authors and general editor accept full responsibility for the final integration of the material presented in this chapter.

A Brief Foreword

ROBERT T. FRANCOEUR

This extensive chapter on sexuality in the United States is unique in this multivolume *International Encyclopedia of Sexuality* for three reasons: (1) the vast amount of research information and data available on American sexuality, (2) the ethnic and religious complexity of the population, and (3) the number of sexologists involved in its preparation. Twenty-three specialists joined me and the chapter coeditors, Drs. Patricia Barthalow Koch and David L. Weis, in writing individual sections. An additional fifteen specialists advised individual writers on topics within their expertise.

Because the editors were very much aware of and sensitive to the diversity of our contributors and their varied and rich perspectives, we felt it was important to let each contributor speak for her or himself. In respecting this freedom and diversity, we feel a strong responsibility to comment on the consequences of this decision for the reader.

The reader should *not* expect to find in this chapter a single, consistent, and coherent picture of sexual attitudes and behaviors in the United States. In some sections, the reader will encounter an insider's or emic view of a particular aspect, e.g., Ariadne Kane offers an insider's view of cross-gender issues, and Mitchell Tepper writes about sexuality and people with physical and developmental disabilities from both his personal experience and professional perspective. Most of the other contributors write from an etic view as outside researchers or observers. To appreciate critically these various views, the reader should consider the perspective of the individual writer. Among the contributors to this chapter, the reader will encounter researchers, therapists, counselors, and educators. Each researcher, therapist, counselor, or educator will be more or less strongly influenced by her or his professional background and training as a psychologist, sociologist, biologist, health-care professional, behavioral biologist, nonverbal behaviorist, social, clinical, or evolutionary psychologist, cultural or evolutionary sociologist, anthropologist, health educator, gender specialist, or activist/advocate.

The reader will encounter research theories and statistics throughout the chapter. These data may represent the results of studies conducted by researchers who might have been constrained by popular interests, political restrictions, or the biases of funding agencies to devote their time and energy to, perhaps, interesting and useful, but trendy research. Thus, they may have had to devote their expertise to more limited, and perhaps chic or politically safe research.

The chapter presented here represents a mosaic that is not always coherent—nor could it be, given the diversity of American sexologists, the funding and support for sexology, and the ever-changing complex of American sexual attitudes, biases, and values. This chapter does, however, present a solid picture of what American sexologists do when they summarize the research and data available on topics in their own domain of interest and specialization.

American Demographics and a Sketch of Diversity, Change, and Social Conflict

DAVID L. WEIS

A. A Demographic Overview

In one sense, great diversity is virtually guaranteed by the sheer size of the United States. The U.S.A. is a union of fifty participating states. It is one of the larger nations in the world, with the forty-eight contiguous states spanning more than three thousand miles across the North American continent, from its eastern shores on the Atlantic Ocean to its western shores on the Pacific Ocean, and more than two thousand miles from its northern border with Canada to its southern border with Mexico and the Gulf of Mexico. In addition, the state of Alaska, itself a large landmass covering thousands of square miles in the northwest corner of North America, and the state of Hawaii, a collection of islands in the mid-Pacific Ocean, are part of the union.

The U.S.A. has a population of more than 260 million racially and ethnically heterogeneous people (Wilkinson 1987; *World Almanac and Book of Facts, 1993*). A majority, about 161 million or two thirds, are white descendants of immigrants from the European continent, with sizable groups from Great Britain, Ireland, Italy, Germany, and Poland. The second-largest group, roughly 29 million or 12 percent, is African-American, most of whose ancestors were brought to North America as slaves before the twentieth century. The third-largest group, 22 million or 9 percent, is comprised of Hispanic-Americans, whose ancestors emigrated from such places as Mexico, Puerto Rico, Cuba, Haiti, and the Dominican Republic, as well as other Central and South American nations. Hispanics represent the fastest-growing minority group in the U.S.A.. There are also more than two million Native Americans—Eskimos, Aleuts, and those mistakenly at one time called Indians—whose ancestors have occupied North America for thousands of years, and whose residence within the boundaries of what is now the U.S.A. predates all of the other groups mentioned.

Another group experiencing rapid growth in recent decades is Asian-Americans; there are now more than three million residents of Asian heritage. Substantial populations of Japanese and Chinese immigrants have been in the U.S.A. since the nineteenth century. More recently, there has been an increase from such nations as India, Vietnam, Korea, the Philippines, Cambodia, Indonesia, and Pakistan. Finally, there are smaller groups of immigrants from virtually every nation, with growing numbers of Moslems in recent decades. The size of the various nonwhite minority groups has been increasing in the last thirty years, both in terms of real numbers and as a percentage of the total U.S.A. population (Wilkinson 1987; *World Almanac 1993*).

It is fair to conclude that the U.S.A. is generally a nation of former immigrants. Moreover, one continuing feature of American history has been the successive immigration of different groups at different points in time (Wells 1985).

Approximately two thirds of the population lives within one hundred miles of one of the coastal shorelines. Most of the largest metropolitan areas lie within these coastal areas, and it is worth noting that most sexologists in the U.S.A. also reside in these same areas.

The U.S.A. is somewhat unique among the world's economies in that it is simultaneously one of the largest agricultural producers as well as one of the largest industrialized nations, exporting manufactured goods and technology to the rest of the world. Historically, the northeast and upper midwest have been the principal industrial centers, and the southeast and the central Great Plains have been the agricultural centers.

One of the economically richest nations in the world, America, nevertheless, has an estimated 500,000 to 600,000 individuals and 125,000 to 150,000 families homeless on any night. Overall, 15 percent of Americans—30 percent of the poor—are without health insurance. Infant-mortality rates and life-expectancy rates vary widely, depending on socioeconomic status and residence in urban, suburban, or rural settings. Fifty-two million American married couples are paralleled by 2.8 million unmarried households and close to 8 million single-parent families.

In summarizing aspects of sexuality in America, it is helpful to keep in mind that the United States of the twenty-first century will look profoundly different from the nation described in this chapter. Four major trends for the future have been detailed in *Population Profile of the United States* (1995), published by the U.S. Census Bureau.

- The average life expectancy for an American in 1900 was 47 years. An American born in 1970 had a life expectancy of 70.8 years. This rose to 76 years in 1993 and is projected to reach 82.6 years by 2050.
- The median age of Americans is currently 34; early in the next century, it will be 39. There are currently 33 million Americans over 65; this number will more than double to 80 million in 2050.
- America's ethnic minorities will continue to grow far more quickly than the majority white population, due to immigration and higher birthrates. In 1994, for the first time, more Hispanics than whites were added to the population. If current trends hold, the percentage of white Americans will decline from 73.7 percent in 1995 to 52.5 percent in 2050.
- In 1994, 24 percent of all children under age 18 (18.6 million) lived with a single parent, double the percent in 1970. Of these single parents, 36 percent had never been married, up 50 percent from 1985. Meanwhile, the number of unmarried cohabiting couples increased 700 percent in the past decade.

There is also great diversity in religious affiliation in the U.S.A. (Marciano 1987; see Section 2A). To a considerable degree, the choice of religious denomination is directly related to the ethnic patterns previously described. The overwhelming majority of Americans represent the Judeo-Christian heritage, but that statement is potentially misleading. Within the Judeo-Christian heritage, there are substantial populations of Roman Catholics, mainstream Protestants (Lutheran, Methodist, Baptist, Episcopalian, and others), and a growing number of fundamentalist Christians. There is no great uniformity in religious practice or sexual mores shared by these various groups. In addition, there is a relatively small percentage of Americans who are Jewish and range from ultra-orthodox to conservative, reformed, and liberal. In recent decades, as immigration from Asia has increased, there has been a corresponding growth in the Moslem and Hindu faiths.

Several trends related to the practice of religion in the U.S.A. have become a source of recent social concern. These trends include: the declining attendance at the traditional Protestant and Catholic churches, in what has been labeled the growing "secularization" of American culture; the "religious revivalism" reflected by the growth of fundamentalist churches; the growth of religious cults (e.g., Hare Krishna and the Unification Church); the growing power of the conservative Christian Coalition; and the emergence of the "Electronic Church" (religious broadcasting) (Marciano 1987). Throughout the history of this nation, diversity of religious beliefs and the separation of church and state have been central elements in conflicts over sexual morality.

The subcultures and peoples of the United States are as varied, diverse, and complex as any other large nation. The unique feature of sexuality in the United States is that we have far more information and data on

American sexual attitudes, values, and behaviors than is available for any other country.

B. A Sketch of Recent Diversity, Change, and Social Conflict

A few examples will illustrate some of the issues that have been affected by this complex of influences.

- Dr. Joycelyn Elders was fired in late 1994 as the Surgeon General of the United States for saying that children perhaps should be taught in school about masturbation. Elders, who was called the "Condom Queen" by conservatives in the United States, had become what the press described as a "political liability" to President Bill Clinton for expressing her views on controversial social issues, such as abortion, condom education for youth, and drug legalization (Cohn 1994). However, her firing was a direct reaction to comments she made about including masturbation as a part of sex-education programs for children. Elders made her comments on December 1, 1994, in an address to a World AIDS Day conference in New York City. In response to a question from the audience about her views on masturbation, Elders said, "I think that is something that is a part of human sexuality, and it's a part of something that perhaps should be taught. But we've not even taught our children the very basics." She added, "I feel that we have tried ignorance for a very long time, and it's time we try education" (Hunt 1994). In announcing her dismissal, the Clinton administration pointedly indicated that the President disagreed with her views.
- After decades of explicitly banning homosexuals from the military, President Clinton proposed ending the ban shortly after he assumed office. Eventually, the policy put into place, popularly known as "Don't ask, don't tell," was one in which the military agreed that they would stop asking recruits to report their sexual orientation. However, gays and lesbians can only serve in the armed forces if they keep their orientation private (*Newsweek* 1993, 6). In 1996, with the state of Hawaii on the verge of granting legal status to same-sex unions, several states moved quickly to enact laws banning the legal recognition of such unions, despite the Constitutional requirement that all states reciprocally recognize the legal acts of other states. In June 1996, a House Judiciary Committee passed a bill that would absolve individual states from recognizing same-sex marriages if legalized in another state. The bill would also bar Federal recognition of such marriages in procedures involving taxes, pensions, and other benefits. Despite emotional debate in Congress, the measure cleared both the U.S. House of Representatives and Senate. Although the President signed the bill into law, this debate remained a lightening-rod issue (Schmitt 1996).

- In late 1993, the book, *Private Parts*, by radio disc-jockey Howard Stern (1993), the inventor of "Shock Rock" radio, was published. Stern's radio shows had had a large audience across the U.S.A. for more than a decade. He had been strongly condemned by some for the sexual explicitness of his shows and criticized by others for the sexist nature of those same shows. On several occasions, his shows had been investigated by the Federal Communications Commission (FCC). *Private Parts*, a lurid account of Stern's shows and his sexual fantasies, was roundly criticized. However, it was also the best-selling book in the U.S.A. in 1993 (Adler 1994).
- In 1993, the state of Idaho passed a law banning thong bikinis at exotic-dancing establishments (topless dancing had already been outlawed). One result was a series of protests outside the state legislature (*Newsweek* 1993, 6).
- There is a growing wave of censorship being engineered by grassroots far-right organizations targeting, in particular, sexuality-education textbooks and programs in local school districts throughout the country. Fear of personal attacks, disruption, controversy, and costly lawsuits have resulted in more teachers, administrators, and school boards yielding to the demands of vocal minority groups. In more than a third of documented incidents, challenged materials and programs were either removed, canceled, or replaced with abstinence-only material or curricula (Sedway 1992). In mid-1996, a three-judge federal panel declared unconstitutional major parts of a new law intended to regulate "indecent" and "patently offensive" speech on the Internet, including information on abortion. Even as the judges described attempts to regulate content on the Internet as a "profoundly repugnant" affront to the First Amendment's guarantee of free speech, the government planned an appeal to the U.S. Supreme Court. Both the Senate and House of Representatives had overwhelmingly passed the bill that included the Communications Decency Act (CDA), and the President signed it into law. As of March 1997, the CDA is going to the Supreme Court, with a decision expected in June.
- The term "sexual harassment" did not appear in American culture until around 1975. In the years since, there has been a tremendous growth in research on the problem and growing social conflict over its prevalence and definition. As late as 1991, when Anita Hill testified against Supreme Court nominee Clarence Thomas, only 29 percent of Americans believed her claims (Solomon and Miller 1994). Yet the number of women filing claims doubled in the 1990s, and the U.S. Supreme Court ruled in 1993 that harassment could be determined if a worker demonstrated that the workplace environment was "hostile" or "abusive" to a "reasonable person" (Kaplan 1993). Workers would no longer have to demonstrate that severe psychological injury had

occurred as a consequence. Similar controversies over definitions, prevalence, and credibility of claims have emerged with the issues of incest, child sexual abuse, and date or acquaintance rape.

- By the middle of the 1990s, seven physicians and clinical staff members had been killed by anti-abortion activists. Over 80 percent of abortion providers in the U.S.A. have been picketed, and many have experienced other forms of harassment, including bomb and death threats, blockades, invasion of facilities, destruction of property, and assaults on patients and staff. The most recent tactic adopted by abortion opponents is to locate women who have had a bad experience with an abortion in order to persuade them to file a malpractice suit against the physician who performed the abortion.
- In mid-1995, Norma Leah McCorvey, the Jane Roe at the epicenter of the 1973 *Roe v. Wade* Supreme Court decision legalizing abortion, announced she had quit her work at a Dallas, Texas, abortion clinic, had been baptized in a swimming pool by a minister of Operation Rescue, a national anti-abortion group, and would be working at the Operation Rescue office next door to the abortion clinic. Although there is "immense symbolic importance" in McCorvey's announcement, it is odd that the born-again-Christian Operation Rescue group would embrace her so enthusiastically, given her declarations that she still believes "a woman has a right to have an abortion, a safe and legal abortion, in the first trimester" of pregnancy, and that she would continue living with her lesbian partner and working for lesbian rights (Verhovek 1995). In mid-1996, abortion again emerged as a major election issue when Robert Dole, the Republican Party candidate for president, called for a statement of tolerance in the Republican platform, a move vehemently opposed by conservative Republicans. Also in mid-1996, the Southern Baptist Convention, the nation's second largest religious denomination, called for a boycott of Walt Disney Company stores and theme parks to protest the company's "anti-Christian and anti-family trend" in extending health benefits to the same-sex partners of employees.

Each of the above incidents serves as an intriguing indicator of the state of sexuality in the United States, and each also reveals much about the interaction of politics and sexual issues as we approach the end of the twentieth century. They demonstrate that, despite the immense social changes that have occurred during this century, a strong element of religious fundamentalism and conservatism remain active within the culture. In fact, a full explanation of sexuality in the United States requires an understanding of the diverse sexual, social, and political ideologies characterizing the culture, and the ongoing conflict between various groups over those ideologies.

In this respect, there is a rather schizophrenic character to sexuality in the United States. On the one hand, the U.S.A. is a country with a multi-billion-dollar-a-year erotica/pornography business; a mass-media system where movies, television, books, magazines, and popular music are saturated with sexually titillating content alongside serious educational material; a high rate of premarital sex (nearly 90 percent by the 1990s); one of the most active and open gay-rights movements in the world; and a continuing public fascination with unusual sexual practices, extramarital sex, and gender-orientation issues, including, most recently, bisexuality.

On the other hand, federal, state, and local governments have invested heavily in recent years in prosecuting businesses for obscenity, allowed discriminatory practices based on sexual orientation, largely failed to implement comprehensive sexuality-education programs in the schools, and refused to support accessibility to contraceptives for adolescents. The consequences of these failures include one of the highest teenage-pregnancy and abortion rates in the world and increasing incidents of gay-bashing that reflect the prevalence of homonegative and homophobic attitudes in the U.S.A.

These examples illustrate one of the major themes in this chapter: the changing nature of sexuality in the U.S.A. throughout the twentieth century. Although accounts of changing sexual norms and practices are frequently portrayed as occurring in a linear process, we would suggest that the more-typical pattern is one reflected by ongoing conflicts between competing groups over sexual ideology and practice. Each of the examples cited is an illustration of how those conflicts are currently manifested in the social and political arenas in the U.S.A.

A focus on the conflict between groups with contrasting ideologies and agendas over sexual issues will be a second theme of this chapter. This process of changing sexual attitudes, practices, and policies in an atmosphere that approaches "civil war" is a reflection of the tremendous diversity within American culture. In many respects, the widespread conflict over sexual issues is a direct outcome of the diversity of groups holding a vested interest in the outcomes of these conflicts, with some groups seeking to impose their beliefs on everyone.

The diversity of these groups will be the third major theme of the chapter. One example that will be apparent throughout this chapter is the question of gender. There is growing evidence that men and women in the U.S.A. tend to hold different sexual attitudes and ideologies, to exhibit different patterns of sexual behavior, and to pursue different sexual lifestyles—frequently at odds with each other (Oliver and Hyde 1993). In some ways, it may even be useful to view male and female perspectives as stemming from distinct gender cultures. In reviewing sexuality in the U.S.A., we will frequently attempt to assess how change occurs in a context of conflict between diverse social groups.

1. Basic Sexological Premises

DAVID L. WEIS

This overall theme of social change occurring in a process of conflict between diverse groups is woven throughout the history of the U.S.A. itself. There are at least two ways in which a study of history is important to an understanding of contemporary sexological premises and sexual patterns in the U.S.A. First, there is a specific history of sexual norms and customs changing over time. To the extent that sexual attitudes and practices are shared by the members of a social group or population in a particular time period, they can be viewed as social institutions. Unfortunately, it is exceedingly difficult to describe such sexual institutions in the U.S.A. prior to the twentieth century, because there are few reliable empirical data sets available for that period. To a large extent, we have to rely on records of what people said about their own or others' sexual attitudes and practices, and such statements may be suspect. Still, it seems reasonable to suggest that current sexual norms and customs have been shaped, at least in part, by earlier patterns.

In addition, there is a second way in which the general social history of the U.S.A. is important to understanding changing sexual institutions. Sexuality, like other social institutions, does not operate in a vacuum. It is related to and influenced by other social institutions, such as the economy, government, marriage and the family, religion, and education, as well as social patterns such as age distributions and gender ratios. As we will discuss in Section 2, a good deal of research evidence indicates that such social institutions are often related to various sexual variables. Researchers have not consistently tested these associations, but the point is a crucial one theoretically for explaining the dynamics of sexual processes in a culture as large and diverse as the U.S.A.

A. From Colonial Times to the Industrial Revolution

In 1776, at the time of the War for American Independence, the U.S.A. became a nation of thirteen states located along the shore of the Atlantic Ocean. Most of the inhabitants of the former British colonies were of English descent, and they tended to be Protestant. Although the first Africans had been brought to America as indentured servants as early as 1620, the practice of slavery quickly evolved. By the time of independence, an active slave trade involving hundreds of thousands of Africans and Caribbeans was well established. Of course, the Africans and Caribbeans brought their own customs with them, although they were frequently prevented from practicing them. West of the thirteen original states, the remainder of the North American continent within the area now constituting the nation was inhabited by several million Native Americans representing hundreds of tribes, each with its own set of customs.

At its birth, the U.S.A. was essentially an agrarian society. More than 90 percent of the population were farmers. There were few cities with as many as 5,000 residents. Boston was the largest city with 16,000, and New York was the second largest with 13,000 (Reiss 1980). The Industrial Revolution had yet to begin. Few men, and virtually no women, were employed outside the family home. Although it has become common to think of the twentieth-century pattern of role specialization, with the man serving as the family provider and the woman as the housekeeper and child-care provider, as the traditional American pattern, it did not characterize this early-American agrarian family. Family tasks tended to be performed out of necessity, with both men and women making direct and important contributions to the economic welfare of their families. Sexual norms and practices in early America arose in this social context.

The images of early-American sexuality in folklore are those of antihedonistic Puritanism and sexually repressed Victorianism. In popular culture, these terms have come to be associated with sexual prudishness. This view is oversimplistic and potentially misleading. Recent scholars (D'Emilio and Freedman 1988; Robinson 1976; Seidman 1991) tend to agree that sexuality was valued by the eighteenth-century Puritans and nineteenth-century Victorians within the context of marriage. To the Puritans, marriage was viewed as a spiritual union, and one that tended to emphasize the duties associated with commitment to that union. Marriage involved mutual affection and respect, and the couple was viewed as a primary social unit. Spouses were expected to fulfill reciprocal duties. One of these was sexual expression. No marriage was considered complete unless it was consummated sexually. The Puritans accepted erotic pleasure, as long as it promoted the mutual comfort and affection of the conjugal pair. The reciprocal duties of marital sexuality were justified, because they were seen as preventing individuals from becoming preoccupied with carnal desires and the temptation to practice improper sex outside of marriage (Seidman 1991). Of course, one of the principal functions of marital sex was reproduction. Pleasure alone did not justify sexual union. Instead, the regulation of sexual behavior reinforced the primacy of marital reproductive sex and the need for children (D'Emilio and Freedman 1988).

Within this context, it is certainly true that the early English settlers tried to regulate nonmarital forms of sexual expression. However, even this point can be exaggerated. Reiss (1980) has noted that Americans have always had a courtship system where individuals were free to select partners of their own choice. To some extent, this may have been due to necessities imposed by immigration to frontier territories, but it also was a consequence of the freedom settlers had from the institutions of social control found in Europe. Elsewhere, Reiss (1960; 1967) has maintained that such autonomy in courtship is associated with greater premarital sexual permissiveness.

In this regard, it is interesting to note that the settlers in New England developed the practice of bundling as a form of courtship. In colonial New

England, settlers faced harsh winters. They commonly faced fuel shortages, and mechanized transportation forms had yet to be developed. Single men would travel miles to visit the home of an eligible female. Typically, they would spend the night before returning home the next day. Few New England homes of the period had multiple rooms for housing a guest, and few could heat the house for an entire twenty-four-hour day. At night, the woman's family would bundle the man and the woman separately in blankets, and they would spend the night together talking to each other as they shared the same bed. It is worth noting that the practice of bundling was restricted to winters. Reiss (1980) has argued that the implicit understanding that the couple would avoid a sexual encounter was not always honored. In fact, a study of marriages in Groton, Massachusetts, from 1761 to 1775 found that one third of the women were pregnant at the time of their weddings (cited in Reiss 1980). This system was acceptable because betrothals were rarely broken at the time and because it served to produce the marital unions the Puritans valued so highly. Eventually, bundling was replaced by visits in the sitting parlors of nineteenth-century homes and by the practice of dating outside parental supervision in the twentieth century (Reiss 1980).

Around 1800, the Industrial Revolution began changing this world, albeit gradually. In the two centuries since, virtually every aspect of American life has been transformed. The nineteenth century was marked by social turmoil, a frontier mentality open to radical change, and a resulting patchquilt of conflicting trends and values. Among the events that left their mark on American culture in the nineteenth century were the following:

- The century started with 16 states and ended with 45 states; the 1803 Louisiana Purchase doubled the country's size. Victory in the War of 1812 with England and a war with Mexico also added territory.
- A Victorian ethic dominated the country. Preachers and health advocates, like Sylvester Graham and John Kellogg, promoted a fear of sexual excesses, such as sex before age 30 or more than once in three years, and a paranoia about the dangers of masturbation.
- Despite a dominant conservative trend and three major economic depressions, small religious groups pioneered a variety of marital and communal lifestyles, and had an influence far beyond their tiny numbers. The Perfectionist Methodists of the Oneida Community (1831-1881) endorsed women's rights and group marriage; the Church of Latter-Day Saints (Mormons) practiced polygyny; Protestant Hutterites celebrated the communal life; and the Shakers and Harmony Community promoted a celibate lifestyle.
- In 1837, the first colleges for women opened.
- In 1848, the first women's rights convention was held in Seneca Falls, New York.
- A midcentury California gold rush and completion of the transcontinental railroad opened the west to an explosive growth. San Francisco,

for example, doubled its population from 400 to 810 between 1847 and 1857; four years later, its population was 25,000. A major shortage of women led to importing thousands of women from Mexico, Chile, China, and the Pacific islands, with widespread prostitution.

- In 1861-1865, a devastating Civil War led to the abolition of slavery, as well as to new opportunities for employment, such as secretaries using the new mass-produced typewriters, and nurses using the skills they developed when they took care of the wounded in the Civil War.
- In 1869, the Territory of Wyoming gave women the vote.
- In 1873, the Comstock Law prohibited mailing obscene literature, including information about marital sex and contraception; it was finally declared unconstitutional a century later.
- In the latter part of the 1800s, a few thousand Americans were part of an influential "free love" movement, which advocated sexual freedom for women, the separation of sex and reproduction, the intellectual equality of women and men, self-health and knowledge of one's own body and its functions, and women's right to the vote, to enjoy sex, and to obtain a divorce.

Pankhurst and Houseknecht (1983) have identified five major trends that they maintain began to change and shape the modern institutions of marriage and the family in the nineteenth century and have continued to impact American culture in the twentieth century. The author of this section suggests that they have had a similar influence on sexual institutions. These trends are:

1. Industrialization, with its consequent process of urbanization and the eventual emergence of suburbs surrounding metropolitan areas;
2. A shift in the family from an economic-producing unit to that of a consumer;
3. The entry of men, and later of women, into the paid labor force;
4. The elongation and expansion of formal education, especially among women and minorities; and
5. Technological change.

We do not have the space to explore fully the impact of each of these trends. However, relevant effects would include increased life spans, decreased maternal and infant mortality at childbirth, the development of effective contraceptives, the emergence of a consumer culture that allows families to purchase most of their goods and services, the creation of labor-saving household technologies, increased leisure time, the development of modern forms of transportation, especially automobiles and airplanes, an increasing divorce rate, the increasing entry of wives and mothers into the labor force, decreasing birthrate and family size, increasing rates of single-parent families and cohabitation, increasing percentages of adults living alone, and increasing proportions of married couples with no children currently living at home (Coontz 1992). Many of these changes have resulted in greater personal autonomy for individuals. As Reiss (1960; 1967) has argued, such autonomy may be a major factor underlying several changes in sexuality throughout American history.

It should be stressed that these changes have not necessarily been linear or consistent throughout the period of the Industrial Revolution. Many began to emerge in the nineteenth century, but accelerated and became mainstream patterns only in the twentieth century. For example, as late as 1900, a majority of Americans were still farmers. The 1920 census was the first to show a majority of the population living in towns and cities. By 1980, only 4 percent of Americans still lived on farms (Reiss 1980). Similarly, women began entering the labor force in the early nineteenth century. However, it was not until 1975 that one half of married women were employed. By 1990, 70 percent of married women between the ages of 25 and 44 were employed (Coontz 1992). Yet another example is provided by the divorce rate. It had been gradually increasing for decades. That rate doubled between 1965 and 1975, and for the first time, couples with children began divorcing in sizable numbers at that time (Coontz 1992; Reiss 1980; Seidman 1991).

Seidman (1991) has described the principal change in American sexuality during the nineteenth century as the "sexualization of love." It could also be described as a shift to companionate marriage. Marriage came to be defined less as an institutional arrangement of reciprocal duties, and more as a personal relationship between the spouses. The modern concept of love as a form of companionship, intimacy, and sharing came to be seen as the primary justification for marriage. As this process continued, the erotic longings between the partners, and the sexual pleasures shared by them, became inseparable from the qualities that defined love and marriage. By the early part of the twentieth century, the desires and pleasures associated with sex came to be seen as a chief motivation and sustaining force in love and marriage (Seidman 1991). This view has come to be so dominant in the contemporary U.S.A. that few Americans today can envision any other basis for marriage.

D'Emilio and Freedman (1988) have argued that what they call the liberal sexual ethic described in the previous paragraph has been the attempt to promote this view of the erotic as the peak experience of marriage while limiting its expression elsewhere. However, as this view became the dominant American sexual ideology of the twentieth century, it also served to legitimate the erotic aspects of sexuality itself (Seidman 1991). Eventually, groups emerged which have sought to value sex for its inherent pleasure and expressive qualities, as well as for its value as a form of self-expression. In effect, as the view that sexual gratification was a critical part of happiness for married persons became the dominant sexual ideology of twentieth-century America, then it was only a matter of time until some groups began to question how it could be restricted only to married persons (D'Emilio and Freedman 1988).

B. The Twentieth Century

The social turmoil and the pace of social change that marked the nineteenth century has accelerated exponentially in the present century. American culture in the twentieth century has been increasingly complicated and changed by often-unanticipated developments in technology, communications, and medicine. Among the events that have been identified as significant in twentieth-century United States are the following:

- In the early 1900s, Sigmund Freud and Havelock Ellis helped trigger the emergence of a more-positive approach to sexuality, especially in recognizing the normal sexuality of women and children, and the need for sex education.
- In 1916, spurred by Havelock Ellis, Margaret Sanger, a New York nurse, launched a crusade to educate poor and immigrant women about contraception, and established the first Planned Parenthood clinics.
- World War I brought women out of their Victorian homes into the war effort and work in the factories; shorter skirts and hair styles were viewed as patriotic fashion and gave women more freedom. American soldiers encountered the more-relaxed sexual mores of France and Europe.
- The "Roarin' Twenties" were marked by the invention of cellulose santitary napkins, the mobility of Henry Ford's affordable automobiles, new leisure and affluence, the advent of movies with female vamp stars and irresistible sex idols, and the appearance of the "Charleston," the "flapper," and cheek-to-cheek, body-clutching dancing.
- From 1929 to 1941, the Great Depression brought a return to sexual conservativism.
- World War II opened new opportunities for women, both at home and in the military support. Interracial marriages set the stage for revoking miscegenation laws later in 1967.
- In the 1940s, the advent of antibiotics brought cures for some sexually transmitted diseases.
- In 1948 and 1953, Alfred Kinsey and colleagues published *Sexual Behavior in the Human Male* and *Sexual Behavior in the Human Female*. They brought sexual topics into widespread public discussion.
- In the 1950s, Elvis Presley became the first major rock 'n' roll star; television became a major influence on young Americans. Senator Joseph McCarthy portrayed sex education as part of a Communist plot to take over the U.S. Coed dormitories appeared on college campuses and bikini swimsuits swept the nation. Motels became popular, provid-

ing comfort for vacationing Americans, as well as for Americans seeking privacy for sexual relations.

- In 1953, the first issue of *Playboy* magazine was published.
- In 1957, the Supreme Court decision in *Roth v. U.S.* set new criteria for obscenity that opened the door to the works of D. H. Lawrence and Henry Miller, and other classic erotic works.
- In the 1950s and 1960s, the beatniks, hippies, flower children, and drug culture emerged.
- In the early 1960s, the hormonal contraceptive pill became available.
- In 1961, Illinois adopted the first "consenting adult" law decriminalizing sexual behavior between consenting adults.
- In 1963, Betty Friedan's *Feminine Mystique* was published, giving voice to the modern feminist movement.
- In 1968, William Masters and Virginia Johnson published *Human Sexual Response*.
- Following the 1969 Stonewall Inn Riot in Greenwich Village, New York City, homosexuals rebelled against police harassment, and launched the gay-rights and gay-pride movement.
- In the 1970s, television talk shows popularized discussions of alternative lifestyles, triggered by the publication of Nena and George O'Neill's *Open Marriage* in 1972.
- In 1970, the White House Commission on Pornography and Obscenity found no real harm in sexually explicit material. President Richard Nixon refused to issue the report.
- In 1972, the first openly gay male was ordained to the ministry of a major Christian church.
- In 1973, the U.S. Supreme Court legalized abortion.
- In the 1980s, openly gay legislators appeared in federal and state governments, and in professional sports.
- In 1983, AIDS was recognized, leading to a new advocacy for sex education in the schools and general public.
- In the late 1980s, conservative Christian activists, including the Moral Majority, the Christian Coalition, Focus on the Family, and similar organizations, emerged as politically and socially powerful groups.

These and other events too numerous to list, let alone analyze here, both contributed to and reflect the tension between the two ideologies mentioned above—one viewing sex as legitimate only in marriage, but as a necessary component of marital happiness, and the other viewing sex as a valid and important experience in its own right. The attempt to reconcile them can be seen as an underlying dynamic for many sexual practices and changes in the twentieth century. These broad-based trends include:

1. The emergence in the 1920s of dating and in the 1940s of "going steady" as courtship forms (Reiss 1980);

2. The rising percentage of young people having premarital sexual experiences (D'Emilio and Freedman 1988; Kinsey, et al., 1948; 1953; Reiss 1980; Seidman 1991);

3. The greater equality between the genders (D'Emilio and Freedman 1988; Reiss 1980; Seidman 1991);

4. The eroticization of the female, including a decline in the double standard and an increased focus on female sexual satisfaction (D'Emilio and Freedman 1988; Seidman 1991);

5. The emergence of professions devoted to sexuality—research, education, and therapy;

6. The expansion of marital sexuality, including increases in frequency, satisfaction, and variation in behavior (Hunt 1974);

7. The emergence of a homosexual identity and subculture, including a gay-rights movement (D'Emilio and Freedman 1988; Seidman 1991);

8. The passage of consenting adult laws;

9. The commercialization of sex, by which we mean the appearance of an "industry" providing sexual goods and services (D'Emilio and Freedman 1988; Seidman 1991).

Reactions to these trends, and the continuing tension between the two major ideologies we have outlined above, lie at the very heart of the ongoing conflicts over sexual issues today. Robinson (1976) has characterized this conflict as a battle between nineteenth-century romanticism and what he calls sexual modernism. Romanticism affirmed the essential worth of the erotic, but only within the context of an intense interpersonal relationship transformed by a spiritual and physical union. Modernism reaffirms this romantic ideal, but also transforms it by acknowledging the value of "an innocent physical need" (p. 194). Although the modernist is glad to be rid of Victorian repression and anticipates the promise of a greater sexual freedom, there is a concomitant fear of a future of emotional emptiness.

Reiss (1981) has characterized this as a conflict between what he calls the traditional-romantic and modern-naturalistic ideologies. He maintains that this distinction can be used to explain current conflicts over such issues as abortion, gender roles and differences, pornography, definitions of sexual exploitation, concepts of sexual normality, and even accounts of sexual history itself. This perspective is useful in interpreting mass-media claims about sexuality in the U.S.A. Thus, Lyons (1983), reporting for *The New York Times*, proclaimed that the "sexual revolution" was over by the 1980s and that America was experiencing a return to traditional values and lifestyles. To support his argument, he claimed that there was a recent decrease in the number of sex partners and a shift away from indiscriminate, casual sexual behavior (Lyons 1983). In contrast, Walsh (1993), writing for *Utne Reader*, proclaimed that the 1990s have been characterized by a re-

newed sexual revolution (second-wavers), with pioneering new philosophies and techniques employing technology (latex, computer imaging,
computer networks, virtual reality sex, phone sex, cathode rays, and group
safe sex) to achieve sensual pleasure in a safe way.

From 1970 to 1990, as these social processes continued, Americans
witnessed: (1) a decrease in the marriage rate; (2) an increase in the divorce
rate; (3) an increase in the birthrate for unmarried mothers (although the
overall adolescent birthrate decreased); (4) an increase in single-parent
families; and (5) an increase in married couples without children at home
(Ahlburg and DeVita 1992). In the next section, we consider the impact
of religious, ethnic, and gender factors on such changes.

2. Religious, Ethnic, and Gender Factors Affecting Sexuality

Social scientists have demonstrated an association between human behavior and such social factors as religion, race, gender, social class, and
education. This is as true of sexuality as of other forms of behavior.
Although sexuality researchers have not always incorporated a recognition
of this principle in their designs and analyses, there is still abundant
evidence that sexual practices in the U.S.A. are strongly related to social
factors. In this section, we examine several examples. First, we review the
general influence of the Judeo-Christian heritage in the U.S.A. and describe the sexual culture of a particular religious group within this tradition, the Church of Jesus Christ of Latter-Day Saints (Mormons). Then we
review the sexual customs of two of the largest minority groups in the
U.S.A., African-Americans and Hispanic-Americans. Finally, we review the
emergence of feminist ideology in the U.S.A., a view constructed around
the concept of gender. These reviews are by no means exhaustive or
complete, but should serve to illustrate both the diversity of social groups
within the U.S.A. and the influence that membership in such groups exerts
on sexual customs and practices.

A. Sources and Character of Religious Values

General Character and Ramifications of American   ROBERT T. FRANCOEUR
Religious Perspectives on Sexuality   AND TIMOTHY PERPER

Sexual science in America is a mid- to late-twentieth-century discipline. By
contrast, Western religious thought about love, sexuality, marriage, the
social and familial roles of men and women, and the emotions and behavioral patterns associated with courtship, pair bonding, conception, and
birth have textual bases in the Jewish *Pentatuch* and other biblical writings.
In pre-Christian Hellenic thought, the first great document of sexology is
Plato's *Symposium* (ca. 400 B.C.E.). Because Judaic and Hellenic thought
have strongly influenced the sexual views of Christianity and all of Western

culture, one must acknowledge that the theological, religious, and secular writings that permeate American conceptions of sexuality are embedded in this 3,500-year-old matrix that gives sexuality its place in life (and unique meanings). This section will explore the sources and character of religious values in the U.S.A. and their impact on sexual attitudes, behaviors, and policies.

Religious Groups in the U.S.A. Statistically, Americans are 61 percent Protestant—21 percent Baptist, 12 percent Methodist, 8 percent Lutheran, 4 percent Presbyterian, 3 percent Episcopalian, and 13 percent other Protestant groups, including the Church of Latter-Day Saints (see Section 2 below for a more in-depth discussion of the sexual doctrines and practices of this religious group), Seventh-Day Adventists, Jehovah's Witnesses, Christian Scientists, and others. Roman and Eastern-rite Catholics account for 25 percent of Americans, Jews 2 percent, 5 percent other religious groups, and 7 percent are not affiliated with any church. Therefore, the two largest denominations in the U.S.A. are the Roman Catholic Church with a membership of over 50 million and Southern Baptist Conventions with between 10 and 15 million members (Greeley 1992). There are also 2.5 million Muslims in the U.S.A.

Because Americans tend to cluster geographically according to both their religious and ethnic heritages, local communities can be much more strongly affected by a small but highly concentrated religious or ethnic tradition than the above percentages might suggest at first sight. With recent public debate focusing on sexual morality (e.g., contraception, abortion, and homosexuality), a paradoxical realignment has occurred, with liberal Roman Catholics, mainstream Protestant churches, and liberal and reformed Jews lining up on one side of these issues, and conservative (Vatican) Roman Catholics, fundamentalist Protestants, including the televangelists and Southern Baptists, Orthodox Jews, and fundamentalist Muslims on the other side.

A Basic Conflict Between Two Worldviews. American religious institutions on the national level, their local religious communities, and individual members are caught in a pervasive tension between the security of traditional unchanging values and the imperative need to adapt perennial religious and moral values to a radically new and rapidly changing environment. This tension permeates every religious group in the United States today, threatening schism and religious "civil war" (Francoeur 1994).

At one end of the spectrum are fundamentalist, evangelical, charismatic factions that accept as word-for-word truth the writings of the Bible as the word of God and advocate the establishment of the United States as a Christian nation. For them, living under God's rule would be evidenced by the man firmly established as the head of each family in the U.S.A. and the woman in her God-given role as submissive wife and bearer of children for the Kingdom of Heaven. Similar fundamentalist strains in the United States are apparent among ultra-orthodox Jews and radical Muslims (LeHaye and LeHaye 1976; Marty and Appleby 1992, 1993, 1994; Penner and Penner 1981; Wheat and Wheat 1981). These embody an absolutist/natural law/ fixed worldview.

On the conservative side, books about sexuality written by married couples dominate the market and sell millions of copies without ever being noticed by the mainstream publishing industry. *Intended for Pleasure* (Wheat and Wheat 1981) and *The Gift of Sex* (Penner and Penner 1981)—the latter couple having been trained by Masters and Johnson—provide detailed information on birth control and express deep appreciation of sex as a gift to be enjoyed in marriage. Tim and Beverly LeHaye's *The Act of Marriage* celebrates marital sexual pleasure, but disapproves of homosexuality and some sexual fantasy. All books in this category stress mutual pleasuring and the importance of female enjoyment of marital sex.

At the other end of the spectrum are various mainstream Protestants, Catholics, Jews, and Muslims who accept a processual/evolutionary worldview (Fox 1983, 1988; Curran and McCormick 1993; Heyward 1989; Kosnick et al. 1977; Nelson 1978, 1983, 1992; Nelson and Longfellow 1994; Ranke-Heinemann 1990; Spong 1988; Thayer 1987; Timmerman 1986) rather than the fixed fundamentalist worldview. In this processual worldview, the sacred divinely revealed texts are respected as

> the record of the response to the word of God addressed to the Church throughout centuries of changing social, historical, and cultural traditions. The Faithful responded with the realities of their particular situation, guided by the direction of previous revelation, but not captive to it. (Thayer et al. 1987)

The most creative and substantive analysis of the evolution and variations in biblical sexual ethics over time is William Countryman's *Dirt, Greed, and Sex: Sexual Ethics in the New Testament and Their Implications for Today.* (For a full annotated list of sexuality texts, see Cornog and Perper 1995.)

The tension between the values and morals derived from fixed worldviews and those derived from processual worldviews is evident in official church debates about sexual morality and is also experienced by church members as they struggle to find their way through the confusion resulting from these two views. But it also affects the lives of secular Americans with no connection with a church, mosque, or synagogue, because the religious debate over sexual values permeates all levels of American society, and no one can escape the impact of this debate and conflict on politics, legislation, and social policies. Table 1 is an attempt to describe in a nondefinitive way the two divergent sets of values derived from the processual and fixed worldviews. Table 2 lists some religious traditions in both the fixed and processual worldviews in the major religions around the world.

Table 1

A Cognitive and Normative Continuum of Sexual Values Derived from Two Distinct Worldviews, Fixed and Process, Within the Christian Tradition

	Christian Religions Type A	Christian Religions Type B
Basic vision	*Cosmos*—a finished universe	*Cosmogenesis*—an evolving universe
Typology	The universe, humankind is created perfect and complete in the beginning.	The universe, humankind is incomplete and not yet fully formed.
	Theological understanding of humans emphasizes Adam.	Theological emphasis has shifted to Christ (The Adam) at the end of time.
Origin of evil	Evil results from primeval 'fall' of a perfect couple who introduce moral and physical evil into a paradisical world.	Evil is a natural part of a finite creation, growth, and the birth pains involved in our groping as imperfect humans struggling for the fullness of creation.
Solution to the problem of evil	Redemption by identification with the crucified Savior. Asceticism, mortification.	Identification with the Adam, the resurrected but still fully human transfigured Christ. Re-creation, growth.
Authority system	Patriarchal and sexist. Male-dominated and ruled. Autocratic hierarchy controls power and all decisions; clergy vs. laity.	Egalitarian—'In his kingdom there is neither male nor female, freeman or slave, Jew or Roman.'
Concept of truth	Emphasis on one true Church as sole possessor of all truth.	Recognition that other churches and religions possess different perspectives of truth, with some elements of revelation clearer in them than in the "one true Church."
Biblical orientation	Fundamentalist, evangelical, word-for-word, black-and-white clarity. Revelation has ended.	Emphasizes continuing revelation and reincarnation of perennial truths and values as humans participate in the creation process.
Liturgical focus	Redemption and Good Friday, Purgatory, Supernatural.	Easter and the creation challenge of incarnation. Epiphany of numinous cosmos.
Social structure	Gender roles clearly assigned with high definition of proper roles for men and women.	There being neither male nor female in Christ, gender roles are flexible, including women priests and ministers.
Goal	Supernatural transcendence of nature.	Unveiling, Revelation of divine in all.

continued

Table 1 continued

	Christian Religions Type A	Christian Religions Type B
Ecological morality	Humans are stewards of the earth, given dominion by God over all creation.	Emphasis on personal responsibility in a continuing creation/incarnation.
Self-image	Carefully limited; isolationist, exclusive, Isaias's 'remnant.' Sects.	Inclusive, ecumenical, catalytic leader among equals.
Human morality	Emphasis on laws and conformity of actions to these laws.	Emphasis on persons and their interrelationships. We create the human of the future and the future of humanity.
Sexual morality	The 'monster in the groins' that must be restrained.	A positive, natural, creative energy in our being as sexual (embodied) persons "Knowing" (*yadah*), Communion.
	Justified in marriage for procreation.	An essential element in our personality in all relationships.
	Genital reductionism.	Diffused, degenitalized sensual embodiment.
	Heterosexual/monogamous.	"Polymorphic perversity," "paneroticism."
	Noncoital sex is unnatural, disordered.	Noncoital sex can express the incarnation of Christian love.
	Contraceptive love is unnatural and disordered.	Contraception can be just as creative and life-serving as reproductive love.
	Monolithic—celibate or reproductive marital sexuality.	Pluralistic—sexual persons must learn to incarnate *chesed/agape* with *eros* in all their relationships, primary and secondary, genital and non-genital, intimate, and passionate.
Energy conception	Competitive.	Synergistic.
	Consumerist.	Conservationist.
	Technology-driven and obsessed.	Concerned with appropriate technologies.

Modern America is a ferment of discourse and debate concerning relationships between sexuality and religion. This occurs on the local and personal level among church members, as well as on the administrative level among the church leadership. The vast majority of local church debates are not reported in the popular press. These debates center on the interpretations of revelation, religious truths, and the nature and place of sexuality within a particular absolutist/natural law/fixed worldview or processual/evolutionary worldview. From time to time, denominational leaders and assemblies issue authoritative statements in denominational

Table 2

A Spectrum of Ethical Systems with Typical Adherents in Different Religious Traditions

This table is an attempt to visualize the range of sexual moralities in different religious traditions and relate them in terms of their basic worldviews. There is often more agreement between different Jews, Protestants, and Catholics at one or the other end of the spectrum, than there is between Protestants, or Catholics, or Jews who disagree in their worldviews. Protestants in the covenant tradition, for instance, have more in common with liberal Catholics who disagree with the Vatican's opposition to such practices as contraception, masturbation, premarital sex, abortion, divorce, and homosexuality, than they do with their fellow Protestants who are members of the fundamentalist Christian Coalition, Eagle Forum, or Focus on the Family.

	A Spectrum or Continuum	
Tradition Source	**Fixed Philosophy of Nature**	**Process Philosophy of Nature**
Roman Catholic tradition	Act-oriented natural law/ divine law order ethics expressed in formal Vatican pronouncements	A person-oriented, evolving ethics expressed by many contemporary theologians and the 1977 Catholic Theological Society of America study of human sexuality.
Protestant nominalism	Fundamentalism based on a literal interpretation of the Bible, as endorsed by the Moral Majority and the religious New Right: Seventh-Day Adventists, Jehovah's Witnesses, and Church of Latter-Day Saints	An ethic based on the covenant announced between Jesus and humans—examples in the 1970 United Presbyterian workstudy document on Sexuality and the Human Community, Unitarian/Universalists, and the Society of Friends (Quakers)
Humanism	Stoicism and epicurean asceticism	Situation ethics, e.g., the 1976 American Humanist Association's "A New Bill of Sexual Rights and Responsibilities"
Judaism	Orthodox and Hasidic concern for strict observation of the Torah and Talmudic prescriptions	Liberal and reformed application of moral principles to today's situations
Islam	Orthodox; observance of female seclusion (*purdah*) and wearing of the veil (*chador*); ritual purifications associated with sexual activities	Secular; more or less adoption of Western gender equality; flexible/lax observance of sex-associated purification rituals

continued

Table 2 continued

While Eastern religions may, in some cases, fit in with this dualism of worldviews, the ascetic traditions of the East are positive traditions and lack the negativism towards sexuality that permeates the history of Christian asceticism and celibacy. Eastern asceticism is seen as a positive balance to the Eastern's embrace of sexuality as both a natural pleasure to be greatly enjoyed and a path to the divine union. Also, the relationship with the dichotomous weltanschauungs evident in Western traditions needs to be explored and explicated.

	A Spectrum or Continuum	
Tradition Source	**Fixed Philosophy of Nature**	**Process Philosophy of Nature**
Hinduism	Ascetic tradition of monks with world-denying sexual abstinence; Yoga; ritual taboos and purification rites associated with sexual activities	Sacramental view of sex with worship of male lingam and female yoni; the *Kama Sutra*
Buddhism	Ascetic tradition of monks with sexual abstinence	Tantric traditions in which sexual relations are a path to divine union

position or workstudy papers. These formal statements are designed to answer questions of sexual morality and set church policy. However, contradictory majority and minority positions rooted in the opposing fixed and processual worldviews accomplish little beyond stirring heated debate and deferring the problem to further committee study (Francoeur 1987, 1994).

However, there is often a great difference between official church doctrine and worldview and the views and practices of its members. For example, the most erotophilic religion in America may be grassroots Roman Catholicism as expressed and lived by the laity. Many rank-and-file American Catholics express great and amused doubt and scorn for the sexual pronouncements of the Vatican (Greeley 1995). Peter Gardella (1985) has made a strong case for the thesis that Christianity has, in fact, given America an ethic of sexual pleasure.

The Conservative Christian Coalition. Among the major forces in the American religious scene that affect public sexual mores is the conservative Christian Coalition. Among the fundamentalist Christians, one finds an extraordinary heterogeneity. There exists a large and virtually unstudied mixture of Pentecostal, fundamentalist, and evangelical/charismatic churches whose preachers expound on sexuality, marriage, family, and morality. Their opinions are diverse, and poorly known or understood by those outside their domain, especially sexologists. Two examples illustrate this: A religious pamphlet published by the Rose of Sharon Press in Tennessee, the buckle of the so-called Bible Belt in the U.S.A., extols the clitoris as the "cradle of love," and the Reverend Timothy LeHaye reminds his followers that God indeed created the delights of oral sex for married couples (only) to enjoy. No statistical data exist concerning these groups, and we know nothing about sexual behavior among individuals within these churches.

The current strength of the power of the American religious right is evident in the wide-reaching branches of Pat Robertson's political machine, the Christian Coalition, and the "electronic churches," including Robertson's cable television Christian Broadcasting Network (CBN), with annual revenues of $140 million (Roberts and Cohen 1995). A parallel conservative culture is James Dobson's multimedia empire, Focus on the Family, which includes ten radio shows, eleven magazines (including speciality publications for doctors, teachers, and single parents), best-selling books, film strips, and videos of all kinds, curriculum guides, church-bulletin fillers, and sermon outlines faxed to thousands of pastors every week. The popularity of Dobson's first book, *Dare to Discipline*—more than 2 million copies sold in 1977—inspired his formation of Focus on the Family, which now has an annual budget of $100 million and a staff of 1,300 workers who answer more than 250,000 telephone calls and letters a month (Roberts and Cohen 1995).

In the late 1980s, Protestant fundamentalist televangelists from the South were reaching millions of listeners. Their influence was weakened by several major sex scandals, but they continue to play a major role in the anti-abortion movement and are part of the Christian Coalition. In the same era, the National Conference of Catholic Bishops tried to establish a cable television network to bring the Catholic faith to the masses. Where they failed, a determined Catholic fundamentalist-charismatic, Mother Angelica, from Mobile, Alabama, succeeded with the Eternal Word Network, which brings ultraconservative interpretations of Catholic sexual and social morality to devoted listeners twenty-four hours a day.

In the southern states, on the east and west coasts, and in the populous midwest states are several hundred "mega-churches," which draw upwards of 5,000 to 20,000 faithful every week to each church. Congregations seated in upholstered theater seats are inspired by the style of a professional theater with a large choir, orchestra, large screens displaying hymn verses for congregational singing, interpretive dance, bible lessons with soft-rock concerts, and morality plays that rival anything on music television (MTV). These mega-churches are usually huge glass and steel shopping-mall-like complexes with large theater-stage sanctuaries, scores of meeting and classrooms for a variety of activities, including aerobics, multimedia Bible classes, counseling centers, and even bowling alleys, accompanied by acres of parking space. Sermons delivered by skilled "teaching pastors" include such topics as: how to find joy in a violent world, create a "happy day" each week, find rhythm between work and rest, handle teenage children, and discipline one's mind to a biblical perspective. Youth, in particular, are attracted to the instant intimacy of this large-group, Disney-World environment. Weekly contributions from 15,000 members at one mega-church averaged $228,000, giving the church an annual budget of almost $12 million (Roberts and Cohen 1995). With the mainstream small local churches suffering a steady decline in attendance and contributions, many of the more-traditional pastors are turning to the mega-churches for pastoral retraining. Thus, the mega-churches are establishing smaller, local congregations. It appears that the way these churches deal with sexual issues may have a major impact on American sexuality because of the large memberships they are attracting.

Emergence of a Sex-Positive Individual-Based Value System. Diotima of Mantinea, Socrates' instructress in the art of love in the *Symposium*, explained that the god Eros provides an avenue or way by which human beings reach upward to the Divine—a view modern classical scholars chauvinistically attribute to Socrates and call the "Erotic Ascent." Historically, Diotima's argument became the basis of the later Christian idea that God is Love. In Eurocentric Christianity, the first great flowering of Eros came between 1050 C.E. and 1200 C.E., when Ovid's *The Art of Love* reached Europe from Arab-Spanish sources. The synthesis of sexuality and spirituality quickly assumed major status as a popular doctrine expressed in the music of the troubadours of "courtly love."

Its most ardent opponents were the faculty of the medieval universities led by Thomas Aquinas, who developed a full and coherent alternative to the theology of the Platonic Erotic Ascent in the thirteenth century. The Thomistic synthesis, with its denunciation of the Erotic Ascent and analysis of the essence and goals of human sexuality in terms of a "natural law," became the official Catholic view. This synthesis is the basis on which the modern magisterium and hierarchy of the Roman Catholic Church grounds its absolute condemnation of contraception, abortion, and the practice of homosexuality. By contrast, Protestantism has been much more accepting of sexuality and sexual pleasure, and more flexible with and accommodating to such issues as divorce, contraception, abortion, masturbation, premarital sex, and even homosexuality.

However, it was not the theory of Thomistic Aristotleanism that ultimately superseded late medieval and Renaissance beliefs in Eros. These dwindled as Europe, staggered under waves of the Black Death, which ultimately killed one quarter of Europe's population; the Crusades, during which 22,000 people were killed in the Provençal city of Bezier alone; endless local wars among nobles, kings, and petty brigands where the peasants were invariably victimized; Turkish invasions; the epidemic of syphilis in 1493; peasant uprisings in Germany and England in the 1300s and 1400s; and the Inquisition, that specifically targeted women as its victims.

Protestant reformers from Luther through Calvin, Knox, and Zwingli, not only rejected the "natural law" approach to sexual morality; but extended, strengthened, and normalized the nuclear family and the blessing of marital sex. This type of marriage was a valuable social institution for assuring the distribution of new wealth from father to son. For example, in northern European merchant families, it replaced the older, southern European models of inheritance by name, and social status by membership in a "house" (e.g., the "house of the Medici"), with this type of lineage system.

An important characteristic of the Renaissance was appreciation and acceptance of individual control of one's own life. Thus, the late 1500s and early 1600s saw a new struggle of the young to wrest control over their love affairs and marriages from their parents and families. Shakespeare's *Romeo and Juliet* epitomizes what was to become the central issue of the modern-American religious debate about sexuality and spirituality. Who is to control the sexuality of the young? Older and more powerful individuals, who have vested interests in the outcome of youthful sexuality, . . . celibate church leaders still convinced of the unchangeable patriarchal sexual values expressed in the Genesis story of creation, . . . or young people, who claim for themselves the right to find the right mates and express their erotic passion in a way that, for them, brings sexuality and transcendence together?

Of growing significance in the 1990s in the U.S.A. is the question of the sacred nature of Eros. Among the liberal religious best-sellers pioneering a new synthesis of sexuality and spirituality are: *Human Sexuality: New Directions in American Catholic Thought* (Kosnick et al. 1977), which was sponsored by the Catholic Theological Society of America, but was condemned by the Vatican; *Original Blessing* (1983) and *The Coming of the Cosmic Christ* (1988) by the Dominican Matthew Fox (censured and expelled from his community by the Vatican); sociologist and erotic-novel author Father Andrew Greeley's *Sex, The Catholic Experience* (1995); lesbian theologian Carter Heyward's 1989 *Touching Our Strength: The Erotic as Power and the Love of God*; Presbyterian seminary professor James Nelson's books *Embodiment* (1978), *Between Two Gardens: Reflections on Sexuality and Religious Experience* (1983), and *Body Theology* (1992); James Nelson and Sandra Longfellow's anthology on *Sexuality and the Sacred* (1994); William Phipps' *Recovering Biblical Sensuousness* (1975); Catholic feminist theologian Joan Timmerman's *The Mardi Gras Syndrome: Rethinking Christian Sexuality* (1986); and Episcopalian Bishop John Shelly Spong's 1988 *Living in Sin? A Bishop Rethinks Human Sexuality*. In addition, some Christians have turned to Eastern religions, particularly in the Tantric and Taoist traditions, to seek the nexus between sexuality and spirituality (Francoeur 1992).

Current and Future Religious Debate. During the 1980s, the most virulently debated issue was abortion. In 1994, between U.S. Supreme Court decisions and violence and murder by extreme anti-abortionists, support for anti-abortion stands stalled. For the majority of Americans, abortion appeared to fade as the central moral dilemma and joined the list of unresolved moral issues that includes war, drugs, crime, capital punishment, discrimination, and related social ills. Certain far-right religious leaders, who still have a devoted and vocal following and claim to speak for Christ, even conceded reluctantly that they could not win their war against abortion, and seemed to refocus their crusade on homosexuality and "the danger of homosexual rights" as their mobilizing issue.

However, with the mid-1995 success of the Republicans' conservative hundred-day Contract with America, the Christian Coalition announced its own Contract with the American Family. Two-dozen legislative proposals were introduced into Congress, including an unprecedented attempt to ban and criminalize some now-legal abortions. A bill to reinstate a ban on abortions at American military hospitals overseas was passed. Other proposed bills would ban family planning programs from including abortion counseling for low-income women and adolescents; refuse funding to institutions that favor requiring obstetric/gynecology programs to provide training in abortion procedures; overturn an executive order lifting a ban against using foreign-aid money for abortion counseling or referrals; end or restrict support for agencies, including the United Nations, that offer family planning programs with abortions funded by private money; limit federal Medicaid money for abortions to situations where the woman's life is threatened and ban it in cases of incest or rape; ban fetal-tissue research; ban clinical testing of RU-486; restore a ban on counseling women about abortion at clinics that receive any federal money; and prohibit the federal employee's health benefit plan from covering abortion. The ultimate goal is to make all abortions under all circumstances a crime.

The list of controversial sexual issues that are religiously debated with little hope of being resolved in the near future includes:

1. Individual sexual choice: Who should be in control of one's sexuality? Should it be church leaders or people themselves, who claim the right to express their sexuality with those of their own choosing in ways that would bring them mutual pleasure, eroticism, and spirituality?
2. Contraception: Should minors have access to contraception? Should condoms be distributed in the schools? Does education about contraception and sexual behaviors outside of marriage promote "promiscuity"? Should people be free to choose the best method of contraception for themselves without religious restriction?
3. Abortion: Should women have control of their own reproductive faculty? Is the embryo/fetus a person with inalienable rights at the moment of conception or does fetal personhood develop over the nine months of gestation? When do fetal rights transcend those of pregnant women, if at all?

4. Nonmarital sexuality: Can sex outside marriage be morally acceptable? If so, under what circumstances? How can it be reconciled with traditional Judeo-Christian morality that limits sexual expression to the marital union?

5. Sexual orientation: Are homosexuality and bisexuality natural and normal states of being? Should sexually active gays, lesbians, and bisexuals be welcomed into church membership? Should they be ordained into the ministry? Should variation in orientation be presented in sex-education curricula as normal, moral, and socially acceptable?

6. Masturbation: Is self-loving and autoeroticism a natural, normal, and morally acceptable expression of human sexuality? (See the first item in Section B of American Demographics at the beginning of this chapter for an illustration of the impact this issue has had on American politics.)

The American religious, and consequent social and political, debates over each of these issues are not likely to be resolved in the near future. The dichotomy of the two worldviews is too deeply embedded in the American culture to allow for a quick resolution. The more likely prognosis is for continued, tension-filled confrontations within the churches, denominations, and political/legislative arenas throughout the United States.

The Religious Right's social and political agenda deeply divides American society. Although 40 percent of Americans express concern about the Democrats' ties to radical liberal groups, 39 percent are worried by Republican ties to conservative special-interest groups like the Religious Right, the Family Research Council, Focus on the Family, Eagle Forum, and the Christian Coalition (Roberts and Cohen 1995). These results reflect the continuing diversity of worldviews within the Judeo-Christian tradition. They also indicate that these religious differences not only result in contrasting sexual ideologies, but also have an important impact on political processes in the U.S.A. more broadly. As such, religion continues to be a major American social influence.

Church of Jesus Christ of Latter-Day Saints   JEANNIE FORREST*

Mormon Origins and Polygyny. One example of a particular religious group within the general Judeo-Christian heritage is provided by the Church of Jesus Christ of Latter-Day Saints (LDS), which is the fastest-growing religion in the world today. The over seven million members are known colloquially as the Mormons. They base their belief system on the Bible and additional

---

*Additional comments by Mark O. Bigler, Ph.D., a lifelong member of the Church of Latter-Day Saints, a graduate of New York University's doctoral program in sexuality, and director of community education programs at the Utah AIDS Foundation, are enclosed in brackets with his name [. . . (Bigler)].

scriptures, most significantly the Book of Mormon, which is understood to be a record of God's dealings with an ancient population of the American continent. The Mormons believe this book came from gold plates revealed to the church founder, Joseph Smith, in Ontario County, New York, in 1823. The church was officially organized in 1829.

The early Mormons were persecuted because their founder claimed the Bible had not been translated properly, that all other religions were false, that religious leaders did not have God's authority—the priesthood—to act in God's name, and finally that the practice of polygyny was a part of the divine plan. There was also the political reality that the tight-knit Mormon communities exercised considerable local power. Interestingly, the term "polygamy" as used in LDS church history and old doctrine means the "condition or practice of having more than one spouse." A more-accurate definition of the Mormon practice of that century lies in the word "polygyny," meaning having more than one wife at one time. The role of polygyny in the church is a source of some embarrassment to mainstream modern-day Mormons, who may discuss the practice somewhat wryly as a revelation designed to build the church population at a time when they literally had to forge new communities under hardship. After several attempts to settle in an area and build a sectarian community, the Mormon pioneers ultimately settled in the Salt Lake City area of Utah, where the church is now headquartered.

Modern Mormon doctrine does not include the practice of polygyny. Church prophet and leader, Wilfred Woodruff, officially eliminated polygyny from doctrine in the Manifesto of 1890 (Ludlow 1992). This proclamation against plural marriage ended a decade of hardship and persecution against the church members, particularly by the Republican Party that had as part of its platform elimination of the "immoral practice of multiple wives." While mainstream Mormons are not held accountable for not practicing plural marriage, they still must "suffer the curse of monogamy." Today, small fundamentalist splinter groups still practice polygyny, despite state laws against it and lack of official church acknowledgment. Even before the church abandoned its practice of plural marriage, only a small fraction of Mormon men, between 3 and 15 percent, had more than one wife (Murstein 1974, 350-364).

Perhaps the persecution faced by the early members of the LDS regarding their marital patterns has contributed to a unique and paradoxical tension around sexuality. On one hand, there is nothing more sacred than sex within the bounds of church-sanctioned marriage. On the other hand, rarely is there found a modern-American subculture more prohibitive and repressive about sexuality.

Salvation and Sex. To further understand this tension, one needs a basic understanding of the Mormon Plan of Salvation. Before birth, the Mormons believe, the soul is alive as an intelligence in a spirit world. During this preexistence, a variety of situations are possible, including acts of valor that would allow the soul to be born into a family of Mormons where opportunities for service abound. At birth, the soul passes through a veil of forgetfulness where all memory of the preexistence is lost (Church of Jesus Christ of Latter-Day Saints, 1989 (Moses 3:5, p. 7; Abraham 3:21-23, pp. 35, 38; Talmage 1977).

During life on this earth, individuals face choices throughout the course of their lives that determine in which of three kingdoms they will spend eternity. The highest kingdom, the Celestial Kingdom, is reserved for those Latter-Day Saints who meet all the requirements of doctrine, one of the most important of which is marriage to another Saint in special temple rites. The exaltation and eternal life in the highest degree of the Celestial Kingdom are achieved only by faithful Mormons through the achievement and building of an eternal marriage, discussed later. (Other good people can only hope to reach the Terrestrial Kingdom, a kind of heaven on earth, while unrepented adulterers, practicing homosexuals, murderers, and other sinners are limited to the Telestial Kingdom, which some describe as a Mormon version of the Christian hell.

[According to Mormon tradition, "hell" is not a place, but rather a state of mind. Those who do not achieve the highest degree of glory (the Celestial Kingdom) will recognize the reward they might have had and live out their eternities with the knowledge of this lost potential. However, the Telestial Kingdom, though typically described in less-than-positive terms, is not generally thought of as the fire and brimstone of the traditional Christian hell. In fact, one prominent Mormon Church leader described the Telestial Kingdom as follows: ". . . all who receive any one of these orders of glory are at last saved, and upon them Satan will finally have no claim. Even the telestial glory 'surpasses all understanding; And no man knows it except him to whom God has revealed it'" (Talmage, 1977, 92-93). (Bigler)]

In Mormon belief, one's marital status is decisive for the life hereafter. Without marriage one can only become a servant angel ministering to those who are far more worthy of glory, the truly married. But most of those who have married on earth are married for *time only* (until death), and not truly married unless they have their marriage sealed in the temple. In heaven, those who are married only for this life will be single, no better than bachelors and spinsters. (In the Mormon view of heaven, one can enjoy all the pleasures of sex, food, and other sensual delights.) Those who are married by a prophet in the temple are sealed to each other and married *for time and eternity*. Couples in a sealed marriage will remain married for eternity, and enjoy reigning in separate kingdoms. It is also possible to marry for eternity and not for time. Thus a kindly man may marry a spinster for eternity but not for time, leaving her to her celibate lifestyle here, but destined for all the delights of the Celestial Kingdom as his mate in eternity (Murstein 1974, 350-362).

Gender Roles. As with all societies, gender roles among Mormons are scripted very early in life. The LDS church plays a distinct role in gender definition and scripting. Church activities segregate children at around the age of 12: boys are guided into vigorous endeavors, such as scouting and outdoor gamesmanship, whereas girls learn household activities and crafts.

[To clarify Forrest's comment above, it is important to note that Mormon adolescents frequently participate in mixed-gender activities. Although young men and young women generally meet separately as a part of the official church youth program (known variously as Mutual Improvement Association (M.I.A.), Mutual, and Young Men's/Young Women's Program), males and females come together for Sunday School and the Mormon worship service known as Sacrament Meeting. In addition, LDS seminaries—religious study programs for high-school-age teens (grades 9 through 12) that operate in virtually every location around the world where congregations of Mormons are found—are always conducted with male and female students meeting together. Furthermore, Mormon youth regularly attend church-sponsored dances and participate together in community activities, including school proms, holiday celebrations, and cultural events. Young Mormon women and men are encouraged to interact, though care is usually taken to provide chaperons or to direct young people into activities where the possibility of sexual contact is limited (e.g., Mormon youths are strongly encouraged by their church leaders and parents to date in groups, and establish curfews that will not keep them out past midnight). (Bigler)]

It is not unusual for a preadolescent girl to have an LDS-designed poster on her bedroom wall urging her to remain "temple worthy," or reminding her of gospel precepts that will keep her safe from worldly situations. For example, one poster is of a young girl looking into a mirror in whose reflection is a vision of herself as a young woman in a bridal scene with a handsome man. The caption says, "looking forward to a temple marriage." Young men are also urged to bridle their carnal urges. Masturbation is expressly forbidden, and moral cleanliness, a requirement for any temple ceremony, essentially equates to abstaining from sexual activity before marriage.

[In Mormon practice, "moral cleanliness" at its most basic level is understood as abstaining from sexual activity before marriage and remaining faithful to one's spouse. It is not at all equated with celibacy, as the author has implied. A pamphlet for youth, recently published by the church, makes this position clear: "Our Heavenly Father has counseled that sexual intimacy should be reserved for his children within the bonds of marriage. . . . Because sexual intimacy is so sacred, the Lord requires self-control and purity before marriage as well as full fidelity after marriage" (Church of Jesus Christ of Latter-Day Saints, 1990, 14-15). (Bigler)]

Gender roles become even more firmly established during transitions into adulthood. Church officials clearly define the position, duties, and destiny of women in the divine plan. Women are to be "copartners with

God in bringing his spirit children into the world" (Tanner 1973); this is generally understood metaphorically without any sexual connotation. Rather than focus on the erotic element of this distinction (having babies does require first having sexual intercourse), the LDS leaders instead urge women to stay home in order to love and care for children to ensure a generation of Mormons who learn about their "duty as citizens and what they must do to return to their Heavenly Father." Women are regarded as sacred vessels, with important roles not only in childbearing, but also as positive influences on men's lives. A "general authority" in the church, Hugh B. Brown, suggests that "women are more willing to make sacrifices than are men, more patient in suffering, and more earnest in prayer" (Relief Society 1965). Women in the Mormon community are indeed known for their good works. The Relief Society is the oldest women's group in the United States and is remarkably active with community support of all kinds.

[Most Mormons, female and male alike, continue to hold traditional views concerning gender and gender roles. In general, Mormon women today still view motherhood and caregiving as fundamental traits of a "righteous" woman. However, it is also fair to say that the beliefs of church officials and the broader membership regarding gender roles have liberalized somewhat since President Hugh B. Brown's statement in 1965. For example, in a recent general conference of the church, Chieko N. Okazaki, First Counselor in the Relief Society General Presidency, urged LDS women to obtain an education and career training:

> [Each year it becomes increasingly important for women to improve their abilities to take care of themselves and their children economically, if circumstances should require. . . . If anything, [the counsel of Elder Howard W. Hunter] has become even more relevant in the almost twenty years that have passed as the national economy has made it increasingly difficult for one wage to support a family, as more mothers are left alone to raise their children, and as more women spend lengthy portions of their lives single. He is telling all of us to use the oar of study to prepare ourselves professionally for worthy and rewarding activities, including paid employment. (Okazaki, 1994) (Bigler)]

LDS men have a clearly defined role as well. Men bear the responsibility and the privilege of the Priesthood, which is a spiritual calling and connection to God specifically not given to women. An exception to this is found in LDS mission work, where young women on evangelical missions for the church have a type of "priesthood calling" on a temporary basis, lasting only for the duration of the mission.

[Throughout the church's history, Mormon women have served missions for the church. Today, young women (typically in their early 20s) are embarking on proselyting and church service missions in ever-increasing numbers. Although Mormon men are encouraged much more strongly than are women to go on missions, teaching and preaching are not restricted to priesthood holders (males) in the church today. In fact, the priesthood is not a prerequisite for participation in most church positions, all of which are filled by lay members. Nevertheless, church leadership at its highest levels, both locally and generally, remains a function of the priesthood (male members). (Bigler)]

Through the priesthood, God governs all things. Priesthood power is considered a vital source of eternal strength and energy; a responsibility delegated to men for the well-being of mankind. Holding the priesthood means having authority to act as God's authorized agent, which includes some church organizational duties. The right of worthy priesthood holders is to preside over their descendants through all ages, achieving its highest function in the family. As the presiding priesthood holder in the home, decisions relating to discipline often fall to the man, and the role of providing for the household is ultimately his, in spite of the presence of more employed Mormon women. Giving righteous advice, loving family members, and the laying-on-of-hands for healing purposes are all rights of the man of the house.

[In the ideal Mormon household, discipline, family decisions, and the day-to-day management of the home are seen as a shared responsibility between a unified husband and wife. Although Mormon fathers have been designated the presiding authority in the family (once again a function of the priesthood), it is the mother who is typically responsible for managing the home and children. However, male church members are counseled against the misuse of their designation as leader in the home, and men have been encouraged by the prophet and president of the church himself to share in parenting and home management:

> [A man who holds the priesthood accepts his wife as a partner in the leadership of the home and family with full knowledge of and full participation in all decisions relating thereto. . . . You share, as a loving partner, the care of the children. Help her to manage and keep up your home. Help teach, train, and discipline your children. (Hunter, 1994, 5-7) (Bigler)]

Body Theology. The Mormon doctrine about the body is worth noting since it creates another element of sexual tension. In many Christian religions, the body is considered simply a vessel housing the spirit/soul for the duration of life. For the Mormons, the body itself is highly revered and serves an eternal function. At the point of resurrection, the body of an individual is returned to "perfection," ridding it of all the faults and defects of this life. A Mormon friend of mine often queries, "Just whose version of perfection will I get in Eternity? I have a list of modifications right here."

One indication of the importance of the body is manifested by the wearing of "garments." During the Temple marriage, a couple is given special "garments" to wear. This special underwear (manufactured by the Mormon church) is designed to serve as a reminder of the sanctity of the covenants made in the temple and to protect the body from harm. A quiet Mormon joke about the garments refers to them as "Mormon contraceptives," since they must be worn next to the skin at all times and are notoriously unsexy in appearance. Women wear their foundation garments, such as brassieres and slips, over the Mormon garments. Because of the design of the garments, only modest clothing can be worn. However, the modern garments are much more relaxed and functional than traditional ones. The old versions are still available, with the tops extending just below the elbows and the bottoms below the knee, but most younger Mormon women opt for the cap sleeve and midthigh cotton versions for comfort and more choice in clothing.

[Mormon garments (which are worn by both women and men) serve as a constant reminder of sacred covenants made in temple ceremonies. Mormons also believe that these undergarments help protect the wearer against physical and spiritual harm. In addition, the design of the underclothing encourages the wearing of modest clothing. Although temple garments are to be worn day and night under normal circumstances, church members are not required by either doctrine or dictum to keep their underclothing on during activities such as bathing or while participating in sporting events. Nor are faithful Mormons required to wear their garments during sexual activity. (Bigler)]

Adolescent Dating. Adolescent dating rituals are very similar to those of other conservative American cultural groups. As LDS children grow older, the church plays more of a role in their lives, interweaving doctrinal and social activities. The transitions through church steps for adolescents are made in tandem with all their church peers. For instance, at 8 years old, children reach the "age of understanding" and are baptized into the church. Many of their peers are also taking this step, which takes on social significance in the form of family gatherings and informal parties. Later, dating is encouraged in group settings around church activities, since this context is most likely to encourage an interfaith marriage. Teens are often told, "if you don't date outside, you won't fall in love outside, and you won't marry outside the faith."

[Dating among Mormon teens is not restricted solely to church activities, although local congregations do often sponsor teen-oriented events, such as dances, firesides (discussions of religious topics especially relevant to teens), and cultural activities (plays, concerts, art exhibits, etc.). While dating outside of the church is not strictly forbidden, it is, as the author states, discouraged by church leaders and parents in an effort to reduce the chances that a member will marry outside of the church. Families of particularly staunch members are likely to view the marriage of a child to someone from outside of the church as a lamentable and perhaps even shameful event. Although Mormons who are married to nonmembers are not excluded from church activity or normal religious practice, one's relationship to the church is undoubtedly affected by the "part-member" status of the family. (Bigler)]

At Brigham Young University, a Mormon-owned and operated institution in Provo, Utah, approximately 45 miles south of Salt Lake City, a subculture of dating reigns. Known to be an ideal place for Mormon youth to find a same-faith marriage partner, it is also a hotbed of sexual exploration. Mormon coeds fine-tune their "NCMOS," (pronounced "nick-moes"), which is an acronym for "noncommittal make-out sessions." These sexual forays include "everything but intercourse": extensive kissing, petting, and "dry humping" (rubbing bodies) is common, but touching of the genitals is typically off-bounds, as is penetration of any kind.

[Brigham Young University, the oldest private university west of the Mississippi River, boasts a student body of more than 30,000, comprised almost entirely of young Mormons who come from every state in the country and many nations outside of the United States. The amount and types of sexual activities that the author reports occur among BYU students are not all that atypical of young college students in general. However, given the strict code of sexual conduct that Mormons have for themselves, even nongenital sex play and sexual activity short of intercourse give BYU the appearance of a "hotbed of sexual exploration." At the same time, such activity also suggests that young Mormons have healthy sexual appetites, and perhaps are not as peculiar as it may first appear when compared to their peers on other American campuses. (Bigler)]

Marriage, Sex, and the Celestial Kingdom. In order to access the Celestial Kingdom, a couple must marry in the temple. These temple rites seal the two partners together not just for life, but for all eternity. When a couple is in the Celestial Kingdom together, they can enjoy the full experience of their resurrected and eternally perfect bodies. The purpose of the sealed marriage is primarily to ensure the eternal connection between partners, allowing them to procreate and populate their own worlds (eternal procreation). An essential precept, "As man is, so God once was; as God is, so man can become," guides heterosexual couples through life with the promise that they, as the God they worship has done, will become creators of their own world (Murstein 1974).

Although not formally prohibited, birth control is regarded with clear reservation by church members, since large families are viewed favorably. Women who leave the Mormon church often refer, "with tongue in cheek," to their loss of opportunity to bear children during the afterlife. One woman commented, "At least I know I won't be barefoot and pregnant through time and eternity."

[While birth control is regarded with reservation by many church members and authorities, various forms of contraception are commonly practiced, even by active, faithful members. Today, the decision to use birth control is left to the discretion of the couple. (Bigler)]

The gender roles established early in the life of the couple are metaphorically established again during the marriage ceremony. The order of the Plan of Salvation is clearly outlined during the ceremony, as is the order of the household that symbolically supports the Divine Order when it is in accord with the Plan of Salvation. An interesting element of the temple marriage is the giving of a name to the bride, known only to her husband. This name is for the use of the husband in calling his wife to him in the afterlife. She does not have access to his secret name—the calling of partners in eternity is purely a masculine prerogative. The giving of the name to the bride is kept secret from outsiders, as is much of the rest of the ceremony, which is closed to all those without special church endowments. Mormon church weddings are different from typical American weddings in that only worthy LDS family members and friends are allowed into the temple to observe the ceremony itself. If a family member is an inactive church member or a nonmember, they will be excluded from the wedding ceremony, joining the party outside the temple or at the reception.

In the face of the lack of sexuality education, the first act of sexual intercourse for a good Mormon is likely to be ill-informed. One contemporary of mine recalls her first sexual experience, which took place after an LDS temple marriage: "We were both virgins, and it literally took us several weeks to consummate the marriage by having intercourse. We had been raised to believe sex was a sacred thing, so we just sat in bed, prayerfully, kissing gently and waiting for something to happen. Obviously, something finally did, but I was dreadfully disappointed. It not only didn't feel sacred, it didn't even feel good." This particular couple did not seek therapy for support or education, relying instead on the Holy Spirit, a decision common among LDS couples.

Because the church operates with a lay ministry, the local bishop has an enormous influence on how issues of sexuality are handled. In most instances in which married couples face difficulty with sexual relations or general marital dissatisfaction, the bishop is the first and most likely source of comfort and counsel. Often the bishop is just a kindly intentioned neighbor with limited or no training. Many times, his response is based on his own experience, attitudes, aversions, and parental training. Some extremely compassionate bishops give forgiving responses to an individual who has erred sexually. Some bishops advise specifically against such behaviors as oral or anal sex. Others, repulsed by the vulgarity of even discussing the topic of sexuality, take refuge in esoteric spiritual or academic language or avoid the topic altogether. Still others may be open-minded and suggest that either the lay ministry has an extremely limited role in the bedroom of other folks or advise liberal measures, such as doing whatever works best for the couple involved. If marriage counseling is clearly needed, a referral may be made by the bishop to the LDS Social Services or to an LDS therapist, who can give professional advice with an empathy for the doctrinal requirements. In sharp contrast, other bishops respond with an injunction to leave the fellowship if someone has premarital intercourse, commits adultery, or engages in homosexual relations, all of which are forbidden by church doctrine.

[Problems that result from limited sexuality education coupled with well intentioned but poorly trained lay clergy are compounded for Mormons by a dearth of LDS therapists and other mental-health professionals who have specific training and experience in the area of sexuality. (Bigler)]

Divorce is discouraged, but not uncommon. The divorce rate in the state of Utah, in spite of a predominantly LDS population, matches those of many states. Even marriages sealed in the temple are now relatively easy to unseal. Remarriage from a doctrinal standpoint is difficult to comprehend in light of the eternal marriage concept, but temple divorces will officially separate the couple for the purposes of the Celestial Kingdom.

[If a temple divorce has been granted, a second marriage can be sealed in a Mormon temple. Marriages that take place outside of the temple are officially recognized by the church as legal and valid, with the understanding that these unions will not carry on into the eternities. (Bigler)]

The Mormon Family. An ideal Mormon family works together, putting the sense of "family" first, honoring the doctrine that families will endure throughout eternity. It is a rare LDS home that lacks some visible reminder of this doctrine in an embroidered or otherwise handcrafted item proclaiming, "Families are Forever." The cultural value placed on family as a priority distinctly impacts those who choose not to have children, making those couples at least the object of social curiosity, if not censure.

Utah, the Mormon Mecca, is culturally oriented toward family because of the LDS church influence. Exemplifying this is Enid Waldholtz, the Republican congresswoman elected to office in 1994 from Utah, who is only the second member of Congress to bear a child while in office. This choice on the part of LDS Congresswoman Waldholtz clearly cemented her popularity among her Mormon constituents. She made a clear statement about her support for family life by meeting one of the most basic expectations of a Mormon couple with this childbirth.

Sex Education. Children are taught about sexuality more by implicit measures than direct and overt messages. Sexual exploration at a very early age is treated with quiet but firm repression. Mormon adults often describe their sense of guilt at their developing sexuality, often beginning at a very early age. These ideas are often disseminated by parents during "morality lessons," which might include the suggestion of singing hymns if "impure thoughts" enter one's mind, or using affirmative reminders that one's primary objective is to reach the Celestial Kingdom, which demands the purity of the body temple. "Impure thoughts" are usually not specifically defined, but are so pervasively assumed to be sexually related that many Mormon adults still claim to equate words such as "purity" and "morality" with specific sexual connotations.

In spite of the importance placed on having babies in a married state, very little formal education is done regarding sexuality and pregnancy. Countless times after I have made a simple junior- or high-school presentation on HIV prevention, students have lined up to ask me other "related" questions, often regarding basic body functioning, for example, "I haven't started my period. . . . How do I know if I'm pregnant? . . . Can I get pregnant from kissing?"

[Mormon families are counseled by their leaders to hold a weekly Family Home Evening each Monday night. This is a specially designated time during the week for the family to join together to study religious topics, enjoy activities outside of the home, or address important family issues. Family Home Evening, as it has been outlined, provides LDS families with a perfect opportunity to provide sexuality education in the home within the framework of the family's own value system. After observing this practice among Mormon families, Dr. Ruth Westheimer and her colleague Louis Lieberman noted:

> [In particular, we have been impressed by the manner in which the Church of Jesus Christ of Latter-day Saints (the Mormons) has approached the difficult task of teaching moral and ethical precepts in the area of sexuality. If Jews, Italians, Chinese, and Japanese, among other groups, may be said to be child-centered societies, the Mormons must be said to be family-centered, par excellence. There appears to be a structured, systematic, integrated and total approach to morality through the family. Thus, sexual morality is taught as part of a system and way of life that focuses on the goal of eternal or celestial marriage. The church reaches out to the family through many media: songs, family meetings, family resource books, television, videos, etc., to provide the Mormon perspective on all aspects of sexuality for all family members. (Westheimer & Lieberman 1988, 109)

[Unfortunately, all too often, Mormon families fail to take advantage of this valuable resource, and miss an obvious opportunity to educate their children about matter related to human sexuality. (Bigler)]

Many couples marry with limited information even about the act of intercourse. If they have been properly parented in the faith, they will have been protected from exposure to sexual or "perverted" images. A Mormon church leader, Dallin Oakes, in a speech at Brigham Young University, said "We are surrounded by the promotional literature of illicit sexual relations on the printed page and on the screen. For your own good, avoid it." He added, "Pornographic or erotic stories and pictures are worse than filthy or polluted food. The body has defenses to rid itself of unwholesome food, but the brain won't vomit back filth."

Biological information about menstruation is disseminated clinically. Some women recall this clinical information as imbued with a sense of shame, in which menstruation is described as a sickness or something one does not discuss in polite company. For example, I dated a Mormon man who was so unfamiliar with menstrual issues and women's bodies—in spite of having several sisters—that he did not know what the purpose of a tampon was or how it functioned.

Abortion. Abortion is considered a most venal sin. Since Mormon doctrine regards the bearing of children as an opportunity to bring "spirit" children into an earthly form, abortion is not only considered murder, but in addition, a denial of a body for a predestined soul.

Gay Culture. Both the San Francisco and New York gay cultures take special note of the Brigham Young University gay underground, famous for its size and covert scope. Many of the returning missionaries come back to BYU to find a mate and resolve the same-sex desires often stirred on the two-year LDS mission strongly encouraged by the Church with strictly enforced male-only companionship.* Sometimes that resolution does not come easily. Support groups for Mormon homosexuals in the Provo and Salt Lake area around BYU give voice to the pain of these men. Lesbians face the same dilemma, since they are surrounded by the cultural pressure to marry and have families.

The divine mandate of heterosexual marriage regards homosexuality as a repudiation of the gift and giver of life. Thus, homosexuality is regarded as a direct violation of God's plan, which is that men should cleave to women. Sexual relations between any nonmarried persons is considered sinful and homosexuality falls into this category. According to Dallin Oaks, one of the church apostles, "Eternal laws that pertain to chastity before marriage and personal purity within marriage apply to all sexual behavior. However, marriage is not doctrinal therapy for homosexual relationships" (Ludlow 1992). Since so much of the restored gospel hinges upon the legally and temple-wedded heterosexual couple, practicing homosexuals are excommunicated.

[*A note on LDS missionary services. Mormon men are strongly encouraged (*not* required) to serve a two-year mission at the age of 19. Formal sanctions are not imposed on those males who choose not to go on a mission. However, in a strong Mormon family or LDS community, social sanctions can be quite severe. The status of "Returned Missionary" is a valuable asset to a young man's marriage potential. In contrast, the decision not to serve a mission—or worse yet, leaving on a mission and returning home early—often brings shame to both the young man and his family. Mormon women, on the other hand, can choose to go on an 18-month mission at the age of 21. However, the expectation of service is not nearly as great for females as it is for males, and the decision not to go, particularly if a young woman opts to get married instead, results in few, if any, negative repercussions. (Bigler)]

Often the feelings of a gay person meet responses of incredulity on the part of parents and church leaders. One parent counseled his son not to act on his "supposed" same-gender feelings, "to date young women seriously, to wait and see" (Schow et al. 1991). Because homosexual couples cannot reproduce, this parent urged his son to "choose otherwise." The church offers "counseling to those who are troubled by homosexual thoughts and actions" in order that they might become acceptable to God. Repentance is offered in these circumstances. "Homosexuality and like practices are deep sins; they can be cured; they can be forgiven" (*Church News* 1978). In order to remain a Mormon in good standing, homosexuals must remain celibate and refrain from all same-gender eroticism. Acceptance is not advocated at any level.

[The current Mormon position on homosexuality can be described as one of limited tolerance. Because sexual activity is reserved for marriage, and same-sex relationships are not recognized by most legal bodies or by the church, homosexual activity is therefore forbidden. As the author correctly notes, to continue to be a Mormon in good standing, homosexual men and women must remain celibate and refrain from all same-sex sexual activity. The church's position officially allows for individuals who are sexually attracted to members of the same gender to remain fully involved in church activities, so long as there is no sexual activity. This stance, though still extremely restrictive, is quite a departure from past policy and practice when virtually any indication of same-sex attraction could be used as grounds for excommunication. However, despite the apparent shift in thinking toward greater acceptance, it remains difficult, if not impossible, for members who feel a same-sex attraction to continue to actively practice Mormonism. Unfortunately, homophobia is often a more-powerful emotion for many church members than the New Testament challenge to "Love thy neighbor as thyself." Frequently, this homophobia is internalized and, despite Ludlow's declaration that "marriage is not doctrinal therapy for homosexual relationships," many gay, lesbian, and bisexual Mormons follow the traditional course that has been set for them by getting married and starting a family. Some carry on with a heterosexual life and take the secret of homosexuality to the grave. Others find their true sexual feelings too powerful to deny and may have clandestine same-sex relationships or seek out friendly advice, often from a bishop or other church authority. For those who acknowledge same-sex attraction, reparative or reorientation therapy is a common recommendation. These programs have demonstrated little lasting success in changing sexual orientation. Participation in reparative or reorientation therapy is often experienced as the ultimate failure, since the promise of change is directly linked to the sincerity and worthiness of one's efforts.

[Change-orientated therapy, therefore, is commonly the final step for many gay, lesbian, and bisexual Mormons before leaving the church or being asked to leave. In the end, homosexual Mormons are often left with a choice between their church and their sexuality. Because the two are diametrically opposed, there is little room for compromise. (Bigler)]

Summary. The Mormon culture is distinct in many ways. Known for hard work, loyal families, and abstinence from alcohol and tobacco, the Mormons are steadfast in their maintenance of traditional family values. Sexually conservative and repressive, Mormon doctrines may be the ideal for people disillusioned with or anxious about the liberalization of sexual attitudes and practices occurring in the United States in recent decades. According to the 1995 United States census, Utah—with a 70 percent Mormon population—ranks first in fertility and last in teen pregnancy. The Mormons, long considered remarkable for their nearly anachronistic traditional values, may actually be on the cutting edge of the Christian Right's abstinence- and morality-based vision of American family life.

B. Racial, Ethnic, and Feminist Perspectives

In addition to the religious factor, two other social factors continue to exert considerable influence on American sexual ideologies and practices, race/ethnicity and gender. In this section, we examine the sexual customs of two of the largest racial and ethnic minority groups in the U.S.A., African-Americans and Latino-Americans, and the effects of feminism and feminist perspectives on sexuality in America and sexological research.

African-Americans   HERBERT SAMUELS

The term African-American is widely and often carelessly used to suggest or imply that the more than 30 million African-Americans constitute some kind of homogeneous community or culture. This is both contrary to reality and dangerous, as the term properly includes a rich diversity of very different, and often distinct, subcultures, each with its own set of sexual values, attitudes, and behavioral patterns. Included under the rainbow umbrella of African-Americans are urban African-Americans in the northeast, ranging from Boston south to Washington, D.C., African-Americans in Los Angeles on the West Coast, and African-Americans in urban centers in the southern states. Rural African-Americans are often quite different from urban African-Americans, even in nearby metropolitan centers. Socioeconomic and educational differences add to the diversity of African-American subcultures. This perspective is essential to avoid overgeneralizations about the observations provided here.

Historical Perspective. A review of the past record reveals that many white Americans have regarded the majority of African-Americans as representing the sexual instinct in its raw state. This belief that African-American sexual behavior is somehow more sordid and crude than the sexual behavior of white Americans is by no means a new concept. Reports dating from the mid-sixteenth century depict the sexual behavior of Africans as bestial. The same descriptions were later applied to the Africans brought to the New World by the slave trade.

Moreover, the folk view of the sexuality of blacks is often hard to distinguish from what appears in the scientific literature. In the guise of science, some investigators have presented such conclusions as: (1) African-American men and women are guided by "bestial instinct" (DeRachewiltz 1964; Jacobus 1937; Purchas 1905); (2) the black man is more animalistic in bed (DeRachewiltz 1964; Jacobus 1937; Purchas 1905); (3) the black man's penis is larger than the penis of the white man (DeRachewiltz 1964; Edwardes and Masters 1963; Jacobus 1937); (4) the black man is a sexual superman whose potency and virility is greater than the white man's (DeRachewiltz 1964; Jacobus 1937; Jefferson 1954); (5) the black man's reproductive capacity is colossal (Jacobus 1937); (6) black men are obsessed with the idea of having sex with white women (Edwardes and Masters 1963; Fanon 1967); (7) all black women want to sleep with anyone who comes along (DeRachewiltz 1964; Jacobus 1937; Rogers 1967); and (8) black women respond instantly and enthusiastically to all sexual advances (DeRachewiltz 1964; Jacobus 1937). Blacks have also been characterized as holding more-permissive attitudes regarding extramarital affairs (Bell 1968; Christensen and Johnson 1978; Houston 1981; Reiss 1964, 1967; Roebuck and McGee 1977; and Staples 1978). This simplistic notion may well misrepresent the complexity of African-American sexual values. According to Robert Staples (1986, 258),

> Blacks have traditionally had a more naturalistic attitude toward human sexuality, seeing it as the normal expression of sexual attraction between men and women. Even in African societies, sexual conduct was not the result of some divine guidance by God or other deities. It was secularly regulated and encompassed the tolerance of a wide range of sexual attitudes and behaviors. Sexual deviance, where so defined, was not an act against God's will but a violation of community standards.

Gender, Gender Role, Sex, Love, and Marriage. Gender and gender roles are culturally defined constructs that determine the boundaries of acceptable and unacceptable behavior for men and women. These notions are often based on stereotypes—a fixed, oversimplified, and extremely distorted idea about a group of people. In the general American culture, the traditional stereotyped female is gentle, kind, dependent, passive, and submissive. The traditional stereotyped male is tough, brutal, independent, aggressive, and intractable. Any deviation from one's expected gender role may be met with skepticism about one's psychological health. For example, the traditional view of the black male—as it relates to gender-role identification—is that he has been emasculated by the experience of slavery and is suffering from gender-identity problems because of absent or inadequate male role models. Moreover, because of these two problems, he has a more-feminine gender identity than white males (Grier and Cobbs 1968; Glazer and Moynihan 1964; Pettigrew 1964; Wilkinson and Taylor 1977). Grier and Cobbs (1968, 59) suggest that:

> For the black man in this country, it is not so much a matter of acquiring manhood as it is a struggle to feel it his own. Whereas the white man regards his manhood as an ordained right, the black man is engaged in a never ending battle for its possession. For the black man, attaining any portion of manhood is an active process. He must penetrate barriers and overcome opposition in order to assume a masculine posture. For the innermost psychological obstacles to manhood are never so formidable as the impediments woven into American society.

Pettigrew (1964) supported the notion that black males are more feminine than white males because of certain responses to items in the masculinity-femininity scale on the Minnesota Multiphasic Personality Inventory (MMPI). Two items that Pettigrew noted were the statements, "I would like to be a singer" and "I think I feel more intensely than most people do." Black males responded more positively to these statements than did white males. This pattern was interpreted to mean that black males are more feminine than white males. Pettigrew based his conclusion regarding the black male's gender identity on two studies. One study included a sample of Alabama convicts; the other was a group of veterans with tuberculosis! As Pleck (1981) notes, these are hardly representative samples.

In contrast to the emasculated, feminine, black-male hypothesis, Hershey (1978) argues that black males have a stronger masculine identity than white males. In her study of sex-role identities and sex-role stereotyping, the black men's mean masculinity score was significantly higher than the mean masculinity score of the white men in her sample.

To the extent that African-American males have been emasculated by gender-role stereotyping, African-American females have been defeminized by gender-role stereotyping. The so-called black matriarchy has been historically blamed for the deterioration of the black family, because black women have greater participation in family decision making in a society where male control is the "normal rule." Because white stereotyped norms are violated, African-American women are seen as being domineering. By virtue of the historical legacy of slavery and discrimination against African-American men, African-American women were in the labor market, received education, and supported their families.

According to Staples,

> Sex relations have a different nature and meaning to black people. Their sexual expression derives from the emphasis in the black culture

on feeling, of releasing the natural functions of the body without artificiality or mechanical movements. In some circles this is called "soul" and may be found among peoples of African descent through the world. (Cited by Francoeur 1991, 90-92)

In a practical sense, this means that black men do not moderate their enthusiasm for sex relations as white men do. They do not have a history of suppressing the sexual expression of the majority of their women while singling out a segment of the female population for premarital and extra-marital adventures (Staples 1977, 141-42).

The major problem with such studies is that few have questioned the stereotyped assumptions regarding gender-role socialization upon which their conclusions are based.

Views and Practices of Sex Education. Black males and females are socialized very early into heterosexual relations by their culture and extended-family system. The less-stringent age and gender-role orientations that are evident in the black community exposes children at an early age to a more permissive sexual ethos. Many African-Americans perceive sex as a natural function; thus, children are not hidden from discussions of a sexual nature.

Academically, many sexuality- or family-life-education programs employ the Health Belief Model, not only as a way to predict sexual behavior, but to facilitate behavior change. This model has certain assumptions that are based on Euro-American social norms. These norms may not be consistent with the beliefs and values of many African-Americans. Mays and Cochran (1990) correctly maintain that such attitude-behavior models

> assume that people are motivated to pursue rational courses of action. They further assume that people have the resources necessary to proceed directly with these rational decisions. . . . Black Americans confront an environment in which much of their surrounding milieu is beyond their personal control. Models of human behavior that emphasize individualistic, direct, and rational behavioral decisions overlook the fact that many blacks do not have personal control over traditional categories of resources—for example, money, education, and mobility.

For many African-Americans, educational models that place emphasis on social norms and the extent of commitment to social responsibilities, rather than those that value individualistic rational reasoning, may be better predictors of future behavior.

Masturbation. Most studies indicate that African-American men and women masturbate less than do white men and women. In a recent national study, *The Social Organization of Sexuality* (Laumann et al. 1994), one third of white men and 56 percent of white women reported that they had not masturbated at all in the past year. However, black men were almost twice as likely to report that they had not masturbated at all during the past year, and about 68 percent of black women reported that they did not masturbate the past year. However, those African-Americans who do masturbate demonstrate the same childhood, adolescent, and adult patterns as their white counterparts. Blacks may not acknowledge that they masturbate as readily as whites, because of the belief that admitting that one masturbates means one is unable to find a sex partner.

Children and Sex. African-American children, according to Staples (1972), are socialized very early into heterosexual relations by their culture and extended-family system. This socialization pattern exposes them at an early age to a more permissive sexual ethos. Thus, African-American children may have a knowledge of sexual intercourse, masturbation, condom usage, and other sexual practices at a younger age.

Adolescents and Sex. Compared to white teenagers, African-American teenagers begin coitus about two years earlier, on the average, and are more likely to progress directly from light petting to sexual intercourse (Brooks-Gunn and Furstenburg 1989). Consequently, African-American females may be at greater risk of pregnancy.

Black men start dating earlier, are more likely to have a romantic involvement in high school, have the most liberal sexual attitudes, and are most inclined to have nonmarital sex without commitment (Broderick 1965; Larson et al. 1976; Johnson and Johnson 1978). (See Section 5B for additional data comparing black and white adolescent sexual patterns).

Adults. In the aftermath of the Civil War, blacks married in record numbers because, under the inhumane institution of slavery, legal marriage had been denied to them. Three out of four black adults were living in intact nuclear families by the early part of the twentieth century, and the overwhelming majority of black children were born to parents who were legally married. Today, an African-American child has but a one-in-five chance of being raised by two parents (Chideya et al. 1993). Out-of-wedlock births have risen since the 1960s, particularly among African-Americans. Two out of three first births to African-American women under the age of 35 are now out of wedlock.

Traditionally, women in American society have tended to marry men in their own social class or to "marry up" to a higher socioeconomic group. This pattern has been substantially disrupted among African-Americans, largely because of a distorted gender ratio among blacks. This imbalance in the proportion of males and females of marriageable age has been present for several decades, but has become exacerbated in recent years. By the 1990s, there were roughly fifty adult African-American women for every forty-two African-American men, largely because of abnormally high rates of black-male mortality and incarceration (Staples and Johnson, 1993). Because the proportion of African-American women who attend college and earn degrees is much higher than the rate for men, this problem is even more severe for higher-status women. As a result, increasing numbers of black women are remaining single or marrying partners from lower-status groups (i.e., less education and/or income). There is no evidence that large groups of black women are choosing to marry outside their race (Staples and Johnson, 1993)

Joseph Scott (1976) has argued that these social conditions are largely responsible for the emergence of a pattern he calls "mansharing." Mansharing is a lifestyle where a number of African-American women, each of whom typically maintains her own separate residence, "share" a man for intimate relationships. Typically, he splits time living with each of the women. Scott (1976) argued that mansharing represented the appearance of a new, polygamous family form in the African-American community. However, we want to stress that this does not mean that black women like or prefer this lifestyle. Cazenave (1979) has noted that lifestyles can sometimes be imposed by external social constraints. There is some evidence (Allen and Agbasegbe 1980) that most black women do not approve of mansharing as a lifestyle, but feel they have reduced options in an environment with few eligible male partners. Scott concluded that:

> Until there is some way to correct the sex ratio imbalance and until blacks control the economic and welfare institutions in such a way to stop the breaking up of black monogamous relationships we cannot be too harsh on black men and women who find some satisfactory adjustments in sharing themselves and their economic resources in a new, at least for this society, family form which meets their most basic needs. (Scott 1976, 80)

Homosexuality and Bisexuality. Attitudes within the African-American community reflect those in the majority culture. According to Staples (1981), homosexuality may be tolerated in the black community but will not be approved openly. Bell and Weinberg (1978), in their study of homosexuality, found that black male homosexuals tended to be younger than their white counterparts, had less education, and were employed at a lower occupational level. Moreover, black male gays more often expressed the belief that their homosexuality and homosexual contacts had helped more than hurt their careers.

Compared to black gay males, black lesbians had fewer transient sexual partners. Most reported that the majority of their sexual encounters were with women for whom they cared emotionally.

Coercive Sex and Pornography. The incidence of rape among African-Americans has been subject to some controversy. According to the Department of Health and Human Services, 683,000 adult women were raped in 1990. By contrast, the National Victim Center estimated that there were 130,236 rapes in 1990 and 207,610 in 1991. Although earlier reports indicated that African-American women were more likely to be sexually assaulted than white women, newer studies do not find any statistically significant differ- ence between African-American and white samples. The historical notion that most rapists are black men is totally without merit; indeed most rapists and their victims are members of the same race or ethnic group.

There is an important difference between the attitudes of those whites who support the antipornography movement in the United States and the lack of interest this issue stirs among African-Americans. For African-Ameri- cans, as Robert Staples (1986, 258) argues, issues of poverty, education, job opportunities, and teenage pregnancy are far more pressing concerns than the crusade against pornography.

> Rather than seeing the depiction of heterosexual intercourse or nudity as an inherent debasement of women as a fringe group as [white religious conservatives and] feminists claim, the black community would see women as having equal rights to the enjoyment of sexual stimuli. It is nothing more than a continuation of the white male's traditional double standard and paternalism to regard erotica as exist- ing only for male pleasure and women only as sexual objects. Since that double standard has never attracted many American blacks, the claim that women are exploited by exhibiting their nude bodies or engaging in heterosexual intercourse lacks credibility. After all, it was the white missionaries who forced African women to regard their quasi-nude bodies as sinful and placed them in clothes. This probably accounts for the rather conspicuous absence of black women in the feminist fight against porn.

Contraception and Abortion. Since the early 1970s, many in the African-Ameri- can community have viewed contraceptive use as a form of genocide advocated by whites. Thus, control over reproduction has had political and social implications.

The majority of women having abortions are white. Although 12 percent of the population is of African-American ancestry, black women constitute approximately 31 percent of the women who seek abortions. There is a history of forced sterilization against African-Americans, which many per- ceive as a form of genocide similar to contraception.

STDs and HIV/AIDS. In 1932, the United States Public Health Service recruited 600 African-American men from Tuskegee, Alabama, to partici- pate in an experiment involving untreated syphilis. The aim of this study was to determine if there were any racial differences in the development of syphilis. The Tuskegee participants were never informed that they had syphilis. This wanton disregard for human life allowed the disease to spread to the sexual partners of these men, as well as their offspring. This experiment continued until 1972! The repercussions from the "Tuskegee Experiment" still resonate strongly through African-American communities, and negatively impact on HIV/AIDS prevention programs.

HIV was the eighth-leading cause of death for all Americans in 1990, but it was the sixth-leading cause of death for African-Americans. It is the leading cause of death for African-American men between the ages of 35 and 44, and the second-leading cause of death for black men and women between 25 and 35. Again this raises the specter of genocide among many members of the African-American community, in that many believe that the virus was man-made!

Sexual Dysfunction. The stereotyped notions about the sexual experiences of African-Americans not only influence the attitudes that whites may have about African-Americans, but also affect the way in which African-Americans perceive themselves. For example, the willingness of an African-American male who is experiencing difficulty in maintaining an erection or ejaculatory control to seek help may be dependent on how closely he identifies with the myth of the "super potent" black man. Any man may feel embarrassment about a sexual problem, but for the African-American male, the embarrassment that he may feel is compounded by the images of the myth.

For clinicians, an awareness of this historical legacy is essential to the treatment process. A key component in the treatment of many sexual problems is the use of self-pleasuring exercises. These exercises are an effective method for a person to learn more about his or her own sex responses. Many African-Americans have negative feelings about masturbation that may infringe on the treatment process. First, changing these negative feelings may take more time than is typical for other clients. Second, African-Americans who do masturbate may be more reluctant to discuss this issue because, for many, admitting that they masturbate indicates that they cannot find a sexual partner.

Latino Perspectives on Sexuality   MIGUEL A. PÉREZ AND HELDA L. PINZÓN

Latinos, like most other ethnic/racial groups residing in the United States, exist in a distinct social environment, have developed a unique culture, and are often disfranchised from mainstream society. The terms "Latino" and "Hispanic" are used interchangeably in this section to describe a heterogeneous group of people representing a kaleidoscope of experiences, educational attainment, acculturation levels, and citizenship status. The term "Latina" pertains specifically to Hispanic women. The heterogeneity of the Latino population residing in the United States of America can be observed in each group's unique culture, beliefs, language, socio-

economic background, family name, racial ascription, and culinary preferences (Castex 1994; Neale 1989; Williams 1989). Although Latinos can be
found in almost every state, more than half of them live in Texas and
California (National Council of La Raza 1992).

Latinos are one of, if not the fastest-growing population groups in the
United States. According to census data, in the last decade, the United
States Latino population increased by 54 percent, a rate of increase more
than twice that of the general population (U.S. Bureau of the Census
[USBC] 1993). Currently, almost nine percent of the U.S. population is
classified as being of Hispanic or Latino descent; this figure is expected to
increase to 21 percent by the year 2050. High fertility rates, high levels of
immigration to the United States, and the relatively young population, are
often cited as reasons for this increase (Brindis 1992). Among Latinos,
persons of Mexican origin form the largest population group, with a
population total of approximately 13.5 million people; Puerto Ricans place
at a distant second with over 2.7 million (USBC 1993).

Overall, U.S. Latinos are a relatively young population with a median
age of 26 years compared to 34 years for non-Latinos; conversely, less than
5 percent of Latinos are aged 65 or older compared to 13 percent for
non-Latinos (USBC 1993). Among U.S. ethnic groups, only Native Americans have a younger population. Further differences among Latinos can
be observed in the age distribution of different Latino groups. Census data
show that Mexican-Americans have the youngest population, with a mean
age of 24 years, and Cuban-Americans have the oldest population—mean
age 40 years (Claude 1993).

The following material describes relevant sexological concepts among
United States Latinos. Although it does not seek to report all sexual-related
knowledge, it will highlight relevant sexological issues and hopefully dispel
some of the stereotypes related to Latino sexuality. Comparisons presented
here represent general data for Latinos, thus the reader needs to understand that there are differences between Latino subpopulation groups. The
truth is that the variety of sexual practices and patterns among Latinos in
the United States, and for that matter in Latin America, are only surpassed
by the limits of human imagination.

Family Issues. Several authors (de la Vega 1990; Lifshitz 1990; Fennelly 1988)
have emphasized the importance of recognizing the differences in family
and cultural expectations regarding sexual behavior for females and males
in the Latino culture. The acknowledgment of these differences allows for
the understanding of the complexity of sexuality-related issues within this
population group. Traditionally, Latinos have placed a high value on the
family, the entity which shapes their earlier views on sexuality (Brindis
1997). Latinos frequently place family over an individual's needs. It is,
therefore, not uncommon for Latinos to reside in multigenerational households with members of their extended families (Alberda and Tilly 1992;

Garcia 1993). This arrangement permits the division of labor, sharing of economic and domestic responsibilities, and most importantly, allows extended-family members to participate in the rearing of children (Kutsche 1983; Leaper-Campbell 1996).

Latino culture has been described as being patriarchal in nature. However, although men are traditionally the family's representative before society, women are the primary caregivers at home; in fact, women in the Latino culture are seen as the base of the family structure. Latinas, according to de la Vega (1990), have an important non-public and non-verbal authority within the family. Females are expected to maintain the equilibrium and smoothness of family relationships. In this role, Latinas traditionally tend to pay more attention to the family's needs than their own. This expectation is most often noted in young women taking care of older relatives, while their male counterparts seek to forge their own future, albeit not too far from the family unit.

Along with family orientation, Latinos often show the closely related concept of *simpatía*. The latter refers to Latinos' willingness to go along with items which may not be understood or that they may disagree with. Szapocznik (1995) has suggested that familism and *simpatía* may now be liabilities for Latinos in the United States, particularly for gay men who attempt to conceal their true HIV-status from their families and friends.

Sexological Concepts: Acculturation and Sexual Practices. Until the advent of the AIDS epidemic, few researchers had systematically documented sexual practices and knowledge among Latinos. Inappropriate application of methodological issues, language difficulties, and cultural insensitivity have all been identified as barriers to data collection among U.S. Latinos (Ford and Norris 1991).

Sexuality is an important life element among Latinos. However, Latino sexuality is not limited or circumscribed to coital activity, but it is rather expressed through a variety of life attitudes which reinforce male and female sexual identities. In the United States, sexual patterns are not only affected by culture, but also by the individual's degree of acculturation and assimilation (Spector 1991).

Acculturation and education also play a pivotal role in the acceptance of new expressions of sexuality. In a 1990 study, Marín, Marín, and Juárez found that Latinas with higher levels of acculturation reported more multiple sexual partners than those with lower acculturation levels. The same study found that less-acculturated males were more likely to carry condoms and report fewer sexual partners. A follow-up study found that less-acculturated Latinas were less likely to carry condoms and experienced higher levels of sexual discomfort (Marín, Gomez, and Hearst 1993). More-acculturated and educated Latinas are also more likely to adopt a leading role during heterosexual activities.

Acculturation notwithstanding, sexuality continues to be a taboo topic for many Latinos, particularly for older, Spanish-speaking Latinos.

Sexual Stereotypes. It is perhaps significant that general knowledge of Latino sexuality is denoted more by stereotypes than factual information. De la Vega (1990) concluded that numerous myths and stereotypes are found among Latinos, as within any group of individuals. It is important that these subtle cultural forms of differentiation not be missed by North American service providers, as they may be the nuances that allow for the development of educational strategies that will effectively reach the Latino "population."

Perhaps the most widely accepted stereotype for Latino males is that of the proverbially promiscuous "Don Juan." This eternally charming individual is known for his ability to sexually conquer and satisfy a large number of females. A second stereotype deals with the erotic nature of some Latino groups as contrasted with more-conservative norms found among more-educated Latinos. Finally, the submissive and passive female stereotype continues to overshadow realities of contemporary Latinas.

Gender and Gender Roles. Worth and Rodriguez (1987) reported that despite the fact some Latinos in the United States have non-traditional lifestyles, they continue to adhere to traditional gender roles. Fennelly (1992) reported on cultural double standards and suggested that, whereas males are encouraged to develop strong self-reliant identities and explore their sexuality, females are taught the value of *etiqueta*, or proper and expected forms of feminine sexual behavior. These, sometimes-conflicting cultural norms contribute to what has been called the "cult of virginity" (Garcia 1980). This "cult of virginity" has its roots in the Catholic Church's teachings and is seen as a sign of purity for women. The basic premise of virginity until marriage has been found to decrease a number of sexual health problems, such as unplanned pregnancies, and to decrease the number of STDs. The primary problem with this concept, at least as practiced among Latinos, is that it is not applied equally to both genders. The literature suggests that these double standards result in either females postponing sexual activities, underreporting of sexual contacts (Taggart 1992), and in some cases, denial of other sexual behaviors, such as anal sex, in order to preserve the "cult of virginity" basic premises. This, however, does not prevent sexual innuendo from taking place.

Coquetería is a term used to describe a group of female behaviors aimed at reinforcing sexual attraction. Some of these behaviors include the use of sexually appealing clothing, the adoption of manners that stimulate sexual attraction, and the use of verbiage that indicate sexual interest. Latinas are not the only ones to discreetly express their sexual or personal interests. *Piropos* are statements generally expressed by men that include a sexual connotation within the context of respect and value for females. Cultural sexual standards are also denoted in language which arbitrarily classifies females as either suitable for marriage, *novias*, or those who can be pursued for sexual conquests, *amantes* (Alexander 1992; Carballo-Diéguez 1989). This dichotomy of sexual and gender roles may explain the reason sexual discussions seldom take place among spouses, since *esposas* (wives) are expected to possess little knowledge about their own sexuality, and even less about their spouse's. It has been suggested that, in some cases, the only Latinas totally in charge of their own sexuality are commercial sex workers, as they can be less constricted to express and fully explore their sexuality.

De la Vega (1990) suggested that sexual double standards are based on the erroneous belief that males are less able than females to control themselves sexually. It is believed that women exercise greater control over their sexual impulses while males appear to be guided by their instincts. In this context, male infidelity is more easily tolerated than female infidelity. Research indicates that Latinos who have poor sexual communication skills engage in extramarital affairs more often then those who have fewer difficulties communicating with their sexual partners. A 1994 study found that infidelity rates were higher among those who attended church infrequently than regular church attenders (Choi, Catalnia, and Docini 1994).

Machismo and Marianismo. *Machismo* has been described as a strong force in most Latino communities, which encourages males to be sexually dominant and the primary providers for their families; it stresses male physical aggression, high risk-taking, breaking rules, and casual, uninvolved sexual relations (de la Vega, 1990). In contrast, *Marianismo* refers to Latino cultural expectations that include the spiritual and moral superiority of women, and encourage Latinas to be virginal, seductive, privately wise, publicly humble, fragile, and yet, provide the glue that holds the family together. It has been argued that while these standards lead to womanizing, they also foster the tenet among males that they are responsible for their family's welfare.

Sexual Education. The AIDS epidemic has spearheaded an emphasis on the need to investigate sexuality education and communication patterns among Latinos in the United States. Family bonds, moral values, *machismo*, *Marianismo*, *etiqueta*, as well as profound religious beliefs, combine to prevent U.S. Latinos from openly discussing sexuality with family members. In some cases, just saying sexual words in front of family members may be difficult for some Latinos (Medina 1987).

The secrecy surrounding sexuality prevents Latinos from receiving adequate, if any, information about sexuality, contraceptives, and HIV/AIDS and other STDs (Amaro 1991; Carrier and Bolton 1991; Mays and Cochran 1988). In 1992, only 67 percent of Latinos said they had communicated with their children about AIDS, as compared to 77 percent of European-Americans and 74 percent of African-Americans (Schoenborn, Marsh, and Hardy 1994).

In traditional Latino families, sexuality education may come from extended-family members rather than nuclear-family members. Aunts, uncles, and grandparents may assume the role of sexuality educators for younger generations. For instance, Marín, Marín, and Juárez (1990) reported that Latinos were more willing than non-Hispanics to discuss certain sexual topics (i.e., drug use and sex) with an older family member. Similarly, data from the National Health Interview Survey found that less than two thirds (59 percent) of Latino parents had discussed AIDS with their children aged 10-17, compared to 72 percent of African-American and 68 percent of European-American parents (Dawson 1990).

In a study of first-generation immigrant adolescents employed in agriculture, Pérez (in press) found that Latino parents failed to adequately educate their children about sexuality-related matters. However, not all Latino parents hesitate to address sexuality-related issues with their offspring. Some researchers have found that 57 percent of Latino parents do communicate with their children about sexuality. In those cases, home-based sexuality education is the primary responsibility of the mother (Biddlecom and Hardy 1991; Dawson and Hardy 1989).

Supporting our earlier assertion that not all Latinos are created equal, Durant (1990) reported that Mexican-American females where less likely than non-Latinas to have communicated with their parents about contraception, sex, and pregnancy. Dawson (1990) found that Mexican-Americans were less likely to broach these topics with their children (50 percent) than were Puerto Ricans (74 percent) and other Latinos (64 percent). In those instances where parents educate their children about sexuality, the responsibility most often lies with the mother. The data suggest that some Latino parents rely on the schools and, in some cases, mass media to educate their children about sexuality-related issues. In a 1994 study, Schoenborn, Marsh, and Hardy found that 46 percent of Latinos had received AIDS information through radio public service announcements (PSAs), compared to 36 percent of European-Americans and 44 percent of African-Americans. An additional 14 percent of Latinos said they had received information through store displays or brochures, compared to 7 percent of European-Americans and 12 percent of African-Americans. Marín, Marín, and Juárez (1990) concluded that this lack of sexual education may contribute to higher rates of childbearing among Latinos. This is among the greatest paradoxes encountered among Latinos, since research suggests that home-based sexuality education plays a key role in decreasing pregnancy rates among Latino adolescents (Brindis 1997) and increasing condom use (Moran and Corley 1991).

Contraception. Throughout Latin America, the number of children in a household assists in establishing a male's role in the community. A large number of children, especially among low-income populations, are sometimes necessary for economic survival; the more hands available for work, the greater the family's income. It is, therefore, not surprising that contraceptive methods are skeptically viewed by some Latinos. This is further compounded by the fact that contraception among Latinos is primarily the responsibility of the woman.

Research indicates that contraceptive use among Latinos is dependent on a number of factors. Attitudes toward contraceptives, religion, condom use during first sexual experience (Marín, Marín, and Juárez, 1990), sexual orientation (Rotheram-Borus et al. 1994), education, and income (Fennelly 1992) have all been identified as being involved with attitudes and likelihood of using contraceptives. Other studies have found that Latino males are less likely to use condoms with their spouses or other primary partners than with other sexual partners (Pérez in press; Sandoval et al. 1995).

In a survey of urban adolescents, Sonestein, Pleck, and Ku (1989) found that Latino males have more-negative attitudes towards condom use than their non-Hispanic counterparts. Although 42 percent of Latina females reported they had used condoms during their first intercourse, Marín, Marín, and Juárez (1990) reported that males still exert a great deal of influence on the decision to use contraceptives. The researchers found that males' attitudes towards condom use determined the likelihood of using them. Latina women whose sexual partners opposed condom use were less likely than those whose partners did not oppose them or voiced no opinion. In a study of 131 bisexual youth in New York City, Rotheram-Borus and colleagues (1994) found that males were more likely to use condoms with a male than with a female sexual partner. The data indicate that more and more Latino men tend to share the decision on whether or not to use contraceptives with their sexual partners. The couple's acculturation and assimilation level, their adherence to Catholic Church doctrine, and their desire for large or small families also play a key in their decision to use contraceptives (Marín, Marín, and Juárez 1990). Furthermore, the data indicate that the proportion of European-Americans who use contraceptive methods at first intercourse is higher than that of Latinos (69 percent and 54 percent, respectively) and that the decision to use condoms during intercourse will be affected by male attitudes towards prophylactics (Forrest and Sing 1990).

Adolescents and Sexuality. One of the pivotal stages in a Latina woman's life is the *quinceañera* celebration—an event that is analogous to the traditional "sweet sixteen" observed in North America. The *quinceañera* party marks a woman's ability to seek a spouse and announces her ability to bear children. During this joyous time, the female is formally introduced to society and is recognized as having achieved full womanhood.

Studies investigating sexual behaviors among Latino adolescents have yielded mixed results. Brindis (1992) found that coital activity rates for Latino youth fall somewhere between that of African-Americans and European-Americans. In contrast to self-reports of lower sexual-activity levels among Latino youth, a national survey found no differences among the proportion of Latino and non-Latino Anglo-American young men who engaged in sexual activities before age 13 (4 percent and 3 percent, respectively) (Sonestein, Pleck, and Ku 1991). Similarly, Forrest and Sing (1990) found that among never-married females 15-19, 49 percent of Latinas reported being sexually active compared to 52 percent of European-Americans and 61 percent of African-Americans.

Differences, however, have been found based on attitudes towards premarital sex (Ginson and Kempf 1990; Padilla and Baird 1991). The data suggest that among adolescents, Latino males tend to engage in sexual intercourse at an earlier age than do females (13 and 15 years of age, respectively). In cross-cultural comparisons, Latino adolescents have been found to have higher sexual risk-taking behaviors (i.e., unprotected sex) than their non-Latino counterparts (Brindis, Wolfe, McCater, Ball, et al. 1995). Brindis (1997) concluded that "acculturation is a key variable influencing adolescent attitudes, behavior, and knowledge about reproduction and contraception" (p. 8).

Latino youths in the United States balance conflicting messages from two cultures regarding their sexuality (Brindis 1992). While the dominant culture appears to promote high levels of non-marital sexual activities, Latino youths, particularly females, must also deal with the more-conservative Latino cultural norms towards sexuality and the "cult of virginity." Some very conservative families see teenage pregnancy, and in some cases pregnancy before marriage, as a "failure." These views are expressed in the often used phrase *fracazó la muchacha*. It is important to clarify that this "failure" does not represent a rejection of the newborn, but rather the woman's limitation to pursue educational goals, employment opportunities, and her possibilities for marriage. Educational level and formal instruction play a role in parental willingness to discuss and educate their adolescent offspring about sexuality. Those with more education have been found to be more willing to educate their children about sexuality-related issues.

Adults and Sexuality. To date, we lack reliable data on the frequency and sexual preferences, masturbatory frequency and techniques, use of pornography, and sexual dysfunctions among Latinos in the United States. Although dialogs about sexual issues are often avoided, Latinos have other more socially acceptable forms to express their sensuality and sexual desire. Some of these mediums include music, dance, art, and poetry. Research indicates that Latino males learn about their sexuality through practical experience rather than through sexual education. Anecdotes suggest that it is not uncommon for young Latinos to lose their virginity through an experience with a sex-industry worker; usually encouraged by older relatives in what could be termed a "sexual rite of passage." Sexual discussions among Latino men tend to occur within same-gender groups while they are under the influence of alcohol, with sex-industry workers, and in the context of jokes (Carrier and Magaña 1991; de la Vega, 1990; Hu and Keller 1989).

In a national survey of sexual behaviors, Billy, Tanfer, Grady, and Klepinger (1992) found that Latino men reported a median of 6.1 sexual partners over a lifetime as compared to 8.0 for African-Americans and 6.4 for non-Latino white males. The same study found that Latinos were more likely than non-Latinos to report four or more sexual partners in the last eighteen months. In a survey of over 1,500 Latinos, Marín, Gomez, and Hearst (1993) found that 60 percent of single Latino males reported multiple sexual partners in the previous 12 months.

Pregnancy. Researchers have identified acculturation level, parental communication, low education, language, and country of origin as a determinant for pregnancy among Latino women (Durant 1990). Given the cultural significance of motherhood, it is not surprising that in the United States Latinas experience more per-capita births than their non-Latina counterparts. In 1990, the average number of children per Latino family was 3.76 compared to 3.43 for African-Americans and 3.11 for European-Americans (USDC 1991). Brindis (1997) has suggested that the higher number of children among Latinas may be a residual effect of an intrinsic belief that developed among immigrants based on economic needs and high mortality rates in their countries of origin.

Garcia (1980) suggested that motherhood serves to secure an identity for the Latino woman. In a 1991 survey, Segura found that the meaning of motherhood among Latinas differed, depending on their country of birth. In his study, Segura surveyed Mexican-born women and American-born Chicanas; the findings indicate that while Mexican-born women viewed motherhood as all-encompassing, Chicanas gave greater meaning to child rearing. Among Latinas, Puerto Rican females have the highest rate of pregnancies. Among Mexican women, those born in Mexico experience more pregnancies than those born in the U.S. (Aneshensel, Becerra, Fiedler, and Schuler 1990). Darabi and Ortiz (1987) concluded that "one plausible explanation of these findings could be that Mexican-origin women marry at very early ages" (p. 27). Further differences were reported by Fennelly (1992), who found birth rates among Latino adolescent females ranging from a high of 21 percent among Mexican-Americans to a low of 6 percent among Cuban mothers. Fennelly-Darabi and Ortiz (1987) reported that Latino women were more likely than non-Latino women to have a second birth shortly after the first, and were less likely to have positive attitudes towards abortions.

Despite higher birth rates than other ethnic groups, lower socioeconomic backgrounds, and fewer prenatal visits to physicians, Latinas as a group have fewer low-birthweight babies. This finding has confused experts who would expect the opposite to be true based on socioeconomic factors. Several explanations have been offered, such as better nutrition in the form of complete proteins, less use of alcohol and other psychoactive drugs during pregnancy, and increased family support during the months preceding childbirth. Other researchers have attempted to link higher birthweights with religiosity and spirituality of Latinas in the United States (Magaña and Clark 1995).

Marriage. Marriage is highly valued among Latino groups; however, in some cases, no difference is made between legal unions and long-term cohabitation. Fennelly-Darabi, Kandiah, and Ortiz (1989) reported that it is not possible to determine the number of couples in informal unions. In a later study, Landale and Fennelly (1992), reported that while the number of non-marital unions has decreased on the island of Puerto Rico, they have greatly increased among Puerto Ricans living on the U.S. mainland.

According to the Census Bureau, in the U.S., Latino marriage rates (62.3 percent) are almost the same for non-Latino whites (64 percent) and are higher than that of African-Americans (46.3 percent). On the other hand, National Council of la Raza data indicate that "The number of Hispanic single parents has increased at a faster rate than Black or White female-headed families" (1993, p.12). According to the U.S. Census Bureau, in 1991, 60 percent of Latino families with a female head-of-household with children under 18 lived under the poverty line (USBC, 1993).

Fennelly, Kandiah, and Ortiz (1989) argued that "A woman's marital status at the time she bears a child is important because of the implications for her later fertility, and for her own and her children's economic and social status" (p. 96). The social and legal implications of out-of-wedlock births have then been used to explain the reasons why there are more premarital pregnancies than premarital births in the Latino culture. It has been a time-honored tradition among some Latinos to marry while the woman is pregnant, in order to provide a stable and legal union for the newborn.

Rape. Few studies have been conducted to investigate sexual activities among Latinos in the United States; however, research findings seem to suggest that acculturation and gender, not culture, are key determinants of attitudes towards forcible sexual activities. In a study of attitudes towards date rape among college students, Fischer (1987) found that Latino students held more-traditional gender roles and had a more-positive attitude towards forcible intercourse under certain circumstances. These included spending a lot of money on the woman, the length of time they had dated, the female "leading" the man on, and the perceived female's previous sexual history.

Acculturation and gender was also found to play a role in the views of college students towards forcible sexual encounters. According to Fischer (1987), "Bicultural and bilingual Hispanic women are less rejecting of forcible rape than assimilated Hispanic and majority women are, while Hispanic males, regardless of degree of acculturation, are less rejecting of forcible date rape than are majority males" (p. 99). Lefley and colleagues (1993) reported that Latinos not only had different definitions of sexual coercion, but also were more likely to blame the victim than were their Anglo-American counterparts. A review of the literature did not support the notion of espousal rape. Males under the influence of alcohol may force their spouses to engage in sexual activities. Forcible sexual intercourse may not be perceived as a violation of a female's body if it happens within the context of marriage. As a result, espousal-rape reports among Latinos in the U.S. are more likely to occur among the acculturated, assimilated second generation, and those with higher educational levels.

Same-Gender Sexual Activities. In a study of African-American, Latino, Asian/Eurasian, and Caucasian gay adolescent males, Newman and Muzzonigro (1993) found that traditional families were less accepting of homosexuality than low-traditional families. Bonilla and Porter (1990) found that Latinos did not differ significantly from their African-American and white counterparts on attitudes toward homosexuality; however, they were less tolerant in their perceptions of civil liberties. This lack of acceptance may force males to hide their sexual orientation or to pursue heterosexual lifestyles (i.e., marriage) while secretly engaging in same-gender sexual activities.

Family acceptance is only part of the equation explaining Latino views toward same-gender sexual activities. Same-gender sex has different meanings and connotations for Latinos than for the non-Latino population in the United States. As a general rule, same-gender relationships are heavily stigmatized among Latinos, even among highly acculturated groups (Fischer, 1987). Homosexuality is not a topic easily discussed among males (Pérez and Fennelly 1996).

Magaña and Carrier (1991) suggested that it is not totally uncommon for Latino males to turn to "effeminate" males to satisfy their sexual needs under certain conditions. They identified lack of a female sexual partner and/or lack the economic resources to visit a sex worker as an acceptable reason for male-male sexual activities. Same-gender sexual behaviors are also more likely to appear while under the influence of alcohol. Same-gender sexual activity perceptions are also affected by Latino cultural norms. Latinos do not necessarily classify the penile inserter during male-male anal sex as homosexual (Amaro 1991; Carrier 1976). As a result, Latino males engaging in same-gender sexual activities may not perceive themselves, or be perceived as, "homosexual" or "bisexual," as long as they play the appropriate dominant sexual role—a role which tends to mirror that of the male in a heterosexual couple (CDC 1993). Carrier (1976) reported that unlike their American "gay" counterparts, Mexican males engaging in same-gender sex prefer anal intercourse over fellatio or other forms of sexual gratification. Also, in contrast to their Anglo-American counterparts, Latino males are more likely to assume only the passive or receptive role during same-gender encounters. Ross, Paulsen, and Stalstrom (1988) concluded that it is not the sexual act itself, but rather the cross-gender behavior which gets labeled and heavily stigmatized among Latinos.

The lack of identification with the homosexual community may explain the inability of Latino men who engage in sex with other men to identify or respond to educational programs targeting homosexuals. But, most importantly, it emphasizes the need for researchers to concentrate more on behaviors than labels when studying sexual interactions (Alcalay et al. 1990; Carrier and Magaña 1991). The labeling-versus-behavior distinction is important in light of the fact that 45 percent of AIDS cases among Latinos are the result of same-gender sex, and that an additional 7 percent of AIDS cases are related to same-gender sex with intravenous drug users (CDC 1994).

Bisexuality. De la Vega (1990) discussed three bisexual patterns among Latino men in the United States. The first type he labeled the closeted, self-identified, homosexual Latino. He described this type as a male with homosexual tendencies, but who lives a heterosexual lifestyle. The second type discussed by de la Vega, is the closeted, latent-homosexual Latino; this type is characterized by a male who describes himself as a heterosexual, but who engages in same-gender sex while under the influence of mind-altering substances, primarily alcohol. Finally, de la Vega described the "super-macho" heterosexual Latino. This man allows himself to have sexual contacts with other males since he considers them to be "pseudo-females." This last type of male will not admit, even to himself, that he may express homosexual tendencies.

HIV/AIDS. Keeling (1993) described the minority experience with AIDS in the United States as follows:

> The factors of social and economic class, poverty, and urban despair
> . . . will continue to result in an increasingly disproportionate impact
> of the epidemic on African-American and Hispanic people during the
> second decade of HIV; it is worth emphasizing as strongly as possible
> that these disproportions occur not because of biologic reality of race,
> but because race is a "front" for class, socioeconomic status, and poverty
> in this context. (p. 264)

This fact could not be of greater truth among Latinos in the United States of America.

The Latino community in the United States has been disproportionately affected by HIV infection. In 1996, Latinos accounted for 17.3 percent of all male AIDS cases in the United States, some 78,926 cases among this population group (CDC 1996). Intravenous drug use (IVDU) is second only to same-gender sex as a transmission mode among Latino males. Latina women account for 20.5 percent of all AIDS cases, a cumulative total of 11,909 Latinas (CDC 1996). Among Latinas, 45 percent contracted AIDS through heterosexual contact, whereas 44 percent of AIDS cases are contracted from IVDU (CDC 1996). Weeks and colleagues (1995) concluded that, although the number of heterosexual cases are increasing among Latinas, the number of AIDS-prevention programs geared towards them continues to be inadequate.

Among Latinos, Puerto Ricans have the highest incidence of HIV infection. Puerto Ricans also have the fourth-highest rate in the nation (NCLR, 1992). According to the Centers for Disease Control and Prevention (1993), up to 70 percent of AIDS cases are related to IVDU in Puerto Rico.

Latino awareness of the disease does not vary greatly from other ethnic groups. Dawson (1990) reported that 41 percent of Latinos said they had some knowledge about AIDS, compared to 39 percent for African-Americans and 48 percent for European-Americans. However, less than half (48 percent) of Latinos understood the connection between HIV and AIDS, compared to 69 percent among European-Americans. These figures did not vary greatly two years later, when Schoenborn, Marsh, and Hardy (1994) reported that 40 percent of Latinos, 47 percent of European-Americans, and 39 percent of African-Americans had "some" knowledge about AIDS.

Latinos are less likely than other ethnic groups to accurately identify HIV-transmission modes. Alcalay, Sniderman, Mitchell, and Griffin (1990) found that Latinos were more likely (36 percent) than European-Americans (15 percent) to believe they could get AIDS from blood donations. The same study found that Latinos were more likely than non-Latinos to believe that HIV transmission could occur through casual contact (e.g., hugging or from water fountains). Dawson (1990) found that 7 percent of Latinos believed it was "very likely" they could become infected with HIV by eating at a restaurant where the cook had AIDS, compared to 5 percent of European-American respondents. The researchers also found that 19 percent of Latinos believed they could catch AIDS from an unclean public toilet, whereas only 8 percent of the European-American respondents and 10 percent of African-Americans believed this to be an exposure category.

Knowledge about AIDS seems to be related to language preference among some Latinos. Research indicates that Spanish-speaking Latinos are more likely than bilingual Latinos to believe AIDS is spread through casual contact (Hu and Keller 1989). Another survey found that 24.1 percent of Spanish-speaking Latinos answered positively to the question, "Do you believe that one can catch AIDS from shaking hands with someone who has AIDS?" in comparison to 1.7 percent of English-speaking Latinos (Alcalay, Sniderman, Mitchell, and Griffin 1990).

Dawson and Hardy (1989) found that Mexican-Americans tended to be less knowledgeable about HIV/AIDS than other Latino groups. Only 50 percent of Mexican-American respondents in their study indicated it is "definitely true" that "AIDS is an infectious disease caused by a virus" compared to 62 percent of other Latinos. Only 46 percent of Mexican-American respondents said they knew that blood transfusions are routinely tested for HIV antibodies, compared to 55 percent of other Latinos, 72 percent of European-Americans, and 53 percent of African-American respondents.

Hu and Keller (1989) found that, despite their lesser knowledge about AIDS, Spanish-speaking Latinos reported a higher interest in learning about AIDS (88 percent) than English-speaking groups (83 percent). Pérez and Fennelly (1996) found that Latino farmworkers are willing to learn about AIDS, even though their reluctance to discuss sex has not decreased. One might expect that lower levels of knowledge about HIV/AIDS among Latinos in the United States would lead to more discrimination towards persons with AIDS. Instead, Alcalay et al. (1990) found no differences between Latinos and non-Hispanics in their likelihood to support AIDS victims' rights.

Summary. Latinos in the United States represent a wide range of educational attainment, socioeconomic levels, and skin color. Sexual practices and knowledge among this population have been found to be heavily influenced by strict cultural norms largely shaped by the Catholic Church. However, the data suggest that Latino sexual norms and behaviors are as varied as the heterogeneous group they represent. Further research is needed to properly investigate sexual attitudes and behaviors among the individual groups.

Feminism and Sexuality in the United States   PATRICIA BARTHALOW KOCH

A Brief History of the Feminist Movements. Earlier in this section, we discussed groups that illustrate ways in which religion and race or ethnicity operate as social factors defining subcultures within the U.S.A. and influence sexuality. Gender can be regarded in a similar manner. Here, we now consider feminist perspectives as reflections of a distinct social group or subculture.

Feminism is defined and implemented in various ways by different people. In its broadest interpretation, feminism represents advocacy for women's interests; in a stricter definition, it is the "theory of the political, social, and economic equality of the sexes" (LeGates 1995, 494). Although the terms "feminism" and "feminist" are only about a hundred years old, advocates for women's interests have been active for centuries throughout the world. As Robin Morgan (1984, 5) wrote in *Sisterhood Is Global,* "An indigenous feminism has been present in every culture in the world and in every period of history since the suppression of women began." Throughout history, women have protested, individually and collectively, against a range of injustices—often as part of other social movements in which gender equality was not the focus of the activity and women were not organized to take action on behalf of their gender.

However, stress on the ideologies of liberty, equality, and emancipation of men in the eighteenth-century political revolutions in Britain, France, and the United States laid the groundwork for these ideologies to be championed in women's lives also. In addition, the Industrial Revolution of the nineteenth century provided educational and economic opportunities supportive of a feminist movement in many societies.

Actual women's movements, or organized and sustained activities for gender equality supported by a relatively large number of people over a period of years, have occurred since the mid-1800s in many countries throughout the world. The United States, as well as most European societies, experienced extensive women's movements in the closing decades of the nineteenth century, with another wave of feminism occurring in the 1960s.

The beginning of an organized women's movement in the United States has been traced to the Seneca Falls Convention of 1848 where a Declaration of Principles called for gender equality (Chefetz and Dworkin 1986). Issues addressed included women's legal rights to property, children, and to their own earnings; equal educational and employment opportunities; the changing of negative feminine stereotypes; and increased opportunities for women to improve their physical fitness and health. These early feminists also addressed more-explicit sexual issues, including the abolition of the sexual double standard of expecting men to be "promiscuous" and women to be "pure"; equality between sexual partners; and the right of married women to refuse sexual activity with their husbands. Yet, although feminist ideology was well developed during these pre-Civil War years, the progressive feminist leaders had few followers. "In the nineteenth and early twentieth centuries the United States was not ready for a mass movement which questioned the entire gender role and sex stratification systems" (Chefetz and Dworkin 1986:112).

Only when the issues were narrowed to focus upon women's right to vote did the movement gain mass following. By 1917, about two million women were members of the National American Woman Suffrage Association, and millions more were supporters of the women's suffrage campaign (Kraditor 1965). The reasons for supporting a woman's right to vote, however, were varied. For some, it was an issue of basic human rights and gender equality. Many others, who believed in gender-role differentiation, supported suffrage on the basis that women would bring higher moral standards into governmental decisions. This more-conservative perspective dominated the movement. After achieving the right to vote in 1920 with the passage of the Nineteenth Amendment to the U.S. Constitution, this first wave of feminism dissipated.

A second wave of feminism developed within the United States, as well as worldwide, in the 1960s. At this time, many women were finding that, while their participation in educational institutions and the labor force was increasing, their political, legal, economic, and social status was not improving. This American feminist movement came on the heels of the black civil rights movement, which had already focused attention on the immorality of discrimination and legitimized mass protest and activism as methods for achieving equality (Freeman 1995). The contemporary women's movement was organized around many interrelated issues, including: legal equality; control over one's own body, including abortion rights; elimination of discrimination based on gender, race, ethnicity, and sexual orientation; securing more political power; and the ending of institutional and social roadblocks to professional and personal achievement. By the mid-1970s, this issue became a mass movement, with over half of American women supporting many of its principles and demands (Chefetz and Dworkin 1986).

The second women's movement had two origins, from two different strata of society, with different styles, values, and forms of organization (Freeman 1995). Although the members of both branches were predominantly white, middle-class, and college-educated, there was a generation gap between them. The younger branch was comprised of a vast array of local, decentralized, grassroots groups that concentrated on a small number or only one issue, rather than the entire movement. Members tended to adjure hierarchical structure and the traditional political system. Some of the activities in which they engaged included: running consciousness-raising groups; providing educational conferences and literature; establishing woman-supporting services (bookstores, health clinics, rape-crisis centers, and battered-women shelters); and organizing public-awareness campaigns and marches. This branch was responsible for infusing the movement with new issues, strategies, and techniques for social change. Many of its projects became institutionalized within American society (e.g., rape-crisis centers) through government funding and entrepreneurship.

These feminists also took their particular perspectives into other arenas, including the prochoice, environmental, and antinuclear movements. They also impacted academia, establishing women's centers and women's studies departments, programs, and courses on campuses throughout the country. By the early 1980s, there were over 300 women's studies programs and 30,000 courses in colleges and universities, and a national professional association, the National Women's Studies Association (Boxer 1982). Many periodicals devoted exclusively to scholarship on women or gender were begun; Searing (1987) listed ninety-four such journals.

The second branch of the women's movement was the older, more-traditional division that formed top-down national organizations with officers and boards of directors, and often paid staffs and memberships. Most of these organizations sought support through contributions, foundations, or government contracts to conduct research and services. Some of these feminist organizations included: the Women's Legal Defense Fund, the Center for Women's Policy Studies, the Feminist Majority Foundation, and the National Coalition Against Domestic Violence; with other previously established groups taking on a more-feminist agenda, such as the National

Federation of Business and Professional Women and the American Association of University Women.

The National Organization for Women (NOW), an action organization
devoted to women's rights, was the primary feminist group to develop a mass
membership. NOW focused its attention at the national level to become
politically powerful. One of its major campaigns was the passage of an Equal
Rights Amendment (ERA) to the U.S. Constitution guaranteeing legal
equality for women. The ERA was endorsed by the U.S. Congress and sent
to the states for ratification in 1972. In 1978, over one hundred thousand
people marched in Washington D.C. in support of the Equal Rights Amendment. But the ERA and feminism were to meet with strong opposition from
well-organized conservative and right-wing political and religious groups
that depicted feminist goals as "an attack on the family and the American
way of life" (Freeman 1995, 525). Stop-ERA campaigns were adeptly organized by these politically savvy groups and, by 1982, the ERA had failed to
pass within the allotted timeframe by seven votes in three states.

Yet, it cannot be said that the feminist movement failed. Many states
passed equal rights amendments of their own, and many discriminatory
federal, state, and local laws were changed with the Supreme Court unanimously ruling in favor of interpreting constitutional law to provide equal
opportunity for women. In addition, a powerful women's health movement
had been spawned, and efforts for reproductive freedom, including abortion rights, would be continued to combat anti-abortion groups throughout
the 1980s and 1990s. As Freeman (1995, 528) concluded: "The real revolution of the contemporary women's movement is that the vast majority of
the [United States] public no longer questions the right of any woman,
married or unmarried, with or without children to work for wages to achieve
her fullest potential."

Although feminists agree there are still many strides to be made in
achieving the goals of legal, economic, political, and social equality for
women in the United States, they are often divided over philosophy, goals,
and strategies for achieving equality in these areas. Feminism is not a
monolithic ideology. There is "not a single interpretation on what feminism
means but a variety of feminisms representing diverse ideas and perspectives radiating out from a core set of assumptions regarding the elimination
of women's secondary status in society" (Pollis 1988, 86-87).

Feminism and Sexuality. Sexuality has always been a critical issue to feminists,
because they see the norms regarding "proper" and "normal" sexual behavior as functioning to socialize and suppress women's expression and
behavior in an effort to control female fertility as socioeconomic and
political assets (Tiefer 1995). "The personal is political," the feminist
rallying cry, applies particularly to sexuality, which is often the most personal, hidden, suppressed, and guilt-ridden aspect of women's lives. Mac-
Kinnon (1982:515) captures this essence well in the analogy that: "Sexuality

is to feminism what work is to Marxism: that which is most one's own, yet most taken away."

Although women are now being seen as sexual beings in their own right, not simply as reproducers or sexual property, Tiefer (1995, 115) describes how women's sexual equality is still constrained by many factors, including:

> Persistent socioeconomic inequality that makes women dependent on men and therefore sexually subordinate; unequal laws such as those regarding age of sexual consent and rights in same-sex relationships; lack of secure reproductive rights; poor self-image or a narrow window of confidence because of ideals of female attractiveness; ignorance of woman-centered erotic techniques, social norms about partner choice; and traumatic scars from sexual abuse.

In general, feminists believe that both women's and men's sexuality is socially constructed and must be examined within its social context (McCormick 1994). Gender-role socialization is viewed as a very powerful process creating unequal power relationships and stereotypic expectations for appropriate sexual feelings and behaviors of women and men. Male gender-role socialization based on male political, social, and economic dominance is likely to result in male sexual control, aggression, and difficulties with intimacy. On the other hand, female gender-role socialization based on political, social, and economic oppression of women is likely to result in disinterest and dissatisfaction with sex, as well as passivity and victimization. Feminists question the assumption of a binary gender system and challenge traditional concepts of masculinity and femininity (Irvine 1990). They politicize sexuality by examining the impact that power inequalities between men and women have on sexual expression.

Although most feminists may agree upon the relevance of socialization and context in the creation of male and female sexuality, they may vehemently disagree about the nature of sexual oppression and the strategies for its elimination (McCormick 1994). This has resulted in the emergence of two major feminist camps: radical feminists and liberal feminists.

As described by McCormick (1994, 211), radical feminists have polarized male and female sexuality—often demonizing men and idealizing women in this process. They view women as victims who must be protected. They use evidence showing girls and women as the predominant victims and boys and men as the perpetrators of rape, sexual harassment, prostitution, domestic violence, and childhood sexual abuse to support their views.

Radical feminists are vehemently opposed to pornography, "likening erotic images and literature to an instruction manual by which men are taught how to bind, batter, torture, and humiliate women" (McCormick 1994, 211). They have spearheaded many efforts to censor pornographic/erotic materials, often joining with right-wing organizations in these efforts. Another goal of radical feminists is the elimination of prostitution, which they view as trafficking in women's bodies. They believe that all women in the sex trades are being victimized.

Because of these beliefs, radical feminists are criticized as treating women as children who are incapable of giving true consent to their choice of sexual activities. In response, these feminists argue that it is our sociopolitical system that treats women as second class and has robbed them of the equality needed for consensual sexual expression. Until this system is changed, true consent from women is not possible. In fact, orthodox radical feminists do not recognize the possibility of consensual heterosexuality, finding little difference between conventional heterosexual intercourse and rape, viewing both acts as representing male supremacy (McCormick 1994, 211). Radical feminists are accused of advocating "politically correct sex" by idealizing monogamous, egalitarian, lesbian sex and celibacy, and rejecting any other forms of consensual relationships or activity.

On the other hand, liberal feminists defend women's rights to sexual pleasure and autonomy. They believe that, if women are viewed only as victims, they are stripped of their adult autonomy and their potential to secure joyous and empowering sexual pleasure and relationships on their own behalf (McCormick 1994, 211). These feminists do not view all erotic material as harmful and believe in women's right to create their own erotic material. They differentiate between the depictions of forced sex in pornography and actual violence against women. Although not always pleased with all types of pornographic material, they believe in the right of free speech and choice, and acknowledge that censorship efforts could never eliminate all pornographic material anyway. In addition, who is to decide what is pornographic and what is erotic? Regarding prostitution, they view sex work as a legitimate occupational choice for some, and acknowledge the tremendous range of experience with sex work primarily based on social class.

Liberal feminism dominated the first phase of the women's movement of the 1960s. The emphasis was on women's empowerment to achieve professional and personal, including sexual, potentials. The expansion of sexual possibilities was explored, with pleasure being emphasized. The strategies of consciousness-raising, education, and female-centered care were used to help eliminate sexual shame and passivity, with women being encouraged to discover and develop new sexual realities for themselves (Tiefer 1995, 115). However, beginning in the 1970s, the pendulum began to swing away from an emphasis on the power of self-definition towards the agendas of the radical feminists who emphasized issues of sexual violence against women, including rape, incest, battery, and harassment. Thus, during this current feminist movement, much more time and emphasis has been devoted to women's sexual victimization, danger, and repression than to women's sexual equality, pleasure, and relationship enhancement.

Today, many in the general public, professionals, and even sexologists fail to distinguish between differences within feminism. They are most aware of and react primarily to the radical-feminist ideologies and strate-gies. Thus, feminism has become stereotyped by the extreme positions of the radicals and seems to have lost much of its overt mass support, with many trying to distance themselves from these extreme positions. For example, it is not unusual to hear someone today say, "I believe in women's rights but I'm not a feminist."

Feminist Critiques of and Contributions to Sexology. Feminist sexology is the scholarly study of sexuality that is of, by, and for women's interests. Employ-ing diverse epistemologies, methods, and sources of data, feminist scholars examine women's sexual experiences and the cultural frame that constructs sexuality. They challenge the assumptions that sexuality is an eternal es-sence, arguing "that a kiss is not a kiss and a sigh is not a sigh and a heterosexual is not a heterosexual and an orgasm is not an orgasm in any transhistorical, transcultural way" (Tiefer 1995, 597). These theories and approaches have resulted in an enormous body of work during the last two decades reexamining theories, methods, and paradigms of gender and sexuality, and contributing to social change (Vance and Pollis 1990).

During this time, feminists and others have challenged the preeminence and validity of traditional science, particularly as it has been applied to human beings and their behaviors. They have argued that traditional science, rather than being objective and value-free, takes place in a particu-lar cultural context (one that is often sexist and heterosexist), which thus becomes incorporated into research, education, or therapy (McCormick 1994). For example, research on unintended and adolescent pregnancy is focused almost exclusively on females, reflecting a double standard requir-ing women to be the sexual gatekeepers while relieving men of such responsibilities.

Another example comes from therapy. Numerous studies have deter-mined that relationship factors, including intimacy, nongenital stimulation, affection, and communication, are better predictors of women's sexual satisfaction than frequency of intercourse or orgasm. Nevertheless, the dominant therapeutic paradigm, as enforced by the *Diagnostic and Statistical Manual of Mental Disorders*, uses physiologically based genital performance during heterosexual intercourse as the standard for determining women's sexual dysfunctions (Tiefer 1995).

Feminist scholarship uses the following principles in overcoming the deficits in understanding of women's experiences, gender and gender asymmetry, and sexuality:

1. Acknowledgment of the pervasive influence of gender in all aspects of social life, including the practice of science;
2. A multifaceted challenge to the normative canons of science, espe-cially the tenet of objectivity, which splits subject from object, and theory from practice;

3. Advocacy of consciousness raising as a research strategy that elevates and legitimates experience as a valid way of knowing, essential to uncovering meaning structures and diversity among individuals;
4. Conceptualization of gender as a social category, constructed and maintained through the gender-attribution process, and as a social structure;
5. Emphasis on the heterogeneity of experience and the central importance of language, community, culture, and historical context in constituting the individual; and
6. Commitment to engage in research that is based on women's experience and is likely to empower them to eliminate sexism and contribute to societal change (Pollis 1986,88).

Sexology has been criticized for being reticent to integrate feminist perspectives and scholarship into its establishment for fear of being perceived as unscientific and radical (Irvine 1990). However, in recent years feminist perspectives have become more visible in the scholarly journals, conferences, and among the membership and leadership of professional sexological organizations. Future goals for feminist sexologists include more attention to understanding the intersections of race, class, and culture within gender, and making the results of their work more usable.

General Summary of Social Factors

This discussion of social factors influencing sexuality in the U.S.A. has selectively focused on religion, race/ethnicity, and gender. Essentially, we have taken the view that such social variables exert influence largely through membership in corresponding social groups. Our review examined the general tradition of the Judeo-Christian heritage of the U.S.A., membership in the Mormon church, African-American, and Latino minority groups, and identification with feminist perspectives as specific examples.

We recognize that this approach omits other important social factors such as education, social class, and size of city of residence. Our purpose has not been to provide an exhaustive review of all pertinent social groups within the U.S.A. Rather, we wished to demonstrate the abundant evidence that a full understanding of sexuality in American culture eventually will require a recognition of the diverse social groups that reside in this nation. As we proceed to examine what sexuality researchers have learned about specific forms of sexual attitudes and behavior, the authors will report, where possible, the results of research which documents an association between sexuality and social variables.

Unfortunately, a recognition of these associations has not always been incorporated into investigations of sexual practices. For example, much of the existing research has been conducted with predominantly white, middle-class, college-educated populations. Researchers have frequently failed to adequately describe the demographic characteristics of their samples, and they have often failed to test possible correlations with social variables. One consequence is that American sexual scientists have yet to develop a full understanding of the very diversity of social groups we have tried to describe. Closing such gaps in our knowledge remains one of the principle tasks of sexual science in the U.S.A.

3. Sexual Knowledge and Education
PATRICIA BARTHALOW KOCH

According to the National Coalition to Support Sexuality Education,

> Sexuality education is a lifelong process of acquiring information and forming attitudes, beliefs, and values about identity, relationships, and intimacy. It encompasses sexual development, reproductive health, interpersonal relationships, affection, intimacy, body image, and gender roles [among other topics]. Sexuality education seeks to assist children [people] in understanding a positive view of sexuality, provide them with information and skills about taking care of their sexual health, and help them to acquire skills to make decisions now and in the future. (SIECUS 1992)

A. A Brief History of American Sexuality Education

Sexuality education in the United States has always been marked by tension between maintaining the status quo of the "acceptable" expression of individual sexuality, and change as precipitated by the economic, social, and political events of the time. The major loci for sexuality education have shifted from the family and the community (in earlier times being more influenced by religion, and in modern times, by consumerism and the media), to schools. Much of the education has been developed by and targeted towards middle-class whites. As will be described in more detail, the two major movements to formalize sexuality education in the United States were spearheaded for the advancement of either "social protection" or "social justice." Throughout history, the goals, content, and methodologies of sexuality education in these two movements have often been in opposition to one another.

According to D'Emilio and Freedman (1988), young people in colonial America learned about sexuality through two primary mechanisms. In these agrarian communities, observation of sexual activity among animals was common. Observation of sexual activity among adults was also common, since families lived in small, often-unpartitioned dwellings, where it was not unusual for adults and children to sleep together. Second, more formal moral instruction about the role of sexuality in people's lives came from parents and clergy, with lawmakers endorsing the religious doctrines. The major message was that sexual activity ought to be limited to marriage and aimed at procreation. However, within the marital relationship, both the man and woman were entitled to experience pleasure during the procreative act.

Ministers throughout the colonies invoked biblical injunctions against extramarital and nonprocreative sexual acts, while colonial statutes in both New England and the Chesapeake area outlawed fornication, rape, sodomy, adultery, and sometimes incest, prescribing corporal or capital punishment, fines, and in some cases, banishment for sexual transgressors. Together, these moral authorities attempted to socialize youth to channel sexual desires toward marriage (D'Emilio and Freedmen 1988,18)

A small minority of colonists also were exposed to a limited number of gynecological and medical-advice texts from London. These underscored the primary goal of sexuality as reproduction, with pleasure only to be associated with this goal.

After the War for American Independence, small autonomous rural communities gave way to more-commercialized areas, and church and state regulation of morality began to decline. Individual responsibility and choice became more emphasized. Thus, instruction on sexuality changed from community (external) control to individual (internal) control. For example, between the 1830s and 1870s, information about contraceptive devices and abortion techniques circulated widely through printed matter (pamphlets, circulars, and books) and lectures. However, peer education was the primary source of sexuality education, with more-"educated" people, especially women, passing along their knowledge to friends and family members.

Increasing secularization and the rise of the medical profession spawned a health-reform movement in the 1830s that emphasized a quest for physical, as well as spiritual, perfection. With advances in publishing and literacy, a prolific sexual-advice literature, written by doctors and health reformers of both genders, emerged. The central message was that, for bodily well-being (as well as economic success), men and women had to control and channel their sexual desires toward procreative, marital relations. "Properly channeled, experts claimed, sexual relations promised to contribute to individual health, marital intimacy, and even spiritual joy" (D'Emilio and Freedman 1988, 72). The popularity of these materials demonstrated Americans' need for and interest in sexuality education. Much of the self-help and medical-advice literature directed at men emphasized the dangers of masturbation. Women were taught that they had less sexual passion than men, and their role was to help men to control their sexual drives. In other words, a standard of female "purity" was the major theme of the sexuality education of the time.

Two studies of women's sexuality conducted in the early 1900s provide insight into the sources of sexual information for women during the nineteenth century. Katharine B. Davis (1929) studied one thousand women (three quarters born before 1890) and Dr. Clelia Mosher (1980) surveyed forty-five women (four fifths born between 1850 and 1880). Over 40 percent of the women in Davis' study and half in Mosher's reported that they received less-than-adequate instruction about sex before marriage. Those who indicated that they had received some sexual information identified Alice Stockham's advice manual, *Tokology*, about pregnancy, child-birth, and childrearing as their chief source.

In the later nineteenth century, a combined health and social-reform movement developed, that attempted to control the content of and access to sexuality education. Middle-class reformers organized voluntary associa-tions, such as the Women's Christian Temperance Union (WCTU), to address issues, including prostitution and obscenity. The social-purity move-ment in the late nineteenth century added the demand for female equality and a single sexual standard to the earlier moral-reform movements. The WCTU spearheaded a sex-education campaign through the White Cross to help men resist sexual temptation. Social-purity leaders authored marital advice books that recognized women's sexual desires and stressed that women could enjoy intercourse only if they really wanted it. Women's rights and social-purity advocates issued the first formal call for sex education in America. They argued that women should teach children about sex: "Show your sons and daughters the sanctities and the terrors of this awful power of sex, its capacities to bless or curse its owner" (D'Emilio and Freedman 1988, 155). They demanded a public discourse of sexuality that emphasized love and reproductive responsibility rather than lust.

An example of the restricted character of sexuality education at the time was the enactment of the 1873 "Comstock Law" for the "Suppression of Trade in, and Circulation of Obscene Literature and Articles of Immoral Use." This revision of the federal postal law forbade the mailing of infor-mation or advertisements about contraception and abortion, as well as any material about sexuality. The Comstock Law was in effect until being overturned by a federal appeals court in 1936 in a decision about contra-ception: *United States v. Dow Package.*

Yet, the turn of the century ushered in a more "progressive" era fueled by industrial capitalism. Progressive reform provoked by the middle class called upon government and social institutions, including schools, to in-tervene in social and economic issues, such as sex education. One of the major movements for sex education was the social-hygiene movement spearheaded by Dr. Prince Morrow to prevent the spread of syphilis and gonorrhea. In 1905, he formed the Society of Sanitary and Moral Prophy-laxis in New York City, later renamed the American Social Hygiene Asso-ciation. This society was joined by the WCTU, YMCA, state boards of health, and the National Education Association in an "unrelenting campaign of education to wipe out the ignorance and the prejudices that allowed venereal diseases to infect the nation" (D'Emilio and Freedman 1988, 205).

They held public meetings and conferences, published and distributed written materials, and endorsed sex education in the public schools. While insisting on frank and open discussions of sexual-health matters, they promulgated the traditional emphasis of sexuality in marriage for reproductive purposes and the avoidance of erotic temptation (like masturbation). More-conservative Americans considered such openness to be offensive. Former-President Howard Taft described sex education as "full of danger if carried on in general public schools" (D'Emilio and Freedman 1988, 207). Others considered this type of education to be too restrictive. For example, Maurice Bigelow, Professor of Biology at Columbia University Teachers' College, objected to the terms "sex" and "reproduction" being used synonymously. Not until after 1920 would these activists see any progress towards the goal of having some basic sex (reproductive) instruction integrated into any school curriculum.

The early 1900s found American minds being expanded by the writings of Sigmund Freud and Havelock Ellis, among others. These psychologists helped popularize the notion of sexuality as a marker of self-identity and a force permeating one's life, which, if repressed, risks negative consequences. In addition, socialist and feminist ideologies and the industrial economy created an environment fertile for the demand of birth-control information and services. These events spearheaded the second major movement for sexuality education, which was based on social-justice issues, particularly for women and the poor.

In 1912, Margaret Sanger began a series of articles on female sexuality for a New York newspaper, which was confiscated by postal officials for violating the Comstock antiobscenity law. Later, to challenge the constitutionality of this law, she published her own magazine, *The Woman Rebel*, filled with information about birth control. She was charged with nine counts of violating the law, with a penalty of forty-five years in prison, after writing and distributing a pamphlet, *Family Limitation*. To avoid prosecution, she fled to Europe; but in her absence, efforts mounted to distribute birth-control information. By early 1915, activists had distributed over 100,000 copies of *Family Limitation*, and a movement for community sexuality education was solidified. Public sentiment in favor of the right to such information was so strong that charges were dropped against Sanger when she returned to America. Community education about and access to birth control, particularly for middle-class women, began to become accepted, if not expected, as a matter of public health, as well as an issue of female equality (social justice).

Premarital experience became a more-common form of sexuality education among the white middle-class, beginning in the 1920s and accelerating as youth became more autonomous from their families (through automobiles, attendance at college, participation in more leisure activities like movies, and war experiences). Dating, necking, and petting among young peers became a norm. "Where adults might see flagrantly loose behavior, young people themselves had constructed a set of norms that regulated their activity while allowing the accumulation of experience and sexual learning" (D'Emilio and Freedman 1988, 261).

Courses on marriage and the family and (sexual) hygiene were being introduced into the college curriculum. Marriage manuals began to emphasize sexual expression and pleasure, rather than sexual control and reproduction, with more-explicit instructions as to how to achieve satisfying sexual relationships (such as "foreplay" and "simultaneous orgasm"). By the end of the 1930s, many marriage manuals were focusing on sexual "techniques." In addition, scientific reports, such as *Sexual Behavior in the Human Male* by Alfred Kinsey and his associates (1948) and the corresponding *Sexual Behavior in the Human Female* (1953), were major popular works primarily read by the middle class. These books provided sexuality education about the types and frequencies of various sexual expressions among white Americans to more than a quarter of a million people. They also are considered landmarks in sexuality education:

> What they [Americans] have learned and will learn may have a tremendous effect on the future social history of mankind. For they [Kinsey and colleagues] are presenting facts. They are revealing not what should be, but what is. For the first time, data on human sex behavior is entirely separated from questions of philosophy, moral values, and social customs. (D'Emilio and Freedman 1988, 286)

As scientific information on sexuality became readily available to the American public, more-explicit presentation of sexual material in printed and audiovisual media became possible through the courts' decisions narrowing the definition of obscenity. The proliferation of such sexually explicit materials was encouraged by the expansion of the consumer-oriented economy. For example, advertising was developing into a major industry, beginning in the 1920s. Sex was used to sell everything from cars to toothpaste. Gender-role education, in particular, was an indirect outcome of the advertising media. A "paperback revolution" began in 1939 placing affordable materials, such as "romance novels," in drugstores and newsstands all over the country.

In December 1953, Hugh Hefner published the first issue of *Playboy*, whose trademark was a female "Playmate of the Month" displayed in a glossy nude centerfold. The early *Playboy* philosophy suggested males should "enjoy the pleasures the female has to offer without becoming emotionally involved" (D'Emilio and Freedman 1988, 302). By the end of the 1950s, *Playboy* had a circulation of 1 million, with the readership peaking at 6 million by the early 1970s. Many a man identified *Playboy* as his first, and perhaps most influential, source of sex education.

By the 1970s, sex manuals had taken the place of marital advice manuals. Popular books like the 1972 *Joy of Sex* by Dr. Alex Comfort encouraged sexual experimentation by illustrating sexual techniques. Sexual references became even more prolific in the mainstream media. For example, the ratio of sexual references per page tripled between 1950 and 1980 in magazines, including *Reader's Digest, Time,* and *Newsweek.* In addition, Masters and Johnson's groundbreaking book, *Human Sexual Response,* emphasizing that women's sexual desires and responses were equal to those of men, was published in 1966. The media were influencing Americans—female and male, married and single—to consider sexual pleasure as a legitimate, necessary component of their lives.

Yet, even with the explicit and abundant presentation of sexuality in the popular media, parents were still not likely to provide sexuality education to their children, nor were the schools.

In 1964, a lawyer, a sociologist, a clergyman, a family life educator, a public health educator, and a physician came together to form the Sex Information and Education Council of the United States (SIECUS). SIECUS is a nonprofit voluntary health organization with the aim to help people understand, appreciate, and use their sexuality in a responsible and informed manner. Dr. Mary Calderone was a co-founder and the first executive director. SIECUS soon became known all over the country as a source of information on human sexuality and sex education.

This private initiative for sexuality education was followed by a governmental one in 1966 when the Office of Education of the federal Department of Health, Education, and Welfare announced its newly developed policy supporting

> family life and sex education as an integral part of the curriculum from preschool to college and adult levels; it will support training for teachers . . . it will aid programs designed to help parents . . . it will support research and development in all aspects of family life and sex education. (Haffner 1989, 1)

In 1967, a membership organization, first called the American Association of Sex Educators and Counselors, was formed to bring together professionals from all disciplines who were teaching and counseling about human sexuality. The organization later expanded to include therapists, and is known today as the American Association of Sex Educators, Counselors, and Therapists (AASECT). Opposition to sexuality education from conservative political and religious groups grew quickly. In 1968, the Christian Crusade published, "Is the Schoolhouse the Proper Place to Teach Raw Sex?" and the John Birch Society was calling sex education a "Communist plot." In response, over 150 public leaders joined the National Committee for Responsible Family Life and Sex Education.

In 1970, Maryland became the first state to mandate family-life and human-development education at all levels in their public schools. However, the new "purity" movement by conservatives was under way, coordinating over 300 organizations throughout the country to oppose sex education in the public schools. Several states passed antisexuality-education mandates, with Louisiana barring sex education altogether in 1968. By the late 1970s, only half-a-dozen states had mandated sex education into their schools, and implementation in the local classrooms was limited.

In 1972, AASECT began developing training standards and competency criteria for certification of sexuality educators, counselors, and therapists. A list of the professionals who have become certified in these three areas is provided in a published register so that other professionals and consumers can locate people who are trained. (Currently this list identifies over 1,000 certified professionals.) AASECT also has developed a code of ethics for professionals working in these fields.

In 1979, the federal government through the Department of Health, Education, and Welfare conducted a national analysis of sex-education programs in the United States. The researchers calculated that less than 10 percent of all students were receiving instruction about sexuality in their high schools. The report's overall conclusion stated:

> Comprehensive programs must include far more than discussions of reproduction. They should cover other topics such as contraception, numerous sexual activities, the emotional and social aspects of sexual activity, values clarification, and decision making and communication skills. In addition to being concerned with the imparting of knowledge, they should also focus on the clarifying of values, the raising of self-esteem, and the developing of personal and social skills. These tasks clearly require that sex education topics be covered in many courses in many grades. (Kirby, Atter, and Scales 1979, 1)

When AIDS burst upon the scene in the 1980s, education with the goal of "social protection" from this deadly disease was targeted for inclusion in public-school curricula. In a relatively short time, most states came to require, or at least recommend, that AIDS education be included in school curricula. The number of states mandating or recommending AIDS education surpassed those mandating or recommending sexuality education. Money and other resources were being infused into AIDS-education initiatives. For example, in 1987-88, 80 percent of the $6.3 million spent nationwide on sexuality education went specifically to AIDS-education efforts. Today, policies and curricula addressing AIDS tend to be much more specific and detailed than those dealing with other aspects of sexuality education, including pregnancy prevention. This may lead to students receiving a narrow and negative view of human sexuality (e.g., "sex kills!").

Throughout this time, SIECUS remained committed to comprehensive sexuality education, as emphasized in its mission statement: "SIECUS affirms that sexuality is a natural and healthy part of living and advocates the right of individuals to make responsible sexual choices. SIECUS develops, collects, and disseminates information and promotes comprehensive education about sexuality" (Haffner 1989, 4). In 1989, SIECUS convened a national colloquium on the future of sexuality education, "Sex Education 2000," to which sixty-five national organizations sent representatives. The mission was to assure that all children and youth receive comprehensive sexuality education by the year 2000. Thirteen specific goals for the year 2000 were set forth as follows:

1. Sexuality education will be viewed as a community-wide responsibility.
2. All parents will receive assistance in providing sexuality education for their child(ren).
3. All schools will provide sexuality education for children and youth.
4. All religious institutions serving youth will provide sexuality education.
5. All national youth-serving agencies will implement sexuality education programs and policies.
6. The media will assume a more proactive role in sexuality education.
7. Federal policies and programs will support sexuality education.
8. Each state will have policies for school-based sexuality education and assure that mandates are implemented on a local level.
9. Guidelines, materials, strategies, and support for sexuality education will be available at the community level.
10. All teachers and group leaders providing sexuality education to youth will receive appropriate training.
11. Methodologies will be developed to evaluate sexuality education programs.
12. Broad support for sexuality education will be activated.
13. In order to realize the overall goal of comprehensive sexuality education for all children and youth, SIECUS calls upon national organizations to join together as a national coalition to support sexuality education (SIECUS 1990).

To aid in the attainment of the third goal of providing comprehensive sexuality education in the schools, a national Task Force with SIECUS's leadership published *Guidelines for Comprehensive Sexuality Education, Kindergarten Through 12th Grade* in 1991. These guidelines, based on six key concepts, provide a framework to create new sexuality-education programs or improve existing ones. The guidelines are based on values related to human sexuality that reflect the beliefs of most communities in a pluralistic society. They represent a starting point for curriculum development at the local level. Currently, another Task Force is working on ways to help providers of preschool education incorporate the beginnings of comprehensive sexuality education into their programs. In 1994, SIECUS also launched an international initiative in order to disseminate information on comprehensive sexuality education to the international community and to aid in the development of specific international efforts in this area.

Yet, in light of progress that has been made, challenges to sexuality programs from conservative organizations have become more frequent, more organized, and more successful than ever before (Sedway 1992). These nationally organized groups, including Eagle Forum, Focus on the Family, American Family Association, and Citizens for Excellence in Education, target local school programs that do not conform to their specific ideology. They attempt to control what others can read or learn, not just in sexuality education (which now is the major target), but in all areas of public education, including science (with the teaching of creationism), history, and literature (with censorship of many classics in children's literature). Although these groups represent a minority of parents in a school district, through well-organized national support, they often effectively use a variety of intimidating tactics to prevent the establishment of sexuality-education programs altogether or establish abstinence-only ones. Their tactics include personal attacks on persons supporting comprehensive sexuality education, threatening and sometimes pursuing costly litigation against school districts, and flooding school boards with misinformation, among other strategies. The greater impact of this anti-sexuality-education campaign on education, in general, and American society, overall, has been poignantly described:

> In another sense, the continuing series of attacks aimed at public education must be viewed in the context of the larger battle—what has come to be known as a "Cultural Civil War"—over free expression. Motion pictures, television programs, fine art, music lyrics, and even political speech have all come under assault in recent years from many of the same religious right leaders behind attacks on school programs. In the vast majority of cases, in the schools and out, challengers generally seek the same remedy, i.e., to restrict what others can see, hear, or read. At stake in attacks on schoolbooks and programs is students' exposure to a broad spectrum of ideas in the classroom—in essence, their freedom to learn. And when the freedom to learn is threatened in sexuality education, students are denied information that can save their lives. (Sedway 1992, 13-14)

B. Current Status of Sexuality Education

Youth-Serving Agencies

National youth-serving agencies (YSAs) in the United States provide sexuality education to over two million youths each year. Over the past two decades, YSAs began developing such programs, primarily in response to the problems of adolescent pregnancy and HIV/AIDS.

> Second only to schools in the number of youth they serve, youth-serving
> agencies are excellent providers of sexuality education programs, both
> because they work with large numbers of youth, including many under-
> served youth, and because they provide an environment that is informal
> and conducive to creative and experiential learning. Some YSAs reach
> youth who have dropped out of school. Others reach youth who have
> not received sexuality education programs in their schools. The people
> who work at YSAs often build close relationships with the youth in their
> programs which allows for better communication and more effective
> educational efforts. (Dietz 1989/1990, 16)

For example, the American Red Cross reaches over 1 million youth each
year in the U.S. with their "AIDS Prevention Program," "Black Youth
Project," and "AIDS Prevention Program for Hispanic Youth and Families."
The Boys Clubs of America has developed a substance abuse/pregnancy
prevention program, called "Smart Moves." The Girls Clubs of America has
a primary commitment to providing health promotion, sexuality education,
and pregnancy-prevention services to its members and reaches over 200,000
youth each year. The Girl Scouts of the U.S.A. developed a curriculum,
"Decision for Your Life: Preventing Teenage Pregnancy," that focuses on
the consequences of teen parenthood and the development of communication, decision-making, assertiveness, and values-clarification skills. The
March of Dimes Birth Defects Foundation developed the "Project Alpha"
sexuality-education program that explores teenage pregnancy from the
male perspective and helps young men learn how to take more responsibility. The National Network of Runaway and Youth Services has developed
an HIV/AIDS education program for high-risk youth, called "Safe Choices."
The program provides training for staff at runaway shelters, residential
treatment facilities, detention facilities, group homes, street outreach programs, hot lines, foster-family programs, and other agencies that serve
high-risk youth.

In addition to the national efforts of YSAs, many local affiliates have
designed their own programs to meet the needs of their local communities
in culturally sensitive ways. For example, the National 4-H Council estimates
that most state extension offices have developed their own programs to
reduce teenage pregnancy in their areas.

Schools

More than 85 percent of the American public approve of sexuality
education being provided in the schools, compared with 76 percent in
1975 and 69 percent in 1965 (Kenney, Guardado, and Brown 1989). Today,
roughly 60 percent of teenagers receive at least some sex education in
their schools, although only a third receive a somewhat "comprehensive"
program.

Each state can mandate or require that sexuality education and/or AIDS education be provided in the local school districts. Short of mandating such educational programs, states may simply recommend that the school districts within their boundaries offer education on sexuality, in general, and/or more-specific AIDS education. In 1992, seventeen states had mandated sexuality education and thirty more recommended it; see Table 3 (Haffner 1992). In addition, thirty-four states had mandated AIDS education, while fourteen more recommended it. Only four states (Massachusetts, Mississippi, South Dakota, and Wyoming) had no position on sexuality education within their schools; whereas Ohio, Wyoming, and Tennessee had no position on AIDS education. In 1995, the NARAL and NARAL Foundation (1995) issued a detailed state-by-state review of sexuality education in America with selected details of legislative action in 1994 and 1995.

Although the majority of states either mandate or recommend sexuality and AIDS education, this does not guarantee that local school districts are implementing the suggested curricula. Inconsistencies in and lack of implementation of these curricula result from: absence of provisions for mandate enforcement, lax regulations regarding compliance, diversity in program objectives, restrictions on course content, lack of provisions for teacher training, and insufficient evaluation.

In 1988, SIECUS conducted a project to examine and evaluate the recommended state sexuality and AIDS-education curricula (Di Mauro 1989-90). Of the twenty-three state curricula that they evaluated for sexuality education, only 22 percent were deemed to be accurate. Although most curricula stated that human sexuality is natural and positive, there was a lack of any content in the curricula to support this concept. Most focused on the negative consequences of sexual interaction, and little attention was paid to the psychosocial dimensions of sexuality, such as gender identification and roles, sexual functioning and satisfaction, or values and ethics. Only one half of the curricula provided thorough information about birth control.

In an evaluation of the thirty-four state-recommended AIDS-education curricula, 32 percent were found to be accurate in basic concepts and presentation. The majority (85 percent) emphasized abstinence and "just say no" skills, whereas only 9 percent covered safer sex as a preventive practice. Thorough information about condoms was provided in less than 10 percent of the curricula. There was no mention of homosexuality in over one third of the curricula. In 38 percent, homosexuals were identified as the "cause of AIDS." The Utah curriculum was especially negative and restrictive:

> Utah's teachers are not free to discuss the "intricacies of intercourse, sexual stimulation, erotic behavior"; the acceptance of or advocacy of homosexuality as a desirable or acceptable sexual adjustment or life-

Table 3

State Requirements for Sexuality, STD, and HIV/AIDS Education in Primary and Secondary Schools

Sexuality Education—Required from Kindergarten Through Senior High School

Alabama, Arkansas, Delaware, District of Columbia, Florida, Georgia, Illinois, Iowa, Kansas, Maryland, Minnesota, Nevada, New Jersey, New Mexico, North Carolina, Rhode Island, Tennessee, Vermont, Virginia, and West Virginia

Sexuality Education—Required for Grades Five or Six Through Senior High School

South Carolina, Texas, and Utah

Sexuality Education—Not Required

Alaska, Arizona, California, Colorado, Connecticut, Hawaii, Idaho, Indiana, Kentucky, Louisiana, Maine, Massachusetts, Michigan, Mississippi, Missouri, Montana, Nebraska, New Hampshire, New York, North Dakota, Ohio, Oklahoma, Oregon, Pennsylvania, South Dakota, Washington, Wisconsin, and Wyoming

STD/HIV/AIDS Education—Required from Kindergarten Through Senior High School

Alabama, Arizona, Arkansas, Connecticut, Delaware, District of Columbia, Florida, Georgia, Idaho, Indiana, Iowa, Kansas, Michigan, Minnesota, Missouri, Nevada, New Hampshire, New Jersey, New Mexico, New York, North Carolina, Ohio, Oregon, Pennsylvania, Rhode Island,[1] Tennessee,[2] Vermont, Virginia, Washington, and Wisconsin

STD/HIV/AIDS Education—Required Grades Five or Six Through Senior High School

California, Illinois, Maryland, Oklahoma, South Carolina, Texas, Utah,[3] and West Virginia

STD/HIV/AIDS Education—Not Required

Alaska, Colorado, Hawaii, Kentucky, Louisiana,[4] Maine, Massachusetts, Mississippi, Montana, Nebraska, North Dakota, South Dakota, and Wyoming

[1] Instruction in sexuality and HIV/AIDS is required at least once a year in all grades.

[2] Instruction in sexuality and HIV/AIDS is required only in counties with more than 19.5 pregnancies per 1,000 females aged 15 to 17. Only one county did not meet this standard.

[3] HIV/AIDS education is required from third to twelfth grades.

[4] Louisiana law prohibits sex education before the seventh grade, and in New Orleans, before the third grade.

Source: *Sexuality Education in America: A State-by-State Review*. NARAL/The NARAL Foundation, 1995.

style; the advocacy or encouragement of contraceptive methods or devices by unmarried minors; and the acceptance or advocacy of "free sex," promiscuity, or the so-called "new morality." This section of their curriculum is replete with warnings of legal violations for instructors crossing prohibition lines; their guidelines indicate that with parental consent it is possible to discuss condom use at any grade level, but without it, such discussions are Class B misdemeanors. (Di Mauro 1989-90, 6; see also the discussion of Mormon sexuality in Section 2A.)

Currently, a broad focus on sexuality education is being supplanted by a narrow focus on AIDS education. Sexuality and AIDS education are being treated independently with separate curricula and teacher training. The report concluded that: "What is needed [for each state] is a comprehensive sexuality education or family-life education curriculum with an extensive AIDS education component that contextualizes preventive information within a positive, life-affirming approach to human sexuality" (Di Mauro 1989-90, 6).

Yet, recommended curriculum content cannot automatically be equated with what is actually being taught in the classroom. To determine what is being taught, a study of public school teachers in five specialty areas (health education, biology, home economics, physical education, and school nursing) in grades seven through twelve was conducted (Forrest and Silverman 1989). It was estimated that nationwide 50,000 public school teachers were providing some type of sexuality education in grades seven through twelve in 1987-88; representing 45 percent of the teachers employed in those areas. Roughly 38.7 hours of sex education were being offered in grades seven through twelve; with 5.0 hours devoted to birth control and 5.9 hours covering STDs.

The teachers cited the encouragement of abstinence as one of their primary goals. The messages that they most want to give included: responsibility regarding sexual relationships and parenthood, the importance of abstinence and ways of resisting pressures to become sexually active, and information on AIDS and other STDs. The teachers agreed that sexuality education belongs in the schools and that students should be taught to examine and develop their own values about sexual behaviors. They reported that there is often a gap between what should be taught, and when and what actually is allowed to be taught. The largest gap concerned sources of birth-control methods; 97 percent of the teachers believed they should be allowed to provide information to students about where they could access birth control, but this was allowed in less than half of their schools. In fact, one quarter of the teachers were permitted to discuss birth control with students only when they are asked a student-initiated question. In addition, over 90 percent of the teachers believed that their students should be taught about homosexuality and abortion, topics that are often restricted by school districts. In addition, the teachers believed that the wide range of sexuality topics should be addressed with students no later than seventh or eighth grade; however, this is not usually done until tenth through twelfth grades, if at all.

The teachers described many barriers to implementing quality sexuality education in their classrooms. The major problem that they identified was opposition or lack of support from parents, the community, or school administrators. They also felt that they lacked appropriate materials because of the difficulties in getting current relevant materials approved for use. They also encountered student-related barriers, such as discomfort, lack of basic knowledge of anatomy and physiology, and misinformation, poor attitudes, and a lack of values and morals reflecting favorable attitudes toward teen pregnancy. Teachers also lacked enough time and training to teach the material effectively. Almost none of them were certified as sexuality or family-life educators by the American Association of Sex Educators, Counselors, and Therapists or the National Council on Family Relations. The level of the teachers' own knowledge on sexual topics was questionable, and some experienced personal conflicts in dealing with certain issues.

The authors concluded that:

> Perhaps the most important step toward improved sex education would be increased, clear support of the teachers. One form this support should take is the development of curricula that provide teachers with constructive, planned ways to raise and deal with the topics on their students' minds, since the data indicate that students will often raise topics even if they are not in the curriculum. Greater support should also help increase the availability of high-quality instructional materials and on-going education and information for teachers. Adequate teaching materials and support for teaching in earlier grades the topics students want to know about might help solve the problem of student inattention and negative reactions, to say nothing of helping with the problems of teenage pregnancy and the spread of AIDS and other STDs. (Forrest and Silverman 1989, 72)

Yet, in recent years, well-organized conservative organizations throughout the United States have been promoting the adoption of their own abstinence-only curricula in the public schools. Since 1985, the Illinois Committee on the Status of Women has received $1.7 million in state and federal funds to promote such a curriculum, called *Sex Respect*. They have been successful in having *Sex Respect* adopted in over 1,600 school systems, even though this curriculum is designed to proselytize a particular conservative sexual-value system. The *Sex Respect* curriculum has been criticized because it:

> (1) substitutes biased opinion for fact; (2) conveys insufficient and inaccurate information; (3) relies on scare tactics; (4) ignores realities of life for many students; (5) reinforces gender stereotypes; (6) lacks respect for cultural and economic differences; (7) presents one side of controversial issues; (8) fails to meaningfully involve parents; [and] (9) is marketed using inadequate evaluations. (Trudell and Whatley 1991, 125)

Careful scientific evaluation of over forty sexuality- and AIDS-education curricula commissioned separately by the Centers for Disease Control and the World Health Organization resulted in the following conclusions:

1. Comprehensive sexuality and HIV/AIDS-education programs do not hasten the onset of intercourse nor increase the number of partners or frequency of intercourse.
2. Skill-based programs can delay the onset of sexual intercourse and increase the use of contraception, condoms, and other safer-sex practices among sexually experienced youth.
3. Programs that promote both the postponement of sexual intercourse and safer-sex practices are more effective than abstinence-only programs, like *Sex Respect* (Haffner 1994).

C. Informal Sources of Sexual Knowledge

Researchers over the past fifty years have consistently found that adolescents identify peers, particularly of their same gender, as their primary source of sexuality education, followed by various types of media, including print and visual media. Parents and schools are usually identified as significantly less-influential sources.

Peers as a Sexual Information Source

Males seem to be more dependent on peers for their sexuality education than are females. One problematic aspect of receiving sexuality education informally from peers is that the information they provide is often inaccurate. However, when peers are formally trained to provide sexuality education, such as on the high school or college level, they are very effective in providing information and encouraging the development of positive attitudes towards responsible and healthy sexual expression. Thus, the peer model is being used more widely in school and community sexuality-education programs.

The Media

The various media are pervasive and influential sources of sexuality education in American culture. Media have been identified by adolescents and college students as being more influential than their families in the development of their sexual attitudes and behaviors. As to television, the radio, and movies, adolescents spend more time being entertained by the media than any other activity, perhaps with the exception of sleeping (Haffner and Kelly 1987).

Television, in particular, has been identified as the most influential source of sexual messages in American society, even though sexual behavior is not explicitly depicted. Yet, in an analysis of the sexual content of prime-time television programming, about 20,000 scenes of suggested sexual intercourse and other behaviors, and sexual comments and innuendos were documented in one year (Haffner and Kelly 1987). These portrayals of sexual interaction are six times more likely to happen in an extramarital, rather than a marital, relationship. In soap operas, 94 percent of the sexual encounters happen between people who are not married to one another. Minority groups are extremely underrepresented on TV, with gay and lesbian characters nearly nonexistent.

In the United States, by the time a child graduates from high school, she or he will have spent more time watching TV than being in a formal classroom setting. There is conflicting evidence as to the impact media portrayals have on youth's developing sexuality (Haffner and Kelly 1987). Gender-role stereotyping is a pervasive aspect of television programming, with children who watch more TV demonstrating more stereotypic gender-role behaviors than those who watch less. Some studies have linked young people's television-viewing habits, including the watching of music videos, to the likelihood that they would engage in sexual intercourse, while others have not supported this relationship. Yet, there is no denying that TV serves as a sexuality educator. Adolescents report that TV is equally or more encouraging about engaging in sexual intercourse than are their friends, and those that have high TV-viewing habits are likely to be dissatisfied about remaining virgins. In addition, those who believe that TV accurately portrays sexual experiences are more likely to be dissatisfied with their own.

Soap operas are one of the most popular television genres. Depictions of sexual behaviors are common. Yet, television censors still establish rules, such as not showing unbuttoning clothes or the characters at the moment of "penetration." Unfortunately, very few references to or depictions of safer sex are part of television programs. As the National Academy of Sciences concluded, the media provide "young people with lots of clues about how to be sexy, but . . . little information about how to be sexually responsible" (Haffner and Kelly 1987, 9).

Sexuality has become a focal point of some newer types of television programming. Sexual topics, such as teenage pregnancy, incest, or AIDS, are often the subject matter of made-for-TV movies and "after-school specials." In addition, the "sexually unconventional," such as transvestites, sex addicts, or bigamists, are often the guests of television talk shows, such as Donahue, Oprah, and Geraldo. Some critics believe that this diversity has encouraged viewers to become more tolerant and open, whereas others believe it has done the opposite, reinforcing negative and hostile attitudes. Among adolescents and young adults, music videos have become one of the most popular forms of television entertainment. Yet, context studies of these music videos indicate that women tend to be treated as "sex objects." Madonna is one exception, depicting a powerful image of female sexuality.

The motto that "Sex Sells" has been generously applied to television advertising. Television uses sexual innuendos and images to sell almost every product from toothpaste to automobiles. The most sexually explicit commercials are generally those for jeans, beer, and perfumes. Paradoxically, commercials and public service announcements for birth control methods are banned from television. Those for "feminine hygiene" products and the prevention of sexually transmissible diseases, including AIDS, are quite restricted.

Subscriber cable television offers more sexually oriented programming, such as the *Playboy Channel*, than does network TV. However, the *Exxxtacy Channel* was forced out of business because of numerous government obscenity prosecutions. Virtual-reality technology is being developed to allow cable subscribers to use goggles, gloves, and body sensors to enjoy their own virtual sexual reality.

Film making is a huge business and American films are marketed worldwide. Movies have been reported as one of the leading sources of sexual information for adolescent Anglo-American, Latino, and Native American males (Davis and Harris 1982). Films are given greater license to depict sexual behavior explicitly than on television; however, they are still censored. In fact, films, such as *Basic Instinct*, have more explicit sex in their uncut versions that are marketed abroad than the "cut" versions that are marketed domestically. Female nudity has become acceptable, whereas male frontal nudity is still censored. Sexual behaviors other than heterosexual intercourse tend to be missing from most films.

Video cassettes and videocassette recorders (VCRs) have revolutionized the viewing habits of Americans. Two hundred million X-rated video cassettes were rented in the U.S. in 1989. One study of college students determined that males viewed about six hours and females two hours of sexually explicit material on their VCRs a month (Strong and DeVault 1994).

Another very popular form of media, directed at females, is the romance novel, comprising 40 percent of all paperback book sales in the U.S. Romance novels are believed to both reflect and create the sexual fantasies and desires of their female American audience. The basic formula of this form of media is: "Female meets devastating man, sparks fly, lovers meld, lovers are torn apart, get back together, resolve their problems, and commit themselves, usually, to marriage" (Strong and DeVault 1994, 22).

Sexual language is disguised by euphemisms. For example, the male penis is referred to as a "love muscle" and the female vagina as a "temple of love." Yet, romance novels are filled with sensuality, sexuality, and passion, with some people considering them soft-core pornography.

Young males in the U.S. tend to learn about sexuality through more-explicit magazines, such as *Playboy* and *Penthouse*. *Playboy* is one of the most popular magazines worldwide, selling about 10 million issues monthly. Half of college men, but much fewer women, report that pornography has been a source of information for them regarding sexual behaviors (Duncan and Nicholson 1991).

Finally, with increased public access to computer technology, sexuality education is now being offered through the computer-based superhighway. This represents the "wave of the future" and is thoroughly discussed in a section at the end of this chapter.

Parents as a Source of Sexual Information

It is widely believed that parents should be the primary sexuality educators of their children. They certainly provide a great deal of indirect sexuality education to their children through the ways that they display affection, react to nudity and bodies, and interact with people of different genders and orientations—as well as the attitudes they express (or the lack of expression) towards a myriad of sexual topics.

However, most parents in the United States provide little direct sexuality education to their children, even though the majority of children express the desire to be able to talk to their parents about sexuality. Studies of American adolescents consistently find that up to three quarters state that they have not discussed sexuality with their parents (Hass 1979; Sorenson 1973). Parents have expressed the following as barriers to discussing sexuality with their children: anxiety over giving misinformation or inappropriate information for the developmental level of their children; lack of skills in communicating about sexuality, since very few parents ever had role models on how to handle such discussions; and fear that discussing sexuality with their children will actually encourage them to become involved in sexual relationships.

When sexuality education occurs in the home, the mother is generally the parent who handles such discussions with both daughters and sons. Studies do indicate that, when parents talk to their children about sexuality, the children are more likely to wait to become involved in sexual behaviors until they are older, than those children who have not talked with their parents (Shah and Zelnick 1981). Further, when parent-educated teens do engage in sexual intercourse, they are more likely to use an effective means of birth control consistently and to have fewer sexual partners. In addition, high family sexual communication seems to be related to similarity in sexual attitudes between parents and their children.

Recognizing the importance of having parents involved in their children's sexuality education, efforts are being made to prepare parents to become better sexuality educators. Sexuality-education programs for parents are offered separate from, and in conjunction with, children's programs in some schools, and through some community and religious organizations. The goals of these programs include developing parents' communication skills so that they can become more "askable," increasing their knowledge about various aspects of sexuality, and exploring their attitudes and values surrounding these issues. For example, the National Congress of Parents and Teachers' Associations (PTA) has created programs and publications on aspects of sexuality and HIV/AIDS prevention for use by local affiliates.

It is clear that we must continue to strive to reach all Americans with positive and comprehensive sexuality education through all of our available informal and formal channels. It is also imperative that sound qualitative and quantitative research methodologies be used to ascertain the impact of differing sexuality education strategies and sources on the diverse groups of people—e.g., gender, age, orientation, race and ethnicity—in the United States.

4. Autoerotic Behaviors and Patterns
ROBERT T. FRANCOEUR*

A. Research Weaknesses and Challenges

Five weaknesses or shortcomings and three challenges can be identified in the current research on autoerotic attitudes and behavior patterns in the U.S.A. The weaknesses are:

1. the virtual absence of recent data on noncollege men and women, especially married women and men;
2. the small sample sizes in available research;
3. a problem with the representativeness of the samples;
4. very limited or no data on African-Americans, Latinos, and other ethnic/racial groups; and
5. a limited use of theory as a driving force in the development of research questions.

The challenges include:

1. finding available research funds;
2. overcoming the negative views in academia toward sex research in general, and especially for research on masturbation; and
3. disseminating the findings to the "consumer" to relieve the guilt feelings that many persons experience as a result of their masturbation practices.

B. Children and Adolescents

In 1985, Mary Calderone, M.D., a pioneer of American sexology and co-founder of the Sex Information and Education Council of the United States, documented the presence of a functioning erectile reflex in a seventeen-week-old male fetus. Considering the homologies of the male and female genital systems, it is logical to assume that females also develop the capacity for cyclical vaginal lubrication while still in the womb. In a 1940 study of boys three to twenty weeks old, seven of nine infants had erections from five to forty times a day. Seven-month-old girls have been observed experiencing what to all appearances can only be judged to be

---

*With input from J. Kenneth Davidson, Sr.

a reflexive orgasm induced by rubbing or putting pressure on their genitals.

The natural reflexes that result in fetal and infant erections and vaginal lubrication are very much like the knee jerk and other reflexes, except that they are accompanied by smiles and cooing that clearly suggest the infant is enjoying something quite pleasurable (Martinson 1990, 1995). Sooner or later, most children learn the pleasures of stimulating their genitals. Once that connection is made, the threat of punishment and sin may not be enough to keep a child from masturbating. Generally, American adults are very uncomfortable with masturbation by infants and children. There are exceptions, of course, as for instance, the practice of indigenous Hawaiian adult caregivers masturbating or fellating infants to calm them at night.

Most children seem to forget their early masturbation experiences. Two thirds of the males in Kinsey's study reported hearing about masturbation from other boys in their prepubescent or early adolescent years before they tried it themselves. Fewer than one in three males reported they rediscovered masturbation entirely on their own. Two out of three females in Kinsey's sample learned about masturbation by accident, sometimes not until after they were married. Some women reported they had masturbated for some time before they realized what they were doing.

In the 1940s, Kinsey and his associates reported that close to 90 percent of males and about 50 percent of females masturbated by the midteens. Studies in the 1980s show an increase in these numbers, with a fair estimate that today nearly three quarters of girls masturbate by adolescence and another 10 percent or so wait until their 20s. About 80 percent of adolescent girls and 90 percent of adolescent boys masturbate with frequencies ranging from once a week to about daily (Hass and Hass 1993, 151, 285).

C. Adults

Race and ethnicity, religion, educational level, and sexual education appear to be important variables that affect the incidence of masturbation. African-Americans engage in masturbation less often than whites and are more negative about it. Very little is known about Latino masturbation attitudes and practices. We are not aware of any studies on masturbation among other major groups, such as Asians and Native Americans. Religion is a key variable, especially given the continuing condemnation of masturbation by the Roman Catholic Church. Granted many Catholics engage in masturbation, but on a continuum, they are more likely to experience guilt feelings than Protestants or Jews. Likewise, persons from fundamentalist-Protestant backgrounds are more likely to have negative attitudes toward masturbation than liberal Protestants. Kinsey and many subsequent researchers have found that, as education level increases, especially among women, the acceptance and approval of masturbation as a sexual outlet increases.

Finally, experience with sex education is an important variable (Heiby and Becker 1980). Persons who have had sex education appear to hold more-tolerant attitudes.

Data indicate that about 72 percent of young husbands masturbate an average of about twice a month. About 68 percent of young wives do so, with an average frequency of slightly less than once a month (Hunt 1974, 86). According to data reported by Edward Brecher in *Love, Sex and Aging* (1984), women in their 50s, 60s and 70s reported a consistent masturbation frequency of 0.6 to 0.7 times a week. In their 50s, men reported masturbating 1.2 times a week with a decline to 0.8 times a week in their 60s, and 0.7 times a week over age 70.

The incidence of masturbation has continued to increase in recent years among both college and postcollege women. During the 1980s, between 46 percent and 69 percent of college women in several surveys reported masturbating. In the 1990s, other surveys have found 45 percent to 78 percent. Postcollege women also became more accepting of masturbation as they received psychological permission, instruction, and support in learning about their own bodies. In fact, in self-reports of masturbation, a majority of postcollege-age, college-educated women indicated this was a sexual outlet. In a large-scale sample of college-educated women, without regard to marital status, frequency of masturbation was 7.1 times per month. By contrast, high-school-educated, married women engaged in masturbation only 3.7 times per month (Davidson and Darling 1993).

Not all women feel comfortable with masturbation. Among college women, 30 percent reported "shame" as a major reason for not engaging in this outlet. Other research indicates that only about half of college women believe that masturbation is a "healthy practice." Even with the apparent increasing incidence of masturbation, considerable data exist that suggest negative feelings toward the practice still deter many college women from choosing this source of sexual fulfillment. And, of those who do engage in masturbation, they do so much less frequently than men, 3.3 times a month for college women compared with 4.8 times for college men (Davidson and Darling 1993).

In general, women are more likely than men to report guilt feelings about their masturbation. Further, substantial evidence suggests that such guilt feelings may interfere with the physiological and/or psychological sexual satisfaction derived from masturbation. In fact, the presence of masturbatory guilt has various implications for female sexuality. Such guilt feelings have been found to inhibit the use of the diaphragm, which necessitates touching the genitals for insertion (Byrne and Fisher 1983). Presumably, this would also affect use of other vaginally inserted contraceptives. Women with high levels of masturbatory guilt experience more emotional trauma after contracting an STD, and exhibit greater fear about telling their sex partner about being infected, than women with low masturbatory guilt. Masturbatory guilt may also inhibit women from experiencing high levels of arousal during foreplay as a prelude to having vaginal intercourse.

One indication of changing attitudes of women toward self-loving is the publication of *Sex for One: The Joy of Selfloving*, by Betty Dodson (1988), and her subsequent appearance on television talk shows. At the same time, the swift dismissal of the U.S. Surgeon General for daring to suggest that masturbation might be mentioned as part of safer-sex education for children indicates that a prevailing negative societal attitude toward masturbation continues.

5. *Interpersonal Heterosexual Behaviors*

A. Childhood Sexuality
DAVID L. WEIS*

Within American culture, childhood sexuality remains an area that has been largely unexplored by researchers. Childhood is widely seen as a period of asexual innocence. Strong taboos continue concerning childhood eroticism, and childhood sexual expression and learning are still divisive social issues. This general ambience of anxiety associated with the sexuality of children is probably understandable, given the general history of sexuality in the U.S.A., with its focus on adult dyadic sex within committed intimate relationships and its opposition to other sexual expressions. This ambience remains, despite the fact that nearly a century has passed since Freud introduced his theory of psychosexual stages with an emphasis placed on the sexual character of childhood development. This reluctance to accept childhood sexuality is somewhat ironic, because Freudian theory, with its concepts of psychosexual stages (oral, anal, phallic, and latency), penis envy, the Oedipus/Electra complexes, repression, and the unconscious, has been immensely popular in the United States throughout much of the twentieth century. Yet, the general American public has been able to ignore the prominence given to childhood sexual development by Freudian theorists and to maintain its central belief that childhood is and ought to be devoid of sexuality.

Perhaps no area reviewed in this section has been the subject of less scientific research than this topic of childhood sexuality. To some extent, the paucity of research has been due to general social concerns about the ethical implications of studying children or assumptions about the possible harm to children that would result if they were to be included in sexuality research. Researchers have frequently had difficulty gaining the permission of legal guardians to ask children questions about their knowledge of sexuality. In this atmosphere, it would be exceedingly difficult to get permission to ask children about their sexual behavior. One consequence of this general social concern has been that most of the relevant research

---

*With input from Paul Okami.

has been confined to asking adults or college students to report retrospectively about events that occurred in their childhood. There are rather clear and obvious limitations to this approach.

On the other hand, we should recognize that many American scientists themselves have been unwilling to study the sexuality of children. A recent review, *Sexuality Research in the United States: An Assessment of the Social and Behavioral Sciences* (di Mauro 1995), is notable for the fact that it never mentions childhood sexuality. It might be interesting to determine the extent to which American researchers accept the premise that scientific explorations of sexuality might be harmful to children. For example, the field of child development, a sizable branch of American psychology, has largely ignored the issue of sexuality in their work (Maccoby and Martin 1983; Mussen 1983). An examination of standard developmental texts or reviews of the child development research literature is striking for its omission of sexuality. Significant bodies of child-development research in such important areas as language acquisition, cognition, communication, social behavior, parent-child interaction, attachment (Allgeier and Allgeier 1988), parenting styles, and child compliance have emerged with scant attention to the possible sexual elements of these areas, or to the ways in which these areas might be related to sexual development (Mussen 1983). As just one example, Piaget never investigated the issue of children's sexual cognition, and there has been little subsequent research exploring the application of his theoretical model to sexual development. Similarly, the emergence of family systems theory has also largely ignored the sexuality of children—except to explain the occurrence of incest.

At the same time, it is just as true that sexuality researchers have largely ignored the work of child developmentalists and other scientific disciplines in their own work. They have speculated about how theories of psychoanalysis, social learning, cognition, attribution, social exchange, and symbolic interactionism might be applied to the sexuality of children or to the process of sexual development, but they have rarely tested such assertions empirically (see Allgeier and Allgeier 1988 and Martinson 1976 for examples). Moreover, sex researchers have largely failed to examine how the various processes studied by developmentalists relate to sexuality.

A third domain of this fractured American approach to child development is the fairly recent emergence of professional fields devoted solely to the issue of child sexual abuse. We present a review of child sexual abuse itself later in this chapter (see Section 8A2). Here, we wish to make the point that professional groups—e.g., social workers and family therapists devoted to the treatment of victims of child sexual abuse—have emerged, largely since the 1970s, with a corresponding body of work devoted to that concern. After having been largely neglected for much of the twentieth century, the treatment of child sexual abuse has become a sizable "industry" in recent years. Unfortunately, much of the work that has been done within this perspective has failed to consider existing data on normative childhood sexuality (Okami 1992, 1995). For example, it is frequently asserted that child sexual abuse has the negative consequence of "sexualizing" the child's world. We do not mean to claim that child sexual abuse is either harmless or nonexistent. However, the notion that a "sexualized" childhood is a tragic outcome of sexual abuse rests on the American premise that child-hood should be devoid of sexuality. It assumes that childhood should not be sexual. From this perspective, the concept of child sexual abuse has been extended to include family nudity—a point certain to shock naturists in many countries around the world—parents bathing with their children, "excessive" displays of physical affection (such as kissing and hugging), and even children of the same age engaging in sex play (Okami 1992, 1995). Thus, we seem to have come full circle. Many professionals have come to accept the premise that childhood ought to be an innocent period, free of sexuality. The fact that this view ignores much of the existing data seems to have had little impact on either the American public or many profes-sionals working with children.

Childhood Sexual Development and Expression

In reviewing the process of child sexual development and the phenomenon of child eroticism, it is crucial to consider the meanings that children attach to their experience. There is a tendency to interpret childhood experiences in terms of the meanings that adults have learned to attach to similar events. This ignores the reality that young children almost certainly do not assign the same meanings to "sexual" events as adults. They have yet to concep-tualize a system of experiences, attitudes, and motives that adults label as "sexual" (Allgeier and Allgeier 1988; Gagnon and Simon 1973; Martinson 1976). A good example is provided by the case of childhood "masturba-tion." Young children often discover that "playing" with their genitals is a pleasurable experience. However, this may well not be the same as "mas-turbating." Masturbation, as adults understand that term, is a set of behav-iors defined as "sexual" because they are recognized as producing "sexual arousal" and typically having orgasm or "sexual climax" as a goal. Young children have yet to construct this complex set of meanings. They know little more than that the experience is pleasurable; it feels good. In fact, it would be useful to see research that examines the process by which children eventually learn to label such self-pleasuring as a specifically sexual behavior called masturbation.

From this perspective, sexual development is, to a considerable extent, a process characterized by the gradual construction of a system of sexual meanings. Gagnon and Simon (1973) have provided a theoretical model of sexual scripting that examines how these meanings are assembled in a series of stages through social interaction with various socialization agents. In their discussion of the model, Gagnon and Simon stressed their intention that it would serve as an organizing framework for future research on the process of sexual development. Although we believe that the model does provide a potentially fruitful framework for thinking about the process of sexual development, and despite the fact that more than twenty years have passed since its original presentation, there is nearly as great a need for research of this type today as when they formulated the model.

One component of the model proposed by Gagnon and Simon (1973) was the concept of assemblies, by which they meant to convey their view that sexual development is actively constructed by humans rather than merely being an organic process. Among the major assemblies they identified were:

1. the emergence of a specific gender identity,
2. the learning of a sense of modesty,
3. the acquisition of a sexual vocabulary,
4. the internalization of mass-media messages about sexuality,
5. the learning of specific acts defined as sexual,
6. the learning of gender, family, and sexual roles,
7. the learning of the mechanisms and process of sexual arousal;
8. the development of sexual fantasies and imagery,
9. the development of a sexual value system,
10. the emergence of a sexual orientation, and
11. the adoption of an adult sexual lifestyle.

Gagnon and Simon maintained that these assemblies were constructed through interactions with a variety of socialization agents, such as parents and family members, same-sex peers, cross-sex peers, and the mass media. To this list, we would suggest adding the church, the school, the neighborhood/community, and boyfriends/girlfriends as potentially important socialization agents. For Gagnon and Simon, the task for researchers was to examine and identify the associations between the activities of various socialization agents and the corresponding construction of specific sexual assemblies. Although a fair amount of research has been conducted on such associations among adolescents (see the following section), sadly there remains relatively little research along these lines for younger children. As such, we will not present a detailed discussion of the activities of each socialization agent here.

Lacking space to review each of the assemblies, we have had to be selective and have chosen to focus on the more explicitly erotic dimensions. However, we do wish to note that each is ultimately important to a full understanding of sexual development, and it is likely that each of these assemblies is related to the others. Although we do not have space to review the research on the development of gender roles and gender identity, it appears that most American children have formed a stable gender identity by the age of 2 or 3 (Maccoby and Martin 1983; Money and Ehrhardt 1972). It also seems likely that, as children acquire sexual information and experience, they filter what they learn in terms of what is appropriate for males and females. Since norms for male and female behavior, both sexual and nonsexual, tend to differ, this filtering process seems likely to lead to differences in the content of and processes of male and female sexual development.

On the other hand, we would caution the reader to resist the temptation to conclude that gender differences in sexuality are invariably large, or that they apply to all dimensions of sexuality. Recent reviews of existing research indicate that many aspects of sexuality are not characterized by male-female differences and that many differences are small in magnitude (Oliver and Hyde 1993). Ultimately, the issue is a matter for empirical investigation. Unfortunately, there has been relatively little empirical research attempting to link gender-role development (of which there has been a great deal of research in the last thirty years) with the processes of more overtly sexual development.

Childhood Sexual Eroticism and Expression. Martinson (1976) has drawn a distinction between what he calls reflexive and eroticized sexual experiences. Reflexive experience is pleasurable and may be a result of learning contingencies, but eroticized experience is characterized by self-conscious awareness and labeling of behavior as sexual. As a general guideline, younger and less-experienced children would seem more likely to react to sexual stimuli in a reflexive manner; older and more-experienced children are more likely to have learned erotic meanings and to define similar behaviors as "sexual." However, there has been virtually no research detailing the process in which this transition occurs or identifying the factors associated with it.

Sexual Capacity and Autoerotic Play. It has been clear for several decades that infants are capable of reflexive sexual responses from birth. Male infants are capable of erections, and female infants are capable of vaginal lubrication (Allgeier and Allgeier 1988; Halverson 1940). Lewis (1965) observed pelvic thrusting movements in infants as early as eight months of age. Generally, these events appear to be reactions to spontaneous stimuli, such as touching or brushing of the genitals. However, the Kinsey research group (1953) did report several cases of infants less than 1 year of age who had been observed purposely stimulating their own genitals. In their cross-cultural survey, Ford and Beach (1951) reported that, in cultures with a permissive norm, both boys and girls progress from absent-minded fingering of their genitals in the first year of life to systematic masturbation by the age of 6 to 8.

With few exceptions, most research on childhood sexual experiences has asked adolescents or adults to describe events in their past. Males participating in such studies commonly report memories of what they call "their first pleasurable erection" at such ages as 6 and 9 (Martinson 1976), although, as we have just seen, studies of infants themselves document the occurrence of erections from birth. Kinsey and his associates (1953) did report that almost all boys could have orgasms without ejaculation three to five years before puberty, and more than one half could reach orgasm by age 3 or 4. Comparable data for females have not been presented. In addition, both boys and girls between the ages of 6 and 10 have reported becoming sexually aroused by thinking about sexual events (Langfeldt 1979).

Much has been made in the U.S.A. of the fact that sexual arousal in boys is readily visible (erections). A number of authors have argued that this increases the probability that young boys will "discover" their penis and are, thus, more likely to stimulate their own genitals than are girls. This idea has become part of the folklore of American culture. We know of no evidence that substantiates this idea. In fact, Galenson and Roiphe (1980) report that there are no gender differences in autoerotic play during the first year of life.

American culture does not encourage such childhood sex play and actively seeks to restrict it. In a study in the 1950s, only 2 percent of mothers reported that they were "permissive" about their own children's sex play (Sears, Maccoby, and Levin 1957). It is also interesting to note that the researchers in this study did not provide a response category that allowed mothers to indicate they "supported" or "encouraged" sex play. Martinson (1973) found this pattern extended well into the 1970s. In a later investigation of parental views toward masturbation, Gagnon (1985) found that the majority (86 percent) of this sample believed that their preadolescent children had masturbated. However, only 60 percent of the parents thought that this was acceptable, and only one third wanted their children to have a positive attitude about masturbation.

Sex Play with Other Children. The capacity to interact with another person in an eroticized manner and to experience sexual feelings, either homosexual or heterosexual, is clearly present by the age of 5 to 6. Langfeldt (1979) did observe both mounting and presenting behaviors in boys and girls at 2 years of age. He also observed that prepubertal boys who engaged in sex play with other children typically displayed penile erections during sex play. Ford and Beach (1951) found that children in cultures, unlike the U.S.A., who are able to observe adult sexual relations will engage in copulatory behaviors as early as 6 or 7 years of age. Moreover, in some cultures, adults actively instruct children in the techniques or practice of sexual relations (Ford and Beach 1951; Reiss 1986). This cross-cultural evidence appears to have had little impact on the way in which most Americans, including many sexuality professionals, think about childhood sociosexual interactions.

Again, most of the research in the U.S.A. has been based on recall data from adolescents or adults. Our impressions of childhood sexual interactions are biased toward periods that such older respondents can remember. A number of studies have examined the frequency of childhood sexual behaviors (Broderick 1965, 1966; Broderick and Fowler 1961; Goldman and Goldman 1982; Kinsey et al. 1948, 1953; Martinson 1973, 1976; Ramsey 1943). Taken together, these studies demonstrate that many American children develop and maintain an erotic interest in the other or same sex, and begin experiencing a wide range of sexual behaviors as early as age 5 to 6. It is not uncommon for Americans to report that they remember "playing doctor" or similar games that provide opportunities for observing and touching the genitals of other children, undressing other children, or displaying their own genitals to others. Many American children also acquire experience with kissing and deep kissing (what Americans call French kissing). In fact, generations of American children have played institutionalized kissing games, such as "spin the bottle" and "post office." These studies also provide evidence that at least some American children experience sexual fondling, oral sex, anal sex, and intercourse prior to puberty. Many of these behaviors are experienced in either heterosexual or homosexual combinations or both.

We have purposely avoided reporting the specific frequencies of the childhood sociosexual experiences in these studies because each possesses severe limitations with respect to generalizability. Most have had small samples drawn from a narrow segment of the total population in a specific geographic region. As early as the 1960s, researchers found evidence of racial and community differences in the rate of such behaviors (Broderick 1965, 1966; Broderick and Fowler 1961). In addition, most have used volunteer samples, with respondents who were trying to recall events that had occurred ten or more years earlier. Moreover, these studies were conducted over a period of five decades, during which there would seem to be great potential for changes. Comparisons among these studies are virtually impossible. As a result, we would have little confidence in the specific accuracy of frequency estimates.

A review of a few of these studies illustrates this point. Interviewing a group of boys in a midwestern city in the early 1940s, Ramsey (1943) found that 85 percent had masturbated prior to age 13, one third had engaged in homosexual play, two thirds had engaged in heterosexual play, and one third had attempted or completed intercourse. The Kinsey group (1948), using a broader sample of adults, reported that 45 percent had masturbated by age 13, 30 percent had engaged in homosexual play, 40 percent had engaged in heterosexual play, and 20 percent had attempted intercourse. For girls, the Kinsey group (1953) reported that roughly 20 percent had masturbated prior to age 13, roughly one third had engaged in both heterosexual and homosexual play, and 17 percent had attempted inter-course. They also reported an actual decline in sexual behaviors after age 10 (Kinsey et al. 1948). The large differences between the Ramsey and Kinsey findings could be due to sample size, differences in geographic region or size of the city, differences in the time period of data collection, or differences in the age range of the samples. Here, it is interesting to note that the Kinsey group (1948) also interviewed a small sample of boys. Roughly 70 percent reported some form of child sex play, a figure that is much closer to Ramsey's findings. In the larger Kinsey sample, only 57 percent of adult males and 48 percent of adult females reported memories of childhood sex play, usually between the ages of 8 to 13 (Kinsey et al. 1948, 1953). It would seem possible, then, that studies with adult samples recalling their childhood experiences might well yield lower estimates than studies of children themselves.

John Money (1976) and Money and Ehrhardt (1972) argue that childhood sex play with other children is a necessary and valuable form of rehearsal and preparation for later adult sexual behavior. He has also suggested that such sex play may occur as part of a developmental stage in childhood. Certainly, this phenomenon has been observed in other primate species, such as the chimpanzee (DeWaal 1982). However, Kilpatrick (1986, 1987) found no differences in various ages of adult sexual functioning between persons who had childhood sexual experiences with other children and those who did not. Given the complexity of the model of sexual assemblies we have presented here, it is not surprising that the effects are not that simple.

Sibling Incest. We discuss incest and child sexual abuse more fully later in Section 8A on coercive sex. Here, we merely wish to note that, in one of the few studies of sibling incest with a nonclinical sample, Finkelhor (1980) found that 15 percent of female and 10 percent of male college students reported having a sexual experience with a brother or sister. Approximately 40 percent of these students had been under the age of 8 at the time of the sexual activity, and roughly 50 percent had been between the ages of 8 and 12. Three quarters of the experiences had been heterosexual. Some type of force had been used in one quarter of the experiences. The most common sexual activities were touching and fondling of the genitals. Only 12 percent of the students had ever told anyone about these sexual activities with a brother or a sister. Interestingly, most of the students reported that they did not have either strong positive or negative feelings about these experiences. Positive reactions were reported by 30 percent, and another 30 percent reported negative reactions. Positive reactions were associated with consensual activities (no force had been used) and an age difference of four or fewer years. For males, there were no correlations between prior sibling experiences and current sexual activity. Among females, those who had had sibling sexual experiences were more likely to be currently sexually active. Those women who had positive sibling experiences after age 9 had significantly higher sexual self-esteem, whereas those who had sexual experiences before age 9 with a sibling more than four years older had lower self-esteem.

Sexual Contacts with Adults. A recent national survey (Laumann et al. 1994) found that 12 percent of men and 17 percent of women reported they had been sexually touched by an older person while they were children. The offender was typically not a stranger, but a family friend or a relative, a finding that is comparable to more-limited samples. We present a more complete review of sexual contacts with adults later in Section 8A2 on child sexual abuse and incest. Relatively few studies of adult-child sexual contacts have been conducted with nonclinical samples. In general, they indicate that children experience a wide range of reactions, from highly negative or traumatic to highly positive, to such contacts in both the short term and long term (Kilpatrick 1986, 1987; Nelson 1986; Farrell 1990). Moreover, there do not appear to be any simple or direct correlations between such childhood experiences and later measures of adult sexual functioning. In her study of incest, Nelson (1986) found no correlation between affective outcomes and type of erotic activity, sexual orientation, or consanguinity. Kilpatrick (1986) did find that the use of force or abuse was significantly related to impaired adult sexual functioning in several areas.

Same-Sex Childhood Experiences. Our discussion to this point has not focused exclusively on heterosexual experience, but it is certainly fair to say that investigations of heterosexual child sex play have dominated existing research. One study of 4- to 14-year-old children found that more than one half of boys and one third of girls reported at least one homosexual experience (Elias and Gebhard 1969). Masturbation, touching of the genitals, and exhibition were the most common activities, although there were also some reports of oral and anal contacts. The fact that children have had such a homosexual experience does not appear to be related to adult sexual orientation (Bell, Weinberg, and Hammersmith 1981; Van Wyk and Geist 1984).

Storms (1981) has hypothesized that such experiences may be related to adult sexual orientation as a function of sexual maturation. He suggests that persons who become sexually mature during the period of homosocial networks (discussed below) may be more likely to romanticize and eroticize these childhood homosexual experiences and, thus, develop a later preference for sexual partners of the same gender. In effect, when sexual maturation, goal-directed masturbation, homosexual explorations, and eroticized fantasies are paired before heterosexual socialization occurs (typically at about age 13), they are more likely to lead to a homosexual orientation later. As far as we know, Storms's ideas have never been directly tested through research.

Childhood Social Networks. During middle childhood (roughly ages 6 to 12), both boys and girls in the U.S.A. tend to form networks of same-sex friends. A pattern of gender segregation, where boys and girls have separate friends and play groups, is central to the daily life of middle childhood. This pattern of homosocial networks is readily observable at elementary schools across the U.S.A. Girls and boys tend to cluster at school into separated, same-sex groups. At lunchtime, they frequently sit at separate "girl's tables" and "boy's tables." On the playground, space and activities tend to be gendered. After school, children tend to associate and play in gender-segregated groupings. In fact, this pattern of gender separation may be more pronounced in middle childhood in the U.S.A. than the more-publicized racial segregation.

It should be acknowledged that these homosocial networks are not characterized by a total separation of the genders. There are some opportunities for heterosocial interactions and play, and children do vary with respect to the extent in which they associate with the other sex. As just one obvious example, some girls, who are known as "tomboys," spend considerable time associating with boys. Still, to a large extent, the worlds of boys and girls in middle childhood in the U.S.A. are separated.

Maltz and Borker (1983) have suggested that these homosocial networks can be viewed as distinct male and female cultures. As cultures, each has its own set of patterns, norms, and rules of discourse. Boys tend to play in groups that are arranged in a hierarchy. They stress a norm of achievement ("doing") and emphasize competitive, physical activities. Conflict is overt and is often resolved directly through physical fighting. Differentiation between boys is made directly in terms of power and status within the group. Since boys belong to more than one such group, and because group memberships do change over time, each boy has an opportunity to occupy a range of positions within these hierarchies. Boys' groups also tend to be inclusive. New members are easily accommodated, even if they must begin their membership in a lower-status position. Courage and testing limits are prime values of boys' groups, and breaking rules is a valued form of bonding. In examining how these patterns influence male communication, Maltz and Borker (1983) report that males are more likely to interrupt others, they are more likely to ignore the previous statement made by another speaker, they are more likely to resist an interruption, and they are more likely to directly challenge statements by others.

Girls tend to associate in smaller groups or friendship pairs. Girls, for example, tend to be highly invested in establishing and maintaining a "best friend" relationship. They stress a norm of cooperation ("sharing") and pursue activities that emphasize "working together" and "being nice." They frequently play games that involve "taking turns." Friendship is seen as requiring intimacy, equality, mutual commitment, and cooperation. However, girls' groups also tend to be exclusive. Membership is carefully reserved for those who have demonstrated they are good friends. Conflict tends to be covert, and it is highly disruptive, leading to a pattern of shifting alliances among associates. Differentiation between girls is not made in terms of power, but rather in relative closeness. Girls are more likely to affirm the value of rules, especially if they are seen as serving group cohesion or making things fair. Girls may break rules, but their gender group does not provide the intense encouragement and support for this behavior seen among boys. Maltz and Borker (1983) note that girls are more likely to ask questions to facilitate conversation, they are more likely to take turns talking, they are more likely to encourage others to speak, and they are more likely to feel quietly victimized when they have been interrupted.

These largely segregated gender networks in middle childhood serve as the contexts for learning about adolescent and adult sexual patterns, as well as for other areas of social life. There is, of course, a certain irony to the fact that homosocial networks serve as a principal learning context for heterosexuality in a culture with such strong taboos against homosexuality as the U.S.A. In fact, Martinson (1973) has argued that these gender networks and this period serve as the settings for a fair amount of homosexual exploration and activity. In one sense, it is almost certainly true that some homosexual activity results from these patterns of social organization. However, this assertion is largely undocumented, and we are not aware of any studies that compare the level of homosexual activity in cultures with homosocial networks with cultures having some other form of childhood networks.

Thorne and Luria (1986) have used this concept of gendered cultures to examine the process of sexual learning in middle childhood. They found that "talking dirty" is a common format for the rule-breaking that characterizes boys' groups. They noted that talking dirty serves to define boys as apart from adults, and that boys get visibly excited while engaging in such talk. Boys also often share pornography with each other and take great care to avoid detection and confiscation by adults. These processes provide knowledge about what is sexually arousing, and they also create a hidden, forbidden, and arousing world shared with other boys, apart from adults and girls. Miller and Simon (1981) have argued that the importance attached to rule violations creates a sense of excitement and fervor about sexual activity and accomplishment.

One other feature of boys' groups is that they serve as a setting for learning both homoeroticism and homophobia. Boys learn to engage in what Thorne and Luria call "fag talk." That is, they learn to insult other boys by calling them names, like "faggot" and "queer." Eventually, they learn that homosexuality is disapproved by the male peer group. Boys at age 5 to 6 can be observed touching each other frequently. By age 11 to 12, touching is less frequent and reduced to ritual gestures like poking each other. On the other hand, much of the time spent with other boys is spent talking about sex. This serves to maintain a high level of arousal within the group. Moreover, the sanctioning of rule-breaking leads to some homosexual experimentation that is kept hidden from the group. Homosexual experiences may become one more form of breaking the rules and one more feature of the secret, forbidden world of sexuality.

In contrast, girls are more likely to focus on their own and their friends' physical appearance. They monitor one another's emotions. They share secrets and become mutually vulnerable through self-disclosure. They have giggling sessions with their friends, with sex often being the source of amusement. Their talks with other girls tend to focus less on physical activities and more on relationships and romance. They also plot together how to get particular boys and girls together in a relationship.

These sexual patterns are largely consistent with the norms of the respective gender cultures. Males tend to focus on physical activities; females on cooperation and sharing. They are also quite consistent with patterns that will become firmly established in adolescent sociosexual patterns. Thus, male and female peer groups become the launching pads for heterosexual coupling as boys and girls begin to "go together." Finally, they serve to heighten the romantic/erotic component of interactions with the other gender.

Professional and Social Issues of Childhood Sexuality

As we stated at the beginning of this section and as should be apparent from the review of sex education in the U.S.A., there are a number of issues concerning childhood sexuality that have been controversial for decades. Moreover, several new issues have become points of social conflict in recent years. We can only briefly mention four here.

The Oedipus and Electra Complexes. The Goldmans' (1982) multinational study of children and sexual learning, including a sizable American sample, raises questions about these complexes. Freud's thesis about castration anxiety and its resolution (typically by the age of 5) would presumably require some awareness of genital differences between males and females, unless one wishes to interpret Freud's terminology strictly as metaphorical. In the Goldman study, the majority of English-speaking children did not understand these differences until they were 7 to 9 years old. Interestingly, a majority of the Swedish children could accurately describe these differences by the age of 5.

Is There a Latency Period? The notion of a latency period, roughly from ages 6 to 11, has had great appeal in American culture. This may be due to the impression that the homosocial networks of middle childhood reflect a lack of sexual interest, and to the fact that many Americans prefer to believe that childhood is a period of sexual innocence. Freud (1938) originally proposed in 1905 that middle childhood is characterized by relative sexual disinterest and inactivity, something like a dormant period. Freud also maintained that latency was more pronounced among boys than girls. The review above should certainly dispel the notion that childhood, at any point, is essentially characterized by sexual disinterest.

In addition, Broderick (1965, 1966) not only provided evidence of active sex play during middle childhood, but also demonstrated that most children indicate they wish to marry as an adult, and that most of these children are actively involved in a process of increasing heterosocial interaction and love involvements during childhood. A majority said they had had a boy-friend or girlfriend and had been in love, and 32 percent had dated by age 13. If anything, we would expect that the age norms for many of these behaviors have actually decreased since that time. Interestingly, those children who indicated that they did not wish to marry eventually were substantially less likely to report any of these activities.

Parental Nudity. Experts have disagreed over the years as to the impact of parental nudity on children (Okami 1995). Some have argued that child-hood exposure to parental/adult nudity is potentially traumatic—largely because of the large size of adult organs. Others have insisted that strong taboos on family nudity may lead to a view that the body is unacceptable or shameful. This group has argued that a relaxed attitude toward nudity can help children develop positive feelings about sexuality. Similar con-cerns have been expressed about the primal scene and sleeping in the parental bed. In a survey of 500 psychiatrists, 48 percent indicated that they believe that children who witness their parents engaging in intercourse do suffer psychological effects (Pankhurst 1979). American experts appear to overlook the fact that most families throughout the world sleep in one-room dwellings. In one study of these issues, Lewis and Janda (1988) asked 200 college students to report their childhood experiences. Exposure to paren-tal nudity for ages zero to 5 and 6 to 11 was generally unrelated to a series of measures of adult sexual adjustment. Sleeping in the parental bed yielded several small, but significant correlations. Persons who had slept in their parents' bed as children had higher self-esteem, greater comfort about sexuality, reduced sexual guilt and anxiety, greater frequency of sex, greater comfort with affection, and a higher acceptance of casual sex as college students.

Okami (1995) reviewed the literature in these same three areas. His review provides a thorough summary of clinical opinions in each area, as well as an assessment of the empirical evidence. Despite the growing number of clinical professionals who label such acts as sexual abuse, there is virtually no empirical evidence of harm. In fact, the only variable found to be associated with harm is cosleeping, which has been found to be associated with sleep disturbances. However, Okami notes that these sleep disturbances may well have preceded and precipitated the cosleeping, rather than vice versa.

Female Genital Cutting. In December 1996, the Center for Disease Control and Prevention (CDC) estimated that more than 150,000 women and girls of African origin or ancestry in the United States were at risk in 1995 of being subjected to genital cutting or had already been cut. This estimate was based on 1990 Census Bureau data gathered before the recent increase in refugees and immigrants from the 28 countries that span Africa's mid-section where female genital cutting varies widely in prevalence and severity (Dugger 1996ab). A second source cites a different estimate from the CDC using data on how much circumcision is practiced in immigrants' home-lands and, making assumptions about sex and age, that about 270,00 African females in the United States were circumcised in their home country or are at risk here (Hamm 1996)

In 1996, Congress adopted a dual strategy to combat the practice here. In April 1996, Congress passed a bill requiring the Immigration and Naturalization Service to inform new arrivals of U.S. laws against genital cutting. It also mandated the Department of Health and Human Services to educate immigrants about the harm of genital cutting and to educate medical professionals about treating circumcised women. A law, which went into effect March 29, 1997, also criminalizes the practice, making it punishable by up to five years in prison and a fine of up to $250,000 for individuals and $500,000 for organizations such as hospitals. Enforcement of the law, however, is problematic for several reasons. First, no one is sure how the law will apply to those immigrants who take their daughters out of the country for the rite. Second, doctors who spot cases of genital mutilation are reluctant to report it for fear of breaking up tight-knit families. Also, when the wounds are healed, it is impossible to ascertain whether the rite was performed here or before arrival in the United States. Finally, there is the secretiveness surrounding this rite of passage, which many African cultures consider essential, and also the hidden nature of the wounds and scars. Sierra Leoneans, for instance, who consider genital cutting part of an elaborate, highly secret initiation rite, view questions about it as a profound invasion of their privacy (Dugger 1996ab).

A government's prevention program focuses on educating both old and recent immigrants in how to survive and assimilate in American society while maintaining their own culture and religion. To this purpose, the U.S. Department of Health and Human Services has organized meetings with advocates for refugees and nonprofit groups that work closely with Africans to develop strategies for combating this practice. Muslim religious leaders, for instance, are invited to explain that the Koran does not require this practice. However, lack of a specific budget hampers this effort.

In one attempt to ameliorate this clash of cultural values, doctors at Harborview Medical Center in Seattle, Washington, persuaded Somali mothers to be satisfied with nicking the clitoral hood without removing any tissue. The ritual usually involves removing the clitoris and sewing the labia closed. The compromise was abandoned in December of 1996 when the hospital was inundated with hundreds of complaints protesting even this compromise, even though the nicking of the clitoral hood has no short- or long-term negative consequences. The massive objection to this compromise raises serious questions of ethnocentrism on the part of the Americans who protested it. It seems somewhat ironic that such complaints would be made in a culture where we routinely circumcise penises. Although some maintained that the compromise of nicking may violate the letter of the law, it remains to be seen what kind of solution will be achieved in this matter (Dugger 1996b).

Child Pornography. It is widely believed, and the Federal Bureau of Investigation (FBI) perpetuates the notion, that child pornography is pervasive and increasing. Several state and federal laws have been enacted in the last twenty years to combat this perceived social problem. The mere possession of a photograph of a naked child has been criminalized in some states. Yet, it is virtually impossible to find any commercial child pornography in the U.S.A. In fact, most of the materials seized by the FBI are private photographs of naked children—with no adults appearing in the photos and no sexual behaviors depicted (Klein 1994; Stanley 1989). Efforts to raid child-pornography businesses have routinely failed to seize any child pornography. FBI sting operations may well have arisen from the corresponding frustrations of government agencies to find any child pornography. One recent legend now circulating is the claim that the U.S. government is now the largest producer of child pornography in the world. This claim is unsubstantiated as far as we know, but, again, it reflects the anxiety of American culture over the sexuality of its children.

B. Adolescent Sexuality
DAVID L. WEIS

Courtship, Dating, and Premarital Sex

In stark contrast to the relative inattention given to childhood sexuality in the U.S.A., Americans have been fascinated by the sexual behavior of adolescents throughout the twentieth century. One is tempted to describe the interest as an obsession. Perhaps no area of sexuality has received as much scrutiny, by both the general public and professionals, as the sexual practices of American teenagers. There have been literally hundreds of scientific studies attempting to determine the rate of adolescent premarital coitus, as well as other aspects of adolescent sexuality. The easy availability of populations to study is only one of the more-obvious reasons for this extensive research.

Since more than 90 percent of Americans ultimately do marry, investigations of adolescent sexual development and premarital sexual practices largely overlap. General trends have been well documented, compared to other areas of sexuality. Given the vast scope of this research, we can review only the highlights here. (For more extensive reviews of research on adolescent and premarital sexuality, see Cannon and Long 1971; Clayton and Bokemeier 1980; and Miller and Moore 1990.)

The issue of premarital sexuality (hereafter PS) and virginity has been a focus of considerable social conflict and concern throughout this century, and remains so to this day. Beginning in the early years of this century, a large literature documents the continuing concern of American adults about the increasing number of teenagers who have experienced sexual intercourse prior to marriage. Interestingly, each successive birth cohort of American adults in this century has been concerned about the tendency of their offspring to exceed their own rate of premarital coitus.

Much of the professional literature has reflected these same concerns. Through much of the twentieth century, the tone of most professional writings has been moralistic. Adults in the U.S.A., including most sexuality researchers, have tended to view adolescent premarital sexual intercourse, PS, as a deviant behavior, as a violation of existing social norms, and as a growing social problem (Spanier 1975). Research has tended to parallel this perspective by emphasizing the costs or negative consequences of adolescent sexuality, such as sexually transmitted disease (venereal disease), "illegitimate" pregnancy, and loss of reputation (Reiss 1960). This tone may have shifted to a less-judgmental, more-analytic perspective in the 1960s and 1970s (Clayton and Bokemeier 1980). However, with the emergence of AIDS and the rise of out-of-wedlock pregnancies in the early 1980s, the general tone has reverted in recent years, with studies of "risk-taking" behavior, "at-risk" youth, and portrayals of adolescent sexuality as a form of delinquency (Miller and Moore 1990).

Trends in Adolescent Sexuality

Despite these adult concerns, it would be fair to suggest that premarital virginity has largely disappeared in the U.S.A., both as a reality and as a social ideal. As we approach the end of the century, the overwhelming majority of Americans now have sexual intercourse prior to marriage, and they begin at younger ages than in the past. "Love" has largely replaced marital status as the most valued criteria for evaluating sexual experience (Reiss 1960, 1967, 1980). Virtually all Americans believe that intimate relationships (like marriage) should be based on love, that love justifies sexual activity, and that sex with love is a more-fulfilling human experience. This view has not only been used to justify PS activity between loving partners, but has also become a criteria for evaluating marital sexuality itself and justifying a pattern of divorce and remarriage.

Premarital Sexual Behavior. These trends may not be quite as dramatic as most Americans imagine. A study of marriages in Groton, Massachusetts, from 1761 to 1775 found that one third of the women were pregnant at the time of their weddings (cited in Reiss 1980), demonstrating that PS was already fairly common in the colonial period (see discussion of bundling in Section 1A). Several early sexuality surveys also document that PS occurred among some groups prior to the twentieth century. Terman (1938) compared groups who were born in different cohorts around the beginning of the century. Of those born before 1890, 50 percent of the men and only 13 percent of the women had premarital coitus. Two thirds of the men who had PS did so with someone other than their future spouse, whereas two thirds of the women who had PS did so only with their future spouse. For those born after 1900, two thirds of the men and nearly half of the women had PS. The relative percentage having PS with their fiance also increased. Fully half of the men and 47 percent of the women had sexual relations with their fiance prior to marriage.

The Kinsey team (1953) found that one quarter of the women born before 1900 reported they had PS, whereas one half of those born after 1900 said they had PS. Like the Terman study, the major change was an increase in the percentage of women born after 1900 who had PS with their fiance. The Kinsey study also indicated that the period of most-rapid change was from 1918 to 1930—the "Roaring Twenties." Burgess and Wallin (1953) reported similar findings for a birth cohort born between 1910 and 1919. These studies indicated that roughly two thirds of the men born after 1900 had PS. The Kinsey studies also found that there had been comparable increases in female masturbation and petting behavior as well.

It is important to note that the growth of PS in the first half of the century occurred primarily within the context of ongoing, intimate relationships. It appears that the percentage of males and females having PS remained fairly stable through the 1950s and early 1960s. In a study of college students during the 1950s, Ehrmann (1959) found rates similar to the Kinsey figures cited above. Ehrmann found that males tended to have greater sexual experience with females from a social class lower than their own, but they tended to marry women from their own social class. Males who were "going steady" were the least likely to be having intercourse. In contrast, females who were "going steady" were the most likely to be having intercourse. In a study comparing college students in Scandinavia, Indiana, and Utah (predominantly Mormon), Christensen (1962) and Christensen and Carpenter (1962) found that rates of PS vary by the norms of the culture and that guilt is most likely to occur when PS is discrepant with those norms.

A second wave of increases in PS seems to have occurred in the period from 1965 to 1980. A number of studies of college students through this period indicated increasing percentages of males and females having premarital coitus (Bauman and Wilson 1974; Bell and Chaskes 1968; Christensen and Gregg 1970; Robinson, King, and Balswick 1972; Simon, Berger, and Gagnon 1972; Vener and Stewart 1974). For example, Bauman and Wilson (1974) found that, for men, the rate having PS increased from 56 percent in 1968 to 73 percent in 1972. For women, the increase was from 46 percent to 73 percent. There was no significant change in the number of sexual partners for either gender. Several of these studies indicate that the increases were still moderate by 1970 (Bell and Chaskes 1968; Simon et al. 1972). In an unusual study of male college students attending an eastern university in the 1940s, 1960s, and 1970s, Finger (1975) found that

45 percent had PS in 1943-44, 62 percent in 1967-68, and 75 percent in 1969-73.

Subsequent studies have indicated that this pattern of increasing PS characterized American youth in general. In a study of urban samples in the mid-1970s, Udry, Bauman, and Morris (1975) found that 45 percent of white teenage women had intercourse by age 20, and 80 percent of black women did. Roughly 10 percent of whites had PS by age 15 and 20 percent of blacks did. Zelnik and Kantner found similar percentages in their studies in 1971 and 1976 (Udry, Bauman, and Morris 1975; Zelnik, Kantner, and Ford 1981).

Reports of increasing sexual activity among adolescents have not been limited to coitus. A number of researchers have reported similar increases in the rate of heavy petting (manual caressing of the genitals) through the late 1960s and 1970s (Clayton and Bokemeier 1980; Vener and Stewart 1974). There have also been reports of increasing levels of oral sex among adolescents (Haas 1979; Newcomer and Udry 1985). In some studies, teenage girls have been more likely to have participated in oral sex than intercourse, and between 16 percent to 25 percent of teens who have never had intercourse have had oral sex (Newcomer and Udry 1985). Weis (1983) has noted that this group may be involved in a transition from virginity to nonvirginity, at least among whites.

Perhaps the single best indicator of the trends occurring from 1965 to 1980 is the series of studies by Zelnik and Kantner in 1971, 1976, and 1979 (Zelnik et al. 1981). These studies, known as the *National Surveys of Young Women*, investigated the sexual histories of 15- to 19-year-old women. The 1971 and 1976 studies were full national probability studies while the 1979 study focused on women living in metropolitan areas. The Zelnik and Kantner research shows a dramatic rise in sexual activity for both black and white women from 1971 to 1976. The pattern of increases continued for white women through 1979, but PS rates for black women remained stable from 1976 to 1979. Among metropolitan women, PS rose from 30.4 percent in 1971 to 49.8 percent in 1979. For blacks, the rate moved from 53.7 percent in 1971 to 66.3 percent in 1976, and was 66.2 percent in 1979. The 1979 study also showed that 70 percent of males had PS intercourse; the figure for black men was 75 percent (Zelnik and Shah 1983; Zelnik et al. 1983).

In a review of these trends, Hofferth, Kahn, and Baldwin (1987) noted that females in the 1980s became sexually active at younger ages and that fewer teenagers married. As a result, the rate of PS increased. The proportion of women at risk of premarital pregnancy increased dramatically from 1965 to the 1980s. The out-of-wedlock pregnancy rate among teenagers increased for both blacks and whites from 1971 to 1976. This trend continued for whites through 1982, but remained level for blacks after 1976. Finally, they noted that, for women born between 1938 and 1940, 33.3 percent had PS by age 20. For women born between 1953 and 1955, the figure was 65.5 percent.

Despite recent claims in some quarters of a return to chastity and abstinence in the late 1980s and 1990s (McCleary 1992), there is no evidence of a decline in PS behavior. National data from 1988 indicate that one quarter of females have PS intercourse by age 15; 60 percent do so by age 19. About one third of United States males have PS intercourse by age 15, and 86 percent by age 19 (Miller and Moore 1990). In fact, a random telephone survey of 100 students attending a midwestern state university in 1994 found that 92 percent had had sexual intercourse; only 8 percent said they were still virgins. Nearly two thirds (63 percent) said that they had participated in what the survey described as a "one-night stand." With respect to their most recent sexual intercourse, 42 percent reported using something to "protect" themselves. Of these, 84 percent reported using condoms; 16 percent said they used the pill (Turco 1994). If anything, the trends that have been well established throughout this century appear to be continuing. Given the continuation of patterns that have been frequently cited as leading to increasing rates of PS, such as industrialization, rapid transportation, dating, and "going steady," we would not expect a reversal in what is now a century-long trend.

Premarital Sexual Attitudes (Permissiveness). There has also been a substantial number of studies examining the attitudes of Americans toward PS, although systematic research in this area began later than research on PS behavior. Reiss (1960) used the term "permissiveness" to describe the extent to which the attitudes of an individual or a social group approved PS in various circumstances. In general, research has found that PS attitudes have become progressively more permissive throughout this century, roughly parallel to the increases in PS behavior (Bell and Chaskes 1970; Cannon and Long 1971; Christensen and Gregg 1970; Clayton and Bokemeier 1980; Glenn and Weaver 1979; Vener and Stewart 1974). Reiss (1967) developed what has come to be called Autonomy Theory to explain this process. According to Reiss, PS permissiveness will increase in cultures where the adolescent system of courtship becomes autonomous with respect to adult institutions of social control, such as the church, parents, and the school. This appears to have happened in the U.S.A. and most other industrialized nations in the twentieth century.

By far, the biggest change has been the growth of a standard that Reiss (1960, 1967, 1980) called "permissiveness with affection," in which PS is seen as acceptable for couples who have mutually affectionate relationships. This standard has grown in popularity in the U.S.A. as the double standard—the view that PS is acceptable for males but not females—has declined (Clayton and Bokemeier 1980; Reiss 1967, 1980). By 1980, a majority of adults as well as young people in the U.S.A. believed that PS is appropriate for couples involved together in a serious relationship (Glenn and Weaver 1979). Moreover, although there has been a historical tendency for males to be more permissive about PS than females, these gender differences have been diminishing in recent decades (Clayton and Bokemeier 1980).

Circumstances of Adolescent Sexual Experiences

Most research on adolescent sexuality has tended to focus on whether or not teenagers or college students have had PS intercourse. Although this allows us to provide reasonable estimates of the percentages of Americans who have had PS in various time periods and to track trends in the rate of virginity and nonvirginity, this same focus has frequently led researchers to ignore the circumstances in which adolescent sexuality occurs (Miller and Moore 1990). As a consequence, we cannot be as confident about the trends in several related areas, and many questions about the specific nature of adolescent sexual experiences and relationships remain to be explored.

First Intercourse. A good example of this lack of perspective is provided by the evidence concerning age at first intercourse. The available research indicates that the average age of first intercourse has been declining since 1970. It seems likely that this trend extends back prior to 1970, but the paucity of relevant data from earlier time periods makes such a conclusion highly tentative. As late as that year, only about one quarter of the males and 7 percent of the females who attended college had intercourse prior to age 18 (Simon et al. 1972). In the Zelnik and Kantner studies, the average age for females dropped from 16.5 in 1971 to 16.2 in 1976 (Zelnik et al. 1981). By 1979, the average age of first intercourse for women was 16.2; for males, it was 15.7. Blacks of both genders tended to experience sexarche at slightly younger ages than whites. Females had first partners who were nearly three years older; whereas males had first partners who were about one year older than they (Zelnik and Shah 1983).

In a study of college females in the 1980s, Weis (1983) found the average age of sexarche to be 16.2. A later study of college students found that the average age was 16.5 (Sprecher, Barbee, and Schwartz 1995). It should be noted, however, that persons who attend college may well be more likely to postpone sexual activity. It is conceivable that a trend of declining age at first intercourse is still occurring among populations that do not attend college, and it is possible that teenagers in the 1990s (who have yet to reach the age of college) may also be having intercourse at younger ages.

Intercourse appears to be, at least among whites, the culmination of a sequence of increasing and expanding experiences with kissing, petting, and possibly oral sex (Spanier 1975; Weis 1983). There is some evidence that women who have rehearsed these noncoital activities extensively, and thus gradually learned the processes of sexual interaction, are more likely to report positive reactions to their first intercourse (Weis 1983). Weis (1983) found that there is great variation as to when people go through these stages and how quickly.

Most authors have stressed the negative aspects of first intercourse for females by citing the finding that females are significantly more likely to report negative affective reactions to their first intercourse than males (Koch 1988; Sprecher et al. 1995). However, the available data strongly suggest that the differences between males and females may not be large in magnitude. It is clear that females report a wide range of affect, from strongly positive to strongly negative (Koch 1988; Schwartz 1993; Weis 1983), but it is also clear that many males report experiencing negative reactions as well. In a study of college students, the males were more likely to report experiencing high levels of anxiety, the females were less likely to report experiencing high levels of subjective pleasure, while sizable numbers of both genders reported experiencing guilt (Sprecher et al. 1995). Positive reactions to first intercourse have been found to be related to prior experience with noncoital sexual activities, having an orgasm in that first intercourse encounter, descriptions of the partner as gentle and caring (for females), involvement with the first partner for more than one month prior to first intercourse, continued involvement with the partner following the first intercourse, and situational factors, such as the consumption of alcohol (Schwartz 1993; Sprecher et al. 1995; Weis 1983). Several researchers have reported that age is associated with affective reactions, but Weis (1983) found that age was not as strongly or directly related as the level of prior noncoital experience. Schwartz (1993) also reported that Scandinavian teenagers were more likely to report positive reactions than a group of American adolescents.

Over the past three decades, a convergence of male and female PS behavior has been identified, with females reporting less emotional attachment to their first coital partners than in the past (Hopkins 1977; Kallen and Stephenson 1982; Koch 1988). Yet, there is still a significant difference between the genders, with males reporting more casual relationships and females more intimate relationships with their first partners (Koch 1988).

In the only national study of first intercourse, Zelnik and Shah (1983) found that more than 60 percent of the females were "going with" or engaged to their first partner. Another third described their first partner as a friend. Roughly a third of the males described their first partner as a friend, and 40 percent were "going with" or engaged to their first partner. The males were twice as likely to have their first intercourse with someone they had just met, although few males or females did this (Zelnik and Shah 1983).

Relationship factors have been reported to be associated with affective reactions to the first intercourse. However, the precise nature of this association remains unclear. There is some evidence that involvement with a partner for longer than one month, and continuing involvement following the first intercourse, are associated with positive affective reactions (Sprecher et al. 1995). There is some evidence that females who are "going with" or engaged to their first partner are more likely to experience positive affect (Weis 1983). However, Weis (1983) also found that attributions that the first partner was caring, considerate, and gentle were more strongly related to affective reactions. Moreover, many women who were "going with" or engaged to their first partner, nonetheless, described their partners as uncaring and inconsiderate. It should be noted that each of these studies found so few participants who were married at the time of their first intercourse that no analyses could be done for that relationship category. For example, not one woman in the Weis (1983) study was married at the time of her first intercourse.

Adolescents appear to have many reasons for becoming involved in PS behavior. Motivations most frequently mentioned by a group of college women for becoming involved in their first intercourse experience included (rank-ordered by declining frequency): love-caring, partner pressure, curiosity, both wanted to, alcohol or other drugs, and sexual arousal (Koch 1988). The comparable rank-ordering of motivations by a group of college men included: both wanted to, curiosity, love-caring, sexual arousal, to "get laid," and alcohol/drug use. Women were four times more likely to report partner pressure than men, whereas men were seven times as likely to say they were looking to "get laid" and twice as likely to report sexual arousal as a motivation for sexarche (Koch 1988).

Most American teenagers describe their first intercourse as an "unplanned, spontaneous" event. Only 17 percent of the females and one quarter of the males in a national study said they had planned their first intercourse (Zelnik and Shah 1983). In the same study, less than one half of the males and females used a contraceptive. Those who had their first intercourse at age 18 or older were more likely to use a contraceptive. White women were more likely to have used some form of contraception, but black women were more likely to use a medically prescribed method. Women who described their first intercourse as planned were more likely to have used a contraceptive—fully three quarters of these women did. However, more than two thirds of these women relied on their partners to use a condom or withdrawal. Black women were more likely to use a contraceptive themselves, rather than rely on their partner.

Finally, various aspects of sexarche have been found to be significantly related to later sexual functioning among college students (Koch 1988). Women who had experienced first coitus at an earlier age had less difficulty reaching orgasm during later sexual interactions than did women who had sexarche at a later age. Men with earlier sexarche had less difficulty in keeping an erection during later sexual interactions than men who had been older at sexarche. Also, women who had reported negative reactions to their first intercourse were subsequently more likely than those who felt more positively to experience: lack of sexual interest, sexual repulsion, inability to reach orgasm, or genital discomfort, pain, or vaginal spasms. Men who reacted negatively to their first intercourse were more likely to ejaculate too quickly during later sexual experiences than men who had positive reactions. Both men and women were more likely to experience subsequent sexual functioning concerns when they were pressured by a close partner to engage in intercourse for the first time.

Number of Premarital Sexual Partners. It is difficult to provide good estimates on the number of PS partners prior to 1950, simply because researchers failed to ask such a question. On the other hand, it does seem clear that the increase in the percentage of American women who reported they had ever had PS after 1900 was due primarily to an increase in the percentage of women who reported they had PS only with their fiance (Kinsey et al. 1953; Terman 1938). In contrast, there is abundant evidence of a significant increase in the number of PS coital partners for females from the late 1960s through the late 1980s (Cannon and Long 1971; Clayton and Bokemeier 1980; Miller and Moore 1990; Vener and Stewart 1974; Zelnik et al. 1983). This finding is, however, potentially misleading. A close inspection of the results of pertinent studies reveals that most of the increase is explained by a shift from zero to one partner and from one to two partners. There were no increases in the percentage with seven or more partners.

Among males, there is some evidence that adolescent boys of recent decades are less likely to use the services of a prostitute than in the past (Cannon and Long 1971). In a unique study of males attending the same eastern university from the 1940s through the 1970s, Finger (1975) actually reported a decline in the number of PS partners with a corresponding increase in the frequency of sexual relations. This was primarily due to an increase in the percentage of men who had PS only with their girlfriends. Finger also reported a decline in the percentage of males reporting they ever had a homosexual experience. However, among those who had a homosexual experience, the frequency of such encounters had increased.

Although there appears to be consistent evidence that there have been significant increases in the number of PS partners throughout this century, at least for females, it should be stressed that, as late as 1990, the majority of American teens had had zero or one PS partner. Only 4 percent of white females, 6 percent of black females, 11 percent of white males, and 23 percent of black males reported six or more partners (Miller and Moore 1990). Thus, the widely held idea that large percentages of American adolescents are now "promiscuous" is greatly exaggerated.

Rates of Teen Pregnancy and Birth. In an examination of how the trends we have been reviewing are related to trends in adolescent pregnancy and birth, it is important to bear in mind that, as late as 1965, several states in the U.S.A. prohibited the sale of contraceptives to married couples. Such laws banning the sale of contraceptives to teenagers and/or single persons were common until 1977 (see Section 9A). Details on out-of-wedlock births, contraception, and abortion are presented later. Here, we want to note that the birthrate among unmarried women has been increasing since 1965, with a notable surge in the rate during the 1980s (Baldwin 1980; Forrest and Fordyce 1988; Miller and Moore 1990). Throughout this period, the percentage of unmarried, adolescent women exposed to the risk of pregnancy has been increasing. One principal reason for this is, of course, the increasing percentage of unmarried persons having PS in the U.S.A. (Forrest and Fordyce 1988).

However, there are several interesting twists among these trends, many of which do not fit with the conventional wisdom in the U.S.A. First, much of the increase since 1980 is attributable to women 20 years of age or older. In fact, the adolescent birthrate has actually been declining since the early 1970s (Baldwin 1980; Forrest and Fordyce 1988). Second, the overall birthrate for adolescent women increased through the late 1940s and 1950s, remained stable in the 1960s, increased in the early 1970s, and has been declining since (Baldwin 1980). The misperception, widespread through the U.S.A., that teen-pregnancy rates have been rising is largely due to two factors: (1) the increasing number of such pregnancies, but not the rate, when the children of the baby-boomer generation began having children, and (2) the fact that, as the average age at first marriage has been increasing, adolescent pregnancies are more likely to occur with unmarried women (Baldwin 1980; Miller and Moore 1990). Finally, the perception that adolescent pregnancy has become a recent social problem has emerged as the out-of-wedlock birthrate has increased more dramatically among white women in the last two decades (Baldwin 1980; Miller and Moore 1990).

Contraceptive Use. To most Americans, an increase in the rate of adolescent pregnancy (widely assumed, though not true) would seem to be an inevitable result of increases in PS activity. However, research in many European countries demonstrates that high rates of adolescent sexual activity can be associated with low rates of adolescent pregnancy, when contraceptives are used widely, consistently, and effectively (Jones et al. 1985). There seems little doubt that the U.S.A. has one of the highest adolescent-pregnancy rates among developed nations, largely because of inconsistent contraceptive use (Forrest and Fordyce 1988; Miller and Moore 1990).

It appears that roughly one half of adolescent women use no contraceptive during their first intercourse (Miller and Moore 1990), and most of the women reporting the use of some contraceptive during their first intercourse note that their partner used a condom (Weis 1983). Moreover, most adolescent girls who seek contraceptive services have been having sexual intercourse for some time, many for more than a year before they seek services (Miller and Moore 1990; Settlage, Baroff, and Cooper 1973). After this delay, it appears that roughly two thirds of American teenagers now use some form of contraceptive (Miller and Moore 1990).

Although these figures certainly indicate that large numbers of American youths continue to experience sexual intercourse with no contraceptive protection, they nonetheless represent an increase in contraceptive use over the last several decades. Research in the early 1970s indicated that two thirds to three quarters of American teens rarely or never used contraceptives (Sorensen 1973; Zelnik et al. 1981). Forrest and Fordyce (1988) report that overall use of medically sound contraceptives remained stable through the 1980s. Of those women age 20 or less who sought family-planning services in 1980, nearly three quarters used the pill. By 1990, this had dropped to 52 percent. In 1980, 14 percent had used no contraceptive at all (Eckard 1982).

By 1990, Peterson (1995) reported that 31.5 percent of 15- to 19-year-old women consistently used some form of contraceptive; 24.3 percent of 15- to 17-year-olds did so, as did 41.2 percent of 18- and 19-year-olds. This behavior appears to be unrelated to social class (Settlage et al. 1973). Among women of childbearing age (15 to 44), Peterson (1995) found that 52.2 percent of Hispanic, 60.5 percent of white non-Hispanic, and 58.7 percent of black non-Hispanic women reported using some form of contraceptive (see Table 6 in Section 9A under current contraceptive behavior).

Despite the popularity of the idea that adolescent pregnancy is a result of poor sexual knowledge, knowledge of one's sexuality or birth control has not been shown to be a strong predictor of contraceptive behavior among teenagers (Byrne and Fisher 1983). No relationship was found between contraceptive use and early sex education by family, or a congruence between attitudes and behavior. Reiss, Banwart, and Foreman (1975), however, reported that contraceptive use among teenagers is correlated with endorsement of sexual choice (permissiveness), self-confidence about desirability, and involvement in an intimate relationship.

Explanations of Adolescent Sexuality

Of course, researchers are not content to provide descriptions of social trends. Instead, they seek to provide theoretically useful explanations of the factors underlying those trends. The essence of scientific analysis is the identification and testing of potential correlates of those trends. There have been thousands of studies of adolescent sexuality testing possible correlates. We cannot review them all here. We will, however, briefly identify several different approaches that have been used to explain the trends we have described above. We have tried to select perspectives that have enjoyed some popularity among sexuality professionals at some point. We have also tried to include explanatory models that represent the diversity of professional opinions about adolescent sexuality.

Changes in Social Institutions. By far, the most common approach to explaining the growing acceptance of PS within American culture and the increasing tendency of adolescents to have PS has been a sociological perspective that locates these trends as part of a series of social changes occurring in response to industrialization and urbanization. (Much of this explanation was presented in Section 1, where we reviewed the sexual history of the U.S.A.) As patterns of residence and community relations changed in the late nineteenth and early twentieth centuries, changes began to occur in most social institutions. These included changes in male-female roles, a lengthening of the period of formal education, and the emergence of new forms of heterosexual courtship (Ehrmann 1964; Reiss 1967, 1976). One example of the complex web of social changes that have occurred in the last century is the increasing average age of first marriage (Surra 1990). In one century, the average age at first marriage has shifted from the late teens to the mid-20s. Combined with the earlier age at which American adolescents reach puberty, this has led to a much longer period between physical maturation and marriage, thus, greatly expanding the probability that sexual activity will occur prior to marriage.

As social institutions changed in response to the growing industrial character of American society and the increasingly urban pattern of residence, new forms of adolescent courtship emerged. The custom of dating appeared in the 1920s following World War I, and the practice of "going steady" emerged in the 1940s following World War II (Reiss 1980). By the 1990s, the practice of "going together" has become so universally common that few American young people can conceive of other courtship forms. Dating provided a forum for adolescents to pursue male-female relationships independent of adult supervision and control. The appearance of modern transportation, such as the automobile, and the development of urban recreational businesses allowed adolescents to interact with each other away from home. Increasingly, decisions about appropriate sexual behavior were made by adolescents themselves. The practice of "going steady" placed adolescents into a relationship with many of the features of marriage. Steady relationships were defined as monogamous and exclusive with respect to sexuality and intimacy. As such, they carried high potential for intimacy, commitment, and feelings of love. Together, the increased independence and greater potential for intimacy led to increased rates of PS behavior (D'Emilio and Freedman 1988; Kinsey et al. 1948, 1953; Seidman 1991). There is evidence that this general pattern has occurred in other countries as a consequence of industrialization as well (Jones et al. 1985).

Reiss (1960, 1967) developed the Autonomy Theory of Premarital Permissiveness, mentioned earlier, to explain the association between social institutions and premarital sexual permissiveness. Essentially, Reiss maintained that, as adolescent courtship institutions (dating and going steady) become independent of adult institutions of social control (parental supervision, the schools, and the church), the level of premarital permissiveness in a culture increases. There has been considerable research testing the specific propositions of the theory since Reiss proposed it (Cannon and Long 1971; Clayton and Bokemeier 1980; Miller and Moore 1990).

Generally, research from this perspective has tended to presume that PS has become normative within American culture.

Sources of Sexual Information and Sexual Knowledge. Several other explanations of PS behavior have been more likely to view it as a social problem and more likely to focus on the individual character of PS attitudes and behavior. One of the more popular and enduring ideas within American culture about adolescent sexual activity is the belief that sexual behavior and pregnancy risk are influenced by knowledge about sexuality and its consequences. In fact, advocates of sex education in the schools have argued for more than a century that American teens typically possess inadequate and inaccurate sexual knowledge. Some have maintained that sex education could solve such social problems as out-of-wedlock pregnancy and sexually transmitted disease by providing thorough and accurate information about sexuality. Embedded in these assertions is an underlying presumption that sexual decision making and behavior are primarily cognitive processes. Operating from this perspective, there have been dozens of studies of the sources of sexual information for children and adolescents in the U.S.A. Generally, these studies have found that young people in the U.S.A. are more likely to receive sexual information from their peers or the mass media than from adult sources, such as parents or the school (Spanier 1975; Wilson 1994). These studies have been used to conclude that peers are a poor source of sexual information, and that such inaccurate information leads directly to unwanted pregnancies and disease. We should note here that few studies of sexual information have sought to demonstrate a correlation between source of information and sexual decisions or outcomes. That connection has typically been assumed. (See also Section 3, which deals with formal and informal sources of sexual knowledge and education.)

However, in a national probability study of American college students, Spanier (1975; 1978) found no differences in premarital sexual behavior between those students who had ever had a sex-education course and those who had not—regardless of who taught the course, when it was offered, or what material was included. Moreover, a number of studies have found a weak correlation between sexual knowledge and sexual behavior or contraceptive use (Byrne and Fisher 1983). More generally, researchers have consistently found a low correlation between knowledge level and a variety of health-related behaviors, such as smoking, drug use, and eating patterns (Kirby 1985).

Cognitive Development. A somewhat similar focus on cognitive processes has been the basis for an argument that adolescents typically lack a sufficient level of cognitive development required for effective sexual decisions. A number of authors have argued that adolescence is characterized by a cognitive level that is inconsistent with sound sexual decision-making and contraceptive use (Cobliner 1974; Cvetkovich, Grote, Bjorseth, and Sarkissian 1975). Within this perspective, it has become common to describe adolescents as having an unreal sense of infallibility that leads them to underestimate the actual risks of sexual experience (Miller and Moore 1990).

Although references to the works of Jean Piaget have been common in this realm, actual empirical tests of a correlation between Piaget's stages of cognitive development and sexual decisions remain to be conducted. Moreover, this explanation has failed to incorporate the cross-cultural evidence that adolescents in many other nations establish high rates of sexual frequency, maintain consistent contraceptive use, and experience low rates of adolescent pregnancy (Jones et al. 1985).

Interaction of Hormonal and Social Determinants. Udry (1990) has attempted to examine how pubertal development, hormones, and social processes may interact to affect the sexual behavior of adolescents. Hormonal studies seem to indicate that androgenic hormones at puberty directly contribute to explaining sexual motivation and noncoital sexual behaviors in Caucasian male and female adolescents (Udry and Billy 1987; Udry et al. 1985, 1986). Because of the differing social encouragement versus constraints for young white males and females, initiation of coitus seems to be strongly hormone dependent for males, whereas for females it seems to be strongly influenced by a wide variety of social sources with no identifiable hormone predictors. The interaction of hormonal and social determinants is unclear for African-American youth and does not fit the models for white youth that emphasize the importance of sociocultural context on sexual behavior.

Delinquency Models. Perhaps the zenith of models which regard adolescent sexuality as a social problem is the emergence of frameworks that explicitly define adolescent sexual behavior as a form of juvenile delinquency (Jessor and Jessor 1977; Miller and Moore 1990). Vener and Stewart (1974) reported that sexual behavior by 15- and 16-year-olds was correlated with the use of cigarettes, alcohol, and illicit drugs, and with less approval for traditional institutions like the police, the school, and religion.

In a subsequent study using this perspective, Jessor and Jessor (1977) conceptualized sexual behavior as a "problem behavior" if it occurred prior to age-appropriate norms. In other words, intercourse was characterized as deviant and delinquent if it occurred prior to the mean age (roughly 17 years of age at the time of the study). Jessor and Jessor found that such early sexual behavior was correlated with other "problem behaviors" such as alcohol use, illicit-drug consumption, and political protest. They concluded that these associations demonstrated that adolescents tend to exhibit multiple forms of delinquency.

By the 1990s, Miller and Moore (1990) reported that a number of studies have found that "early" sexual behavior is associated with a variety of "criminal" behaviors such as those described above. Some authors have overlooked the fact that these studies have found this association with delinquent behaviors only for early sexual behavior and have tended to characterize all adolescent sexual behavior as delinquent. These studies do suggest the possibility that developmental issues may be relevant to these findings.

Sexual Affect. A different approach has been taken by a group of researchers interested in examining the role of affective reactions to sexual stimulation, both as a factor that may influence sexual decisions and behavior and as an outcome of sexual experience. Sorensen (1973) reported that 71 percent of teenagers agreed with the view that using the birth-control pill indicates that a girl is planning to have sex. This has been offered as evidence that adolescents are unwilling or unable to accept responsibility for contraceptive use, and thus lack cognitive development. However, affective theorists would argue that it is just as likely that sexual guilt, fear, or embarrassment prevent such a decision.

In the early 1960s, Christensen (1962) conceptualized sexual guilt as a variable response to sexual experience. He found that adolescents are more likely to report experiencing guilt in cultures with restrictive PS norms. He called this a value-behavior discrepancy. Schwartz (1973) found that persons with high sex guilt retain less information in a birth-control lecture, especially when aroused by a sexually stimulating condition. In the Schwartz study, females retained more information than males across all conditions.

Donn Byrne and his associates have maintained that individuals can be placed on a continuum ranging from erotophilic, reacting to sexual stimuli with strongly positive emotions, to erotophobic, reacting to sexual stimuli with strongly negative emotions. Erotophobic persons have been shown to be less likely to seek contraceptive information, to have lower levels of contraceptive knowledge, and to be less likely to purchase contraceptives or use those contraceptive methods that require them to touch themselves (Byrne and Fisher 1983; Goldfarb, Gerrard, Gibbons, and Plante 1988). However, they are no less likely to retain information about contraceptives, even though they become more sexually aroused by a lecture (Goldfarb et al. 1988).

There is a need for much future research on the association between adolescent sexuality and affective variables. However, the studies just mentioned suggest that affective variables may prove to be a fruitful way of explaining adolescent sexual behavior and its consequences. This approach seems particularly suited to examining the variety of ways that adolescents behave and the diverse consequences of such behavior.

Reference Group. Yet another approach to explaining adolescent sexuality has been the attempt to identify persons or groups who have influenced teenagers. Perhaps the most developed theoretical perspective of this type is known as Reference Group Theory. There is some evidence that, as adolescents progress from age 12 to 16, they shift their primary reference-group identification from their parents to their peers. Peer orientation has been shown to be related to sexual intercourse. Moreover, association with peers who are seen as approving PS is correlated with PS permissiveness and PS behavior (Cannon and Long 1971; Clayton and Bokemeier 1980; Floyd and South 1972; Reiss 1967; Teevan 1972). Similarly, Fisher (1986) found that the correlation between the attitudes of teenagers and their parents decreased as adolescence progressed. However, females who cited their mothers as their major source of sexual information were less likely to engage in intercourse and more likely to use contraceptives when they did.

These results should not be interpreted to mean that parents or families do not or cannot exert influence on the sexuality of adolescents. There have been relatively few scientific studies of the influence of differing parental styles and the PS behavior of children. One study (Miller, McCoy, Olson, and Wallace 1986) found that adolescents were least likely to have PS or to approve of PS when their parents were moderately strict. Teenagers who described their parents as very strict or not at all strict were more likely to have had PS. This correlation also held when parents were asked to describe the rules they set for their children. There is some evidence that the age of a mother's first intercourse is related to the age of her daughter's first intercourse (Miller and Moore 1990). Miller and Moore (1990) also showed that girls from single-parent families tend to have sex at younger ages.

Thus, there appears to be two conflicting sets of empirical findings. One set of studies finds evidence that adolescent sexuality is most strongly related to peer influences, especially as age increases. Another set of studies provides evidence that families and parents can exert influence in various ways. Obviously, important questions remain to be resolved.

Rehearsal. A more direct perspective views adolescent sexuality as a developmental process, in which intercourse is seen as the culmination of a sequence of progressively sexual behaviors (Miller and Moore 1990; Simon et al. 1972; Weis 1983). Adolescents appear to move through a series of stages, from kissing to petting of the female's breasts to genital petting to intercourse. There is evidence that, among white adolescents, this pattern is strongly consistent. White adolescents appear to take an average of two years to move through this sequence (Miller and Moore 1990; Weis 1983). In contrast, blacks appear to move through the stages more quickly, and there is greater variability in the actual sequence of behaviors (Miller and Moore 1990). Within this perspective, each subsequent sexual behavior can be viewed as a rehearsal for the next behavior in the sequence.

Not only is there evidence that adolescent sexual experience is acquired in a process that produces an escalating and expanding repertoire of sexual behaviors, but dating and "going steady" appear to serve as the key social contexts in which this process occurs (Clayton and Bokemeier 1980; Reiss 1967; Spanier 1975). The age of onset of dating and the frequency of dating appear to be major factors in the emergence of sexual behavior (Spanier 1975). In fact, adolescent experiences with intimate relationships (dating and "going steady") and the sequencing of sexual behaviors have been shown to be more influential in predicting PS intercourse than general social background variables, parental conservatism or liberalism, or religiosity (Herold and Goodwin 1981; Spanier 1975).

As dating frequency and noncoital experiences increase, exposure to eroticism, sexual knowledge, and interest in sex are all likely to increase concomitantly. Male behavior appears to be more strongly related to the sequencing of behaviors. In contrast, female behavior seems to be more a result of involvement in affectionate relationships. Increased dating interaction and frequency increase sexual intimacy, since opportunities and desire increase. This process is likely to overshadow the influence of prior religious, parental, or peer influences. Thus, adolescent courtship provides the context for the general process of sexual interaction. As Reiss (1967, 1980) has noted, such adolescent courtship also serves as a rehearsal experience for adult patterns of intimate involvement. It is also possible that such adolescent rehearsal experiences are a more powerful and direct explanation of adolescent sexual behavior (Spanier 1975; Weis 1983).

Multivariate Causal Models. An important trend in American research on adolescent sexuality has been the growing recognition that several of the factors reviewed here will eventually need to be included in a sound theory of adolescent sexual development and expression. Reiss (1967) was one of the first to test competing hypotheses in an attempt to identify the strongest predictors of PS permissiveness. Since then, a number of researchers have used multivariate techniques to examine the relative strength of PS correlates (Byrne and Fisher 1983; Christopher and Cate 1988; DeLamater and MacCorquodale 1979; Herold and Goodwin 1981; Reiss et al. 1975; Udry 1990; Udry, Tolbert, and Morris 1986; Weis 1983).

A few examples should illustrate the potential usefulness of this multivariate approach. Herold and Goodwin (1981) found that the best predictors of the transition from virginity to nonvirginity for females were perceived peer experience with PS, involvement in a steady, "committed" relationship, and religiosity. In contrast, parental education, grade-point average, sex education, and dating frequency failed to enter the multivariate equation.

Udry and his associates (1990; Udry et al. 1986) have investigated the relative influence of hormonal and social variables in explaining adolescent sexual behavior. Several studies demonstrate that androgenic hormones present at puberty directly contribute to the sexual motivation and precoital sexual behavior of white males. For white males, the initiation of coitus seems to be strongly related to androgen levels. Female initiation of coitus seems, on the other hand, to be strongly related to a series of social variables, but not to any hormonal predictors. Udry has argued that these results reflect the differing social encouragement versus constraints placed on males and females respectively. Interestingly, the behavior of African-American youth does not appear to fit with these same explanations, so that the exact interaction between social factors and hormonal variables remains unclear.

Adolescent Sexual Relationships: The Neglected Research

Before moving to the issue of adult heterosexuality, we wish to make a few comments about the nature of intimacy in adolescent sexual relationships and the process of relationship formation. Most of the research on adolescent sexuality reviewed here has tended to focus on the specifically and explicitly sexual elements of such experiences and to ignore the broader relational aspects. In one sense, this is understandable, given the fact that Americans have generally viewed adolescent sexuality, especially its premarital forms, as a social problem. Consistent with this perspective, Americans have tended to deny the possibility that any genuine intimacy occurs in sexual experiences involving adolescents. This is unfortunate in at least two respects. First, it tends to ignore the fact that most adolescent sexual encounters in the U.S.A. occur within the context of what the participants define as a meaningful, intimate relationship. It also ignores the reality that sexual expression within loving, intimate relationships (rather than marital status) has become the dominant attitudinal standard for Americans of all ages. Second, the tendency to ignore the relational character of adolescent sexuality means that researchers have tended to overlook the reality that patterns of sexual and intimate interactions are largely learned within the context of adolescent experiences, and these are likely to be extended well into adulthood. Thus, the failure to investigate these larger relational questions probably impairs our ability to fully understand adult intimate relationships as well. This is not meant to denigrate other forms of sexual expression or to deny that other forms of expression do occur, both in adolescence and later. Rather, it is to suggest that one strong characteristic of American sexuality is the tendency to associate love and sexuality. Any attempt to understand or explain American sexual expression must acknowledge that it generally occurs within the context of ongoing, intimate relationships. This is as true for adolescents as for adults.

The separation of sexuality and relational concerns is well reflected by the emergence of two independent bodies of research within the American academy. On the one hand, there is a well-established field of research on the formation of adolescent intimate relationships, dating and courtship, and mate selection. This tradition extends back to the 1920s and has largely been explored by family sociologists. Social exchange theory has become the dominant perspective in this tradition in recent decades. Surra (1990) provides an excellent review of such research through the 1980s. However, this tradition has largely failed to consider sexuality as an issue in courtship and mate selection, although it ought to be apparent that sexual dynamics and processes are key components of adolescent attraction, dating, courtship, and mate selection. Sexuality carries the potential both for increasing intimacy between teenagers or young adults and for creating intense relationship conflict and, possibly, termination. Yet, Surra's (1990) review is notable precisely for the fact that there is not one single citation of a study including sexuality variables. This is not an indictment of Surra per se. Her goal was to review the field of mate selection as it stood at the beginning of the 1990s. Her assessment serves to document that researchers in this area continue to ignore the role of sexuality in adolescent relationship processes after seven decades of empirical research.

This tendency to ignore sexuality within the courtship process is unfortunate, because of the growing evidence that one of the major influences on PS behavior is the intimate relationship in which most adolescent sexual activity occurs. Being involved in a loving and caring relationship increases the probability of a decision to engage in intercourse (Christopher and Cate 1985) and contributes to sustained activity once it begins (DeLamater and MasCorquodale 1979; Peplau, Rubin, and Hill 1977). In fact, most adolescent sexual experiences in the U.S.A., especially for females, occur within the context of an ongoing intimate relationship. It does appear, however, that as the general rates of PS have increased and as the average age of first intercourse have declined throughout this century, intercourse has tended to occur at earlier stages in a relationship (Bell and Chaskes 1970; Christensen and Carpenter 1962; Christensen and Gregg 1970). With respect to attitudes, Americans are more likely to approve of PS in the context of a relationship. This permissiveness-with-affection-and/or-commitment standard has increasingly become the norm for both adults and young people (Christensen and Carpenter 1962; Christensen and Gregg 1970; Reiss 1960, 1967).

A second body of research examining the formation of sexual relationships has begun to emerge in recent decades. Much of this work has been done by biologists or evolutionary social psychologists and extends a model of mammalian mating first presented by Beach (1976). We discuss it here because it also reflects the separation of the sexual and intimate domains of relationships, and because much of the pertinent human research has been done with samples of college students. Essentially, this body of work forms the foundation for what might be called female selection theory.

The traditional view had always been that males are the aggressors and initiators of sexual involvement. From this perspective, females were seen as sexual "gatekeepers." Their role supposedly was to regulate male access by accepting or rejecting male advances (Perper 1985; Perper and Weis 1987). Beginning with Beach (1976), a growing number of researchers have provided evidence that this traditional view is highly flawed. Instead, females select desirable partners and initiate sexual interaction by proceptively signaling selected males (Fisher 1992; Givens 1978; Moore 1985; Moore and Butler 1989; Perper 1985; Perper and Weis 1987). Males, in turn, respond to these proceptive signals. Moore (1985; Moore and Butler 1989) has demonstrated that, not only do women use such signaling, but that men are more likely to "approach" women who do. Perper (1985; Perper and Weis 1987) has provided evidence that American women employ a variety of complex strategies to arouse male interest and response. Finally, Jesser (1978) has provided some evidence that males are just as likely to accept direct initiations from women as they are to respond to more covert strategies, although females tend to believe that men are "turned off" by female sexual assertiveness.

This new line of research raises fundamental questions about the roles of males and females in the formation and maintenance of sexual relationships—for both adolescents and adults. It indicates a need for research that is focused on the dynamics within and the processes of sexual relationships themselves. As just one example, Christopher and Cate (1988) found that, early in a relationship, the level of conflict was positively related to a greater likelihood of intercourse. As the relationship progressed, love and relationship satisfaction eventually became significant predictors of sexual involvement. In the case of adolescence, we need to move beyond "social bookkeeping," counting the number of American teenagers who have PS, to examine what actually happens in their relationships with each other.

C. Adult Heterosexuality

DAVID L. WEIS

The National Health and Social Life Survey

Strangely, there has been considerably more research on the sexual conduct of American adolescents than of adults, and much of the existing research on adults has tended to focus on sexual "problems" such as extramarital sex (ES) and sexual dysfunction (see Section 12 on sex dysfunctions and therapies). There has been little research on the patterns of sexual interactions within nonclinical marital relationships. This is striking, precisely because of the fact that marriage is the most widely accepted setting for sexual relations in the U.S.A. and because more than 90 percent of Americans do marry. Taken together, the preponderance of research on adolescent sexuality, ES, and dysfunction indicates the tendency of American sexuality professionals to focus on sexual behaviors that have been defined as social problems, rather than on "normal" sexuality.

In October 1994, a national survey of adult sexual practices was released with great media fanfare (Laumann, Gagnon, Michael, and Michaels 1994). The survey, titled the *National Health and Social Life Survey* (NHSLS), randomly sampled 3,432 persons, aged 18 to 50. It was touted as the most comprehensive American sex survey ever, and the first national study of adult sexuality. However, Reiss (1995) has noted that this claim is misleading, as there have been more than a dozen national surveys of a more-limited scope. Given our interest in reviewing the nature of American sexuality research, it is interesting to note that the survey was originally planned and approved as a government-sponsored project. Funding was denied for this project and a similar study of teens (the Udry study) when conservatives in the U.S. Congress objected to the studies. Conservatives argued that the government should not use taxpayer money to study private matters like oral sex—clearly rejecting the significance of the health concerns involved. The researchers found private funding instead. Also interesting is the fact that conservatives hailed the findings when the study was released (Peterson 1994).

There is little doubt that the NHSLS is the most comprehensive study of adult sexuality to date, with literally hundreds of variables assessed. Among the key findings are the following:

- Most Americans report that they are satisfied with their sex life—even those who rarely have sex. Among married persons, 87 percent reported they were satisfied with their sex life.
- For the entire sample, 30 percent of men and 26 percent of women have sex two or three times a week; 36 percent of men and 37 percent of women have sex a few times a month; and 27 percent of men and 30 percent of women have sex a few times a year. Married persons have sex more often than single people, and persons who are cohabiting have sex more often than marrieds.
- Approximately 80 percent of married women and 65 percent of married men have never had ES. The majority of those who are cohabiting also have never "cheated." The group most likely to have extradyadic sex is unmarried men, aged 42 to 51, who have lived with a woman for three years or less (32 percent).
- There has been a slight increase in the number of lifetime sexual partners, largely because people now have intercourse earlier, marry later, and are more likely to get divorced.
- Among marrieds, 94 percent had sex only with their spouse in the last year; 75 percent of cohabiting persons had sex only with their partner in the last year. About 80 percent of American adults have had either one or no sexual partners in the last year. Only 3 percent have had five or more partners in the last year. About 50 percent of men and 30 percent of women have had 5 or more partners since age 18.
- Most Americans have a fairly limited sexual "menu" of activities. Roughly 80 percent of both men and women reported that sexual intercourse is very appealing; only 50 percent of men and 33 percent of women find receiving oral sex appealing; 37 percent of men and 19

percent of women describe giving oral sex as appealing. About 25 percent of both men and women have tried anal sex at least once.

- People who already have an active sex life with a current sexual partner are more likely to masturbate. Among married people, 57 percent of husbands and 37 percent of wives have masturbated in the last year.
- About 2.8 percent of men and 1.4 percent of women identified themselves as homosexual or bisexual. Only 9 percent of men and 4 percent of women reported ever having a homosexual experience. These rates are considerably higher in the twelve largest U.S. cities.
- Most heterosexuals are not at risk of contracting AIDS, because they are not part of social networks with high risk.

The NHSLS has sparked considerable controversy among sexuality professionals. Questions have been raised, primarily about the legitimacy of the prevalence estimates for such behaviors as number of sexual partners, homosexual experience, and ES. In general, the NHSLS estimates tend to be lower than those found in most prior sex research—including prior national studies (Billy, Tanfer, Grady, and Klepinger 1993). It should be noted that the NHSLS estimates are remarkably similar to findings in a series of studies conducted by the National Opinion Research Center using similar national probability samples (Davis and Smith 1994; Greeley et al., 1990; Smith 1990, 1991). These national samples have been carefully constructed to be representative of gender, age, race, education, marital status, size of city of residence, and religion in the U.S.A. The NHSLS did obtain a 79 percent response rate, probably because participants were financially reimbursed. Few prior studies have had comparable response rates, and few have reimbursed participants. Questions about how this impacted the results are a legitimate matter for future research.

In a review of the NHSLS, Reiss (1995) credits the study for its comprehensiveness, the richness of the data generated, the theoretical nature of the investigation, and the high quality of the sampling techniques. However, he also raises several questions that may influence the validity of the findings. Here, we will focus on a few of the more serious. One concerns the fact that 21 percent of the respondents were interviewed with someone else present during the interview. As Reiss notes, a person with an intimate partner or a family member present may well have answered questions differently for obvious reasons. For example, only 5 percent of persons interviewed with another person present reported that they had two or more sexual partners in the last year. In contrast, 17 percent of those interviewed with no one else present reported two or more partners in the last year. This is a sizable difference, and it raises questions about the validity of responses to many questions in the survey. Similarly, the NHSLS asked respondents to report the number of sexual partners they have had since age 18. Most previous studies asked respondents to report their lifetime number of sexual partners. Here, one half of the sample did have sexual relations prior to age 18. This reduced estimates for lifetime number of partners. The NHSLS reported a median number of six sexual partners for men and and two for women. Reiss notes that these estimates are lower than comparable studies (Billy et al., 1993), and that this reported gender difference cannot possibly be true in the real world.

To this critique, we can add that it is possible that prevalence estimates have been inflated by the volunteer bias of most sex research. There are unexamined questions about the effects of volunteer bias and response rates. Paul Gebhard (1993), a member of the original Kinsey research team, has argued that estimates of lifetime prevalence rates for homosexual behavior have been remarkably similar when adjusted for sampling weaknesses. Gebhard also criticized the NORC and NHSLS studies for failing to use trained sex researchers to conduct their interviews, and for their own sampling flaws that overrepresented rural populations. In fairness, it is appropriate to note that several of the volunteer samples overrepresent urban populations, and there is evidence that urban-rural differences in sexual attitudes remain substantial (Weis and Jurich 1985). Finally, although there is a general consensus that persons who agree to participate in sex research are more permissive and more sexually experienced, two recent studies strongly suggest that persons who decline to answer particular items in a sex survey are attempting to hide behavior in which they have engaged (Wiederman 1993; Wiederman, Weis, and Allgeier 1994).

Although these questions will require considerable future research to resolve, it should be acknowledged that the NHSLS is a major contribution to the field of sex research in the U.S.A. It is a landmark study with important new information about the sexual practices of the vast and diverse American adult population, and it will set the parameters for questions yet to be explored. Finally, it provides important data on each of the topics we will explore further in this section.

Sexuality and Single Adults

Practically every American spends at least a portion of his or her adult life unmarried. At any one point in time, more than 20 percent of the U.S. population is single, and this percentage has been increasing for several decades (Francoeur 1991; Shostak 1987). The chief reasons for this are the greater tendency to postpone marriage (median age is now in the late 20s), the increasing divorce rate (5 per 1,000 by the 1980s and fairly stable thereafter), and the increasing rate of cohabitation (which tripled since 1960), both as an alternative to marriage and as a form of courtship prior to marriage (Glick 1984; Norton and Moorman 1987; Shostak 1987). Glick (1984) has speculated that the prolongation of formal education, the increasing acceptability of premarital sexuality, the growing independence of women, and the earlier mortality of males may also be factors promoting the growth of singlehood.

Actually, the single adult population contains three groups who may share little in common: Those who have never married, those who have divorced, and those who are widowed. Persons within each group may or may not have chosen to be single, and they may or may not intend to remain single. Also, persons in each group may be living alone, may be living with roommates who are not intimate or sexual partners, or may be cohabiting with an intimate partner. By 1980, it was estimated that close to 2 percent of the adult U.S. population was cohabiting (Glick and Norton 1977; Yllo 1978). Of course, some single persons are gay or lesbian, although they are not typically included in estimates of cohabitation, even when they live with their partners.

It should be stressed that the population of single adults is a fluid one. The U.S.A. has high rates of marriage, divorce, and remarriage (Glick 1984; Norton and Moorman 1987). Most of those who are classified as having never married at any one point will eventually marry. This is especially true for the growing group who have remained unmarried well past the age of 20. Approximately three quarters of women who get divorced, and more men, eventually remarry (Glick 1984; Norton and Moorman 1987). Thus, the composition of the single population is always shifting as some marry and others divorce or are widowed. We are not aware of any research examining the impact of this shifting character on the sexual lifestyles of single persons. Some singles become involved in intimate relationships that lead to cohabitation or marriage, although we know little about whether these processes are similar to adolescent courtship. For those singles who are not involved in an ongoing intimate relationship, it is possible that finding sexual partners can be problematic.

It is popularly believed that being single in adulthood has become more acceptable in the U.S.A. today. There is, however, some evidence that married couples continue to associate primarily with other couples. Certainly, it is more acceptable to be sexually active while single today. Singles have greater social and sexual freedom than ever before to pursue a variety of lifestyles. In fact, the labeling of a category of "single adults" may serve to obscure the fact that the range of sexual and intimate lifestyle options is just as wide as for married persons.

Despite the large number of single adults in the U.S.A., there has been virtually no research on the sexual practices or attitudes of these groups. The NHSLS (Laumann et al. 1994) did distinguish between "single" and cohabiting respondents, an important distinction. As we discussed earlier, the NHSLS did find that "single" persons had sex less frequently than married persons, and that cohabiting persons had sex more often than married persons.

The Never Married. We know of no research that has focused on the population of never-married adults who are not cohabiting. Of course, this group does include persons in their early 20s who have yet to marry. A portion of that group is included in many of the studies of premarital sexuality, although that group is not isolated for separate analysis. There is virtually no scientific information on how never-married persons find or meet sexual partners, establish sexual encounters, or maintain sexual relationships.

Divorced (Postmarital Sex). Divorce has increased in the U.S.A. dramatically throughout the twentieth century (Berscheid 1983). The rate has leveled since 1980 (*Current Population Reports* 1985; Glick 1984; Norton and Moorman 1987; Shostak 1987). Of the roughly 40 percent of the American population that gets divorced, about 70 percent eventually remarry, often within a few years (Glick 1984; Norton and Moorman 1987).

Again, there has been little research on this group. It appears that about 80 percent of women, and nearly all men, remain sexually active following a divorce (Gebhard 1968; Hunt 1974). Most persons have sex with a new partner within the first year following a divorce (Hunt, 1974). In the 1970s, Hunt (1974) reported that divorced women averaged four sexual partners a year, and had a higher frequency of orgasm in their postmarital sex than they had had in their marriage. Men averaged nearly eight partners a year.

Again, there has been little research on the process by which divorced persons form or maintain sexual relationships. However, it is fair to suggest that, as the title of an American novel and corresponding movie implies, most divorced persons find that they must "start over." After a period of marriage, they find themselves in the position of dating and courting again. Some have anecdotally reported that they find this anxiety-provoking, whereas others find it exhilarating.

Widowed. This process of "starting over" may be relevant to those persons who are widowed as well. Our review of the research literature identified only one study of the sexual practices of widowed persons. Nearly three decades ago, Gebhard (1968) reported that widowed persons were less likely to have sexual experiences than divorced persons. Francoeur (1991) has suggested that this may be due, in part, to a sense of loyalty to the former spouse or to perceived and real pressure from kin members.

Marital Sex

By far, the most common adult sexual lifestyle in the U.S.A. is legal marriage, and marriage is the context for the overwhelming majority of sexual experiences in the U.S.A. In fact, marriage is the only context in which sexuality is universally approved. Despite this, researchers have investigated marital sexuality less than nonmarital forms of sexual expression. Greenblat (1983) has suggested that sex within marriage is more likely to be the object of jokes than of scientific investigation. Strong and DeVault (1994) report that only nine of 553 articles on sexuality that appeared in scholarly journals between 1987 and 1992 were devoted to marital sexuality.

This pattern of research is somewhat odd in light of the widespread belief that effective sexual functioning is indispensable to a good marriage (Frank and Anderson 1979). In this regard, it is striking that much of the research conducted on couples has utilized clients in sex therapy. Here we review works on nonclinical samples.

Sexual Frequency and Practices. Most of the research on sexual relations within marriage has assessed the frequency of sexual relations. Many of these studies have also examined how that frequency is related to marital satisfaction. Americans seem to be fascinated with comparing their own frequency to other couples. Until recently, this research was based on volunteer samples, which typically were also quite small.

Perhaps the first sex survey ever conducted in the U.S.A. was done by Clelia Duel Mosher (1980), who investigated the sexual practices and attitudes of forty-five women between 1890 and 1920. Most of these women reported that they found sex to be pleasurable and believed that it was "necessary" for both men and women. The women who were interviewed before 1900 were less likely to describe sex as important or enjoyable, and they were less likely to associate sex with the expression of love. The Mosher survey documents the first signs of a shift to a post-Victorian culture.

In a study of more than 1,000 men and women, Dickinson and Bean (1932) reported that sexual dissatisfaction was more important in explaining marital difficulties than disputes over work, money, and children. Davis (1929) drew similar conclusions in her study of 2,200 women. Sexual satisfaction within marriage had clearly become a norm in the U.S.A. by the early twentieth century. Somewhat later, Hamilton (1948) interviewed a hundred married men and women and concluded that an unsatisfactory sex life is the principal cause of marital dysfunction. Without addressing the validity of that particular claim, the Hamilton data do demonstrate that, in the small sample surveyed in the 1930s and 1940s, sex was considered to be an important part of a marriage.

The Kinsey group (1953) reported that married couples in the 1940s had sex an average of two times a week in the early years of marriage, declining to about once a week after ten years of marriage. By comparing those born before 1900 and those born after 1900, they found that the frequency of marital coitus had remained the same. However, virtually every other aspect of marital sex had changed. Couples born after 1900 engaged in more and longer foreplay, used more coital positions, were more likely to have oral sex, were more likely to use French (deep) kissing and manual caressing of genitals, and had sex more often naked.

More-recent studies have tended to fit two patterns. Small samples with volunteers have found a general average of three to four times a week in early marriage with a decline to twice a week in later years. However, studies with national samples have tended to get lower figures more like Kinsey's (Bell and Bell 1972; Blumstein and Schwartz, 1983; Call, Sprecher, and

Schwartz 1995; Hite 1976; 1983; Hunt 1974; Sarrel and Sarrel 1980; Tavris and Sadd 1974; Trussell and Westoff 1980; Udry 1980; Westoff 1974). Interestingly, married women tend to report lower frequencies than married men (Call et al. 1996).

A few researchers have asked respondents to report their ideal or preferred frequency. Hite (1976) found that one third of married women would like to have sex at least daily, another third wanted it two to five times a week, and a final third less often.

(1) Changes Throughout Marriage. The evidence of a decrease over time or length of marriage is strong and consistent (Blumstein and Schwartz 1983; Edwards and Booth 1976; Greeley 1991; Hunt 1974; Kinsey et al. 1953; Michael et al. 1994; Trussell and Westoff 1980; Westoff 1980). Longitudinal studies of the same couples over time have also documented this pattern (James 1981; Udry 1980), as have retrospective studies of couples looking back over the course of their marriage (Greenblat 1983).

In a national study of the 1988 *National Survey of Families and Households* (Call et al. 1995), frequency decreases over the length of marriage were correlated with biological aging, diminished health, and habituation. In a multivariate analysis, age was most strongly related to frequency, followed by marital happiness, and factors that reduce the opportunity for sex (such as pregnancy and small children). Couples who had not cohabited prior to marriage and who were still in their first marriage had less-frequent sex than cohabitors, married persons who had cohabited prior to marriage, and those who were in their second or later marriage.

These findings are largely consistent with prior research. Decreasing frequency of marital sex has been found to relate to age-related reductions in the biological capacity for sex, including declines in male motivation and physical ability, declines in women's testosterone levels, and increases in illness (Greenblat 1983; Hengeveld 1991; James 1983; Udry, Deven, and Coleman 1982). Negative social attitudes about sex and the elderly may also lead some to believe that their interest and capacity should decline (Masters and Johnson 1970; Riportella-Muller 1989). However, these aging factors do not explain the decline in frequency that occurs within the first several years of marriage (Jasso 1985; Kahn and Udry 1986). James (1981) found that the coital rate dropped by one half during the first year of marriage. Some have suggested that there is a honeymoon effect early in the marriage. As the honeymoon period ends, habituation occurs and frequency declines (Blumstein and Schwartz 1983; Doddridge, Schumm, and Berger 1987). Habituation may be seen as a decreased interest in sex that occurs with the increased accessibility of a regular sexual partner and the routine predictability of behavior with that partner over time (Call et al. 1995).

Other reasons that have been cited as influencing a decrease in frequency include fatigue, work demands, child care, and management of complex schedules (Michael et al. 1994).

(2) Effects of Children. A few comments on the effects of children are worth special note. There is some evidence that sexual frequency declines by the third trimester of pregnancy—prior to the actual birth of a child (Kumar, Brant, and Robson 1981). The birth of a child introduces parental roles into the marital relationship. The child increases fatigue, reduces time alone together for the couple, and decreases time in situations that are conducive to sexual encounters (Blumstein and Schwartz, 1983; Doddridge, et al. 1987; Greenblat 1983).

(3) Association with Sexual and Marital Satisfaction. A majority of Americans report that they are satisfied with their marital sex life (Hunt 1974; Lauman et al. 1994). In general, researchers have not found frequency to be related to sexual or marital satisfaction (Blumstein and Schwartz 1983; Frank, Anderson, and Rubinstein 1978). However, there is evidence that the congruence between ideal and actual frequency is related (Frank and Anderson 1979). There is some evidence that sexual problems are likely to occur fairly early in a marriage (Brayshaw 1962; Murphy et al. 1980).

Some studies have found social factors associated with relationship satisfaction. Rainwater (1964) found, in a study of couples in poverty in four different cultures, that lower-class couples were more likely to have highly gender-segregated role relationships (traditional gender roles); they were less likely to have close sexual relationships, and the wife was not likely to view sex with her husband as gratifying.

Several studies have found that sexual satisfaction is related to both sexual and nonsexual aspects of the marriage. The Kinsey group (1953) found that divorce was related to decreases in the wife's orgasm rate. Hunt (1974) reported a strong correlation between marital closeness and sexual satisfaction. He found that the most important predictor was the extent to which couples share similar sexual desire. Thornton (1977) found that couples who spend more time having sex than they do fighting tend to have happier marriages. Sarrel and Sarrel (1980) found that couples who talk with each other about sex often, who rate their communication about sex as good, where the wife likes oral sex, and where the man believes the women's movement has been good for women tend to have more satisfying sexual relationships.

Hite (1976) asked women to identify what aspect of their marital sex gave them the greatest satisfaction. Responses given by 20 percent or more included closeness, orgasm, coitus, and foreplay. In response to what they liked least, more than 10 percent said oral or anal sex, lack of orgasm, the "messiness" following sex, excessive or rough foreplay, and the routine nature of their activities.

In the *Redbook* magazine surveys (Tavris and Sadd 1975; Tavris 1978), marital satisfaction did not decline with length of marriage or age. The majority reported enjoying oral sex. Most respondents believed that good communication is an important ingredient of marital and sexual happiness. The most common complaint was that they had sex too infrequently. For women, religiosity was related to a happier sex life and marital satisfaction.

In an unusual study of a hundred mostly white and well-educated couples who were happily married (selected because none had ever had ES or been in therapy), Frank and Anderson (1979) found that 85 percent described themselves as sexually satisfied. One half of the wives reported they had difficulty becoming aroused or reaching orgasm. Roughly 10 percent of the husbands reported they had experienced erectile difficulties. One third of the couples expressed complaints about such things as anxiety, too little foreplay, and low sexual desire. There was no correlation between sexual dysfunctions and marital satisfaction, but complaints by the wife were associated with reduced marital happiness.

(4) Unexplored Issues. This review of research on marital sexuality serves to confirm the narrow range of the questions researchers have investigated. We know little about the dynamics of sexual relationships in marriage— about the ways couples interact sexually, about how they transact or negotiate sexual encounters, or about how they initiate and terminate encounters. Little is known about how sexuality in marriage is affected by power dynamics between the couple. There has been little study of sexual coercion in marriage. Perhaps it is time to end the focus on counting episodes and begin to examine what happens within marital sexual relationships.

Extramarital Sexual Relationships. Researchers have been studying ES for decades, although the range of the questions they have examined has been fairly narrow (For more-thorough reviews of ES research and nonexclusive lifestyles, see Macklin 1980; Thompson 1983; Weis 1983).

(1) ES Attitudes. One focus of concern has been the degree of normative consensus reflected by ES attitudes. A series of national surveys indicate that ES has consistently been disapproved by 75-85 percent of the adult American population (Glenn and Weaver 1979; Greeley, Michael, and Smith 1990; Reiss, Anderson, and Sponaugle 1980; Weis and Jurich 1985). Weis and Jurich (1985) found that nearly one third of residents in the twelve largest cities found ES acceptable, the only locations in the U.S.A. where as many as 20 percent approved. In small towns and rural areas, fewer than 10 percent approved. The norm of sexual exclusivity within marriage is so widespread in American culture that few question it.

Approval of ES has been found to be related to (1) being male, (2) young age, (3) being nonwhite, (4) living in a large city, (5) high levels of education, (6) low religiosity, and (7) being unmarried (Glenn and Weaver 1979; Reiss et al. 1980; Weis and Jurich 1985; Weis and Slosnerick 1981). Although a number of researchers have reported that approval of ES is related to lower levels of marital happiness, Weis and Jurich (1985) found that marital happiness was less strongly related to ES attitudes than several of these other variables.

(2) ES Incidence/Prevalence. A second major concern of researchers has been the attempt to establish estimates of the prevalence and/or incidence of ES behavior. Generally, this has taken the form of asking respondents to indicate whether or not they have ever had ES. Authors have regularly claimed that roughly one half of married persons in the U.S.A. have had at least one ES experience, citing the Kinsey research (1948, 1953) as the basis for this claim. Although the point is often ignored, the Kinsey team actually found that 33 percent of husbands and 26 percent of wives reported having ES. Because of suspicions of underreporting, they raised the estimate for male—but not female—ES to 50 percent. Several researchers have reported that the figures for husbands have remained "fairly stable" since then, but that the rate for wives has increased to approximately that of husbands (Blumstein and Schwartz 1983; Hunt 1974; Levin 1975). Researchers have reported lifetime prevalence rates from as low as 20 percent (Johnson 1970) to nearly 75 percent (Hite 1981).

Several recent studies by the National Opinion Research Center (Smith 1990; 1991; Greeley et al. 1990) have found that only 2 to 3 percent of American married men and women have ES each year. Further, they reported that 65 percent of wives and 30 percent of husbands have the same number of lifetime sexual partners as spouses. According to these researchers, the increases in premarital sex and cohabitation, the rising rate of divorce, and the later age at first marriage that have characterized the last forty years have resulted in less sexual exclusivity among the unmarried, but no such trend has occurred among married persons in the U.S.A. The Greeley group concluded that Americans are overwhelmingly "monogamous" [sic] and that rates of ES have been overestimated by previous researchers. *The National Health and Social Life Survey* (Laumann et al. 1994), also conducted by the NORC, found that only 35 percent of men and 20 percent of women reported ever having ES, and 94 percent had sex only with their spouse in the last year.

As we have already discussed, making comparisons between the results of the NORC national probability samples and previous studies is most difficult. Most previous studies have reported lifetime prevalence rates. The NORC studies have generally reported annual incidence rates. It seems likely that the conditions surrounding the collection of data and the greater representation of rural respondents in the NORC studies led to low estimates. On the other hand, the volunteer nature of most previous studies and their greater inclusion of urban respondents may well have led to high estimates. For the time being, we must conclude that questions about the incidence and prevalence of ES in the U.S.A. remain largely unanswered.

(3) Marital Happiness. The third major focus of ES research has been the attempt to demonstrate an association between ES behavior and marital happiness/satisfaction. By far, this has been the most frequently tested hypothesis. As a consequence, there has been little research exploring the circumstances or conditions surrounding ES behavior itself or testing alternative hypotheses. A number of researchers have found that ES behavior is significantly related to lower levels of marital happiness (Bell et al. 1975; Edwards and Booth 1976; Glass and Wright 1977; 1985; Prins, Buunk, and Van Yperen 1993; Saunders and Edwards 1984). Lower marital happiness has also been found to be related to ES attitudes (Reiss et al. 1980; Weis and Jurich 1985).

However, the association may not be as strong as these findings imply. The research by Glass and Wright (1977, 1985) suggests that the actual association between ES and marital happiness may be quite complex. In their earlier study, Glass and Wright (1977) found that husbands who had ES in the early years of marriage did have lower marital satisfaction. However, there were no differences in marital satisfaction between husbands who had never had ES and those who began ES later in their marriages. Interestingly, exactly the reverse was true for wives. There were no differences in marital satisfaction between wives who had never had ES and those who began it early in their marriages. Yet, wives who began their ES experiences later in marriage did have significantly lower marital satisfaction. In their later study, Glass and Wright (1985) found that ES was related to lower marital happiness only for wives. They concluded that male ES is likely to be more strongly associated with individual factors, rather than marital issues.

The Glass and Wright studies represent a level of complexity that has rarely been seen in ES research. Few studies have examined the possibility that marital happiness might relate to different types of ES experiences. As just one example, we can take the case of consensual ES. In one of the few comparisons of couples who had made an agreement to include ES in their marriage with couples who did not have this agreement and had a sexually exclusive relationship, there were no significant differences in marital stability, marital happiness, or level of jealousy (Rubin and Adams 1986). Similarly, Gilmartin (1978) found no differences in marital happiness between a group of couples who participated in swinging and a control group of nonswinging couples.

Moreover, Ellis (1969) has made the obvious point, substantiated by all the studies cited here, that some people who have ES also report high marital satisfaction. In fact, although the two variables have been consistently found to be significantly related, the proportion of ES variance explained by marital quality variables has tended to be rather small. This may be due, in part, to the tendency to dichotomize ES into "ever versus never" categories, thus ignoring the diversity of ES types. This treatment of ES as a simplistic construct that uniformly reflects poor marital dynamics may reduce our ability to establish better explanations of ES. For example, Weis and Jurich (1985) did report that ES attitudes and marital happiness were significantly related in a series of national probability samples, but they also found that marital happiness was more weakly related to ES attitudes than several background variables.

(4) Exploring the Diversity of ES Experience. This failure to recognize the diversity of ES experience may be the single greatest obstacle to the development of sound research and theory. ES experiences are, in fact, a class of relationship types, every bit as complex as other relationship forms. With few exceptions, American researchers have failed to recognize the historical and cross-cultural evidence that male and female ES behavior is universal, despite the strong normative traditions and sanctions against it. They have also largely ignored the cross-cultural evidence that amply demonstrates a wide variety of ES patterns and normative responses to it (Buss 1994; Fisher 1992; Ford and Beach 1951; Frayser 1985; Murdock 1949).

(5) Specific Aspects of ES. Ultimately, a full understanding of ES will require more-thorough investigation of the myriad ways in which ES experiences vary. Several factors require additional research. These include:

- *Specific Sexual Behaviors Involved.* ES can range from flirting,kissing, and petting to intercourse (Glass and Wright 1985; Hurlbert 1992; Kinsey et al. 1948; 1953).
- *Specific Relationship Behaviors Involved.* ES relationships vary from those in which sexual interaction is nearly the sum total of the relationship to those where sexuality is a minimal component (Hurlbert 1992; Richardson 1985; Thompson 1983, 1984).
- *Number of ES Partners.* In general, the scant evidence available suggests that most Americans have a small number of ES partners (Bell et al. 1975; Greeley et al. 1990; Kinsey et al. 1953; Pietropinto and Simenauer 1977).
- *Length of ES Relationship.* It appears that most, but certainly not all, ES relationships are of relatively short duration and entail less than ten actual sexual encounters, with some evidence that females tend to be involved for longer periods (Bell et al. 1975; Gagnon 1977; Hall 1987; Hunt 1974; Hurlbert 1992; Kinsey et al. 1953; Pietropinto and Simenauer 1977).
- *Level of Involvement.* ES ranges from single sexual encounters in which partners know little of each other to highly intimate affairs with characteristics that are quite similar to intimate marriages.
- *Consensual Versus Secretive.* Although most ES is secretive or clandestine (Gagnon 1977; Hunt 1974), it is important to recognize that some spouses do know about their partner's ES activities and expressly agree

to permit ES (see section below on alternatives to traditional marriage) (Blumstein and Schwartz 1983; Thompson 1983; Weis 1983).

- *Motives and Meanings.* There are dozens of motives for ES. Weis and Slosnerick (1981) demonstrated that a distinction between individual motives (such as adventure, variety, romance, or pleasure) and marital motives (such as revenge against a spouse, marital hostility, marital sex problems, or as an alternative marriage form) was useful in explaining differences in ES attitudes.
- *Bisexual/ Homosexual.* ES has usually been assumed to be heterosexual, but there is evidence that, at least some ES is homosexual (D. Dixon 1985; J. K. Dixon 1984).

(6) Gender Issues. Before discussing theoretical factors for ES, we want to note that the available evidence strongly suggests that researchers explore the possibility of separate predictive models for men and women. There is evidence that men are more likely to have ES than women and to have more numerous ES encounters (Buss 1994; Glass and Wright 1985), more likely to report ES relationships with limited involvement (Glass and Wright 1985; Spanier and Margolis 1983), and tend to have more partners (Buss 1994; Thompson 1983). Men and women may also experience different outcomes. There is some evidence that women are more likely to report experiencing guilt as a result of ES (Spanier and Margolis 1983). It is possible that women, as a group, are more likely to be motivated to engage in ES activities by marital factors and may be more likely to seek intimacy as a primary goal in ES (Reibstein and Richards 1993). Several studies have found that marital variables are more strongly related to ES for women than for men (Glass and Wright 1985; Saunders and Edwards 1984). All of these findings indicate that the ES experiences of men and women may differ substantially.

(7) Building Theoretical Models. Edwards and Booth (1976) have argued that the context of marital interaction is more important than background factors in explaining the process leading to ES involvement. However, Weis and Slosnerick (1981) have maintained that individuals enter marriage with internalized scripts for sex, love, and marriage. Ultimately, the scripts of married persons stem from an interaction of marital dynamics and background factors. Each of these, in turn, is likely to be influenced by one's position within the social structure.

As just noted, there is evidence of a significant correlation between marital happiness and both dichotomous measures of ES experience and ES attitudes, although this association has not always been a strong or robust one. In a study of ES attitudes (approval), Weis and Slosnerick (1981) isolated two orthogonal factors of justifications for ES. One was a set of motivations for ES that mentioned aspects of the marital relationship. The other was a set of individual motives for ES. Both factors were significantly related to approval of ES, but the individual motivations were more strongly related than the marital motivations.

These findings suggest two possible paths for future research that seeks to elaborate the complex nature of the association between ES and marital satisfaction. One is to contrast the types of ES experiences that persons with individual versus marital motivations tend to have and to explore how these relate to marital satisfaction and, perhaps, to outcomes of ES relationships. The other is to separate happily and unhappily married persons and to investigate the types of ES experiences and outcomes for each group. It seems reasonable to expect that the two groups might well pursue different kinds of ES experiences under different circumstances, with different outcomes.

A second theoretical factor may be background variables. A number of researchers have reported that premarital sexual attitudes and behavior are related to ES attitudes and behavior, several arguing that it is the best predictor of ES involvement (Bukstel et al. 1978; Christensen 1962, 1973; Glenn and Weaver 1979; Medora and Burton 1981; Reiss et al. 1980; Singh et al. 1976; Thompson 1983; Weis and Jurich 1985; Weis and Slosnerick 1981). ES variables have been found to correlate with premarital sexual permissiveness, number of premarital sexual partners, and early premarital sexual experience (low age). Weis and Jurich (1985) found premarital sexual permissiveness was the strongest and most consistent predictor of ES attitudes in a series of regression analyses with national probability samples throughout the 1970s.

Several questions remain to be explored. Do these findings suggest that there is something particular about premarital sexual interactions with partners that is associated with ES, or are measures of premarital sex merely indicative of a broader interest in and history of sexual pleasure in various forms? Which of these will prove to be more useful in explaining various types of ES activities? For example, Joan Dixon (1984) found that female swingers tend to have early and continuing histories of heterosexual involvement, but that they also tend to have early and continuing histories of masturbation and high current sexual frequencies with partners. Gilmartin (1978) also found that swingers tend to have early heterosexual experiences and high sexual frequencies with their spouses. One might conceivably argue that such persons like sex, and ES is an extension of a broader orientation to pleasure.

A third factor has been suggested by Cazenave (1979), who has criticized work in the area of alternative lifestyles for its emphasis on ideological preference and its failure to explore how structural variables (such as age, gender, and race) may impose external constraints. In fact, there is evidence that ES behavior and ES permissiveness (attitudes) are related to (1) young age, (2) being nonwhite, (3) low education for behavior and high education for attitudes, (4) low religiosity, and (5) residence in a large city (Fisher 1992; Greeley et al. 1990; Smith 1990, 1991). Several of these associations may, in fact, be quite complex. For example, the Kinsey group (1948, 1953) found that blue-collar males tend to have ES in their 20s and their behavior diminishes by their 40s. White-collar males with college educations tended to have little ES in their 20s. This rate gradually increased to an average of once a week by age 50. In contrast, female ES peaked in the late 30s and early 40s. Finally, there is a need for research that explores the role of such American social trends as the increasing age at first marriage, the growing divorce rate, the unbalanced gender ratio, and greater mobility and travel in ES behavior.

(8) Unexplored Issues. There has been little research to this point on the process of ES relationships. For example, there has been little investigation of how opportunities for ES involvement occur in a culture with strong prohibitions against ES. Cross-sex friendships and interactions have been frequently cited as creating the opportunity for ES (Johnson 1970; Saunders and Edwards 1984; Weis and Slosnerick 1981), although this has not been empirically tested. The matter is somewhat complicated by the evidence that friendships outside of marriage are associated with higher levels of marital satisfaction (Weis and Slosnerick 1981). Wellman (1985, 1992) has documented how the friendship networks of men have shifted from public spaces (bars, cafés, and clubs) to private homes. This has led to a narrowing of the concept of friendship to emotional support and companionship. Husbands' and wives' networks are now both based in private, domestic space, and many wives actively maintain their husbands' ties to friends and kin. Men get much of their emotional support from women, as well as men, and women get almost all of their support from women. Wellman argues that marriage may impose constraints on men's ability to spend time and be intimate with other men or women. Whether this is related to ES remains to be explored.

Similarly, little is known about the outcomes of ES involvement. Generally, it is assumed that ES relationships are short in duration, exploitive in character, and tragic in outcome. For example, it is generally assumed that ES and cross-sex friendships will be a source of jealousy in a marriage. Although there is a growing body of evidence about jealousy, little research has specifically investigated jealousy in the context of ES (Bringle, 1991; Bringle & Boebinger, 1990; Buunk, 1981; 1982; Denfeld, 1974; Jenks, 1985).

Alternatives to Traditional Marriage. Although most ES is secretive, some couples do pursue lifestyles that permit ES (Blumstein and Schwartz 1983; Thompson 1983; Weis 1983). There is some evidence that consensual ES is unrelated to marital satisfaction (Gilmartin 1978; Ramey 1976; Rubin and Adams 1986; Wachowiak and Bragg 1980), suggesting there might be different outcomes for the consensual and nonconsensual forms of ES.

A number of models for consensual ES have been proposed, particularly during the 1970s. These include swinging (recreational and shared ES)

(Bartell 1971; Gilmartin 1978; Jenks 1985), comarital sex (Smith and Smith 1974), open marriage (O'Neill and O'Neill 1972), intimate friendship networks (ES within context of friendship) (Francoeur and Francoeur 1974; Ramey 1976), and group marriage (Constantine and Constantine 1973; Rimmer 1966). Certainly, there are differences among these various nonexclusive lifestyles. We do not have the space to review fully the distinctions among them here (see Libby and Whitehurst 1977; Weis 1983). What unites them for the discussion here is that they all represent a consensual agreement to allow multilateral sexual involvement. As such, ES is assigned a different set of meanings from betrayal.

Consensual agreements can vary in terms of the degree of sexual involvement desired, the degree of intimate involvement desired, the degree of openness with the spouse, and the amount of time spent with the ES partner (Sprenkle and Weis 1978). Buunk (1980) studied the strategies couples employ in establishing ground rules for sexually open marriages. The five most common were: (1) primary value placed on maintaining the marriage, (2) limiting the intensity of ES involvements, (3) keeping the spouse fully informed of ES relationships, (4) approving ES only if it involves mate exchange, and (5) tolerating ES if it is invisible to the spouse. It would be useful to see research on the association between the types of strategies employed and outcomes of ES.

Interestingly, husbands tend to initiate swinging (Bartell 1971; Weis 1983). There is some evidence that most couples swing for a few years, rather than pursuing it for a lifetime (Weis 1983). Dropouts from swinging report problems with jealousy, guilt, emotional attachment, and perceived threat to the marriage (Denfeld 1974). As far as we know, there have been no studies comparing dropouts and those who enjoy and continue swinging.

The Constantine study (1973) is virtually the only source of data on group marriage in contemporary America. They report that the typical relationship includes four adults. Most enter a group with their spouses, and if the group dissolves, most of the original pair bonds survive. In fact, the original pair bonds retain some primacy after the formation of the group, and this may be a factor working against the success of the group. Jealousy between male partners appears to be a common problem.

Studies of marital models that permit ES have tended to employ small, volunteer samples with no control or contrast groups for comparison. There is no basis for a firm estimate of the incidence or prevalence of such alternative lifestyles, although Blumstein and Schwartz (1983) suggested that as many as one of seven marriages in the U.S.A. may have some agreement allowing ES. Despite the vast attention given to these alternative lifestyles in the 1970s, and despite the more recent claims that Americans are "returning to traditional models of monogamous marriage," there is no scientific basis for concluding that these patterns increased in popularity earlier or that they have become less common in the 1980s and 1990s.

Sexuality and People with Physical and   MITCHELL S. TEPPER
Developmental Disabilities

Government Policies Affecting Sexuality and Disability. Over the past twenty years, pivotal legislation has been enacted in the United States that enables people with disabilities to gain their rightful place as equal members of American society. These changes have been led by spirited people with disabilities and their advocates. The Rehabilitation Act of 1973, the 1975 Education for All Handicapped Children Act (Public Law 94-142), and the Americans with Disabilities Act passed in 1990 have all added opportunities for inclusion and integration into the community for people of all abilities. With inclusion and integration have come greater opportunities for social interaction and sexual expression. The same spirit that has raised disability-rights issues to a national priority is now demanding that people with disabilities be recognized as sexual beings with a right to sexual education, sexual health care, and sexual expression afforded under the law.

Demands for the sexual rights of people with disabilities have resulted in a resurgence of research interest in the area of sexuality and disability in the 1990s. Notably, the National Center for Medical Rehabilitation Research (NCMRR) of the National Institute of Child Health and Human Development under the National Institutes of Health has identified sexuality as a priority issue that impacts the quality of life of people with disabilities. It subsequently issued a Request for Applications on Reproductive Function in People with Physical Disabilities in February of 1992. The purpose of the request was to develop new knowledge in the areas of reproductive physiology, anatomy, and behavior that are common to people with disabilities with the goal of restoring, improving, or enhancing reproductive function lost as a consequence of injury, disease, or congenital disorder. The request for applications included a specific objective to characterize the effect of impairments of sexual function on psychosocial adaptation, emotional state, and establishment of intimate relationships. Special focus was placed on research with women and minorities who have disabilities. NCMRR has funded six studies on sexuality and disability over the last three years. Two of the studies were with women who have spinal cord injury, and a third was a study of women with a variety of disabilities.

Consumers with Disabilities Leading the Way. Research, education, and advocacy efforts in the area of sexuality and disability are being led by people with disabilities (consumers). A review of the most recent annotated bibliography on sexuality and disability published by the Sexuality Information and Education Council of the United States (SIECUS, 1995) reveals a growing number of books, newsletters, special issues of publications, and curricula on sexuality and disability written by people with disabilities. In addition, national consumer-based organizations like the National Spinal Cord Injury Association, the National Multiple Sclerosis Foundation, and the Arthritis Foundation are beginning to publish self-help brochures on the specific effects of particular disabilities on sexuality. Most recently, self-help groups have been appearing on the Internet, computer bulletin-board services, and commercial computer services like American Online.

Health-Care Professionals Involved in Sexuality and Disability. In addition to the work by people with disabilities and nonprofessional advocates, health-care professionals are also taking an increased interest in sexuality and disability. The American Association of Physical Medicine and Rehabilitation has a Sexuality Task Force; the American Association of Sexuality Educators, Counselors, and Therapists has a special-interest group that focuses on educating medical and allied help professionals in the area of sexuality and disability; the Society for the Scientific Study of Sexuality includes presentations and workshops in the area of sexuality and disability for its members; and Planned Parenthood agencies around the country have increased education and services in the area of sexual health care to people with disabilities. More rehabilitation hospitals are including "privacy" rooms to give patients an opportunity to experiment sexually while still in the hospital, and many are adding specialty programs in the area of fertility and erectile function for men, obstetric and gynecological care for women, and parenting for both men and women with disabilities.

Portrayals of Sexuality and Disability in the Popular Media. The portrayal of people with disabilities as sexual beings has improved over time in the popular media. Movies that include a focus on the sexuality and relationships of people with disabilities, such as *Forest Gump, Passion Fish, Water Dance, Regarding Henry, My Left Foot, Children of a Lesser God,* and *Born on the Fourth of July* have dealt with the issue of sexuality and disability with varying degrees of sensitivity, and have enjoyed success at both the box office and in video stores. TV shows have also included people with disabilities and sexuality themes. One show, *LA Law,* where one of the stars portrayed a person with a developmental disability who had a sexual relationship with another person with a developmental disability, was honored by the Coalition of Sexuality and Disability for the positive portrayal of sexuality and disability in the media. There has also been an increase in TV commercials that include people with disabilities in relationships or with children. Popular magazines ranging from *Bride* to *Penthouse* and *Playboy* are also beginning to include feature articles on sexuality and disability. Efforts to portray people with disabilities as part of everyday life in the media are slowly helping to explode the myth that people with disabilities are asexual.

Problems, Controversies, and Hurdles. Two of the most serious sexual problems facing people with disabilities are (1) the high rate of sexual abuse, exploitation, and unwanted sexual activity, especially among women with physical disabilities and all people with developmental disabilities, and (2) the risk of STDs, including HIV, among people with cognitive impairments who are sexually active. Two leading areas of controversy are (1) the issue of what constitutes informed consent for sexual activity in people with serious cognitive impairments, and (2) the area of reproductive rights, eugenics, abortion, and prenatal testing for disabilities. As far as hurdles, there is still a need for greater access to information and educational material that affirms the sexuality of people of all abilities, including people with early- and late-onset disabilities, physical, sensory, and mental disabilities, and disabilities that hinder learning. Despite the positive current trends in sexuality and disability, we still have a long way to go in increasing the number of sexuality education and training programs for teachers, health-care workers, and family members to help them understand and support the normal sexual development and behavior of persons with disabilities. A goal is that all social agencies and health-care delivery systems develop policies and procedures that will insure sexual-health services and benefits are provided on an equal basis to all persons without discrimination because of disability.

Sexuality and Older Persons   ROBERT T. FRANCOEUR

In 1860, over half of the American population was under 20 years of age and only 13 percent over age 45. In 1990, less than a third were under age 20 and 21 percent were over age 45. The so-called Baby Boomers born between 1945 and 1965 are now in their middle years. With the birthrate less than 15 per 1,000, America has become a graying society.

Although Americans over age 50 are the fastest-growing segment of our population, research on their lifestyles and patterns of intimacy has been almost exclusively limited to studies of the chronically ill, the socially isolated, and the poor. Edward Brecher (1984) was one of the first to study older healthy Americans. His sample of 4,246 persons between ages 40 and 92 was largely white and affluent, although he did include a low-income group. His overall conclusion was that the sexual interests and activities of older persons are the best-kept secrets in America. Although there is a common belief that the elderly are no longer interested in sexual intimacy, older persons were just as affected as young people by the social turmoil and changing attitudes of the 1960s and 1970s.

Brecher found that healthy, older person today are "enormously differ-ent from the older person of forty or fifty years ago," and very much interested in intimacy and sexual relations. Not one of Brecher's 4,246 respondents was sexually inactive, although masturbation was the most common sexual outlet. Forty-four percent rated their sexual satisfaction as most enjoyable; less than 1 percent rated their sexual activity as not enjoy-able (Table 4). Poor health was a major determinant in hindering older persons from maintaining an active sexual life.

Table 4

Sexual Activity Among 4,246 Americans, Ages 45 to 92, in the Brecher 1984 Survey

	Age Group		
	50s	**60s**	**70+**
Women			
Orgasms while asleep or awakening	26%	24%	17%
Women who masturbate	47%	37%	33%
Masturbation frequency for women who masturbate	0.7/week	0.6/week	0.7/week
Wives having sex with husband	88%	76%	65%
Frequency of marital sex	1.3/week	1.0/week	0.7/week
Men			
Orgasms while asleep or awakening	25%	21%	17%
Men who masturbate	66%	50%	43%
Masturbation frequency for men who masturbate	1.2/week	0.8/week	0.7/week
Men having sex with wife	87%	78%	59%
Frequency of marital sex	1.3/week	1.0/week	0.6/week

About half of these couples reported engaging in oral-genital sex and did not limit their sexual activities to nighttime. Most of the men and women were usually orgasmic. About one in fifteen had participated in group sex after age 50. One in five couples had engaged in extramarital sex; 1 percent of couples had a mutually accepted "open marriage." Forty percent of older single women reported a relationship with a married man. A third thought it was acceptable for an older man or woman to have a much younger lover.

In another study of healthy, upper-middle-class men and women, ages 80 to 102 living in residential retirement communities, 14 percent of the men and 29 percent of the women were still married. Sexual touching and caressing, followed by masturbation and then intercourse were the most common sexual activities. Of these outlets, only touching and caressing declined with age, a decline more evident in men than in women. Those who had been sexually active earlier in life tended to remain sexually active in their 80s and 90s, although the frequency of sexual intercourse was sometimes limited by their current physical health and by social circumstances including the lack of an available partner (Bretschneider and McCoy 1988).

The Starr-Weiner Report on Sex and Sexuality in the Mature Years (1981) examined the sexual lives and attitudes of 800 persons, aged 60 to 91, from four regions of the country. When the sexual activities of these 60- to 90-year-olds were compared with the 40-year-olds Kinsey studied thirty-five years earlier, there was no significant decline when opportunities for sexual activity existed. "Sex remains pretty much the same unless some outside event intrudes, such as a health problem, the loss of a spouse, impotence, or boredom." A reliable predictor of the sexually active life of older persons is their acceptance or rejection of the social stereotype of the dependent, sickly older person. Older persons who maintain an active participation in life in general tend to be more sexually active in their later years.

Starr and Weiner also identified two major problems with no easy remedy. First is the tendency for older men to become asexual when they encounter an occasional erection or orgasmic problem. Instead of exploring noncoital pleasuring, many older men simply give up all interest in sex. The second problem is the ever-growing number of older women who are without sexual partners and, thus, deprived, against their will, of sexual intimacy and pleasure. (See Section 6B below on sexuality among older homosexual men and women.)

A Closing Comment

Throughout this section, we have noted the tendency of sexuality researchers in the U.S.A. to focus on the incidence and/or frequency of sexual behaviors in various lifestyles. There has been little corresponding research on the process of sexual relationships or the dynamics within them. This is precisely the same point we made in summarizing the section on adolescent sexuality. Suffice it to say that American researchers need to move beyond asking how many people "do it" and how often they "do it" to more fully investigate the contexts surrounding adult sexual lifestyles, and to identify the social, psychological, and biological factors associated with sexual practice.

6. Homoerotic, Homosexual, and Ambisexual Behaviors

To this point, we have examined the general socio-historical context of sexuality in the U.S.A. and reviewed evidence concerning what may be called mainstream sexual behaviors, in the sense that a majority of Americans engage in these activities. Our review of autoerotic behaviors and the development of heterosexual patterns throughout the life cycle may be seen in this light. We did occasionally mention less-common patterns. For example, the review of childhood sexuality did note that homosexual activities do occur in childhood, and research that examined the development of homosexual behavior was briefly discussed. However, the focus of the chapter so far has clearly been on mainstream, and essentially heterosexual, patterns.

Our review will now shift to an examination of a variety of sexual patterns that are less common, as this has also been a prime concern of sexuality professionals in the U.S.A. We hope that the reader will note that many of the general themes we have stressed so far—change and diversity, for example—are applicable to these patterns as well. In reviewing heterosexual lifestyle patterns, we stressed that researchers have tended to focus on the incidence or frequency of sexual behaviors and less likely to investigate relationship dynamics or theoretical explanations of behavior. These same trends also tend to characterize the study of less-conventional sexual behavior.

A. Children and Adolescents   ROBERT HAWKINS AND WILLIAM STACKHOUSE

Although research on childhood sexual activity in the United States is limited, what little we know (and can remember on a personal level) indicates that a great deal of same-gender sex play takes place among children, usually of an exploratory nature. Occasionally a lesbian, gay, or bisexual adult will recall such childhood activity as being different from exploratory activity with someone of the other gender, and therefore indicative of an early awareness of orientation. But it appears that, for the majority of people, childhood sexual play, while it includes same-gender activity, has little implication for adult orientation.

Some research shows a relationship for males between cross-gender behavior as a child (known as "sissy" behavior) and homoeroticism as an adult, but that relationship has not been shown to be causal and may be more a result of the patriarchal homophobic character of the culture than any innate biological characteristic of the child. This is more apparent when one compares the research on females who engage in cross-gender role behavior as a child (known as "tomboy" behavior), wherein the same relationship is not present. Even the labels for the person engaging in cross-gender role behavior carry different connotations in the culture. For a boy, being called "sissy" is considerably more detrimental to healthy development than is being called "tomboy" for a girl (Green 1987).

When the American child is developing a lesbian, gay, or bisexual identity, the heterosexism and homophobia of the culture dictates that this is not an acceptable orientation, and it becomes difficult at best for the child to develop into an adolescent or adult with a positive self-image. Lesbian and gay youth, particularly those from small communities, seldom receive support from their peers or from the sex education and family life courses in their school. Books that could be supportive, such as Leslea Newman's *Heather Has Two Mommies* (1989), or *Gloria Goes to Gay Pride* (1991), are usually banned from school curricula or simply not considered appropriate for children, even though they were written specifically for all children to read. Counselors and teachers generally assume that all of their students are heterosexually oriented, even though some students in any school will have a same-gender orientation.

As children grow into adolescents and attempt to deal constructively with the tensions and uncertainties of adolescence, gay, lesbian, and bisexual teenagers have to confront the question of the gender of the person to whom they find themselves sexually attracted. Do they surrender to peer and cultural pressure and date only members of the other gender? Do they tell a best friend of their orientation and risk losing that friend or being ostracized or physically attacked? Should they get sexually involved with someone of the other gender to attempt to prove that they really are "straight"? Just what do they do when they find themselves sexually attracted to someone of the same gender? Fortunately, the number and quality of resources that lesbian and gay teens can use are increasing, both on national and local levels. During the late 1980s and early 1990s, many books, pamphlets, and other resources have been published, providing practical guidelines and insights into what lesbian and gay youth should know about dating, living together, and coping in a hostile world.

However, the resources that are available for them are usually available only through homophile groups and a few commercial bookstores, and are generally not available through school libraries or other youth agencies. For example, the Boy Scouts organization has been explicitly noninclusive for both homosexual youth members and adult leaders. In rare cases, such as in New York City, a special high school has been established for gay and lesbian youth who are unable to cope with the discrimination that they face in a regular school setting. This discrimination comes from other students, as well as teachers, administrators, and counselors, making it difficult for these students to obtain an education.

Although this discrimination is still rampant in elementary and secondary schools, it is lessening somewhat in colleges and universities. Most American public and large private colleges and universities recognize and fund student organizations such as a Gay and Lesbian Alliance (GALA) or a Lesbian and Gay Organization (LAGO). Several chapters of gay fraternities and lesbian sororities have been organized. However, even where such organizations exist, many lesbian and gay collegians avoid them or keep their membership quiet. Even at religiously based institutions of higher education, there are differences with respect to the acceptance of these organizations. As late as 1995, one university, the Roman Catholic-affiliated Notre Dame, refused to allow any homophile organizations, and even denied the availability of counseling-center-sponsored group-support activities for lesbians, gays, and bisexuals. At the same time, a large Jewish orthodox-affiliated university, Yeshiva, provides numerous opportunities and funding for gay and lesbian organizations at both the graduate and undergraduate levels.

Even though information on issues confronting lesbian, gay, and bisexual adolescents may be available in printed form, the difficulty in gaining access to such materials, the anti-homoeroticism that is rampant in the media, the negative stereotypes that are still being touted as representative of all who are homoerotic, and the silence on ambieroticism or bisexuality all combine to make life unnecessarily difficult for the adolescent lesbian, gay, or bisexual person in this country. One result is that almost one third of adolescent suicides are related to the issue of homoeroticism. The data on attempted suicide among adolescents are also informative. About 10 percent of heterosexual male and female adolescents attempt suicide, while twice as many lesbian adolescents and three to four times as many gay adolescents attempt suicide (Youth Suicide National Center Report, 1989). The lack of support and acceptance of these young people is undoubtedly a factor in this difference.

B. Adults   ROBERT HAWKINS AND WILLIAM STACKHOUSE

Research on Gender Orientation

The question of gender orientation and the definition of orientation is complex and confusing for both sexuality researchers and the layperson alike. Several researchers have concluded, after extensive study, that there is no clinical description that can be applied to the label "homosexual"— that there is virtually no single phenomenon that can be labeled "homo-sexuality" and then described in clinical terms. Yet, some theorists have suggested models to define and categorize. When researchers then indicate that they are using a specific model, usually there is no internal consistency. Take, for example, the Kinsey continuum of orientation. After interviewing 5,300 men and 5,940 women in the 1940s, Kinsey and associates developed a continuous scale based on the ratio of sexual fantasies and physical contacts with one's own gender and with the other gender. Along this continuum are seven points, labeled from 0 to 6, with a "Kinsey 0" being a person whose behavior and fantasies have always involved persons of the other gender, and a "Kinsey 6" being a person whose behavior and fantasies have always involved persons of their own gender.

Even where researchers have indicated their use of the Kinsey scale, the actual definitions of research subjects have varied significantly from the original and also varied from study to study. In some instances, fantasy data are not available and consequently not considered; in other instances, behavior alone is the criteria for being placed in a "Kinsey" category, with no recognition of the difference in subjective experience of the sexual activity. In other studies, subjects are placed on the continuum solely according to the gender of the partner with whom they are living.

There are other models available that begin to reflect some of the complexities of gender orientation. Moses and Hawkins (1982; 1986) indicated that the minimum data necessary for identifying orientation in subjects were an assessment of the gender of emotional relationship part-ners, the gender of sexual attraction partners, and the gender of partners in sexual fantasy content, and that all three of these should be considered from a past and a present perspective, implying that although orientation may be consistent throughout one's life, it is not necessarily so. It is seen as a potentially dynamic characteristic.

An even more complex model was developed by Fred Klein, a physician and gender-orientation researcher. Klein indicated that an assessment of orientation needed to consider seven criteria over three time periods, resulting in a Sexual Orientations Grid of 21 cells. The criteria are: (1) sexual attraction; (2) sexual behavior; (3) sexual fantasies; (4) emotional/affectional relationship preference; (5) social relationship preference; (6) lifestyle; and (7) self-identification, with each of these criteria being assessed over three time periods: the past, the present, and the future ideal. This was the first model to present the notion that one's self-label might be an important facet of one's orientation, and the time factor was an acknowledgment of the potentially dynamic character of orientation. Research subjects can rate themselves on these criteria using a three-by-seven grid and the Kinsey ratings, summing the ratings, and then dividing by 21 to produce a position on a scale identified popularly as "The Kinsey Scale" (Klein 1978; Klein, Sepekoff, and Wolf, 1985). Although the initial response to Klein's model was that it was more comprehensive and realistic, its complexities have kept most researchers from using or disseminating it widely. It has thus remained unfamiliar to many.

Developmental Biological Insights

Several studies in the past decade have attempted to identify biological determinants for adult homoeroticism from a heterosexist theoretical base, in which heterosexual behavior is viewed as the basic, natural human behavior, and anything else is deviant. There is usually little recognition of definitional complexity or the possibility of precursors rather than determinants. Subjects are typically placed in the dichotomous classification so prevalent in the culture—that one is either gay or straight, homosexual or heterosexual—with no recognition of the Kinsey continuum, and especially no recognition of Klein's model. Researchers have purported to examine twins, siblings, adopted children, and brains of people who are homosexual and those who are not.

For example, Simon LeVay (1991) reported finding a portion of the hypothalamus that was smaller in homosexual men than in heterosexual men and was equal in size to that portion in heterosexual women. There were no lesbian brains identified as such in this study. The "finding" was quickly seized by the popular media and soon became what is called "common knowledge." There were many problems with the study, but these were generally ignored, even in the scientific press. The definitional problem, whereby subjects were classified according to whether they were known to be gay or not (obviously all subjects were no longer living, so no information could be garnered from the subjects), has been ignored. The size of the sample (nineteen men previously identified as gay, sixteen men identified as not known to be gay and, therefore, heterosexual; one man known to be identified as bisexual and included in the study as such; and six women, all classified as heterosexual) has also generally been ignored. The fact that the size of another part of the hypothalamus in the women's brains did not coincide with other research on women's brains was ignored in discussions, and the possibility that what was found may have had something to do with body build and general physical characteristics rather than directly with sexual orientation was also never discussed. The overly simplistic design was convenient, because including even a few of the other variables, such as body build or sexual history, would mean that the sample size would have to be considerably larger to enable any conclusions to be drawn.

Dean Hamer and his research team (1993) have reported the discovery of a genetic region, the Xq28 region on the X chromosome, that is claimed to be associated with male homosexuality in about three quarters of gay men and inherited on the maternal side of the family. Similar research on lesbian women does not show similar findings. There is also no attempt in all of this research to explain the "exceptions" that are reported. If there is a "gay" gene, then why is it that all men who are gay do not show it? Most biologically focused studies suffer from similar problems, first with the issue of definition, then with the exclusion or nonsimilarity of research on women who are attracted to women, and finally with assumptions, conclusions, and discussions of results that assume the "natural" state of the human being is exclusively heterosexual.

Although the question of a biological basis for homoeroticism has, in recent years, seen increased interest and attention, such research consistently does not consider the complexities of orientation, such as emotional attraction, behavior, and other criteria that constitute sexual orientation in Klein's model. Most of the classification methods for identifying orientation of subjects in these studies are overly simplified. Although there may be biological precursors to orientation, no well-designed, appropriately controlled study has been done to support that conclusion.

One positive side effect of the popular interpretation of research into possible biological roots of homoerotic orientation has been in easing the acceptance of gay and lesbian persons by some churches. One can paraphrase a common response among some mainstream Protestant church people and leaders: "If homosexual orientations are not a freely chosen preference but in some way rooted in prenatal genetic, hormonal, and/or neural templates, then God and nature made them this way, and we and the church must accept that reality."

Bisexuality Research

The research on bisexuality or ambieroticism is even more scant. It is very difficult to do research on bisexuality if one cannot define it, and there is no simple, dichotomous cultural model as is available with research on homosexuality. In a 1994 book, *Dual Attraction*, Weinberg, Williams, and Pryor report that using the Kinsey scale with sexual behaviors, sexual feeling, and romantic feelings, they identified five different types of bisexuals in their study of 435 men and 338 women:

1. The Pure Type, scoring at least 3 on all criteria;
2. The Mid Type, scoring 3 on one criteria and 2 to 4 on the other two;
3. The Heterosexual-Leaning Type, scoring 0-2 on each of the three criteria;
4. The Homosexual-Leaning Type, scoring 4 to 6 on each dimension; and
5. The Varied Type, whose scores did not fit any of the first four categories or types.

Additionally, it is only in the recent past that models for development of a bisexual identity have been proposed, and further research into ambieroticism, such as was begun by Fred Klein, has moved very slowly. The heterosexist nature of the culture, combined with the indigenous psychological and sociological perspectives of many researchers, has precluded the acceptance of a somewhat radical notion that the basic state of the human sexual orientation is ambierotic and mutable, with exclusive heterosexual or exclusive homosexual behavior being equally deviant from the biological norm. Further research on bisexuality appears to be moving in that direction. (See Section C below for more on bisexuality.)

Incidence

In much of the public discussion of homoeroticism, there is a preoccupation with the general question, "How many are there?" The answer to this question carries political and economic implications, and there is a need to understand the extent of the economic power and political power that this group wields. For example, is the culture required, in policy decisions, to provide for this group, or is it such a small number that policymakers are not required to respond to identified needs of this population? Commerce is in a strategic position to profit from this population, and economically driven decisions in the marketplace are taking these numbers into serious account. For example, in 1994, advertisements focusing directly on lesbian women and gay men as consumers were introduced in popular television and print media, and more mainstream commercial advertisements were being placed in homoerotically focused magazines, such as *The Advocate*, and in programs for fund-raising benefits for homoerotic communities.

Another area where numbers are considered in policy decisions is the increasing recognition and development of domestic-partner benefits, such as health insurance and death benefits. This began in the early 1990s when some employers became aware that lesbians, gay men, and bisexuals comprise enough of the work force to have an effect on productivity and efficiency, and that accommodating their needs is beneficial to the company so that it can have and keep well-qualified people.

Ignoring the basic fact that there is no definition of what "a homosexual" or "a bisexual" person is, until the mid-1990s the most-often cited figure for incidence of homosexuality came from the research of Kinsey and associates carried out in the 1940s. These data have been used to estimate the number of homoerotic people in the population without any indication of the simplistic nature of the definition. The commonly cited figure that 10 percent of American men are homosexual is a combination of Kinsey's finding that 4 percent of his sample were exclusively homosexual (Kinsey 6) and 6 percent were predominantly homosexual (Kinsey 5) (Kinsey et al. 1948). His data on homosexual activity in women indicated approximately 9 percent were either exclusively or predominantly homosexual (Kinsey 5 or 6) (Kinsey et al. 1953).

Laumann et al. (1994) found that almost 3 percent of their subjects were homosexual. Although these two sets of figures may, at first, seem at odds, the 1994 figure had a 1 percent error rate, and the Kinsey figure for exclusive homosexuality was 4 percent, so the two major studies do not differ greatly. There were some other problems with the 1994 study, such as the use of females as interviewers and the tendency of males in this culture to deny homosexual activity, even in anonymous questionnaires, but especially in face-to-face contact with anyone else; however, even with those design problems, the numbers are similar (Schmalz 1993).

Clinical View

In 1973, the American Psychiatric Association removed homosexuality from the *Diagnostic and Statistical Manual of Mental Disorders*. This was a major turning point, both in the United States and worldwide, in the clinical acceptance of homosexuality. Homosexuality was no longer to be viewed as an illness. The impact within psychology and psychiatry was profound, and has influenced many aspects of society. The basis for this change was the scientific conclusion that, among individuals who were not in clinical treatment, it was impossible to distinguish heterosexual and homosexual persons. Evelyn Hooker first arrived at this conclusion in 1957 with the first controlled study to include a comparison on a non-clinical sample of heterosexual and homosexual men.

Since then, research designs employing the principle that such non-clinical participants exist have resulted in many studies confirming that, in itself, homosexuality is not an illness. The illness model of homosexuality that had existed as the basis for so much discrimination is no longer supported by the psychiatric and psychological establishments. In 1973, the *Compre-*

hensive Textbook of Psychiatry was revised to state: "many homosexuals, both male and female, function responsibly and honorably, often in positions of high trust, and live emotionally stable, mature, and well adjusted lives, psychodynamically indistinguishable from well-adjusted heterosexuals, except for their alternative sexual preferences."

This has led clinicians to change their point of reference regarding homosexuals, from a pathological frame to a counseling frame, from looking at persons as sick to looking at how persons may maximize their human potential in society. Since then, many studies and books have examined aspects of the development of gay men and lesbian women, looking at identity development (social, sexual, and psychological), family issues, relationship issues, work and career development, and other dimensions of identity and lifestyle. There now exists a large body of American literature, in both the professional and general press aimed at maximizing the health and wholeness of gay men and lesbians.

Still, gay and lesbian individuals often have difficulty with their own self-acceptance and the process of deciding just how to live as gay or lesbian persons. Mental-health professionals who specialize in working with gay and lesbian clients offer individual and group counseling throughout the U.S.A. Various organizations also routinely offer support groups for a wide range of concerns. In addition, counseling is now available to the family members and friends of gay and lesbian persons who have difficulty in accepting the homosexuality of their loved ones.

Legal Perspectives

In examining the legal status of lesbians, gays, and bisexuals, one needs a rudimentary understanding of the legal system in the United States. There are levels of jurisdiction throughout the country; each jurisdiction, from local villages, to city, county, state, and the federal governments, has its own legal codes. In addition, the military has its own legal code. The issue of rights for lesbians and gays has been raised at all levels of jurisdiction. Supposedly, all of these laws are subject to the provisions of the Constitution of the United States, which provides consistency. Each state has its own state constitution, which is also to be consistent with the federal Constitution, as are the governing documents of cities and local communities.

Generally, lesbian women and gay men have no protection against discrimination based on orientation or the perception of orientation, and in 1995, only nine states had laws including sexual orientation as a minority protected from discrimination. Historically, attempts to obtain protection have followed the patterns of other oppressed groups in the United States. First, there were attempts to gain protection against discrimination in public accommodations and employment. More recently, this has expanded to include equal treatment with regard to employment-related benefits accorded to married heterosexual relationships. Examples include the benefits accrued to persons by their legally married status (as of 1995 same-gender partners are not allowed to marry legally in any state in the U.S.), as well as benefits in relation to parental status (such as adoption or custody issues), and bereavement leave with respect to family members.

Opposition to these attempts to expand discrimination protection either takes the stance that homosexual activity is immoral and, therefore, not deserving of consideration for equal protection, or suggests that lesbian women and gay men are seeking "special treatment." There is even an argument put forth that suggests that lesbian women and gay men are not an oppressed minority and should not be treated as such. Where legal protections have been instituted, it has usually been based on the need for equal treatment.

In the past decade, some local jurisdictions have passed laws recognizing the civil rights of same-gender couple relationships and of homoerotic individuals. Similarly, many corporations, of all sizes, have granted gay and lesbian couples the same benefits as heterosexual couples. For example, in Dallas, Texas, a major corporation threatened not to locate a new corporate facility in that city if the corporation's policy on domestic partnership benefits for same-gendered couples was declared illegal by virtue of the city's discriminatory laws. The economic impact of this decision caused the city government to rescind the law.

In May 1993, a court case highlighted a conflict between the antidiscrimination clause in the Constitution of the State of Hawaii and that state's ban on the recognition of same-gender unions. The state's Supreme Court asked the state to prove its "compelling interest" for continuing the discrimination or to end it. Lawyers generally admit that it will be very difficult to prove a "compelling interest," and if it cannot be done, the state will be forced to grant legal recognition of same-gender partnerships. Currently, all fifty states grant reciprocal recognition of the legality of heterosexual marriage, but if Hawaii legalizes homosexual marriages, the other forty-nine states will have to decide whether to continue that reciprocity. In early 1995, several states sought to pass legislation that would limit their reciprocity to heterosexual marriage, in the event that Hawaii recognized same-gender marriages (Rotello 1996; Eskridge 1996; Sullivan 1996).

Lesbians and gays are also treated differently with respect to serving in the United States armed forces. For many years, they were specifically excluded in official policy, yet were differentially managed in individual cases. For example, when the war in Kuwait broke out, some lesbians and gays who were scheduled for separation from the service were required to serve until the end of the conflict. In another instance, an enlisted man, Perry Watkins, repeatedly told the military that he was gay, but they kept reenlisting him until someone finally decided that he should be separated from the service, and the legal process to do so was instituted (Shilts, 1993).

In 1994, the military instituted a policy called "Don't ask, Don't tell," in which recruits were no longer to be asked if they had "homosexual tendencies," but were also forbidden from telling anyone if they were homoerotic. Prior to this, the official policy being enforced was one in which activity was not a requirement for dismissal; simply acknowledging one's homo-erotic orientation was enough to cause separation from the service. For example, Joseph Stephan, a midshipman at the United States Naval Academy, was only three months from graduation when he was asked if he was a homosexual. He indicated that he was, but never was asked, nor did he ever acknowledge any homosexual activity. He was separated from the navy and was denied his bachelor's degree from the Naval Academy (Rotello 1996; Eskridge 1996; Shilts 1993; Sullivan 1996).

Lesbians and gays have to pay special attention to wills, as biological families have successfully contested wills that left nothing to the blood relatives and everything to the person's life partner. This situation has led to the development of agencies and books focusing specifically on estate planning for lesbian and gay couples and individuals.

The legal issues for bisexuals generally focus on that part of their lives that includes someone of the same gender, so it is the homoerotic aspect of their ambieroticism that suffers from the lack of legal protection. Additionally, there is no legal option for triangular relationships that provides legitimacy, so if a bisexual person has a primary relationship simultaneously with a man and a woman, that relationship cannot be legitimized as a marriage.

Religious Issues

With the removal of homosexuality from the category of mental illness in 1973, the major foundation for legal discrimination against homosexuality was removed. As a result, religious intolerance of homosexuality, which had always been present, took on a more significant role in the debate on homosexuality within American social and political dialogue. Those who believe homosexuality to be immoral on religious grounds have since become more vocal in their quest to have their particular moral positions on homosexuality and other religious and moral issues inserted into the nation's laws (see also Section 2 of this chapter).

At the same time as Americans witnessed the radical change in the clinical view of homosexuality and the emergence of the gay-liberation movement, religious bodies in the U.S. were challenged on their stances with regard to homosexuality. Within Christian and Jewish sects, the debate generally has centered on the interpretation of sacred Biblical texts (Boswell 1980; Countryman 1988; Curran 1993; Francoeur in Gramick and Furey 1988; Gold 1992; Kosnick et al. 1977; Helminiak 1994; McNeill 1976; Presbyterian Church 1991; Thayer et al. 1987). The central locus of the debate is concerned with certain Old Testament texts, particularly the story of Sodom and Gomorrah, and the New Testament comments of the Apostle Paul in 1 Corinthians 6:9 and I Timothy 1:9-10 (Helminiak 1994), which appear to condemn homosexuality. In actuality, the debate is waged on the basis of how ancient texts are interpreted and used for modern guidance. Many "fundamentalist" and traditional sects accept the ancient texts for their literal meaning and condemn all homosexual expression (Presbyterian Church, Part 2, 1991). These sects, however, generally do not address the extent to which they completely ignore many other Biblical texts and do not use them for modern guidance. Other, liberal, bodies interpret the ancient texts in their historical context in the light of current biological and psychological knowledge about the origins and nature of homosexual and other orientations. These bodies, particularly liberal reformed—and to some extent conservative—Judaism, the Episcopal Church, and the United Church of Christ, frequently welcome homosexual men and women to membership, and even to the ministry (Heyward 1989; Presbyterian Church 1991; Thayer 1987). Within the Catholic Church in America, there is a quite-visible split that, on the grassroots level, constitutes a silent schism on the issue of homosexuality. On the pastoral level, many, perhaps a majority of the clergy, accept the tolerant and liberal position expressed by the Catholic Theological Society of America (Kosnick et al. 1977), and quietly ignore the dogmatic condemnation of homosexuality by the Vatican (Curran 1993; Francoeur in Gramick and Furey 1988; McNeill 1976).

Among American religious bodies, the major continuing issues regarding homosexuality center on welcome, support, and affirmation of members within congregations and on the presence of openly gay and lesbian persons in religious leadership. Recently, support for gay and lesbian members has often led to performing "holy unions" for gay and lesbian partners. Given that the legal option of marriage has not been available, religious bodies have been the logical place for couples to seek such recognition and support. Many congregations have offered these services to both their members and to gay and lesbian persons in their communities. Although there are gays and lesbians in leadership in some religious bodies, they are few and often do not receive the support of predominantly heterosexual congregations. The one religious place where gay and lesbian persons have found a guaranteed welcome has been in the special ministries that exist for gay and lesbian persons. This includes a variety of individual denominations and individual congregations with a special outreach to gay and lesbian persons.

Social Issues

The growing visibility of homosexuals in American society and the scrutiny of the press probing the private lives of public figures have led some politicians to acknowledge publicly their homoerotic orientation. In 1980, Robert E. Bauman, a leading conservative Republican Congressman from Maryland, lost his bid for reelection after revealing his homoerotic orientation. About the same time, Congressman Gerry E. Studds from Massachusetts revealed his homoeroticism and he served in the House of Representatives until 1996. Elaine Noble was the first openly lesbian legislator in the state of Massachusetts. On the federal level, Representative Barney Frank, also from Massachusetts, disclosed his homoerotic orientation in 1987, and also continues to serve. In 1994, President Bill Clinton named Roberta Achtenberg as his highest-ranking lesbian appointee, and she was confirmed by the Congress as assistant secretary for fair housing and equal opportunity in the Department of Housing and Urban Development. In 1995, she announced that she was leaving that post to run for mayor of San Francisco.

Thanks to the political and educational activism of a wide variety of gay and lesbian individuals and groups, American society is becoming increasingly sensitized to the prevailing discrimination of heterosexism and homophobia. On the negative side, there has been an apparent increase in violence against people perceived to be homosexual. Studies have indicated increases in the reporting of violent crimes that are based on the perceived homosexuality of the victim, and students have reported witnessing harassment of students and teachers thought to be homosexual. In some instances, the growing hostility is purported to be linked with fear and anxiety about AIDS, but lesbian and gay leaders suggest that this is simply a convenient new excuse to further hate and discrimination. Lesbians, gays, and bisexuals see themselves as the last large minority that is not legally protected from discrimination, and thus, as a group, they fulfill the need of some people to find scapegoats for whatever social ills occur. The other negative aspect of this increased visibility is that it causes the opposition to become aggressive. Observing the progress made by lesbians and gays in attempting to obtain equal rights, those opposed have taken a proactive approach in attempting to limit the rights and opportunities for lesbians and gays to enjoy a full and unrestricted life. This has taken many forms, including the development and dissemination of a video filled with partial truths and false information designed to arouse fear of and hatred toward homoerotic individuals and groups. There have also been referendums on ballots to deny homosexuals equal protection. While some of these have been passed in several jurisdictions, some of them have subsequently been declared unconstitutional by state and federal courts. That has not deterred others from developing similar referendums. In September 1996, Congress voted to deny Federal benefits to married people of the same sex and to permit states to ignore such marriages sanctioned in other states. A separate bill that would have banned for the first time discrimination against homosexuals in the workplace was defeated by a single vote.

On the positive side, openly gay or lesbian people have been elected to almost every level of government, with the exception of the executive branch of the state and federal governments (governors and the president and vice president). Voters in several jurisdictions have enacted legislation to protect the civil rights of lesbians and gays. The amount of literature and published research on lesbian and gay issues has increased exponentially in recent years, and the arts have moved to include lesbian, gay, and bisexual subjects in other than classically stereotypic and tragic roles. Research and commentary regarding gay, lesbian, and bisexual issues in the academic disciplines has become acceptable, and the result has been a concomitant exponential increase in published works in all the academic disciplines. There are even a few departments in universities specifically devoted to studies of lesbian, gay, and bisexual issues. In all the arts and literature, there are more and more instances of openly lesbian and gay themes, stories, and characters. And there are more openly gay, lesbian, and bisexual people in professional and amateur sports (such as Martina Navratalova in tennis, and Greg Louganis, the Olympic multiple-gold-medal diver), and in commerce (billionaire David Geffan).

Some people who are known privately but widely to be lesbian or gay are challenged by the gay and lesbian communities to be open. On occasion they are "outed," that is, they are publicly announced to be lesbian or gay. Whether this is appropriate and ethical, given the extent of the homophobia in the culture, is a question. Originally, this practice was instituted only in cases where a person was widely known to be homoerotic and was not only keeping that information secret, but also was engaging in antihomosexual activity, such as gay public officials supporting antigay, antilesbian legislation. It later developed into a more-general application of "outing," which many have questioned and challenged.

One of the major problems for lesbian, gay, and bisexual adolescents is the lack of positive role models available in the homophobic, heterosexist culture. This lack contributes to the lowered self-esteem of lesbian and gay youth. The increased visibility of lesbian women and gay men throughout all levels of the society means that younger lesbians and gays are able to see others of identical orientation who have succeeded in whatever their chosen career. This has a positive effect on ego and the development of self-image.

Family Issues

Gay and lesbian people have been at the forefront of defining operative, nontraditional, nonbiological family concepts. Although this may have grown from the difficulties of association with biological families and the impracticality of the "heterosexual husband-wife with children" relationship model, it has resulted in the active development and maintenance of alternative family structures of great depth and commitment that have subsequently provided an alternative model for the heterosexual society. This includes not only nonmarital couples and their children, but also committed long-standing friendship circles that constitute a chosen extended family, a set of associations often with stronger bonds than those that may exist through the unchosen avenue of blood relatives.

The depth and extent of these intentional relationships have become dramatically evident in the caring provided to those within such networks in the HIV/AIDS epidemic. The depth and extent of this caring has provided incontrovertible evidence of the wholesomeness and loving nature of these associations, and has significantly challenged the remainder of society.

The social, familial, and internalized heterosexist homophobia sometimes creates a situation in which the lesbian or gay man sees heterosexual marriage as the only public option for life. They may or may not include secret homosexual activity while married. With the increased visibility of lesbians, gays, and bisexuals, this pattern of behavior is less likely to occur without conscious awareness and dissonance on the part of both marital partners. Sometimes, but rarely, the only way a gay man or lesbian can cope successfully with the social pressures is to find a homoerotic person of the other gender to agree to a "marriage of convenience," in which they might live as roommates and have separate sexual lives.

Some lesbians and gay men choose to have children. Women have the option of childbearing through the medically established procedure of donor insemination available in this country, or they can, and sometimes do, seek and find a man who will biologically impregnate them. Men obviously do not have this option. Therefore, the issues for lesbians who want a child are different from those for a gay man who wants one. In keeping with the resourcefulness and creativity of many lesbians and gay men, there are many patterns that have been developed to achieve biological parenthood.

Support organizations for the heterosexual relatives of homoerotic individuals have formed and become available. Most notable is the organization Parents and Friends of Lesbians and Gays, (PFLAG), with headquarters in Washington, D.C. and groups throughout the United States. Where there are lesbian and gay community centers, usually one finds programs for children of lesbian and gay parents, such as The Center Kids, a program at the Lesbian and Gay Community Center in New York City. These centers also usually have support groups and education sessions for the biological families of lesbians and gays, as well as for the chosen families.

Health Issues

American lesbian women and gay men have many of the same health issues as their heteroerotic counterparts, but there are some issues that are unique, including the fact that the assumption of heterosexuality for individuals in the culture in general continues into the sphere of the health-care consumer. When the health-care professional is taking a history and asks, "Are you married or single or divorced?" there is little room for the lesbian or gay individual to indicate that she or he is in a long-term relationship with another person. And if the person is bisexually active, the answer to that question could be very misleading to the professional who should be concerned with whatever may impact the patient's health.

Lesbian women and gay men also have to interact with hospitals and other health-care facilities that often do not recognize the rights of a nonmarital partner to determine the course of treatment or to visit in an intensive-care unit unless they have obtained either a power of attorney or have officially been designated as a "health-care proxy."

Although lesbians have the lowest rates of sexually transmitted diseases of any orientation group, they also have some special concerns that would not apply to heteroerotic women, but would apply to bisexual women. Those issues are related to the fact that this person is sexually active with another woman. There is some debate concerning whether lesbians who are not sexually active with a man should have a Pap smear as often as a woman who is sexually active with a man. Additionally, if a patient tells the health-care professional that she is a lesbian, the assumption is then made that she is not being sexually active with a man. This assumption should always be checked, because it is not necessarily true. A comprehensive sex history is needed to avoid incorrect assumptions, but is seldom done.

Gay men, on the other hand, have a high rate of sexually transmitted diseases. Prior to the 1980s, there was no major push for these men to wear condoms to prevent STDs, because most of the diseases could be cured by medical intervention. However, with the advent of HIV/AIDS, that situation changed, and the increased use of condoms in this population has significantly decreased the incidence of other STDs. The high frequency of sexual activity in many gay men means that their health care needs include concerns for the many diseases that can be transmitted sexually—and a comprehensive sex history is mandatory if the professional is to provide appropriate health care.

In the early 1980s, what we now know as AIDS was called GRID, Gay Related Immunodeficiency Disease, and it was believed that gay men were the only people who had it. While that has changed, the largest percentage of cases of AIDS in the United States continues to be among gay men, and part of gay-male identity is now referenced to HIV status, i.e., whether he is HIV-positive or HIV-negative. There is some concern about the effect that this has on one's psychological health, with some people questioning the acceptance of that reference to "Gay Related" when the infectious potential of HIV is not influenced by a person's sexual orientation.

Additionally, gay men have been likened in a psychological manner to Vietnam veterans in that both have experienced the death of many people with whom close bonds had been established. There has been a suggestion that many gay men, particularly in the regions of the country that are hardest hit by the HIV/AIDS epidemic, are suffering from post-traumatic stress disorder, and are in need of psychological treatment. Those lesbians who are very involved in the care of and are friends of HIV-positive gay men, are also experiencing trauma associated with multiple bereavement.

Another group that is receiving little attention in this epidemic are those gay men who are HIV-negative, who have lost partners to AIDS, and who are having to deal with survivor guilt and associated issues. Many of these men must also cope with the very strong feelings of pleasure that were associated with sexual activity before HIV became a threat. These men are at great risk for HIV infection; yet in the mid-1990s, the public-health focus has turned to women and children at risk, generally ignoring gay men.

Homosexuality in the Later Years

Very little is known about sexuality and aging among the estimated 3.5 million American men and women over age 60 who are homosexual. For gay men and lesbians, aging can create unique conflicts and problems. The death of a partner in a long-term relationship may bring out homophobic reactions among family members that lead these relatives to ignore the bereaved partner or contest a will and estate. Gay men and lesbians who decide to acknowledge their orientation after years of passing as heterosexual face the possibility of quite different outcomes when loved ones, children, and grandchildren, learn of their relative's sexual orientation. Gay men, who are fearful that their orientation will be discovered as it becomes evident they are not going to marry, may adopt a loner life with relatively little sexual and social intimacy. Lesbian couples have to cope with two female incomes, which would usually be lower than most dual-career gay male or heterosexual couples (Friend 1987).

By necessity, gay men and lesbians develop skills in coping and crisis management, which give them an advantage in the aging process. More-flexible gender roles may allow older homosexuals to take aging more in stride and develop ways of taking care of themselves that seem comfortable and appropriate. "These skills may not be developed to the same degree among heterosexual men or women, who may be used to having or expecting a wife or husband to look after them" (Friend 1987, 311). Gay people tend to plan ahead for their own independence and security, whereas heterosexuals are more likely to assume that their children will take care of them in their old age. Homosexual men and women have significantly more close friends who serve as a "surrogate family" than do heterosexuals. In larger urban areas, organizations like Senior Action in a Gay Environment (SAGE) provide a variety of social and support services for older homosexuals.

Gay Men, Lesbian Women, and Bisexuals—Comparisons

Because gay men are socialized as males and generally perceive themselves as males, their socialization process is somewhat different from that of lesbian women, who are socialized as females and generally perceive themselves as being female. This means that, from a general perspective, just as there are differences in male and female socialization, there are differences between lesbians and gay men, as well as differences among them. For example, in general analyses of gay and lesbian relationships, one difference often noted between the two is the role of sexual activity and sexual exclusivity. Generally, lesbian relationships are sexually exclusive and gay male relationships are not. This appears to be especially true of long-term relationships, and can be explained by the differences in socialization of women and men around sexual activity issues.

When gay men and lesbian women join together to form groups working toward a common goal, sometimes there are issues of power differentials and attitudes toward sexual activity that prevent the original goals from being reached by dividing the group along gender lines. Again, this can be explained by the differential socialization process.

It was not until the late 1980s that people identified as bisexual were welcomed into what were previously lesbian and gay organizations, and they are still viewed with caution in many circles. Bisexuals are sometimes accused by heterosexual people of being gay or lesbian and are labeled homophobic and fake by some homoerotic people. There are few bisexual support groups, most of them in large cities. The United States is only just beginning to attempt to understand the bisexual phenomenon.

C. Bisexuality   CAROL QUEEN WITH ROBERT MORGAN LAWRENCE

The ambivalence about bisexuality is reflected in the history of the concept. For several years after the terms homosexuality and heterosexuality were coined in the late 1800s, bisexuality was largely ignored by the physicians and sex researchers who had newly medicalized sex. Sigmund Freud, with his theory of sexual development borrowed from Darwinian evolutionary models, helped to change that. By the 1920s, when Wilhelm Stekel wrote *Bi-Sexual Love*, the erotic capacity to desire both males and females could be envisioned as universal, if likely to be outgrown by adulthood. Havelock Ellis, by contrast, viewed bisexuality as a distinct sexual-orientation category, comparable to both homo- and heterosexuality.

Alfred Kinsey (1948, 1953) conceptualized bisexuality not in evolutionary terms, as the Freudians tended to do, but in simple behavioral terms. In his sexual-orientation scale, bisexuality was represented on a continuum between exclusive heterosexuality (the 0 end of Kinsey's scale) and exclusive homosexuality (at 6), with a Kinsey 3 equally attracted to or having had sexual experience with males and females.

Since most humans experience their erotic desires and relationships in a social context, many (perhaps most) bisexuals have more sexual experience with one or the other gender, depending upon whether their social affiliations tend to be mostly heterosexual or homosexual. Indeed, researchers have noted that many people who have displayed "bisexual" behavior over the lifespan—that is, people who have had sexual experience with both males and females—tend to identify sexually according to the gender of their current partner (Blumstein and Schwartz 1983). This is reported as especially true of women. When the current partner is female, women are more likely to identify themselves as lesbian, and when the current partner is male, as heterosexual. Factors such as political or social affiliation can also lead an individual to—or away from—a bisexual identity.

One common stereotype about bisexuals suggests a person is not "really" bisexual unless he or she is a Kinsey 3. This is related to the presumption that the individual is "really" homosexual but hiding behind a heterosexual relationship. The notion that all, or most, people are "really" homosexual or heterosexual has been termed "monosexuality." Monosexuals are individuals who desire members of only one gender, whereas bisexuals desire both. The term was apparently first used to describe hetero- and homosexuals by Stekel (1922). Today this term has gained new currency in the American bisexual community as bisexuals seek to understand and combat the sources of stereotyping and social opprobrium they term "biphobia" (Hutchins and Kaahumanu 1991). Expressions of biphobia encompass caustic dismissals, such as Bergler's (1956) "Nobody can dance at two different weddings at the same time"; difficult relations between bisexual women and some lesbians (Weise 1992); and media-fed concerns that bisexual men are "spreading AIDS" into the heterosexual population. (The latter concern ignores the possibility that bisexual men can be as responsible about safe-sex practices as anyone else, that heterosexuals may also contract HIV from other heterosexuals, and that bisexual men may choose to live monogamous lives with female—or male—partners.)

Until recently, American bisexuals had few sources of support for their sexuality unless they derived it from the gay community—which has been far from uniformly supportive. In fact, it should be noted that many gays deny the reality and/or possibility of bisexuality. In the 1970s, a few support groups for bisexuals were formed; the best known of these was San Francisco's Bisexual Center. By the late 1980s, groups and organizations had emerged that aimed specifically to develop a supportive bisexual community; at the time of this writing, these are extensively networked and are producing their own publications and conferences.

Due to insufficient support, the influence of negative and alienating stereotypes, and the apparent fact that many bisexuals have lived as lesbians, gay men, or heterosexuals, it has been difficult to estimate what percentage of the population is, or has been, bisexual. It is probable that many more people have bisexual histories than would answer affirmatively to a survey researcher asking "Are you bisexual?" Too, many researchers have conflated or collapsed homosexuality and bisexuality (for a recent example, see Laumann et al. 1994), a further indication that many still consider one a variant of the other.

To stress the multidimensional nature of sexuality, Fred Klein (1985) developed his Sexual Orientation Grid, which expands Kinsey's concept of the continuum. He considers not only experience and desire, but also dreams, fantasies, social networks, relationships, ideal sexual orientation, and other variables. Additionally, Klein breaks the scale into temporal units (adolescence; early adulthood; present) so it can better reflect changes in behavior and sexual identity over the lifespan. Coleman (1987) has also developed a scale that takes factors like these into account and that serves as a clinical interview tool. Researchers using these scales, as well as Kinsey's, find that, although some display continuity of sexual identity over the lifespan, other individuals change identity over time. Many rate themselves near the middle of the Kinsey scale when asked their ideal, but report their relationships fall closer to one or the other end.

That behavior and identity are not fixed (and are sometimes not even consonant) is of special interest and relevance to researchers of bisexuality. The differences between homosexual and heterosexual may be less important and intriguing than those between monosexual and bisexual. Why, for example, is a prospective partner's gender of primary importance to some (monosexuals) and not to others (many bisexuals)? Other researchers note that bisexuality assumes different forms in different cultures, subcultures, and individuals. Klein (1978) suggests four primary types: (1) sequential (in which an individual will alternately partner or engage in sex with only men, then only women); (2) concurrent (in which an individual partners and/or engages in sex with both genders during the same period of time); (3) historical (bisexual behavior in an individual's past, especially adolescence); and (4) transitional (through which a heterosexual moves toward homosexuality or a homosexual moves toward heterosexuality).

Other American researchers have concentrated not on the taxonomy of bisexuality, but on the development and adjustment of bisexuals in day-to-day life. Some of this research has been incidental to studies done on gay and lesbian or heterosexual populations; other researchers have looked at self-identified bisexual populations. Just as estimates on the percentage of bisexuals in the population are inconclusive, so is information about what percentage of people who have a history of sexual experience with both genders defines themselves as bisexual. What differentiates those who do from those who do not is still a matter of speculation, although research into the formation of bisexual identity suggests that, at least for them, identity formation is more open-ended than linear.

A common monosexual accusation is that bisexuals are "confused." Although this may be descriptive of some bisexuals before they find the label with which to self-identify, and some may also experience ongoing distress or uncertainty due to the dearth of societal validation (Weinberg and Williams 1994), some research has indicated that self-identified bisexuals are high in self-esteem, self-confidence, and independence of social norms (Rubenstein 1982; Twining 1983).

Much more attention has been given to bisexuals, especially males, who are heterosexually married than to those whose primary relationships are homosexual. These marriages are most successful when the partners communicate openly, the spouse is aware and accepting of the bisexual partner's sexuality, and both partners are committed to the relationship. Especially as the bisexual community brings self-identified bisexual people together, more bisexuals are choosing to partner with other bisexuals. These relationships may be monogamous, open, polyamorous, or—much more rarely—triadic.

Bisexuals bringing issues related to their sexual identities into therapy may seek help in interpreting their attractions to both genders; other issues are isolation and alienation, fears about coming out or about nonvoluntary disclosure of their sexuality, and relationship concerns.

What bisexual community spokespeople call "bisexual invisibility" hinders many individuals from easily resolving their concerns about adopting a non-normative sexual identity. Many do not know about the existence of a community of peers. While some individuals move towards a bisexual identity after considering themselves heterosexual, others have previously been gay- or lesbian-identified. As such, diversity in the bisexual community is broad, and will undoubtedly become broader as more people gain access to its institutions.

7. *Cross-Gendered Persons*

ARIADNE KANE

A. Conceptualizations

[On March 12, 1993, the "Op-Ed" page of *The New York Times* carried a full-page reflection on "How Many Sexes Are There?" The March/April issue of *The Sciences*, published by the New York Academy of Sciences, featured an article on "The Five Sexes: Why Male and Female Are Not Enough." These articles, by biologist Anne Fausto-Sterling, are evidence of a trend in changing definitions of gender roles over the past decade that is echoed in the appearance in 1995 of *Hermaphrodites with Attitudes*, a newsletter published by cross-gendered persons who endorse Fausto-Sterling's call for the medical profession to recognize gender diversity and cease using surgery and gender reassignment to force true hermaphrodites ("herms"), female pseudohermaphrodites ("ferms"), and male pseudohermaphrodites ("merms") into the dichotomous mold of male or female. (Editor)]

An Indigenous View

American society, with its cultural diversity, has long assumed that one's gender perception, role, and presentation are all a function of biological anatomy, as visually ascertained at birth. This biocentric viewpoint served as the basis for looking at sexual and gender variations for both sexologists and therapists. Until the mid-1970s, many sexual and gender options were seen and diagnosed as deviations of the male/female gender dichotomy

1540 · *International Encyclopedia of Sexuality*

and/or as types of sexual dysfunction. Gender options, as style modes of clothing and accouterment, gender shifts, and transsexualism were viewed as dis-eases [sic] of the psyche. Those who chose such options were considered "gender-conflicted" and were treated on the basis of known medical or psychological modalities (Pauly 1994).

Factors contributing to the current trend of changing gender roles include the rise and powerful articulation of feminism among both women and men; the knowledge explosion in molecular biology, specifically genetics and endocrinology, artistic diversity in both the visual arts and music with their individual styles and presentations (with cinema, television, and music increasingly dealing with gender and cross-gender issues), the emergence of an articulate, vocative, and visible gay-lesbian-cross-gender "community," and the influence of computer technology and its application in almost all sectors of American life. The impact of these factors on the daily lives of Americans—how they think, how they feel both about themselves as well as society, and how they act and present themselves to each other—has been awesome.

In this social context, there is a powerful drive to question the biocentric notion about gender being a derivative of the biomorphic nature of *Homo sapiens*, i.e., two sexes implies only two gender forms. This challenge to gender rigidity, in roles and presentations, is seen in many areas of American social and economic life. Women as bus drivers and heavy-equipment operators and men as nurses and secretaries represent only one aspect of the varied paradigm shift occurring in America in the nature of gender identity and its concomitant behaviors. Instead of a two-sexes/two-genders model, one needs a model of two or more sexes and many genders. This gives rise to a sociocentric view of gender, in which one can think of gender in terms of three basic parameters: perception (Jungian constructs of anima/animus), social role (cuing, interactions, and gender-role inventories), and presentation (modes of presenting one's self, for whom, when, motivations, etc.). A person is then seen as a composite of these three parameters, with the gender composite time-dependent and always subject to some change in one or more component over the lifespan.

The shift from focusing on individual gender conflict to looking at facets of gender diversity is evident in the "gender rainbow" paradigm suggested by gender counselors Leah Schaefer and Constance Wheeler, June Reinisch's concept of "gender flavors," and James Weinrich's model of "gender landscapes" (Francoeur 1991, 100-101). In these paradigms, the notion of conflict is broadened to include gender explorations and gender clarifications and how an individual can access these avenues in their search for personal growth in a tolerant and more nurturant society. Armed with this sociocentric model of gender, one can study CD/CG (cross-dressing/cross-gender) behaviors and conflicts with a more-sensitive approach to the issues and problems of gender expression in an ethnoculturally diverse American society.

Traditionally, the terms "transvestite" (TV) and "transsexual" (TS) have been used to label individuals, mostly males, who wear apparel usually associated with the other sex, or who want to cross a gender boundary and seek anatomical congruity with the other sex. These terms are too inclusive and stigmatize the person, who may be on a gender exploration, or who sees personal gender expression as only one piece in their total personality matrix. To deal with this limitation, the following new glossary has been proposed, with the terms serving as "mileposts" on the road to gender "happiness:"

- A "cross-dresser" (CD) is a person, male or female, who wears an item or items of apparel usually worn by the other gender; it is a descriptor of behavior and includes previously used terms like TV (transvestite), FI (female impersonator), and DQ (drag queen).
- "Cross-gender" (CG) refers to a person, male or female, who desires to cross and explore a gender role different from typical gender roles associated with their biologic sex. It can also be used as a behavior descriptor.
- A "transsexual" (TS) is a person, male or female, who has chosen a preferred gender role and wants anatomical congruity with that gender-role preference. This is achieved with an appropriate sex-hormone-therapy program and sex-reassignment surgery (SRS).
- "New Women/Men" refer to persons, male or female, who have transited to a preferred gender role, i.e., transgenderist, and have had sex-reassignment surgery.
- The "CD/CG/TS paraculture" refers to the community of people, males and females, whose general behavior patterns include a major component of gender-diverse activity.

The term "transgender" indicates that a person is crossing gender boundaries usually associated with traditional gender traits of one or the other sex. Transgender, transgendered, and transgenderist are also used to indicate transcending—rising above—traditional gender forms and expressions, a usage that has gained popularity both within the paraculture, as well as in the health-care and academic professions.

A Clinical View

The term "transsexualism" was coined by D. O. Cauldwell, an American sexologist, and popularized by Harry Benjamin in the 1950s and 1960s. Research on this phenomenon was facilitated in 1980 when the concepts of transsexualism and gender disorders were recognized in the American Psychiatric Association's *Diagnostic and Statistical Manual III*. In 1988, transsexualism was defined by the *DSM-III-R* as having the following diagnostic criteria:

1. persistent discomfort and sense of inappropriateness about one's assigned sex;
2. persistent preoccupation for at least two years with getting rid of one's primary and secondary sex characteristics and acquiring the sex characteristics of the other sex; and
3. having reached puberty (otherwise, the diagnosis would be childhood gender identity disorder).

DSM-IV has replaced the term "transsexual" with the generic term "gender disorder."

Transsexualism is estimated to affect at least 1 in 50,000 individuals over the age of 15 years, with a 1:1 male-to-female ratio. The greater visibility of male-to-female transsexuals may reflect a more-negative bias toward male homosexuality or a lack of available female-to-male treatment in a society. Whatever the real incidence, this disorder carries more social significance and impact than the actual prevalence might suggest because of the questions raised for anyone who watches and listens to transsexuals (and transvestites) in their frequent appearances on television talk shows (Pauly 1994, 591).

An individual's perception of his or her own body, and the way she or he feels about these perceptions, are important in the clinical diagnosis of gender disorders. In 1975, Lindgren and Pauly introduced a Body Image Scale, a thirty-item list of body parts, for which the individual is asked to rate her or his feelings on a five-point scale ranging from (1) very satisfied to (5) very dissatisfied. This scale is useful in following the progress and evaluating the success of sex-reassignment treatment.

Evaluating the outcome of sex-reassignment surgery is complicated and difficult. The most recent evaluation leaves little question that the vast majority of post-operative transsexuals claim satisfaction and would pursue the same course if they had to do it again. Post-operative satisfaction ranged from 71.4 percent to 87.8 percent for post-operative male-to-female transsexuals, with only 8.1 percent to 10.3 percent expressing dissatisfaction. Among female-to-male transsexuals surveyed, 80.7 percent to 89.5 percent were satisfied with their outcome, compared with only 6.0 percent to 9.7 percent who are not satisfied. The difference between male-to-female and female-to-male satisfaction was not statistically significant (Pauly 1994, 597).

The publicity that followed the American, Christine Jorgenson's sex-change surgery in Denmark in 1953, led to widespread public and professional discussion, and ultimately a distinction between transsexualism and transvestism. Harry Benjamin developed a three-point scale of transvestism, with transsexuals viewed as an extreme form of transvestism; he later came to regard the two as different entities.

The variety of cross-dressers includes fetishistic males and females who cross-dress for erotic arousal and those who enjoy cross-dressing to express their female persona; it includes individuals who cross-dress and live full-time in the other gender role, and those who cross-dress only occasionally and partially, with the whole range between these two ends of the spectrum.

In the 1960s, Virginia (Charles) Prince, a Los Angeles transvestite, began publishing *Transvestia*, a magazine for heterosexual cross-dressers. Encouraged by the response, Prince organized a "sorority without sisters," the Society for the Second Self or Tri-Ess (SSS), with chapters in several major cities. As a result of her worldwide travels, lectures, and television appearances, research on transvestism increased significantly because of the availability of research subjects.

As the cross-gender movement grew and became more visible, dissident and new voices appeared. At present, there are a variety of support groups for cross-dressers; some accept only heterosexual or homosexual and bisexual members, while others are not concerned with orientation. Some CD groups include transsexuals, others do not. In addition, there is a small industry, including "tall or big girl" fashion shops and mail-order catalogs, that cater to the clothing and other needs of cross-gendered persons.

B. Current Status of American CD/CG Paraculture

It is apparent that many more American males and females are openly cross-dressing than at any other time in this century. The motivations for this activity are quite varied, ranging from female- or male-impersonation (FI, MI) as "Miss Coquette" or "Mr. Baggypants" at a Halloween party, to lip-synching performances at FI and MI reviews (i.e., "La Cage aux Folles" or Mr. Elvis Presley look-alike shows), to femme expressions in daily activities such as work or socializing. While it appears less obvious, there are many more females who cross-dress with the intent of expressing some part of their masculine persona (animus).

In the last decade, there has been a dramatic increase in the number of social contact groups, both for males who cross-dress and want social contact with others of similar persuasion in a secure setting, and for females who want to explore more fully the dimensions of their masculinity. Both female and male adolescents are cross-dressing to reflect feelings of their favorite musical stars, e.g., k.d. lang, RuPaul, Boy George, Melissa Etheridge, Michael Jackson, or the Erasure or Indigo Girls rock groups. (It should be noted that several of these performers are also known to be gay or lesbian, perhaps creating some public confusion about the association between cross-dressing and sexual orientation.) There are also young people who show some affinity for atypical gender-role expression. These may be early phases of mixing aspects of traditional gender norms with explorations of the limits of gender duality, that may benefit from appropriate professional help.

One segment of this paraculture is definitely exploring gender options with the aim of resolving gender conflict. Such conflicts may not be limited to the intrapsychic, but extend into resolving tensions between the rights of individual expression and the norms of conventional gender roles and presentations. When the desire to shift gender is experienced, there is a need for professional help in understanding the motivation for the gender shift and to develop a program that will clarify some of the important questions that individual may have to address in pursuing such a choice. Such a program of gender exploration or gender shift may involve the use of hormones and also the decision to have sex-reassignment surgery. Some of these people label themselves transgenderists, in the sense noted above, and can fully develop and express an alternate gender role and lifestyle. Some may be satisfied with this shift and not want to pursue sex-reassignment surgery. For others, after living full-time for one-and-a-half to two years in the preferred gender role, the decision is to complete the shift with surgery; in which case, the label "transsexual" is appropriate.

Currently, more and more people are challenging the binary gender forms and want to explore other gender options. If surgery is not the ultimate objective, these individuals may choose to blend traits and become more androgynous or gynandrous, expressing a feminine-masculine or masculine-feminine gender. This segment of the paraculture is also receiving some attention.

As for legal issues involving CD/CG behaviors, most states do not have statutes that specifically prohibit the practice of CD/CG presentation in public. However, there may be some local ordinances that restrict this behavior in their jurisdiction. If tested in the judicial system, such laws would probably be ruled unconstitutional. Obtaining a legal change of name is not a problem in most areas of the country, and should be accompanied by some form of public notice for creditors, usually in the classified section of a local newspaper. Change of birth certificate may pose some problems; again each state has its own guidelines.

With regard to sex-reassignment surgery, a medical group created a pamphlet of guidelines for the preoperative transsexual about 1980. *Standards of Care* details guidelines for the client, health-care counselor/therapist, and the surgeon for handling the process of gender shift prior to surgery. This document is available from any of the organizations listed at the end of this section. Few, if any medical-insurance plans pay for this surgery, which for a male-to-female runs about $8,000 to $10,000. In recent years, several reputable gender clinics have discontinued providing this surgery.

For health-care professionals, sex educators, counselors, therapists, physicians, nurses, and sexologists, there are two major programs available to update one's knowledge about gender or to facilitate change in attitudes about gender issues. Segments in the standard Sexual Attitudes Reassessment (SAR) Workshop focus on CD/CG behaviors and lifestyles. In the Gender Attitude Reassessment Program (GARP), the focus is on all aspects of gender and its diversity; ten to fifteen units deal with specific topics in the phenomenon of gender. Both of these programs are given at national professional meetings and in continuing education programs at major universities and mental health centers in the U.S.A.

Within the paraculture structures, there are several programs for CD/TG/TS/AN Americans. Two of the oldest and "personal-growth-oriented" are Fantasia Fair and Be All. Fantasia Fair, founded twenty years ago, provides a living/learning experience for adult male cross-dressers who want to explore the many dimensions of their femme persona in a tolerant open community. Fantasia events, often held at Provincetown on Cape Cod, Massachusetts, emphasize personal growth in all aspects of their programming. Be All, an offshoot of Fantasia Fair, focuses on the practical and social aspects of femme persona development. It is usually held in a motel/inn near a major city and is sponsored by a regional group of social contact organizations.

Organizations providing information on gender issues include:

American Education and General Information Service, P. O. Box 33724, Decatur, Georgia 33033.

Harry Benjamin International Gender Dysphoria Association, P. O. Box 1718, Sonoma, California 95476.

I.C.T.L.E.P., Inc., 5707 Firenza St., Houston, Texas 77035-5515.

Outreach Institute of Gender Studies (OIGS), 126 Western Ave., Suite 246, Augusta, Maine 04330.

The Society for the Second Self (Tri-Ess) (for heterosexual cross-dressers only), P. O. Box 194, Tulare, California 93275. (Publishes a quarterly magazine, *Femme Mirror*, and other support material.)

8. Significant Unconventional Sexual Behaviors

In this section, we consider a group of "other" sexual behaviors. These include sexual coercion (rape, sexual harassment, and child sexual abuse), prostitution, pornography, paraphilias, and fetishes. As a general rule, Americans tend to view heterosexual relations between consenting adults in an ongoing relationship, such as marriage, as the norm. It is true that such sexual relations are the modal pattern in the U.S.A. (Laumann, et al., 1994), as is true of every culture. However, the earlier reviews of extramarital sex, alternative lifestyles, homosexuality, and bisexuality all serve to illustrate that sizable percentages of Americans engage in sexual behavior which departs from this assumed norm. American sexologists have struggled for some time to develop acceptable terminology to describe other sexual practices. The concept of sexual orientation has allowed us to view homosexuality and bisexuality as variations in orientation. Similarly, the concept of gender transposition has provided a terminology for examining cross-gender behaviors.

Typically, non-marital sexual practices have been labeled as sexual deviance or sexual variance. There are, however, at least two problems with such terms. First, no matter what the proper sociological conceptualization, these terms inevitably convey a sense of pathology, dysfunction, or abnormality to behaviors which are situationally defined. For example, consider the act of exhibitionism, exposing one's genitals to another. When practiced in the streets, the act is defined as a crime and is quite rare. When practiced in certain business establishments, the practitioner is paid for the act and clients pay to see it; and when practiced in the privacy of one's home with an intimate partner, it is seen as normal and healthy sexual interaction. Second, some of these behaviors are, in fact, quite common. Muehlenhard reviews evidence that shows many women are victims of sexual coercion. Several recent surveys provide evidence that nearly one quarter of Americans view pornographic video tapes each year (Davis 1990; Laumann, et al. 1994). It appears that relatively small percentages of Americans participate in any one of the various fetish groups reviewed below. However, taken together and added to the forms of non-marital sexual expression we have already reviewed, it seems clear that rather large percentages of Americans do participate in some "other" form of sexual practice [D. L. Weis, Coeditor].

A. Coercive Sex

Sexual Assault and Rape   CHARLENE MUEHLENHARD AND BARRIE J. HIGHBY

Basic Concepts. The conceptualization of rape and the treatment of rapists and rape victims in the United States have changed substantially since the 1970s, largely due to the work of feminists. The situation is complex, however; there are many perspectives on these issues. Even the terminology related to rape is at issue. Some persons have suggested that the term "rape" be replaced by "sexual assault" in order to emphasize the violent nature of the act and to place greater emphasis on the behavior of the perpetrator; recent reforms in the criminal codes of some states no longer speak of rape, but of varying degrees of sexual assault (Estrich 1987; Koss 1993a). Others, however, prefer to retain the term rape "to signify the outrage of this crime" (Koss 1993a, 199). Some regard rape as different and more serious than assault and contend that "to label rape as a form of assault . . . may obscure its unique indignity" (Estrich 1987, 81). There is no clear consensus in the law, the popular media, research literature, or feminist writings. We will use the term rape.

Similarly, some persons have suggested that the term "rape victim" be replaced by "rape survivor." Each term has advantages. The term "victim" highlights the harm that rape causes. The term "survivor" has more optimistic connotations and, thus, may empower someone who has been raped; it also highlights similarities between people who have survived rape and people who have survived other life-threatening events. The term "survivor," however, may perpetuate the stereotype that only rapes that are life-threatening—that is, that involve a great deal of extrinsic violence—are worthy of being regarded as "real rape." Thus, we will use the term rape victim.

Definitions. Rape can generally be defined as one person's forcing another to engage in sex against that person's will. This general definition, however, leaves many questions unanswered (Muehlenhard et al. 1992b). What behaviors count as sex? Whom do these definitions cover? What counts as force? In the United States, thinking about each of these questions has changed since the 1970s, and controversy remains.

Defining rape is complicated by the fact that there are many types of definitions. In the legal domain, the federal government and all fifty states each have their own definition. Legal definitions are written by legislatures, which are composed primarily of men; thus, these definitions are likely to be written from men's perspectives (Estrich 1987). The definitions held by the general public are influenced by the law, the media, folk wisdom, jokes, and so forth. Some researchers base their definitions on legal definitions, which makes them subject to the same biases as legal definitions; others make conscious decisions to deviate from legal definitions, which they find biased or inadequate. Finally, there are political definitions, written by activists wanting to make various political points. For example, MacKinnon (1987, 82) wrote,

> Politically, I call it rape whenever a woman has sex and feels violated. You might think that's too broad. I'm not talking about sending all of you men to jail for that. I'm talking about attempting to change the nature of the relations between women and men by having women ask ourselves, "Did I feel violated?"

Persons who regard legal definitions as the most valid criticize such political definitions as being too broad (e.g., Farrell 1993). Based on the assumption that language is power, however, political activists have resisted the status quo by challenging widely held definitions and encouraging people to think about the assumptions behind these definitions.

Prior to the 1970s, rape definitions of sex often included only penile-vaginal sexual intercourse. This definition has been criticized as too phallocentric, promoting the ideas that an act must involve a man's penis and must have the potential for reproduction to count as "real sex" (Muehlenhard, et al. 1992b; Rotkin 1972/1986). Currently, most definitions of rape use a broader conceptualization of sex, including many kinds of sexual penetration (e.g., penile-vaginal intercourse, fellatio, cunnilingus, anal intercourse, or penetration of the genitals or rectum by an object). Some definitions are even broader, including behaviors such as touching someone's genitals, breasts, or buttocks (Estrich 1987; Koss 1993a).

Another contentious question involves whom these definitions cover. If rape is defined as forced penile-vaginal intercourse, then by definition an act of rape must involve a woman and a man; this definition would exclude coercive sex between two individuals of the same sex. In requiring the perpetrator to penetrate the victim sexually, such definitions would exclude

1548 · *International Encyclopedia of Sexuality*

situations in which a woman forced a man to engage in penile-vaginal intercourse, because such situations would involve the victim penetrating the perpetrator (Koss 1993a). Some definitions of rape include only the experiences of adolescents and adults (e.g., Koss et al. 1987), whereas others also include the experiences of children (e.g., Russell 1984).

Prior to the 1970s, rape laws in the U.S. included a "marital exclusion," exempting husbands from being charged with raping their wives. As of the mid-1990s, this marital exclusion has been removed from the laws of all fifty states, as well as from federal law (X 1994). In some states, however, laws still define rape between spouses more narrowly than rape between non-spouses, giving married women less legal protection than unmarried women. Furthermore, some state laws still treat rape less seriously if it occurs between two people who have previously engaged in consensual sex (X 1994).

Yet another contentious question involves what counts as force. Most definitions include physical force and threats of physical force. Many also include sex with someone who is unable to consent due to being intoxicated, asleep, or otherwise unable to consent. There is disagreement, however, regarding how intoxicated one needs to be, whether the alcohol or drugs need to be administered to the victim by the perpetrator, what happens if both persons are intoxicated, and so forth. This is particularly relevant in cases of date or acquaintance rape (Muehlenhard et al. 1992b).

Even regarding threats of physical force, there is disagreement about how direct such threats need to be. For example, in some court cases, appellate judges have made it clear that a woman's acquiescing to sex with a man because she is afraid that he will harm her (e.g., because he has harmed her in the past, or because they are in an isolated location and he is behaving in a way she regards as threatening) is not sufficient to define the incident as rape. Instead, these judges interpreted the law to mean that a woman should not cry and give in; she should fight like a "real man" (Estrich 1987).

Conceptualizations of Rape and Rapists. Prior to the changes initiated by feminists in the 1970s, rape was commonly conceptualized as a sexual act in which a man responded to a woman's sexual provocations. Rapists were often assumed to be either black men who raped white women or else men who were lower class or crazy and who were provoked by women who dressed or behaved too provocatively (Davis 1981; Donat and D'Emilio 1992; Gise and Paddison 1988; LaFree 1982; Mio and Foster 1991). Amir (1971, 273), for example, discussed "victim precipitated rape," which he conceptualized as rape incited by female victims who spoke, dressed, or behaved too provocatively (e.g., who went to a man's residence or who attended "a picnic where alcohol is present." MacDonald (1971, 311) wrote that

> the woman who accepts a ride home from a stranger, picks up a hitchhiker, sunbathes alone or works in the garden in a two-piece bathing suit which exposes rather than conceals her anatomy invites

rape. The woman who by immodest dress, suggestive remarks or behavior flaunts her sexuality should not be surprised if she is attacked
sexually. These ladies are referred to as "rape bait" by police officers.

Female victims were often thought to have desired or enjoyed the
experience (Gise and Paddison 1988; Griffin 1971; Mio and Foster 1991;
Muehlenhard et al. 1992a). For example, Wille (1961, 19) wrote about the
typical rape victim's "unconscious desires to be the victim of a sexual
assault." Husbands, in effect, "owned" their wives and were entitled to their
sexuality; thus, the concept of marital rape was nonexistent (Clark and
Lewis 1977; Donat and D'Emilio 1992). Sexual acts that occurred between
acquaintances or on dates were often assumed to be sexual encounters that
the woman had let get out of hand (Amir 1971).

In the 1970s, feminist writers began to conceptualize rape as violence
(e.g., Brownmiller 1975; Griffin 1971). In a classic article, Griffin (1971,
312) wrote that

> rape is an act of aggression in which the victim is denied her self-deter-
> mination. It is an act of violence which, if not actually followed by
> beatings or murder, nevertheless always carries with it the threat of
> death. And finally, rape is a form of mass terrorism, for the victims of
> rape are chosen indiscriminately.

Griffin also emphasized that the fear of rape limits women's freedom,
and as such, rape functions as do other forms of violence. Conceptualizing
rape as violence has numerous advantages: acknowledging the serious
consequences of rape; highlighting the similarities between the effects of
rape and the effects of other kinds of violence; taking the emphasis of rape
prevention off restricting women's sexual behavior; and acknowledging
that rape affects all women, even those who have not actually been raped,
by instilling fear and, thus, restricting women's freedom.

Currently, in the United States, it is common to hear people say, "Rape
isn't sex; it's violence." Nevertheless, many writers, both feminist political
activists and researchers, have found value in conceptualizing rape as
having elements of sex as well as violence (Muehlenhard et al. in press).
Feminists have discussed similarities between rape and other sexual situations, which may also be coercive:

> So long as we say that [rape involves] *abuses of violence, not sex*, we fail
> to criticize what has been made of sex, what has been done to us through
> sex, because we leave the line between rape and intercourse . . . right
> where it is. (MacKinnon 1987, 87, emphasis in original)

Understanding rapists has been enhanced by investigating both the
sexual and the violent aspects of their behavior and attitudes. Rapists are

more likely than nonrapists to become sexually aroused by depictions of sexual violence, as well as to feel hostile toward women, to accept rape myths and violence against women, and to view heterosexual relationships as adversarial. They drink more heavily and are more likely to have drinking problems, which may serve as a release or an excuse for sexually violent behavior. They are also more likely to have witnessed parental abuse or to have been physically or sexually abused in their childhoods. They begin having sexual experiences, either consensual or nonconsensual, earlier than nonrapists (Berkowitz 1992; Burt 1991; Koss and Dinero 1988; Finkelhor and Yllo 1985; Malamuth 1986; Russell 1982/1990).

Drawing on over thirty years of rehabilitation work with convicted sex offenders at the New Jersey State facility, William Prendergast (1991) has described a developmental-descriptive profile of typical compulsive-repetitive sex offenders. This profile involves two childhood experiences or characteristics: an unresolved inadequate personality and an unresolved preadolescent or early adolescent sexual trauma. Rapists try to cope with these unresolved personality traits by denial and overcompensating. In seeking to control their victims, they use terror, physical force, and any behavior that will degrade the victim. Pedophiles, on the other hand, accept their unresolved traits and seek to control their victims by seduction.

Current research has also dispelled other myths about rape. Rapists represent all ethnic groups and social classes (Russell 1984, 1990), and the overwhelming majority of rapes occur between acquaintances (Kilpatrick et al. 1987; Koss et al. 1988; Russell 1984) and between members of the same race or ethnicity (Amir 1971; O'Brien 1987). Research shows that men can be raped and women can be rapists (Brand and Kidd 1986; Muehlenhard and Cook 1988; Sarrel and Masters 1982; Waterman et al. 1989). Still, because rape and the fear of rape affects women more than men, and because of the differences in how women's and men's sexuality is conceptualized in the United States, some claim it would be a mistake to treat rape as a gender-neutral phenomenon (MacKinnon 1990; Rush 1990). Finally, "thanks to the feminist movement, no one any longer defends the dangerous claim that rape is a sexually arousing or sought-after experience on the part of the victim" (Palmer 1988, 514).

Prevalence. How prevalent is rape? Estimates of prevalence depend not only on how rape is defined, but also on the methodology used. Telephone surveys consistently result in lower prevalence estimates than do questionnaires or face-to-face interviews. Conducting interviews in the presence of family members yields low prevalence estimates, which is understandable given that many rape victims do not tell their families about having been raped, and some rape victims have been raped by family members. Asking respondents if they have been "raped" yields low prevalence estimates because many rape victims do not label their experience as "rape." Asking respondents a single question about their experiences generally yields low estimates, perhaps because asking only one such question fails to elicit memories of rapes that may have occurred in numerous contexts (e.g., with strangers, casual acquaintances, dates, or family members, obtained by force or threats of force or when the victim was unable to consent, and so forth; Koss 1993a).

Two sources of information on rape published by the government are generally inadequate: The *Uniform Crime Reports*, published by the Federal Bureau of Investigation (FBI 1993), include only rapes that were reported to the police—a small minority of all rapes (Russell 1984). The *National Crime Victimization Surveys*, conducted by the government's Bureau of Justice Statistics (BJS), also have serious methodological flaws (BJS 1993; Koss 1992; Russell 1984).

The best approach to studying the prevalence of rape involves confidentially asking respondents a series of questions about various experiences that meet the definition of rape. Studies using this procedure have found that approximately 20 percent of adult women in the United States have been raped (see Koss 1993b, for a review). As mentioned previously, most of these rapes occur between acquaintances of the same race. Percentages of men who report being raped or otherwise sexually victimized are generally lower than the percentages of women who report such experiences (Koss 1993a), although because most prevalence studies have focused on female respondents, information on men's being raped is scant.

Consequences for Rape Victims. American research on the consequences of rape has improved dramatically in the past several decades. Prior to the 1970s, studies of rape victims consisted of occasional case studies of victims who sought psychotherapy, a biased sample because most rape victims do not seek therapy and those who do are likely to be atypical (e.g., to be in greater distress, to be of higher socioeconomic status, etc.). The next generation of studies involved assessing rape victims who reported the rapes to police or emergency-room personnel; this practice allowed longitudinal assessment of the effects of rape, but the samples were still biased because most rapes are never reported. Currently, the consequences of rape are often studied by surveying random samples of people; this practice allows comparisons of rape victims with nonvictims, regardless of whether the rape victims had reported the rapes to authorities or had labeled their experiences as rape. Some researchers even conduct prospective studies, in which members of a high-risk group (e.g., first-year college students) are assessed annually; if someone in the sample is raped during the time span of the study, their pre- and postrape adjustment can be compared (Muehlenhard et al. 1992a).

Research shows that most rape victims experience psychological, physical, and sexual problems after being raped. It is important to remember, however, that not all rape victims experience all of these consequences;

some experience many consequences, whereas others experience relatively few consequences.

The psychological consequences of rape can include: depression; fear; anxiety; anger; problems with self-esteem and social adjustment; feeling betrayed, humiliated, or guilty; and experiencing problems with trust (Lystad 1982; Muehlenhard et al. 1991; Resick 1993). Recently, some of these psychological consequences have been conceptualized as post-traumatic stress disorder (PTSD) (American Psychiatric Association 1994). This symptom constellation includes reexperiencing the rape (such as in dreams or flashbacks), feeling numb and avoiding reminders of the rape, and experiencing hyperarousal (such as insomnia, difficulty concentrating, outbursts of anger, or an exaggerated startle response; see Herman 1992; Resnick et al. 1993).

Sexual problems resulting from rape can include avoidance of sex, decreased sexual satisfaction, sexual dysfunctions, and flashbacks to the rape during sex (Kilpatrick et al. 1987; Lystad 1982; Warshaw 1988). Some rape victims engage in sex more than before, perhaps because the rape made them feel devalued, as if "they now have nothing left that's worth protecting" (Warshaw 1988, 74).

The physical consequences of rape can include physical injuries (including injuries from weapons or fists, as well as vaginal or anal injuries), sexually transmitted diseases, pregnancy, reproductive problems causing infertility, and various psychosomatic problems. Physical consequences can also include alcohol and drug abuse and dependency (Koss 1993b; Resick 1993; Warshaw 1988).

Divulging the rape to someone else may result in various problems: feeling embarrassed or uncomfortable; reliving aspects of the experience; being disbelieved or blamed; and being questioned about one's behavior and dress, which might lead victims to feel as if they are "on trial," needing to prove their innocence to others. When rape victims report the rape to the police, their report may be disbelieved or trivialized, although police attitudes and sensitivity have improved during the last several decades. Should the case go to trial, recent "rape shield laws" generally prohibit defense attorneys from inquiring about the victim's sexual past; nevertheless, defense attorneys typically try to discredit victims (Allison and Wrightsman 1993; Estrich 1987; Gelles 1977; Griffin 1971; Roth and Lebowitz 1988).

Contrary to stereotypes, acquaintance or date rape is as traumatic as stranger rape. Victims of acquaintance rape are as likely as victims of stranger rape to experience depression, anxiety, problems with relationships, problems with sex, and thoughts of suicide (Koss et al. 1988). Women who are raped by acquaintances they had trusted may doubt their ability to evaluate the character of others and may be reluctant to trust others. Women raped by acquaintances are less likely than women raped by strangers to be believed and supported by others. If the victim and rapist have mutual friends, the friends may be reluctant to believe that a friend of theirs could be a rapist; they may thus be reluctant to take the victim's side against the perpetrator, and the victim may feel unsupported. If the rapist goes to the same school, workplace, or social functions as the victim, the victim may feel uncomfortable and withdraw from these activities (Kilpatrick et al. 1987; Koss et al. 1988; Russell 1982/90; Stacy et al. 1992; Warshaw 1988). There has been considerable controversy about the prevalence of date or acquaintance rape, especially on college campuses (Roiphe 1993).

People raped by their spouses or cohabiting partners may experience consequences that other rape victims do not experience. Whereas stranger rape is typically a one-time occurrence, the rape of wives and other partners is likely to occur repeatedly and may last for years. The more frequently women are raped by their husbands or partners, the more likely they are to suffer from grave long-term consequences. Many victims of marital or partner rape are also physically abused. Victims raped by a spouse or partner must decide either to live with the perpetrator and risk subsequent rapes or to divorce or separate, which requires many lifestyle adjustments, and which does not guarantee that they will not be raped by their ex-spouse or ex-partner (Koss et al. 1988; Lystad 1982; Russell 1982/90). The consequences may also extend to children living in the household (Mio and Foster 1991). Children may be aware of the problem and may even witness the rapes. They may fear the parent or stepparent who is the perpetrator and may develop negative views of sex and relationships.

Boys and men who have been raped experience many of the same consequences that girls and women do, although being a male victim may result in additional consequences that female victims do not encounter. Being forced into submission is incongruous with the male sex-role stereotype that espouses control and dominance. Males raped by females often confront beliefs that they must have desired and enjoyed the act and that male victims are less traumatized than are female victims. Males raped by other males, regardless of their sexual orientation, often confront homophobic attitudes. Males also confront the belief that, if they had an erection, they must have wanted sex (Groth and Burgess 1980; Russell 1984; Smith et al. 1988; Sarrel and Masters 1982; Warshaw 1988).

Lesbian and gay rape victims may encounter difficulty in attempting to obtain services from crisis-intervention and social-service centers, as these agencies are not prepared to serve lesbian and gay clients (Waterman et al. 1989). Obtaining services may require that gay or lesbian rape victims "come out," revealing their sexual orientation and risking possible discrimination, possibly even losing their jobs, housing, or children should others find out (legal protection of lesbians and gays in the United States varies from city to city and state to state). If rape occurs in a lesbian or gay relationship in which the perpetrator is the biological parent of the children, if the victimized partner leaves the relationship, she or he will probably have to leave the children with the perpetrator. Furthermore, the gay and lesbian community is often tight-knit, so lesbian or gay rape victims may be reluctant to tell mutual friends or to participate in the community's social functions (Grover 1990; Muehlenhard et al. 1991).

Punishment of Rapists. The modal punishment for rapists is no penalty, given that most rapes are not reported to the police (Koss et al. 1988; Russell 1984). Even those that are reported rarely result in arrest and conviction (Allison and Wrightsman 1993). Among those who are convicted of rape, punishment varies from merely being placed on parole to life in prison.

Until the 1970s, the penalty for rape included the death penalty; 89 percent of the men executed for rape in the United States from 1930 to 1967 were African-American (Estrich 1987, 107). In 1977, the U.S. Supreme Court found the death penalty for rape to be unconstitutional (*Coker v. Georgia*, 433 U.S. 584, 1977; see Estrich 1987). Studies of actual sentences given to convicted rapists reveal that the harshest penalties for rape are still imposed on African-American men accused of raping white women (Estrich 1987; LaFree 1980). There is also a bias against convicting affluent, successful men and men who rape women they know or who rape women who do not conform to cultural expectations of how a "good woman" should behave (Estrich 1987; LaFree et al. 1985).

Prevention. Prior to the 1970s, rape prevention was generally regarded as women's responsibility. Because rape was regarded as an act of sex incited by provocative women, rape prevention consisted largely of expecting women to restrict their behavior (expecting women not to talk or dress provocatively, not to go out at night, etc.).

Currently, a variety of prevention strategies are common in the U.S. (Muehlenhard et al. 1992a). There are still those who urge women to restrict their behavior, and research shows that women do indeed restrict their behavior due to the fear of rape: Women report avoiding going outside alone at night, not talking to strangers, wearing bulky clothing, having unlisted phone numbers, and so on (Gordon and Riger 1989). These efforts limit women's freedom and diminish women's quality of life. Furthermore, this approach focuses on stranger rape, a minority of all rapes, and does not address the causes of rape.

There are other prevention strategies that are not predicated on women's restricting their behavior. For instance, many universities have installed extra lighting and emergency telephones (often marked by blue lights) to help women feel safer. These strategies are aimed primarily at preventing stranger rape, however, and will not help women who are raped indoors by husbands, partners, dates, or other acquaintances. To address these problems, many universities have initiated lectures and workshops presented to college dormitory residents, fraternities, sororities, and athletic groups; some high schools and even junior high schools have also initiated such programs, although they sometimes meet resistance from parents and school boards (Donat and D'Emilio 1992). There is evidence that such programs can lead to attitude change (Jones and Muehlenhard 1990), although the effectiveness of these strategies in actually preventing rape is unknown.

Some women take self-defense classes. For example, Model Mugging or En Garde programs teach women self-defense strategies that utilize women's physical strengths, such as lower-body strength (Allison and Wrightsman 1993). Research shows that active-resistance strategies (e.g., physically fighting, screaming, and running away) are generally more effective than the passive-resistance strategies (e.g., coaxing, begging, crying, reasoning, or doing nothing), and active strategies do not increase the risk of physical harm (Bart and O'Brien 1984; Ullman and Knight 1992; Zoucha-Jensen and Coyne 1993). Unfortunately, no strategy is effective all of the time or for all people, and even experiencing an attempted rape can be traumatic. Furthermore, many feminist theorists have argued that, because most rapists are men, it is unfair to place the burden of rape prevention on women (Berkowitz 1992; Koss 1993b).

The most important strategies for preventing rape involve working for broader social change: changing men's and women's attitudes about rape, sex, and gender roles; working toward gender equality; discouraging violence as a problem-solving technique; and emphasizing that coercive sex in any context, whether with a stranger or acquaintance, is never acceptable.

Child Sexual Abuse and Incest   DIANE BAKER AND SHARON E. KING

Knowledge of child sexual abuse (CSA) has undergone cycles of awareness and suppression, as both professionals and the general public have struggled to come to terms with its existence since CSA first gained widespread attention in the 1890s, when Freud proposed that it was at the root of hysterical neurosis. Although modern clinical work tends to confirm the link between CSA and various neuroses, Freud quietly abandoned his early belief in response to the strong opposition from Victorian attitudes of that era. Linking neuroses with repressed childhood sexual conflict, Freud's Oedipal and Electra complexes, was revolutionary, but at least much more acceptable than admitting the reality and prevalence of child sexual abuse.

During the past twenty years, CSA has received renewed attention from American clinicians, researchers, and the general public. Recently, CSA has been the focus of a substantial amount of American research that has, in turn, led to broader recognition of the initial and long-term problems associated with CSA.

Definitions. The definition presented by the National Center on Child Abuse and Neglect is "Contact and interactions between a child and an adult when the child is being used for the sexual stimulation of the perpetrator or another person." This definition is problematic, however, in that it leaves key terms open to question. For example, in considering who is a child, researchers have employed cutoff ages anywhere between 12 and 17 years for victims of CSA. In deciding who is an adult, some researchers have required perpetrators to be at least 16 years of age; others have required age differences between victim and perpetrator of five years or ten years; still others have not required any age difference at all if force or coercion was used. In determining what is sexual stimulation, some authors include noncontact experiences, such as exhibitionism or propositioning, whereas others require manual contact, and still others, genital contact. In a 1987 study designed to determine the effect of varying the operational definition of CSA on its prevalence, the percentage of college men identified as victims ranged from 24 percent to 4 percent based on how restrictive the criteria used were. The parameters defining CSA, therefore, will have strong implications for how widespread a problem society considers it.

A second major issue is determining, in the absence of physical injury, what has been damaged. This issue is complicated by a consistently identified minority of victims who report such experiences as having been positive. Some authors have pointed to this subset and wondered whether the abuse was against the individual or societal values, and further, whether in defining CSA, consideration should be given to the victim's view of the experience as negative or positive. Yet, a victim's view of a CSA experience as positive does not preclude the possibility that it was a harmful or damaging one.

A cogent argument against using the victim's assessment of the experience as positive or negative in defining abuse is that the inequalities of knowledge, sophistication, and power inherent in any child-adult relationship prevent the child from giving informed consent to engage in sexual behavior. From this perspective, it is the emotional and intellectual immaturity of the child that causes the developmentally inappropriate exposure to adult sexuality to be harmful and abusive.

These issues of definition influence the composition of the groups studied by researchers and, thereby, the results obtained. As yet, there has been no completely satisfactory way to define CSA to ensure that the research results are relevant and helpful to the greatest number of people. Currently, the most widely used set of criteria for defining CSA are contact experiences between a child aged 12 or younger with an individual five or more years older, or between a child aged 13 to 16 with an individual ten or more years older. These criteria emphasize the differences in developmental maturity between the victim and perpetrator, while minimizing the inclusion of age-appropriate sexual exploration between peers as sexual abuse.

Prevalence of CSA. Accurate estimates of the prevalence of CSA in either the general population or clinical populations have been difficult to obtain, due in part to the differences in operational definitions discussed above, in part to the sensitive nature of the topic, and in part to differing methods of assessment (e.g., questionnaire, face-to-face interview, or telephone interview). Estimates of the percentage of adult women who have experienced CSA vary from 6 percent to 62 percent and of adult men from 3 percent to 31 percent. In general, percentages are higher among clinical samples than among community-based samples. Additionally, more people disclose abuse histories when information is gathered via an interview rather than by questionnaire, when specific questions about childhood sexual experiences are asked, and when such terms as "sexual abuse" and "molestation" are avoided (see also Prendergast 1993).

More confidence can be placed in the accuracy of prevalence rates when the samples used are large, random, and community-based. In a 1990 random sample of over 2,000 adults across the United States, 27 percent of women and 16 percent of men reported having experienced such abuse as children. In other large-scale studies, about 25 percent of women and 17 percent of college men have been identified as having histories of CSA. The majority of CSA cases are perpetrated by a nonrelative, generally an acquaintance or family friend; about 30 percent of girls are abused by a relative (with about 4 percent involving father-daughter incest), whereas about 10 percent of boys are abused by a relative. Finally, the prevalence of CSA does not seem to vary with social class or ethnicity (Hunter 1990).

Theories Explaining CSA. Upon hearing of CSA, people generally react strongly, wondering how such abuse could occur. Originally, professionals held a simplistic view of CSA, considering it to be the result of the isolated actions of a depraved and flawed perpetrator. In the past several decades, however, two more-complicated theories of CSA have dominated the field.

Family systems theory posits that families function as integrated systems and that irregularities in the system are displayed through symptomatic behavior in one or more family members. From this perspective, the occurrence of incest reflects a distortion in the family system, specifically in the marital subsystem, that is being expressed through a parent's (usually the father's) sexual behavior with a child. This model proposes, then, that CSA occurs as a misguided attempt to cope with problems in the family. Treatment, therefore, involves recognition of the underlying problems and the institution of changes by all family members rather than through removal of the perpetrator.

Although less simplistic than earlier proposals, this model has been criticized for seeming to blame the victims for the abuse and by removing responsibility from the perpetrator. Additionally, the model is relevant only to incest, which is a relatively small fraction of the CSA cases.

In order to address these concerns, Finkelhor proposed a four-factor model of CSA incorporating some aspects of the family systems' perspective, but shifting responsibility for the abuse back to the perpetrator. He conceptualized CSA as resulting from an interaction between environmental circumstances and the personality of the perpetrator, rather than simply as inherent in the perpetrator or in the family system.

In this model, four preconditions must be met for CSA to occur. First, the offender must have some motivation to abuse sexually; thus, CSA satisfies some emotional or sexual need in the perpetrator that is not readily satisfied in other ways. Second, the offender must overcome his or her inhibitions against CSA. Inhibitions may be overcome in a variety of ways, such as substance use, rationalization, the influence of stressors, or personality factors (e.g., impulsivity). Third, environmental impediments to the abuse must be removed; the offender must have private access to a child. Therefore, she or he may target children who are without consistent adult supervision or obtain employment that provides contact with children. Fourth, the offender capitalizes on the lowered resistance of the child; children who are insecure, needy, uneducated about sexuality, and/or have a trusting relationship with the offender have lowered resistance. These children are less likely to be assertive in refusing abusive overtures or to disclose immediately that the abuse took place. All of these factors, working in concert, allow CSA to occur.

Some people remain uncomfortable with the third and fourth preconditions of this model, because they appear to place some responsibility for the CSA outside the perpetrator and onto the child and his or her non-offending parent(s). Finkelhor stresses, however, that without the first and second preconditions, qualities, and behaviors of the offender alone, CSA would never occur. These preconditions place responsibility for the act squarely with the perpetrator.

Who Is at Risk for CSA? The environmental circumstances in which boys are sexually abused versus those in which girls are sexually abused differ in some important ways. Some of these differences were highlighted by Tzeng and Schwarzin (1987), who compared the demographic characteristics of boys and girls in over 15,000 substantiated cases of sexual abuse in Illinois. They found that girls who had been sexually abused tended to live in homes that did not differ from those of the general population in the numbers and kinds of parents/caretakers present, whereas boys who had been sexually abused were significantly more likely to come from single-parent homes and/or from families with either new or many children/dependents. On the other hand, the girls' families tended to display significantly more dysfunction, and caretakers were more physically and/or mentally impaired than caretakers in the boys' families. These results are similar to those of Finkelhor, who found the risk of CSA among girls increased approximately twofold when a mother was absent from the home. These findings point to an increased risk of sexual abuse when parents are absent, impaired, or overworked (see also Prendergast 1993).

Some differences in the perpetrators of abuse of boys versus girls have also been identified. Tzeng and Schwarzin (1987) and others reported that sexual abuse of boys is more likely to be perpetrated by a stranger, whereas abuse of girls is more likely to be perpetrated by a relative. Further, when boys are abused by a relative, these relatives are more likely to be within five years of age of the boys, whereas relatives who abuse girls are more likely to be ten or more years older than the girls. Although the vast majority of perpetrators of both boys and girls are men, boys are more likely to be abused by women than are girls (17 percent versus 2 percent). Thus, for boys, CSA experiences tend to occur outside the home and to be perpetrated by a nonfamily member or, if inside the home and perpetrated by a relative, the relative is less likely to be a parent-figure or to have adult status. Girls are more likely to be abused within the home by a relative ten or more years older. Risk to girls is increased by sevenfold for girls with a stepfather. A general consensus among researchers is that more boys are somewhat more likely to experience severe abuse (actual intercourse) than are girls.

These differences suggest boys and girls may be experiencing CSA situations that require differing coping skills. Girls may, more typically, need to adjust to the notion that an adult in a position of trust has been abusive, and boys may, more typically, need to adjust to the notion that the world outside the home is not safe and may need to react to a more-severe physical experience. It should be stressed that all of these differences are generalizations, and there is substantial overlap in the nature of the CSA experiences of boys and girls.

Initial Effects of CSA. Although researchers have identified a wide array of problems occurring among children who have been sexually abused, most have failed to find any substantial differences in symptomatology between male and female victims. When studying these initial effects, researchers have recently begun to divide subjects into three groups based on their stage of development: preschool (ages 3 to 6), school age (ages 7 to 12), and adolescent (ages 13 to 17). By using these groupings, the presence and frequency of various behaviors and symptoms can be compared to those considered developmentally appropriate for the stage.

Among both preschool boys and girls, the most frequent behavioral symptom associated with CSA experiences is an increase in sexualized behaviors (Beitchman et al. 1991). This increase has been noted in a number of studies using a variety of methodologies, including chart review, parent rating, observed play with anatomically correct dolls, and human-figure drawing. However, the prevalence of this behavior varies widely depending on the context, from 10 percent of the sample in the case of human-figure drawing to 90 percent of the sample in play with anatomically correct dolls; still, this finding is among the most robust in the literature. [*Note:* These studies do not make conparisons to groups of "normal" children and their rate of sexual behavior. (D. L. Weis, Coeditor)]

Emotionally, preschool children are likely to respond to sexual abuse with anxiety, signs of post-traumatic stress (e.g., nightmares, vigilance, or bed wetting), and depression (Kendall-Tackett et al. 1993). These children are also likely to exhibit greater immaturity than nonabused controls, showing increases in both dependency and impulsivity relative to physically abused and nonabused age peers.

Among school-age children, researchers have focused on behavioral problems that interfere with academic and social success. Sexually abused children have been assessed by their teachers as significantly less able than their nonabused peers to learn in the school environment. This difficulty may be a function of the wide range of behavioral and emotional problems they display. For example, approximately half of the school-age girls with histories of CSA show high levels of immaturity and aggression (Kendall-Tacketts et al. 1993). Similarly, both parents and teachers rated sexually abused children as more emotionally disturbed and neurotic than their classmates, displaying both depression and a wide range of fears (Beitchman et al. 1991; Browne and Finkelhor 1986; Kendall-Tackett et al. 1993). Additionally, like preschool children, the sexually abused school-age boys and girls display clear-cut increases in sexualized behaviors, including such problems as excessive and inappropriate masturbation and sexual aggression (Browne and Finkelhor 1986; Kendall-Tackett et al. 1993). All of these symptoms would be expected to lead to problems in school for children, regardless of their intelligence.

A somewhat different presentation has been observed among adolescents with a history of sexual abuse. Although acting-out behaviors, such as running away, substance use, and sexual promiscuity were more common in these adolescents than their nonabused peers, they were less common than among clinical groups of adolescents (Beitchman et al. 1991). The predominant finding among sexually abused adolescents is an increase in depressive symptomatology, such as low self-esteem and suicidal ideation. This depression may be expressed through self-injurious behaviors, as exhibited by more than two thirds of sexually abused adolescents (Kendall-Tackett et al. 1993), or through suicide attempts made by a third of these adolescents in a clinical sample.

Although there is an extensive list of symptoms and problems associated with the initial effects of sexual abuse, it should be noted that not all children display such effects. Indeed, 20 percent to 40 percent of sexually abused children have been found to be asymptomatic at the time of initial assessment (Kendall-Tackett et al. 1993). Unfortunately, some of these children have become symptomatic by the time of later assessments. There is fairly consistent evidence that from a third to a half of sexually abused children show improvement in symptom presentation twelve to eighteen months after the abuse, although another quarter to a third show deterioration in function.

Long-Term Effects of CSA. Although the long-term effects of CSA experiences have been studied in both men and women, the majority of the work has been done with women. Reviews of this research have been conducted by Browne and Finkelhor (1986) and Beitchman et al. (1992). The results vary somewhat, depending on whether the samples were community-based or clinically based; still, there is substantial overlap across the two populations.

In both clinical and community-based surveys of women with histories of CSA, the most common long-term effect is depression. Depression is particularly striking among the community-based samples of victims, in which significantly more women with a history of CSA report both more-severe and more-frequent episodes of depression compared to those without such experiences. Almost one in five college women reporting a history of CSA had been hospitalized for depression compared to one in twenty-five women who had not been abused. In a community-based study of the Los Angeles area, researchers found that a history of CSA was associated with a fourfold increase in the lifetime prevalence rate for major depression among women. Other prominent depression-related symptoms include problems with self-esteem, which appear to intensify as time elapses from the abuse, and an increased risk for self-injurious or destructive behaviors (Browne and Finkelhor 1986).

Increases in problems with anxiety occur among some women with sexual abuse histories. Problems with anxiety are more prominent among clinical samples than community samples (Beitchman et al. 1992; Brown and Finkelhor 1986). Anxiety seems to be particularly prevalent among women sexually abused by a family member and in cases in which force was used during the abuse.

Relationship difficulties are more common among women with histories of CSA compared to nonabused women. Abused women are more likely to fear intimacy and to have sexual dysfunctions, particularly when the abuse was more severe and/or was perpetrated by a father or stepfather (Beitchman et al. 1992). A history of CSA in women is also associated with an increased risk of further revictimization in the forms of rape and domestic violence.

Much less research has been conducted on the long-term effects of sexual abuse in men; much of the information available has been based on clinical case studies or extrapolated from studies with some adult male victims, but in which the majority of the subjects were women. Therefore, conclusions are much more tentative. Several community-based surveys found that men who reported CSA experiences exhibited a higher rate of psychopathology (e.g., depression, anxiety, or symptoms of post-traumatic stress) than those who did not report such experiences. Men who have been sexually abused have reported significant problems with poor self-esteem and self-concept. Men may respond to such feelings by self-medicating with alcohol and drugs, as indicated by the large degree of substance abuse and dependence among male victims; sexually abused women, on the other hand, report greater levels of depression and anxiety.

Clinicians suggest that intense anger, sexual dysfunction, problems with intimacy, gender-identity confusion, and substance abuse are prominent symptoms for males with a history of CSA seeking therapy. Additionally, disclosure of sexual abuse is particularly difficult for men. Issues related to disclosure include fears of not being believed (particularly if the perpetrator was female), fears others will consider them homosexual, concerns that they are homosexual because they have been abused by a man, and issues related to masculine identity.

Correlates of More-Severe Effects. Although the preceding paragraphs present a grim picture of the aftereffects of CSA, not all individuals suffer such severe effects. In fact, in a given sample of abuse survivors, a quarter to a third of the individuals can be expected to appear symptom-free on the chosen assessment instruments (Kendall-Tackett et al. 1993). About one third of these asymptomatic individuals may become symptomatic at later assessments. Still, these differences in outcome have led researchers to examine variables associated with more-severe effects.

One variable consistently associated with more-severe effects is the use of force (Beitchman et al. 1992; Browne and Finkelhor 1986; Kendall-Tackett et al. 1993). This finding has been most robust in studies of the initial effects of CSA among children (Kendall-Tackett et al. 1993). A number of researchers also have identified an association between the use of force and victims' reports of the degree of trauma experienced among adult survivors as well (Beitchman et. al. 1992; Browne and Finkelhor 1986). There is also some evidence that family-background variables, such as high levels of conflict and low levels of support, are related to more-severe effects. The situation is further complicated in that, for some individuals, the use of force has been associated with a decrease in self-blame, thereby reducing the severity of effects.

The relationship of the perpetrator to the victim has also been examined. Among children, the initial effects of abuse are more severe when the perpetrator has a closer relationship to the child (Kendall-Tackett et al. 1993). The situation is less clear for the long-term effects among adults. In general, whether the perpetrator was a family member has little impact on later outcome among adults (Beitchman et al. 1992; Browne and Finkelhor 1986) with one important caveat: Trauma and psychopathology effects are more severe if the abuse was perpetrated by a father or stepfather (Beitchman et al. 1992; Browne and Finkelhor 1986). This difference may represent a greater degree of family dysfunction and a more significant breach of trust when a father perpetrated the abuse (Beitchman et al., 1992). The lack of a general effect of intrafamilial versus extrafamilial abuse among adults may be a reflection that it was the quality of the relationship with the abuser (i.e., how much he was trusted) that influenced outcome rather than whether he was a relative. Finkelhor has extended this notion by proposing that the important variable is the degree to which the child was seduced and persuaded by the perpetrator, whether or not the child had a prior relationship with the perpetrator.

A third major variable examined to determine its relationship to long-term effects has been the duration of the abuse. This variable has been difficult to assess for a number of reasons. First, the criterion for CSA of long duration varies among researchers, from abuse that occurred for more than six months to abuse that occurred for more than five years. Second, as noted by Beitchman et al. (1992), researchers have tended to use very different measures, some assessing a subjective sense of harm, and others assessing a more objective degree of psychopathology. There is some evidence, however, that CSA of longer duration leads to an increase in psychopathology in community-based samples. The two major reviewers of long-term effects of CSA (Beitchman et al. 1992; Browne and Finkelhor 1986) have both concluded that more research must be conducted before firm conclusions can be drawn, whereas reviewers of initial effects have suggested that longer duration is associated with a worse outcome (Kendall-Tackett et al. 1993).

The severity of the CSA experience has also been examined in relation to psychopathology and harm in adulthood; here again, the results are mixed. There is general agreement that increased trauma and maladjustment are associated with contact abuse versus noncontact abuse, both initially and in the long term. Further, abuse involving genital contact, whether manual, oral, or invasive, is associated with more-serious outcomes than kissing or clothed contact. Researchers differ, however, in whether invasive contact as compared to manual contact is associated with increased trauma in the long term. Initially, invasive contact is associated with a worse outcome (Kendall-Tackett et al. 1993). Further research is necessary to determine the long-term effects of invasive contact.

One nonabuse-related variable, family support, has also been consistently identified as contributing significantly to both the initial and long-term effects of CSA. Kendall-Tackett et al. (1993) reviewed three studies examining the relationship of maternal support to symptom outcome in children who had been sexually abused. All three studies concluded that children whose mothers were low in support exhibited worse outcomes following the abuse. This conclusion was supported by the findings of other researchers who examined long-term coping among college women with histories of CSA.

Theories about the Nature of the Effects. Researchers have cataloged a multitude of symptoms associated with CSA that therapists have, in turn, attempted to address in treatment. Therapeutic treatment of any type is greatly facilitated by a theory or framework to organize and to approach symptoms. Many clinicians note that it is an impaired trust in self and others that underlies many of the symptoms associated with CSA.

This difficulty with trust has led some researchers and therapists to conceptualize the symptoms associated with CSA as a function of post-traumatic stress disorder (PTSD). This disorder encompasses some of the more-troubling symptoms experienced by sexual abuse survivors, such as depression, nightmares, and affective numbing. All of the PTSD conceptualizations of sexual abuse incorporate the idea that exposure to the abuse is experienced by the victim as overwhelming, due to intense fear and/or to extreme violations of beliefs about the way the world operates. When confronted with the abuse then, the child is unable to cope, given his or her current level of internal resources, and so must distort cognitions and/or affect in an effort to adjust to the experience. These distortions are, then, the basis for the symptoms that appear following the abuse.

However, there are some limitations to the application of PTSD to sexual abuse symptomatology. Among the most compelling of these limitations is the fact that the symptoms of PTSD do not encompass all of the problems associated with CSA. Also, many survivors do not meet the criteria for PTSD. In one group of survivors, only 10 percent could be diagnosed with PTSD at the time of the survey, and only 36 percent could have ever been diagnosed with the disorder. Clearly, more work is needed in the conceptualization of the symptoms associated with a history of CSA.

Toward this end, Finkelhor has proposed a theory of CSA symptomatology, the Traumagenic Dynamics Model of Child Sexual Abuse (TD), which attempts to address the empirical findings more fully. The TD model emphasizes that the trauma associated with CSA may be due to the stress of the ongoing nature of the abuse situation, rather than an isolated event that is overwhelming and far removed from usual human experience (as described by the PTSD criteria in the *Diagnostic and Statistical Manual III Revised (DSM III-R)*. This differentiation does not suggest that one type of trauma is more harmful than another; it simply highlights a qualitative difference in events that may lead to different coping responses and/or symptomatology.

The TD model includes four dynamics that occur to varying degrees in any CSA situation and that are postulated to contribute to the symptoms identified in the research literature. These dynamics include: (a) Traumatic Sexualization, which occurs when the child is taught distortions about his or her sexuality, and may lead to the increase in sexual dysfunctions observed among adult survivors; (b) Betrayal, which occurs in two ways, either when the child finds that an adult she or he trusted has hurt him or her or when the child discloses the abuse to an adult who refuses to believe or help the child. Finkelhor characterized the increased depression and revictimization seen among survivors as a result of the lost trust and unmet dependency needs. It can also lead to increased anger and hostility as a mechanism of keeping others at a distance; (c) Powerlessness, which occurs in a variety of ways in the CSA situation; for example, when the child finds himself or herself incapable of physically warding off the perpetrator. Powerlessness is further manifest when the child is unable to extricate himself or herself from the abuse situation or unable to do so in a satisfactory way (e.g., without being removed from the home). This powerlessness dynamic leads to anxiety and fear in adult survivors as well as a decreased coping ability; (d) Stigmatization, which occurs either directly through the labeling of the child by others as bad or dirty following disclosure of the abuse or indirectly through the sneaking behavior of the perpetrator and the admonitions that the abuse be kept secret. Stigmatization may be associated with the low self-esteem and the self-destructive behaviors, such as substance abuse and suicide attempts, observed among survivors.

However the effects are conceptualized, recent evidence has demonstrated that CSA is prevalent and commonly results in harmful effects. Finkelhor and others have attempted to make sense of a confusing array of symptoms presented by many, but not all, victims of CSA. More-sophisticated research designs (e.g., involving structural equation modeling) are required before the relationship between various experiences of CSA and outcomes become more clear.

Clergy Sexual Abuse

SHARON E. KING

In the past ten years, sexual abuse of minors by clergy has become a major public scandal and crisis for all the churches, although the public attention is often focused on the Catholic clergy because of their requirement of celibacy. Until recently, charges of sexual abuse by clergy were treated as an internal problem within Church jurisdiction and not reported to police. The main issue for Church officials was to control damage to their institution's image. That silence exploded with national media coverage of the case of James Porter, a Massachusetts priest, who victimized, often sadistically, over 200 minors in several states between 1960 and 1972, and a similar case in Louisiana. Media coverage triggered a flood of new charges of abuse. Ten of 97 priests in a southwestern diocese, nine of 110 in a midwestern diocese, seven of 91 in a southern diocese, and fifteen of 220 and forty of 279 in the eastern United States were charged in civil and criminal suits. In December 1993, twelve of 44 priests in a California minor seminary were charged with having been sexually active with 11- to 17-year-old boys between 1964 and 1987. Between 1984 and 1994, an estimated 5,000 survivors reported their abuse to Church authorities. By early 1995, over 600 cases were pending (Sipe 1995, 26-28). Meanwhile, the Catholic dioceses of Sante Fe and Chicago admitted being in danger of bankruptcy; between 1984 and 1994, Catholic officials admitted to paying out over a half billion dollars in damages to survivors (Rossetti 1991).

Sipe (1995, 26-27) estimates that, at any one time, 6 percent of Catholic clergy are sexually involved with minors; the situation does not appear to be as serious in Protestant and Jewish circles. One third of the cases of abuse by priests can be classified as true pedophiles, with a three-to-one preference for boys. Two thirds of the abusive priests are involved with adolescents with a more even gender distribution. Four times as many priests are involved with adult women as with minors.

"The crisis of image has been compounded by church authorities who were slow, defensive, and even duplicitous in their public response as abuse by clergy became public and other indications of trouble mounted" (Sipe 1995, 8). Even as late as 1992, fully two thirds of the American Catholic bishops were confused or unconvinced that there is a problem of sexual abuse by the clergy, although even the Pope has acknowledged the crisis.

Civil authorities have responded by extending the statutes of limitations on reporting such abuse. New laws in all states require any professional to report suspected sexual abuse of a minor; in many states, any person is required to report suspected abuse. However, such laws are often vague in defining "reasonable suspicion."

The year 1990 was a watershed as confused Church authorities began losing their damage-control efforts to the rising tide of victims' voices expressed in civil and criminal lawsuits against priests, dioceses, and religious orders. Support groups for survivors spread across the nation: Victims of Clergy Abuse LINKUP, Survivors Connections, American Coalition for Abused Awareness, and Survivors Network of Those Abused by Priests (SNAP).

In 1992, the Catholic Archdiocese of Chicago adopted a model plan for processing allegations of clergy abuse; unfortunately, it remains incompletely and unevenly implemented. In 1993, St. John's (Benedictine) Abbey and University in Collegeville, Minnesota, established an ecumenical Interfaith Institute to study this problem.

How survivors are treated by a religious community varies greatly, and survivors should be reminded that, when they set out to seek legal action against anyone, the course may be extremely difficult. Far too often, survivors feel that they are revictimized by a system that protects the abuser, rather than one that is sensitive to the trauma of the victim.

Satanic Ritual Abuse   SHARON E. KING

"Satanic" ritual abuse is another area of recent concern. As the 1989 report by the ritual abuse task force by the Los Angeles County Commission for Women shows, it is a controversial area that requires careful and serious attention. Books and groups dealing with cult and ritual abuse continue to expose this alarming and controversial topic. Unfortunately, it often takes on the atmosphere of a circus and witch hunt. There is no scientific evidence that this type of CSA is widespread or common.

Recovered Memories and False Memory Syndrome   DIANE BAKER AND
                                                       SHARON E. KING

Of great concern recently are a number of cases involving children in day-care centers reporting that they were sexually abused by their caretakers.

Although some investigations have led to convictions, other cases have been found to lack any substance at all. In one case, a middle-aged male retracted his charge that a prominent Catholic cardinal archbishop had sexually abused him when he was in the seminary, claiming that his lawyer had probably prompted or influenced his "recovered memory" of being abused.

Concern over false reporting is not limited to young children. Teachers all over the country report that they no longer touch their students as they once did. Hugging a child, allowing a young child to sit on one's lap, or being alone in a room with a child are just some of the things that teachers must now monitor. Cases in which children have projected sexual abuse that was happening at home onto a teacher, and the false reporting of sexual abuse by a teacher in order to get back at the teacher are now issues that mental-health workers and the legal system must unravel in some of the more unusual cases placed before the courts.

Better questioning of young victims by mental-health and legal workers is one area that continues to improve. As with any inquiry, it has become evident that the invitation to tell what happened cannot, in any way, be colored by suggestive questioning on the part of the interviewer.

Increasing numbers of adult women and men have begun to disclose incidents of sexual abuse that happened to them when they were children. Their sexual abuse occurred during a time when it was not safe for children to disclose such information and when the support systems of the state and therapeutic communities were not in place.

In some incidents where adults disclose what happened to them as children, they have always known what happened to them, but they have never before spoken out or sought help. In some instances, however, adults report "remembering" or retrieving lost memories of childhood sexual abuse. Remembering and dealing with unresolved issues of childhood sexual abuse can often explain to a victim how and why his or her life has been affected by the abuse. Weight problems, depression, sleep disturbances, intimacy and sexual disorders, unexplained fears, compulsive behaviors, self-esteem issues, and psychosomatic disorders are just a few of the symptoms that can be resolved when an adult finally confronts the repressed and unresolved trauma of childhood sexual abuse.

In a response to their own daughter's accusation of being sexually abused by her father, the Freyds' of Philadelphia started an organization that examines the False Memory Syndrome. Dr. Pamela Freyd and her husband have been most public in their denial of their daughter's accusations, basing their response on a belief that her "memories" were suggested by her therapist. After a period of silence on her part, Dr. Jennifer Freyd publicly countered her parents' denial of what happened to her, citing her mother's public debate as yet another example of her intrusiveness. Whatever the struggle between the members of the Freyd family, this small organization has brought forth a concern about the authenticity and reliability of retrieved memories.

Sexual Harassment   ROBERT T. FRANCOEUR

Public awareness of sexual harassment is also a recent phenomenon in American culture, even though sexual discrimination was prohibited by federal law over thirty years ago by Title VII of the 1964 Civil Rights Act. In 1979, Stanford University Law School professor Catharine MacKinnon broadly defined sexual harassment as "the unwanted imposition of sexual requirements in the context of a relationship of unequal power." More-recent definitions include unwanted sexual advances, touches, and actions between peers and coworkers. Sexual harassment can also occur when a subordinate offers sexual favors in return for a promotion, better evaluation, or grade.

A 1976 *Redbook* magazine survey reported that 88 percent of the more than 9,000 women responding reported having experienced overt sexual harassment and regarded it as a serious work-related problem. A 1988 *Men's Health* survey reported 57 percent of the magazine's male readers stated they had been sexually propositioned at work, and 58 percent admitted they had at least occasional sexual fantasies about coworkers.

In a broad survey of over 20,000 federal government workers, 42 percent of the women and 15 percent of the men reported having been sexually harassed at work in the preceding two years. Most of the harassers, 78 percent, were male. Both women and men victims reported that the harassment had negative effects on their emotional and physical condition, their ability to work with others on the job, and their feelings about work. Women were considerably more likely than men to have been harassed by a supervisor, 37 percent versus 14 percent (Levinson et al. 1988).

A random-sample survey of undergraduate women at the Berkeley campus of the University of California found that 30 percent had received unwanted sexual attention from at least one male instructor during their undergraduate years. Examples of harassment included: verbal advances and explicit sexual propositions; invitations to date or to one's apartment; touches, kisses, and fondling; leering or standing too close; writing emotional letters; being too helpful; and offering grades in exchange for sexual favors (see Table 5).

Table 5

Varieties of Sexual Harassment in the Workplace

Type of Harassment	% of Males Reporting	% of Females Reporting
Uninvited sexual attention	20	50
Touching	16	45
Suggestive invitations, talk, joking	15	42
Harassed by same sex	12	7

Based on De Witt 1991; U.S. Merit Systems Board, 1981, 1988, and other sources.

It took over 15 years for the government to identify the sexual-harassment implications of the 1964 Civil Rights Act, and even longer for business corporations to understand the law. In a 1981 *Redbook–Harvard Business Review* survey, 63 percent of the top-level managers and 52 percent of middle managers believed that "the amount of sexual harassment at work is greatly exaggerated." Although the amount of sexual harassment in the workplace has probably decreased because of the growing awareness of its risks, *Working Woman* reported that at least some business managers believe that "More than 95 percent of our complaints have merit" (Gutek 1985).

Although most research on sexual harassment has focused on its occurrence in the workplace and academia, sexual harassment has also been studied in the relationship between psychologists or psychotherapists and their clients, and between physicians and other health-care workers and their patients.

In 1991, televised hearings of Supreme Court nominee Clarence Thomas and Anita Hill captured the nation's attention and sparked considerable debate and a growing awareness of sexual harassment. About the same time, the United States Navy became the focus of congressional investigations and media headlines when close to a hundred male pilots and officers at an annual Tailhook convention were charged with blatant examples of sexual harassment. Sexual harassment was also the subject of *Disclosure*, a popular and powerful 1994 film dealing with a female executive sexually harassing a male employee. As a result, practically every American corporation, professional organization, and educational institution has been forced to develop and adopt a statement defining the nature of sexual harassment and its policies for responding to it.

The "interim guidelines" issued by the Equal Employment Opportunity Commission in 1980, established that "unwelcome sexual advances, requests for sexual favors, and other verbal or physical conduct of a sexual nature constitute sexual harassment" when

1. submission to such conduct is made either explicitly or implicitly a term or condition of an individual's employment,
2. submission to or rejection of such conduct by an individual is used as the basis for employment decisions affecting such individual, or when
3. such conduct has the purpose or effect of substantially interfering with an individual's work performance or creating an intimidating, hostile, or offensive working environment.

In 1985, sociologist Barbara Gutek explained the occurrence of sexual harassment in the workplace in terms of a gender-role spillover model. She defined a work role as "a set of shared expectations about behavior in a job," and a gender role as "a set of shared expectations about the behavior of women and men." Gender-role spillover occurs when gender roles are carried into the workplace, often in inappropriate ways; for example, when the woman in a work group is expected to make coffee or take notes at the meeting. Despite many attitudinal changes in American society, women are still often seen as subservient and sex objects. When these aspects of gender roles spill over into the workplace, sexual harassment can easily occur, despite its negative effects on the employees and organization (Gutek 1985, 17).

B. Prostitution-Sex Workers

ROBERT T. FRANCOEUR AND
PATRICIA BARTHALOW KOCH

Historical Perspective

In the American colonies and early days of the United States, prostitution did not thrive in the sparse rural population. Despite a shortage of women, there were still women on the financial fringe in the small cities—recent immigrants and unattached, single women with few skills—for whom prostitution provided a way of survival and, at times, a way to find a husband or other male supporter. Female servants, apprentices, and slaves were not allowed to marry—a custom that encouraged prostitution. In contrast, indentured male servants are apprentices and could earn money to support themselves and their families, although they received no salary. Until the end of the American Civil War, African and Caribbean women brought to the United States in the slave trade were frequently and regularly exploited sexually by their owners (Barry 1984).

In the nineteenth century, the Industrial Revolution in New England and Middle Atlantic cities precipitated a massive influx of women from rural areas and from abroad looking for work and other opportunities. For example, women preferred the freedom that textile-mill work gave them to the tightly regulated life of a domestic servant, even though the wages were lower. There was little, if any, social life available after work hours for these single persons living apart from their families. Since they often shared a boarding house room with six to eight women, sometimes sleeping three to a bed, they frequently found their only relief at the local tavern. With men moving to the western frontier and a surplus of women, some women turned to prostitution for escape or affection. Too often they found that only sex work offered them a living wage (D'Emilio and Freedman 1988).

Throughout the mid-1800s, waves of immigration created a surplus of males who left their wives and families in Europe. In each new wave of immigration, some of the unattached immigrant women turned to prostitution in an effort to survive; some were already involved in "the trade." Males far outnumbered women in the western frontier towns and mining camps. Thousands of women were imported from Mexico, Chile, Peru, the South Pacific, and China to work in the flourishing brothels. After the Civil War, American cities followed the European practice of segregating prostitutes to certain areas of the city, which came to be known as "red-light" districts, and requiring them to register or be licensed. Regular physical examinations were required of all sex workers.

Between 1880 and 1920, prostitution was commonplace and legal. Since few prostitutes bothered to register, licensing was not effective in controlling disease. Police supervision only spawned crime and corruption via bribes for protection or "looking the other way." In 1910, Congress passed the Mann Act, which forbade the transportation of women across state lines for "immoral" purposes. In the decade before World War I, the Social Hygiene Movement, Women's Christian Temperance Union, Young Men's Christian Association, and other "purity" organizations worked for the criminalization of prostitution. By the end of World War I, these efforts were successful in ending politicians' tolerance of prostitution. "Legal brothels were destroyed and prostitutes were dispersed from stable homes in red-light districts to the city at large where they were less likely to be self-employed or work for other women and more likely to be controlled by exploitive men including pimps, gangsters, slum landlords, unscrupulous club owners, and corrupt politicians" (McCormick 1994, 91).

Currently, prostitution is illegal in all states except Nevada, where a 1971 court decision allowed counties with a sparse population the discretion of legalizing and licensing prostitution. State legal codes forbid making money from the provision of sexual services, including prostitution, keeping a brothel, and pandering, procuring, transporting, or detaining women for "immoral" purposes. Patronizing a prostitute is illegal in some states; a convicted offender may face a fine of $500 or more and a year or more in jail. In some states, pimps may be sentenced to ten to twenty years in jail and fined $2,000 or more.

The Spectrum of Sex Workers and Their Clients

Sex workers vary greatly in status, income, and working conditions, as well as in the services they offer—oral sex being the most common sexual practice offered. The vast majority of sex workers are females with male customers. Most prostitutes view their work as temporary, often on a part-time basis to supplement their traditionally female, poorly paid employment, and to support themselves and their families (McCormick 1994). The average prostitute's career lasts five years since youthful attractiveness is valued by customers. The sexual orientation of female sex workers reflects that of the larger population, and includes heterosexual, lesbian, and bisexual women. While sex workers are predominantly female, the "managers," at all levels, are predominantly male. Pimps—those who live off the earnings of a sex worker—often exploit the workers' romantic feelings, emotional needs, or fear of violence, and often come from disenfranchised groups themselves.

On one hand, many believe that females turn to prostitution because of dysfunctional families and individual psychopathology. The belief that female prostitutes are more likely than other women to be depressed, alienated, emotionally volatile, or engage in criminal activities and excessive use of alcohol and street drugs are often based on small, specialized samples (McCormick 1994). Research is also inconclusive as to the proportion of sex workers who abuse alcohol and other drugs. At least one study has indicated that call girls were as well adjusted as a control group of nonsex-worker peers who were matched for age and educational level (McCormick 1994). Yet, for many juveniles, sexual and physical abuse seems to be related, at least indirectly, to their becoming involved with prostitution.

On the other hand, economic survival, not psychopathology, may be the most important contributing factor to engaging in prostitution. Poor and disadvantaged women may engage in sex work because it is the best paying or only job available. More-advantaged women may also engage in sex work because of the often unparalleled economic rewards, coupled with the flexibility in working hours, and the sense of control over clients. Although noncommercial sex is described as more satisfying by most sex workers, many report achieving satisfaction and orgasm though their work (Savitz and Rosen 1988).

On the lowest rung of female and male sex workers are those who solicit on the street; above them are those working in bars and hotel lobbies. Their limited overhead is matched by their low fees. Streetworkers, usually from the lower-socioeconomic class or run-away teenagers, face high risks of violence, robbery, and exploitation, as well as drug addiction, STDs, and HIV infections. Approximately 35 percent of streetwalkers have been physically abused and 30 to 70 percent raped while on the job (Delacoste and Alexander 1987). In addition, because of their visibility, streetworkers are the most vulnerable to harassment and arrest by law enforcement agents. While 10 to 20 percent of sex workers are streetwalkers, they constitute 90 percent of sex-worker arrests. Prostitution is the only crime in America in which the majority of offenders are female. In dealing with prostitutes, the courts often become a "revolving door system," with the sex worker posting bail and back on the street shortly after being arrested. Paradoxically, she is often fined, making it financially important for her to turn again to sex work to survive.

Government estimates suggest that half of the five million teenagers who run away from their homes each year spend at least some time as sex workers. Poor self-images, rejection by peers, few friends, unsupervised homes, and emotional, if not sexual, abuse in the home make them susceptible to the lure of big-city glamor where their survival needs force them to find work on the streets.

Houses of prostitution are less common today than they were in the past. The famous houses of the Storyville area of New Orleans or San Francisco's Barbary Coast were often very luxurious, and women both lived and worked in the same brothel for many years. Because of legal problems, most brothels today are run-down and in disrepair. If tolerated by the local police, they may be better maintained. In many places, regular, "go-go," and "topless" bars and massage parlors double as "fast-service" brothels. Brothels sometimes advertise their services in "underground" newspapers or in the "free press."

Escorts and call girls are at the upper level of sex workers. Young, slender, attractive, middle- and upper-class white women command the highest fees and the best working conditions among sex workers. Call girls typically see a small number of regular, scheduled clients. For them, sex work provides a much higher income than they would earn in almost any other profession, plus better control over their working hours.

The typical customer of a female sex worker, a "john," appears indistinguishable from the average American male. They are often involved in sexual relationships with another woman and report that they purchase sex by choice—perhaps for the adventurous, dangerous, or forbidden aspects of sex with a prostitute. Some frequent prostitutes because their usual sexual partners are unwilling to participate in certain sexual behaviors (like oral or anal sex). Other men frequent prostitutes because they have difficulty in establishing an ongoing sexual relationship because of lack of opportunity or physical or emotional barriers.

Most heterosexual male prostitutes are not street hustlers, but have steady customers or relationships that are ongoing and similar to those of a high-priced call girl. Their clients are often wealthy older women. Much more common are males who sell their sexual services to other males. In fact, most male prostitutes identify themselves as homosexual or bisexual. In large cities, gay male prostitutes cruise gay bars, gay bath houses, public toilets, bus and train stations, and other areas known to local clients.

Sex work also includes a variety of erotic entertainment jobs, including erotic dancing, live pornography or "peep shows," and acting in pornographic films and videos. Female burlesque shows have long been part of the American scene. However, the professional burlesque queens of the past have been replaced by amateur, poorly paid "table dancers." Feminists Barbara Ehrenreich, Gloria Hass, and Elizabeth Jacobs (1987) maintain that male go-go dancers play a role in advancing the rights of women and in breaking down patriarchal biases, because their female viewers treat them as sex objects and reduce their phallic power to impotence within bikini shorts.

The incidence of HIV infection and AIDS varies among sex workers and is increased by IV drug use, untreated STDs, and unsafe-sex practices. In general, it is high among female and gay male sex workers on the street, and lowest among high-priced call girls and heterosexual male prostitutes.

Economic Factors

In the early 1990s, there were an estimated 450,000 female prostitutes working in the United States, a profession lacking job security and fringe benefits, such as health insurance and social security. Most working outside the high-class escort services do not pay taxes. Nor are taxes paid on any of the monies that are exchanged in the underground economy associated with prostitution, such as: the monies that pass between prostitutes and their pimps; the hotel, motel, massage parlor, or bar owners and clerks; or the recruiters like cab drivers and doormen who make prostitution possible.

A 1985 survey of the cost of enforcing antiprostitution laws in the sixteen largest cities of the U.S. estimated police enforcement costs at $53,155,688, court costs at $35,627,496, and correction costs at $31,770,211, for a total 1985 cost of $119,553,395. In 1985, Dallas, Texas, police made only 2,665 arrests for the 15,000 violent crimes reported. They made 7,280 prostitution arrests at a cost of over $10 million and almost 800,000 hours of police work. In 1986, Boston, Cleveland, and Houston police arrested twice as many people for prostitution as they did for all homicides, rapes, robberies, and assaults combined. Meanwhile, 90 percent of perpetrators of violent crimes evaded arrest. Between 1976 and 1985, violent crimes in the sixteen largest cities rose by 32 percent while arrests for violent crimes rose only 3.7 percent, and arrests for robbery and homicide actually dropped by 15 percent. Equally important, the sixteen largest cities continue to spend more on enforcing prostitution laws than they do on either education or public welfare (Pearl 1987).

Working in pairs, police spend an average of twenty-one hours to obtain a solicitation, make an arrest, transport the prostitute to the detention center, process her papers, write up a report, and testify in court. Undercover police cruising the street looking to get a solicitation need frequent changes of disguises and rented cars. Making an arrest of a call girl is even more difficult, requiring greater expense for false identification and credit cards, hotel room, luggage, and other paraphernalia to convince the call girl this is a legitimate customer and not a policeman. The hotel room is usually wiretapped and the solicitation videotaped.

Arrests of prostitutes working in massage parlors present their own difficulties. It usually takes half an hour for an undercover policeman to undress, shower, and get into the massage, before an illegal service is offered. For a while, Houston police ran their own parlor. When that was declared entrapment by the courts, teams of 10 undercover officers began working existing modeling studios as customers. "Ten officers at a time, at $60 each, with no guarantee that we'd get solicited. . . . We could spend $3000 or $4000 and not make a case" (Pearl 1987).

Current and Future Status

Historically, sex workers have been blamed for the spread of sexually transmissible diseases (STDs). However, recent research has indicated that sex workers are much more likely to practice safer sex than the "average teenager" (McCormick 1994). While prostitutes are being blamed for transmitting HIV to their clients, data from the Centers for Disease Control indicate that only a small proportion of persons with AIDS contracted HIV from a prostitute. However, rates of HIV infection are quite high—up to 80 percent—among sex workers who also use intravenous drugs. Unfortunately, sex workers are usually at higher risk of contracting an STD, including HIV, from their lovers with whom they do not use a condom than from their clients with whom they use a condom.

Today in the United States, religious and political conservatives and radical feminists continue to oppose prostitution through such groups as WHISPER (Women Hurt in Systems of Prostitution Engaged in Revolt), an organization devoted to rescuing women and children from sex work. On the other hand, sex workers have begun to organize and advocate better working conditions and treatment through such groups as COYOTE (Call Off Your Old Tired Ethics), Scapegoat, and U.S. PROStitutes. These groups lobby for the decriminalization and legalization of prostitution, inform the public about the realities of prostitution, and offer various services to sex workers. In addition, liberal feminists inside and outside of the sex industry have founded the International Committee for Prostitutes' Rights (ICPR) in order to preserve their rights to life, liberty, and security.

In spite of continued economic inequities in the United States, some observers believe prostitution will decline because of the availability of effective contraceptives, a continued liberalization of sexual attitudes and divorce, a decline in the double standard in employment and sexual expression between the genders, and the risk of AIDS. In the Kinsey study of male sexuality in the late 1940s, 69 percent of white males reported having had at least one experience with a prostitute. The recent national study of 18- to 59-year-olds, *Sex in America*, found that only 16 percent of the men ever paid for sex (Gagnon, Laumann, and Kolata 1994). Yet, it seems that prostitution will continue to exist in some form or another. Although some people support the decriminalization of sexual activity between consenting adults, whether or not money is exchanged, this is not likely to happen in the United States.

C. Pornography and Erotica   ROBERT T. FRANCOEUR

The Legal Context

A landmark legal definition of obscenity was established by the Supreme Court in the 1957 *Roth v. the United States* decision. For a book, movie, magazine, or picture to be legally obscene,

- the dominant theme of the work, as a whole, must appeal to a prurient interest in sex;
- the work must be patently offensive by contemporary community standards; and

- the work must be devoid of serious literary, artistic, political, or scientific value.

This ruling permitted the publication in the U.S.A., for the first time, of such works as D. H. Lawrence's *Lady Chatterly's Lover*, James Joyce's *Ulysses*, and works by Henry Miller. However, this definition left the meaning of the term "community standards" unclear.

In the 1973 *Miller v. the United States* decision, the Supreme Court attempted to tighten the restrictions on obscene material by requiring that defenders of an alleged obscene work prove that it has "serious literary, artistic, or scientific merit." Despite this clarification, the courts still faced the near-impossible task of determining what has "literary, artistic, or scientific merit," who represents the "average community member," and what the "community" is. In 1987, the Supreme Court attempted to refine the *Roth* and *Miller* decisions by saying "a reasonable person," not "an ordinary member of the community," could decide whether some allegedly obscene material has any serious literary, artistic, political, or scientific value. Justice Potter Stewart further confused the situation when he remarked that "You know it when you see it."

In 1969, the Supreme Court ruled that private possession of obscene material was not a crime and is not subject to legal regulation. However, federal laws continue to prohibit obscene material from being broadcast on radio and television, mailed, imported, or carried across state lines. In recent years, pornographic material of any kind involving underaged children has been the target of repeated federal "sting" operations, raising issues of police entrapment.

Research Models

For at least two decades, there has been often-heated debate among the public, among feminists groups, and among scientists regarding the social and psychological impact of pornography, particularly materials that link sex with the objectification of women and with violence. A psychological research theory, the catharsis model, assumes that pornography and other sexually explicit materials provide a "safety valve" in a sexually repressive society. This model views pornography and other sexually explicit materials as "not so good, perhaps disgusting, but still useful" in diverting tensions that otherwise might trigger aggressive antisocial behavior. A different hypothesis suggests an imitation model in which sexually explicit books, pictures, and movies provide powerful role models that can, by conditioning and scripting, promote antisocial, sexually aggressive behavior. A third model of pornography addresses the personal and societal uses of pornography in different cultures, as a product designed as an alternative source of sexual arousal gratification and a way of enhancing masturbation. There are also models of pornography based on communication,

Marxist, psychoanalytic, feminist, and religious theories (Francoeur 1991, 637).

Commission Studies

A 1970 White House Commission funded research by experts in the field and concluded that neither hard-core nor soft-core pornography leads to antisocial behavior and recommended that all obscenity laws except those protecting minors be abolished. The majority of the commission concluded that pornography provides a useful safety valve in an otherwise sexually repressive culture. President Richard Nixon refused to officially accept the commission's report.

A 1986 investigation by then-Attorney General Edwin Meese did not sponsor any new research and took a different approach in reaching its conclusion. This commission reexamined the alleged connection between pornography and child abuse, incest, and rape by inviting anyone interested in speaking to the issue. The commission was widely criticized for having a preset agenda, for appointing biased commission members, and for relying on "the totality of evidence," which gave equal weight to the testimony of fundamentalist ministers, police officers, antipornography activists, and putative victims of pornography. This allowed the commission to conclude there is a "proven" causal connection between violent pornography and sexual assaults. This commission concluded that there is a causal connection between viewing sexually explicit materials, especially violent pornography, and the commission of rape and other sexual assaults. The commission recommended stricter penalties to regulate the pornography traffic, enactment of laws to keep hard-core pornography off home cable television and home telephone service, more vigorous prosecution of obscenity cases, and encouraged private citizens to use protests and boycotts to discourage the marketing of pornography. Among the many criticisms of the Meese Commission, Robert Staples, a black sociologist, pointed out that in the black community, pornography is a trivial issue. It is "a peculiar kind of white man's problem," because blacks see the depiction of heterosexual intercourse and nudity, not as a sexist debasement of women, but as a celebration of the equal rights of women and men to enjoy sexual stimuli and pleasure (Nobile and Nadler 1986).

Concurrent with the *Meese Commission Report*, the 1986 *Report of the U.S. Surgeon General* concluded that we still know little about the patterns of use or the power of attitudes in precipitating sexually aggressive behavior. Much research is still needed in order to demonstrate that the present knowledge of laboratory studies has significant real-world implications for predicting behavior. This report did not call for censorship, boycotts, and other tactics advocated by the Meese Commission. Rather, it recommended development of "street-based, innovative approaches" to educate the public about the different types of sexually explicit material and their possible effects.

Local Efforts at Regulation

In 1985, Andrea Dworkin, Catherine MacKinnon, and Women Against Pornography joined forces with local citizens' groups in Minneapolis, Minnesota, and Long Island, New York, to promote a new kind of pornography legislation. Using a civil rights argument, the proposed legislation stated that

> Pornography is sex discrimination. [Where it exists, it poses] a substantial threat to the health, safety, peace, welfare, and equality of citizens in the community . . . . Pornography is a systematic practice of exploitation and subordination based on sex that differentially harms women. The harm of pornography includes dehumanization, sexual exploitation, forced sex, forced prostitution, physical injury, and social and sexual terrorism and inferiority presented as entertainment.

The proposed legislation would have made producing, selling, or exhibiting pornography an act of sex discrimination. Women forced to participate in pornographic films, exposed by force of circumstances to view pornography in any place of employment, education, home, or public place, or assaulted by a male inspired by pornography could sue in civil court for damages based on sex discrimination. The American Civil Liberties Union (ACLU), Feminist Anti-Censorship Taskforce (FACT), and others challenged this kind of legislation. After considerable nationwide debate about civil rights, sex discrimination, and the constitutional right to free speech, these legislative efforts were abandoned.

Contemporary Aspects

The availability of sexually explicit, X-rated videocassette rentals and sales has become a major factor in American home entertainment. In the past decade, feminist soft-core pornography or erotica has made its mark in the popular media by portraying women as persons who enjoy sexual pleasure as much as men. This material appears in the pages of such mainstream women's magazines as *Cosmopolitan.* It is promoted by sex boutiques, with names like Eve's Garden, Adam and Eve, and Good Vibrations, catering to women. Another growing phenomenon is a variation on the Tupperware and Mary Kay Cosmetics home parties that bring women the opportunity to examine and, of course, purchase sex toys, love lotions, and lingerie in the privacy of their homes, surrounded by other women with whom they are friends. Exotic lingerie is also available in specialty stores in major shopping malls and by mail order from Victoria's Secret and Frederick's of Hollywood. Since 1992, Feminists for Free Expression, opposed to censorship and supported by such notables as Betty Friedan, Erica Jong, and Nancy Friday, has countered the efforts of some feminists to suppress pornography with an alternative view for the feminist community.

Erotic romance novels have become an acceptable form of soft-core pornography for women. Far outselling gothic novels, science fiction, self-help, and other books aimed at women, erotic romances often center around a traditional rape myth, a story in which the woman is at first unwilling, but finally yields in a sensual rapture to a man. In nonsexual characteristics, women who read erotic romantic novels are very much like women who do not. However, they appear to enjoy sex more and have a richer sexual fantasy life (Coles and Shamp 1984; Lawrence and Herold 1988).

Researchers and theorists, both feminist and nonfeminist, have almost completely ignored the existence of gay pornography. Lesbian pornography tends towards two extremes, about evenly divided in popularity, with little middle ground. Small independent presses publish soft-core pornography or erotica. Erotica on audiocassettes are very popular among lesbians. On the other side is a hard-core lesbian literature with a strong SM character that makes some feminists uncomfortable. *On Our Backs*, a tabloid magazine, is the largest publication of this type. *Eidos*, another tabloid, carries numerous ads for lesbians who desire bondage and dominance or sado-masochistic relations.

Considerably more pornography designed for homosexual men is available. Most of this genre is hard-core pornography with an emphasis on leather, SM, and younger males. At the same time, gay videos have pioneered in eroticizing the condom, nonoxynol-9, and safer-sex practices.

Dial-a-porn, or telephone sex, is a multimillion-dollar-a-year business producing massive profits for telephone companies and the companies providing phone-in services. In one year, dial-in services, including dial-a-porn, earned Pacific Bell $24.5 million and the phone-in companies $47.2 million. Because of constitutional concerns, the Public Utilities Commission and Federal Communications Commission (FCC) do not allow telephone companies to censor telephone messages or to discriminate among dial-for-a-message 1-900 services on the basis of content. Telephone companies cannot legally deny telephone lines to adults willing to pay the bill, although at least one court has ruled that it is not unlawful discrimination for a telephone company to refuse to provide services for dial-a-porn services. The FCC does require dial-a-porn services to screen out calls by minors by supplying their customers with special access numbers or having them pay by credit card. Concerned parents may pay a one-time fee to block all phones in a residence from access to dial-a-porn.

D. Paraphilias and Unusual Sexual Practices   BRENDA LOVE

In 1990, a Los Angeles man named Jeff Vilencia formed a group called Squish Productions. Through magazine articles, television appearances, and radio interviews, Vilencia had attracted more than 300 members to his group by 1995, all of whom shared the fetish of becoming aroused by the sight of others stepping on small living things such as snails and insects.

Although the fetish shared by Vilencia and his fellow members in Squish Productions may seem—and may in fact be—novel, paraphilias are nothing new. Paraphilias and fetishes have most likely been in existence in the U.S. for as long as there have been inhabitants on the Western continents. Although while a few immigrants may have brought sexual preferences, such as autoerotic asphyxiation, sadomasochism (SM), foot fetishes, and bestiality with them, other paraphilias have unquestionably developed here. In the world of paraphilias and fetishes, there is always something new. And thanks to increased awareness of and access to information about unorthodox sexual practices and their practitioners, interest in paraphilias appears to be growing in the United States.

Definitions

"Fetish," as defined for the American health professional by the *Diagnostic and Statistical Manual of Mental Disorders III* (*DSM III*), "is the use of nonliving objects (fetishes) as a repeatedly preferred or exclusive method of achieving sexual excitement." Such objects "tend to be articles of clothing, such as female undergarments, shoes, and boots, or, more rarely, parts of the human body, such as hair or nails" (American Psychological Association 1980).

The manual also states that the fetish object "is often associated with someone with whom the individual was intimately involved during childhood, most often a caretaker.... Usually the disorder begins by adolescence, although the fetish may have been endowed with special significance earlier, in childhood. Once established, the disorder tends to be chronic" (APA 1980).

"Paraphilias," on the other hand, are defined by *DSM III* as recurrent, fixed, compulsive, sexually motivated thoughts or actions by a personally or socially maladjusted individual that interfere with the individual's capacity for reciprocal affection. It is important to note that a paraphilia is not merely an activity that may appear strange or disgusting to an observer; rather, the activity or compulsion must meet all of the above criteria to be considered a problem requiring therapy.

It is also important to note in the area of paraphilias that many patients mention their unusual sexual interest simply to receive validation. The therapist can do much for the mental health of a patient by mentioning a support group or club for people with the interest, or by giving the patient the clinical name for the practice, stressing that the term paraphilia only applies when the above *DSM III* criteria apply. This can be followed by therapy to improve the person's self-esteem, communication, and social skills. The confession of activities involving minors or nonconsensual activities, however, of course requires immediate intervention by health professionals.

Background on Fetishes and Paraphilias in the U.S.A.

Fetishes change according to current fashions and customs. A hundred years ago, fetishists were aroused by such things as handkerchiefs, gloves, black rubber aprons, garters, corsets, enemas, seeing females wring the necks of chickens, or whipping horses. Today many of these stimuli have been replaced by pantyhose, high heels, tennis shoes, cigarettes, escalators, latex, or phone sex.

In addition, today's technology adds to the variety of ways a fetishist can pursue his or her predilection. In the past, one had either to create one's own drawings, or hope to catch a glimpse of an arousing person, object, or situation. Today, the fetishist has access to television, photographs, Internet newsgroups, clubs, videos, and magazines. Membership in fetish groups has increased during the last decade. And as computer technology has descreased the cost of publishing, groups or individuals have been increasingly able to print their own sex magazines, books, and newsletters, thereby avoiding the censorship imposed by mainstream publications.

At the same time, even the more straitlaced mainstream media have helped to increase the information available about fetishes and paraphilias. Unfortunately, many national television talk shows have "cashed in" on fetishes and victims of sexual trauma by sensationalizing their lives, rather than trying to educate the public. Hollywood also sensationalizes the issue, portraying erotic asphyxia, lust murder, sadomasochism, and nipple piercing. An example of the media's exploitation and sensationalization of unusual sex practices was the hundreds of hours of air time devoted to keeping the public informed of the status of John Wayne Bobbit, the circumstances leading to his castration at the hands of his wife, the subsequent surgical reattachment of his penis, and his appearance in an X-rated video.

Perhaps the most important development in the growth of interest in paraphilias and fetishes has been the Internet, the worldwide computer network through which up to 500,000 "lurkers" a month enter the "alt.sex" newsgroups. Users of these newsgroups, which offer uncensored forums devoted to a wide variety of sexual interests, can exchange or download photos and information, including what would normally be considered illegal in the United States, with other Internet users.

While the Internet has played an increasing role in the lives of fetishists in recent years, it would not be correct to attribute the growing popularity of fetishism and other unorthodox forms of sexuality to the Internet alone, as those in Washington who seek to censor the Internet seem to believe. The role of the Internet is more modest according to Robin Roberts, an Internet guru in California and founder of Backdrop, one of America's oldest fantasy and bondage clubs. Established in 1965, Backdrop promoted itself with discreet ads in the *Berkeley Barb* with post office boxes or mail-drop services as the method of contact. Today, Backdrop has about 5,700 members, but Roberts does not attribute the club's growth to exposure on the Internet.

Roberts explains that Internet lurkers rarely participate in dialog and tend not to join sex clubs. They are typically readers of *Forum* magazine or

"Letters to the Editor" columns. For those users who do participate in sex on-line, computers provide anonymity, and a way to explore taboos in a safe, non-threatening environment. Roberts does note, however, that for those who are active participants in computer sex, rather than just lurkers, the Internet provides twenty-four-hour access to other users, an equal chance to express one's opinions, and an unlimited number of fantasies. At the same time, Roberts does not feel computer sex will replace fetish clubs, due to the simple fact that electronic mail does not provide touch, intonation of the voice, nuances of speech, or visual impressions.

The Growing Popularity of Fetishes and Paraphilias

Not everyone who accesses information about paraphilias and fetishes through these new technological avenues is a fetishist. Many are among the growing number of experimenters who, even though they do not have a fetish, will join groups or purchase sex toys and SM paraphernalia. Such experimentation seems to be on the increase; a 1994 survey conducted in two San Francisco sex boutiques indicated that approximately 55 percent of their customers had at least experimented with SM (Love 1994).

Ann Grogan, owner of San Francisco's Romantasy boutique, has seen an increase in such experimentation among the customers who frequent her sex-accessory establishment, one of two operating in San Francisco in 1995 geared toward women customers.

"Gender play is becoming more and more popular among customers of all ages, primarily ages 30-50 years," Grogan says. "Couples now buy matching corsets and wrist restraints." During the last five years, females in increasing numbers have shown an interest in transgender play, assuming the dominant role in the sexual relationship. Many men are also expressing an interest in anal sexuality, measured in part by the purchase of dildoes and harnesses to be used on men by the women. And a growing number of recently divorced female customers in their 50s have shown a curiosity about safe sex and pleasuring themselves.

Grogan can also testify to the increasing influence of the Internet:

> The latest trend seems to be the appearance of couples who have met on the Internet. They appear together at Romantasy after only one or two meetings, because in previous communications they have gotten far beyond the awkward preliminary dialog about each other's sexual preferences and have jumped into a willingness to act out each other's fantasies. Meeting on the Internet seems to be a "fast track to intimacy." (Grogan 1995)

Ted McIlvenna, president of the Institute for the Advanced Study of Human Sexuality, expects that interest and participation in paraphilias and fetishes will continue to grow. "In the next five years," McIlvenna believes, we will see a group of people seeking information and support groups for their sex interests which, in the past, people have considered excessive or compulsive. This is not an evil path; instead it is remedial sex education. Because of the massive number of people involved—in the U.S. the estimate is forty million people—I have labeled this the "sexual accessories movement." Mental health professionals, including sexual health professionals, must monitor and study but leave this movement alone; their sexuality belongs to them. We can expect people to buy more, join more, and experiment more, and we can only hope that out of this will emerge societal control methods that will enable people to have better and more fulfilling sex lives. (McIlvenna 1995)

Given the recent and anticipated growth of many of the fetish clubs described below, it is important to ask about what causes paraphilias. Although there has been much scientific interest in this question, science has not yet discovered the etiology of fetishes or "paraphilic lovemaps," according to John Money (1988), the leading expert on paraphilias. It does appear, however, that, as is the case with substance abuse and addiction, a small percentage of the population seems more predisposed toward the development of paraphilias, often due to childhood trauma. Money says,

The retrospective biographies of adolescent and adult paraphiles point to the years of childhood sexual rehearsal play as the vulnerable developmental period. . . . The harsh truth is that as a society we do not want our children to be lustfully normal. If they are timorous enough to be discovered engaging their lust in normal sexual rehearsal play or in masturbation, they become, in countless numbers, the victims of humiliation and abusive violence. (Money 1988)

Money has explained how these early traumas can lead to paraphilias:

They [adults who subject sexually curious children to abuse] do not know that what they destroy, or vandalize, is the incorporation of lust into the normal development of the lovemap. The expression of lust is diverted or detoured from its normal route. Thus, to illustrate: those adults who humiliate and punish a small boy for strutting around with an erected penis, boasting to the girls who watch him, do not know that they are thereby exposing the boy to risk of developing a lovemap of paraphilic exhibitionism. (Money 1988)

Fetish and Paraphilia Clubs

The United States is probably home to more fetish clubs than any other country. As Brenda Love (1992) wrote in *The Encyclopedia of Unusual Sex Practices*, which catalogs over 700 sexual practices,

international advertising is fairly inexpensive and computerized printing of newsletters has made it simpler to form clubs. People with fetishes
as obscure as large penises, big balls, hairy bodies, mud wrestlers,
shaving, cigars, used condoms, genital modification, and throwing pies
have been able to find others with similar interests willing to form clubs.

Sadomasochist (SM) clubs are probably the most prevalent type of fetish
clubs in the U.S.A. today, although very few of the members could be
defined as having a true SM fetish or paraphilia.

SM has become an umbrella term for many sexual activities, and because
of its accouterments and role playing, people wanting to experiment with
or improve their sexuality join these groups. "It was only in the late fifteenth
century that the first unambiguous case report of SM was reported, and
then as a medical curiosity rather than a problem" (Ellis 1936). William
Simon has eloquently described the allure of SM:

> The sadomasochistic script plays upon the potential absolutism of
> hierarchy, not merely to experience hierarchy with the relief accompa-
> nying the elimination of its ambiguities but to experience the danger-
> ous emotions that invariably accompany acknowledgment of its exer-
> cise, the rage and fear of rage in both the other and ourselves. (Simon
> 1994)

Charles Moser (1988) estimates that approximately 10 percent of the
adult population are SM practitioners. This estimate is based on Kinsey's
report that approximately 50 percent reported some erotic response to
being bitten (Kinsey 1953). However, there is no direct empirical evidence
verifying this estimate. Moser divides SM behaviors

> into two types, physical and psychological. . . . Physical behaviors may
> be further subdivided into the following categories: bondage, physical
> discipline, intense stimulation, sensory deprivation, and body altera-
> tion. . . . Psychological pain is induced by feelings of humiliation,
> degradation, uncertainty, apprehension, powerlessness, anxiety, and
> fear. . . . Both physical and psychological behaviors are devised to
> emphasize the transfer of power from the submissive to the dominant
> partner. SM practitioners often report it is this consensual exchange of
> power that is erotic to them and the pain is just a method of achieving
> this power exchange. (Moser 1988)

Moser lists the common types of clinical problems presented by SM
practitioners to their therapists as: "1) Am I normal? 2) Can you make these
desires go away? 3) SM is destroying our relationship; 4) I cannot lead this
double life anymore; 5) I cannot find a partner; and 6) Is it violence or SM?"
(Moser 1988). All but the last question are also the concern of most fetishists.

Foot-fetish club members have a more focused interest than do SM practitioners. Weinberg et al. (1994) conducted a survey of 262 members of a gay foot-fetishist group called the Foot Fraternity that had approximately 1,000 members in 1990, but had grown to over 4,000 by 1995. These sexologists also compared the ratio of self-masturbation during sexual encounters to that of oral-genital activity and to anal intercourse. Fetishists tended to masturbate to orgasm while engaging in foot play rather than experiencing orgasm as a result of some type of penetrative sex with a partner. Furthermore, the researchers discovered that 76 percent responded that they masturbated themselves to orgasm frequently, whereas 48.1 percent performed oral-genital activity, and only 9.55 percent performed anal intercourse.

Weinberg et al. (1994) reported that their research highlighted the psychological importance a support group or club has for fetishists.

> Despite the lack of a widespread fetish subculture, the Foot Fraternity itself can be considered an embryonic subculture. Almost 70 percent of the respondents said membership in the Foot Fraternity allowed them to pursue their fetish interests more easily. Some 66 percent said membership increased their interest in feet and footwear, and over 40 percent said that they learned new ways of expressing their sexuality. Thus, the organization helped to sustain, as well as expand, its members' unconventional sexual interest. Almost 70 percent said the Foot Fraternity got them to correspond with others with similar interests, 50 percent that it got them to meet others with similar interests, and 40 percent that this led them to engage in foot play with another member. Finally, over 40 percent said that membership in the Foot Fraternity helped remove confusion about their interest in feet and footwear and almost 60 percent that it increased their self-acceptance. (Weinberg et al. 1994)

These statistics regarding benefits of membership can most likely be applied to other sexual interest groups as well.

Doug Gaines, founder of this Cleveland-based club, estimates that 15 percent of the U.S. population has a foot or related fetish, an opinion based on the fact that he has received 80,000 requests for club information. He promotes the group in magazines, radio interviews, and a foot-fetish Internet newsgroup.

Interestingly, Gaines seconded the findings of researchers on the genesis of fetishes by identifying childhood experiences, such as being tickled, riding on the foot of a parent ("playing horsey"), or seeing a parent's foot immediately prior to being picked up and nurtured, as predominant memories of most of his members. The Foot Fraternity offers a newsletter, glossy magazine, and videos of men modeling their feet. The selection of photos is determined by a detailed membership questionnaire which asks what type of shoe, sock, or foot the new member finds erotic.

The activities in which foot enthusiasts participate include masturbation while looking at photos of feet, slipping off a partner's shoes in order to smell the stockings and foot, or placing oneself underneath the foot in a submissive posture. The foot is massaged and licked completely (toes, between toes, bottom, etc.). SM dominance and submission scenes, for example, where a partner takes on the role of a policeman and the fetishist must kiss his boot to get out of being given a traffic ticket, are popular.

Another common scene consists of acting out the roles of principal and student. Foot fetishists rarely use pain in their dominance/submission; rather, these scenes simply serve as an excuse for foot worship. A few foot fetishists attend auctions where they are able to purchase shoes once belonging to their favorite sports figures or movie stars hoping that the "scent" of the person remains in the shoe.

Squish Productions, mentioned earlier, can also be viewed as a foot-fetish club. Unlike the Foot Fraternity, Squish has yet to be the subject of any in-depth survey by sexologists. Even so, the genesis of the Squish fetish appears to be similar to that found in other fetishes, as evidenced by Squish founder Jeff Vilencia's recollections of his childhood. Identifying what he considers to be his childhood trigger point in the development of his fetish, Vilencia recalled that, as the younger of two children, he was the "victim" of an older sister who enjoyed kicking and stepping on him. Upon reaching puberty, he discovered feeling aroused when seeing females step on bugs. The bug apparently only serves as a projection of himself, because his fantasy involves taking the bug's place under the woman's foot.

Cross-dressing and other forms of transgender activity are found in many countries. The new *DSM IV* no longer lists this activity as a paraphilia, but rather as "gender dysphoria." Clubs such as ETVC in San Francisco have an extensive library for members, social outings, support-group hot line, newsletter, make-up classes, and lingerie modeling. Membership in ETVC increased from 329 in 1988 to a total of 433 in 1995.

Another group, Texas Tea Party, sponsors an annual party that, after eight years of existence, drew about 400 people in 1995. Estimates on the percentage of the population who have ever cross-dressed range from 1.5 to 10 percent. Groups attract new members with newspaper and magazine advertisements, appearances on television and radio, magazine articles on the subject, and by staffing a booth at the annual San Francisco Lesbian and Gay Freedom Day Parade and Celebration.

A recent survey of 942 transgenderists by Linda and Cynthia Phillips indicates that most members experienced cross-dressing in puberty, although one member did not begin cross-dressing until the age of 72. The average transgenderist did not seek out a transgender club until his early 40s. Sexual arousal while cross-dressing is also more common during adolescence, and appears to diminish as the boy grows older. Therefore, an adult male transgenderist dresses to feel "feminine," whereas an underwear fetishist uses the lingerie for sexual arousal. (Females who cross-dress do not tend to experience arousal while cross-dressing) (Phillips 1994).

No one knows how many cross-dressers or clubs exist in the U.S., but it is known that many people purchase special-interest cross-dressing magazines. One of these, *Tapestry*, had a 1995 quarterly distribution of 10,000 issues compared to 2,000 five years earlier. And a fairly new magazine, *Transformation*, had an international distribution of 50,000 in 1995.

Infantilism is fairly unique to the U.S. and growing in popularity. Its practitioners take on the persona of infants or young children. They may wear diapers under their business suits, drink from a baby bottle, use an assortment of toys and baby furniture, and, if they have a partner, they may participate by reading bedtime stories, diapering, spanking, or using other forms of affection or punishment.

One practitioner, who asked to be identified only as Tommy, is the founder of Diaper Pail Friends. Inside his home in a prestigious San Francisco suburb, a visitor will find an adult-sized high chair, bibs, and numerous baby bottles in the kitchen. Downstairs, Tommy's bedroom features a large crib with a view of the Bay area, a collection of adult-sized baby clothes, and a trail of toys leading to a train set that fills the center of an adjacent room.

Diaper Pail Friends is about 15 years old, and grew from about 1,000 members in 1990 to more than 3,000 in 1995. Most of the members discovered the group through articles in magazines or books, television talk shows, or an Internet newsgroup. The club publishes a newsletter, short stories, videos, and distributes adult-sized baby paraphernalia.

A group of sexologists conducted an extensive survey of the Diaper Pail Friends, but had not yet published their findings as of 1995. Tommy, however, concluded from an informal survey of the group's members that

> Even a casual review of infantilists in the DPF Rosters show that there are tremendous differences between one infantilist and another. In fact, there would seem to be as many personal, individual variations as there are people. Nevertheless, certain patterns do seem to become evident, patterns that seem to encompass a very large percentage of the environmental and inborn factors that are involved with the creation of Infantilism in human personality. These patterns are [in order of prevalence] (1) deficient early nurturing, (2) rejection of Softness, (3) childhood sexual abuse [primarily in female members], and (4) bed wetting. Every infantilist probably has one or more of these patterns in their history, and each infantilist combines them in varying degrees. The variations are limitless. (Tommy 1992)

A Chicago-based national acrotomophile club (people aroused by seeing amputees) has a membership of about 300. They sponsor an annual conference during the first week of June and have spawned local chapters that also hold meetings. Quarterly pamphlets are sent to members and a couple of Internet newsgroups exist. New membership is not aggressively recruited, but the number of self-identified acrotomophiles has increased since 1989 publication of Grant Riddle's book, *Amputees and Devotees*, which examines the psychological basis of this phenomenon.

According to Riddle, many "devotees" are aware of this preference as a child, but there seems to be a wide variety of reasons for its development. One of these is being overly criticized by parents and wishing to be like a handicapped neighbor, assuming this would relieve some of the pressure. Another cause is being taught that sex is dirty, and from there, having to rationalize that if one cares for someone handicapped, one can justifiably ask for sex in return. Activities of acrotomophiles include having a healthy partner pretend to limp or use crutches; most acrotomophiles, however, content themselves with viewing photos (mostly of clothed females) or possibly catching a glimpse of an amputee on the street (Riddle 1989).

Autoerotic asphyxia (self-strangulation) seems originally to have been carried to Europe by French Foreign Legionnaires returning from war in Indochina (Michaldimitrakis 1986). Erotic asphyxia involves using a pillow, gag, gas mask, latex or leather hood, plastic bag, or other object to block oxygen intake. It may also involve strangulation by a partner's hands, or with a scarf or Velcro blood-pressure cuff. Corseting of the waist is another less obvious method of impeding oxygen intake.

This practice takes the lives of an estimated 250 to 1,000 Americans each year. It is believed that many more people experiment with asphyxia safely alone and/or with a partner, but because this act carries great legal liability if things go wrong, it is impossible to estimate the number of people who engage in it. During the early 1990s, a Seattle man made an effort, through workshops and lectures, to teach safety techniques to practitioners. Although he found many interested parties, he had to limit his public appearances and advice due to legal concerns.

Although there is little information available about the asphyxiphile's childhood, John Money has described one case in his book, *Breathless Orgasm*. This subject recalled first becoming interested in asphyxia when his childhood sweetheart drowned. He began by thinking of her drowning experience and soon discovered he was becoming aroused by visualizing her nude body under water and thinking about her suffocating (Money et al. 1991).

Another asphixiphile, who related his experience to the audience at a San Francisco lecture on the subject, described being raised as a Jehovah's Witness and taught that masturbation was a sin. This did not deter him from engaging in masturbation, but rather made it much more exciting, because he felt he could be "struck by lightning." After giving up his religious practice in his late teens, he immediately discovered that masturbation lost its intensity. He then found that by putting himself in a life-or-death situation, i.e., asphyxia, he could recover this lost intensity.

Most data on asphyxiphiles have been collected from the death scene of the victims. Ray Blanchard and Stephen J. Hucker have collected a vast data bank of coroner's reports and other materials on the subject. In their study of 117 incidents, they discovered that older men

> were more likely to have been simultaneously engaged in bondage or transvestitism, suggesting elaboration of the masturbatory ritual over time. The greatest degree of transvestitism was associated with intermediate rather than high levels of bondage, suggesting that response competition from bondage may limit asphyxiators' involvement in a third paraphilia like transvestitism. (Blanchard et al. 1991).

Sexual asphyxia is rarely depicted in print media, but has been shown in a few films, such as the 1993 movie, *The Rising Sun*, and also in the 1976 French-Japanese movie, *In the Realm of the Senses.*

Chubby Chasers, a San Francisco club of men attracted to the obese, almost doubled in membership between 1990 and 1995 and grew to include 50 different international groups. This club was involved on the Internet early and recruited many of its members there. This club also staffs a booth at the annual San Francisco Lesbian and Gay Freedom Day Parade. Membership in the organization includes a newsletter and invitation to many social activities. Many, but not all, "chasers" had a parent or close relative who was very obese, and recall having a preference for "chubbies" when they were as young as 4 or 5. For those with this interest, there are full-color commercial magazines depicting obese nude females, sometimes with a slender male partner, available in adult book stores.

There are a number of food fetishists or "piesexuals," a word coined by a well-known pie enthusiast, Mike Brown, who began his affair with pies at age 13. Mr. Brown produces pie videos and also hosts annual "bring your own pie" throwing parties, where couples undress and hit each other with pies. There is an Internet newsgroup and also several clubs catering to this interest. *Splosh* magazine, although not sexual, features attractive females smeared with an assortment of food and mud, another messy fetish.

Other more obscure fetish/paraphilia organizations include WES (We Enjoy Shaving) of Reno, Nevada; the Wisconsin STEAM journal for agoraphiles, who enjoy engaging in sex in public; and Hot Ash, a New York club for people aroused by partners who smoke. Hot Ash publishes a newsletter and sells videos for those with this interest.

New York is also the home of a vampire sex club whose members make small cuts on others and rub or lick the blood off. Blood sports are also common among some SM practitioners in forms of caning, cutting, or piercing. San Francisco had coprophilia (feces) and urophilia (urine) clubs before the AIDS epidemic. Some of the newest groups include Fire Play, whose members drip hot wax on their partners, rub lit cigarettes on their bodies, and/or use chemical irritants. Some with this interest rub a small part of the body with diluted alcohol and ignite it.

In another new paraphilic activity, some men catch bees and use them to sting the penis. The venom not only doubles the size of the penis for a few days, but also seems to bring about a change in the neural system that enhances the arousal stage.

The foregoing are but a few of the many unorthodox sexual practices now being pursued in the United States. Many more exist, and new ones are being invented all the time. And thanks to technology, including the Internet, advances in the quality and availability of home-based desktop publishing, and the rise of sensationalist television talk shows, interest and participation in these activities is on the increase.

In the coming years, the continuing growth of fetish/paraphilia sex groups will require therapists to learn to make clear determinations among people who experiment with various activities, those who self-report to have a fetish but five years later become bored with it, and the few clinically defined paraphiles who truly need some type of intervention or treatment.

9. Contraception, Abortion, and Population Planning
PATRICIA BARTHALOW KOCH

[In the final sections of this review of sexuality in American culture, we consider several areas which are concerned with health and/or technology. The areas of contraception, abortion, and sexually transmitted disease each have rather obvious health implications, but each is also influenced by growing medical technology and illustrates a relationship between sexual conduct and technological advances. We would note that the question of effective social policy in each of these areas remains a matter of considerable social conflict within the U.S.A. The identification and treatment of sexual "dysfunctions" reflect these same concerns. In fact, the growing recognition that various sexual conditions can be diagnosed and treated, and the growing public acceptance of the legitimacy of such treatment, may be one of the more profound, if subtle, changes in American sexuality in the last century. In no small way, this process has served to fuel the growth of an array of sexual professions with a corresponding need to provide graduate education for such professionals and the emergence of professional organizations. We provide a brief review of each of these professional developments. Finally, we close with a brief review of how one recent technological development, the Internet, may be changing the way that at least some Americans receive sexual information and communicate with each other about sexuality. Some mention of this was already made earlier in the section on fetishes and paraphilias (see Section 8D). As always seems to be the case with sexual issues within the U.S.A., this technology has already generated a fair amount of political activity and social conflict over its use. (D. L. Weis, Coeditor)]

A. Contraception

PATRICIA BARTHALOW KOCH

A Brief History

"The struggle for reproductive self-determination is one of the oldest projects of humanity; one of our earliest collective attempts to alter the biological limits of our existence" (Gordon 1976, 403). Throughout U.S. history, as elsewhere, many have been desperate to learn safe and effective ways to prevent conception and induce abortion, while others have believed artificial contraception is unacceptable because it interferes with the course of nature.

Brodie (1994) conducted a historical analysis of efforts for reproductive control in colonial and nineteenth-century America. New England fertility rates in colonial times were higher than those in most of Europe. Colonists had little real ability, and perhaps little will, to intervene in their reproduction. It has been estimated that one third of the brides of this time were pregnant. Although the Puritans viewed marriage with children as the highest form of life, the prevalence of premarital pregnancy was not viewed as a threat to this value, because virtually all such pregnancies led to marriage (Reiss 1980).

On the other hand, Native Americans seemed to possess knowledge and cultural practices—breast-feeding, periodic abstinence, abortion, and infanticide—specific to their particular tribes, enabling them to maintain small families. Fertility among the African and Caribbean women brought as slaves varied widely, depending on the region of the United States—in some places, fecundity reaching human capacity and in other places, fertility rates decreasing. According to Brodie (1994, 53): "Fecundity assured slave women that they were valuable to the master and offered some hope against being sold. Yet preventing the birth of new slaves for the master could be a form of resistance to slavery."

The three most common forms of birth control during this time were coitus interruptus (withdrawal), breast-feeding, and abortion. The effectiveness of breast-feeding in preventing another pregnancy depended on how long the woman breast-fed, on when her menstruation resumed after childbirth, and on how long and how often the infant suckled. However, by the nineteenth century, the option of bottle feeding infants was becoming more available and popular.

Abortion methods included violent exercises, uterine insertions, and the use of drugs. These methods may have been no more dangerous than the pregnancy and childbirth complications of the time, but it has been suggested that these methods were also a common cause of death for women. American folk medicine was evolving from the knowledge and indigenous practices of the Native Americans, European settlers, and African/Caribbean slaves. Many abortificients were made from plants, such as pennyroyal, tansy, aloe, cohash, and squaw root. Such "remedies" were often passed down through family Bibles and cookbooks. Over 1,500 medical almanacs, many containing herbal remedies to "bring on a woman's courses," were circulated before the American Revolution. Yet there was little public discussion of birth control and no laws or statutes governing information or practice.

Brodie documents that reproductive control during most of the nineteenth century in America was neither rare nor taboo. Information was available about withdrawal, douching (the "water cure"), rhythm (although the information was not very accurate), condoms, spermicides, abortion-inducing drugs, and early varieties of the diaphragm. When other contraceptive options were available, couples seemed to prefer them over withdrawal; sexual abstinence was not one of the chief means of controlling birth rates. Abortion was not illegal until "quickening" (movement of the fetus).

Beginning in the 1830s, reproductive control became a commercial enterprise in the expanding American market economy. Douches and syringes, vaginal sponges, condoms, diaphragms (or "womb veils"), cervical caps, and pessaries (intravaginal and intrauterine devices) began to be widely advertised through a burgeoning literature on the subjects of sexuality and reproductive control, euphemistically called "feminine hygiene." Education through this means was made possible by the technological improvements in printing and the increased basic literacy of the American public.

The self-help literature instructed readers on how to make contraceptive and abortion agents at home from products readily available in the household or garden. Douching was the most frequent method for reproductive control used by middle- and upper-class women. The invention of the vulcanization process for rubber by Goodyear in the 1840s enabled condoms to be made more cheaply. In addition, the appearance of the mail-order catalog allowed the public to "shop" for contraceptive devices confidentially.

The birthrate of white native-born married women was reduced almost by half between 1800 and 1900, coinciding with the major social upheaval of industrialization and urbanization. Many American couples wanted fewer children and greater spacing between them. This became possible with the evolving availability of information about and access to more-effective contraceptive techniques.

By the mid-1800s, the abortion rate among the white middle class increased sharply with greater access to diverse sources of information about abortion, abortion drugs and instruments, and persons offering abortion services. There was little outcry about abortion being "immoral" until the American Medical Association launched a campaign to curb it at mid century. Historians have debated whether the new opposition to abortion by male physicians was due more to the threat of competition from female midwives or to a concern about the dangers of unsafe abortion.

As reproductive control became commercialized after 1850, and as some women became increasingly able to assert a degree of independent control over their fertility through contraception and abortion, the deep ambivalences with which many Americans regarded such changes came increasingly into play. In the second half of the nineteenth century, diverse groups emerged to try to restore

> American "social purity," and one of the issues they focused on was restricting sexual freedom and control of reproduction. . . . All branches of government were their allies; their goals were won through enactments of federal and state legislation and sustained by judicial decisions that criminalized contraception and abortion, both of which had in earlier decades been legal. (Brodie 1994, 253)

Laws began to alter two hundred years of American custom and public policy towards contraception and abortion. Federal and state laws made it a felony to mail products or information about contraception and abortion. Such materials were then labeled "obscene." In 1873, Congress passed "The Act for the Suppression of Trade in, and Circulation of Obscene Literature and Articles of Immoral Use," which tightened the loopholes on interstate trade and importation of birth-control materials from abroad. This law was better known as the Comstock Law, named after Anthony Comstock, a leading "social purity" proponent and crusader against "obscenity." Comstock was even appointed a special agent of the U.S. Post Office and allowed to inspect and seize such "illegal" material until his death in 1915.

> The combined force of the social purity legions and of overwhelming public acquiescence overrode a generation of commercialization and growing public discourse and drove reproductive control, if not totally back underground, at least into a netherworld of back-fence gossip and back-alley abortion. (Brodie 1994, 288)

The Comstock Law would stand until a federal appeals court would overturn its anticontraceptive provisions in 1936 (*United States v. One Package*) on the grounds that the weight of authority of the medical world concerning the safety and reliability of contraception was not available when the law was originally passed. (The anti-obscenity provisions of the Comstock Law remained intact for several more decades.)

What is referred to as "the birth-control movement" was begun in the United States shortly before World War I, primarily by socialists and sexual liberals as both a political and moral issue. Margaret Sanger's leadership, in the early 1900s, was responsible for gaining support from mainstream America and centralizing the cause through her American Birth Control League. Sanger attributed her indomitable dedication to making birth-control information and methods available to American women, particularly of the working class, to her nursing experiences with poor women during which they would beg her to tell them the "secrets" of the rich for limiting children.

In 1915, she began publishing *Woman Rebel*, a monthly magazine advocating birth control. She was indicted for violating the Comstock Law, but the case was dropped and she continued dispensing birth-control information through lectures and publications. In 1916, she was arrested again for opening the first birth-control clinic in the United States in a poor slum in Brooklyn, New York. She served thirty days in jail; however, the testimonials of her poor birth-control clients at the trial helped to fuel the birth-control movement.

Gordon (1976) documents the birth-control movement throughout the twentieth century in the United States. In the early 1920s, most doctors were opposed to contraception. However, through the efforts of Margaret Sanger and Dr. Robert Latou Dickenson, contraception was scientifically studied and became accepted as a health issue, not simply a moral one. Clergy, particularly of the Protestant and Jewish faiths, also began to view contraceptive choice as an individual moral decision when it affected the health of a family. To this day, however, the Catholic Church has remained staunch in its opposition to "artificial birth control." Yet, this opposition has not deterred Catholic women in the United States from using birth-control methods as frequently as women of other or no faiths.

The Great Depression of the 1930s forced many more Americans into accepting and practicing birth-control measures. Social workers, based on their interactions with many poor and struggling families, became proponents in support of better education about, and access to, birth control for all women, not just the middle class and wealthy. The manufacturing of condoms became a large industry. In the 1930s, with the formation of the American Birth Control League, over three hundred clinics throughout the United States were providing contraceptive information and services; this increased to more than eight hundred clinics by 1942.

Yet, despite the fact that a 1937 poll indicated that 79 percent of American women supported the use of birth control, those who did not have access to private doctors were limited in their access to birth-control information and devices. However, judges, doctors, government officials, entrepreneurs, and others were beginning to respond to grassroots pressure. For example, in 1927, the American Medical Association officially recognized birth control as part of medical practice. In 1942, Planned Parenthood Federation of America (PPFA) was founded with a commitment to helping women better plan family size and child spacing. PPFA was greatly responsible for making birth control more accessible to women of various backgrounds, particularly those of lower-socioeconomic levels, throughout the United States.

Development of the Oral Contraceptive Pill and IUD

During the 1950s, research was progressing in the United States that would transform contraceptive technology and practice worldwide. Asbell (1995) details the biography of the "drug that changed the world." The quest for a female contraceptive that could be "swallowed like an aspirin" began when Margaret Sanger and Katherine McCormick, a wealthy American woman dedicated to the birth-control movement, enlisted Gregory Pincus, an accomplished reproductive scientist, to develop a contraceptive pill. Applying the basic research findings of others, particularly Russel Marker, who produced a chemical imitation of progesterone from the roots of Mexican yam trees, Pincus developed just such a pill combining synthetic estrogen and progesterone.

With the help of John Rock, a noted Harvard gynecologist and researcher, the oral contraceptive was initially given to fifty Massachusetts volunteers, and then field tested with approximately 200 women in Puerto Rico in 1956, where it was believed opposition to such a drug would be less than in the United States. However, the pill was heartily condemned by the Catholic Church, leaving Puerto Rican women to face the dilemma of choosing to be in the trials (and committing a mortal sin) or bearing more children which they could not adequately support. In addition, the standards for informed consent for research subjects were not as strict as they are today, so that participants in these trials were not thoroughly informed as to the experimental procedures being used and the potential risks involved (which were generally unknown).

In 1957, the pill was first approved by the Food and Drug Administration (FDA) for treatment of menstrual disorders. At this time, it was observed that many women who had never before experienced menstrual disorders suddenly developed this problem and sought treatment with the pill. By 1960, the pill was formally approved by the FDA as a contraceptive following double-blind clinical trials with 897 Puerto Rican women. Such a procedure would well be considered ethically questionable today.

The pill was extremely attractive to many potential users because of its convenience and efficacy. Women now had the option of engaging in intercourse with minimal threat of pregnancy. This method separated the act of coitus from the action taken to restrict fertility (ingestion of the pill). In addition, the woman was in sole charge of this method of birth control and did not need any cooperation from her male partner. Many believed this innovation in birth control was responsible for a "sexual revolution" in which women were to become more "sexually active," displaying patterns of sexual attitudes and behaviors more like men, although there is little scientific evidence to support this claim. As Ira Reiss explained the evolutionary changes taking place in American sexual expression:

> Sexual standards and behavior seem more closely related to social structure and cultural and religious values than to the availability of contraceptive techniques . . . [increased premarital sexuality] was promoted by a courtship system that had been evolving for a hundred years in the United States permitting young people to choose their own marriage partners, and which therefore encouraged choice of when as well as with whom to share sex. (Asbell 1995, 201)

By 1967, the Population Council estimated that 6.5 million women were using the birth-control pill in the U.S., while 6.3 million women were using it in other parts of the world. Some were concerned as to whether millions of women were serving as guinea pigs in a massive experiment, since careful large-scale studies of its safety had not been conducted before it was marketed (Seaman 1969). Disturbing side effects, including deep-vein thrombosis, heart disease and attacks, elevated blood pressure, strokes, gallbladder disease, liver tumors, and depression, were being reported. In the first few years of use in the U.S., more than one hundred court claims were filed against its manufacturer. Some countries, including Norway and the Soviet Union, banned the pill. Some American women mobilized to create a women's health movement, spearheaded by the National Women's Health Network, to help the public become better informed about the benefits and risks of pill use, as well as other medical procedures and drugs. Yet, accurate information about the benefits and risks of pill use was often unavailable, difficult to access, and distorted and sensationalized. In the 1970s, pill sales dropped 20 percent.

Twenty-five years later, oral contraception has become one of the most extensively studied medications ever prescribed. Today, pills with less than 50 micrograms of estrogen are associated with a significantly lower risk of serious negative effects and are as effective in preventing pregnancy as the higher-dose pills of the past (Hatcher et al. 1994).

The intrauterine device (IUD) also became popular in the United States as the "perfect" alternative to the pill because of its effectiveness and convenience. However, the Dalkon Shield, which was marketed from 1971 to 1975, was implicated in a number of cases of pelvic inflammatory disease and spontaneous septic abortions resulting in the deaths of at least twenty women. In 1974, the Shield was taken off the U.S. market, although it was still distributed abroad. Currently, there are only two IUDs for sale in the United States, the TCu-380A (ParaGard) and the Progesterone T device (Progestasert).

Government Policy and Legal Issues

While research was expanding birth-control options, the 1950s and 1960s saw the development and implementation of federal policies supporting population control programs designed to deal with overpopulation throughout the world. Birth control was offered as a "tool" for economic development to Third World countries. The 1960 budget of $2 million for family-planning programs grew to $250 million in 1972 (Asbell 1995). However, American goals were often in conflict with the cultural beliefs of the people in various countries. Reproductive options cannot be separated from the economic options and social mores of a culture.

Governmental policies on birth control were also changing at home. In 1964, President Lyndon B. Johnson, over strong political opposition, provided federal funds to support birth-control clinics for the American poor. These efforts were continued by President Richard M. Nixon, who in 1970 declared "a new national goal: adequate family-planning services within the next five years for all those who want them but cannot afford them" (Asbell 1995).

Important legal changes were also occurring in the U.S. during this time. In 1965, the Supreme Court decided, in *Griswold v. Connecticut,* that laws prohibiting the sale of contraceptives to married couples violated a constitutional "right of privacy." Writing the majority opinion, Justice William O. Douglas declared:

> we deal with a right of privacy older than the Bill of Rights—older than our political parties, older than our school system. Marriage is a coming together for better or worse, hopefully enduring and intimate to the degree of being sacred. (Asbell 1995, 241)

The court asked, "Would we allow the police to search the sacred precincts of marital bedrooms for telltale signs of the use of contraceptives?" The judges responded, "The very idea is repulsive to the notions of privacy surrounding the marital relationship."

In 1972, the Supreme Court extended this "right to privacy" for contraceptive use to unmarried people (*Eisenstadt v. Baird*) on the basis that a legal prohibition would violate the equal protection clause of the 14th Amendment. A 1977 Supreme Court decision (*Carey v. Population Services*) struck down laws prohibiting the sale of contraception to minors, the selling of contraception by others besides pharmacists, and advertisements for or displays of contraceptives.

Recent Developments in Birth Control

More-recent developments in contraceptive technology receive tougher scrutiny than in the past before winning FDA approval. For example, Norplant was developed by the international nonprofit Population Council, which began clinical trials including half a million women in 46 countries, not including the U.S.

However, Norplant was not approved for use in the United States by the Food and Drug Administration (FDA) until 1990. This approval was opposed by the National Women's Health Network because the long-term safety of Norplant had not been established. Wyeth-Ayerst, the U.S. distributor, is required by law to report any unusual events associated with Norplant use to the FDA, while an internationally coordinated surveillance of Norplant use and its effects is being conducted by the World Health Organization and others in eight developing countries. Currently, a class-action suit is being formulated by a group of Norplant users in the U.S., primarily because of the difficulties they experienced in having the Norplant rods removed. Such complications are a serious impediment keeping American pharmaceutical companies from researching and developing new contraceptives.

Depro-Provera (Depo-medroxyprogesterone acetate or DMPA) is the most commonly employed injectable progestin used in over ninety countries worldwide. However, it was not approved for use in the U.S. by the FDA until 1992. Women's health activists, organized by the National Women's Health Network, had opposed its approval in the absence of more long-term studies of its safety.

In 1993, the FDA approved the first female condom, called Reality, for over-the-counter sale in the United States. The female condom, or vaginal pouch, is a polyurethane lubricated sheath that lines the vagina and partially covers the perineum. Although the method failure rate of the female condom (5 percent) is similar to that of the male condom (3 percent), it has a higher failure rate with typical use (21 percent) than does the male condom (12 percent) (Hatcher et al. 1994). This may reflect the "newness" of this female method and inexperience with its use. Yet, in a study of 360 women using female condoms, only 2 discontinued its use.

Although a combination of RU-486 (mifespristone) and prostaglandin has been tested in over a dozen countries, particularly in France, it has generated controversy in the U.S. and was only approved for use here in 1996. Because RU-486, when combined with a prostaglandin, is an effective early abortifacient, its use has been opposed by anti-abortion proponents, even for research purposes or its potential use in the treatment of breast cancer, Cushing's syndrome, endometriosis, and brain tumors. Because it was so politically controversial, RU-486 had not been expected to be approved for any use in the United States, which turned out not to be the case.

What is the future for the development of new birth-control methods in the United States? Contraceptive-vaccine researchers acknowledge that a new form of birth control for men is badly needed. Yet, it is believed that immunizing men against their own sperm would risk destroying the testes. However, researchers in the U.S. are talking with the FDA to test a vaccine with women that induces the woman's immune system to attack sperm. Previously, such vaccines have been tested on mice, rabbits, and baboons with an effectiveness rate of 75 to 80 percent.

In the past, Federal agencies have shied away from supporting such work because "right-to-lifer" advocates view such a vaccine as abortive and, therefore, unacceptable. In addition to the possibility of medical liability, American pharmaceutical companies are unlikely to market such a vaccine because of the protests and boycotts that "right-to-life" groups threaten to organize. Because of the threat of boycotts from adversarial groups and lawsuits from persons claiming to be harmed by new contraceptive technologies, only one American company remains active in contraceptive research and development. In the late 1960s, nine American drug companies were competing to find new and better birth-control methods.

Current Contraceptive Behavior

Between 1988 and 1990, the proportion of women in the United States, from the age of 15 to 44, who had never had vaginal-penile intercourse declined from 12 percent to 9 percent. (Data used in this section are based on the 1982 and 1988 *National Survey of Family Growth* (*NSFG*) and the 1990 *NSFG Telephone Reinterview*) (Peterson 1995). The proportion of 15- to 44-year-olds who were at risk for unintended pregnancy but were not contracepting increased from 7 percent to 12 percent. This increase was most pronounced among 15- to 44-year-olds (8 percent to 22 percent), never-married women (11 percent to 20 percent), and non-Hispanic white women (5 percent to 11 percent).

In 1990, 34.5 million women, or 59 percent of those aged 15 to 44, in the United States were using some type of contraception—with almost three quarters (70.7 percent) of married women using contraception; see Table 6. There is little difference in contraceptive use based on religious background between Catholic, Protestant, and Jewish women. The leading methods used by contraceptors were female sterilization (29.5 percent), the contraceptive pill (28.5 percent), and the male condom (17.7 percent). (Information on the use of three newer methods—Norplant, the female condom, and Depo-Provera—was not available at the time of the surveys). Overall, the use of female and male sterilization, the condom, and periodic abstinence had increased from 1988, whereas the use of the pill, IUD, and diaphragm had decreased.

Female sterilization is most widely used among older and less-educated women who have completed their childbearing, with over one half (52.0 percent) of female contraceptors age 40 to 44 having been sterilized. Anglo-American women are much more likely to have male partners with a vasectomy (15.5 percent) than are African-American women (1.3 percent). The aging of the baby-boom generation in the United States portends a continued rise in female sterilization rates throughout the next decade and a rise in vasectomies among the better educated.

The increased use of the condom was most pronounced among young (aged 15 to 44), African-American, never-married, childless, or less-educated women, and those living below the poverty level. For example, condom use among never-married women tripled between 1982 and 1990 (4 percent to 13 percent). The percentage of adolescents using condoms rose from 33 percent to 44 percent between 1988 and 1990. Almost all contracepting teenagers used either the pill (52 percent) or condom (44 percent) in 1990. However, it must be kept in mind that only 56 percent of condom users report using them consistently every time they have intercourse.

The use of contraception at first intercourse by adolescents has increased significantly since the early 1980s. For example, during 1980-1982, 53 percent of unmarried women aged 15 to 19 used contraception during their first intercourse experience. By 1988-1990, this percentage rose to 71

Table 6

Number of Women 15-44 Years of Age, Percent Using Any Method of Contraception, and Percent Distribution of Contraceptors by Method, According to Age, Race and Origin, and Marital Status, 1988 and 1990

Age, Race, and Marital Status	Number of Women Using a Method (in Thousands)	Percent Using Any Method	Female Sterilization	Male Sterilization	Pill
				Read across >>>>>	
1990[2]					
All women	34,516	59.3	29.5	12.6	28.5
Age					
15-19	2,623	31 5	0.0	0.0	52.0
15-17	1,165	24.3	0.0	0.0	41.1
18-19	1,458	41.2	0.0	0.0	60.7
20-24	5,065	55.3	8.0	1.8	55.4
25-29	6,385	60.0	17.4	5.0	47.3
30-34	7,344	66.2	32.7	13.0	23.9
35-39	7,138	70.6	44.2	19.8	10.6
40-44	5,962	66.9	52.0	26.5	2.2
Race and Origin					
Hispanic	2,856	52.2	33.1	6.4	31.4
White non-Hispanic	25,928	60.5	27.3	15.5	28.5
Black non-Hispanic	4,412	58.7	41.0	1.3	28.5
Marital Status					
Currently married	21,608	70.7	33.5	33.5	19.2
Divorced, separated, widowed	4,026	57.3	52.1	2.8	22.4
Never married	8,882	43.0	9.6	1.1	50.5
1988					
All women	34,912	60.3	27.5	11.7	30.7
Age					
15-19	2,950	32.1	1.5	0.2	58.8
15-17	1,076	19.9	0.0	0.0	53.3
18-19	1,874	49.6	2.4	0.4	61.9
20-24	5,550	59.0	4.6	1.8	68.2
25-29	6,967	64.5	17.0	6.0	44.5
30-34	7,437	68.0	32.5	14.0	21.5
35-39	6,726	70.2	44.9	19.7	5.2
40-44	5,282	66.0	51.1	22.2	3.2

<<<<< Read across

Age, Race, and Marital Status	IUD	Diaphragm	Condom	Periodic Abstinence[1]	Other
1990[2]					
All women	1.4	2.8	17.7	2.7	4.8
Age					
15-19	0.0	0.0	44.0	1.0	3.0
15-17	0.0	0.0	51.9	2.2	4.7
18-19	0.0	0.0	37.6	0.0	1.7
20-24	0.8	0.6	25.3	2.8	5.3
25-29	0.4	2.3	19.0	2.7	5.9
30-34	0.9	4.7	15.9	3.5	5.4
35-39	3.3	3.3	10.3	3.4	5.2
40-44	1.8	3.8	9.2	1.6	2.9
Race and Origin					
Hispanic	1.9	1.5	17.1	3.7	5.1
White non-Hispanic	1.3	3.0	17.0	2.7	4.7
Black non-Hispanic	1.4	1.6	19.4	1.2	5.6
Marital Status					
Currently married	20.6	1.4	14.0	3.5	3.8
Divorced, separated, widowed	2.5	0.9	9.7	0.6	9.0
Never married	0.8	0.6	30.1	1.8	5.5
1988					
All women	2.0	5.7	14.6	2.3	5.4
Age					
15-19	0.0	1.0	32.8	0.8	4.8
15-17	0.0	0.7	40.4	0.9	4.7
18-19	0.0	1.2	28.4	0.8	4.9
20-24	0.3	3.7	14.5	1.7	5.2
25-29	1.3	5.5	15.6	2.4	7.6
30-34	2.9	8.9	12.0	2.7	5.5
35-39	2.7	7.7	11.8	3.0	5.1
40-44	3.7	3.9	10.5	2.2	3.2

continued

Table 6 continued

Age, Race, and Marital Status	Number of Women Using a Method (in Thousands)	Percent Using Any Method	Female Sterilization	Male Sterilization	*Read across* >>>>> Pill
1988					
Race and Origin					
Hispanic	2,799	50.4	31.7	4.3	33.4
White non-Hispanic	25,799	62.9	25.6	14.3	29.5
Black non-Hispanic	4,208	56.8	37.8	0.9	38.1
Marital Status					
Currently married	21,657	74.3	31.4	17.3	20.4
Divorced, separated, widowed	4,429	57.6	50.7	3.6	25.3
Never married	8,826	41.9	6.4	1.8	59.0

[1] Includes natural family planning and other types of periodic abstinence.

[2] Percentages for 1990 were calculated excluding cases for whom contraceptive status was not ascertained. Overall, contraceptive status was not ascertained for 0.3 percent of U.S. women in 1990.

Source: Peterson, L. S. (1995, February). "Contraceptive Use in the United States: 1982-1990." From *Vital and Health Statistics. Advanced Data No. 260*, Hyattsville, MD: National Center for Health Statistics.

percent, mainly attributable to rising condom use (from 28 percent to 55 percent). The increase in condom use was particularly striking among Hispanic teens, with a threefold increase from 1980 to 1990 (17 percent to 58 percent).

Table 7 depicts the latest estimates of pregnancy prevention with typical use (indicating user failure) and perfect use (indicating method failure) among the contraceptive methods currently available in the United States (Hatcher et al., 1994). The most effective methods are Norplant, the oral contraceptive pill, male and female sterilization, Depo-Provera, and IUDs.

B. Childbirth and Single Women

Each year, one million American teenage girls become pregnant, a per-thousand rate twice that of Canada, England, and Sweden, and ten times that of the Netherlands. A similar disproportionately high rate is reported for teenage abortions (Jones et al. 1986).

The birthrate for unmarried American women has surged since 1980, with the rate for white women nearly doubling, and the rate for teenagers dropping from 53 percent of the unwed births in 1973, to 41 percent in 1980, and 30 percent in 1992. One out of every four American babies in 1992 was born to an unmarried woman. The unwed birthrate rose sharply for women 20 years and older. The highest rates were among women ages 20 to 24 (68.5 births per 1,000), followed by 18- and 19-year olds (67.3 per

<<<<< *Read across*

Age, Race, and Marital Status	IUD	Diaphragm	Condom	Periodic Abstinence[1]	Other
1988					
Race and Origin					
Hispanic	5.0	2.4	13.6	2.5	7.1
White non-Hispanic	1.5	6.6	15.2	2.3	5.0
Black non-Hispanic	3.2	2.0	10.1	2.1	5.9
Marital Status					
Currently married	2.0	6.2	14.3	2.8	5.6
Divorced, separated, widowed	3.6	5.3	5.9	1.9	3.8
Never married	1.3	4.9	19.6	1.3	5.7

1,000) and 25- to 29-year-olds (56.5 per 1,000). Overall, according to a 1995 report from the National Center for Health Statistics, the unmarried birthrate rose 54 percent between 1980 and 1992, from 29.4 births per 1,000 unmarried women ages 15 to 44 in 1980 to 45.2 births per 1,000 in both 1991 and 1992 (Holmes 1996a).

In 1970, the birthrate for unmarried black women was seven times the rate for white women, and four times the rate for white women in 1980. Since 1980, the white unmarried birthrate has risen by 94 percent while the rate for blacks rose only 7 percent. By 1992, the birthrate for single black women was just 2.5 times the rate for white women. In 1992, the out-of-wedlock birthrates were 95.3 for Hispanic women, 86.5 for black women, and 35.2 for white women (Holmes 1996a).

Commenting on the social implications of these statistics, Charles F. Westoff, a Princeton University demographer, said they "reflect the declining significance of marriage as a social obligation or a social necessity for reproduction." Poorly educated, low-income teenage mothers and their children are overwhelmingly likely to experience long-term negative consequences of early childbearing as single parent (Associated Press News Release, June 7, 1995). A 1996 study, sponsored by the charitable Robin Hood Foundation, estimated the public cost of unwed teenage pregnancy at $7 billion. The study looked at the consequences for teenage mothers, their children, and the fathers of the babies, compared with people from the same social background when pregnancy was delayed until the woman

Table 7

Percentage of Women Experiencing a Birth Control Failure During the First Year of Typical Use and the First Year of Perfect Use and the Percentage Continuing Use at the End of the First Year

Method	% of Women Experiencing an Accidental Pregnancy Within the First Year of Use		% of Women Continuing Use at One Year
	Typical Use	**Perfect Use**	
Chance	85	85	
Spermicide	21	6	43
Periodic Abstinence	20		67
Calendar		9	
Ovulation Method		3	
Sympto-Thermal		2	
Post-Ovulation		1	
Withdrawal	19	4	
Cap (with spermicide)			
Parous Women	36	24	45
Nulliparous Women	18	9	58
Sponge			
Parous Women	36	20	45
Nulliparous Women	18	9	58
Diaphragm (with spermicide)	18	6	58
Condom			
Female (Reality)	21	5	56
Male	12	3	63
Pill	3		
Progestin Only		0.5	N.A.
Combined		0.1	N.A.
IUD			
Progesterone T	2.0	1.5	81
Copper T 380A	0.8	0.6	78
Depo-Provera	0.3	0.3	70
Norplant (6 Capsules)	0.09	0.09	85
Female Sterilization	0.4	0.4	100
Male Sterilization	0.15	0.10	100

Source: Hatcher, R. et al. (1994). *Contraceptive Technology* (16th rev. ed.) p. 13. New York: Irvington.

was 20 or 21. The breakdown of annual costs included $2.2 billion in welfare and food-stamp benefits, $1.5 billion in medical-care costs, $900 million in increased foster-care expenses, $1 billion for additional prison construction, and $1.3 in lost tax revenue from the reduced productivity of teenage women who bear children (Holmes 1996a).

At the present rate, something like 50 percent or more of America's children will spend at least part of their childhood in a single-parent family. About half of this number will be the result of divorce or separation; the rest will be born to a mother who has never been married (Luker 1996).

In any given year, roughly 12 percent of American infants are born to teenage mothers. However, the vast majority of these teenage mothers are 18 or 19 years old, and thus only technically teenagers. American teenagers have been producing children at about the same rate for most of this century. Fewer than a third of all single mothers are teenagers, even when we include the 18- to 19-year-olds. And this proportion is declining. What is different in recent decades is that increasing numbers of teenage mothers are unmarried when they give birth. In 1970, only 30 percent of teenage mothers had never been married; by 1995, 70 percent of teenage mothers had never been married (Luker 1996).

While there is no good reason to suppose that the teenage birthrate is going up in any significant way—it was, in fact, higher in the 1950s—one must admit that the rate of single parenting is going up. In 1947, virtually all single mothers were widows, or living apart from their mate after separation or divorce. In 1947, fewer than one in a hundred had never been married. Today, overall, never-married single mothers account for one in three, and the percentage is rising. The number of single teenage mothers is going up at a rapid rate, but so is the number of single mothers at every age.

These data suggest that we are participants in, or at least witness to, an important shift in the nature of American family life that is echoing throughout the industrialized world. According to Luker (1996), the last years of this century may turn out to be the beginning of a time when the very notions of childrearing on the one hand and family life on the other are increasingly disconnected. While the rate of out-of-wedlock births is clearly on the way up, the rate of marriage may be declining, and the age of first marriage is clearly being delayed. In 1995, 60 percent of American families were headed by a single parent, half of them never-married. Luker (1996) suggests two possible outcomes. The present situation may prove to be only a temporary deviation from a stable pattern of long-standing. Or it may mark the first hesitant appearance of an important new pattern.

If the latter interpretation turns out to have substance, one can ask why this is happening. Luker cites several influential shifts in social attitudes and behavior. First, "illegitimacy" has lost its moral sting. Second, many women are realizing that they do not need to put up with the abuse, domination, and other burdens they associate with married life. This has special resonance for women in poverty, who ask why they should live with a male who is unreliable and has no skills or job. Third, although welfare benefits are declining throughout the industrialized world, teenage pregnancies are on the rise regardless of the level of welfare benefits. Finally, the vast majority of teenage pregnancies are unintended and not linked with the availability of welfare aid.

So long as teenagers are sexually active, the most effective way to reduce the incidence of childbearing is to assure that they have access to contraception before the fact, and abortion, if needed, after the fact. The many Americans who oppose sexuality and contraceptive education in the schools, distribution of contraceptives in schools, and abortion can only hope that someone discovers a way to reduce teenage sexual activity itself. That seems unlikely, given the decreasing age of puberty among American youth, the declining age of first sexual intercourse, and the clear trend to delay marriage well into the 20s or even 30s. Admonitions to "Just say 'No'" are scarcely going to suffice as a workable national policy. In analyzing the politics of teenage pregnancy and single mothers in the United States, Kristin Luker (1996) concluded that:

> Americans have every right to be concerned about early childbearing and to place the issue high on the national agenda. But they should think of it as a *measure*, not a cause, of poverty and other social ills. A teenager who has a baby usually adds but a slight burden to her life, which is already profoundly disadvantaged. . . . Early childbearing may make a bad situation worse, but the real causes of poverty lie elsewhere.

C. Abortion

In America today, it seems that two camps are at war over the abortion issue. "Pro-choice" supporters advocate the right of the individual woman to decide whether or not to continue a pregnancy. They contend that the rights of a woman must take precedence over the "assumed" rights of a fertilized human egg or fetus. They believe that a woman can never be free unless she has reproductive control over her own body. Pro-choice advocates in the United States include various Protestant and Jewish organizations, Catholics for Free Choice, Planned Parenthood, the National Organization for Women (NOW), National Abortion Rights Action League (NARAL), and the American Civil Liberties Union (ACLU), among others.

Anti-abortion groups have politically identified themselves as "pro-life" supporters of "the right to life" for the unborn. This coalition involves such constituents as Eastern Orthodox, charismatic and conservative Roman Catholics, fundamentalist Protestants, and Orthodox Jews, in influential groups like Operation Rescue, Focus on the Family, and the Christian Coalition. These groups use various methods in order to prevent women from being able to have abortions, including, in some cases, personal intimidation of abortion providers and clients and political action.

The basic motivation of the protection of human life of those in the anti-abortion movement has, however, been questioned. For example, an analysis of the voting records of U.S. senators who are anti-abortion advocates indicates that they had the lowest scores on votes for family-support issues, bills for school-lunch programs, and for aid to the elderly (Prescott and Wallace 1978).

A Brief Legal History

As documented by Brodie (1994), early American common law accepted abortion up until "quickening" (movement of the fetus). Not until the early 1800s did individual states begin to outlaw abortion at any stage of pregnancy. By 1880, most abortions were illegal in the United States, except those "necessary to save the life of the woman." However, since the right and practice of early abortion had already taken root in American society, abortionists openly continued to practice with public support and little legal enforcement. In the 1890s, doctors estimated that there were approximately two million abortions performed each year in the U.S. (Brodie 1994).

Before 1970, legal abortion was not available in the United States (Gordon 1976). In the 1950s, about one million illegal abortions were performed a year, with more than one thousand women dying each year as a result. Three quarters of the women who died from abortions in 1969 were women of color. Middle- and upper-class women, often with difficulty and great expense, could get "therapeutic abortions" from private physicians. By 1966, four fifths of all abortions were estimated to be for married women, and the ratio of legal to illegal abortions was 1 to 110.

In 1970, New York State passed legislation that allowed abortion on demand through the twenty-fourth week if it was done in a medical facility by a physician. However, on January 22, 1973, the U.S. Supreme Court decided a landmark case on abortion—*Roe v. Wade*. The Court stated the "right of privacy . . . founded in the Fourteenth Amendment's concept of personal liberty . . . is broad enough to encompass a woman's decision whether or not to terminate her pregnancy" (Tribe 1992). The major points of this decision were:

1. An abortion decision and procedure must be left up to the pregnant woman and her physician during the first trimester of pregnancy.
2. In the second trimester, the state may choose to regulate the abortion procedure in order to promote its interest in the health of the pregnant woman.
3. Once viability occurs, the state may promote its interest in the potentiality of human life by regulating and even prohibiting abortion except when judged medically necessary for the preservation of the health or life of the pregnant woman.

Although induced abortion is the most commonly performed surgical procedure in the United States, various restrictions continue to be placed upon the accessibility of abortion for certain groups of women. For example, in 1976, the Hyde Amendment, implemented through the United States Congress, prohibited federal Medicaid funds from being used to pay for abortions for women with low incomes. This is believed to contribute to the fact that low-income women of color are more likely to have second-trimester abortions, rather than first-trimester ones, since it takes time for them to save enough money for the procedure.

In addition, the Supreme Court has upheld various state laws that have been instituted to restrict abortions. In 1989, a Missouri law prohibiting the use of "public facilities" and "public employees" from being used to perform or assist abortions not necessary to save the life of the pregnant woman was upheld (*Webster v. Reproductive Health Services*). The court also upheld one of the strictest parental notification laws in the country in 1990 (*Hodgson v. Minnesota*). This law required notification of both of a minor's parents before she could have an abortion, even if she had never lived with them. Along with this restriction came a "waiting period" provision. A court decision in *Rust v. Sullivan* (1991) upheld a "gag rule" that prohibited counselors and physicians in federally funded family-planning clinics from providing information and making referrals about abortion. In 1992, the court upheld many restrictions set forth in a Pennsylvania law (*Planned Parenthood v. Casey*). These restrictions included requiring physicians to provide women seeking abortions with pro-childbirth information, followed by a twenty-four-hour "waiting period," and parental notification for minors (Tribe 1992).

Nineteen years after the *Roe* decision, the *Casey* decision demonstrated that the Supreme Court was divided more sharply than ever over abortion. While a minority of justices wanted to overturn the *Roe* decision outright, the majority did not allow a complete ban of abortion. However, by enacting the "undue burden" standard, they did lower the standard by which abortion laws are to be judged unconstitutional. This standard places the burden of proof on those challenging an abortion restriction to establish that it is a "substantial obstacle" to their constitutional rights.

The various state laws now restricting abortion are particularly burdensome for younger and poorer women, and open the way for the creation of increasing obstacles to women's access to abortion. Currently, only thirteen states provide funding for poor women for abortions, and thirty-five states enforce parent-notification/consent laws for minors seeking abortions. At the same time, the Supreme Court has upheld the right to abortion in many cases.

The recent murders of physicians and staff at abortion clinics, arson and bombing of abortion clinics, and the blocking of abortion clinics by anti-abortion protesters have contributed to women's difficulty in receiving this still-legal medical procedure. Over 80 percent of all abortion providers have been picketed, and many have experienced other forms of harassment, including bomb threats, blockades, invasions of facilities, property destruction, assault of staff and patients, and death threats.

In 1988, Operation Rescue, the term adopted by anti-abortion groups, brought thousands of protesters to Atlanta to blockade the abortion clinics. Using an 1871 statute enacted to protect African-Americans from the Ku Klux Klan, the federal courts invoked injunctions against the protesters. However, in 1993, this decision was overturned, leading to Operation Rescue blockades of abortion clinics in ten more U.S. cities. The federal government moved to apply the Racketeer Influenced and Corrupt Organization (RICO) Act against such blockades on the grounds that it was a form of extortion and part of a nationwide conspiracy. This application of the RICO Act was upheld unanimously by the Supreme Court in 1994. Despite this protection, there has nevertheless been a serious decline in the number of facilities and physicians willing to perform abortions.

Current Abortion Practice

Legally induced abortion has become the most commonly performed surgical procedure in the United States. In 1988, 6 million pregnancies and 1.5 million legal abortions were reported. One in five women (21 percent) of women of reproductive age have had an abortion (Hatcher et al. 1994). If current abortion rates continue, nearly half of all American women will have at least one abortion during their lifetime.

Women having abortions in the United States come from every background and walk of life (Koch 1995). Abortion rates are highest among 18- to 19-year-old women, with almost 60 percent being less than 25 years old. One in eight (12 percent) are minors, aged 17 or younger. Of these minors, over 98 percent are unmarried and in school or college, with fewer than one tenth having had any previous children.

The vast majority (80 percent) of adult women having abortions are separated, divorced, or never married, with 20 percent currently married. One third of American women seeking abortions are poor. Almost half are currently mothers, with most of them already having two or more children. Half of the women seeking abortions were using a form of birth control during the month in which they conceived. About one third of abortion clients are employed, one third attend public school or college, and the other third are unemployed. The majority of women (69 percent) getting abortions are Anglo-American. Latinas are 60 percent more likely than Anglos to terminate an unintended pregnancy, but are less likely to do so than are African-American women.

Women with a more-liberal religious or humanist commitment are four times more likely to get an abortion than those adhering to conservative religious beliefs, according to Alan Guttmacher Institute surveys in 1991 and 1996. Catholic women are just as likely as other women to get abortions.

Catholic women, who constitute 31% of the female population, had 31 percent of the abortions in 1996. In 1991, one sixth of abortion clients in the U.S. were born-again or evangelical Christians (Alan Guttmacher Institute 1991). In a similar 1996 survey, evangelical or born-again Christians, who account for almost half the American population, had 18% of the abortions.

Women give multiple reasons for their decision to have an abortion, the most important reasons being financial inability to support the child and inability to handle all the responsibilities of parenting. Three quarters of abortion clients believe that having a baby would interfere with work, school, or their other family responsibilities. Over half are concerned about being single parents and believe that the relationship with the father will be ending soon. Adolescent women, in particular, usually believe that they are not mature enough to have a child. One fifth of the women seeking an abortion are concerned that either the fetus or they, themselves, have a serious health problem which necessitates an abortion. One in a hundred abortion clients are rape or incest survivors. Most abortion clients (70 percent) want to have children in the future.

Half of the abortions in the U.S. are performed before the eighth week of gestation and five out of six are performed before the thirteenth week (Hatcher et al. 1994). The safest and easiest time for the procedure is within the first three months. Most (97 percent) women receiving abortions during this time have no complications or postabortion complaints. Vacuum curettage is the most widely used abortion procedure in the United States, accounting for 97 percent of abortions in 1989. Intra-amniotic infusion is the rarest form of abortion performed, accounting for only 1 percent of abortions in 1989.

The weight of research evidence indicates that legal abortion, particularly in the first trimester, does not create short or long-term physical or psychological risks for women, including impairment of future fertility (Russo and Zierk 1992). In 1985, the maternal death rate for legal abortions was 0.5 per 100,000 for suction methods, 4.0 for induced labor, and one in 10,000 for childbirth (Hatcher et al. 1994).

Attitudes Toward Abortion

The National Opinion Research Center has been documenting attitudes toward abortion since 1972 (Smith 1996). Throughout this time period, public support for abortion under various circumstances has increased (see Table 8). The vast majority of Americans approve of abortion if a pregnancy seriously endangers the health of the mother, if the fetus has a serious defect, or if the pregnancy resulted from a rape or incest. Approximately half of the American public approves of abortion if the woman does not want to marry the father or if the parents cannot afford a child or do not want any more children. Close to half of Americans approve of abortion if

Table 8

Percentage of U.S.A. Adults Approving of
Legal Abortion for Various Reasons

Reason	1972	1985	1996
Pregnancy poses serious health endangerment for woman	87.4	89.9	91.5
Strong chance of serious defect of fetus	78.6	78.9	81.1
Pregnancy resulted from rape	79.1	81.5	83.7
Parent(s) low income—cannot afford a child	48.9	43.2	45.7
Unmarried woman who does not want to marry father	43.8	41.2	44.3
Married woman who does not want more children	40.2	40.7	46.2
Woman wants an abortion for any reason	N.A.*	37.0	44.6

*Not asked

Source: Smith, T. W. (1996, December). Unpublished data from 1972-1996. *General Social Surveys.* Chicago: National Opinion Research Center.

the woman wants it for any reason. Level of education has the strongest effect on people's attitudes, with college-educated people being significantly more approving than those who are less educated. Catholics, fundamentalist Protestants, and Mormons who have a strong religious commitment are the most likely to disapprove of abortion. Anglo-Americans are somewhat more approving than African-Americans; men and adults under 30 are slightly more approving than women and adults over 65. In general, approval of legal abortion and the right of women to control their reproductive ability is associated with a broad commitment to basic civil liberties.

America is at a crossroads in terms of protecting the access of all women to abortion (Tribe 1992, 6). (See comments on efforts of the Christian Coalition to enact laws that restrict and limit access to abortion and abortion information in Section 2A). The era of absolute judicial protection of legal abortion rights that began with the Supreme Court's 1973 decision in *Roe v. Wade* ended with that Court's 1989 decision upholding certain state regulations of abortion in the case of *Webster v. Reproductive Health Services.* Thus, a woman's right to decide whether to terminate a pregnancy was placed in the arena of rough-and-tumble politics, subject to regulation, and possibly even prohibition, by federal and state elected representatives. The range of abortion rights that many Americans have taken for granted are now in jeopardy. Even as the public agenda is stretched to address such new questions as the right to die, the use of aborted fetal tissue in treating disease, and the ethics and legal consequences of reproductive technologies, no issue threatens to divide Americans politically in quite as powerful a way as the abortion issue still does.

10. Sexually Transmitted Diseases

ROBERT T. FRANCOEUR

It is impossible to obtain reliable statistics about the incidence of STDs, because American physicians are only required by law to report cases of HIV and syphilis to the Centers for Disease Control and Prevention (CDC). Public clinics keep fairly reliable statistics, but many private physicians record syphilis and other STDs as urinary infections and do not report them to the CDC. A second, equally important factor leading to the lack of data is the number of persons infected with various STDs who are without symptoms and do not know they are infectious. This "silent epidemic" includes most males infected with candidiasis, 10 percent of males and 60 to 80 percent of females infected with chlamydia, 5 to 20 percent of males and up to 80 percent of females with gonorrhea, and many males and females with hemophilus, NGU, and trichomonas infections.

In 1995, the nation's three most commonly reported infections were sexually transmitted, according to statistics from the federal Centers for Disease Control and Prevention released in October 1996. Chlamydia, tracked for the first time in 1995, topped the list with 477,638 cases. Gonorrhea, the most commonly reported infectious disease in 1994 with 418,068 cases dropped to second in 1995 with 392,848 cases. AIDS dropped from second place in 1994 (78,279 cases) to third place in 1995 (71,547 cases). In 1995, five sexually transmitted diseases, chlamydia, gonorrhea, AIDS, syphylis, and hepatitis B, accounted for 87 percent of the total number of infectious cases caused by the top ten maladies. Chalmydia was more commonly reported among women, striking 383,956 in 1995; gonorrhea and AIDS were more common with men, with 203,563 and 58,007 cases, respectively.

The latest data suggest that the national incidence of gonorrhea and syphilis has continued to decline (U.S. Department of Health and Human Services 1994). Reported cases of gonorrhea peaked at a million cases in 1978 and declined to about 700,000 cases in 1990. With a realistic estimate suggesting two million new cases annually, gonorrhea is one of the most commonly encountered STDs, especially among the young. About 50,000 new cases of syphilis are reported annually; an estimated 125,000 new cases occur annually. Syphilis is primarily an adult disease, mostly concentrated in larger cities, and one of the least common STDs. The incidence of syphilis rose sharply between the late 1980s and the early 1990s, and then continued its more long-term decline. Congenital syphilis rates have decreased in parallel to declining rates of syphilis among women. Infants most at risk were born to unmarried, African-American women who receive little or no prenatal care. Syphilis and gonorrhea have consistently been more common in the southern states. Reasons for this are not well understood, but may include differences in racial and ethnic distribution of the population, poverty, and the availability and quality of health-care services.

Chlamydia is the most prevalent bacterial STD in the United States, with four million adults and possibly 10 percent of all college students infected. It is more common in higher socioeconomic groups and among university students. Prevention and control programs were begun in 1994, and are a high priority because of the potential impact on pelvic inflammatory disease (PID) and its sequelae, infertility and ectopic pregnancy. Twenty to 40 percent of women infected with chlamydia develop PID. Many states have implemented reporting procedures and begun collecting case data for chlamydia.

Three million new cases of trichomonas are reported annually, but probably another six million harbor the protozoan without symptoms. Fifteen million Americans have had at least one bout of genital herpes. About a million new cases of genital warts are reported annually.

STD rates continue to be much higher for African-Americans and other minorities than for white Americans, sixtyfold higher for blacks and fivefold higher for Latinos. About 81 percent of the total reported cases of gonorrhea occur among African-Americans, with the risk for 15- to 19-year-old blacks more than twentyfold higher than for white adolescents. Similarly, the general gonorrhea rate is fortyfold higher for blacks and threefold higher for Latinos than it is for white Americans. There are no known biologic reasons to explain these differences. Rather, race and ethnicity in the United States are risk markers that correlate with poverty, access to quality health care, health-care-seeking behavior, illicit drug use, and living in communities with a high prevalence of STDs.

11. HIV/AIDS

A. A National Perspective   ANDREW D. FORSYTH

In a single decade, human immunodeficiency virus (HIV), the agent that causes acquired immunodeficiency syndrome (AIDS), has become one of the greatest threats to public health in the United States. By 1992, AIDS surpassed heart disease, cancer, suicide, and homicide to become the leading cause of death among men between ages 25 and 54 (CDC 1993a). Similarly, AIDS became the fourth leading cause of death among women between ages 25 to 44 in 1992 and the eighth leading cause of death among all United States citizens. Over one million people are estimated to be infected with HIV in the United States—approximately 1 in 250—and over 441,528 cases of AIDS have been diagnosed, 62 percent of which have already resulted in death (CDC, 1994a).

Trends suggest that AIDS will continue to have significant impact in the United States in coming years. Throughout the 1980s and early 1990s, there was a steady increase in the number of documented AIDS cases. However, between 1993 and 1994, the number of AIDS cases reported to public health departments nationwide dramatically increased due to the implementation of an expanded surveillance definition of AIDS, which included cases of severe immunosuppression manifesting in earlier stages of HIV infection. Although the number of AIDS cases declined in 1994 relative to the previous year, it still represents a considerable increase over cases reported in 1992 (CDC 1995a).

Consistent with previous years, the most severely affected segment of the U.S. population in 1994 was men who have sex with men. Although men constitute 82 percent of all AIDS cases reported among adults and adolescents (13 years or older), men who have sex with men represent the single largest at-risk group, constituting 44 percent of all nonpediatric AIDS cases (CDC 1994a). Young men who have sex with men (between ages 20 and 24) constitute a particularly salient at-risk group for HIV infection, representing 60 percent of AIDS cases among all men of that same age. In contrast, 53 percent of all men with AIDS occur in men who have sex with men.

Even so, the number of AIDS cases reported among men who have sex with men decreased by 1.1 percent for the second consecutive year in 1992, suggesting that infection rates among this segment of the population may be leveling off (CDC 1993a). The same cannot be said for heterosexual men who inject drugs and men who inject drugs and have sex with men; they represent the second and third largest at-risk groups among men, explaining 24 percent and 6 percent of AIDS cases, respectively (CDC 1994b). Newly reported AIDS cases for these groups continue to increase sharply. Although only 4 percent of all men diagnosed with AIDS by 1994 were infected via sexual contact with an infected woman, they had the largest proportionate increase in AIDS cases among all men in recent years (CDC 1994a).

The proportion of AIDS cases reported among women has more than doubled since the mid-1980s (CDC 1994b). In 1994, 58,448 cumulative cases of AIDS were documented among women, comprising 13 percent of all adults and adolescents (13 years or older) diagnosed with AIDS in the United States (CDC 1994a). Although they represent a minority of all AIDS cases, the incidence of AIDS among women has increased more rapidly than have rates for men, with over 24 percent of all cases of AIDS among women reported in the last year alone (CDC 1994b). The impact of the CDC's implementation of the expanded case definition for AIDS is particularly salient for incidence rates among women: In 1994, 59 percent of cases of women with AIDS were reported based on the revised surveillance definitions. Correspondingly, the incidence of AIDS opportunistic illness (AIDS-OI) has increased more rapidly among women than it has for men. Overall, the modes of HIV transmission for women also differ considerably from those for men: Women are most likely to be infected via intravenous drug use (41 percent) or sex with infected men (38 percent). Although 19 percent of women with AIDS reported no risk of exposure to HIV, follow-up data from local public health departments suggested an inverse trend. Most of those with previously unidentified risk exposure were infected via heterosexual contact (66 percent) or intravenous drug use (27 percent (CDC 1994b).

Because women of childbearing age (i.e., 15 to 44 years old) represent 84 percent of AIDS cases among women, perinatal transmission of HIV presents itself as a serious problem (CDC 1994b). In comparison with the statistics for HIV transmission for all women cited above, the most frequently reported modes of HIV transmission for seropositive new mothers were by heterosexual contact with infected male partners (36 percent) and injection drug use (30 percent) (CDC 1994a). However, it is often impossible to separate these two avenues of infection, because women may be having sex with of an infected male while also using IV drugs, both before and during pregnancy. According to recent trends, approximately 7,000 HIV-infected women gave birth to infants in the United States in 1993; about 30 percent of these infants may have contracted HIV perinatally (Gwinn et al. 1991). In 1994, 1,017 cases of AIDS were documented among children less than 13 years of age, an increase of 8 percent from 1993. In 92 percent of these cases, children contracted HIV perinatally (CDC 1994a). Demographically, there were no apparent differences in perinatal transmission rates between boys and girls; however, most newly reported cases of pediatric AIDS occurred among African-American (62 percent) and Hispanic (23 percent) children (CDC 1995a). By December 1994, a cumulative total of 6,209 AIDS cases were documented among children 13 years or younger (CDC 1994a).

In any discussion of incidence, etiology, and the avenues of infection for HIV/AIDS, the official CDC statistics are quite misleading, especially when comparing figures for different years. The clinical definition of the AIDS syndrome has been expanded several times, making the incidence seem comparatively lower in earlier years. In addition, the CDC has not been consistent in studying modes of infection, especially for women. The intake interview questions asked of men and women seeking HIV testing have changed significantly over the years; they also differ significantly for men and women, with several possible avenues of infection left out in the questions for women. In the 1980s, being born in a developing country could be listed as an avenue for men and women testing HIV-positive; women, but not men, were asked if they had had sex with a person from a developing nation. Also, the criteria for assignment to the "unidentified risk" category has changed back and forth, which in turn raises or lowers the number of infected individuals in other categories.

Clearly, adolescents and young adults are at-risk for HIV infection as well, although modes of transmission for them vary considerably. In 1994, there was a cumulative total of 1,965 cases of AIDS among adolescents between ages 13 and 19 years (CDC 1994a). For this age group, males represented 66 percent of AIDS cases and most frequently contracted HIV through receipt of infected blood products (44 percent), through sex with men (32 percent), or through injection drug use (7 percent). In contrast, females between the ages of 13 and 19 most frequently contracted HIV through sexual contact with infected men (52 percent) or injection drug use (18 percent); 22 percent of these young women failed to identify an exposure category. For young adults between the ages of 20 and 24, men represented 77 percent of AIDS cases, most of whom contracted HIV through sex with men (63 percent), injection drug use (13 percent), or sex with men and injection drug use (11 percent). Young women in this group were most likely to be infected with HIV through sexual contact with infected men (50 percent) or injection drug use (33 percent). Another 14 percent of women in this age group failed to identify an exposure category, although it is possible that the most frequent mode of transmission for them and their younger peers parallels that of older women who initially failed to report an exposure category, most of whom were infected via sexual contact with infected men (CDC 1994a).

The impact of the AIDS epidemic has been especially devastating in communities of color in the United States, largely due to a number of socioeconomic factors that disproportionately affect racial and ethnic minorities (CDC 1993b). Although they represent only 21 percent of the population, racial and ethnic minorities presently constitue 47 percent of cumulative AIDS cases among adult and adolescent men, 76 percent of cases among adult and adolescent women, and 81 percent of all pediatric AIDS cases (CDC 1994a). In 1994, African-Americans and Hispanics alone represented 58 percent of the 80,691 reported AIDS cases for that year, and they had the highest rates of infection per 100,000 people (100.8 and 51.0, respectively). In contrast, Asian/Pacific Islanders and American Indians/Alaska Natives comprised 577 (0.007 percent) and 227 (0.003 percent) of AIDS cases, respectively, reported in 1994 and had the lowest rates of infection per 100,000 people (6.4 and 12.0 percent, respectively). Whites comprirsed 33,193 (41 percent) of AIDS cases reported in 1994 and had the third highest infection rate per 100,000 people (17.2 percent).

The disproportionate effects of AIDS on racial minorities in the U.S. are most salient among women and children. In 1994, infection rates among African-American and Hispanic adult and adolescent women (i.e., 13 years and older) were 16.5 and 6.8 times higher than were rates for white women of the same ages, respectively (CDC 1994a). Likewise, infection rates among African-American and Hispanic children (i.e., less than 13 years old) were 21 and 7.5 times higher than were rates for white children, respectively. Although racial and ethnic status do not themselves confer risk for HIV/AIDS, a number of sociocultural factors inherent to many communities of color increase the risk of HIV infection, including chronic under-employment, poverty, lack of access to health-education services, and inadequate health care (CDC 1993b).

Clearly, AIDS has quickly emerged as a leading threat to public health facing United States citizens. Although there appear to be trends indicating that the impact of AIDS is leveling off in some risk groups (e.g., men who have sex with men), it is increasing steadily in others (e.g., African-American and Hispanic women and children). Furthermore, it is possible that additional segments of the population are currently "at risk" for HIV infection, including the severely mentally ill, older adults, and women who have sex with women. AIDS cases among them may constitute a third wave in the AIDS epidemic.

Because there is no cure for AIDS, behavioral change that reduces risk of exposure to HIV (e.g., unprotected sex and sharing of needles while injecting drugs) is paramount. Interventions focusing on AIDS education, self-protective behavioral change, and utilization of existing medical and testing services together represent the most promising course of action in the prevention of HIV infection and AIDS in the United States.

The clinical definition of AIDS has been revised twice by the Centers for Disease Control, first in 1987 and then in 1993, when new female symptoms for invasive cervical (stage 4) and other disease were added, along with a revision in the T4 (helper) cell count. These redefinitions need to be considered when interpreting statistics on the rates of AIDS infection.

Confidential testing for HIV status is available nationwide, with a free or sliding-scale fee and counselors available to assist in informing partners of HIV-positive persons. Several states have won the right to test all prospective employees for HIV and share this information with related agencies. The American Civil Liberties Union has won a court decision denying mandatory testing. Legal and ethical challenges posed by HIV/AIDS are far-reaching, and it may be another decade before consistent, reasonable, and effective guidelines emerge.

Although African-Americans constitute 12 percent of the population, they represent 27 percent of the reported AIDS cases (CDC 1992), these infections being due more to heterosexual intercourse and IV drug use than to gay and bisexual men. Hispanics are also overrepresented, with 16 percent of reported cases. Consequently, there is an urgent need for development of the education and prevention programs in the African-American and Latino communities.

College students pose a particular problem. Changes in college-student behaviors between 1982 and 1988 were not encouraging. In a comparison of student behavior among 363 unmarried students in 1982 (when the term AIDS was coined and few articles were published on the subject) and 273 students in 1988, the number of students having intercourse, the number of partners, and the lifetime incidence of intercourse all increased. In 1988, 72 percent of men and 83 percent of women had received oral sex, and 69 percent of males and 76 percent of females had given oral sex; 14 and 17 percent respectively had engaged in anal sex. Twenty percent of males and 12 percent of females in 1988 had four or more partners. Students with multiple or casual partners were less likely to use condoms; there also was no increase in condom use from first to most recent intercourse (Bishop and Lipsitz 1991).

Despite the need and proven effectiveness of sterile needle-exchange programs for IV drug users and the free distribution of condoms in high schools, both programs have met considerable opposition from conservative groups and the religious right. At the same time, the need for safer-sex education for all segments of the population has allowed educators to make considerable progress in general sexuality education that might not have been possible if AIDS did not pose such a major public health problem.

B. Five Specific Emerging Issues   LINDA L. HENDRIXSON

AIDS as a Family Dilemma

As the AIDS pandemic continues through its second decade in the United States, unforeseen issues have emerged as important considerations in attempts to meet the needs of people living with AIDS (PLWAs).

What began as a disease syndrome affecting individuals has become a problem which confronts whole families in America. Researchers, health providers, and policymakers have had to re-work their approaches to take into account the impact that AIDS has on family members, both immediate and extended. Our definition of "family" has undergone much change throughout this pandemic. As we consider the people who care for PLWAs, and those who care about them, family has come to be defined much more broadly than before. The family of origin has been replaced or extended to include non-blood-related friends, lovers, AIDS buddies, and others who provide emotional and instrumental support.

For many PLWAs, estrangement from birth families is a way-of-life. AIDS exacerbates those earlier problems. Others become estranged after their diagnosis is discovered. Families who have not disclosed the illness of their family member live with fear of ostracism and discrimination. If an AIDS diagnosis is kept secret within the family, social isolation becomes a continuing problem. Family pressures escalate if children are involved, especially if those children are infected. The financial strain of caring for adults and/or children with AIDS can be considerable. Finding competent doctors is an additional serious challenge throughout the country. Medical costs, health insurance, adequate health care, and social support, caregiving, child custody, disclosure, stigma, discrimination, loss, and grieving are among the troubling issues facing families and others living with AIDS (Macklin 1989).

Emerging Populations and Changing Locales

AIDS is no longer found in what were originally perceived to be the only affected American AIDS populations—white, middle-class gay men and minority intravenous drug users in the inner cities (Voeller 1991; Wiener 1991). AIDS is now found in:

- people who live in rural locations;
- middle- and upper-class women, many of whom do not misuse drugs or alcohol;
- women who have only vaginal sex with men;
- women who have rectal sex with men, but do not report this behavior;
- women who have received contaminated donor semen;
- women who have had oral sex with other women;
- middle- and upper-class men;
- men who have only vaginal sex with women, and do not have sex with other men;
- black, Hispanic, and Asian gay and bisexual men;
- teenagers who have been sexually abused as children;
- people who use drugs, such as heroin, but do not use needles;
- athletes who use contaminated needles while injecting illegal steroids;
- women with blood-clotting disorders;
- people who have received contaminated organ transplants and other body tissues;
- senior citizens; and
- babies who nurse from infected mothers

There is no longer a statistically precise AIDS profile or pattern. To a great extent, epidemiological categories have become meaningless.

The spread of AIDS to rural and small-town locations is worth noting. Most people still equate AIDS with major urban areas, and, true, the numbers of cases are highest there. However, the pandemic has diffused from urban epicenters, past suburbia, and into small, rural enclaves in the U.S. (Cleveland and Davenport 1989) The spread of AIDS in Africa along truck routes, as men seek sex away from home, is not unlike the spread of AIDS along major highways in the U.S., as people travel in and out of metropolitan AIDS epicenters. The government is paying little attention to rural AIDS in America; it is the least understood and least researched part of our national epidemic, with numbers of infected rising dramatically.

Limited research shows that some PLWAs who left their rural birthplaces for life in the city, are now returning to their rural families to be cared for. But many PLWAs who grew up in cities are leaving their urban birthplaces and moving to the country where they believe it is healthier for them, mentally and physically. This is especially true for recovering addicts whose city friends have died of AIDS, and who hope to escape a similar fate.

Besides the "in-migration" of people with AIDS to rural locations, there are many indigenous people in small towns who are infected as well. The numbers of cases of HIV/AIDS is increasing rapidly in rural America, where social services are inadequate, medical care is generally poor, and community denial is a reality. Federal and state monies continue to be channeled to inner-city agencies, leaving rural and small-town providers with scant resources to ease increasing caseloads (Hendrixson 1996).

Complexion of the Pandemic

The face of AIDS is changing in other ways, as well. There is now a considerable number of infected people who have outlived medical predictions about their morbidity and mortality. These are divided into two groups: asymptomatic non-progressors, and long-term survivors. Both groups test HIV-antibody-positive, indicating past infection with human immunodeficiency virus.

Despite being HIV-antibody-positive, the first group shows no other laboratory or clinical symptoms of HIV disease. The second group has experienced immune suppression and some opportunistic infections, and is diagnosed as having AIDS, but continues to live beyond its expected lifespan (Laurence 1994). In addition, there are others who are inexplicably uncharacteristic:

- people who have been diagnosed with AIDS, but who do not test HIV-antibody-positive, meaning that there is no indication of previous exposure to the virus, despite their illnesses
- people who have "retro-converted" from testing HIV-antibody-positive to now testing HIV-antibody-negative
- people who are repeatedly exposed to HIV through sex or contaminated blood and who do not become infected

Scientists have no explanation for these anomalies. Little research has been done on people who do not fit the accustomed pattern physicians look for. Yet, the very fact that they challenge medical expectations is a clue that they hold answers that may help thousands of others in this country.

In many ways, some new drug treatments have helped infected people forestall serious illnesses, turning AIDS into more of a chronic than an acute-illness syndrome. Yet many PLWAs have renounced AZT and other toxic anti-retroviral drugs, because of their serious side effects. Increasing numbers of patients are embracing alternative therapies—physical, mental, and spiritual—rather than taking potent AIDS drugs. Others are combining the best of conventional and unconventional medicine in their own self-styled treatment plans. The new protease inhibitors offer much promise, but it is too early to know what side effects they may produce. The bottom line is that AIDS no longer automatically equates with death ("The End of AIDS" 1996).

HIV-Positive Children Coming of Age

As life is extended, more and more children born with the virus are moving through late childhood and early adolescence in relatively good physical health. New challenges await them and their families. Some children may know they are infected with HIV; others may not. They continue to grow socially, with sexual feelings beginning to emerge. How do we help them fit in with their uninfected peers? How do we teach them about their sexuality? How do we prepare them for dating situations? What do we say when they speak of marriage hopes? How do we teach them about safer sex? What new approaches in HIV/AIDS education should health teachers consider as these children enter their classes? Parents, teachers, and youth leaders are wrestling with new questions that were unanticipated ten years ago when we believed that HIV-antibody-positive children would not live much beyond toddlerhood.

New Paradigms, New Theories

At least one revolutionary theory about AIDS is gaining prominence, as a cure for the syndrome continues to elude us. Dr. Peter Duesberg, a cancer geneticist, virologist, and molecular biologist at the University of California–Berkeley, and a member of the elite National Academy of Sciences, along with other well-established scientists, has challenged the standard medical and scientific HIV hypothesis. He maintains that AIDS researchers have never definitively proven that HIV alone causes AIDS. He theorizes that HIV cannot be the sole cause of such a complex cascade of physiological events as the complete suppression of the entire human immune system, eventually leading to fatal opportunistic infections and conditions such as cancer and dementia.

Duesberg, one of the first scientists to discover retroviruses, the family of viruses to which HIV belongs, contends that HIV is a benign "carrier" retrovirus which a healthy immune system inactivates as it would any intruder. HIV antibodies result from this normal defense response. Being HIV-antibody-positive only means that a person's immune system is working properly. It does not mean that the person will develop AIDS.

Duesberg and others believe that the serious immune suppression which manifests as severely lowered T-cell counts and opportunistic infections that may become fatal, can result from one or more of the following factors, all of which are immune-suppressive:

- continuous, long-term misuse of legal and illegal recreational drugs, including sexual aphrodisiacs such as nitrite inhalants, used by men to facilitate rectal sex with other men;
- over-use of prescription drugs, including antibiotics, anti-virals, and anti-parasitics, often taken for repeated sexually transmitted infections;
- toxic effects of AZT and other anti-retroviral drugs, which are intended to interfere with cell DNA replication ("DNA chain terminators"), and, therefore, kill *all* body cells without discrimination;
- malnutrition, which often accompanies long-term illicit drug and alcohol use; or
- untreated sexual diseases and other recurring illnesses, which also suppress immunity.

One or a combination of these factors eventually brings on the potentially fatal condition which the CDC arbitrarily calls "AIDS."

Duesberg points to the number of people with AIDS who do not test HIV-antibody-positive, as well as those who are HIV-antibody-positive but are not symptomatic. He questions why scientists are not interested in studying these people who defy the accepted AIDS dogma. Duesberg's efforts to have his research papers published by the mainstream American scientific press, to present his views at scientific AIDS conferences, and to be awarded funding to do additional AIDS research have met with virtual failure in this country.

Duesberg (1996) has been shut out by the powerful medical/scientific establishment which pretends to be open to new ideas and theories, but which, he maintains, is chained to the HIV-equals-AIDS hypothesis. He presented his challenge in a 1996 book entitled *Inventing the AIDS Virus.*

Conclusion

In the fifteenth year of the AIDS pandemic, we have no cure and no vaccine for this disease. Thousands have died in our country, most of them young people. Thousands more have died in other countries. New advances in drug treatments and alternative/holistic modalities have helped some American PLWAs, but many families continue to silently mourn the death of their loved ones. The stigma of AIDS is ever-present; the fear continues. Yet, compassion and love have emerged, as well, as caring people reach out to help those who are suffering. AIDS appears to have "dug in" for the long term while science looks for answers. In the meanwhile, we need to ask two questions. First, as scientists search for the truth of AIDS, are they asking the right questions? Second, as the disease shifts from its former pattern of early, premature death to a more manageable long-term chronic illness, are we meeting the needs of all the people infected and affected by this disease—PLWAs, their families, and their loved ones?

C. The Impact of AIDS on Our Perception of Sexuality

RAYMOND J. NOONAN

Little has been written on the impact that AIDS has had and continues to have on our collective sensibilities about sexuality and our innate needs to express aspects of our sexual selves. Research has been sparse, if non-existent, on the various meanings ascribed—both by professionals in the sexual sciences and members of the general public—to either sexuality itself or to the disease complex of AIDS.

Professionals in any field often serve to support and maintain the various cultural norms of any given society. As such, with the exception of the safety-valve role of those who might be referred to as the "loyal opposition," rarely are there expressions of sentiments or ideas that seriously challenge widely held beliefs and assumptions. Within the various disciplines encompassing the sexual sciences, the struggling theory, for example, that HIV may not be the direct cause of AIDS (see previous section), is one of the few examples of such reassessments. Among the popular press, nevertheless, various accounts have sporadically appeared with critical appraisals of either our general or specific approaches to current AIDS perspectives, including Farber (1993; 1993a; 1993b), Fumento (1990), Patton (1990), and others.

Current Trends

It cannot be denied that AIDS is a serious, debilitating, and potentially deadly disease. Yet, the American response to it has often been one in which the reality of the disease, as well as myths promoted as facts, have been appropriated to further some related or unrelated political aim. Metaphorical allusions are often used to discuss the issue, not to impart factual information about or to motivate persons to AIDS prevention, but to further a political agenda or even to attack some political group(s) perceived as adversaries. Such political goals and targets have included:

- claims that AIDS is God's punishment for sexual impropriety made by some homophobic religious leaders and others;
- instituting and promoting sex education by supporters;
- the promotion of male contraceptive responsibility by some health and sexuality professionals;
- AIDS used as a scare tactic to discourage sexual activity, particularly among the young, by some parents and others;
- providing the "scientific" reason for postponing sexual activity, being more selective about who one's sexual partners are, and reducing the number of sexual partners, by some educational, political, and health authorities;
- the promotion of monogamy and abstinence;
- the promotion of community and solidarity among compatriots, from gays to fundamentalist Christians, who perceive they are under attack;
- the use of AIDS to promote anti-male, anti-white, and/or anti-Western attitudes; and
- the advocacy of some noncoital sex practices to communicate covert negative (heterophobic) views of heterosexuality and penile-vaginal intercourse (see Noonan 1996, pp. 182-185).

For most sexologists and sexuality educators, the co-opting of the issues of protection and responsibility, especially for young people, reflects the intrinsically good part of human nature that seeks to find the "silver lining" in the dark cloud of HIV/AIDS. Although these political goals and targets probably do not apply to all people who are concerned about HIV/AIDS, these philosophies have had a more profound effect on overall public and professional approaches to sexuality and related issues than the number of their supporters would suggest. Some examples follow.

Although it is well known that anal intercourse offers the most effective way for HIV to be transmitted sexually, and that vaginal-penile intercourse is far less risky, rarely have investigators asked those whose infections are suspected to have been heterosexually transmitted, particularly women, whether and how often they engaged in anal intercourse. Instead, heterosexually transmitted HIV infections are assumed to be vaginally transmitted, although this is generally unlikely on the individual scale, and not likely to result in an HIV epidemic in the heterosexual population (Brody 1995; National Research Council 1993).

Concentrating only on the condom for both contraception and STD/AIDS prevention ignores the effectiveness of spermicidal agents with nonoxynol-9 in the prevention of pregnancy and infection as a reasonable alternative for couples who object to condom use (North 1990) (see Table 7 in Section 9A). It also ignores the negative impact condoms have on sexual intimacy for some couples (Juran 1995).

In addition, our terminology with respect to AIDS has had a profound impact on our perception of sexuality. For example, the well-known slogan, "When you sleep with someone, you are having sex with everyone she or he has slept with for the last x-number of years," is believed to be literally true by many people. The effectiveness of this slogan is seriously undermined when questions are raised about the kind of statistical and/or epidemiological evidence available to support this statement. To many, such slogans imply a view of sexuality that denigrates *all* sexual experiences, no matter how valid or valuable they are or have been. The "epidemic" of AIDS is another phrase that many, if not most, people believe to be literally true. They fail to realize that the word is being used in its metaphorical sense, with its emotional connotations being more important than its literal truth. The same can be said for the statement, "Everyone is equally at risk for AIDS." Granted this statement is true, but only in the trivial sense that we are all, as mortal human beings, prone to sickness and death. The fact that ethnic and racial minorities in the U.S. are disproportionately represented in the AIDS and HIV-positive statistics (CDC 1996) should dispel that myth completely. Brandt (1988) has insightfully analyzed the notion of AIDS-as-metaphor:

> At a moment when the dangers of promiscuous sex are being empha-
> sized, it suggests that every *single* sexual encounter is a promiscuous
> encounter. . . . As anonymous sex is being questioned, this metaphor
> suggests that no matter how well known a partner may be, the relation-
> ship is *anonymous*. Finally, the metaphor implies to heterosexuals that
> if they are having sex with their partner's (heterosexual) partners, they
> are in fact engaging in homosexual acts. In this view, every sexual act
> becomes a homosexual encounter. (p. 77, emphasis in original)

In fact, our very use of the terms "safe" or "safer sex" implies that all sex is dangerous, when in fact it usually is not (Noonan 1996a).

It is typical within the American culture to ignore the chronic problems that result from the general American uncomfortableness with sexuality and sexual pleasure. In terms of responding to the health issues surrounding AIDS, Americans have two choices:

1. We can continue to respond as we have to other sexual issues, by spotlighting them and ignoring the broader issues of sane healthy sexuality, which includes the celebration of sexual intimacy and pleasure. This narrow panic response is typical of American culture and its dealing with such issues as teenage pregnancy, child sexual abuse, satanic ritual practices, sexual "promiscuity," the "threats" to heterosexual marriage and the family posed by recognition of same-sex marriages, and the "epidemics" of herpes and heterosexual AIDS; or
2. We can respond to the AIDS crisis within the context of positive broad-based accommodation to radical changes in American sexual behavior and relationships. This broad-based, sex-positive approach could well include: the availability of comprehensive, more affordable, and more reliable sexual-health and STD evaluations for men, comparable to the regularly scheduled gynecological exams generally encouraged for women; the development of effective alternatives to the condom, including the availability of effective male contraceptives that are separated from the sexual act of intercourse, easy to use, and reliable; making birth control as automatic for men as the pill has been for women (ideally, they would also work to prevent STDs); the expansion of research to make all contraceptives safe for both women and men; the elimination of fear as a method to induce the suppression of sexual behavior; and sex-positive encouragement for making affirmative intentional decisions to have sex, in addition to the "traditional" support for deciding not to do so (Noonan 1996a).

At this time, it remains unclear whether the American response to AIDS will follow its customary pattern of initial panic in the mass media, followed by a benign neglect and silence prompted by our traditional discomfort with sex-positive values, or whether this country will, at long last, confront the issue of AIDS, and deal with it in the broader context of a safe, sane, and healthy celebration of sexuality.

12. Sexual Dysfunctions, Counseling, and Therapies

A. Brief History of American Sexual Therapy   WILLIAM HARTMAN AND
MARILYN FITHIAN

The scientific study of sexual dysfunctions and the development of therapeutic modalities in the United States started with Robert Latou Dickinson (1861-1950). Born and educated in Germany and Switzerland, he earned his medical degree in New York and began collecting sex histories from his patients in 1890. In the course of his practice, he gathered 5,200 case histories of female patients, married and single, lesbian and heterosexual, and published extensively on sexual problems of women (Brecher 1979; Dickinson and Beam 1931, 1934; Dickinson and Person 1925).

The turn-of-the-century popularity of Sigmund Freud's psychoanalysis strongly influenced early American sexual therapy. Although its popularity has faded significantly, the psychoanalytic model is still practiced or integrated with other modalities by some therapists working with sexual problems. The 1948 and 1953 Alfred Kinsey studies brought an increased awareness of human sexuality as a subject of scientific investigation that could include the treatment of sexual disorders as part of psychiatry and medicine. The pioneering work of Joseph Wolpe and Arnold Lazarus (1966) in adapting behavioral therapy, shifted sexual therapy away from the analytical and medical model, as therapists began to view dysfunctional sexual behavior as the result of learned responses that can be modified.

William Masters and Virginia Johnson began their epoch-making study of the anatomy and physiology of human sexual response in 1964. Their initial research with 312 males and 382 females, published as *Human Sexual Response* (1966), remains the keystone of modern sex therapy, not just in the United States, but anywhere sex therapy is studied or practiced. *Human Sexual Inadequacy* followed in 1970. Masters and Johnson used a male-female dual-therapy team, and a brief, intensive, reeducation process that involved behavior-oriented exercises like sensate focus. It appeared to be highly successful because they worked with a select population of healthy people in basically solid relationships. After their success with relatively simple cases, they and other therapists began to encounter more difficult cases, which could not be solved with the original behavioral approach.

In the early 1970s, Joseph LoPiccolo advocated the use of additional approaches designed to reduce anxiety within the behavioral therapy model suggested by Masters and Johnson (LoPiccolo and LoPiccolo 1978; LoPiccolo and Lobitz 1973; Lobitz and LoPiccolo 1972). LoPiccolo's (1978) analysis of the theoretical basis for sexual therapy identified seven major underlying elements in every sex therapy model: (1) mutual responsibility, (2) information, education, and permission giving, (3) attitude change, (4) anxiety reduction, (5) communication and feedback, (6) intervention in destructive sex roles, lifestyles, and family interaction, and (7) prescribing changes in sex therapy.

John Gagnon and William Simon (1973) stressed the importance of addressing social scripting in sex therapy. Harold Lief, a physician and family therapist, pointed out the importance of nonsexual interpersonal issues and communications problems as factors in sexual difficulties. Lief (1963, 1965) also advocated incorporating the principles of marital therapy into sex therapy. As therapists began to integrate other modes of psychotherapy, such as cognitive, gestalt, and imagery therapies, it soon became apparent that there was no single "official" form of sex therapy. In addition, some sex therapists became sensitive to the impact and influence of ethnic values on some sexual problems (McGoldrick et al. 1982).

Helen Singer Kaplan, a psychiatrist at Cornell University College of Medicine, made an important and profound contribution to sex therapy when she blended traditional concepts from psychotherapy and psychoanalysis with cognitive psychology and behavioral therapy. Kaplan's *New Sex Therapy* (1974) explored the role of such important therapeutic issues as resistance, repression, and unconscious motivations in sex therapy. This new approach focused not only on altering behavior with techniques like the sensate-focus exercises, but also with exploring and modifying covert or unconscious thought patterns and motivations that may underlie a sexual difficulty (Kaplan 1974, 1979, 1983).

Specific areas of sexual therapy have been developed, including Lonnie Barbach's (1980) and Betty Dodson's (1987) independent work with non-orgasmic women, Bernard Apfelbaum and Dean Dauw's use of surrogates in their work with single persons, William Hartman and Marilyn Fithian's (1972) integration of films, body imagery, and body work with dysfunctional couples, and Bernie Zilbergeld's (1978, 1992) focus on male sexual health and problems.

There have been no major innovative treatments developed in sex therapy programs in recent years, although new refinements continue to occur. Some would comment that one does not have to reinvent the wheel when the results are good, but the early success rates have declined as the presenting problems have become more complicated and difficult to treat. Nevertheless, self-reported success rates from reputable sex therapy clinics run between 80 percent and 92 percent. However, critical reviews of sex therapy treatment models emphasize the paucity of scientific data in determining the effectiveness of such programs.

Today, few professionals who counsel clients with sexual difficulties see themselves as pure sex therapists. More and more, the term "sex therapy" refers to a focus of intervention, rather than to a distinctive and exclusive technique. Individual psychologists, psychotherapists, marriage counselors, and family therapists may be more or less skilled in providing counseling and applying therapeutic modalities appropriate to specific sexual problems, but each tends to apply those interventions and techniques with which they are more comfortable.

Informal support groups also provide opportunities for dealing with sexual problems and difficulties. Many hospitals and service organizations provide workshops and support groups for patients recovering from heart attacks, for persons with diabetes, emphysema, multiple sclerosis, cystic fibrosis, arthritis, and other chronic diseases. These support groups usually include both patients and their partners.

B. Current Status   JULIAN SLOWINSKI AND WILLIAM R. STAYTON

Recently, American sex therapy has incorporated important advances in medicine and pharmacology. More-precise knowledge and techniques now allow a therapist to develop a hormone profile for a patient, monitor nocturnal penile tumescence, and check penile and vaginal blood flow. With patients now reporting the negative side effects of medications on their sexual responses, doctors have developed strategies for altering the course of medication. New surgical methods improve penile blood supply. Moreover, prosthetics and other aids, like injections and electrical devises to stimulate erection, have been developed.

Breakthroughs are also occurring in female sex research with direct implications for sex therapy. Examples include the efforts of sex-affirming women to redefine sexual satisfaction in women's terms and expand our appreciation of the spectrum of erotic/sexual responses beyond the phallic/coital (Ogden 1995), Joanne Loulan's (1984) exploration of lesbian sexual archetypes, sexual responses of women with a spinal cord injury, the effects on women's libido of homeopathics to increase the bioavailability of testosterone, and work combining testosterone with estrogen replacement to increase both sexual desire and pleasure in perimenopausal women.

One sidelight in this exciting female sex research is that the old methods of sensate focus and pleasuring exercises are still working successfully. For example, the self-help materials are still very useful in working with preorgasmic women. The traditional sensate-focus exercises are still effective in working with desire issues, painful intercourse, and vaginal spasms.

More good news are the trends in treating male sexual dysfunction today. For the motivated and cooperative male, there is treatment for virtually every dysfunction. In addition to the ever-helpful sensate-focus exercises, we have medications for increasing desire and arousal, such as yohimbe, a bark extract of the African tree yohimbe, and a combination of green oat and palmetto-grass extract. These are available through a physician's prescription, at health food stores, or through mail-order catalogs. As of mid-1995, there is enthusiastic anecdotal feedback from individual therapists who are using yohimbe and oat extract with their clients, but what is anxiously awaited—and needed—in this area are the results of controlled clinical studies to document the actual therapeutic effects, if any.

The vacuum pump for erections has been much improved with automatic monitoring of blood flow. With some clients, penile injections produce remarkable results. Monoxydyl and nitroglycerin are being used as topical preparations, as are prostaglandin E1 suppositories inserted into the urethral meatus. Taken alone, these medications are not effective. Without therapy, the person will often stop using the medication or method. However, when sex therapy is added, the success rate increases dramatically, because both the relationship and the dysfunction are being treated.

Problems

Several problems currently impede the delivery of sex therapy to clients. Primary among these is the state of flux in the insurance industry (third-party payers) with the shift toward managed care, health maintenance organizations, and provider networks. The availability of third-party payment makes it much more feasible for patients to avail themselves of sex therapy. The insurance industry has changed the entire health-care-provider field by creating the impression that therapists, like others in the medical field, are not to be trusted to know how long therapy should last, or what methods should be used to treat psychodynamic problems. This has created the image that all psychological problems can be treated by brief therapy within a predetermined number of sessions. The insurance industry has also made confidentiality problematic, because clients must sign away the right to confidentiality in order to receive mental-health coverage. Increasingly, insurance plans refuse to pay for sex therapy. This has prompted many therapists to give a diagnosis that is acceptable to the plan, and then include sex therapy as an Axis II diagnosis.

Secondly, the rise of the religious right appears to have had a negative impact on sex therapy in America. Although there has been no general decline in premarital sex in America, the "abstinence only until marriage" ethic can be a considerable barrier to normal adolescent sexual rehearsal explorations for some people, and may well result in trauma and dysfunction when newlywed couples confront their sexuality and sexual functioning on the wedding night. Thirty years ago, Masters and Johnson found that religious orthodoxy was a primary cause of sexual dysfunction. Two responses are likely, the individuals and/or couple may become so stressed that it is difficult for them to function naturally within the permitted circumstances, or they may rebel even before marriage and get involved in promiscuous and/or risky practices.

A third concern is a growing challenge as to whether sex therapy is even a separate discipline. There are those who believe that sex therapy needs to be subsumed under psychology, marriage and family therapy, social work, or psychiatry. The fact is that few of these disciplines have educational or training programs that teach about the healthy aspects of sex and sexuality or the creative treatment of sexual problems.

Finally, the amount of money and effort given to research on female sexuality significantly lags behind research on male sexuality (di Mauro 1995).

Because humans are born sexual but not lovers, sex therapy is increasingly seen as including good sex education, good medicine, and good psychotherapy/counseling. In the last ten years, sex therapy has added important concerns related to gender-identity dysphoria, sexual (gender) orientations, and lifestyle issues.

C. Recent Developments JULIAN SLOWINSKI AND WILLIAM R. STAYTON

Psychotropic Drugs

Antidepressants, antianxiety, and antipanic medications are being used with psychotherapy in treating desire-phase problems and in treating paraphilic compulsive-obsessive behaviors (Coleman 1991). Recent anecdotal reports and some early controlled studies are finding a category of antidepressant medications useful in treating sexual disorders. SSRIs, such as Zoleft, Paxix, and Prozac, are useful in increasing the latency time for ejaculation, and thus are helping some men who present with problems of ejaculatory control (early ejaculation). Another medication, Anafranil, and antidepressants used in treating obsessive-compulsive disorders, have been demonstrated in at least one study to help in the treatment of premature ejaculation. Of course, these results occur when therapy is provided, for if medication is discontinued, there can be a resumption of symptoms. That suggests the presence of untreated anxiety, relationship problems, or a constitutional tendency towards difficulty with ejaculation control.

An unfortunate side effect of SSRIs is the frequent complaint by patients of some loss of sexual desire. This has been reported by patients on these medications for depression. In some patients, however, the lifting of their depression symptoms alone is enough to increase their libido, despite the use of medication. Wellbrutrin, a relatively recent antidepressant, is claimed to have few negative effects on sexual desire. A newly marketed antidepressant, Serzone, is also being hailed for having no negative effects on libido.

Vulvodynia, a Newly Identified Syndrome

One of the new challenges facing American sex therapists and gynecologists today is the occurrence in many women of a painful burning sensation in the vulvar and vaginal area. This condition, recently named vulvodynia, or burning vulva syndrome, is a form of vestibulitis that can have a number of causes, from microorganisms that cause dermatosis to inflammation of the vestibular glands. The presenting complaint of these women is burning and painful intercourse. Some women develop secondary vaginismus. Discomfort varies from constant pain to localized spots highly sensitive to touch. In many cases, the psychological and relationship consequences are grave. Many women become depressed as a result and frustrated by attempts at treatment.

Current treatment includes topical preparations, laser surgery to ablate affected areas, dietary restrictions, and referral to a physical therapist to realign pelvic structure and reduce pressure on the spinal nerves serving the genital area. Some affected women have sought relief with acupuncture. Therapy may be enhanced by focusing on the effects of the condition on the sexual functioning of the patient, her relationship with her partner, and self-image. Pain-reduction techniques, including self-hypnosis, have proven valuable in some cases. Low doses of an antidepressant, including some SSRIs, may reduce the pain.

There is much work to be done in the treatment of vulvodynia, including making the public aware of this condition and educating physicians in the role that sex therapists can play in supporting these women and their partners.

The Medicalization of Sex Therapy

There is an increasing medicalization in sex therapy today. Although this may at first seem to benefit many patients—and it does—there is a concern among sex therapists that many conditions will be summarily treated through medications by primary physicians, with a corresponding failure to address the dynamic and interpersonal aspects of the patient. In short, there is a danger of incomplete evaluation of the patient's status if only the medical aspects are considered and the therapist is left out of the process. In the ideal situation, the sex therapist and physician would collaborate on the treatment plan, using medication as indicated.

D. Education and Certification of Sex Therapists JULIAN SLOWINSKI AND WILLIAM R. STAYTON

Since American sex educators, counselors, and therapists are not licensed by any government agency, reputable professionals in the field operate under one of several traditional professional licenses, as part of their practice as a physician, psychologist, psychoanalyst, social worker, marriage and family counselor, or pastoral counselor.

The American Association of Sex Educators, Counselors, and Therapists (AASECT) does offer its own certification for sex educators, counselors, and therapists following successful completion of specified training programs that include supervised practice. Continuing education credits are required for renewal of this certification.

E. Sex Surrogates: The Continuing Controversy RAYMOND J. NOONAN

Three decades after Masters and Johnson pioneered modern sex therapy, the use of sexual partner surrogates continues despite a long history of controversy, largely because it has been found by some professionals to be an effective therapeutic modality in certain circumstances for persons without partners and for specially challenged persons with physical limitations. Still, as Dauw (1988) has noted, little in-depth research has been conducted about surrogates, their effectiveness, or their appropriateness in working with specific sexual dysfunctions. Misconceptions about surrogates are widespread (Apfelbaum 1984), in part, because of a common confusion between the roles of sex surrogates and prostitutes, based on the potential for intimate sexual interaction and the surrogate being paid for her or his work. Roberts (1981) has suggested that "the most common misconception" is of the surrogate as "an elitist type of prostitute." In addition, some authors have commented on the effects of media accounts of sex surrogates, which have tended to focus on the bizarre, the sensational, and even the untrue (Braun 1975; Lily 1977).

The distinction commonly noted between surrogates and prostitutes usually relies on the intent of the sexual interaction: the prostitute's intent being immediate gratification localized on genital pleasure, whereas the surrogate's intent is long-term therapeutic reeducation and reorientation of inadequate capabilities of functioning or relating sexually (Brown 1981; Jacobs et al.,1975; Roberts 1981). In 1970, Masters and Johnson noted that ". . . so much more is needed and demanded from a substitute partner than effectiveness of purely physical sexual performance that to use prostitutes would have been at best clinically unsuccessful and at worst psychologically disastrous."

IPSA, the International Professional Surrogates Association (n.d.), wrote,

> A surrogate partner is a member of a three-way therapeutic team consisting of therapist, client and surrogate partner. The surrogate participates, as a partner to the client, in experiential exercises designed to build the client's skills in the areas of physical and emotional intimacy. This partner work includes exercises in communication, relaxation, sensual and sexual touching and social skills training.

Others, including Allen (1978), Apfelbaum (1977, 1984), Brown (1981), Dauw (1988), Masters and Johnson (1970), Roberts (1981), Symonds (1973), Williams (1978), and Wolfe (1978) have described, either briefly or in part, typical surrogate sessions or alternative models. According to Jacobs, et al. (1975): "The usual therapeutic approach is slow and thorough. Exercises are graduated and concentrate on body awareness, relaxation and sensual/sexual experiences that are primarily non-genital." Where appropriate, the surrogate also teaches "vital social skills and traditional courtship patterns which finally include sexual interaction." However, none of these writers gave a perspective of the relative amount of time or importance that each aspect of the surrogate therapy session or program places on the entire process. Such a perspective would give a clearer understanding of the true functions of a sex surrogate that would allow the integration of the use of surrogate therapy into a useful theoretical perspective relative to clinical sexology, as well as to normative sexual functioning.

The use of sex surrogates was introduced by Masters and Johnson (1970) as a way to treat single men who did not have partners available to participate in their couple-oriented sex-therapy program. As the practice evolved, surrogates sometimes specialized in working with specific populations, such as single heterosexual or homosexual men, with couples as a coach, or with people with physical disabilities.

Today, the use of surrogates remains controversial with complex legal, moral, ethical, professional, and clinical implications. Although Masters and Johnson abandoned the practice (Redlich, 1977), the use of professional sex surrogates has been ethically permissible as part of the sex therapist's armamentarium, according to the American Association of Sex Educators, Counselors, and Therapists (AASECT 1978, 1987). Still, the most recent version of AASECT's (1993) *Code of Ethics* has ceased to mention the use of surrogates explicitly. Instead, the 1993 code merely states that a member of AASECT should not make a "referral to an unqualified or incompetent person" (p. 14), which would presumably refer to surrogates, among others.

In their 1987 *Code of Ethics*, however, and in at least one earlier version, AASECT addressed the issue of surrogates directly, and promulgated the parameters for their ethical use, including the understanding that the surrogate is not a sex therapist or psychotherapist, and that the therapist must protect the dignity and welfare of both the client and the surrogate. In addition, it outlined how issues of confidentiality and consent should be addressed. In many ways, this document is similar in putting the client's welfare first to the *Code of Ethics* espoused by the International Professional Surrogates Association (IPSA, 1989). Among IPSA's strict requirements for members are the necessity that surrogates practice only within the context of the therapeutic triangle consisting of the client, surrogate, and supervising therapist, that the relationship with the client always be within the context of the therapy, that the surrogate recognize and act in accordance with the boundaries and limitations of her competence, and that the surrogate be responsible for all precautions against pregnancy and disease. Confidentiality and continuing-education requirements are also among the seventeen items listed in the code, although the surrogate's primary role as a co-therapist or substitute partner in any given therapeutic situation is left open to agreement between the therapist and surrogate.

In 1997, there are estimated to be fewer than 200 surrogates worldwide, according to Vena Blanchard, president of IPSA (personal communication, March 15, 1997), with maybe 100 practicing in the U.S.A. This number is down by about two thirds from the 300 estimated to be practicing in the U.S.A. in 1983-1984 (Noonan 1995/1984), a time when the number of surrogates peaked. However, the downward trend of the subsequent decade, caused primarily by fears surrounding AIDS, has been showing signs of reversing since the mid-1990s, according to Blanchard, who pointed to the number of new surrogates being trained and requesting training by IPSA. Still, according to Blanchard, only a few urban areas, primarily on the two coasts, have surrogates working, with most of the country not being served.

Noonan (1995/1984) surveyed fifty-four sex surrogates who were part of a surrogates' networking mailing list representing about 65 to 70 percent of all known legitimate trained surrogates in 1983-1984. The fifty-four surrogate respondents represented about 36 percent of the 150 estimated known surrogates, who were estimated to be approximately one half of all surrogates practicing in the U.S. at the time. In addition to demographic data, the instrument asked respondents to estimate the percentage of time they spent in each of seven activities with clients. The data gathered seemed to support strongly the hypothesis that sex surrogates provide more than sexual service for their clients, spending about 87 percent of their professional time doing non-sexual activities. In addition to functioning as a sexual intimate, Noonan found that the surrogate functions as educator, counselor, and co-therapist, providing sex education, sex counseling, social-skills education, coping-skills counseling, emotional support, sensuality and relaxation education and coaching, and self-awareness education. The results indicated that a majority of time is spent outside of the sexual realm, suggesting further that surrogate therapy employs a more holistic methodological approach than previous writings, both professional and lay, would seem to indicate. Clearly, the sex surrogate functions far beyond the realm of the prostitute.

Specifically, Noonan's (1995/1984) results showed that the surrogate spends much of her or his time talking with the client, with approximately 34 percent of the time spent giving sexual information, as well as reassurance and support. Almost one half of the surrogate's time (48.5 percent) is spent in experiential exercises involving the body non-sexually, with the majority of that time devoted to teaching the client basically how to feel—how to be aware of what is coming in through the senses. Combining the two averages, we find that the surrogate typically spends 82.5 percent of the therapeutic time enhancing the cognitive, emotional, and sensual worlds of the client. Only after this foundation is developed does the surrogate spend almost 13 percent of the time focusing on erotic activities, including sexual intercourse, cunnilingus, and fellatio, and teaching sexual techniques. The remaining 4.5 percent focuses on social skills in public settings, clearly the least important aspect of what the surrogate deals with.

Finally, a profile emerged of the "average" sex surrogate in 1983-1984: she is a white female, in her late 30s/early 40s, and not very religious. She is one way or another single with 1.4 children, college-educated, lives in California, has been practicing as a surrogate for four years three months, and sees twenty-seven clients per year. Finally, she is a heterosexual who does not need to concern herself or her partner with chemical or mechanical methods of contraception, because she has been sterilized (Noonan 1995/1984). It is interesting to note that among the fifty-four respondents, six of the surrogates had earned doctorates, with the average being a bachelor's degree plus some advanced study, indicating the atypically high level of educational achievement in this group.

Present and Future Issues

Surrogate therapy has no doubt changed somewhat over the past decade and a half for various reasons. These changes need to be elucidated, documented, and incorporated into our collective knowledge about normative sexuality and how to address the various problems we have created or maintained around its expression.

Since 1983, the impact of AIDS has become a deep concern of both surrogates and therapists. Exactly how it has affected the work of surrogates remains to be studied. Certainly in the years immediately following Noonan's (1995/1984) study of the functions of sex surrogates, many surrogates, who in retrospect were not particularly at risk for HIV infection, stopped practicing or modified their practice as surrogates out of fear. Many therapists also stopped referring clients to surrogates out of fear of legal liability. As the reality of HIV infection has become better known, surrogates, who are mostly female working with heterosexual males, are continuing to help clients function better sexually while promoting responsible sexual behavior at all levels. Little or no research exists that has investigated how gay male surrogates, who worked mostly with gay male clients in the 1980s, have changed their practice.

Since the 1980s, women have become more aware of how surrogates might help them effectively deal with various sexual dysfunctions. Some female clients will ask their therapists, or seek out therapists who are open to the possibility, to find a male surrogate with whom they might work. Largely because of the sexual double standard that continues to operate in many, if not most, therapists, however, most clients of surrogates continue to be male. The degree to which women have begun to work with surrogates to solve their sexual problems, or who consider it a viable option, are questions that require additional research. In addition, the differences that may exist in the design of the therapy program itself and how a female client might work with a surrogate, as compared to how males work with surrogates, is also a topic open to research. It appears that heterosexual male surrogates remain today the rarest of sex surrogates, as in the early 1980s.

Despite these research needs, the population of surrogates is likely to remain resistant to study, both because of the legal ambiguities often involved with their practice and the fact that the use of surrogates retains a relatively high visibility in public consciousness, although surrogates themselves are usually quite invisible. Because they are a small group, they will be difficult to study with any reasonable assurances of confidentiality.

The most troubling aspect of research on sex surrogates may be the indication, yet to be verified by any research, that there are probably many more surrogates working with clients and therapists in the United States, who are independently trained by varying standards by the therapists with whom they may be working, and who are both isolated from other surrogates and from researchers. This leaves them unaware of the most recent knowledge and advances in the field, because rarely are therapists trained in working with surrogates. It also deprives us of the knowledge gained from experience that these "hidden" surrogates may have learned.

13. Research and Advanced Education

A. A Research Assessment   ROBERT T. FRANCOEUR

The United States has a long tradition and unequaled wealth of sexological research. The survey work of Alfred Kinsey and his colleagues in the 1940s and 1950s and the clinical/therapeutic research of William Masters and Virginia Johnson are but tips of the iceberg, referred to and cited in almost any discussion of sexological research anywhere in the world (Brecher 1979; Bullough 1994; Pomeroy 1972).

Sexological research in the United States today is vital to the management of many social and public health problems. Each year, one million teenage girls become pregnant, a per-thousand-rate twice that of Canada, England, and Sweden, and ten times that of the Netherlands; the disproportion is similar for teenage abortions (Jones et al. 1986). The nation spends $25 billion on families begun by teenagers for social, health, and welfare services. One million Americans are HIV-positive and almost one quarter of a million have died of AIDS. Yet only one in ten American children receives sexuality education that includes information about HIV/AIDS transmission and prevention. One in five adolescent girls in grades eight through eleven is subject to sexual harassment, while three quarters of girls under age 14 who have had sexual relations have been raped. These and other public health problems are well documented and increasingly understood in the context of poverty, family trauma, ethnic discrimination, lack of educational opportunities, and inadequate health services. However, there is little recognition of the need for sexological research to deal effectively with these problems. Congress has several times refused or withdrawn funding for well-designed and important surveys because of pressure from conservative minorities (di Mauro 1995).

In 1995, the Sexuality Research Assessment Project of the Social Science Research Council (605 Third Avenue, 17th Floor. New York, New York 10158) published a comprehensive review of *Sexuality Research in the United States: An Assessment of the Social and Behavioral Sciences* (di Mauro 1995). This report identified and described major gaps and needs in American sexological research. There is a serious lack of a framework for the analysis of sexual behaviors in the context of society and culture. This framework is needed to examine how sexual socialization occurs in families, schools, the media, and peer groups, and to address the complex perspectives of different situations, populations, and cultural communities. Areas of need identified by the project include: gender, HIV/AIDS, adolescent sexuality, sexual orientation, sexual coercion, and research methodology. Three major barriers hindering sexuality research are (1) the lack of comprehensive research training in sexuality, (2) inadequate mechanisms and efforts to disseminate research findings to policymakers, advocates, practitioners, and program representatives in diverse communities who need this information, and (3) the lack of federal, private-sector, and academic funding for research.

B. Advanced Sexological Institutes, Organizations, and Publications

MARTHA CORNOG

Advanced Sexuality Education and Institutes

The premier American sexological research institute is the Kinsey Institute for Research in Sex, Gender and Reproduction, based at Indiana University, Bloomington, Indiana. Two other major institutes are: the Institute for the Advanced Study of Human Sexuality (Address: 1525 Franklin Street, San Francisco, CA 94109); and the Mary Calderone Library at the Sexuality Information and Education Council of the United States). A more complete selection of libraries specializing in various sexuality topics may be found by consulting the index to the *Directory of Special Libraries and Information Centers* (Gale Research).

About two dozen universities grant degrees with majors or concentrations in sexology and/or sex education, counseling, or therapy. These include Indiana University, the University of Minnesota, New York University, and the University of Pennsylvania. A full list is available from the national office of the Society for the Scientific Study of Sexuality (see address below).

In the late 1960s, several medical schools introduced programs in human sexuality into their curricula for training physicians. These programs reached their zenith in the early 1980s. By the late 1980s, many of them were under fire from newly appointed conservative administrators, and threatened with cutbacks and elimination. Indications suggest a significant decline in sexuality training for physicians and other health-care professionals, but the picture is not clear because no one has studied the situation nationwide (see Section E below). Likewise, students seeking an advanced degree or major concentration in sexology find the current situation of prospects for the future of individual graduate study cloudy.

Sexological Organizations

There are four major American sexological organizations:

The Society for the Scientific Study of Sexuality (SSSS). Founded in 1957; currently over 1,000 members. Address: P. O. Box 208, Mt. Vernon, Iowa 52314.

The American Association of Sex Educators, Counselors, and Therapists (ASSECT). Founded in 1967; currently over 3,000 members. Address: 435 North Michigan Avenue, Suite 1717, Chicago, Illinois 60611.

The Sexuality Information and Education Council of the United States (SIECUS). Founded in 1964; currently about 3,600 members. Address: 130 West 42nd Street, Suite 350, New York, NY 10036.

The Society for Sex Therapy and Research (SSTAR). Founded in 1974; currently about 300 members. Address: c/o Candyce Risen, The Center for Sexual Health, 2320 Chagrin Boulevard, 3 Commerce Park, Beachwood, Ohio 44122.

Several dozen other groups are oriented to various types of professionals concerned with sexuality. Typical among these are: Association for the Behavioral Treatment of Sexual Abusers, Association of Nurses in AIDS Care, National Council on Family Relations, Society for the Psychological Study of Lesbian and Gay Issues, and Society for the Study of Social Problems. (For addresses of many of these groups, see the listing in the Directory of Sexological Organizations at the end of this volume.)

There are at least one hundred advocacy and common-interest organizations that deal in one way or another with advocacy for gay and lesbian viewpoints, or provide a vehicle for the gay and lesbian practitioners of a profession or hobby to socialize or work together. The largest and most comprehensive are the National Gay Rights Advocates, the Lambda Defense and Education Fund, and the National Gay and Lesbian Task Force, each with 15,000 or more member-contributors and budgets in the millions of dollars. Typical of smaller special-interest groups are: Federal Lesbians and Gays (federal government workers), International Gay Travel Association, Good Gay Poets, Lesbian and Gay Bands of America, Girth and Mirth (overweight gay men), and Gay and Lesbian History on Stamps Club.

Similar organizations exist for many sexual viewpoints and behaviors other than homosexuality—and for sexual matters perceived as problems. An all-too-brief sampling from the *Encyclopedia of Associations* (*EoA*) (Gale Research Publications) includes: Americans for Decency, American Coalition for Traditional Values, American Sunbathing Association (nudism), Adult Video Association (pro-pornography/erotica), Christian Voice, Eagle Forum, Focus on the Family, North American Swing Club Association and Lifestyles (both recreational nonmonogamy), National Clearinghouse on Marital and Date Rape, National Task Force on Prostitution (pro-prostitution, formerly COYOTE), PONY (Prostitutes of New York), Society's League Against Molestation (child sexual abuse), Society for the Second Self (TRI-Ess) (transvestites), Sexaholics Anonymous, Impotents Anonymous, People with AIDS Coalition, Women Exploited by Abortion, Renaissance (Philadelphia-based with a dozen local chapters for transvestites and transsexuals), and Women Against Pornography. Check *EoA* for a full listing. Other special-interest groups are not listed in the *EoA* but can be located by scanning sex-related publications. Such groups include: Club Latexa (rubber fetishists), DPF (Diaper Pail Friends; infantilism and nepiophilia), Janus (bisexuals), SAMOIS (lesbian sadomasochism), and Eulenspiegel (sadomasochism).

Sexological Journals and Sexually-Oriented Magazines

Professional journals that publish sexuality-related research include: *Archives of Sexual Behavior, Annual Review of Sex Research, Journal of Gay and Lesbian Psychotherapy, Journal of Gender Studies, Journal of Homosexuality, Journal of Marriage and the Family, Journal of Psychology and Human Sexuality, Journal of Sex and Marital Therapy, Journal of Sex Education and Therapy, Journal of Sex Research, Marriage and Family Review, Journal of Social Work and Human Sexuality, Journal of the History of Sexuality, Maledicta* (language), *Medical Aspects of Human Sexuality,* and the *SIECUS Report.*

Major popular magazines that publish sexually oriented nonfiction and sometimes fiction include: *Eidos, Frighten the Horses, Libido, Penthouse, Playboy, Screw, Tantra,* and *Yellow Silk* (entirely literary). Resource directories include: *Gayellow Pages, Gaia's Guide,* and *Gay and Lesbian Library Service.* The major gay/lesbian nationwide periodicals are: *Advocate* (out of Los Angeles) and *Blade* (out of Washington, D.C.). Dozens of other publications exist, such as *Deneuve* and *On Our Backs* (for lesbians). Addresses for these and similar journals and magazines can be found in the *Gale Directory of Publications and Broadcast Media, Ulrich's International Periodical Directory, The Standard Periodical Directory,* or other directories.

C. Sexuality Education of Physicians and Clergy

Medical School Sexuality Education   RICHARD J. CROSS

Medical schools have always taught certain aspects of sexuality, e.g., the anatomy of the male and female sex organs, the menstrual cycle, basic obstetrics, and some psychology and psychiatry. That picture began to change about thirty years ago when Harold I. Lief (1963, 1965), a psychiatrist at Tulane University Medical School in Louisiana, wrote articles pointing out that most Americans regarded physicians as authorities on human sexuality, that the field of sexology was changing fast, and that only three medical schools in the country were even trying to teach modern sexology. The situation gradually improved, and when Harold Lief and Richard J. Cross, a physician who had introduced sexology education at the Robert Wood Johnson Medical School at Rutgers University in New Jersey, sent a questionnaire to all medical schools in the U.S. and Canada in 1980, they found only three schools that said they did not teach sexuality. However, they did not publish their results because of the poor response rate and apparent unreliability of self-serving responses from medical school administrators. It was clear, however, that the improvement was limited; part of the change reported was due to different interpretations of the questionnaire and differing definitions of "sexuality." No one knows just what is being taught in the different medical schools today.

Part of the problem is that medical schools have traditionally defined education as the acquisition of factual information and certain skills by students. In the field of sexuality education, affective learning is also important. The greatest shortcoming of most practicing physicians is their discomfort. Since early childhood, they have been taught that sex is a private subject and that it is impolite and/or improper to talk about it. Physicians, who have not learned to confront and overcome their discomfort in talking about sex, transmit to their patients nonverbal, and sometimes verbal, messages that they do not want to hear about sexual problems. Their patients, who are often equally uncomfortable, cooperate by not raising any sexual issues. The result, too often, is "a conspiracy of silence," in which sexual issues that sometimes have a great impact on health never get discussed.

A number of medical schools have instituted courses or short programs in sexuality that emphasize attitudes, values, and feelings, rather than the memorization of factual information. These courses make extensive use of sexually explicit, educational films and videos and panels of people who are willing and able to talk about their personal sexual experiences. Following each large-group session, the students break into smaller groups who meet with facilitators to process what they have heard and seen with an emphasis on their personal feelings and reactions. Such programs seem to give medical students a better understanding of their own sexuality, a greater tolerance for unusual sexual attitudes they may encounter in their patients, and greater comfort in dealing with and discussing sexual issues.

Unfortunately, these programs rarely elicit enthusiastic support from the medical school faculties, who, after all, have been selected for their expertise in analyzing scientific data. Time is jealously guarded in the medical school curriculum. Money has always been a concern in higher education, but money gets tighter year by year, and small groups are expensive to organize and run. Many sexuality programs in medical schools are elective, which is sad, because the students who need these courses most are often the least likely to register for them.

Despite thirty years of improved sexuality education, most American doctors still do an inadequate job of helping patients with sexual problems. Comprehensive courses seem to help, but in the current conservative political and economic climate, it seems unlikely that they will be greatly expanded in the near future. In fact, there are indications that some programs are in danger of being cut back. There is, on the other hand, a small but growing move in the Association of American Medical Colleges to go beyond stuffing facts into students by dealing with attitudes and feelings in the medical school curricula. If this takes hold, sexuality courses may lead the way. Time alone will tell.

Sexuality Education for Clergy in   PATRICIA GOODSON AND
Theological Schools and Seminaries   SARAH C. CONKLIN

History. Protestantism has historically enjoyed the status of dominant religion in this country, but democracy, with its emphasis on religious freedom
and pluralism, has nourished the establishment of countless religious
groups. Because these groups are numerous, and the education of their
leadership varies considerably, a discussion of clergy training in sexuality
requires qualification.

The main focus here will be on the seminaries and students included in
the studies conducted by Conklin (1995) and Goodson (1996). Denomi-
nationally, the emphasis in these studies was mainly on Protestant and
Roman Catholic clergy, although Jewish seminary faculty members were
interviewed for the study by Conklin. By including both conservative and
liberal schools and denominations, the largest religious groups are represented, but the samples are neither random nor the results generalizable.

Seminaries and theological schools are defined, here, as institutions of
higher education accredited by the Association of Theological Schools
(ATS). They offer post-baccalaureate degrees leading to ordination and
licensure of pastors, priests, ministers, rabbis, chaplains, and pastoral counselors (categories broadly referred to as clergy).

Traditionally, clergy students have been characterized as young, white,
and male, but this profile is slowly changing. First, it is becoming an older
population composed of more part-time and second-career students. Second, diversity in both ethnicity and gender is increasing. In a comparison
of motivations, women were more inclined to report entering seminary to
discover "ways to best serve Christ in the church and the world" or "personal
spiritual growth and faith development" rather than "preparing to be a
parish minister," which was the overwhelmingly reported motivation for men
entering seminary (Aleshire in Hunter 1990, p. 1265). In terms of sexuality
education, seminary students are now perceived as being "more diverse in
attitudes, more willing to share personal experiences, and more open about
sexual orientation" than in previous generations (Conklin 1995, p. 231).

Conflict over whether seminary education accents professional training
or personal formation may be a factor accounting for the apparent lack of
emphasis on sexuality content (Kelsey 1993). As the percentage of female
students has increased, greater awareness and sensitivity about the negative
sexual experiences of women has been accompanied by curricular changes.
As clinical settings for counseling practice have been included in most
seminary curricula, less emphasis has been placed on foundational education (languages, such as Latin, Greek, and Hebrew, are less often required),
but issues of training remain problematic, especially concerning sexuality
education.

The scientific literature contains abundant evidence of the positive role
that clergy may have in health promotion generally and in sexual health

promotion, specifically. One study affirmed, for instance, that nearly half of all referrals made by clergy to mental-health professionals "involved marriage and family problems" (Weaver 1995, p. 133).

Recently, however, this supportive role has come into question as trust in clergy generally has been undermined by the misconduct of a few. Fortune (1991) contends that omission of sexuality components in professional training misses an intervention opportunity for clergy students to explore ethical boundary issues concerning what appropriate sexual conduct consists of prior to entering the profession. Such evidence clearly points to the appropriateness of marriage, family, and sexuality content in clergy training, but such content seems lacking or is limited by various internal and external restrictions.

Prevalence. When seminary course offerings were surveyed in the early 1980s, only a small number of courses included the term sex or sexuality in their title or description (McCann-Winter 1983). It might be assumed that sexual content is included in courses not so named, but this low prevalence still indicates that sexuality content is not prevalent in most clergy training programs.

A review of literature on training in pastoral counseling cites one study in which 50 to 80 percent of the sampled clergy thought their training in pastoral counseling was inadequate and did not equip them to deal with marital counseling issues (Weaver, 1995). A study by Allen and Cole (1975) comparing samples of Protestant seminary students in 1962 and 1971 found that the students in the more recent sample did not perceive themselves as better trained in family-planning issues than those students in 1962. A recent study by Goodson (1996) documented that 82 percent of the Protestant seminary students surveyed declared having had zero hours of training in family planning in their seminaries, and 66 percent expressed desire for more training on this topic.

When seminary faculty members who include some aspect of sexuality in their courses were interviewed (Conklin, 1995), they indicated that they did not identify themselves as sexuality educators, and they expressed anxiety about how their teaching of sexuality content would be viewed by others. Yet, they expressed optimism and hope, because sexuality content and courses are sought and positively evaluated by students, even though not required. There is eagerness and enthusiasm by students, congregants, and clergy to have sexuality issues addressed openly and to move in the direction of health, justice, and wholeness.

Content. Profound changes have occurred in the past four decades regarding sexuality education in seminaries. Resources which were once viewed as advantageous are now seen as outdated. More use is being made of commercial films, literature, and case studies. Printed materials with sexuality content have vastly increased in both quantity and quality. The Sexual

Attitude Reassessment (SAR) model, providing intense and condensed exposure to a range of explicit materials, panels, and speakers interspersed with small-group processing, is still viewed with both affirmation as effective and with suspicion as risky (Rosser et al. 1995).

Increased awareness of the pervasiveness of negative outcomes related to sexuality has provided the impetus for continuing-education require- ments, mandatory screening of various sorts, development of training programs, trainers, centers, and professional counselors, therapists, and consultants focusing on prevention of various kinds of violations. An un- derstanding of sexuality based upon the content of sexual relationships, rather than the form of sexual acts, is described as a paradigmatic change now underway.

In the Conklin study (1995), sexual orientation and related terms were included, either as central concerns or peripherally, in all but one of the thirty-nine interviews with seminary faculty. Prevention of harm seemed a more common goal than promotion of sexual health, and resources, language, and experiences for classroom use which focus on positive aspects of sexuality seem to be lacking. Examples of content frequently mentioned in the interviews included sexual violence, such as rape, abuse, and incest, sexual harassment and misconduct, sexually transmitted diseases, and sexual compulsivity. Content having religious connections included ordi- nation, celibacy, incarnation, sexual theology, and sacrament.

Support and Resistance. While the need for professional sexuality education within seminaries has been documented in a few studies, and Conklin's qualitative assessment has indicated strong faculty support for teaching sexuality content, some resistance is still expected. Limitations may arise from diverse sources, such as denominational executives and curriculum committees, seminary reward and assignment systems for faculty, financial restrictions, and students' reluctance to deal with sexual issues or be in value conflict with their institution or instructor's teaching.

Goodson's survey (1996) of the attitudes of Protestant seminary stu- dents toward family planning identified 4.5 percent of conservative stu- dents, as compared to 0.9 percent of non-conservative students ($p < .05$), espousing unfavorable views of family planning, and potentially opposing its teaching in seminary. With this same sample, when analyzing a statistical model to predict intention to promote family planning in their future careers, the variable "attitudes toward sexuality" emerged as a strong mediator of the relationship between the variables "religious beliefs" and "attitudes toward family planning." While "religious beliefs" exhibited a correlation of 0.81 with the "attitudes toward sexuality" variable, conser- vative students had, on average, more negative views of sexuality when compared to their non-conservative counterparts. The difference was statistically large: 1.04 standard deviation units, and significant at the 0.001 level of probability.

Resources and Intervention Needs. Given these findings, it is clear that religious beliefs need to be considered when selecting resources and planning interventions. At present, it seems broad-based support for sexuality education comes from insurers encouraging risk-reduction measures to prevent actionable behaviors which could lead to claims or litigation. Some administrative encouragement of faculty efforts has been reported, especially in response to student pressure or suggestions from peers or superiors. However, this support seems to be far outweighed by administrative indifference or caution, although perceived hostility has decreased.

A high standard has been set by faculty members who have taught and written about sexuality. Impetus to do more, not less, seems dominant, especially among faculty. However, no one has clearly articulated as a unified plan of action what there should be more of in this area. There is, however, some openness toward planning and development rather than a rigid adherence to an already conceived plan or model. A current resource encouraging the development of plans or models is the Center for Sexuality and Religion in Wayne, Pennsylvania.

As we see it, a two-pronged approach to sexuality education is needed, in which promotion of assets and prevention of deficits are both necessary (Conklin 1995). Clearly, the main assets of Protestant and Catholic churches include their nurturing, caring, and supportive environments, as well as maintenance of centers for dissemination of knowledge and training of their leaders. Nevertheless, such training has been characterized as deficient, and the need to plan, implement, and evaluate appropriate sexuality programs is notorious. The outcomes of a successful two-pronged intervention, which balances emphasis on both sexual health and sexual harm, may be worth pursuing, if we consider the important role clergy and churches have had and may continue to have in promoting the health and well-being of people in this country.

A Door to the Future: Sexuality on the Information Superhighway

Sexuality and the Internet   SANDRA BARGAINNIER

People interested in sexual topics have always been quick to explore a new mode of communication—from graffiti on a prehistoric cave wall, movable type, photography, and radio, to video cameras, VCRs, and videocassette rentals and sales—as a way around the censorship society uses to regulate and limit the dissemination of sexual information. The most recent new mode of communication, the computer-based "information superhighway," the Internet or simply "the Net," is no exception. From its birth, the Net has raised images of erotica, pornography, and cybersex available in the privacy of one's home. The Net does provide sexuality information for the general "on-line" public, but it can also provide a wealth of reliable information for sex researchers, sex educators, and sex therapists. However, the use of the Net to access sexuality information has also brought the inevitable sequel of society's effort to regulate this new avenue of sex information.

The Internet is not a physical or tangible entity, but rather a giant network which interconnects innumerable smaller groups of linked computer networks. In early 1995, the global network of the Internet had 2 million Internet hosts; in late 1995-1996, 5 million hosts; and in early 1996, 9.5 million hosts. This is expected to double to 20 million hosts sometime in 1997. However, the number of Internet hosts is misleading, because many hosts limit access of their users with firewalls and other electronic barriers.

Gateways to a variety of electronic messaging services allow Internet users to communicate with over 15 million educational, commercial, government, military, and other types of users throughout the worldwide matrix of computer networks that exchange mail or news. These rapidly developing, and constantly changing, network information and retrieval tools are transforming the way people learn, interact, and relate. These networks provide users with easy access to documents, sounds, images, and other file-system data; library catalog and user-directory data; weather, geography, and physical-science data; and other types of information (Schwartz and Quarterman 1993). Professional journals, papers, conferences, courses, and dialogues are increasingly delivered electronically.

Although the federal government initiated the Internet during the "Cold War" as a way to send top-secret information quickly and securely, no government or group controls or is in charge of the Internet today. The Internet depends on the continuing cooperation of all the interconnected networks (Butler 1994). Because there is no proprietary control, anyone can send e-mail (electronic mail), start a newsgroup, develop a listserv, download files, and/or have their own World Wide Web (WWW) home page or Web site. This freedom has opened the cyberspace doors to the sexuality arena.

For sexuality professionals, the opportunities in cyberspace are limitless. E-mail is just one of many functions. This one-on-one mode of electronic communication allows colleagues to communicate and collaborate in their research worldwide, pursue new leads quickly, test new ideas and hypotheses immediately, and build networks of like-minded colleagues. Whole documents can be attached to e-mail, sent electronically around the globe, and downloaded by the recipients almost instantly. Both time and money can be saved by editing on-line and bypassing postal delays and costs.

Many American university professors communicate with their students by e-mail. Lessons, syllabi, and homework are passed back and forth with e-mail. E-mail can also provide the shy or quiet students in a class another venue for participation.

Listserv mailing lists are similar to e-mail, but instead of communicating with only one other person, communication takes place between many. Many Americans of all ages subscribe to a mailing list and use it as a good place to debate issues, share professional ideas, and try out new concepts with others. Subscribers automatically receive correspondence from others who belong to the list. It is like reading everyone's e-mail about a particular topic. Hundreds of listservs exist, including those that address rape, gay and bisexual issues, feminist theory, women's health, AIDS, addictions, survivors of incest, and advocacy, to name a few.

In addition to sending e-mail to individuals or to a mailing list, Americans are increasingly meeting people and sharing interests through newsgroups. Like listservs, newsgroups are open discussions and exchanges on particular topics. Users, however, need not subscribe to the discussion mailing list in advance, but can instead access the database at any time (Butler 1994). One must access a special program called a news reader to retrieve messages/discussions from a newsgroup. A local site may have many newsgroups or a few.

Newsgroups are as diverse as the individuals posting on them. Usenet newsgroups are arranged in a hierarchical order, with their names describing their area of interest. The major hierarchies are talk, alt, biz, soc, news, rec, sci, comp, and misc. Some examples of newsgroups in the field of sexuality are: sci.med.aids, talk.abortion, soc.women, soc.men, soc.bi, alt.sex, alt.transgendered, alt.sexual.abuse.recovery, and alt.politics.homosexuality. This hierarchy and system of naming help the user decide which groups may be of interest.

Many groups provide informative discussions and support. Other groups are often magnets for "flamers" (those who insult) or people posing as someone else (i.e., a young adult male posing on-line as a lesbian). One benefit of the newsgroup is that anyone can read the articles/discussions but not participate. These voyeurs are called "lurkers." This may be a safe starting point for a few months until one has an understanding of the group, their history, and past discussions. "Newbies" (newcomers to groups) are often flamed if they ask neophyte questions in some newsgroups. Reading a newsgroup's "FAQ" (frequently asked questions) page prior to inquiring on-line is one way newbies can avoid being flamed for naive or inappropriate inquiries.

In addition to transmitting messages that can be read or accessed later, Internet users can also engage in an immediate dialogue (called "chat") in "real time" with other users. Real-time communication allows one-to-one communication, and "Internet Relay Chat" (IRC) allows two or more people to type messages to each other that almost immediately appear on the other's computer screen. IRC is analogous to a telephone party line. In addition, most commercial on-line services have their own chat systems allowing members to converse. An example of a chat system is the Human Sexuality Forum on CompuServe, a proprietary on-line network that also offers members access to the Internet.

In addition to e-mail, newsgroups, listservs, and chats, one can access information by transferring files from one computer to another with FTP (file transfer protocol). One important aspect of FTP is that it allows files to be transferred between computers of completely dissimilar types. It also provides public file sharing (*The Internet Unleashed*, 1994). These files may contain text, pictures, sound, or computer programs.

Another method of connecting with remote locations is through Telnet. Telnet allows the user to "log in" on a remote machine in real time. For example, a student can use Telnet to connect to a remote library to access the library's online card catalog.

American sexuality professionals now communicate, collaborate, and discuss issues with colleagues around the globe. They can also access information from around the world. Two of the more common methods for accessing information are Gopher and the World Wide Web (WWW). A user can collect data, read conference proceedings, tap into libraries, and even search for jobs on-line.

Gopher guides an individual's search through the resources available on a remote computer. It is menu driven and easy to use. Most American colleges and universities have a local Gopher menu. Gopher can also be accessed through most commercial on-line services. Gopher allows users to access information from various locations. The National Institute for Health, the Centers for Disease Control and Prevention, and the National Library of Medicine are just a few examples of sites that are accessible via Gopher.

Most information sites that can be reached through Gopher can also be accessed via the World Wide Web (WWW). The "Web" uses a "hypertext" formatting language called hypertext markup language (HTML). Programs called Web browsers that "browse" the Web can display HTML documents containing text, images, sound, animation, and moving video. Any HTML document can include links to other types of information or resources. These hypertext links allow information to be accessed and organized in very flexible ways, and allow people to locate and efficiently view related information, even if the information is stored on numerous computers all around the world.

Many organizations now have "home pages" on the Web. The home page typically serves as a table of contents for the site, and provides links to other similar sites. Some Web sites that may be of interest to the sexuality professional are: the Society for the Scientific Study of Sexuality (SSSS) [http://www.ssc.wisc.edu/ssss/]; the Kinsey Institute [http://www.indiana.edu/~kinsey/]; the Sexuality Information and Education Council of the United States (SIECUS) [http://www.siecus.org/]; the Queer Resources Directory [http://www.qrd.org/qrd/]; and Tstar [http://travesti.geophys.mcgill.ca/~tstar/]. TStar provides resources and information for the transgendered community. The TStar home page is also a gateway to other resources on the Web, such as the Lesbian, Gay, Transgendered Alliance, and the Gay, Bi-Sexual, Lesbian, and Transgender

Information from the United Kingdom. [*The SexQuest Web Index for Sexual Health* provides links to most sexuality research, education, and therapy sites on the Web: http://www.SexQuest.com/SexQuest.html. (Editor)]

Sex researchers, educators, and therapists can use e-mail, listservs, newsgroups, and the WWW for updated information and resources. Sexuality professionals can also use the Internet as a new frontier for sex research. Approximately 200 active Usenet newsgroups deal with sex and variations of some sexual theme (Tamosaitis 1995). Very few have researched who these newsgroup users are, what sexuality knowledge they possess, what sexual attitudes they hold, or in which types of behavior they engage.

In the fall of 1994, a modified version of the Kinsey Institute Sex Knowledge Test was distributed to 4,000 users on-line (Tamosaitis 1995). The results showed that over 83 percent were male, white, highly educated, single, middle- to upper-class, and not afraid of technology. The majority were in their 20s and 30s and predominantly bicoastal, with 63 percent living either on the West or East coasts. The survey demonstrated that both the sexually oriented and general on-line user group respondents are more knowledgeable about women's sexuality issues than they are about comparable men's issues when compared to the general off-line population polled (Tamosaitis 1995). This study, the first of its kind, could provide the impetus for further on-line research. Of the twenty most popular Usenet newsgroup forums, half are on sex-related topics (Lewis 1995).

Several universities are also concerned about sexually explicit material and are limiting or prohibiting access to certain newsgroups. In November 1994, Carnegie Mellon University moved to eliminate all sexually oriented Usenet newsgroups from its computers. Stanford, Penn State, Iowa State and other universities have also attempted to limit access (Tamosaitis 1995).

Legal Challenges to Free Speech on the Internet   BARBARA GARRIS

Politically, any mention of sexuality in international cyberspace, from the most benign to the most perverse, is currently under scrutiny in the Supreme Court. In June 1995, Senator James Exon offered the Communications Decency Act of 1995 as an amendment to the Telecommunications Act of 1996, which was then included in the Telecom Act as Title 5, Section 507. The Communications Decency Act (CDA) expands regulations on obscene and indecent material to minors which would be transmitted to them through the telephone lines by way of the worldwide Internet, or any other on-line service (Itialiano 1996; Lewis 1995; Lohn 1996).

The bill included, in a very subtle unthreatening way, elements of the old Comstock Act of 1873 which, in the past, made it a crime to send material on birth control and abortion through the postal service (Schwartz 1996a). This archaic act, inserted by Representative Henry J. Hyde, a longtime abortion foe, remains on the legislative books today as 18 U.S.C. Sec. 1462. Elements of the Comstock Act prohibiting dissemination of contraceptive information and the sale of contraceptives to married and single women had been declared unconstitutional in various decisions, the last two in 1966 and 1972. However, the prohibition against providing information about abortion remains on the books to the present. In the new Communications Decency Act, the maximum fine for providing information about abortion has been raised from $5,000 to $250,000 for anyone convicted of knowingly transmitting any "obscene, lewd, lascivious, filthy, or indecent" communications on the nation's telecommunications networks including the Internet. Meanwhile, other legislators sponsored legislation, the Comstock Clean-up Act of 1996, to repeal completely the remnants of the Comstock Act.

The Telecommunications Act of 1996 was signed by President Clinton on February 8, 1996. Although the President signed the bill into law, he immediately issued a disclaimer, saying that

> I do object to the provision in the Act concerning the transmission of abortion related speech and information. . . . The Department of Justice has advised me of its long-standing policy that this and related abortion provisions in current law are unconstitutional and will not be enforced because they violate the First Amendment [protecting freedom of speech].

The CDA was included in the Telecommunications Act supposedly to squelch on-line pornography and make the World Wide Web and the Internet, as well as other on-line services, "safe" for children. But the wording crafted by Internet-illiterate congressmen was so vague and overly broad that even the most innocent use of health-related information could result in a $250,000 fine and two years in prison. Free-speech activists, spearedheaded by the American Civil Liberties Union, Electronic Freedom Foundation, American Library Association, and many others, were appalled and filed suit to keep at bay any prosecution and punishment for this alleged on-line crime until the case can be heard by the United States Supreme Court.

Suit was immediately filed by the American Library Association and the Citizen's Internet Empowerment Coalition in the United States District Court for the Eastern District of Pennsylvania seeking a preliminary injunction against the CDA on the constitutional grounds of the right to free speech. "Plaintiffs include various organizations and individuals who, inter alia, are associated with the computer and/or communications industries, or who publish or post materials on the Internet, or belong to various citizen groups." The case was heard before Judge Sloviter, Chief Judge, United States Court of Appeals for the Third Circuit, and Judges Buckwalter and Dalzell, Judges for the Eastern District of Pennsylvania.

An injunction was granted on June 11, 1996, after all three judges had schooled themselves with hands-on experience with the Internet. The basis for the injunction was three-fold:

1. That whatever previous decisions had been handed down limiting indecent expression on other media (such as cable television and radio) could not be applied to cyberspace,
2. Control over pornography aimed at children rested with the parents and schools, not with the government nor with on-line services transmitting the offensive material, and
3. There was no technological way available to the Internet of checking the age of Internet users, except the use of credit card numbers, to access hard-core pornography.

All three judges saw the CDA as patently unconstitutional and asked the Supreme Court for a final ruling (EPIC 1996; McCullaugh 1996; *The New York Times* 1996; Quinttner 1996; Schwartz 1996b).

On July 1, 1996, the U.S. Department of Justice officially filed an appeal. In its September 30, 1996, edition, *HotWired* magazine reported that the U.S. Department of Justice was stalling for time, and the U.S. Supreme Court granted them an extra month to submit filings. The case was supposed to have been heard in the Supreme Court in October 1996, but no new hearing date had been published as of November 1996. As of March 1997, the CDA was going to the Supreme Court, with a decision expected in June.

Judge Dalzell's opinion sums up the on-going debate over sex on the Internet:

> True it is that many find some of the speech on the Internet to be offensive, and amid the din of cyberspace many hear discordant voices that they regard as indecent. The absence of govermental regulation of Internet content has unquestionably produced a kind of chaos, but as one of plaintiffs' experts put it with such resonance at the hearing: "What achieved success was the very chaos that the Internet is. The strength of the Internet is that chaos."
>
> Just as the strength of the Internet is chaos, so the strength of our liberty depends upon the chaos and cacophony of the unfettered speech the First Amendment protects.
>
> For these reasons, I without hesitation hold that the CDA is unconstitutional on its face.

Since the filing of this case, three other state cases have been brought to court. A New York City case, filed April 30, 1996, by Joe Shea, reporter for the *American Reporter*, sought to overturn the CDA, claiming that the law limits freedom of speech for the press. On July 29, 1996, the court ruled in favor of Shea. This case is expected to be folded into the primary case brought to the Supreme Court by the American Civil Liberties Union (ACLU) et al. suit mentioned above. At the same time, journalism professor Bill Loving of the University of Oklahoma filed suit against the university charging that it blocked access on April 1, 1996 to a newsgroup, "alt.sex," after the university received complaints from a fundamentalist religious organization. Loving claimed that restricting students' access to the Internet is a violation of their First Amendment rights. (As of late 1996, he was awaiting the University's response.) Finally, effective July 1, 1996, the Georgia State General Assembly passed a law providing criminal sanctions against anyone falsely identifying themselves on the Internet. A suit (*ACLU of Georgia et al. vs. Miller et al.*), seeking a preliminary injunction against the Georgia statue, was filed September 24, 1996, by the ACLU, Electronic Frontiers Georgia, Georgia State Representative Mitchell Kaye, and others. As of late 1996, the hearing had not been held.

Summing Up   SANDRA BARGAINNIER

What is considered sexually explicit? Are safe-sex guidelines considered sexually explicit? Obviously, this type of law could disband the educational and informative sex-related Internet resources and the sex-related newsgroups.

Another concern associated with the Internet is the loss of community in the real world and the formation of on-line communities. Opponents believe that people are not honest about who they are in cyberspace, which is a fantasy land. Proponents say that virtual communities provide a place for support, information, and understanding. Many feel that gender, race, age, orientation, and physical appearance are not apparent in cyberspace unless a person wants to make such characteristics public. People with physical disabilities or less-than-glamorous appearances find that virtual communities treat them as they always wanted to be treated—as thinkers and transmitters of ideas and feelings, not just an able body or a face (Rheingold 1995). Many young people can be part of a community for the first time in their life by interacting with an on-line community. An on-line community might, for example, provide a teenage lesbian who feels alienated at school and home with a sense of self-worth and understanding.

Not since the invention of television has a technology changed how a nation and a world spend their time, gather information, and communicate, as has the Internet. Sexuality professionals and the public have the capacity to access tremendous amounts of sexual information, some of it valid and educational, some of it entertaining, and some that others might label "obscene." But who is to judge? Sexuality professionals need to get involved before others judge what is deemed acceptable sexuality information. The Internet will also serve as a new frontier for sex research, sex education, sex information, collaboration, and communication (Tamosaitis 1995).

References and Suggested Readings*

Adler, J. 1994 (January 10). "Farewell, Year of the Creep." *Newsweek*, 59.

Ahlburg, D. A., and C. J. DeVita. 1992. "New Realities of the American Family." *Population Bulletin*, 47(2).

Alan Guttmacher Institute. 1991. *Abortion in the United States: Facts in Brief.* New York: Alan Guttmacher Institute.

Alberda, R., and C. Tilly. 1992. "All in the Family: Family Types, Access to Income, and Family Income Policies." *Policy Studies Journal*, 20(3):388-404.

Alcalay, R., P. M. Sniderman, J. Mitchell, and R. Griffin. 1990. "Ethnic Differences in Knowledge of AIDS Transmission and Attitudes Among Gays and People with AIDS." *International Quarterly of Community Health Education*, 10(3):213-222.

Alcorn, R. C. 1990. *Is Rescuing Right? Breaking the Law to Save the Unborn.* Downers Grove, IL: InterVarsity Press.

Alexander, J. M. 1992 (April). "Meeting Changing STD Counseling Needs: A Glossary of Contemporary Mexican Sexual Terms." Prepared for the Resource Book of the Third Annual New Orleans HIV/AIDS Conference for Primary Health Care Providers.

Allen, J. E., and L. P. Cole. 1975. "Clergy Skills in Family-Planning Education and Counseling." *Journal of Religion and Health*, 14(3):198-205.

Allen, N. 1978 (June). "Sex Therapy and the Single Woman." *Forum*, pp. 44-48.

Allen, W. R., and B. A. Agbasegbe. 1980. "A Comment on Scott's 'Black Polygamous Family Formation.'" *Alternative Lifestyles*, 3:375-381.

Allgeier, A. R., and E. R. Allgeier. 1988. *Sexual Interactions* (2nd ed.). Lexington, MA: D. C. Heath.

Allison, J. A., and L. S. Wrightsman. 1993. *Rape: The Misunderstood Crime.* Newbury Park, CA: Sage Publications.

Altman, L. K. 1997 (February 28). "U.S. Reporting Sharp Decrease in AIDS Deaths." *The New York Times*, pp. A1 and A24.

Amaro, I. 1991. *Hispanic Sexual Behavior: Implications for Research and HIV Prevention.* Washington, DC: National Coalition of Hispanic Health and Human Services Organizations.

American Association of Sex Educators, Counselors, and Therapists (AASECT). 1978 (March, rev.). *AASECT Code of Ethics.* Washington, DC: Author.

American Association of Sex Educators, Counselors, and Therapists (AASECT). 1987. *AASECT Code of Ethics.* Washington, DC: Author.

American Psychiatric Association. 1980. *Diagnostic and Statistical Manual of Mental Disorders III (DSM III)* (3rd ed. 302.81, pp. 268). Washington, DC: American Psychiatric Association.

American Psychiatric Association. 1994. *Diagnostic and Statistical Manual of Mental Disorders* (4th ed.). Washington, DC: American Psychiatric Association.

Amir, M. 1971. *Patterns in Forcible Rape.* Chicago: University of Chicago Press.

Anderson, P. B., D. de Mauro, and R. J. Noonan, eds. 1996. *Does Anyone Still Remember When Sex Was Fun? Positive Sexuality in the Age of AIDS* (3rd ed.). Dubuque, IA: Kendall/Hunt Publishing Co.

Aneshensel, C. S., R. M. Becerra, E. P. Fiedler, and R. H. Schuler. 1990. "Onset of Fertility Related Events during Adolescence: A Prospective Comparison of Mexican American and Non-Hispanic White Females." *American Journal of Public Health*, 80(8):959-963.

Annon, J. S. 1974. *The Behavioral Treatment of Sexual Problems Volume 1: Brief Therapy.* Honolulu, HI: Kapiolani Health Services.

*Acknowledgment: The *Encyclopedia* editor appreciates the assistance of William Taverner, M.Ed., in checking many of the bibliographic references in this and other chapters of the *Encyclopedia*.

Ansen, D. 1994 (April 18). "Boy Meets Girl Meets Boy." *Newsweek*, p. 60.

Apfelbaum, B. 1977. "The Myth of the Surrogate." *Journal of Sex Research*, 13(4):238-249.

Apfelbaum, B. 1984. "The Ego-Analytic Approach to Individual Body-Work Sex Therapy: Five Case Examples." *Journal of Sex Research*, 20(1):44-70.

Asbell, B. 1995. *The Pill: A Biography of the Drug that Changed the World*. New York: Random House.

Atwater, L. 1982. *The Extramarital Connection: Sex, Intimacy, and Identity*. New York: Irvington.

Baldwin, W. 1980. "The Fertility of Young Adolescents." *Journal of Adolescent Health Care*, 1:54-59.

Barbach, L. 1980. *Women Discover Orgasm: A Therapist's Guide to a New Treatment Approach*. New York: Free Press.

Barry, K. 1984. *Female Sexual Slavery*. New York: New York University Press.

Bart, P. B., and P. H. O'Brien. 1985. "Stopping Rape: Effective Avoidance Strategies." *Signs*, 10:83-101.

Bartell, G. D. 1971. *Group Sex: A Scientist's Eyewitness Report on the American Way of Swinging*. New York: Wyden.

Bauman, K. E., and R. R. Wilson. 1974. "Sexual Behavior of Unmarried University Students in 1968 and 1972." *Journal of Sex Research*, 10:327-333.

Beach, R. A. 1976. "Sexual Attractivity, Proceptivity and Receptivity in Female Mammals." *Hormones and Behavior*, 7:105-138.

Beitchman, J. H., K. Zucker, J. Hood, G. DaCosta, and D. Akman. 1991. "A Review of the Short-Term Effects of Childhood Sexual Abuse." *Child Abuse and Neglect*, 15:537-556.

Beitchman, J. H., et al. 1992. "A Review of the Long-Term Effects of Child Sexual Abuse." *Child Abuse and Neglect*, 16:101-118.

Belcastro, P. A. 1985. "Sexual Behavior Differences Between Black and White Students." *Journal of Sex Research*, 21:56-67.

Bell, A. P.1968 (October). "Black Sexuality: Fact and Fancy." Paper presented to Focus: Black American Series, Indiana University, Bloomington, IN.

Bell, A. P., and M. Weinberg. 1978. *Homosexualities: A Study of Diversity Among Men and Women*. New York: Simon and Schuster.

Bell, A. P., M. S. Weinberg, and S. K. Hammersmith. 1981. *Sexual Preference: Its Development in Men and Women*. Bloomington, IN: Indiana University Press.

Bell, R. R., and P. I. Bell. 1972 (December). "Sexual Satisfaction Among Married Women." *Medical Aspects of Human Sexuality*, 136-144.

Bell, R., and J. B. Chaskes. 1968. "Premarital Sexual Experience Among Coeds, 1958 and 1968." *Journal of Marriage and the Family*, 30:81-84.

Bell, R. R., S. Turner, and L. Rosen. 1975. "A Multivariate Analysis of Female Extramarital Coitus." *Journal of Marriage and the Family*, 37(2):375-384.

Berger, R. J., P. Seales, and C. E. Cottle. 1991. *Pornography*. New York: Praeger.

Bergler, E. 1956. *Homosexuality: Disease or Way of Life*. New York: Collier.

Berkowitz, A. 1992. "College Men as Perpetrators of Acquaintance Rape and Sexual Assault: A Review of Recent Research." *Journal of American College Health*, 40:175-181.

Bernstein, A. C., and P. A. Cowan. 1975. "Children's Concepts of How People Get Babies." *Child Development*, 46:77-91.

Berscheid, E. 1983. "Emotion." In H. H. Kelley, et al., eds. *Close Relationships* (pp. 110-168). New York: W. H. Freeman and Co.

Biale, D. 1992. *Eros and the Jews: From Biblical Israel to Contemporary American*. New York: Basic Books.

Biddlecom, A. E., and A. M. Hardy. 1991. "AIDS Knowledge and Attitudes of Hispanic Americans: United States, 1990." *Advance Data. Number 207*. Washington, DC: U.S. Department of Health and Human Services.

Billy, J. O. G., K. Tanfer, W. R. Grady, and D. H. Klepinger. 1992. "Sexual Behavior of Men in the United States." *Family Planning Perspectives*, 25(2):52-60.

Bishop, P. D., and A. Lipsitz. 1991. "Sexual Behavior Among College Students in the AIDS Era: A Comparative Study." *Journal of Psychology and Human Sexuality*, 4:467-476.

Blanchard, R. and S. J. Hucker. 1991 (September0. "Age, Transvestism, Bondage, and Concurrent Paraphilic Activities in 117 Fatal Cases of Autoerotic Asphyxia." *British Journal of Psychiatry*, 159:371-377.

Blumstein, P., and P. Schwartz. 1983. *American Couples*. New York: William Morrow.

Bolin, A. 1988. *In Search of Eve: Transsexual Rites of Passage*. South Hadley, MA: Bergin and Garvey Publishers.

Bonilla, L., and J. Porter. 1990. "A Comparison of Latino, Black, and Non-Hispanic White Attitudes Toward Homosexuality. Hispanic." *Journal of Behavioral Sciences*, 12(4):437-452.

Boswell, J. 1980. *Christianity, Social Tolerance, and Homosexuality*. Chicago: University of Chicago Press.

Boswell, J. 1994. *Same-Sex Unions in Premodern Europe*. New York: Villard Books.

Brand, P. A., and A. H. Kidd. 1986. "Frequency of Physical Aggression in Heterosexual and Female Homosexual Dyads." *Psychological Reports*, 59:1307-1313.

Brandt, A. M. 1988. AIDS and Metaphor. *Social Research*, 55(3, Autumn), p. 430. Cited in M. Fumento, 1990, *The Myth of Heterosexual AIDS*. New York: Basic Books.

Braun, S. ed. 1975. *Catalog of Sexual Consciousness* (pp. 135-137). New York: Grove Press.

Brayshaw, A. J. 1962. "Middle-Aged Marriage: Idealism, Realism, and the Search for Meaning." *Marriage and Family Living*, 24:358-364.

Brecher, E. M. 1979. *The Sex Researchers*. San Francisco: Specific Press.

Brecher, E. M., and the Editors of Consumer Reports Books. 1984. *Love, Sex, and Aging: A Consumer Union Report*. Boston: Little, Brown.

Bretschneider, J. G., and N. L. McCoy. 1988. "Sexual Interest and Behavior in Healthy 80- to 101-year-olds." *Archives of Sexual Behavior*, 17(2):109-129.

Brett, G. H. 1993. "Networked Information Retrieval Tools in the Academic Environment: Towards a Cybernetic Library." *Internet Research*, 3(3):26-36.

Brindis, C. 1992. "Adolescent Pregnancy Prevention for Hispanic Youth: The Role of Schools, Families, and Communities." *Journal of School Health*, 62(7):345-351.

Brindis, C. 1997. "Adolescent Pregnancy Prevention for Hispanic Youth. *The Prevention Researcher*, 4(1):8-10.

Brindis, C., A. L. Wolfe, V. McCater, and S. Ball. 1995. "The Association Between Immigrant Status and Risk-Behavior Patterns in Latino Adolescents." *Journal of Adolescent Health*, 17(2):99-105.

Bringle, R. G. 1991. "Psychosocial Aspects of Jealousy: A Transactional Model." In P. Salovey, ed. *The Psychology of Jealousy and Envy* (pp. 103-131). New York: Guilford Press.

Bringle, R. G., and K. L. G. Boebinger. 1990. "Jealousy and the 'Third' Person in the Love Triangle." *Journal of Social and Personal Relationships*, 7:119-133.

Broderick, C. B. 1965. "Social Heterosexual Development Among Urban Negroes and Whites." *Journal of Marriage and the Family*, 27(2):200-203.

Broderick, C. B. 1966a. "Socio-Sexual Development in a Suburban Community." *Journal of Sex Research*, 2:1-24.

Broderick, C. B. 1966b. "Sexual Behavior Among Pre-Adolescents." *Journal of Social Issues*, 22:6-21.

Broderick, C. B., and S. E. Fowler. 1961. "New Patterns of Relationships Between the Sexes Among Preadolescents." *Marriage and Family Living*, 23:27-30.

Brodie, J. F. 1994. *Contraception and Abortion in Nineteenth-Century America*. Ithaca, NY: Cornell University Press.

Brody, S. 1995. "Lack of Evidence for Transmission of Human Immunodeficiency Virus Through Vaginal Intercourse." *Archives of Sexual Behavior*, 24(4):383-393.

Brooks-Gunn, J., and F. F. Furstenberg. 1989. "Adolescent Sexual Behavior. *American Psychologist*, 44:249-259.

Brown, D. A. 1981. "An Interview with a Sex Surrogate." In D. A. Brown & C. Chary, eds. *Sexuality in America* (pp. 301-317). Ann Arbor, MI: Greenfield Books.

Browne, A., and D. Finkelhor. 1986. "Impact of Child Sexual Abuse: A Review of Research." *Psychological Bulletin*, 99:66-77.

Brownmiller, S. 1975. *Against Our Will: Men, Women, and Rape* New York: Bantam.

Bukstel, L. H., G. D. Roeder, P. R. Kilmann, J. Laughlin, and W. M. Sotile. 1978. "Projected Extramarital Sexual Involvement in Unmarried College Students." *Journal of Marriage and the Family*, 40:337-340.

Bullough, V. L. 1994. *Science in the Bedroom: A History of Sex Research.* New York: Basic Books.

Bullough, V. L., and B. Bullough. 1987. *Women and Prostitution: A Social History.* Buffalo, NY: Prometheus Press.

Bullough, V. L., and B. Bullough. 1992. *Annotated Bibliography of Prostitution, 1970-1992.* New York: Garland.

Bullough, V. L., and B. Bullough. 1993. *Cross Dressing, Sex, and Gender.* Philadelphia: University of Pennsylvania Press.

Bullough, V. L., and B. Bullough. 1994a. "Prostitution." In V. L. Bullough and B. Bullough, eds. *Human Sexuality: An Encyclopedia.* New York: Garland Publishing.

Bullough, V. L., and B. Bullough. 1994b. "Cross-dressing." In V. L. Bullough and B. Bullough, eds. *Human Sexuality: An Encyclopedia* (pp. 156-160). New York: Garland Publishing.

Bureau of Justice Statistics. 1993. *Sourcebook of Criminal Justice Statistics—1992.* Washington, DC: U.S. Government Printing Office.

Burgess, E. W., and P. Wallin. 1953. *Engagement and Marriage.* Philadelphia: Lippincott.

Burt, M. R. 1991. "Rape Myths and Acquaintance Rape." In A. Parrot and L. Bechhofer, eds. *Acquaintance Rape: The Hidden Crime.* New York: Wiley.

Buss, D. M. 1994. *The Evolution of Desire: Strategies of Human Mating.* New York: Basic Books.

Butler, M. 1994. *How to Use the Internet.* Emeryville. CA: Ziff & Davis Press.

Buunk, B. 1980. "Sexually Open Marriages: Ground Rules for Countering Potential Threats to Marriage." *Alternative Lifestyles*, 3:312-328.

Buunk, B. 1981. "Jealousy in Sexually Open Marriages." *Alternative Lifestyles*, 4:357-372.

Buunk, B. 1982. "Strategies of Jealousy: Styles of Coping with Extramarital Involvement of the Spouse." *Family Relations*, 31:13-18.

Byrne, D., and W. A. Fisher. eds. 1983. *Adolescents, Sex, and Contraception.* Hillsdale, NJ: Erlbaum.

Call, V., S. Sprecher, and P. Schwartz. 1995. "The Incidence and Frequency of Marital Sex in a National Sample." *Journal of Marriage and the Family*, 57:639-652.

Cannon, K. L., and R. Long. 1971. "Premarital Sexual Behavior in the Sixties." *Journal of Marriage and the Family*, 33:36-49.

Carballo-DiÉguez, A. 1989. "Hispanic Culture, Gay Male Culture, and AIDS: Counseling Implications." *Journal of Counseling and Development*, 68:26-30.

Carrier, J. M. 1976. "Cultural Factors Affecting Urban Mexican Male Homosexual Behavior." *Archives of Sexual Behavior*, 5(2):103-124.

Carrier, J. M., and R. Bolton. 1987. "Anthropological Perspectives on Sexuality and HIV Prevention." *Annual Review of Sex Research*, 2:49-75.

Carrier, J. M., and J. R. Magaña. 1991. Use of Ethnosexual Data on Men of Mexican Origin for HIV/AIDS Prevention Programs. *Journal of Sex Research*, 28(2):189-202.

Castex, G. M. 1994. "Providing Services to Hispanic/Latino Populations: Profiles in Diversity." *Social Work*, 39(3):288-296.

Cazenave, N. A. 1979. "Social Structure and Personal Choice: Effects on Intimacy, Marriage and the Family Alternative Lifestyle Research." *Alternative Lifestyles*, 2:331-358.

Cazenave, N. A. 1981. "Black Men in America: The Quest for Manhood." In H. P. McAdoo, ed. *Black Families* (pp. 176-185). Beverly Hills: Sage.

Centers for Disease Control. 1992. "HIV Infection, Syphilis, Tuberculosis, Screening Among Migrant Farm Workers—Florida 1992." *Morbidity and Mortality Weekly Report*, 41(39):723-725.

Centers for Disease Control. 1993a. "The Scope of the HIV/AIDS Epidemic in the United States." *Fact Sheet. (Publication no. D-534).* Rockville, MD: CDC National AIDS Clearinghouse.

Centers for Disease Control. 1993b. "HIV/AIDS and Race/Ethnicity." *Fact Sheet. (Publication no. D-293).* Rockville, MD: CDC National AIDS Clearinghouse.

Centers for Disease Control. 1993c, August. "Study of Non-Identifying Gay Men." *HIV/AIDS Prevention Newsletter*, 4(2):6-7.

Centers for Disease Control. 1994a. *HIV/AIDS Surveillance Report*, 6(2):1-39.

Centers for Disease Control. 1994b. *HIV/AIDS Surveillance Report. Year-End Edition*, 6:11.

Centers for Disease Control. 1994c. "Women and HIV/AIDS." *Fact Sheet. (Publication no. D-290).* Rockville, MD: CDC National AIDS Clearinghouse.

Centers for Disease Control. 1995a. "Update: Acquired Immunodeficiency Syndrome—United States, 1994." *Morbidity and Mortality Weekly Report*, 44(4):64-67.

Centers for Disease Control. 1995b. "Update: AIDS Among Women." *Morbidity and Mortality Weekly Report*, 44(5):81-84.

Centers for Disease Control and Prevention (CDC). 1996. *HIV/AIDS Surveillance Report, Year-End 1995 Edition*, 7(2):1-18.

Chefetz, J. S., and A. G. Dworkin. 1986. *Female Revolt: Women's Movements in the World and Historical Perspective.* New Jersey: Rowman & Allanheld.

Chideya, F., et al. 1993 (August 30). "Endangered Family." *Newsweek*, 17-27.

Choi, K. H., J. A. Catania, and M. Dolcini. 1994. "Extramarital Sex and HIV Risk Behavior Among U.S. Adults: Results from the National AIDS Behavior Survey." *American Journal of Public Health*, 84(12):2003-2007.

Christensen, F. M. 1990. *Pornography: The Other Side.* New York: Praeger.

Christensen, H. T. 1962a. "Value-Behavior Discrepancies Regarding Premarital Coitus in Three Western Cultures. *American Sociological Review*, 27:66-74.

Christensen, H. T. 1962b. "A Cross-Cultural Comparison of Attitudes Toward Marital Infidelity." *International Journal of Comparative Sociology*, 3:124-137.

Christensen, H. T. 1973. "Attitudes Toward Infidelity: A Nine-Culture Sampling of University Student Opinion." *Journal of Comparative Family Studies*, 4:197-214.

Christensen, H. T., and G. R. Carpenter. 1962. "Timing Patterns in the Development of Sexual Intimacy: An Attitudinal Report on Three Modern Western Societies." *Marriage and Family Living*, 24:30-35.

Christensen, H. T., and C. F. Gregg. 1970 (November). "Changing Sex Norms in America and Scandinavia." *Journal of Marriage and the Family*, 616-627.

Christensen, H., and L. Johnson. 1978. "Premarital Coitus and the Southern Black: A Comparative View." *Journal of Marriage and the Family*, 40:721-732.

Christopher, F. S., and R. M. Cate. 1985. "Premarital Sexual Pathways and Relationship Development." *Journal of Social and Personal Relationships*, 2:271-288.

Christopher, F. S., and R. M. Cate. 1988. "Premarital Sexual Involvement: A Developmental Investigation of Relational Correlates." *Adolescence*, 23:793-803.

Church of Jesus Christ of Latter-Day Saints. 1989. *Pearl of Great Price.* Salt Lake City, UT.

Church of Jesus Christ of Latter-Day Saints. 1990. *For the Strength of Youth.* Salt Lake City, UT.

Church News. 1978, December 16. Volume 6. Salt Lake City: Church of Jesus Christ of the Latter-Day Saints Publication.

Clark, L., and D. J. Lewis. 1977. *Rape: The Price of Coercive Sexuality.* Toronto: Women's Press.

Claude, P. 1993. "Providing Culturally Sensitive Health Care to Hispanic Clients." *Nurse Practitioner*, 18(12):40-51

Clayton, R. R., and J. L. Bokemeier. 1980. "Premarital Sex in the Seventies." *Journal of Marriage and the Family*, 42:759-776.

Cleveland, P. H. and J. Davenport. 1989 (Summer). "AIDS: A Growing Problem for Rural Communities." *Human Services in the Rural Environment*, 13(1):23-29.

Clunis, D. M., and G. D. Green. 1988. *Lesbian Couples.* Seattle, Washington: Seal Press.

Cobliner, W. G. 1974. "Pregnancy in the Single Adolescent Girl: The Role of Cognitive Functions." *Journal of Youth and Adolescence*, 3:17-29.

Cohn, B. 1994 (December 19). "Goodbye to the 'Condom Queen.'" *Newsweek*, 26-27.

Coleman, E. 1987. "Assessment of Sexual Orientation." *Journal of Homosexuality*, 14(1/2):9-24.

Coleman, E. 1991. "Compulsive Sexual Behavior: New Concepts and Treatments." *Journal of Psychology and Human Sexuality*, 4(2):37-52.

Coles, C. D., and M. J. Shamp. 1984. "Some Sexual, Personality, and Demographic Characteristics of Women Readers of Erotic Romances." *Archives of Sexual Behavior*, 13:187-209.

Conklin, S. C. 1995. *Sexuality Education of Clergy in Seminaries and Theological Schools: Perceptions of Faculty Advocates Regarding Curriculum Implications.* Unpublished doctoral dissertation. University of Pennsylvania, Philadelphia.

Constantine, L. L. 1973. *Group Marriage: A Study of Contemporary Multilateral Marriage.* New York: Macmillan.

Coontz, S. 1992. *The Way We Never Were: American Families and the Nostalgia Trap.* New York: Harper Collins Basic Books.

Cornog, M. 1994. "Appendix on Sexological Research." In V. L. Bullough and B. Bullough, eds. *Human Sexuality: An Encyclopedia* (pp. 607-617). New York: Garland Publishing.

Cornog, M., and T. Perper. 1996. *For Sex Education, See Librarian.* New York: Greenwood Press.

Countryman, L. W. 1988. *Dirt, Greed and Sex: Sexual Ethics in the New Testament and Their Implications for Today.* Philadelphia: Fortress Press.

Curran, C. E., and R. A. McCormick, eds. 1993. *Dialogue about Catholic Sexual Teaching.* Mahwah, NJ: Paulist Press.

Current Population Reports. 1985. *Marital Status and Living Arrangements. March, 1984.* United States Department of Commerce, Bureau of the Census.

Darabi, K. F., and V. Ortiz. 1987. "Childbearing Among Young Latino Women in the United States." *American Journal of Public Health*, 77(1):25-28.

Dauw, D. C. 1988. "Evaluating the Effectiveness of the SECS' Surrogate-Assisted Sex Therapy Model." *Journal of Sex Research*, 24:269-275.

Davidson, J. K., and C. Anderson Darling. 1993. "Masturbatory Guilt and Sexual Responsiveness Among Post-College-Age Women: Sexual Satisfaction Revisited." *Journal of Sex and Marital Therapy*, 19(4):289-300.

Davis, A. Y. 1981. *Women, Race and Class.* New York: Vintage Books.

Davis, J. A. 1990. *General Social Surveys, 1972-1990: Cumulative Codebook.* Chicago: National Opinion Research Center, University of Chicago.

Davis, J. A., and T. W. Smith. 1994. *General Social Surveys, 1979-1994: Cumulative Codebook.* Chicago: National Opinion Research Center.

Davis, K. B. 1929. *Factors in the Sex Life of Twenty-Two Hundred Women.* New York: Harper and Row.

Davis, S. M., and M. B. Harris. 1982. "Sexual Knowledge, Sexual Interest, and Sources of Sexual Information of Rural and Urban Adolescents from Three Cultures." *Adolescence,* 17:471-492.

Dawson, D. A. 1990. "AIDS Knowledge and Attitudes for January-March 1990. Provisional Data from the National Health Interview Survey." *Advanced Data from Vital and Health Statistics. Number 193.* Hyattsville, MD: National Center for Health Statistics.

Dawson, D. A., and A. M. Hardy. 1989. *AIDS Knowledge and Attitudes of Hispanic Americans. Provisional Data from the 1988 National Health Interview Survey. Advanced Data from Vital and Health Statistics. Number 166.* Hyattsville, MD: National Center for Health Statistics.

de la Cancela, V. 1989. "Minority AIDS Prevention: Moving Beyond Cultural Perspectives Towards Sociopolitical Empowerment." *AIDS Education and Prevention,* 1(2):141-153.

Delacoste, F., and P. Alexander. 1987. *Sex Work: Writings by Women in the Sex Industry.* Pittsburgh, PA: Cleis Press.

de la Vega, E. 1990. "Considerations for Reaching the Latino Population with Sexuality and HIV/AIDS Information and Education." *SIECUS Report,* 18(3).

DeLamater, J. D., and P. MacCorquodale. 1979. *Premarital Sexuality: Attitudes, Relationships, Behavior.* Madison, WI: University of Wisconsin Press.

D'Emilio, J., and E. B. Freedman. 1988. *Intimate Matters: A History of Sexuality in America.* New York: Harper and Row.

Denfeld, D. 1974. "Dropouts from Swinging." *Family Coordinator,* 23:45-59.

DeRachewitz, B. 1964. *Black Eros: Sexual Customs of Africa from Prehistory to the Present Day.* New York: Lyle Stuart.

DeWaal, F. 1982. *Chimpanzee Politics: Power and Sex Among Apes.* New York: Harper Colophon Books.

DeWitt, K. 1991 (October 13). "As Harassment Plays, Many U.S. Employees Live It." *The New York Times,* p. 24.

Dickinson, R. L., and L. Bean. 1931/1932. *A Thousand Marriages: A Medical Study of Sex Adjustment.* Baltimore: Williams & Wilkins.

Dickinson, R. L., and L. Bean. 1934. *The Single Woman.* Baltimore: Williams and Wilkins.

Dickinson, R. L., and H. H. Pierson. 1925. "The Average Sex Life of American Women." *Journal of the American Medical Association,* 85:1113-1117.

Dietz, P. 1989/1990 (December/January). "Youth-Serving Agencies as Effective Providers of Sexuality Education." *SIECUS Report,* 18:16-20.

di Mauro, D. 1995. *Sexuality Research in the United States: An Assessment of the Social and Behavioral Sciences.* New York: Social Sciences Research Council.

di Mauro, D. 1989/1990 (December/January). "Sexuality Education 1990: A Review of State Sexuality and AIDS Education Curricula." *SIECUS Report,* 18:1-9.

Dixon, D. 1985. "Perceived Sexual Satisfaction and Marital Happiness of Bisexual and Heterosexual Swinging Husbands." Special Issue: Bisexualities: Theory and Research. *Journal of Homosexuality,* 11(1-2):209-222.

Dixon, J. K. 1984. "The Commencement of Bisexual Activity in Swinging Married Women over Age 30." *Journal of Sex Research.* 20:71-90.

Docter, R. F. 1988. *Transvestites and Transsexuals: Toward a Theory of Cross-Gender Behavior.* New York: Plenum Press.

Doddridge, R., W. Schumm, and M. Berger. 1987. "Factors Related to Decline in Preferred Frequency of Sexual Intercourse Among Young Couples." *Psychological Reports*, 60:391-395.

Dodson, B. 1987. *Sex for One: The Joy of Selfloving.* New York: Harmony Books. Published in 1974 and 1983 under the titles of *Selflove and Orgasm* and *Liberating Masturbation.*

Donat, P. L. N., and J. D'Emilio. 1992. "A Feminist Redefinition of Rape and Sexual Assault: Historical Foundations and Change." *Journal of Social Issues*, 48(1):9-22.

Donnerstein, E., D. Linz, and S. Penrod. 1987. *The Question of Pornography: Research Findings and Policy Implications.* New York: The Free Press.

Duberman, M., M. Vicinus, and G. Chauncey, eds. 1989. *Hidden from History: Reclaiming the Gay and Lesbian Past.* New York: New American Library.

Duesberg, P. H. 1996. *Inventing the AIDS Virus.* Washington, DC: Regnery Press.

Dugger, Celia W. 1996a (December 28). "Tug of Taboos: African Genital Rite vs. U.S. Law." *The New York Times*, pp. 1 and 9.

Dugger, Celia W. 1996b (October 12). "New Law Bans Genital Cutting in United States." *The New York Times*, pp. 1 and 28.

Duncan, D. F., and T. Nicholson. 1991. "Pornography as a Source of Sex Information for Students at a Southeastern State University." *Psychological Reports*, 68:802.

Durant, R. 1990. "Sexual Behaviors Among Hispanic Female Adolescents in the U. S." *Pediatrics*, 85(6):1051-1058.

Eckard, E. 1982. *Contraceptive Use Patterns, Prior Source, and Pregnancy History of Female Family Planning Patients: United States, 1980.* Washington, DC: United States Department of Health and Human Services, Public Health Service, Vital Statistics, No. 82.

Edwardes, A., and R. E. L. Masters. 1963. *The Cradle of Erotica: A Study of Afro-Asian Sexual Expression and an Analysis of Erotic Freedom in Social Relationships.* New York: The Julian Press.

Edwards, J. N., and A. Booth. 1976. "Sexual Behavior In and Out of Marriage: An Assessment of Correlates." *Journal of Marriage and the Family*, 38(1):73-81.

Ehrenreich, B., G. Hass, and E. Jacobs. 1987. *Remaking Love: The Feminization of Sex.* New York: Doubleday/Anchor.

Ehrmann, W. W. 1959. *Premarital Dating Behavior.* New York: Holt, Rinehart and Winston.

Ehrmann, W. W. 1964. "Marital and Nonmarital Sexual Behavior." In H. T. Christensen, ed. *Handbook of Marriage and the Family* (pp. 585-622). Chicago: Rand McNally.

Elias, J., and P. Gebhard. 1969. "Sexuality and Sexual Learning in Childhood." *Phi Delta Kappan*, 50:401-405.

Ellis, A. 1969. "Healthy and Disturbed Reasons for Having Extramarital Relations." In G. Neubeck, ed. *Extramarital Relations* (pp. 153-161). Englewood Cliffs, NJ: Prentice-Hall.

Ellis, H. 1936. *Love and Pain, Studies in the Psychology of Sex.* Vol. 1 (originally published 1903). New York: Random House.

EPIC (on-line) 1996 (September 30). "CDA Ruled Unconstitutional?".

Eskridge, W. N. 1996. *The Case for Same-Sex Marriage.* New York: Free Press.

Estrich, S. 1987. *Real Rape.* Cambridge, MA: Harvard University Press.

Faderman, L. 1991. *Odd Girls and Twilight Lovers.* New York: Columbia University Press.

Fanon, F. 1967. *Black Skin, White Mask.* New York: Grove Press.

Farber, C. 1993 (March). "Out of Africa." *Spin*, pp. 60-63, 86-87.

Farber, C. 1993a (April). "Out of Africa: Part Two." *Spin*, pp. 74-77, 106-107.

Farber, C. 1993b (April). "Sex in the '90s." *Spin*, p. 15.

Farrell, W. 1990. "The Last Taboo?: The Complexities of Incest and Female Sexuality." In M. Perry, ed. *Handbook of Sexology: Volume 7: Childhood and Adolescent Sexology.* New York: Elsevier.

Farrell, W. 1993. *The Myth of Male Power: Why Men Are the Disposable Sex.* New York: Simon & Schuster.

Federal Bureau of Investigation. 1993. *Uniform Crime Reports for the United States 1992.* Washington, DC: U.S. Government Printing Office.

Fennelly, K. 1988. *El Embarazo Precoz: Childbearing Among Hispanic Teenagers in the United States.* New York: Columbia University, School of Public Health.

Fennelly, K. 1992. "Sexual Activity and Childbearing Among Hispanic Adolescents in the United States." In R. Lerner, et al., eds. *Early Adolescence: Perspectives on Research, Policy and Intervention.* Hillsdale, NJ: Eldbaum Press.

Fennelly, K., V. Kandiah, and V. Ortiz. 1989. "The Cross-Cultural Study of Fertility Among Hispanic Adolescents in the Americas." *Studies in Family Planning,* 20(2):96-101.

Fennelly-Darabi, K., and V. Ortiz. 1987. "Childbearing Among Young Latino Women in the United States." *American Journal of Public Health,* 77(1):25-28.

Fine, M., and A. Asch, eds. 1988. *Women with Disabilities: Essays in Psychology, Culture, and Politics.* Philadelphia: Temple University Press.

Finger, F. W. 1975. "Changes in Sex Practices and Beliefs of Male College Students Over 30 Years." *Journal of Sex Research,* 11:304-317.

Finkelhor, D. 1980. "Sex Among Siblings: A Survey on Prevalence, Variety, and Effects." *Archives of Sexual Behavior,* 9:171-194.

Finkelhor, D., and K. Yllo. 1985. *License to Rape: Sexual Abuse of Wives.* New York: Free Press.

Fischer, G. J. 1987. "Hispanic and Majority Student Attitudes Towards Forcible Date Rape as a Function of Differences in Attitudes Towards Women." *Sex Roles,* 17(2):93-101.

Fisher, H. E. 1992. *Anatomy of Love: The Natural History of Monogamy, Adultery, and Divorce.* New York: Norton.

Fisher, T. D. 1986. "An Exploratory Study of Parent-Child Communication About Sex and the Sexual Attitudes of Early, Middle, and Late Adolescents." *Journal of Genetic Psychology,* 147:543-557.

Floyd, H. H. Jr., and D. R. South. 1972. "Dilemma of Youth: The Choice of Parents or Peers as a Frame of Reference for Behavior." *Journal of Marriage and the Family,* 34:627-634.

Ford, C. S., and F. A. Beach. 1951. *Patterns of Sexual Behavior.* New York: Harper and Brothers.

Ford, K., and A. Norris. 1991. "Methodological Considerations for Survey Research on Sexual Behavior: Urban African American and Hispanic Youth." *Journal of Sex Research,* 28(4):539-555.

Ford, K., and A. E. Norris. 1993. "Urban Hispanic Adolescents and Young Adults: Relationship of Aculturation to Sexual Behavior." *Journal of Sex Research,* 30(4):316-323.

Forrest, J. D., and R. R. Fordyce. 1988. "U.S. Women's Contraceptive Attitudes and Practices: How Have They Changed in the 1980s?" *Family Planning Perspectives,* 20(3):112-118.

Forrest, J. D., and J. Silverman. 1989. "What Public School Teachers Teach about Preventing Pregnancy, AIDS and Sexually Transmitted Diseases." *Family Planning Perspectives,* 21:65-72.

Forrest, J. D., and S. Singh. 1990. "The Sexual and Reproductive Behavior of American Women, 1982-1988." *Family Planning Perspectives,* 22(5):206-214.

Fortune, M. M. 1991. *Is Nothing Sacred? When Sex Invades the Pastoral Relationship.* San Francisco: Harper.

Fox, M. 1983. *Original Blessing.* Sante Fe, New Mexico: Bear and Company.

Fox, M. 1988. *The Coming of the Cosmic Christ: The Healing of Mother Earth and the Birth of a Global Renaissance.* San Francisco: Harper and Row.

Fox, R. 1995. "A History of Bisexuality Research." In Anthony D'Augelli and Charlotte Patterson, eds. *Lesbian, Gay and Bisexual Identities Over the Lifespan.* New York: Oxford University Press.

Francoeur, R. T. 1987. "Human Sexuality." In M. B. Sussman and S. K. Steinmetz, eds. *Handbook of Marriage and the Family.* New York: Plenum Press.

Francoeur, R. T. 1988. "Two Different Worlds, Two Different Moralities." In: Jeannine Gramick and Pat Furey, eds. *The Vatican and Homosexuality.* New York, NY: Crossroads.

Francoeur, R. T. 1990. "Current Religious Doctrines of Sexual and Erotic Development in Childhood." In M. Perry, ed. *Handbook of Sexology: Volume 7: Childhood and Adolescent Sexology.* New York: Elsevier.

Francoeur, R. T. 1991a. *Becoming a Sexual Person* (2nd ed.). New York: Macmillan.

Francoeur, R. T. 1991b. *Taking Sides: Clashing Views on Controversial Issues in Human Sexuality* (3rd ed.). Guilford, CT: Dushkin Publishing Group.

Francoeur, R. T. 1992 (April/May). "Sexuality and Spirituality: The Relevance of Eastern Traditions." *SIECUS Report,* 20(4):1-8.

Francoeur, R. T. 1994. "Religion and Sexuality." In V. L. Bullough and B. Bullough, eds. *Human Sexuality: An Encyclopedia* (pp. 514-520). New York: Garland.

Francoeur, A. K., and R. T. Francoeur. 1974. *Hot and Cool Sex: Cultures in Conflict.* New York: Harcourt, Brace, Jovanovich.

Frank, E., and C. Anderson. 1979 (July/August). "Sex and the Happily Married." *The Sciences,* 10-13.

Frank, E., C. Anderson, and D. Rubinstein. 1978. "Frequency of Sexual Dysfunction in 'Normal' Couples." *New England Journal of Medicine,* 299:111-115.

Frayser, S. 1985. *Varieties of Sexual Experience: An Anthropological Perspective on Human Sexuality.* New Haven, CT: HRAF Press.

Freeman, J. 1995. "From Suffrage to Women's Liberation: Feminism in Twentieth-Century America." In J. Freeman, ed. *Women: A Feminist Perspective.* Mountain View, CA: Mayfield.

Freud, S. 1938. Three Contributions to the Theory of Sex. In A. A. Brill, ed. *The Basic Writings of Sigmund Freud* (originally published in 1905). New York: The Modern Library.

Friend. R. A. 1987. "The Individual and Social Psychology of Aging: Clinical Implications for Lesbians and Gay Men." *Journal of Homosexuality,* 14(1-2):307-331.

Fumento, M. 1990. *The Myth of Heterosexual AIDS.* New York: Basic Books [A New Republic Book].

Gagnon, J. H. 1977. *Human Sexualities.* New York: Scott, Foresman.

Gagnon, J. H. 1985. "Attitudes and Responses of Parents to Preadolescent Masturbation." *Archives of Sexual Behavior,* 14:451-466.

Gagnon, J. H., and W. Simon. 1973. *Sexual Conduct: The Social Sources of Human Sexuality.* Chicago: Aldine.

Gaines, D. 1995 (June 30). *Founder of the Foot Fraternity.* Interview with Brenda Love. San Francisco.

Galenson, E. 1990. "Observation of Early Infantile Sexual and Erotic Development." In M. Perry, ed. *Handbook of Sexology: Volume 7: Childhood and Adolescent Sexology.* New York: Elsevier.

Galenson, E., and H. Roiphe. 1980. "Some Suggested Revisions Concerning Early Female Development." In M. Kirkpatrick, ed. *Women's Sexual Development: Exploration of Inner Space* (pp. 83-105). New York: Plenum.

Garcia, C. 1993. "What Do We Mean by Extended Family? A Closer Look at Hispanic Multigenerational Families." *Journal of Cross Cultural Gerontology*, 8(2):137-146.

Garcia, F. 1980. "The Cult of Virginity." In *Program on Teaching and Learning: Conference on the Educational and Occupational Needs of Hispanic Women* (pp. 65-73). Washington, DC: National Institute of Education.

Gardella, P. 1985. *Innocent Ecstasy: How Christianity Gave America an Ethic of Sexual Pleasure.* New York: Oxford University Press.

Gebhard, P. H. 1968. "Postmarital Coitus Among Widows and Divorcees." In P. Bohannan, ed. *Divorce and After* (pp. 81-96). New York: Doubleday.

Gebhard, P. H. 1993 (September/October). "Kinsey's Famous Figures." *Indiana Alumni Magazine*, p. 64.

Gelles, R. J. 1977. "Power, Sex, and Violence: The Case of Marital Rape." *Family Coordinator*, 26:339-347.

Gibson, J. W., and J. Kempf. 1990. "Attitudinal Predictors of Sexual Activity in Hispanic Adolescent Females." *Journal of Adolescent Research*, 5(4):414-430.

Giles, J., and C. S. Lee. 1994 (August 15). "There's Nothing Like a Dame." *Newsweek*, p. 69.

Gilmartin, B. G. 1978. *The Gilmartin Report.* Secaucus, NJ: Citadel.

Gise, L. H., and P. Paddison. 1988. "Rape, Sexual Abuse, and Its Victims." *Psychiatric Clinics of North America*, 11:629-648.

Givens, D. 1978. "The Nonverbal Basis of Attraction: Flirtation, Courtship, and Seduction." *Psychiatry*, 41:346-359.

Glass, S. P., and T. L. Wright. 1977. "The Relationship of Extramarital Sex, Length of Marriage and Sex Differences on Marital Satisfaction and Romanticism: Athanasiou's Data Reanalyzed." *Journal of Marriage and the Family*, 39:691-703.

Glass, S. P., and T. L. Wright. 1985. "Sex Differences in Type of Extramarital Involvement and Marital Dissatisfaction." *Sex Roles*, 12:1101-1120.

Glazer, N., and D. P. Moynihan. 1964. *Beyond the Melting Pot: The Negroes, Puerto Ricans, Jews, Otawoams, Italians, and Irish of New York City.* Cambridge, MA: MIT Press.

Glenn, N. D. and C. N. Weaver. 1979. "Attitudes Toward Premarital, Extramarital, and Homosexual Relations in the U. S. in the 1970s." *Journal of Sex Research*, 15:108-118.

Glick, P. C. 1984. "Marriage, Divorce, and Living Arrangements: Prospective Changes." *Journal of Family Issues*, 5:7-26.

Glick, P. C., and A. Norton. 1977. *Marrying, Divorcing, and Living Together in the U.S. Today.* Washington, DC: Population Reference Bureau.

Gold, Rabbi Michael. 1992. *Does God Belong in the Bedroom?* Philadelphia: The Jewish Publication Society.

Goldfarb, L., M. Gerrarc, F. X. Gibbons, and T. Plante. 1988. "Attitudes Toward Sex, Arousal, and the Retention of Contraceptive Information." *Journal of Personality and Social Psychology*, 55:634-641.

Goldman, R. J., and J. G. D. Goldman. 1982. *Children's Sexual Thinking.* Boston: Routledge & Kegan Paul.

Goodson, P. 1996. *Protestant Seminary Students' Views of Family Planning and Intention to Promote Family Planning Through Education.* Unpublished doctoral dissertation. The University of Texas at Austin, TX.

Gordon, L. 1976. *Woman's Body, Woman's Right: A Social History of Birth Control in America.* New York: Penguin.

Gordon, M. T., and S. Riger. 1989. *The Female Fear.* New York: Free Press.

Greeley, A. 1995. *Sex: The Catholic Experience.* Allen, TX: Thomas More Press.

Greeley, A. M. 1991. *Faithful Attraction: Discovering Intimacy, Love, and Fidelity in American Marriage.* New York: Doherty.

Greeley, A. M., R. T. Michael, and T. W. Smith. 1990. "Americans and Their Sexual Partners." *Society*, 27(5):36-42.

Green, R. 1987. *The "Sissy Boy Syndrome" and the Development of Homosexuality.* New Haven, CT: Yale University Press.

Greenblat, C. S. 1983. "The Salience of Sexuality in the Early Years of Marriage." *Journal of Marriage and the Family,* 45:289-299.

Grier, W., and W. Cobbs. 1968. *Black Rage.* New York: Basic Books.

Griffin, S. 1971. "Rape: The All-American Crime." *Ramparts,* 10:26-35.

Griffit, W. September 1985. "Some Prosocial Effects of Exposure to Consensual Erotica." Paper presented at annual meeting of the Society for the Scientific Study of Sex, San Diego, CA.

Grogan, Ann. 1995 (July 5). Owner of Romantasy Boutique. Interview with Brenda Love. San Francisco.

Groth, A. N., and A. W. Burgess. 1980. "Male Rape: Offenders and Victims." *American Journal of Psychiatry,* 137:806-810.

Grover, J. 1990. "Is Lesbian Battering the Same as Straight Battering? Children from Violent Lesbian Homes. Battered Lesbians Are Battered Women." In: *Confronting Lesbian Battering: A Manual for the Battered Women's Movement* (pp. 41-46). St. Paul, MN: Minnesota Coalition for Battered Women.

Gutek, B. A. 1985. *Sex and the Workplace.* San Francisco, CA: Jossey-Bass.

Gwinn, M., M. Pappaioanou, J. R. George, et al. 1991. "Prevalence of HIV Infection in Childbearing Women in the United States." *Journal of the American Medical Association,* 265(13):1704-1708.

Haffner, D. W. 1989 (March/April). "SIECUS: 25 Years of Commitment to Sexual Health and Education." *SIECUS Report,* 17:1-6.

Haffner, D. W. 1992 (February/March). "1992 Report Card on the States: Sexual Rights in America." *SIECUS Report,* 20:1-7.

Haffner, D. W. 1994 (August/September). "The Good News about Sexuality Education." *SIECUS Report,* 17-18.

Haffner, D. W., and M. Kelly. 1987 (March/April). "Adolescent Sexuality in the Media." *SIECUS Report,* 9-12.

Hahn, H. and R. Stout. 1994. *The Internet Yellow Page.* Berkeley, CA: Osborne McGraw-Hill.

Hall, T. 1987 (June 1). "Infidelity and Women: Shifting Patterns." *The New York Times.*

Halverson, H. M. 1940. "Genital and Sphincter Behavior of the Male Infant." *Journal of Genetic Psychology,* 56:95-136.

Hamer, D., S. Hu, V. Magnuson, N. Hu, and A. Pattatucci. 1993. "A Linkage Between DNA Markers on the X Chromosome and Male Sexual Orientation." *Science,* 261:321-327.

Hamilton, G. V. 1948. *A Research in Marriage.* New York: Lear Publications.

Hamm, Lisa M. (Associated Press). 1996 (November 4). "Not Just Africa: Female Circumcision Even Happens in U.S." *New Jersey On-Line—Newark Star Ledger's Electronic Edition.*

Hartman, W. E., and M. A. Fithian. 1972. *Treatment of Sexual Dysfunction: A Bio-Psycho-Social Approach.* Long Beach, CA: Center for Marital and Sexual Studies.

Haseltine, F. P., S. S. Cole, and D. B. Gray, eds. 1993. *Reproductive Issues for Persons with Physical Disabilities.* Baltimore: Paul H. Brookes Publishing Co.

Hass, A. 1979. *Teenage Sexuality.* New York: Macmillan.

Hass, K., and A. Hass. 1993. *Understanding Sexuality.* St. Louis: Mosby.

Hatcher, R., J. Trussell, F. Stewart, G. Stewart, D. Kowal, F. Guest, W. Cates, Jr., and M. Pokicar. 1994. *Contraceptive Technology* (16th rev. ed.). New York: Irvington.

Hawkins, G., and F. E. Zimring. *Pornography in a Free Society.* Cambridge: Cambridge University Press.

Heiby, E., and J. D. Becker. 1980. "Effect of Filmed Modeling on the Self-Reported Frequency of Masturbation." *Archives of Sexual Behavior*, 9(2):115-120.

Helminiak, D. A. 1994. *What the Bible Really Says about Homosexuality.* San Francisco: Alamo Press.

Hendrixson, L. L. 1996. *The Psychosocial and Psychosexual Impact of HIV/AIDS on Rural Women: A Qualitative Study.* Unpublished doctoral dissertation, New York University.

Hengeveld, M. W. 1991. "Erectile Disorders: A Psychological Review." In U. Jonas, W. F. Thon, C. G. Stief, eds. *Erectile Dysfunction* (pp. 207-235). Berlin: Springer-Verlag.

Herman, J. L. 1992. *Trauma and Recovery.* New York: Basic Books.

Herold, E. S., and M. S. Goodwin. 1981. "Adamant Virgins, Potential Nonvirgins and Nonvirgins." *Journal of Sex Research*, 17:97-113.

Hershey, M. 1978. "Racial Differences in Sex-Role Identities and Sex Stereotyping: Evidence Against a Common Assumption." *Social Science Quarterly*, 58:584-596.

Heyward, C. 1989. *Touching Our Strength: The Erotic as Power and the Love of God.* San Francisco: HarperSanFrancisco.

Hite, S. 1976. *The Hite Report* New York: Dell.

Hite, S. 1983. *The Hite Report on Male Sexuality.* New York: Knopf.

Hofferth, S. L., J. R. Kahn, and W. Baldwin. 1987. "Premarital Sexual Activity Among U.S. Teenage Women over the Past Three Decades." *Family Planning Perspectives*, 19(2):46-53.

Holmes, S. A. 1996a (June 13). "Public Cost of Teen-Age Pregnancy Is Put at $7 Billion This Year." *The New York Times*, p. A19.

Holmes, S. A. 1996b (October 5). "U.S. Reports Drop in Rate of Births to Unwed Women." *The New York Times*, pp. 1 and 9.

Holzman, H., and S. Pines. 1982. "Buying Sex: The Phenomenology of Being a John." *Deviant Behavior*, 4:89-116.

Hooker, E. E. A. 1957. "The Adjustment of the Male Overt Homosexual." *Journal of Projective Techniques*, 21:17-31.

Hopkins, J. 1977. "Sexual Behavior in Adolescence." *Journal of Social Issues*, 33:67-85.

Houston, L. 1981. "Romanticism and Eroticism Among Black and White College Students." *Adolescence*, 16:263-272.

Hu, D. J., and R. Keller. 1989. "Communicating AIDS Information to Hispanics: The Importance of Language in Media Preference." *American Journal of Preventive Medicine*, 54:196-200.

Hunt, M. 1974. *Sexual Behavior in the 1970s.* Chicago: Playboy Press.

Hunt, T. 1994 (December 10). "Clinton Fires Surgeon General" (AP News Service). *Bowling Green Sentinel Tribune*, p. 3.

Hunter, H. W. 1995. *Being a Righteous Husband and Father.* Salt Lake City, UT: Church of Jesus Christ of Latter-Day Saints.

Hunter, M. 1990. *The Sexually Abused Male.* Lexington, MA: Lexington Books.

Hunter, R. J., ed. 1990. *Dictionary of Pastoral Care and Counseling.* Nashville, TN: Abingdon Press.

Hurlbert, D. F. 1992. "Factors Influencing a Woman's Decision to End an Extramarital Sexual Relationship." *Journal of Sex and Marital Therapy*, 18(2):104-113.

Hutchins, L. and L. Kaahumanu, eds. 1991. *By Any Other Name: Bisexual People Speak Out.* Boston: Alyson.

International Professional Surrogates Association (IPSA). 1989 (June). *Code of Ethics* [Brochure]. Los Angeles: Author.

International Professional Surrogates Association (IPSA). n.d. "General Information about IPSA and Surrogates." *Surrogate Partner Therapy* [Brochure]. Los Angeles: Author.

The Internet Unleashed. 1994. Indianapolis, IN: SAMS Publishing.

Irvine, J. 1990. *Disorders of Desire: Sex and Gender in Modern American Sexology.* Philadelphia: Temple University Press.

Itialiano, Laura. 1996 (March). "Communications Decency Act: Threat to Cyber Space? Or Much Ado About Nothing?" *NJ Online.*

Jacobs, M., L. A. Thompson, and P. Truxaw. 1975. "The Use of Sexual Surrogates in Counseling." *The Counseling Psychologist,* 5(1):73-77.

Jacobus, X. 1937. *Untrodden Fields of Anthropology.* New York: Falstaff Press.

James, W. H. 1981. "The Honeymoon Effect on Marital Coitus." *Journal of Sex Research,* 17:114-123.

James, W. H. 1983. "Decline in Coital Rates with Spouses' Ages and Duration of Marriage." *Journal of Bioscience,* 15:83-87.

Jasso, G. 1985. "Marital Coital Frequency and the Passage of Time: Estimating the Separate Effects of Spouses' Ages and Marital Duration, Birth, and Marriage Cohorts, and Period Influences." *American Sociological Review,* 50:224-241.

Jefferson, T. 1954. *Notes on the State of Virginia.* Chapel Hill, North Carolina: University of North Carolina Press.

Jenks, R. J. 1985. "Swinging: A Test of Two Theories and a Proposed New Model." *Archives of Sexual Behavior,* 14:517-527.

Jesser, C. J. 1978. "Male Responses to Direct Verbal Sexual Initiatives of Females." *Journal of Sex Research,* 14:118-128.

Jessor, S. L., R. Jessor. 1977. *Problem Behavior and Psychosocial Development: A Longitudinal Study of Youth.* New York: Academic Press.

Johnson, L. B. 1978. "Sexual Behavior of Southern Blacks." In R. Staples, ed. *The Black Family: Essays and Studies.* Belmont, CA: Wadsworth Press.

Johnson, L. B. 1986. "Religion and Sexuality: A Comparison of Black and White College Students in Three Regions of the U.S." Unpublished manuscript.

Johnson, R. E. 1970. Some correlates of extramarital coitus. *Journal of Marriage and the Family,* 32:449-456.

Jones, E., J. Forrest, N. Goldman, S. Henshaw, R. Lincoln, J. Rossoff, C. Westoff, and D. Wulf. 1985. "Teenage Pregnancy in Developed Countries: Determinants and Policy Implications. *Family Planning Perspectives,* 17:53-63.

Jones, E. F., et al. 1986. *Teenage Pregnancy in Industrialized Countries.* New Haven, CT: Yale University Press.

Jones, J., and C. L. Muehlenhard. 1990 (November). "Using Education to Prevent Rape on College Campuses." Presented at the annual meeting of the Society for the Scientific Study of Sex, Minneapolis, MN.

Joseph Smith's Testimony. Salt Lake City: Church of Jesus Christ of the Latter-Day Saints Publication.

Juran, S. 1995. The 90's: Gender Differences in AIDS-Related Sexual Concerns and Behaviors, Condom Use and Subjective Condom Experience. *Journal of Psychology & Human Sexuality,* 7(3):39-59.

Kahn, J. R., and J. R. Udry. 1986. "Marital Coital Frequency: Unnoticed Outliers and Unspecified Interactions Lead to Erroneous Conclusions." *American Sociological Review,* 51:734-737.

Kallen, D., and J. Stephenson. 1982. "Talking about Sex Revisited." *Journal of Youth and Adolescence.* 11:11-23.

Kaplan, D. A. 1993 (November 22). "Take Down the Girlie Calendars." *Newsweek,* p. 34.

Kaplan, H. Singer. 1979. *Disorders of Sexual Desire and Other New Concepts and Techniques in Sex Therapy.* New York: Brunner/Mazel.

Kaplan, H. Singer. 1983. *The Evaluation of Sexual Disorders: Psychological and Medical Aspects.* New York: Brunner/Mazel.

Kaplan, H. Singer. 1974. *The New Sex Therapy: Active Treatment of Sexual Dysfunctions.* New York: Brunner/Mazel.

Kelsey, D. H. 1993. *Between Athens and Berlin: The Theological Education Debate.* Grand Rapids, MI: Eerdmans.

Kendall-Tackett, K., L. A. Williams, and D. Finkelhor. 1993. "Impact of Sexual Abuse on Children: A Review and Synthesis of Recent Empirical Studies." *Psychological Bulletin,* 113:164-180.

Kenney, A., S. Guardado, and L. Brown. 1989. "Sex Education and AIDS Education in the Schools: What States and Large School Districts Are Doing. *Family Planning Perspectives,* 21:56-64.

Kilpatrick, D. G., C. L. Best, B. E. Saunders, and L. J. Veronen. 1987. "Rape in Marriage and in Dating Relationships: How Bad Is It for Mental Health?" *Annals of the New York Academy of Sciences,* 528:335-344.

Kinsey, A. C., W. Pomeroy, and C. Martin. 1948. *Sexual Behavior in the Human Male.* Philadelphia: Saunders.

Kinsey, A. C., W. Pomeroy, C. Martin, and P. Gebhard. 1953. *Sexual Behavior in the Human Female.* Philadelphia: Saunders.

Kirby, D. 1985. "Sexuality Education: A More Realistic View of Its Effects." *Journal of School Health,* 55(10):421-424.

Kirby, D., J. Atter, and P. Scales. 1979. *An Analysis of U.S. Sex Education Programs and Evaluation Methods: Executive Summary.* Atlanta, GA: U.S. Department of Health, Education, and Welfare.

Kirkendall, L. A., and I. G. McBride. 1990. "Preadolescent and Adolescent imagery and Sexual Fantasies: Beliefs and Experiences." In M. Perry, ed. *Handbook of Sexology: Volume 7: Childhood and Adolescent Sexology.* New York: Elsevier.

Kilpatrick, A. C. 1986. "Some Correlates of Women's Childhood Sexual Experiences: A Retrospective Survey." *Journal of Sex Research,* 22:221-242.

Kilpatrick, A. C. 1987. "Childhood Sexual Experiences: Problems and Issues in Studying Long-Range Effects." *Journal of Sex Research,* 23:173-196.

Klein, M. 1994. "Response to the FBI—The Rest of the 'Child Porn' Story." *AASECT Newsletter.*

Klein, F. 1978. *The Bisexual Option: A Concept of One Hundred Percent Intimacy.* New York: Arbor House.

Klein, F., B. Sepekoff, and T. J. Wolf. 1985. "Sexual Orientation: A Multi-Variable Dynamic Process." *Journal of Homosexuality,* 11(1/2):35-50.

Koch, P. B. 1988. "The Relationship of First Sexual Intercourse to Later Sexual Functioning Concerns of Adolescents." *Journal of Adolescent Research,* 3:345-352.

Koch, P. B. 1995. *Exploring Our Sexuality: An Interactive Text.* Dubuque, IA: Kendall/Hunt.

Kosnick, A., W. Carroll, A. Cunningham, R. Modras, and J. Schulte. 1977. *Human Sexuality: New Directions in American Catholic Thought.* New York: Paulist Press.

Koss, M. P. 1992. "The Underdetection of Rape: Methodological Choices Influence Incidence Estimates." *Journal of Social Issues,* 48(1):61-75.

Koss, M. P. 1993a. "Detecting the Scope of Rape: A Review of Prevalence Research Methods." *Journal of Interpersonal Violence,* 8:198-222.

Koss, M. P. 1993b. "Rape: Scope, Impact, Interventions, and Public Policy Responses." *American Psychologist,* 48:1062-1069.

Koss, M. P., and T. E. Dinero. 1988. "Predictors of Sexual Aggression Among a National Sample of Male College Students." In R. A. Prentky and V. L. Quinsey, eds. *Human Sexual Aggression: Current Perspectives* (pp. 133-147). New York: New York Academy of Sciences.

Koss, M. P., T. E. Dinero, C. A. Seibel, and S. L. Cox. 1988. "Stranger and Acquaintance Rape: Are There Differences in the Victim's Experience?" *Psychology of Women Quarterly*, 12:1-24.

Koss, M. P., C. A. Gidycz, and N. Wisniewski. 1987. "The Scope of Rape: Incidence and Prevalence of Sexual Aggression and Victimization in a National Sample of Higher Education Students." *Journal of Consulting and Clinical Psychology*, 55:162-170.

Kraditor, A. 1965. *The Ideas of the Women's Suffrage Movement.* New York: Columbia University Press.

Krivacska, J. J. 1990. "Child Sexual Abuse and Its Prevention." In M. Perry, ed. *Handbook of Sexology: Volume 7: Childhood and Adolescent Sexology.* New York: Elsevier.

Kutsche, P. 1983. "Household and Family in Hispanic Northern New Mexico." *Journal of Comparative Family Studies*, 14(2):151-165.

LaFree, G. D. 1982. "Male Power and Female Victimization: Toward a Theory of Interracial Rape." *American Journal of Sociology*, 88:311-328.

LaFree, G. D., B. F. Reskin, and C. A. Visher. 1985. "Jurors' Responses to Victims' Behavior and Legal Issues in Sexual Assault Trials." *Social Problems*, 32:389-407.

Langfeldt, T. 1979. "Processes in Sexual Development." In M. Cook and G. Wilson, eds. *Love and Attraction.* Oxford: Pergamon Press.

Larson, D. L., E. A. Spreitzer, and E. E. Snyder. 1976. "Social Factors in the Frequency of Romantic Involvement Among Adolescents." *Adolescences*, II:7-12.

Laumann, E. O., J. H. Gagnon, R. T. Michael, and S. Michaels. 1994. *The Social Organization of Sexuality: Sexual Practices in the United States.* Chicago: University of Chicago Press.

Laurence, J. 1994 (March/April). "Long-Term Survival Versus Nonprogression." *The AIDS Reader*, 4(2):39-40, 71.

Lawrence, K., and E. S. Herold. 1988. "Women's Attitudes Toward and Experience with Sexually Explicit Materials." *Journal of Sex Research*, 24:161-169.

Lawrence, R. J. 1989. *The Poisoning of Eros: Sexual Values in Conflict.* New York: Augustine Moore Press.

Leaper-Campbell, V. D. 1996. "Predictors of Mexican American Mothers' and Fathers' Attitudes Toward Gender Equality. Hispanic." *Journal of Behavioral Sciences*, 18:343-355.

Lefley, H. P., C. S. Scott, M. Llabre, and D. Hicks. 1993. "Cultural Beliefs about Rape and Victims' Response in Three Ethnic Groups." *American Journal of Orthopsychiatry*, 63(4):623-632.

LeGates, M. 1995. "Feminists Before Feminism: Origins and Varieties of Women's Protests in Europe and North America before the Twentieth Century. In: J. Freeman, ed. *Women: A Feminist Perspective.* Mountain View, CA: Mayfield.

LeHaye, T., and B. LeHaye. 1976. *The Act of Marriage: The Beauty of Sexual Love.* Grand Rapids, MI: Zondervan.

Leiblum, S. R., and L. A. Pervin, eds. 1980. *Principles and Practice of Sex Therapy.* New York: Guilford Press.

Leiblum, S. R., and R. C. Rosen, eds. 1988. *Sexual Desire Disorders.* New York: Guilford Press.

LeVay, S. 1991. "A Difference in Hypothalamic Structure Between Heterosexual and Homosexual Men." *Science*, 253:1034-1037.

Levin, R. J. 1975 (October). "The Redbook Report on Premarital and Extramarital Sex." *Redbook*, 38-44 and 190-192.

Levinson, D. R., M. L. Johnson, and D. M. Devaney. 1988. *Sexual Harassment in the Federal Government: An Update.* Washington, DC: U.S. Merit Systems Protection Board.

Lewis, P. H. 1995 (March 26). "Cybersex Stays Hot, Despite a Plan for Cooling It Off." *The New York Times News Service* (on-line).

Lewis, R. J., and L. H. Janda. 1988. "The Relationship Between Adult Sexual Adjustment and Childhood Experiences Regarding Exposure to Nudity, Sleeping in the Parental Bed, and Parental Attitudes Toward Sexuality." *Archives of Sexual Behavior*, 17:349-362.

Lewis, W. C. 1965. "Coital Movements in the First Year of Life." *International Journal of Psychoanalysis*, 46:372-374.

Libby, R. W. and R. N. Whitehurst, eds. 1977. *Marriage and Alternatives: Exploring Intimate Relationships*. Glenview, IL: Scott-Foresman.

Lief, H. I. 1963. "What Medical Schools Teach About Sex." *Bulletin of the Tulane University Medical Faculty*, 22:161-168.

Lief, H. I. 1965. "Sex Education of Medical Students and Doctors." *Pacific Medical Surgery*, 73:52-58.

Lifshitz, A. 1990. "Critical Cultural Barriers that Bar Meeting the Needs of Latinas." *SIECUS Report*, 18(3):16-17.

Lily, T. 1977 (March). "Sexual Surrogate: Notes of a Therapist." *SIECUS Report*, 12-13.

Lobitz, W. C., and J. LoPiccolo. "New Methods in the Behavioral Treatment of Sexual Dysfunction." *Journal of Behavior Therapy and Experimental Psychiatry*, 3(4):265-271.

Lohr, S. 1996 (June 13). "A Complex Medium That Will Be Hard to Regulate." *The New York Times*.

LoPiccolo, J., and W. C. Lobitz. 1973. "Behavior Therapy of Sexual Dysfunction." in L. A. Hammerlynck, L. C. Handy, and E. J. Mash, eds. *Behavior Change: Methodology, Concepts and Practice*. Champaign, IL: Research Press.

LoPiccolo, J., and L. LoPiccolo, eds. 1978. *Handbook of Sex Therapy*. New York: Plenum Press.

Lorch, D. 1996 (February 1). "Quinceañera" A Girl Grows Up. *The New York Times*, pp. C1 and C4.

Loulan, J. 1984. *Lesbian Sex*. San Francisco: Spinsters/Aunt Lute.

Love, B. 1992. *The Encyclopedia of Unusual Sex Practices*. New York: Barricade Books.

Love, B. 1994. "Interviews and Surveys of 200 Adult Book Store Customers and Analysis of Same, 1994." In: *A Longitudinal Study of Sexuality*. San Francisco: The Institute for the Advanced Study of Sexuality, (in press).

Ludlow, D. H., ed. 1992. *The Encyclopedia of Mormonism*. New York: McMillan Publishing Co.

Luker, K. 1996. *Dubious Conceptions: The Politics of Teenage Pregnancy*. Cambridge, MA: Harvard University Press.

Lyons, R. D. 1983 (October 4). "Sex in America: Conservative Attitudes Prevail." *The New York Times*.

Lystad, M. H. 1982. "Sexual Abuse in the Home: A Review of the Literature." *International Journal of Family Psychiatry*, 3:3-31.

Maccoby, E. E., and J. A. Martin. 1983. "Socialization in the Context of the Family: Parent-Child Interaction." In P. H. Mussen, ed. *Handbook of Child Psychology: Volume 4* (4th ed., pp. 1-101). New York: J. Wiley.

MacDonald, J. M. 1971. *Rape Offenders and Their Victims*. Springfield, IL: Thomas.

MacKinnon, C. 1982. "Marxism, Method, and the State: An Agenda for Theory." *Signs*, 7:515-544.

MacKinnon, C. A. 1987. *Feminism Unmodified: Discourses on Life and Law*. Cambridge, MA: Harvard University Press.

MacKinnon, C. A. 1990. "Liberalism and the Death of Feminism." In D. Leidholdt and J. G. Raymond, eds. *The Sexual Liberals and the Attack on Feminism* (pp. 3-13). New York: Pergamon.

Macklin, E. D. 1980. "Nontraditional Family Forms: A Decade of Research." *Journal of Marriage and the Family*, 42:905-920

Macklin, E. D. ed. 1989. *AIDS and Families: Report of the AIDS Task Force*. *Groves Conference on Marriage and the Family*. Binghamton, NY: Harrington Park Press.

Magaña, A., and N. M. Clark. 1995. "Examining a Paradox: Does Religiosity Contribute to Positive Birth Outcomes in Mexican American Populations?" *Health Education Quarterly*, 22(1):96-109.

Malamuth, N. M. 1986. "Predictors of Naturalistic Sexual Aggression." *Journal of Personality and Social Psychology*, 50:953-962.

Malin, M. H. 1987 (June 14-20). "A Preliminary Report of a Case of Necrophilia." Paper presented at the Eighth World Congress for Sexology, Heidelberg.

Maltz, D. N., and R. A. Borker. 1983. "A Cultural Approach to Male-Female Miscommunication." In J. J. Gumperz, ed. *Language and Social Identity* (pp. 195-216). New York: Cambridge University Press.

Mansfield, P. K., A. Voda, and P. B. Koch. 1995. "Predictors of Sexual Response Changes in Heterosexual Midlife Women." *Health Values*, 19:10-20.

Marciano, Teresa Donati. 1987. "Families and Religion." In M. B. Sussman and S. K. Steinmetz, eds. *Handbook of Marriage and the Family* (pp. 285-316). New York: Plenum Press.

Marcus, I. M., and J. F. Francis, eds. 1975. *Masturbation from Infancy to Senescence*. New York: International Universities Press.

Marín, B. V., C. A. Gomez, and N. Hearst. 1993. "Multiple Heterosexual Partners and Condom Use Among Hispanics and Non-Hispanic Whites." *Family Planning Perspectives*, 25:170-174.

Marín, B. V., G. Marín, and R. Juárez. 1990. "Differences Between Hispanics and Non-Hispanics in Willingness to Provide AIDS Prevention Advice." *Hispanic Journal of Behavioral Sciences*, 12(2):153-164.

Martinson, F. M. 1973. *Infant and Child Sexuality: A Sociological Perspective*. St. Peter, MN: The Book Mark.

Martinson, F. M. 1976. "Eroticism in Infancy and Childhood." *Journal of Sex Research*, 12:251-262.

Martinson, F. M. 1990. "Current Legal Status of the Erotic and Sexual Rights of Children." In M. Perry, ed. *Handbook of Sexology: Volume 7: Childhood and Adolescent Sexology*. New York: Elsevier.

Martinson, F. M. 1995. *The Sexual Life of Children*. Westport, CT: Greenwood Press.

Marty, M. E., and R. Scott Appleby, eds. 1992. *Fundamentalisms Observed, Volume 1*. Chicago: University of Chicago Press.

Marty, M. E., and R. Scott Appleby, eds. 1993. *Fundamentalism and Society, Volume 2*. Chicago: University of Chicago Press.

Marty, M. E., and R. Scott Appleby, eds. 1993. *Fundamentalism and the State, Volume 3*. Chicago: University of Chicago Press.

Marty, M. E., and R. Scott Appleby, eds. 1994. *Accounting for Fundamentalism, Volume 4*. Chicago: University of Chicago Press.

Masters, W. H., and V. E. Johnson. 1966. *Human Sexual Response*. Boston: MA: Little Brown.

Masters, W. H., and V. E. Johnson. 1970. *Human Sexual Inadequacy*. Boston, MA: Little Brown.

Mays, V. M. and S. D. Cochran. 1988. "Issues in the Perception of AIDS Risk and Risk Reduction by Black and Hispanic/Latino Women." *American Psychologist*, 43(11):949-957.

Mays, V. M. and S. D. Cochran. 1990. "Methodological Issues in the Assessment and Prediction of AIDS Risk-Related Sexual Behaviors Among Black Americans." In B. Voeller, J. M. Reinisch, and G. M. Gottlieb, eds. *AIDS and Sex: An Integrated Biomedical and Biobehavioral Approach*. New York: Oxford University Press.

McCann, J., and M. K. Biaggio. 1989. "Sexual Satisfaction in Marriage as a Function of Life Meaning." *Archives of Sexual Behavior*, 18:59-72.

McCann-Winter, E. J. S. 1983. *Clergy Education about Homosexuality: An Outcomes Analysis of Knowledge, Attitudes, and Counseling Behaviors*. Unpublished doctoral dissertation, University of Pennsylvania, Philadelphia.

McCleary, K. 1992 (May). "The Chastity Revolution." *Reader's Digest*, 69-71.

McCormick, N. B. 1994a. "Feminism and Sexology." In V. L. Bullough and B. Bullough, eds. *Human Sexuality: An Encyclopedia* (pp. 208-212). New York: Garland Publishing, Inc.

McCormick, N. B. 1994b. *Sexual Salvation: Affirming Women's Sexual Rights and Pleasures*. Westport, CT: Praeger.

McCullagh, Declan. 1996 (August 20). "CDA Update." *The Netizen.*

McGoldrick, J. K. Pearce, and J. Giordano, eds. 1982. *Ethnicity and Family Therapy*. New York: Guilford Press.

McIlvenna, T. 1995 (July 3). Telephone interview with Brenda Love, Palo Alto, California.

McNeil, J. 1976. *The Church and the Homosexual*. Kansas City, Missouri: Sheed Andrews and McMeel.

McWhirter, D., and A. Mattison. 1984. *The Male Couple: How Relationships Develop*. Englewood Cliffs, NJ: Prentice-Hall.

Medina, C. 1987. "Latino Culture and Sex Education." *SIECUS Report*, 15(3):1-4.

Medora, N., and M. Burton. 1981. "Extramarital Sexual Attitudes and Norms of an Undergraduate Student Population." *Adolescence*, 16:251-262.

Michael, R. T., J. H. Gagnon, E. O. Laumann, and G. Kolata. 1994. *Sex in America: A Definitive Survey*. Boston: Little, Brown.

Michaldimitrakis, M. 1986. "Accidental Death During Intercourse by Males." *American Journal of Forensic Medicine and Pathology*, 7:74.

Mikawa, J. K., et al. "Cultural Practices of Hispanics: Implications for the Prevention of AIDS." *Hispanic Journal of Behavioral Sciences*, 14(4):421-433.

Miller, B. C., J. K. McCoy, T. D. Olson, and C. M. Wallace. 1986. "Parental Discipline and Control Attempts in Relation to Adolescent Sexual Attitudes and Behavior." *Journal of Marriage and the Family*, 48:503-512.

Miller, B. C., and K. A. Moore. 1990. "Adolescent Sexual Behavior, Pregnancy, and Parenting: Research Through the 1980s." *Journal of Marriage and the Family*, 52:1025-1044.

Miller, P. Y., and W. Simon. 1981. "The Development of Sexuality in Adolescence." In J. Adelson, ed. *Handbook of Adolescent Psychology* (pp. 383-407). New York: J. Wiley.

Mio, J. S., and J. D. Foster. 1991. "The Effects of Rape upon Victims and Families: Implications for a Comprehensive Family Therapy." *American Journal of Family Therapy*, 19:147-159.

Money, J. 1976. "Childhood: The Last Frontier in Sex Research." *The Sciences*, 16:12-27.

Money, J. 1985. *The Destroying Angel*. Buffalo, NY: Prometheus Press.

Money, J. 1986/1994. *Lovemaps: Sexual/Erotic Health and Pathology, Paraphilia, and Gender Transposition in Childhood, Adolescence, and Maturity* Buffalo, NY: Prometheus.

Money, J. 1988. *Gay, Straight, and In-Between: The Sexology of Erotic Orientation*. New York: Oxford University Press.

Money, J. 1995. *Gendermaps: Social Constructionism, Feminism, and Sexosophical History*. New York: Continuum.

Money, J., and A. A. Ehrhardt. 1972. *Man & Woman, Boy & Girl*. Baltimore: Johns Hopkins University Press.

Money, J., and R. W. Keyes. 1993. *The Armed Robbery Orgasm*. Amhearst, NY: Prometheus Books.

Money, J., and M. Lamacz. 1989. *Vandalized Lovemaps: Paraphilic Outcome of Seven Cases in Pediatric Sexology.* Buffalo, NY: Prometheus Press.

Money, J., G. Wainwright, and D. Hingsburger. 1991. *The Breathless Orgasm: A Lovemap Biography of Asphyxiophilia.* Buffalo, NY: Prometheus Books.

Moore, M. M. 1985. "Nonverbal Courtship Patterns in Women: Context and Consequences." *Ethology and Sociobiology,* 6:201-212.

Moore, M. M., and D. L. Butler. 1989. "Predictive Aspects of Nonverbal Courtship Behavior in Women." *Semiotica,* 76:205-215.

Moran, J. R., and M. D. Corley. 1991. "Source of Sexual Information and Sexual Attitudes and Behaviors of Angle and Hispanic Adolescent Males." *Adolescence,* 26(104):857-864.

Morgan, R. 1984. *Sisterhood Is Global.* Garden City, NY: Anchor Press.

Moser, C. 1988. *"Sadomasochism" The Sexually Unusual Guide to Understanding and Helping.* New York: Harrington Park Press.

Moses, A. and R. Hawkins, Jr. 1982/1986. *Counseling Lesbian Women and Gay Men: A Life-Issues Approach.* Englewood Cliffs, NJ: Paramount Publishing.

Mosher. Clelia Duel. 1980. *The Mosher Survey: Sexual Attitudes of Forty-Five Victorian Women.* James Mahood and Kristine Wenburg, eds. New York: Arno Press.

Mosher, D. L. 1994. "Pornography." In V. L. Bullough and B. Bullough, eds. *Human Sexuality: An Encyclopedia.* New York: Garland Publishing.

Muehlenhard, C. L., and S. W. Cook. 1988. "Men's Self-Reports of Unwanted Sexual Activity." *Journal of Sex Research,* 24:58-72.

Muehlenhard, C. L., S. Danoff-Burg, and I. G. Powch. 1996. "Is Rape Sex or Violence? Conceptual Issues and Implications." In D. M. Buss and N. Malamuth, eds. *Sex, Power, Conflict: Evolutionary and Feminist Perspectives.* New York: Oxford University Press.

Muehlenhard, C. L., M. F. Goggins, J. M. Jones, and A. T. Satterfield. 1991. "Sexual Violence and Coercion in Close Relationships." In K. McKinney and S. Sprecher, eds. *Sexuality in Close Relationships.* Hillsdale, NJ: Lawrence Erlbaum Associates.

Muehlenhard, C. L., P. A. Harney, and J. M. Jones. 1992. From "Victim-Precipitated Rape" to "Date Rape": How Far Have We Come? *Annual Review of Sex Research,* 3:219-253.

Muehlenhard, C. L., I. G. Powch, J. L. Phelps, and L. M. Giusti. 1992. "Definitions of Rape: Scientific and Political Implications." *Journal of Social Issues,* 48(1):23-44.

Murdock, G. P. 1949. *Social Structure.* New York: Macmillan.

Murphy, G. J., W. W. Hudson, and P. L. Cheung. 1980. "Marital and Sexual Discord Among Older Couples." *Social Work Research and Abstracts,* 16:11-16.

Murry, V. M. 1995. "An Ecological Analysis of Pregnancy Resolution Decisions Among African American and Hispanic Adolescent Females." *Youth and Society,* 26(3):325-360.

Murstein, B. I. 1974. *Love, Sex, and Marriage Through the Ages.* New York: Springer.

Mussen, P. H., ed. 1983. *Handbook of Child Psychology: Volume 1, History, Theory, and Methods* (4th ed.). New York: J. Wiley.

NARAL. 1995. *Sexuality Education in America: A State-by-State Review.* Washington, DC: NARAL and the NARAL Foundation.

National Council of la Raza. 1992 (February). *State of Hispanic America 1991: An Overview.* Washington, DC: National Council of la Raza.

National Council of la Raza. 1993. *State of Hispanic America: Toward a Latino Anti-Poverty Agenda.* Washington, DC: National Council of la Raza.

National Research Council. Panel on Monitoring the Social Impact of the AIDS Epidemic. 1993. *The Social Impact of AIDS in the United States.* Washington, DC: National Academy Press.

Neale, T. H. 1989. *Hispanic Heritage in the U.S.: Tradition, Achievement, and Aspiration. CRS Report for Congress 89-532 Gov. Congressional Research Service.* Washington, DC: The Library of Congress.

Nelson, J. B. 1978. *Embodiment.* Minneapolis: Augsburg Publishing House.

Nelson, J. B. 1983. *Between Two Gardens: Reflections on Sexuality and Religious Experience.* New York: Pilgrim Press.

Nelson, J. A. 1986. "Incest: Self-Report Findings from a Nonclinical Sample." *Journal of Sex Research,* 22:463-477.

Nelson, J. B. 1992. *Body Theology.* Louisville, Kentucky: Westminster/John Knox.

Nelson, J. B., and S. P. Longfellow, eds. 1994. *Sexuality and the Sacred: Sources for Theological Reflection.* Louisville, Kentucky: Westminster/John Knox Press.

NetGuide. 1995 (April). "Millions Hooked on the Net," p. 139.

Newcomer, S. F., and J. R. Udry. 1985. "Oral Sex in an Adolescent Population." *Archives of Sexual Behavior,* 14:41-46.

Newman, B. S., and P. G. Muzzonigro. 1993. "The Effects of Traditional Family Values on the Coming Out Process of Gay Male Adolescents." *Adolescence,* 28(109):213-226.

Newman, L. 1989. *Heather Has Two Mommies.* Northampton, MA: In Other Words Publishers.

Newman, L. 1991. *Gloria Goes to Gay Pride.* Boston: Alyson Publications.

Newsweek. 1996 (December 2). "The End of AIDS", pp. 64-73.

The New York Times. 1996 (June 13. "Panel of Three Judges Turns Back Federal Law Intended to Regulate Decency on Internet."

Newsweek. 1993 (August 2). "A Cheeky Protest," p. 6.

Newsweek. 1993 (August 2). "Aspin on Gays in the Military," p. 4.

Newsweek. 1994 (March 14). "Was It Real or Memories?" pp. 54-55.

Nobile, P., and E. Nadler. 1986. *United States of America vs. Sex.* New York: Minotaur Press.

Noonan, R. J. 1995/1984. *Sex Surrogates: A Clarification of Their Functions.* Master's thesis, New York University. Available at World Wide Web site: http://www.SexQuest.com/surrogat.htm. New York: SexQuest/The Sex Institute.

Noonan, R. J. 1996a. "New Directions, New Hope for Sexuality: On the Cutting Edge of Sane Sex." In P. B. Anderson, D. de Mauro, and R. J. Noonan, eds. *Does Anyone Still Remember When Sex Was Fun? Positive Sexuality in the Age of AIDS* (3rd ed.; pp. 144-221). Dubuque, IA: Kendall/Hunt Publishing Co.

Noonan, R. J. 1996b. "Survival Strategies for Lovers in the 1990s." In P. B. Anderson, D. de Mauro, and R. J. Noonan, eds. *Does Anyone Still Remember When Sex Was Fun? Positive Sexuality in the Age of AIDS* (3rd ed.; pp. 1-12). Dubuque, IA: Kendall/Hunt Publishing Co.

North, B. J. 1990. Effectiveness of Vaginal Contraceptives in Prevention of Sexually Transmitted Diseases. In N. J. Alexander, H. L. Gabelnick, & J. M. Spieler, eds. *Heterosexual Transmission of AIDS: Proceedings of the Second Contraceptive Research and Development (CONRAD) Program International Workshop, held in Norfolk, Virginia, February 1-3, 1989* (pp. 273-290). New York: Wiley-Liss.

Norton, A. J., and J. E. Moorman. 1987. "Current Trends in Marriage and Divorce Among American Women." *Journal of Marriage and the Family,* 49:3-14.

O'Brien, R. M. 1987. "The Interracial Nature of Violent Crimes: A Reexamination." *American Journal of Sociology,* 92:817-835.

Ogden, G. 1995. *Women Who Love Sex.* New York: Pocket Books.

Okami, P. 1992. "Child Perpetrators of Sexual Abuse: The Emergence of a Problematic Deviant Category." *Journal of Sex Research,* 29:109-130.

Okami, P. 1995. "Childhood Exposure to Parental Nudity, Parent-Child Co-Sleeping, and 'Primal Scenes:' A Review of Clinical Opinion and Empirical Evidence." *Journal of Sex Research*, 32:51-64.

Okazaki, C. N. 1994 (November). "Rowing Your Boat." *Ensign*. 24(11):92-94.

Oliver, M. B., and J. S. Hyde. 1993. "Gender Differences in Sexuality: A Meta-Analysis." *Psychological Bulletin*, 114:29-51.

O'Neill, N., and G. O'Neill. 1972. *Open Marriage: A New Lifestyle for Couples.* New York: M. Evans.

Padilla, A. M., and T. L. Barids. 1991. "Mexican-American Adolescent Sexuality and Sexual Knowledge: An Exploratory Study." *Hispanic Journal of Behavioral Sciences*, 13(1):95-104.

Palmer, C. T. 1988. "Twelve Reasons Why Rape Is Not Sexually Motivated: A Skeptical Examination." *Journal of Sex Research*, 25:512-530.

Paluszny, M. 1979. "Current Thinking on Children's Sexuality." *Medical Aspects of Human Sexuality*, 13:120-121.

Pankhurst, J., and S. K. Houseknecht. 1983. "The Family, Politics, and Religion in the 1980s." *Journal of Family Issues*, 4:5-34.

Patton, C. 1990. *Inventing AIDS.* New York: Routledge.

Pauly, I. B. 1994. "Transsexualism." In V. L. Bullough and B. Bullough, eds. *Human Sexuality: An Encyclopedia* (pp. 590-598). New York: Garland Publishing.

Pauly, I., and T. Lindgren. 1976. "Body Image and Gender Identity. *Journal of Homosexuality*, 2:133-142.

Pearl, J. 1987. "The Highest Paying Customers: America's Cities and the Costs of Prostitution Control." *Hastings Law Journal*, 38:769-800.

Penner, C., and J. Penner. 1981. *The Gift of Sex: A Guide to Sexual Fulfillment.* Dallas: Word.

Peplau, L. A., Z. Rubin, and C. T. Hill. 1977. "Sexual Intimacy in Dating Relationships." *Journal of Social Issues*, 33:86-109.

Pérez. M. A. In press. "Sexual Communication Among Hispanic Farmworker Adolescents."

Pérez, M. A. and K. Fennelly. 1996. "Risk Factors for HIV and AIDS Among Latino Farmworkers in Pennsylvania." In S. I. Misha, R. F. Conner, and J. R. Magana, eds. *AIDS Crossing Borders: The Spread of HIV Among Migrant Latinos* (pp. 137-156). Boulder, CO: Westview Press.

Perper, T. 1985. *Sex Signals: The Biology of Love.* Philadelphia: ISI Press.

Perper, T., and D. L. Weis. 1987. "Proceptive and Rejective Strategies of U.S. and Canadian College Women." *Journal of Sex Research*, 23:455-480.

Peterson, K. S. 1994 (October 7). "Turns Out We Are 'Sexually Conventional.'" *USA Today*, pp. 1-2A.

Peterson, L. S. 1995 (February). "Contraceptive Use in the United States: 1982-90." *Advance Data, No. 260.* Hyattsville, MD: Centers for Disease Control, U.S. Department of Health and Human Services.

Pettigrew, T. 1964. *A Profile of the Negro American.* Princeton, NJ: Van Nostrand.

Phillips, L., and C. Phillips. 1994. *Survey of Transgenderists.* Bulverde, TX 78163: P.O. Box 17.

Phipps, W. E. 1975. *Recovering Biblical Sensuousness.* Philadelphia: Westminster Press.

Pietropinto, A., and J. Simenauer. 1977. *Beyond the Male Myth: A Nationwide Survey.* New York: New American Library.

Pleck, J. 1981. *The Myth of Masculinity.* Cambridge, MA: MIT Press.

Pomeroy, W. B. 1972. *Dr. Kinsey and the Institute for Sex Research.* New York: Harper and Row.

Prendergast, W. E. 1991. *Treating Sex Offenders in Correctional Institutions and Outpatient Clinics: A Guide to Clinical Practice.* Binghamton, NY: Haworth Press.

Prendergast, W. E. 1993. *The Merry-Go-Round of Sexual Abuse: Identifying and Treating Survivors.* Binghamton, NY: Haworth Press.

Prescott, J. W., and D. Wallace. 1978 (July-August). "Abortion and the 'Right-to-Life.'" *The Humanist,* 18-24.

Prins, K. S., B. P. Buunk, and N. W. VanYperen. 1993. "Equity, Normative Disapproval and Extramarital Relationships. *Journal of Social and Personal Relationships,* 10:39-53.

Purchas, S. 1905. *Haklutus Posthumus, or Prchas His Pilgrimes: Contayning a History of the World in Sea Voyages and Land Travells by Englishmen and Others.* Glascow, Scotland: J. Maclehose and Sons.

Quinttner, Joshua. 1996 (June 24). "Free Speech for the Net." *Time Magazine,* 147(26).

Rainwater, L. 1964. "Marital Sexuality in Four Cultures of Poverty." *Journal of Marriage and the Family,* 26:457-466.

Ramey, J. W. 1976. *Intimate Friendships.* Englewood Cliffs, NJ: Prentice-Hall.

Ramsey, G. V. 1943. "The Sexual Development of Boys." *American Journal of Psychology,* 56:217-233.

Ranke-Heinemann, U. 1990. *Eunuchs for the Kingdom of Heaven: Women, Sexuality, and the Catholic Church.* New York: Doubleday.

Redlich, F. 1977. "The Ethics of Sex Therapy." In W. H. Masters, V. E. Johnson, and R. C. Kolodny, *Ethical Issues in Sex Therapy and Research.* Boston: Little, Brown and Company.

Reibstein, J. A., and M. Richards. 1993. *Sexual Arrangements: Marriage and the Temptation of Infidelity.* New York: Scribner.

Reichelt, P. A., and H. H. Werley. 1975. "Contraception, Abortion and Venereal Disease: Teenagers' Knowledge and the Effect of Education." *Family Planning Perspectives,* 7(2):83-88.

Reiss, I. 1960. *Premarital Sexual Standards in America.* New York: Free Press.

Reiss, I. 1964. "Premarital Sexual Permissiveness Among Negroes and Whites." *American Sociological Review,* 29:688-698.

Reiss, I. 1967. *The Social Context of Premarital Sexual Permissiveness.* New York: Holt, Rinehart and Winston.

Reiss, I. L. 1976/1980. *Family Systems in America* (2nd ed./3rd ed.). New York: Holt, Rinehart and Winston.

Reiss, I. 1981. "Some Observations on Ideology and Sexuality in America." *Journal of Marriage and the Family,* 43(2):271-283.

Reiss, I. L. 1986. *Journey into Sexuality: An Exploratory Voyage.* Englewood Cliffs, NJ: Prentice-Hall.

Reiss, I. L. 1995. "Is This the Definitive Sexual Survey?" Review of E. O. Laumann, J. H. Gagnon, R. T. Michael, and S. Michaels. The Social Organization of Sexuality: Sexual Practices in the United States. *Journal of Sex Research,* 32:77-85.

Reiss, I. L., R. E. Anderson, and G. C. Sponaugle. 1980. "A Multivariate Model of the Determinants of Extramarital Sexual Permissiveness." *Journal of Marriage and the Family,* 42:395-411.

Reiss, I. L., A. Banwart, and H. Foreman. 1975. "Premarital Contraceptive Usage: A Study and Some Theoretical Explorations." *Journal of Marriage and the Family,* 37:619-630.

Relief Society Conference, 1965 (September 29). Salt Lake City: Church of Jesus Christ of the Latter-Day Saints Publication.

Resick, P. A. 1993. "The Psychological Impact of Rape." *Journal of Interpersonal Violence*, 8:223-255.

Resnick, H. S., D. G. Kilpatrick, B. S. Dansky, B. E. Saunders, and C. L. Best. 1993. "Prevalence of Civilian Trauma and Posttraumatic Stress Disorder in a Representative National Sample of Women." *Journal of Consulting and Clinical Psychology*, 61:984-991.

Rheingold, H. 1995 (March/April). "The Virtual Community." *Utne Reader*, 68:61-64.

Richardson, L. W. 1985. *The New Other Woman: Contemporary Single Women in Affairs with Married Men.* New York: Free Press.

Riddle, G. 1989. *Amputees and Devotees.* Sunnyvale, CA: Halcyon Press.

Rimmer, R. H. 1966. *The Harrad Experiment.* New York: Bantam.

Riportella-Muller, R. 1989. "Sexuality in the Elderly: A Review." In K. McKinney and S. Sprecher, eds. *Human Sexuality: The Societal and Interpersonal Context* (pp. 210-236). Norwood, NJ: Ablex.

Roberts, B. 1981. "Surrogate Partners and Their Use in Sex Therapy." In D. A. Brown & C. Chary, eds. *Sexuality in America* (pp. 283-300). Ann Arbor, MI: Greenfield Books.

Roberts, S. V., and G. Cohen. 1995 (April 24). "The Religious Right: Church Meets State; On God's Green Earth; The Heavy Hitter." *U.S. News and World Report*, pp. 26-39.

Robinson, I. E., K. King, and J. O. Balswick. 1972. "The Premarital Sexual Revolution Among College Females." *Family Coordinator*, 21:189-194.

Robinson, P. 1976. *The Modernization of Sex.* New York: Harper and Row.

Roebuck, J. and M. McGee. 1977. "Attitudes Toward Premarital Sex and Sexual Behavior Among Black High School Girls." *Journal of Sex Research*, 13:104-114.

Rogers, J. A. 1967. *Sex and Race: Negro-Caucasian Mixing in All Ages and All Lands.* 9th ed. New York: J. A. Rogers.

Roiphe, K. 1993. *The Morning After: Sex, Fear and Feminism on Campus.* Boston: Little Brown.

Rosen, R. C., and J. G. Beck. 1988. *Patterns of Sexual Arousal: Psychophysiological Processes and Clinical Applications.* New York: Guilford Press.

Ross, M. W., J. A. Paulsen, O. W. Stalstrom. 1988. "Homosexuality and Mental Health: A Cross-Cultural Review." *Journal of Homosexuality*, 15(1):131-152.

Rosser, B. R. S., S. M. Dwyer, E. Coleman, M. Miner, M. Metz, B. Robinson, and W. O. Bockting. 1995. "Using Sexually Explicit Material in Sex Education: An Eighteen Year Comparative Analysis." *Journal of Sex Education and Therapy*, 21(2):118-128.

Rossetti, S. J. 1991. *Slayer of the Soul: Child Sexual Abuse and the Catholic Church.* Mystic, CT: Twenty-Third Publications.

Rotello, G. 1996 (June 24). "To Have and To Hold: The Case for Gay Marriage." *The Nation*, pp. 11-18.

Roth, S., and L. Lebowitz. 1988. "The Experience of Sexual Trauma." *Journal of Traumatic Stress*, 1:79-107.

Rotheram-Borus, M.J., M. Rosario, et al. 1994. "Sexual and Substance Use Acts of Gay and Bisexual Male Adolescents in New York City." *Journal of Sex Research*, 31(1):47-57.

Rotkin, K. 1986. "The Phallacy of Our Sexual Norm." In S. Bem, ed. *Psychology of Sex Roles* (pp. 384-391). Acton, MA: Copley Publishing. (Reprinted from *RT: A Journal of Radical Therapy*, 1972, p. 3.)

Rubenstein, M. 1982. *An In-Depth Study of Bisexuality and Its Relationship to Self-Esteem.* Unpublished doctoral dissertation, The Institute for Advanced Study of Human Sexuality, San Francisco.

Rubin, A. M., and J. R. Adams. 1986. "Outcomes of Sexually Open Marriages." *Journal of Sex Research*, 22:311-319.

Rush, F. 1990. "The Many Faces of Backlash." In: D. Leidholdt and J. Raymond, eds. *The Sexual Liberals and the Attack on Feminism* (pp. 165-174). New York: Pergamon.

Russell, D. E. H. 1990. *Rape In Marriage* (rev. ed.; originally published in 1982). Bloomington: Indiana University Press.

Russell, D. E. H. 1984. *Sexual Exploitation: Rape, Child Sexual Abuse, and Workplace Harassment.* Newbury Park, CA: Sage.

Russo, N., and K. Zierk. 1992. "Abortion, Childbearing, and Women's Well-being." *Professional Psychology: Research and Practice*, 23:269.

Samuels, H. P. 1994. "Race, Sex, and Myths: Images of African-American Men and Women." In V. L. Bullough and B. Bullough, eds. *Human Sexuality: An Encyclopedia.* New York: Garland Press.

Samuels, H. P. 1995. "Sexology, Sexosophy, and African-American Sexuality: Implications for Sex Therapy and Sexuality Education." *SIECUS Report*, 23:3.

Sandoval, A., R. Duran, L. O'Donnel, and C. R. O'Donnell. 1995. "Barriers to Condom Use in Primary and Nonprimary Relationships Among Hispanic STD Clinic Patients." *Hispanic Journal of Behavioral Sciences*, 17(3):385-397.

Sarrel, P. M, and W. H. Masters. 1982. "Sexual Molestation of Men by Women. *Archives of Sexual Behavior*, 11:117-231.

Sarrel, P., and L. Sarrel. 1980 (October) and 1981 (February). "The Redbook Report on Sexual Relationships, Parts 1 and 2." *Redbook*, pp. 73-60 and 140-145.

Saunders, J. M., and J. M. Edwards. 1984. "Extramarital Sexuality: A Predictive Model of Permissive Attitudes. *Journal of Marriage and Family*, 46:825-835.

Savitz, L., and L. Rosen. 1988. "The Sexuality of Prostitutes: Sexual Enjoyment Reported by 'Streetwalkers.'" *Journal of Sex Research*, 24:200-208.

Schmitt, E. 1996 (June 13). "Panel Passes Bill to Let States Refuse to Recognize Gay Marriage." *The New York Times*, p. A15.

Schmalz, J. 1993 (April 16). "Survey Stirs Debate on Number of Gay Men in U.S." *The New York Times*, p. 20.

Schoenborn, C. A., S. L. Marsh, and A. M. Hardy. 1994 (February). "AIDS Knowledge and Attitudes for 1992: Data from the National Health Interview Survey." *Advance Data from Vital and Health Statistics #243. National Center for Health Statistics.* Hyattsville, MD: Government Printing Office.

Schwartz, I. 1993. "Affective Reactions of American and Swedish Women to Their First Premarital Coitus: A Cross-Cultural Comparison." *Journal of Sex Research*, 30:18-26.

Schwartz, John. 1996a (February 9). "Abortion Provision Stirs On-Line Furor." *Washington Post.*

Schwartz, John. 1996b (June 13). "Court Upholds Free Speech on Internet, Blocks Decency Law." *Washington Post.*

Schwartz, M. F. and J. S. Quarterman. 1993. "The Changing Global Internet Service Infrastructure." *Internet Research*, 3(1):8-25.

Schwartz, S. 1973. "Effects of Sex Guilt and Sexual Arousal on the Retention of Birth Control Information." *Journal of Consulting and Clinical Psychology*, 41:61-64.

Scott, J. W. 1976. "Polygamy: A Futuristic Family Arrangement for African-Americans." *Black Books Bulletin*, p. 4.

Scott, J. W. 1986. "From Teenage Parenthood to Polygamy: Case Studies in Black Polygamous Family Formation." *Western Journal of Black Studies*, 10(4):172-179.

Schow, R., W. Schow, and M. Raynes. 1991. *Peculiar People: Mormons and Same-Sex Orientation.* Salt Lake City, UT: Signature Books.

Seaman, B. 1969. *The Doctor's Case Against the Pill.* New York: Peter H. Wyden.

Sears, R. R., E. E. Maccoby, and H. Levin. 1957. "Patterns of Child Rearing." Evanston, IL: Row, Peterson.

Sedway, M. 1992 (February/March). "Far Right Takes Aim at Sexuality Education. *SIECUS Report*, 20(3):13-19.

Segura, D. A. 1991. "Ambivalence or Continuity? Motherhood and Employment Among Chicanas and Mexican Immigrant Women Workers." *Aztlan*, 20(2):150.

Seidman, S. 1991. *Romantic Longings: Love in America, 1830-1980.* New York: Routledge.

Settlage, D., S. Fordney, S. Baroff, and D. Cooper. 1973. "Sexual Experience of Younger Teenage Girls Seeking Contraceptive Assistance for the First Time." *Family Planning Perspectives*, 5:223-226.

Shapiro, L. 1994 (January 24). "They're Daddy's Little Girls." *Newsweek*, p. 66.

Shah, R., and M. Zelnick. 1981. "Parent and Peer Influence on Sexual Behavior, Contraceptive Use, and Pregnancy Experience of Young Women." *Journal of Marriage and the Family*, 43:339-348.

Shilts, R. 1993. *Conduct Unbecoming: Gays and Lesbians in the U.S. Military.* New York: St. Martin's Press.

Shilts, R. 1987. *And the Band Played On: Politics, People, and the AIDS Epidemic.* New York: St. Martin's Press.

Shostak, A. B. 1987. "Singlehood." In M. B. Sussman and S. K. Steinmetz, eds. *Handbook of Marriage and the Family* (pp. 355-368). New York: Plenum.

SIECUS. 1990. *Sex Education 2000. A Call to Action.* New York: SIECUS.

SIECUS. 1991. *Comprehensive Sexuality Education, Kindergarten-12th Grade.* New York: SIECUS.

SIECUS Fact Sheet #2 (on comprehensive sexuality education). 1992. National Coalition to Support Sexuality Education.

Simon, W. 1994. "Deviance as History: The Future of Perversion." *Archives of Sexual Behavior*, 23(1):16.

Simon, W., A. S. Berger, and J. H. Gagnon. 1972. "Beyond Anxiety and Fantasy: The Coital Experiences of College Youth." *Journal of Youth and Adolescence*, 1:203-222.

Singh, B. K., B. L. Walton, and J. J. Williams. 1976. "Extramarital Sexual Permissiveness: Conditions and Contingencies." *Journal of Marriage and the Family*, 38:701-712.

Sipe, A. W. Richard. 1995. *Sex, Priests, and Power: Anatomy of a Crisis.* New York: Brunner/Mazel.

Slowinski, J. W. 1994. "Religious Influence on Sexual Attitudes and Functioning." In V. L. Bullough and B. Bullough, eds. *Human Sexuality: An Encyclopedia* (pp. 520-522). New York: Garland.

Smedes, L. B. 1994. *Sex for Christians: The Limits and Liberties of Sexual Living* (rev. ed.) Grand Rapids, MI: William B. Erdsman.

Smith, L. G., and J. R. Smith. 1974. "Co-Marital Sex: The Incorporation of Extramarital Sex into the Marriage Relationship." In J. R. Smith and L. G. Smith, eds. *Beyond Monogamy* (pp. 84-102). Baltimore: Johns Hopkins Press.

Smith, R. E., C. J. Pine, and M. E. Hawley. 1988. "Social Cognitions about Adult Male Victims of Female Sexual Assault." *Journal of Sex Research*, 24:101-112.

Smith, T. W. 1987 (August). *Unpublished Data from 1972-1987 General Social Surveys* Chicago: National Opinion Research Center.

Smith, T. W. 1990 (February). "Adult Sexual Behavior in 1989: Number of Partners, Frequency, and Risk." Paper presented at the annual meeting of the American Association for the Advancement of Science, New Orleans, LA.

Smith, T. W. 1991. "Adult Sexual Behavior in 1989: Number of Partners, Frequency of Intercourse and Risk of AIDS." *Family Planning Perspectives*, 23(3):102-107.

Smith, T. W. 1996 (December). *Unpublished Data from 1972-1994. General Social Surveys.* Chicago: National Opinion Research Center.

Solomon, J., and S. Miller. 1994 (September 12). "'Hero' or 'Harasser'?" *Newsweek*, pp. 48-50.

Sonestein, F. L., J. H. Pleck, and L. C. Ku. 1991. "Levels of Sexual Activity Among Adolescent Males in the United States. *Family Planning Perspectives*, 23(4):162-167.

Sorensen, R. C. 1973. *Adolescent Sexuality in Contemporary America.* New York: World.

Spaccarelli, S. 1994. "Stress, Appraisal, and Coping in Child Sexual Abuse: A Theoretical and Empirical Review." *Psychological Bulletin,* 116:340-362.

Spanier, G. B. 1975. "Sexualization and Premarital Sexual Behavior." *Family Coordinator,* 24:33-41.

Spanier, G. B. 1976. "Formal and Informal Sex Education as Determinants of Premarital Sexual Behavior." *Archives of Sexual Behavior,* 5:39-67.

Spanier, G. B. 1978. "Sex Education and Premarital Sexual Behavior Among American College Students." *Adolescence,* 8:659-674.

Spanier, G. B., and R. L. Margolis. 1983. "Marital Separation and Extramarital Sexual Behavior." *Journal of Sex Research,* 19:23-48.

Spector, R. E., ed. 1991. *Cultural Diversity in Health and Illness.* Norwalk, CA: Appleton and Lange.

Spong, J. S. 1988. *Living in Sin? A Bishop Rethinks Human Sexuality.* San Francisco: HarperSanFrancisco.

Sprenkle, D. H. and D. L. Weis. 1978. "Extramarital Sexuality: Implications for Marital Therapists." *Journal of Sex and Marital Therapy,* 4:279-291.

Stacy, R. D., M. Prisbell, and K. Tollefsrud. 1992. "A Comparison of Attitudes Among College Students Toward Sexual Violence Committed by Strangers and by Acquaintances: A Research Report." *Journal of Sex Education and Therapy,* 18:257-263.

Stanley, L. A. 1989. "The Child Porn Myth." *Cardozo Arts and Entertainment Law Journal,* 7:295-358.

Sprecher, S., A. Barbee, and P. Schwartz. 1995. "'Was It Good for You, Too?': Gender Differences in First Sexual Intercourse Experiences." *Journal of Sex Research,* 32:3-15.

Staples, R. 1972. "Research on Black Sexuality: Its Implications for Family Life, Sex Education and Public Policy." *The Family Coordinator,* 21:183-188.

Staples, R. 1974. "Black Sexuality." In: M. Calderone, ed. *Sexuality and Human Values* (pp. 62-70). New York: Association Press.

Staples, R. 1977. "The Myth of the Impotent Black Males." In D. Y. Wilkinson and R. L. Taylor, eds. *The Black Male in America.* Chicago: Nelson-Hall.

Staples, R., ed. 1978. *The Black Family: Essays and Studies.* Belmont, CA: Wadsworth Publishing Co.

Staples, R. 1981. *The World of Black Singles: Changing Patterns of Male/Female Relations.* Westport: CT: Greenwood Press.

Staples, R. 1982. *Black Masculinity: The Black Male's Role in American Society.* San Francisco: The Black Scholar Press.

Staples, R. 1986. "The Black Response." In R. T. Francoeur, ed. *Taking Sides: Clashing Views on Controversial Issues in Human Sexuality.* Guilford, CT: Dushkin Publishing.

Staples, R., and L. Boulin Johnson. 1993. *Black Families at the Crossroads: Challenges and Prospects.* San Francisco: Jossey-Bass.

Starr, B. D., and M. Bakur Weiner. 1981. *The Starr-Weiner Report on Sex and Sexuality in the Mature Years.* Briarcliff Manor, NY: Stein and Day.

Stekel, W. 1922. *Bi-Sexual Love.* New York: Emerson Books.

Stern, H. 1993. *Private Parts.* New York: Simon and Schuster.

Stine, G. J. 1995. *AIDS Update: 1994-1995.* Englewood Cliffs, NJ: Prentice-Hall.

Storms, M. D. 1981. "A Theory of Erotic Orientation Development." *Psychological Review,* 88:340-353.

Strong, B., and C. DeVault. 1994. *Human Sexuality.* Mountain View, CA: Mayfield.

Sullivan, A. 1996. *Virtually Normal: An Argument about Homosexuality.* New York: Knopf.

Surra, C. A. 1990. "Research and Theory on Mate Selection and Premarital Relationships in the 1980s." *Journal of Marriage and the Family,* 52:844-865.

Symonds, C. 1973 (September). "Sex Surrogates." *Penthouse Forum.* Quoted in S. Braun, ed. 1975, *Catalog of Sexual Consciousness* (p. 137). New York: Grove Press.

Szapocznik, J. 1995. "Research on Disclosure of HIV Status: Cultural Evolution Finds an Ally in Science." *Health Psychology*, 14(1):4-5.

Taggart, J. M. 1992. "Gender Segregation and Cultural Constructions of Sexuality in Two Hispanic Societies." *American Ethnologist*, 19:75-96.

Talmage, J. E. 1977. *A Study of the Articles of Faith.* Salt Lake City, UT: Church of Jesus Christ of Latter-Day Saints.

Tamosaitis, N. 1995. *net.sex.* Emeryville, CA: Ziff-Davis Press.

Tangri, S., M. R. Burt, and L. B. Johnson. 1982. "Sexual Harassment at Work: Three Explanatory Models." *Journal of Social Issues*, 38(4):33-54.

Tanner, President N. Eldon. 1973. *The Role of Womanhood.* Salt Lake City: Church of Jesus Christ of the Latter-Day Saints Publication.

Tavris, C. 1978, February. "40,000 Men Tell About Their Sexual Behavior, Their Fantasies, Their Ideal Women, and Their Wives." *Redbook*, pp. 111-113 and 178-181.

Tavris, C., and S. Sadd. 1975. *The Redbook Report on Female Sexuality.* New York: Delacorte.

Teevan, J. J. Jr. 1972. "Reference Groups and Premarital Sexual Behavior." *Journal of Marriage and the Family*, 34:283-291.

Terman, L. M. 1938. *Psychological Factors in Marital Happiness.* New York: McGraw-Hill.

Thayer, N. S. T., et al. 1987 (March). "Report of the Task Force on Changing Patterns of Sexuality and Family Life." *The Voice.* Newark, NJ: Episcopal Diocese of Northern New Jersey.

Thompson, A. P. 1983. "Extramarital Sex: A Review of the Research Literature." *Journal of Sex Research*, 19:1-22.

Thompson, A. P. 1984. "Emotional and Sexual Components of Extramarital Relations." *Journal of Marriage and the Family*, 46:35-42.

Thorne, B., and Z. Luria. 1986. "Sexuality and Gender in Children's Daily Worlds." *Social Problems*, 33(3):176-190.

Thornton, B. 1977. "Toward a Linear Prediction Model of Marital Happiness." *Personality and Social Psychology Bulletin*, 3:674-676.

Tiefer, L. 1995. *Sex Is Not a Natural Act and Other Essays.* San Francisco: Westview.

Time Magazine. 1995 (Spring). Special Issue: "Welcome to Cyberspace."

Timmerman, J. 1986. *The Mardi Gras Syndrome: Rethinking Christian Sexuality.* New York: CrossRoads.

Tommy. 1992. "A Theory on Infantilism." Reprint available from DPF. Suite 127. 38 Miller Avenue. Mill Valley, CA 94941.

Tribe, L. H. 1992. *Abortion: The Clash of Absolutes.* New York: W. W. Norton.

Trudell, B., and M. Whatley. 1991. "Sex Respect: A Problematic Public School Sexuality Curriculum." *Journal of Sex Education and Therapy*, 17:125-140.

Trussell, J., and C. Westoff. 1980. "Contraceptive Practice and Trends in Coital Frequency." *Family Planning Perspectives*, 12: 246-249.

Turco, S. A. 1994 (September 22). "Students Admit Sexual Activity." *BG News*, 80(22):1 and 5.

Twining, A. 1983. *Bisexual Women: Identity in Adult Development.* Unpublished Doctoral dissertation, Boston University School of Education.

Tzeng, O. C. S., and H. J. Schwarzin. 1987. "Gender and Race Differences in Child Sexual Abuse Correlates." *International Journal of Intercultural Relation*, 14:135-161.

Udry, J. R. 1980. "Changes in The Frequency of Marital Intercourse from Panel Data." *Archives of Sexual Behavior*, 9:319-325.

Udry, J. R. 1990. "Hormonal and Social Determinants of Adolescent Sexual Initiation." In J. Bancroft and J. M. Reinisch, eds. *Adolescence and Puberty* (pp. 70-87). New York: Oxford Press.

Udry, J. R., K. E. Bauman, and N. M. Morris. 1975. "Changes in Premarital Coital Experience of Recent Decade of Birth Cohorts of Urban American Women." *Journal of Marriage and the Family*, 37:783-787.

Udry, J. R., F. R. Deven, and S. J. Coleman. 1982. "A Cross-National Comparison of the Relative Influence of Male and Female Age on the Frequency of Marital Intercourse." *Journal of Biosocial Science*, 14:1-6.

Udry, J. R., L. M. Tolbert, and N. M. Morris. 1986. "Biosocial Foundations for Adolescent Female Sexuality." *Demography*, 23:217-230.

Ullman, S. E., and Knight, R. A. 1992. "Fighting Back: Women's Resistance to Rape." *Journal of Interpersonal Violence*, 7:31-43.

United Presbyterian Church in the U.S.A. General Assembly Special Committee on Human Sexuality. 1991. *Part 1: Keeping Body and Soul Together: Sexuality, Spirituality, and Social Justice. Part 2: Minority report of the Special Committee on Human Sexuality* (Report to the 203rd General Assembly). Baltimore: Presbyterian Church (U.S.A.).

U.S. Bureau of the Census. 1993. *Hispanic Americans Today. Current Population Reports, P23-183*. Washington, DC: Government Printing Office.

U.S. Department of Commerce. 1991. *Statistical Abstract of the United States 1991. 111th edition. Bureau of the Census*. Washington, DC: Government Printing Office.

U.S. Department of Health and Human Services. 1994 (December). *Sexually Transmitted Disease Surveillance 1993*. Atlanta, GA: Public Health Service, Centers for Disease Control and Prevention.

U.S. News and World Report. 1995 (April 24). "The Religious Right: Church Meets State," pp. 26-39.

Vance, C. S., and C. A. Pollis. 1990. "Introduction: A Special Issue on Feminist Perspectives on Sexuality. *Journal of Sex Research*, 27:1-5.

Van Wyk, P. H. and C. S. Geist. 1984. "Psychosexual Development of Heterosexual, Bisexual, and Homosexual Behavior." *Archives of Sexual Behavior*, 13:505-544.

Vener, A. M., and C. S. Stewart. 1974. "Adolescent Sexual Behavior in Middle America Revisited: 1970-1973." *Journal of Marriage and the Family*, 36:728-735.

Verhovek, S. H. 1995 (August 12). "New Twist for a Landmark Case: Roe v. Wade Becomes Roe v. Roe." *The New York Times*, pp. 1, 9.

Voeller, B. 1991. "AIDS and Heterosexual Anal Intercourse." *Archives of Sexual Behavior*, 20(3):233-276.

Wachowiak. C., and H. Bragg. 1980. "Open Marriage and Marital Adjustment." *Journal of Marriage and the Family*, 42(1):57-62.

Walsh, J. 1993 (July/August). "The New Sexual Revolution: Liberation at Last? or the Same Old Mess?" *Utne Reader*, No. 58:59-65.

Warshaw, R. 1988. *I Never Called It Rape*. New York: Harper & Row.

Waterman, C. K., L. J. Dawson, and M. J. Bologna. 1989. "Sexual Coercion in Gay Male and Lesbian Relationships: Predictors and Implications for Support Services." *Journal of Sex Research*, 26:118-124.

Weaver, A. J. 1995. "Has There Been a Failure to Prepare and Support Parish-Based Clergy in Their Role as Front-Line Community Mental Health Workers: A Review." *Journal of Pastoral Care*, 49(2):129-147.

Weeks, M. R., J. J. Schensul, S. S. Williams, M. Singer, and M. Grier. 1995. "AIDS Prevention for African-American and Latina Women: Building Culturally and Gender-Appropriate Interventions." *AIDS Education and Prevention*, 7(3):251-264.

Weinberg, M., and C. J. Williams. 1994. *Dual Attraction.* New York: Oxford University Press.

Weinberg, M. S., C. J. Williams, and C. Calham. 1994. "Homosexual Foot Fetishism." *Archives of Sexual Behavior,* 23(6):611-626.

Weis, D. L. 1983. "Affective Reactions of Women to Their Initial Experience of Coitus." *Journal of Sex Research,* 19:209-237.

Weis, D. L. 1983. "Open Marriage and Multilateral Relationships: The Emergence of Nonexclusive Models of the Marital Relationship." In E. D. Macklin and R. H. Rubin, eds. *Contemporary Families and Alternative Lifestyles: Handbook on Research and Theory* (pp. 194-216). Beverly Hills, CA: Sage.

Weis. D. L., and J. Jurich. 1985. "Size of Community of Residence as a Predictor of Attitudes Toward Extramarital Sexual Relations." *Journal of Marriage and the Family,* 47(1):173-179.

Weis, D. L., and M. Slosnerick. 1981. "Attitudes Toward Sexual and Nonsexual Extramarital Involvement Among a Sample of College Students." *Journal of Marriage and the Family,* 43:349-358.

Weise, E. R., ed. 1992. *Closer to Home: Bisexuality and Feminism.* Seattle: Seal Press.

Wellman, B. 1992. "Men in Network: Private Communities, Domestic Friendships." In P. M. Nardi, ed. *Men's Friendships* (pp. 74-114). Newbury Park, CA: Sage.

Wellman, B. 1985. "Domestic Work, Paid Work and Net Work. In S.W. Duck and D. Perlman, eds. *Understanding Personal Relationships* (pp. 159-191). Newbury Park, CA: Sage.

Wells, R. V. 1985. *Uncle Sam's Family: Issues and Perspectives on American Demographic History.* Albany, NY: State University of New York Press.

Westheimer, R., and L. Lieberman. 1988. *Sex and Morality: Who Is Teaching Our Sex Standards?* Boston, MA: Harcourt, Brace, Jovanovich.

Westoff, C. 1974. "Coital Frequency and Contraception." *Family Planning Perspectives,* 6:136-141.

Wheat, E., and G. Wheat. 1981. *Intended for Pleasure* (rev. ed.) Grand Rapids, MI: Fleming H. Revell/Baker Book House.

Wheeler, D. L. 1995 (April 7). "A Birth-Control Vaccine." *The Chronicle of Higher Education,* 41(A8):9 & 15.

Whitley, M. P., and S. B. Poulsen. 1975. "Assertiveness and Sexual Satisfaction in Employed Professional Women." *Journal of Marriage and the Family,* 37:573-581.

Wiederman, M. W. 1993. "Demographic and Sexual Characteristics of Nonrespondents to Sexual Experience Items in a National Survey." *Journal of Sex Research,* 30:27-35.

Wiederman, M. W., D. L. Weis, and E. R. Allgeier. 1994. "The Effect of Question Preface on Response Rates to a Telephone Survey of Sexual Experience." *Archives of Sexual Behavior,* 23:203-215.

Wiener. L. S. 1991 (September). "Women and Human Immunodeficiency Virus: A Historical and Personal Psychosocial Perspective." *Social Work,* 36(5):375-378.

Wilkinson, D. 1987. "Ethnicity." In M. B. Sussman & S. K. Steinmetz, eds. *Handbook of Marriage and the Family* (pp. 183-210). New York: Plenum Press.

Wilkinson, D. Y., and R. L. Taylor. 1977. *The Black Male in America.* Chicago: Nelson-Hall.

Wille, W. S. 1961. "Case Study of a Rapist: An Analysis of the Causation of Criminal Behavior." *Journal of Social Therapy,* 7:10-21.

Williams, J. D. 1989. *U.S. Hispanics: A Demographic Profile. CRS Report for Congress 89-460 Gov. Congressional Research Service.* Washington, DC: The Library of Congress.

Williams, M. H. 1978. "Individual Sex Therapy." In J. LoPiccolo & L. LoPiccolo, eds. *Handbook of Sex Therapy* (pp. 477-483). New York: Plenum Press.

Wolfe, L. 1978. "The Question of Surrogates in Sex Therapy." In J. LoPiccolo & L. LoPiccolo, eds. *Handbook of Sex Therapy* (pp. 491-497). New York: Plenum Press.

Wolpe, J., and A. A. Lazarus. 1966. *Behavior Therapy Techniques.* New York: Pergamon Press.

World Almanac and Book of Facts, 1993. New York: World Almanac, Pharos Books.

World Almanac and Book of Facts, 1996. New York: World Almanac, Pharos Books.

Worth, D. and R. Rodriquez. 1987, January/February. "Latina Women and AIDS." *SIECUS Report,* 25(3):5-7.

Wyatt, G. E., and G. J. Powell, eds. 1988. *Lasting Effects of Child Sexual Abuse.* London: Sage Publications.

X, L. 1994. "A Brief Series of Anecdotes about the Backlash Experienced by Those of Us Working on Marital and Date Rape." *Journal of Sex Research,* 31:141-143.

Yllo, K. A. 1978. "Nonmarital Cohabitation: Beyond the College Campus." *Alternative Lifestyles,* 1:37-54.

Zelnik, M., J. F. Kantner, and K. Ford. 1981. *Sex and Pregnancy in Adolescence.* Beverly Hills, CA: Sage.

Zelnik, M., and F. K. Shah. 1983. "First Intercourse Among Young Americans." *Family Planning Perspectives,* 15(2):64-70.

Zilbergeld, B. 1978. *Male Sexuality: A Guide to Sexual Fulfillment.* Boston, MA: Little Brown.

Zilbergeld, B. 1992. *The New Male Sexuality.* New York: Bantam Books.

Zoucha-Jensen, J. M., and A. Coyne. 1993. "The Effects of Resistance Strategies on Rape." *American Journal of Public Health,* 83:1633-1634.

Contributors

ROBERT T. FRANCOEUR, PH.D., A.C.S. (General Editor) Trained in embryology, evolution, theology, and the humanities, Dr. Francoeur's main work has been to synthesize and integrate the findings of primary sexological researchers. He is the author of twenty-two books, contributor to seventy-eight textbooks, handbooks, and encyclopedias, and the author of fifty-eight technical papers on various aspects of sexuality. His books include *The Scent of Eros: Mysteries of Odor in Human Sexuality* (1995), *Becoming a Sexual Person* (1982, 1984, 1991) and *Taking Sides: Clashing Views on Controversial Issues in Human Sexuality* (1987, 1989, 1991, 1993, 1997)—two college textbooks, *Utopian Motherhood: New Trends in Human Reproduction* (1970, 1974, 1977), *Eve's New Rib: 20 Faces of Sex, Marriage, and Family* (1972), *Hot and Cool Sex: Cultures in Conflict* (1974), and *The Future of Sexual Relations* (1974). He is editor-in-chief of *The Complete Dictionary of Sexology* (1991, 1995). A fellow of the Society for the Scientific Study of Sexuality and past president of the Society's Eastern Region, he is also a charter member of the American College of Sexology. He is currently professor of biological and allied health sciences at Fairleigh Dickinson University, Madison, New Jersey, U.S.A., adjunct professor in the doctoral Program in Human Sexuality at New York University, and professor in the New York University "Sexuality in Two Cultures" program in Copenhagen.

Authors of Individual Chapters

Preface:

TIMOTHY PERPER, PH.D. Dr. Perper is a Philadelphia-based, independent sex researcher and writer. Trained as a biologist, with his doctorate from City University of New York, he has studied human courtship and flirtation behaviors for over a decade, assisted by full-support grants from the Harry Guggenheim Foundation. He is author of *Sex Signals: The Biology of Love* (1985), coauthor of *For Sex Education, See Librarian* (1996), author of numerous articles on human and animal sexual behavior, and coeditor of *The Complete Dictionary of Sexology* (1991, 1995). He has served variously as associate, consulting, and book review editor for the *Journal of Sex Research*. He is a long-time member of the Society for the Scientific Study of Sexuality and an elected fellow of the American Anthropological Association.

Introduction:

IRA L. REISS, PH.D. Professor of sociology at the University of Minnesota, Dr. Reiss is the former president of the International Academy of Sex Research, the National Council on Family Relations, and the Society for the Scientific Study of Sexuality, recipient of the 1990 Kinsey Award for Distinguished Scientific Achievement, and author of eleven books and more than a hundred professional articles. His latest books are *Journey Into Sexuality: An Exploratory Voyage* (1986) and *An End to Shame: Shaping Our Next Sexual Revolution* (1990).

Argentina:

SOPHIA KAMENETZKY, M.D. Early in her work as a gynecologist in her native Argentina, Dr. Kamenetzky dedicated herself to increasing the sexual knowledge of women. Teaching biology at an Argentine university, she collaborated with other educators in organizing sexual education courses. Post-graduate studies in France and study visits to African, Asian, and Latin American countries provided her with an understanding of the roles and problems of women in different societies. Her acquaintance with contraceptive practices led her to become medical advisor and director of public relations with Latin American Universities for the Population Information Program then based at the George Washington University in Washington, D.C. Her further studies at the Institute for the Advanced Study of Human Sexuality in San Francisco were guided by Dr. John Money. Now retired, Dr. Kamenetzky facilitates seminars on sexuality and the role of emotions in the health of the immune system.

Australia:

ROSEMARY COATES, PH.D. An honorary life member for the Western Australia Sexology Society, Dr. Coates is an associate professor of physiotherapy in the Division of Health Sciences at Curtin University in Western Australia. She is vice-president of the Family Planning Association of Western Australia and also founding member, inaugural president, and an honorary life member of the Western Australia Sexology Society. The author of *Sexual Awareness Manual, Teacher's Survival Manual,* and comparative studies of sexual knowledge, attitudes, and behavior among college-aged people, she is also interested in transvestism, transsexualism, and medical ethics.

Acknowledgments: ANN RITCHIE, librarian at the PIVET Medical Centre and former librarian for the Family Planning Association of Western Australia, provided research and editorial assistance. ROBERT TONKINSON, PH.D., provided advice on Australian aboriginal cultures, and editorial assistance.

Bahrain:

JULANNE MCCARTHY, M.A. M.S.N., holds a master's degree in anthropology from Indiana University (Bloomington campus) where she took her first course in human sexuality. She also holds a master's degree in adult health nursing from the University of Illinois (Urbana campus). For nine years, between 1988 and 1996, she lived and worked in the State of Bahrain. The author of several articles and a monograph on nursing care for Japanese patients, she now resides in Bloomington, Illinois. In writing this chapter, she supported her comprehensive literature of sexual customs and behavior in Bahrain and neighboring Arabic and Islamic countries with insights and observations provided by twenty Bahraini professionals and eight expatriates in a variety of disciplines, as well as with anecdotal insights from personal contacts and local popular print media.

Brazil:

SÉRGIO LUIZ GONÇALVES DE FREITAS, M.D. President of Associação Brasileira de Sexologia (AB-SEX), scientific director of the Sociedade Brasileira de Estudos da Impotência Sexual, Dr. Freitas has also organized three national sexological conferences in Brazil and the First Pan-American Congress of Sexology in 1986. A gynecologist and surgeon, he has served for twenty-two years in the National Institute of Public Health (INSS) in which he founded the Department of Sexology in 1986. In 1984, Dr. de Freitas founded *The Journal of Sexology*, serving five years as its editor. Among his many publications on sex therapy and sexology, Dr. de Freitas is the author-editor of *Sangue no Chao* and *Os Especiais*.

ELÍ FERNANDES DE OLIVEIRA Reverend de Oliveira combines his theological and psychological training as a counselor working with couples, children, and homosexuals. He is president of the São Paulo Baptist Convention, second vice-president of the Brazilian Baptist Convention, and pastor of the Baptist Church of Liberty in São Paulo, Brazil.

LOURENÇO STÉLIO REGA, M.TH. Professor Stelio Rega's research interest is in the anthropological perspectives of sexual ethics. His recent publications in this area include *Perspectiva Crista do Sexo* (1990), *Libertação e Sexualidade, uma Abalise* (1991), *Aspectos Éticos da Pena de Morte* (1991), and *Avaliação Ética do Jeito Brasileiro* (1992). He is a professor of sexual and medical ethics and dean of the Baptist Theological Faculty of São Paulo, Brazil.

Translated by LUIS CARREGA, who is a native of Portugal and a former student of the *Encyclopedia*'s editor. Additional information by RAYMOND J. NOONAN, whose biographical sketch can be found in the U.S.A. section, and SANDRA ALMEIDA, who is a Brazilian lawyer and women's rights advocate currently living in New York.

Canada:

MICHAEL BARRETT, PH.D. Dr. Barrett is a professor in the Department of Zoology, University of Toronto, Ontario, Canada; executive director of the Sex Information and Education Council of Canada (SIECCAN); editor of the *Canadian Journal of Human Sexuality*; and the author of *Population and Canada* (1982).

ALAN KING, ED.D. Dr. King is director of the Social Policy Evaluation Group at Queen's University, Kingston, Ontario, Canada.

JOSEPH LÉVY, PH.D. Dr. Lévy is a professor in the Department of Sexology at the University of Quebec, Montreal, Quebec, Canada.

ELEANOR MATICKA-TYNDALE, PH.D. Dr. Maticka-Tyndale is a professor in the Department of Sociology and Anthropology at the University of Windsor, Ontario, Canada.

ALEX MCKAY, PH.D. Dr. McKay is research coordinator for the Sex Information and Education Council of Canada, and associate editor of the *Canadian Journal of Human Sexuality*.

China:

FANG-FU RUAN, M.D., PH.D. A physician and medical historian, Dr. Fang-fu Ruan was on the faculty at the Beijing Medical University until 1985. Editor and major author of *Xingzhishi Shiuce (Guide to Sexuality)* (1985), prepared for the People's Republic of China, he has also written *Sex in China: Studies in Sexology in Chinese Culture* (1991) and coauthored with Professor Vern Bullough *Chinese Erotic and Sexual Classics in Translation, Book 1: The Fragrant Flower: Classic Chinese Erotic in Art and Poetry* (1990). He has also published on sex education, transsexualism, sexual repression, and gender orientations in China in such journals as *Archives of Sexual Behavior, Journal of Gender Studies, Health Education, Journal of Sex Research, Health Education, Journal of Homosexuality,* and *Medical Aspects of Human Sexuality.* A visiting professor at several American universities, Dr. Ruan is currently chairperson of the department of Oriental Studies at the Institute for the Advanced Study of Human Sexuality in San Francisco, and professor and dean of instruction at the Academy of Chinese Culture and Health Sciences in Oakland, California. He is also a diplomate of the American Board of Sexology, and a founding fellow of the American Academy of Clinical Sexologists.

M. P. LAU, M.D. A psychiatrist, Dr. Lau was born and lived in Hong Kong for thirty years, before moving to Canada, where he has lived for the past three decades while maintaining close ties with colleagues in China. Dr. Lau, the author of a major analysis of the nationwide survey conducted in China by Professor Liu Dalin included in this *Encyclopedia* chapter, is a faculty member in the Department of Psychiatry at the University of Toronto, Ontario, Canada, and an active member of the Culture, Community, and Health Program at Toronto's Clarke Institute of Psychiatry. His research interests range from psychiatry, geriatrics, epidemiology, and substance abuse to sexology, Sinology, and cultural anthropology. A member of the Society for the Scientific Study of Sexuality, he was also an executive of the Section of Sexology at the Ontario Psychiatric Association from 1979 to 1988.

The Czech Republic and Slovakia:

JAROSLAV ZVERINA, M.D. Dr. Zverina is director of the Institute of Sexology and a member of the First Medical Faculty at Charles University, Prague, in the Czech Republic. President of the Sexological Society of Prague and member of the executive committee of the European Federation of Sexology, he has authored *Advice for Intimate Life* (1991) and *Medical Sexology* (1992), both in Czech. His research focuses on the behavioral and biological aspects of sexology and reproductive medicine, mainly andrology. He has published in *Archives of Sexual Behavior* and authored a chapter on "Sexuelle Teaktionen auf Optische Stimuli bei Frauen" in *Prakitische Sexual-medizin*, edited by W. Eicher (Weisbaden, 1988).

ANTON ROS, a native of the Czech Republic and physician in Weirton, West Virginia, and LYNNE ROS, a former student of the editor of this *Encyclopedia* with extensive experience in the health-care professions, worked together to provide a translation of difficult sections in Dr. Zverina's manuscript.

Finland:

OSMO KONTULA, D.SOC.SCI., PH.D. As research director of Docent at the Department of Public Health, the University of Helsinki, Dr. Kontula had directed two national surveys of sexual life in Finland. He is coauthor, with Elina Haavio-Mannila, of *Suomalainen Seksi: Tietoa Suomalaisten Suku-puolielämän Muutoksesta (Finnish Sex: Information of Changes in Sexual Life in Finland)* (WSOY, Juva 1993). Since 1986, Dr. Kontula has authored or coauthored about 25 books on sexology, drug use, and the health impacts of economic recession.

ELINA HAAVIO-MANNILA, PH.D. Dr. Haavio-Mannila is coauthor with Osmo Kontula of *Suomalainen Seksi: Tietoa Suomalaisten Sukupuolielämän Muutok-sesta (Finnish Sex: Information of Changes in Sexual Life in Finland)* (1993-1994, published in both Finnish and English), *Tyopaikan Rakkausuhteet (Love Relations in the Work Place)* (1987), and *Unfinished Democracy—Women in Nordic Politics* (with Drude Dahberup and others, 1985). Her many publications cover her research on drug and alcohol use and gender roles in family, work, politics, and dancing. With Osmo Kontulo, she was responsible for national sociological surveys of sexual life in Finland. She is currently professor of sociology at the University of Helsinki, vice president of the Finnish Sociological Association (Westermarck Society), board member of the European Sociological Association Steering Group, and vice chairperson of the Finnish Academy of Science and Letters.

Germany:

RUEDIGER LAUTMANN, PH.D. Professor of sociology and sociology of law at the University of Breman, Dr. Lautmann has published widely on the social controls of sexual behavior in Germany since the Nazi period.

KURT STARKE, PH.D. Dr. Starke, a sociologist and political scientist, has served for twenty years as department head, head of research in sexology, and vice-director of the Central Institute of Youth Research in Leipzig.

Ghana:

AUGUSTINE K. ANKOMAH, PH.D. A graduate of the University of Ghana and the University of Ife, Nigeria, Dr. Ankomah received a doctorate from the Institute of Population Studies, the University of Exeter (U.K.), where he currently is a lecturer. Between 1986 and 1989, he taught sociology at the University of Cape Coast in Ghana. His research has focused on the sexual behavior of young women in Ghana and its implications for AIDS, family planning service provision, contraceptive use, and reproductive health as they relate to sexual behavior and HIV infection. He is currently comparing sociocultural determinants of induced abortion in Kenya, Peru, and the Philippines. As a consultant for the Population Council (New York), he trains health personnel for the Ministry of Health in Nigeria.

Greece:

DIMOSTHENIS AGRAFIOTIS, PH.D. Dr. Agrafiotis, a sociologist, teaches and conducts sexological research at the Athens School of Public Health. He also works with the Collaborating Center for the Global Program on AIDS and the Sociology of AIDS of the World Health Organization.

PANGIOTA MANDI, PH.D. Dr. Mandi, a sociologist, teaches and conducts sexological research at the Athens School of Public Health. She also works with the Collaborating Center for the Global Program on AIDS and the Sociology of AIDS of the World Health Organization.

Reading and comments by MARIA BAKAROUDIS. A native of Greece, Ms. Bakaroudis earned a Master of Arts degree in the Human Sexuality Program at New York University and is currently a community health educator for Planned Parenthood in Jamaica, New York.

India:

JAYAJI K. NATH, M.D., is the director of the National Institute for Research in Sex Education, Counseling, and Therapy (NIRSECT–India). A fellow of the Indian Academy of Juvenile and Adolescent Gynaecology and Obstetrics and the International Council of Sex Education and Parenthood of the American University, Dr. Nath is also a consultant on sexual medicine at the Mahatma Gandhi Mission Hospital in Bombay. He is working with his coauthor of the chapter on India, Vishwarath R. Nayar, on a training curriculum for sexuality teachers in India.

VISHWARATH R. NAYAR is the founder-director of the National Institute for Research in Sex Education, Counseling, and Therapy (NIRSECT–India), organizer of two national sexological conferences in India, and editor of the English news fortnightly *Raigad Observer*. He is working with his coauthor of the chapter on India, J. K. Nath, on a training curriculum for sexuality teachers in India.

Indonesia:

WIMPIE PANGKAHILA, M.D. Dr. Wimpie Pangkahila, a lecturer in the Medical School and secretary of the Study Group on Human Reproduction of Udayana University (Bali, Indonesia), is also chairperson of the Indonesian Society of Andrology in Bali. As an andrologist and sexologist, he specializes in infertility, adolescent sexuality, and sexual dysfunctions. He is author of *What You Should Know about Sex* (1981), *About the Sexual Problem in the Family* (1988), *Discussing Sexual Problems in the Family* (1991), *We and Sex* (1991), and *Some Sexual Problems in the Female* (1991).

J. ALEX PANGKAHILA, M.D. Dr. J. Alex Pangkahila is a medical sexologist at the Institute of Family and Sexological Sciences at the Catholic University of Louvain, Belgium, an andrologist, and a lecturer in the Medical School at Udayana University in Bali, Indonesia. His research focuses on sexual fitness and perineometry. He is the author of *Gymnastics and Sexual Impotency* (1986), *Premature Ejaculation* (1979), *Misorgasm (Anorgasm) Among Balinese Women* (1979), and *Impotentia Erectionis* (1979).

Iran:

PAULA E. DREW, PH.D. Dr. Paula Drew, a British-born cultural anthropologist, held consecutive tenured positions at the University of Tabriz in northern Iran and the National University of Tehran for fourteen years between 1964 and the fall of the Shah in 1978. In these universities, she taught Iranian women French, German, English, and psychology in Persian. For three years, she served as academic and personal advisor to female students in the humanities. She also ran a clinic for mothers and babies in an Iranian oasis community for almost ten years. Field-note observations formed the basis for her doctoral thesis in anthropology, *Arranging Marriages in Iran*, at Rutgers University, New Jersey. At present, she teaches anthropology and a cross-cultural humanities core course at Fairleigh Dickinson University, Madison, New Jersey.

Ireland:

THOMAS PHELIM KELLY, M.B. A physician and medical coordinator for Family Planning Services in Dublin, Dr. Kelly also has a private practice as a psychosexual therapist.

Additional comments by HARRY A. WALSH. Born and raised in Ireland, Dr. Walsh is a Catholic priest, and the executive director of the Institute for Child and Adolescent Sexual Health, in Monticelle, Minnesota.

Israel:

RONNY A. SHTARKSHALL, PH.D. Dr. Shtarkshall is a professor in the Department of Social Medicine, the Hebrew University, and Hadassah, Braun School of Public Health and Community Medicine, in Jerusalem. He is also a member of the board of directors for the Israeli Family Planning Association, and an honorary member of the Polish Academy of Sexual Medicine. He is coauthor of *Avoiding AIDS: Preventing AIDS While Preserving Sex and Youth, Sexuality and Relations Between the Sexes: A Facilitator's Handbook*, and program modules, published by the Israeli Ministry of Education and Culture (1987). He is currently researching sexual function and dysfunction in old age in Israel, the sexual attitudes and behaviors of adolescents, and sex, sexuality, and relationships in a national Israeli sample.

MINAH ZEMACH, PH.D., a native of Israel, holds bachelor's degrees in statistics and psychology from the Hebrew University of Jerusalem, and master's and doctoral degrees in psychology from Yale University. She is currently the director and senior researcher at the Dachaf Research Institute in Tel Aviv (since 1979). She is an expert in developing surveys and making population analyses and predictions for social, political, and commercial purposes. She coauthored the chapter on "Surveys" in *Research Methods in Social Sciences* (The Open University, 1986), and *Zug O Peret* (*Odds or Even*), an analysis of relationships among Israeli couples (Am Oved, 1990).

Japan:

YOSHIRO HATANO, PH.D. received his Ph.D. degree from the University of Oregon in the United States and is currently a professor at Tokyo Gakugei University. He is also a board member and director of the Japanese Association for Sex Education, an advisory committee member of W.A.S. (the World Association of Sexology), secretary general of W.A.S. Organizing Committee for the Twelfth World Congress of Sexology, vice president of the Asian Federation of Sexology, International vice president of ICHPER-ESD (International Council for Health, Physical Education, Recreation, Sport and Dance), and a member of the National Committee of Japanese YMCAs.

TSUGUO SHIMAZAKI is a graduate of Waseda University and a journalist and staff member of Shogakukan Press, Tokyo. He serves as secretary general and a board member and director of the Japanese Association for Sex Education, and deputy secretary general of Twelfth World Congress of Sexology (W.C.S.) Organizing Committee. In addition to being editor of *Monthly Report Sex Education Today,* he is a visiting professor at Chiba University and an adjunct professor at Roanoke College in the state of Virginia in the United States.

Additional comments by YOSHIMI KAJI, M.A., who is an educator working to promote knowledge about gay and lesbian issues in the Japanese community in both Japan and the United States.

Kenya:

NORBERT BROCKMAN, PH.D. Associate professor of politics and AASECT-certified sex educator, Dr. Brockman teaches at St. Mary's University in San Antonio, Texas. His research interests focus on African studies and political psychology. In sexology, he concentrates on the relationship between power and sexual behavior, professional incest, and power and sex roles in the women's and men's movements. He has taught in Kenya and worked at the Amani Counselling Centre in Nairobi.

Mexico:

EUSEBIO RUBIO, PH.D. Dr. Rubio is founder of Asociacion Mexicana para la Salud Sexual A.C., Mexico City, Mexico, a non-profit organization that provides low-cost medical and psychological help to low-income persons, and training in sex therapy for professionals. He also conducts some research projects at AMSSAC.

The Netherlands:

JELTO J. DRENTH, PH.D. Dr. Drenth, president and chairman of the Dutch Society for Sexology (Nederlandse Vereniging voor Seksuologie), is a member of the Sexology Department of the Rutgers Foundation and Consultation Bureau for Contraceptive and Sexological Advice in the Hague, the Netherlands.

A. KOOS SLOB, PH.D. Dr. Slob is senior scientist and professor of pathophysiology of sexuality in the Department of Endocrinology and Reproduction, the Faculty of Medicine, Erasmus University, Rotterdam, the Netherlands. Editor-in-chief of the *Dutch Journal of Sexology (Tijdschrift voor Seksuologie)*, Dr. Slob was the first recipient of the "Van Emde Boas-Van Ussel" Award (1987) from the Dutch Society for Sexology. He also holds the special chair for physiology and pathophysiology of sexuality, the Trustfund, Erasmus University. He is coeditor of *Facetten van Seksualiteit: Een Inleiding tot de Seksuologie* (1990), *Seksuologie voor de Arts* (1992), and numerous professional articles.

Poland:

ANNA SIERZPOWSKA-KETNER, M.D., PH.D. A psychiatrist and sexologist, Dr. Sierzpowska-Ketner is senior lecturer and consultant forensic expert in sexology in the Department of Sexology at the Postgraduate Medical Education Center. She is also the vice-president of the Polish Sexological Society and secretary of the Sexological Section of the Polish Medical Association. Specializing in sexual dysfunctions, paraphilias, sexual fantasies, and sex offenders and their victims, Dr. Sierzposka-Ketner is also coauthor of a just-published *Encyclopedia of Sexology.*

Polynesia:

ANNE BOLIN, PH.D. A cultural anthropologist, Dr. Bolin is assistant professor of anthropology at Elon College, North Carolina. Her book, *In Search of Eve: Transsexual Rites of Passage*, won the Choice Award for Outstanding Academic Book for 1988-1989. Coauthor of a college text, *The Anthropology of Human Sexuality* (1992), Dr. Bolin has done extensive fieldwork and published on male-to-female transsexual and transvestite subcultures, ethnomedicine in the Marshall Islands, and ethnographic research in a gay community and among competitive women and men bodybuilders. She is currently working on a textbook on the anthropology of human sexuality.

Puerto Rico (The United States of America)

LUIS MONTESINOS, PH.D. Dr. Montesinos is an assistant professor at Montclair State College in New Jersey, where he teaches undergraduate and graduate courses in human sexuality, health psychology, and behavioral modification. His major research interest is in the area of health psychology applied to different ethnic groups and cultures.

JUAN PRECIADO, PH.D. Dr. Preciado, an associate professor in the Department of Urban and Community Health at Hostos Community College of the City University of New York, has given numerous presentations on sexual health and cultural issues in Europe and Latin America. His research interests are in the area of health education and bilingualism.

Russia:

IGOR S. KON, PH.D. Dr. Kon, sociologist, psychologist, and anthropologist, has been chief researcher at the Institute for Ethnography and Anthropology, the Russian Academy of Sciences, since 1974. A member of the Russian Academy of Education, Dr. Kon was also A. D. White Professor-at-Large at Cornell University (1990-1995), a member of the International Academy of Sex Research, and a member of the Polish Sexological Academy. In addition to over 300 professional articles, he has authored *Introduction to Sexology*, published in Hungarian, German, Ukrainian, Estonian, and Chinese. A Russian edition was published in 1988 after being banned for ten years. Among his numerous other books are *Taste of the Forbidden Fruit* (1992 in Russian), *Sex and the Soviet Society* (1993; coeditor with James Riordan), and *The Sexual Revolution in Russia* (1995). Between 1985 and the present, he held short-term lecture appointments at the universities of Stanford, Johns Hopkins, Minnesota, Chicago, Harvard, Princeton, Indiana, Rutgers, Notre Dame, Paris, London, Kent, Oslo, Helsinki, Amsterdam, Berlin, Leipzig, Tubingen, Tel Aviv, Prague, Budapest, Warsaw, Krakow, Beijing, and others.

South Africa:

LIONEL JOHN NICHOLAS, PH.D. Dr. Nicholas is senior psychologist and senior lecturer at the University of the Western Cape, Bellville, South Africa, and an adjunct professor at the Institute for the Advanced Study of Human Sexuality in San Francisco. He earned his master's degree in psychology at Boston University and his doctorate at the University of the Western Cape. His main research interests are in political psychology, sexual counseling, racism, and AIDS. Since 1990, he has conducted an annual survey of sexual experience, attitudes, and AIDS knowledge among black South African first-year university students. In addition to these annual survey reports, his 1994 journal publications include: "The Experience of Black South African First-Year Students of First Intercourse and Contraception" (*International Journal for the Advancement of Counseling*), "Lying as a Factor in Sexuality Research" (*Psychological Reports*), and "AIDS Knowledge and Attitudes Toward Homosexuality of Black South African Freshmen 1990-1992." (*Psychological Reports*). The author/editor of *Sex Counseling in Educational Settings* (1994), he is coeditor of *Psychology and Apartheid* (1990) and editor of *Psychology and Oppression: Critiques and Proposals* (1993).

PRISCILLA SANDRA DANIELS, M.S. Ms. Daniels is senior lecturer and departmental chairperson of Human Ecology and Dietetics, as well as vice-dean of the Faculty of Community and Health Sciences at the University of the Western Cape in Bellville, South Africa. She holds a master's degree in science from Cornell University in the United States. Her research interests are in sexuality, family, and women's issues. She is coauthor of chapters on "Sexual Harassment and Rape in Educational Settings," "Sexual Attitudes and Behaviours of University Students," and "Sex in South Africa" in *Sex Counseling in University Settings* (1994). Among her journal publications, she coauthored "AIDS, Knowledge and Attitudes Towards Homosexuals of Black First-Year Students, 1990-1992" (*Psychological Reports*).

MERVYN BERNARD HURWITZ, M.D. A diplomate and fellow of the South African College of Gynaecologists and fellow of the Royal College of Obstetricians and Gynaecologists, Dr. Hurwitz is head of the Sexual Dysfunction Clinic at Johannesburg Hospital in South Africa, and lecturer and examiner in the Department of Obstetrics & Gynecology, University of Witwatersrand, Johannesburg. A member of the editorial board of the *Medical Sex Journal of South Africa*, Dr. Hurwitz is the author of *Educating the Doctor and Patient in Human Sexuality* (1986), *The Problem of Deep Dyspareunia* (1986), *Sexuality in the Professional-Patient Relationship* (1987), *Sex and the Disabled* (1987), *Sexual Dysfunction Associated with Infertility* (1989), and *Breast Feeding and Sexuality* (1992).

Spain:

JOSE ANTONIO NIETO, PH.D. (Chapter Coordinator) Since receiving his doctorate from the New School for Social Research in New York, Dr. Nieto has specialized in the anthropology of sexuality. Currently head professor and director of the Human Sexuality Program at the Universidad Nacional de Educacio a Distancia, he has authored *Cultura y Sociedad en las Practicas Sexuales* (1989), *La Sexualidad en la Sociedad Contemporanea: Lecturas Antropologicas* (1991), and *Sexualidad y Deseo: Critica Anthropologica de la Cultura* (1992). Among his research interests are Polynesian sexual customs, and sexual behavior and HIV infections in Europe.

JOSE ANTONIO CARROBLES, PH.D. Dr. Carrobles is full professor and director of the Department of Biological Psychology and Health at the Universidad Autonoma in Madrid, and professor of sexology and sexual therapy in the Master's Program in Human Sexuality at the Universidad Nacional de Educacio a Distancia in Madrid. His publications include *Biologia y Psicofisiologia de la Conducta Sexual* (1990), *Terapia Sexual* (1991), *Analisis y Modificatcion de la Conducta* (1985, 1991), and *La Practica de la Terapia de Conducta* (1978, 1991). His interests focus on sexual dysfunctions, sexual differences, sex therapy, and the psychology of health.

MANUEL DELGADO RUIZ, PH.D. Dr. Delgado Ruiz is professor of anthropology at the University of Barcelona and the Master's Program in Human

Sexuality at the Universidad Nacional de Educacio a Distancia in Madrid. His publications include *De la Muerta de un Dios* (1986), *La Festa de Catalunya* (1992), *La Ira Sagrada* (1992), and "La Reconquista del Cuerpo, Ideologias Sexuales" in *La Sexualidad en la Sociedad Contemporanea* (1991).

FELIX LOPEZ SANCHEZ, PH.D. Dr. Lopez Sanches, a full professor of psychology of sexuality and director of the Sexology Doctoral Program at the University of Salamanca, is also a professor in the Master's Program in Human Sexuality at the Universidad Nacional de Educacio a Distancia in Madrid and director of the Center for Sexual Documentation in Salamanca. His publications include *Principios Basicos de Educacion Sexual* (1984), *Educacion Sexual en la Adolescencia* (1986), *Para Comprender la Sexualidad* (1989), and *Educacion Sexual en el Aula* (1990).

VIRGINA MAQUIEIRA D'ANGELO, PH.L.D. Dr. Maquieira D'Angelo, Doctor of Philosphy and Letters, is professor in the Department of Sociology and Social Anthropology at the Universidad Autonoma de Madrid, and a professor in the Master's Program in Human Sexuality at the Universidad Nacional de Educacio a Distancia in Madrid. A member of the Consejo del Instituto Universitario de Estudio de la Mujer and an international editor for *Gender and Society*, she is also editor of *Mujer y Hombres en la Formacion del Pensamiento Occidental* (1989) and coeditor of *Violencia y Sociedad Patriarcal* (1990).

JOSEP-VICENT MARQUES, PH.D. Dr. Marques is professor in the Department of Sociology and Social Anthropology at the University of Valencia, and a professor in the Master's Program in Human Sexuality at the Universidad Nacional de Educacio a Distancia.

FERNARDO MORENO JIMINEZ, PH.D. Dr. Moreno Jimenez, a psychologist with a Licenciado in Philosophy and Letters, studies sexology at the Interdisciplinary Institute of Ciencias Sexologicas at Louvain, Belgium. He is professor of biological psychology and health at the Universidad Autonoma in Madrid and a professor in the Master's Program in Human Sexuality at the Universidad Nacional de Educacio a Distancia. He is author of *La Sexualidad Humana: Estudio y Perspectiva Historica* (1990).

RAQUEL OSBORNE VERDUGO, PH.D. Dr. Osborne Verdugo is professor of sociology at the Universidad Nacional de Educacio a Distancia and in the Master's Program in Human Sexuality at the same university. Her publications include *Las Prostitutas* (1978), *Las Mujeres en la Encrucijada de la Sexualidad* (1989), and *Sexualidad y Sexismo* (1991; in collaboration with Josep V. Marques).

CARMELA SANZ RUEDA, PH.D. Dr. Sanz Rueda is a professor in the Department of Social Psychology at the Universidad Complutense in Madrid, and a professor in the Master's Program in Human Sexuality at the Universidad Nacional de Educacio a Distancia. A founding member of the Instituto de

Investigaciones Feministas de la Universidad Complutense, she has also been a visiting scholar at Wellesley College in Boston. She has authored *La Comunicacion Interpersonal en el Matrimonio: El Punto de Vista de la Mujer* (1982), *Nuevas Perspectivas Sobre la Mujer* (1982), and *Genero y Sexualidad* (1991).

CARMELO VASQUEZ VALVERDE, PH.D. Dr. Vasquez Valverde is professor of psychology at the Universidad Complutense in Madrid and a professor in the Master's Program in Human Sexuality at the Universidad Nacional de Educacio a Distancia. He was a Fulbright Visiting Scholar in the Psychology Department at Northwestern University in Illinois (1984-1986).

Translation by LAURA BERMAN and JOSE NANIN. Ms. Berman earned a master's degree in the Human Sexuality Program at New York University, and has traveled extensively in Spain and Gibralta. She works as a health educator and counselor at the Hunter College Center on AIDS, Drugs and Community Health in New York City. A Cuban by birth, Mr. Nanin also earned a master's degree in the Human Sexuality Program at New York University and works in AIDS-education programs on the university level.

Sweden:

JAN TROST, PH.D. Professor of sociology at Sweden's Uppsala University, Dr. Trost has served on the editorial staffs of numerous professional publications, including *Nordisk Sexologi, Journal of Marriage and the Family*, and *Alternative Lifestyles*, as an expert on revision of Family Law for the Swedish Government. He has edited seven books, including *The Family in Change*, and authored or coauthored 11 books, including *To Cohabit and to Marry: Facts and Foibles.*

MAI-BRIHT BERGSTROM-WALAN, PH.D. Dr. Berstrom-Walan, a psychologist, is founder and director of the Swedish Institute for Sexual Research, a diplomate of sexology, and certified sex therapist. She organized the 1976 International Symposium of Sex Education and Therapy in Stockholm and is currently vice-president of the European Federation of Sexology. A registered midwife, she has been involved in films and has authored several books on sex education, including *The Swedish Hite Report.*

Thailand:

KITTIWUT JOD TAYWADITEP, M.D., M.A., is currently a doctoral candidate in clinical psychology at the University of Illinois at Chicago (U.I.C.). He grew up in northern Thailand and received an M.D. from the Chiang Mai University (C.M.U.) in 1989 where, during his work as a faculty member in immunology, he became involved in HIV/AIDS education, prevention, counseling, and research on human sexuality and HIV-risk. His work in Thailand has been funded by the Center for AIDS Prevention Studies (C.A.P.S.) at the University of California in San Francisco. After attending the graduate program at U.I.C. in 1992, he has worked in a series of C.D.C.-funded studies focusing on the sexual behavior of behaviorally bisexual men and African-American men who have sex with men in the Chicago area. During his training as a clinical psychologist, he has worked as a psychotherapist and diagnostician at a U.I.C.-based clinic for psychological services and at the HIV Primary Care, Cook County Hospital. More recently, he has worked as a group facilitator in a NIDA-funded research project at the Howard Brown Health Center in Chicago which assesses the impact of cognitive-behavioral workshops designed to address substance use and sexual risk in men at risk for HIV. His clinical interests are on applying cognitive-behavioral theories and technology to various health-risk behaviors, such as cigarette smoking and HIV infection, and his dissertation on the automatic cognitive processes in depression reflects such interface between social-cognitive and clinical psychology.

ELI COLEMAN, PH.D. Dr. Coleman is director and professor in the Program in Human Sexuality at the University of Minnesota Medical School. He is a past president and fellow of the Society for the Scientific Study of Sexuality, secretary of the World Association for Sexology, and editor of the *Journal of Psychology and Human Sexuality*. In addition to many professional papers, Dr. Coleman has authored or edited *Psychotherapy for Homosexual Men and Women* (1988), *Chemical Dependency and Intimacy Dysfunction* (1987), *Sex Offender Treatment: Approaches for Clinical Practice* (1992), and *Sex Offender Treatment: Interpersonal Violence, Intrapsychic Conflict, and Biological Dysfunction* (1995). He has done field research in sexology in Thailand.

PACHARIN DUMMRONGGITTIGULE, M.SC. has been an instructor in biology at Payap University, Thailand, since 1986. She began researching gender and sexuality in 1991 and has been the principle investigator on an HIV-prevention project among married couples in northern Thai villages. Currently she is a senior program officer at the Thailand Research Fund in Bangkok. In addition, she continues her research on HIV prevention and women's sexuality.

Ukraine:

TAMARA GOVORUN, PH.D. Dr. Gorovun is chair of the psychology department, assistant professor, and post-doctoral researcher at the Ukrainian Pedagogical University in Kiev, Ukraine. She is also the head of the psychological department of Kiev's Research Sexology and Andrology Center, a member of the Ukrainian Psychologists' Society, and chairman of Sexual Education in the Ukrainian Sexologists Society. Her major degree is from the Department of Psychology at Kiev's State University and her Ph.D. from the Ukrainian Institute of Psychology. Her research in sex education, psychosexual development, and psychotherapy of sexual disorders has led to many publications.

BORYS M. VORNIK, PH.D. Dr. Vornik is director of Kiev's Research Sexology and Andrology Center, vice-president of the All-Union Sexologists' Association (Ukraine), and chief of the Ukrainian Commission for Transsexual Persons. He is a graduate of the Medical University of the Ukraine (Kiev) and the Institute of Andrology.

The United Kingdom of Great Britain and Northern Ireland

KEVAN R. WYLIE, M.B., CH.B., M.MED.SC., M.R.C.PSYCH., D.S.M., the coordinator and author of several sections for this chapter, is a consultant psychiatrist at the Whiteley Wood Clinic and specialist in sexual medicine at the Clinic, Community Mental Health Care Directorate in Sheffield. An honorary (clinical) lecturer in the Department of Psychiatry at Sheffield University, his current in-press publication is *Physical Treatments of Sexual Dysfunction* in the Royal College of Psychiatry Monograph Series. In addition to recruiting and coordinating the specialists who contributed to this chapter, Dr. Wylie authored Section 5C5 on heterosexual behaviors, Section 8 on significant unconventional sexual behaviors, Section 12 on sexual dysfunctions and therapies, and Section 13 on advanced education, research, and sexological organizations.

ANTHONY BAINS, B.A., is a gay men's community worker at the Centre for HIV and Sexual Health in Sheffield. His interests include HIV prevention in gay and bisexual men. He authored Section 6 on homosexual, lesbian, and bisexual issues.

TINA BALL, PH.D., is a consultant clinical psychologist in learning disabilities at the Sheffield Consulting and Clinical Psychologists, Community Health, Sheffield. She also works as a member of the clinical team at the Porterbrook Clinic, a National Health Service for sexual and relationship difficulties. A specialist working with people with disabilities and sexual problems, she authored Section 5D on sexuality and persons with disabilities.

PATRICIA BARNES, M.A., C.Q.S.W., BASMT (ACCRED.), UKCP-registered psychotherapist, is director and clinician of the sex and marital therapy clinic at the Psychiatric and Psychological Consultant Service in London. Editor of a 1994 special issue of the journal of the British Association for Sex and Marital Therapy on sex education, she also coauthored *Woman's Guide to Loving Sex.* She coauthored Section 3 on sexual knowledge and education.

ROHAN COLLIER, PH.D., principal women's advisor at the London Borough of Hendon, specializes in issues of sexual harassment and domestic violence. She coauthored Section 8B of sexual harassment

JANE CRAIG, M.B., CH.B., MRCP (UK), is registrar in genitourinary medicine. Her work at the Royal Hallamshire Hospital in Sheffield focuses on the clinical aspects of genital herpes and HIV/AIDS. She coauthored Section 11 on HIV/AIDS.

LINDA DELANY, L.L.B., M.JUR., Solicitor, is a senior lecturer in the School of Law at Manchester Metropolitan University, where her interests focus of legal issues of health care. She coauthored Section 9C on abortion.

JULIA FIELD, B.A., works at Social and Community Planning Research in Northampton Square, London, and is one of four authors of *Sexual Behaviour in Britain: The National Survey of Attitudes and Lifestyles* (1994). She coauthored Section 5C on interpersonal heterosexual adult behavior.

DANYA GLASER, MBBS, D.CH., FRCPSYCH, is a consultant child and adolescent psychiatrist working with the victims of child sexual and emotional abuse. Her publications include coauthoring *Child Sexual Abuse* (1993), as well as authoring Section 5A/B on heterosexual behavior of children and adolescents.

PETER GREENHOUSE, M.A., MRCOG, MFFP, is a consultant in sexual health at Ipswich Hospital where he develops and integrates sexual health education with holistic clinical care, particularly in the management of sexually transmitted diseases. He authored Section 10 on sexually transmitted diseases.

MARY GRIFFIN, M.B., M.SC., MFFP, is joint academic coordinator in the diploma program in couple relationship and sexual dysfunction at London's Institute of Psychiatry, and clinical assistant in the Sexual Therapy Clinic at the Maudsley Hospital. In addition to publishing on the sexual health of women and sexuality training, she authored Section 9B on teenage pregnancy.

MARGOT HUISH, B.A., BASMT (ACCRED.), holds a diploma in human sexuality from St. George's Hospital Medical School, the University of London, where she continues her work as a course tutor and a sexual relationship therapist at Barnet General Hospital. She authored Section 4 on autoerotic behaviors and patterns.

ANNE M. JOHNSON, M.A., M.SC., M.D., MRCGP, FFPHM, is a staff member of the Academic Department of Genitourinary Medicine, Mortimer Market Centre, in London and one of the four coauthors of *Sexual Behaviour in Britain: The National Survey of Attitudes and Lifestyles* (1994). Section 5 on Interpersonal Heterosexual Adult Behavior.

GEORGE KINGHORN, M.D. FRCP, is clinical director for communicable diseases in the Central Sheffield University Hospitals. Chairman of the Royal College of Physicians Genitourinary Medicine Committee, he has published widely and has broad research interests, particularly in genital ulcer diseases, the control of sexually transmitted diseases, and the treatment of HIV infection and AIDS. He coauthored Section 11 on HIV/AIDS.

HELEN MOTT earned her B.A. (Hons.) in social psychology at the University of Sussex and is currently a doctoral student in psychology at Lancaster University, specializing in sexual harassment. She coauthored Section 8B on sexual harassment, a topic she has published on professionally.

PAULA NICOLSON, PH.D., lectures in health psychology in the Department of Psychiatry, the Centre for Health and Related Research, at Sheffield University. Chair-elect of the British Psychological Society's Psychology of Women Section, she coauthored *Applied Psychology for Social Workers* (1990), and coedited *The Psychology of Women's Health and Health Care* (1992) and *Female Sexuality* (1994). She authored Section 2 on ethnic and religious influences.

JANE READ, B.A. (HONS.), a U.K.C.P. registered psychotherapist accredited by the British Association for Sexual and Marital Therapy, holds diplomas in counseling and in human sexuality. Her publications include *Counseling for Fertility Problems* (1995) and a 1995 article on "Female Sexual Dysfunction" in the *International Review of Psychiatry*. She coauthored of Section 9C on abortion.

FRAN READER, FRCOG, MFFP, BASMT (ACCRED.), is a consultant in family planning and reproductive health in the Reproductive and Sexual Health Care Centre at Ipswich Hospital, NHS Trust, Ipswich, Suffolk. She authored Section 9A on contraception.

GWYNETH SAMPSON, DPM, MRCPSYCH., is an honorary lecturer at the University of Sheffield and a consultant psychiatrist at the Porterbrook Clinic in Sheffield. She coauthored Section 7 on gender-conflicted persons.

PETER SELMAN, PH.D., DPSA, is senior lecturer and head of the department of social policy at the University of Newcastle upon Tyne. He has published extensively on family planning services, population studies, demographic analysis, and comparative social policy. In addition to the books *Society and Fertility* (1979) and *Family Planning* (1987), he authored Section 9D on population planning.

JOSÉ M. A. HERBERT-PARDO VON BÜHLER, R.M.N., CPN, DIP.H.S., is a specialist in human sexuality and relationship psychotherapy at the Cardinal Clinic, Bishops Lodge, Oakley Green, Berkshire. Author of *Human Sexuality and Relationship Psychotherapy*, he also coauthored Section 3 on sexual knowledge and education.

JANE WADSWORTH, B.SC., M.SC., is on staff at the Department of Epidemiology and Public Health, St. Mary's Hospital Medical School, London. She is also coauthor of *Sexual Behaviour in Britain: The National Survey of Attitudes and Lifestyles* (1994), as well as Section 5 on Interpersonal Heterosexual Adult Behavior.

KAYE WELLINGS, M.A., M.SC., works in the AIDS Public Education in Europe department at the London School of Hygiene and Tropical Medicine. She is one of the four authors of *Sexual Behaviour in Britain: The National Survey of Attitudes and Lifestyles* (1994), and coauthored Section 5 on Interpersonal Heterosexual Adult Behavior.

STEPHEN WHITTLE, PH.D., M.A., L.L.B., is a lecturer in law at the School of Law, Manchester Metropolitan University, where he specializes in issues of gender, sex, sexuality, and the law. Vice-president of Press for Change, he coauthored Section 7 on gender-conflicted persons.

The United States of America:

DAVID L. WEIS, PH.D., coeditor, received his Ph.D. in family studies in 1979 from Purdue University. He has taught at Rutgers University, and is currently an associate professor of human development and family studies at Bowling Green State University in Ohio. A member of and officer for the National Council on Family Relations, the Society for the Scientific Study of Sexuality, and the International Network on Personal Relationships, he is also an associate editor for the *Journal of Sex Research.* Weis has published numerous research articles in professional journals in such areas as adolescent sexuality, marital exclusivity, marital and sexual belief systems, sexual interaction processes, peer education programming, social services for the homeless and mentally ill, and adolescent drug use. He has also taught and conducted workshops in these areas, as well as in interpersonal communications, intimacy, flirtation behavior, dual-career marriages, and black families. Weis received the Hugo Beigel Award for Outstanding Sexuality Research for his study of the emotional reactions to first intercourse. (Introduction; Section 1 Basic Sexological Premises; and Section 5 Interpersonal Heterosexual Behaviors.)

PATRICIA BARTHALOW KOCH, PH.D., coeditor of the United States of America chapter, is an associate professor of biobehavioral health and health education at Pennsylvania State University. She earned a master's degree in the Program in Human Sexuality, Marriage and Family Life Education at New York University, during which time she studied in Japan and Sweden. Her doctorate is in health education from Pennsylvania State University, specializing in sexuality education, sexual health issues, human development, and counseling. She has authored over fifty chapters and scientific articles and contributed to several textbooks on sexual topics.

She recently authored a textbook, *Exploring Our Sexuality: An Interactive Text* (Kendall/Hunt). She has conducted numerous research studies in the areas of sexuality education, sexual health issues, and women's health. She is also past president of the Society for the Scientific Study of Sexuality, Eastern Region, and has served on the board of directors of SSSS and the Foundation for the Scientific Study of Sexuality. (Section 2C Sexological Research and Advanced Education—Feminist Issues; Section 3 Sexuality Knowledge and Education; and Section 10 Contraception and Abortion.)

Biographical Sketches for Section Authors:

Most of the following contributors are active members of the Society for the Scientific Study of Sexuality, and several have held national or regional offices in the Society.

DIANE E. BAKER, M.A., PH.D. (cand.) is completing her doctoral dissertation on child sexual abuse in the Psychology Department at Syracuse University, Syracuse, New York. (Section 7A Incest and Child Sexual Abuse.)

SUSAN BARGAINNIER, ED.D., is a certified athletic trainer and assistant professor at the State University of New York in Oswego specializing in wellness promotion. (A Door to the Future: Sexuality on the Information Superhighway.)

SARAH C. CONKLIN, PH.D., received her first three degrees in her native state of Minnesota, a bachelor of science from the University of Minnesota, a master's degree in guidance and counseling from the University of St. Thomas, and a master's degree in theology from United Theological Seminary of the Twin Cities (Minneapolis–St. Paul). She earned her doctorate in human sexuality education from the University of Pennsylvania. She is currently an assistant professor of health and sexuality education at the University of Wyoming (Laramie), College of Health Sciences, School of Physical Health Education, and has done adjunct education in sexuality in Pennsylvania and Minnesota seminaries. (Section 13 Clergy Education.)

MARTHA CORNOG, M.A., M.S., is a linguist and librarian at the American College of Physicians. Her recent work includes a long article on conducting sexological research in *Human Sexuality: An Encyclopedia*, coeditor of *The Complete Dictionary of Sexology*, and coauthoring *For Sex Education: See Librarian.* (Section 13 Sexuality Research and Advanced Education.)

RICHARD CROSS, M.D., pioneered medical school sexuality education while he was a professor at the Robert Wood Johnson School of Medicine at Rutgers University, New Brunswick, New Jersey. (Section 13E Medical School Education.)

MARILYN A. FITHIAN, PH.D., is cofounder of the Center for Marital and Sexual Studies, Long Beach, California, and coauthor of *Treatment of Sexual Dysfunction, Any Man Can,* and other works. (Section 12 Sexual Dysfunctions and Therapies.)

JEANNIE FORREST, M.A., worked for seven years as a family educator with the Church of the Latter-Day Saints and was married to a Mormon. She earned a master's degree in health education in the Human Sexuality Program at New York University. (Section 2A Sexuality and the Church of the Latter-Day Saints.)

ANDREW D. FORSYTH, M.S., is a fifth-year graduate student in clinical psychology in the Department of Psychology at Syracuse University, Syracuse, New York, whose interests include the assessment of high-risk sexual behaviors among at-risk groups. (Section 11 HIV/AIDS.)

ROBERT T. FRANCOEUR, PH.D., A.C.S., worked with coeditors David L. Weis and Patricia Barthalow Koch to integrate the input of some fifty scholars who wrote or consulted on different sections in this chapter. In addition to contributing several sections of his own to this chapter, Dr. Francoeur is General Editor for this *International Encyclopedia of Sexuality*. His fuller biographical sketch appears at the beginning of this Contributors' section. (Section 2 Religious Values, Section 4 Autoerotic Behavior, Section 5 Sexuality and Older Persons, Section 8 Sexual Harassment, Prostitution, and Pornography, Section 10 STDs, and Section 13 Research Assessment).

BARBARA GARRIS, M.A., earned a bachelor's degree in anthropology and sociology at Mountclair State University and did graduate studies at New York University in women's studies. She works for AT&T. (A Door to the Future: Sexuality on the Information Superhighway.)

PATRICIA GOODSON, PH.D., obtained her bachelor's degree from the Universidade de Campinas, Brazil, and a master's degree in philosophy of education from the Pontificia Universidade Catolica de Campinas, Brazil. After earning a Master of Arts degree in general theological studies from Covenant Theological Seminary in St. Louis, Missouri, she completed her doctorate in health education at the University of Texas at Austin. At present, she is an assistant professor in health at the University of Texas at San Antonio, in the Division of Education. (Section 12 Clergy Education.)

WILLIAM E. HARTMAN, PH.D. is cofounder of the Center for Marital and Sexual Studies, Long Beach, California, and coauthor of *Treatment of Sexual Dysfunction, Any Man Can,* and other works. (Section 12 Sexual Dysfunctions and Therapies.)

ROBERT O. HAWKINS, PH.D., former associate dean of the School of Allied Health Professions at the Health Sciences Center of the State University of

New York at Stony Brook, is also coauthor of *Counseling Lesbian Women and Gay Men: A Life-Issues Approach.* (Section 6 Homosexual and Lesbian Issues.)

LINDA L. HENDRIXSON, PH.D., completed her undergraduate studies and master's degree in health education at Montclair State University in New Jersey. She did her doctoral studies in the Human Sexuality Program in the Department of Health Education at New York University. Her dissertation examined issues of HIV-positive women in rural northwestern New Jersey. She has taught at various New Jersey universities and colleges, and published on issues related to sexuality and health education. (Section 11B Emerging Issues in HIV/AIDS.)

BARRIE J. HIGHBY, M.A., is a graduate student in clinical psychology at the University of Kansas, where her research has focused on rape. She has worked at several shelters for battered women. (Section 8A Sexual Coercion and Rape.)

ARIADNE KANE, M.ED., is a nationally known gender specialist, author, and educator, as well as a diplomate of the American Board of Sexology. (Section 7 Cross-Gender Issues.)

SHARON KING, M.S.ED., graduated from the Human Sexuality Program at the University of Pennsylvania where she completed all but her dissertation for the doctorate. Her specialty is survivor therapy. (Section 8A Child Sexual Abuse and Incest.)

ROBERT MORGAN LAWRENCE, D.C., is on the board of advisors of San Francisco Sex Information. He lectures extensively about sexuality and health. (Section 6B Bisexuality.)

BRENDA LOVE is author of the *Encyclopedia of Unusual Sex* and has worked at the Institute for the Advanced Study of Human Sexuality in San Francisco. (Section 8D Paraphilic Behaviors.)

CHARLENE MUEHLENHARD, PH.D., is an associate professor of psychology and women's studies at the University of Kansas. Her research focuses on rape and other forms of sexual coercion, as well as on communication and miscommunication about sex. (Section 8A Sexual Coercion and Rape.)

RAYMOND J. NOONAN, M.A., PH.D. (cand.), is an adjunct instructor of human sexuality and health education at the Fashion Institute of Technology, State University of New York, in Manhattan. He is also director of SexQuest/The Sex Institute, providing educational consulting in human sexuality and educational content for the World Wide Web. He is coeditor and author of *Does Anyone Still Remember When Sex Was Fun? Positive Sexuality in the Age of AIDS* (3rd edition, 1996). He is completing his doctoral dissertation in the Human Sexuality Program at New York University. (Section 11C Impact of AIDS on the Perception of Sexuality and Section 12E Sex Surrogates.)

MIGUEL A. PERÉZ, PH.D., teaches kinesiology at the University of North Texas, where he also pursues an interest in sexuality. (Section 2B Latino Sexuality.)

TIMOTHY PERPER, PH.D., is a Philadelphia-based, independent sex researcher and writer. Trained as a behavioral biologist, he wrote about his extensive research on human courtship and flirtation in *Sex Signals: The Biology of Love.* He is also coauthor of *For Sex Education: See Librarian* (1996) and coeditor of *The Complete Dictionary of Sexology* (1995). (Section 2A Religious Values and Sexuality.)

HELDA L. PINZÓN, PH.D. is a Colombian-born nurse with wide experience in public health. A professor at Pennsylvania State University, her research interests include Latino health issues, community health, and Latino adolescent health. (Section 2B Latino Sexuality.)

CAROL QUEEN, PH.D. (cand.), has written extensively on bisexuality and other topics related to sexual diversity, including *Exhibitionism for the Shy: Show Off, Dress Up, and Talk Hot* (1995). She is a cultural sexologist in the doctoral program at the Institute for Advanced Study of Human Sexuality. (Section 6B Bisexuality.)

HERBERT P. SAMUELS, PH.D., is assistant professor of natural and applied sciences at the City University of New York/Laguardia Community College. (Section 2B African-American Sexuality.)

JULIAN SLOWINSKI, PSY.D., is a marital and sex therapist at Pennsylvania Hospital and faculty member at the University of Pennsylvania School of Medicine, Department of Psychiatry. (Section 12 Sexual Dysfunctions and Therapies.)

WILLIAM STACKHOUSE, PH.D., is director of the HIV Prevention Program for the Bureau of HIV Program Services at the New York City Department of Health. He is also an adjunct assistant professor in the Graduate Department of Applied Psychology at New York University and maintains a private psychotherapy practice. (Section 6 Male Homosexuality and Lesbianism.)

WILLIAM R. STAYTON, TH.D., is assistant professor of psychiatry and human behavior at Jefferson Medical College and an adjunct professor in the Human Sexuality Program at the University of Pennsylvania. (Section 12 Sexual Dysfunctions and Therapies.)

MITCHELL S. TEPPER, M.P.H., is completing work on a doctorate at the University of Pennsylvania, Program in Human Sexuality. (Section 5D Sexuality and People with Disabilities.)

Acknowledgments

An impressive list of 170 dedicated scholars on six continents gener-ously contributed their expertise, energy, and enthusiasm to these volumes. Their careful research, analysis, and integration of information from a wide variety of sources have resulted in the unique, richly detailed, and comprehensive portraits of sexual attitudes, values, and behavior of people in thirty-two countries that appear in these three volumes. As the editor and catalyst for these volumes, I was constantly inspired by the enthusiasm and scholarship they brought to their work. By all rights, I should say something special about each and every contributor. Unfortu-nately limited space will not allow me to comment on their individual contributions in helping create these volumes, although I do mention some of them in my Foreword. Here I can only add that every person mentioned as an author, advisor, or otherwise acknowledged by individual contributors in their chapters has played an important role in these volumes, and can be quite proud of their contribution. I thank them, one and all.

However, I must mention here a few individuals who played pivotal roles as we approached publication.

Jack Heidenry, my editor and good friend, deserves my hearty thanks for recognizing the importance of this unique reference work when it was little more than a fast-growing embryo. I thank Jack for his steady, patient support and especially his crucial advice in bringing about a firm publica-tion date after considerable, unavoidable delays. Working with the Contin-uum staff, Evander Lomke, Ulla Schnell, Martin Rowe, and Gene Gollogly, has been both supportive and an education because of the problems we faced and solved together.

Ray Noonan—In late November 1996, the graphic design skills of a long-time friend and former student unexpectedly came to the fore. For a dozen years, I have known Ray Noonan as a colleague, roommate at conferences, and mentor for his doctoral research in the Human Sexuality Program at New York University. My vague awareness that Ray works in graphic design suddenly solved some major problems. Without Ray's fast, reliable, and creative graphics work, and his constant devotion to additional copyediting, we could not have moved from my computer text files to camera-ready page proofs in the phenomenal two months time Ray took to accomplish this crucial step.

As the work with Ray Noonan on repros raced along, Kittiwut Jod Taywaditep and Eli Coleman completely rewrote the Thailand chapter, tripling its length with invaluable new material. Michael Barrett and his team of Canadians valiantly pushed to come in at the very last minute with a marvelous early-1997 update for Canada. Osmo Kontula and Elina Haavio-Manila provided last-minute updates for Finland; Thomas Phelim Kelley updated Ireland. Julanne McCarthy, whom I met by chance while on a July 1996 vacation in France, created a gem of a chapter on Bahrain in four months time. Thanks to Maria Bakaroudis and James Shortridge for finding Kevan Wylie, and to Dr. Wylie and his team of British colleagues who produced an excellent chapter on the United Kingdom in record time. I also thank Tim Perper for putting me in contact with Dr. M. P. Lau, who happily agreed to our including his brilliant analysis of the nationwide *"Sex Civilization" Survey of 20,000 Subjects in China.*

My thanks to Dr. Paul S. Boyer, professor of earth sciences at Fairleigh Dickenson University, for his cartography skills.

In the United States entry, several key updates and important additions came in on very short notice from Barbara Garris on sex on the information superhighway, Patricia Goodson and Sally Conklin on sexuality education for the clergy, added material for the Latino section from Miguel Pérez and Helda Pinzón, and Linda Hendrixson on AIDS, women, children, and families. I also want to thank David Weis for his thoughtful summaries and introductions linking sections of the United States entry, his meticulous additional last-minute copyediting of the long United States entry, and his critical, constructive input along the way to production.

To all who contributed in whatever way to these three volumes, my sincere thanks. It has been a wonderful experience working with all of you on this unique sexological research project.

Geographic Locations of the
Countries in This Encyclopedia

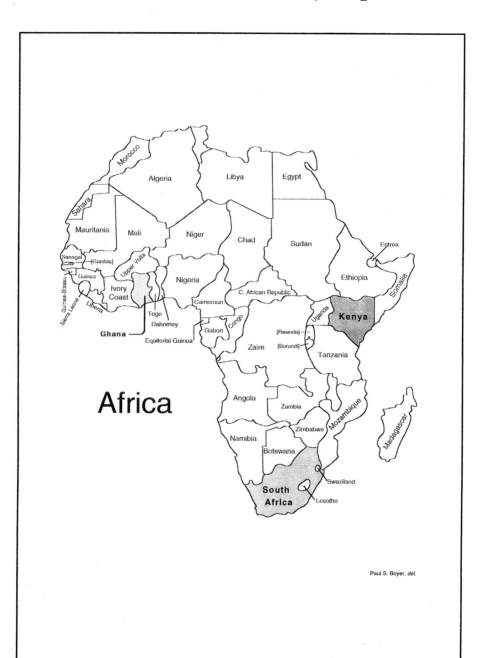

Paul S. Boyer, *del.*

Americas

P. S. Boyer, *del.*

Asia

and the Near East

Is: Israel
Th: Thailand

P. S. Boyer, *del.*

Europe

Cz: Czech Republic
Sl: Slovakia

Paul S. Boyer, *del.*

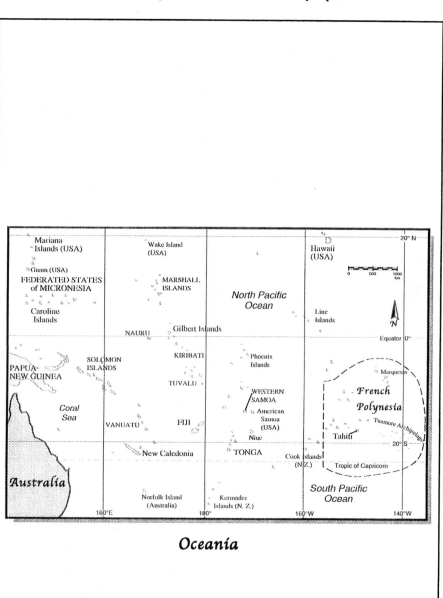

Oceania

Directory of Sexuality Organizations

Argentina

Sociedad Argentina de Sexualidad
Humana
Dr. León Guimdim, Director
Darragueira 2247, P.B. "B"
1425 Buenos Aires, Argentina

Australia

Australian Association of Sex Educators
Counselors, and Therapists (AASERT)
P. O. Box 346 Lane Cove
New South Wales 2066 Australia
Telephone: 61-2-427-1292
Also: 21 Carr Street
Coogee, New South Wales 2034 Australia

Family Planning Australia, Inc.
Lua Building, Suite 3, First Floor
39 Geils C, P. O. Box 9026
Deakin, ACT 26000 Australia
Telephone: 61-6/282-5298
Fax: 61-6/285-1244

Family Planning Victoria
266-272 Church Street
Richmond 3121 Australia
Telephone: 61-3/429-1868

Western Australian Sexology Society
c/FPA 70 Roe Street
Northbridge, Western Australia 6000
Australia

Brazil

Brazilian Association of Sexology
(AB-SEX)
Associação Brasileira de Sexologia
Dr. Sergio Luiz G. de Freitas, M.D.,
President
Rua Tamandare, 693 - Conj. 77
01525-001 Sao Paulo - SP - Brasil

Brazilian Sexual Impotency
Research Society
Sociedade Brasileira de Pesquisa
sobre Impotencia Sexual
Roberto Tullii, M.D., Director
Alameda Gabriel Monteiro da Silva, 1719
01441-000 São Paulo - SP - Brasil

Brazilian Sexual Education Association.
Associação Brasileira de Educação Sexual
Alameda Itu, 859 - Apto 61
01421-000 São Paulo - SP - Brasil

Brazilian Society of Sexology
Isaac Charam, M.D., President
Pca Serzedelo Correia, 15 - Apto 703
22040-000 Rio de Janeiro - RJ - Brasil

Brazilian Society of Human Sexuality
Sociedade Brasileira de Sexualidade
Humana
Av. N.S. Copacabana, 1072 - s. 703
22020-001. Rio de Janeiro - RJ - Brasil

Sexology Nucleus of Rio de Janeiro
Nucleo de Sexologia do Rio de Janeiro
(NUDES)
Av Copacabana, 1018 - Grupo 1109
22060-000. Rio de Janeiro - RJ - Brasil

National Sexology Commission of
The Brazilian Federation of the
Societies of Gynecology and Obstetrics
Comission Nacional de Sexologia da
Federação Brasileira das Sociadades
de Ginecologia e Obstetricia
(FEBRASGO)
Edf. Venancio 2000, Bloco 50 - Sala 137
70302-000 Brasilia - DF - Brasil

Paranaense Commission of Sexology
Comissal Paranaense de Sexologia
Rua General Carneiro, 181 - 4° andar
Maternidade do Hosp. de Clinicas
80060-000 Curitiba - PR - Brasil

Department of Sexology - ARE
Varzea do Carmo
Departamento de Sexologia
Rua Leopoldo Miguez, 257
01518-000. São Paulo - SP - Brasil

Canada

L'Association des Sexologues
du Quebec
695 St. Denis, Suite 300
Montreal, Quebec
H2S 2S3 Canada

Sex Information and Education
Council of Canada (SIECCAN)
850 Coxwell Avenue
East York, Ontario
M4C 5RI Canada
Telephone: 416/466-5304
Fax: 416/778-0785

Canadian Sex Research Forum
c/o Pierre Assalian, M.D.,
Executive Director
1650 Cedar Avenue, Room B6-233
Montreal, Quebec
H3G 1A4 Canada

The Department of Sexology
University of Quebec at Montreal
455 Boulevard Rene Levesque East
Montreal, Quebec
H3C 3P8 Canada

Planned Parenthood Federation
of Canada
1 Nicolas St., Suite 430
Ottawa, Ontario
K1N 7B7 Canada
Telephone: 613/238-4474

International Academy of Sex
Research (IASR)
Clarke Institute of Psychiatry,
Child and Family Studies Centre
250 College Street
Toronto, Ontario
M5T IR8 Canada
Telephone: 416/979-2221
Fax: 416/979-4668
E-Mail: zucker@cs.clarke-inst.on.ca

China

Chinese Association of Sex Education
Mercy Memorial Foundation
11F, 171 Roosevelt Road, Section
Taipei Taiwan
Republic of China
Telephone: 886-2/369-6752
Fax: 886-2/365-7410

Chinese Sex Education
Research Society
Director: Dr. Jiahuo Hong
The Shanghai College of
Traditional Chinese Medicine
530 Ling Ling Road
Shanghai 200032
People's Republic of China

China Family Planning Association
1 Bei Li, Shengguzhuang,
He Ping Li, Beijing
People's Republic of China

China Sexology Association
Number 38, Xue Yuan Lu, Haidion
Beijing 100083
People's Republic of China
Telephone: 86-1/209-1244
Fax: 86-l/209-1548

Shanghai Family Planning
Association
122 South Shan Xi Road
Shanghai 200040
People's Republic of China
Telephone: 86-21/279-4968
Fax: 86-21/247-2262 extension 18

Shanghai International Center for
Population Communication China
(SICPC)
122 South Shan Xi Road
Shanghai 200040
People's Republic of China
Telephone: 86-21/247-2262
Fax: 86-21/247-3049

Shanghai Sex Education
Research Association
122 South Shan Xi Road
Shanghai 200040
People's Republic of China

State Family Planning Commission
IEC Dept., 14 Zhichun Road
Haidian District
Beijing 100088
People's Republic of China
Telephone: 86-1/204-6622
Fax: 86-1/205-1847

Institute for Research in
Sexuality and Gender
Professor Sui-ming Pan, Director
Post Office Box 23
Renmin University of China
39# Hai Dian Road
Beijing 100872
People's Republic of China
Fax: 86-1/256-6380

Hong Kong Sex Education Association
P. O. Box 50419, Sai Ying Pun
Hong Kong
Telephone: 852/819-2486

Family Planning Association of
Hong Kong (FPAHK)
Tenth Floor, Southern Centre
130 Hennessy Road, Wanchai
Hong Kong
Telephone: 852/575-4477
Fax: 852/834-6767

Asian Federation for Sexology (AFS)
Dr. M. L. Ng, Chairman
Department of Psychiatry
University of Hong Kong
Queen Mary Hospital
Pokfulam Road
Hong Kong
Telephone: 852/855-4486
Fax: 852/855-1345

The Czech Republic and Slovakia

Sexuologigky Ustav
Czechoslovak Sexological Society
1. Lekarske Fakulty
Univerzity Karlovy
Karlovo namesti, 32
120 00 Praha 2, Czech Republic
Telephone: 42-2/297-285
Fax: 42-2/294-905

Spolecnost pro Planovani Rodiny a
Sexualni Vychovu (SPRSV)
National Family Planning Association
Podoske nabrezi 157
140 00 Praha 4, Czech Republic

The Sexological Institute and
The Slovak Sexological Society
Polna 811-08
Bratislava 1, Slovak Republic

The School of Medicine
Comenius University, Bratislava
Sasinkova 4, 811 08
Bratislava 1, Slovak Republic

Finland

Seksuaalipoliittinen yhdistys Sexpo ry
Sexual Policy Association
Malminkatu 22E, 00100
Helsinki, Finland

Seksuaalinen Tasavertaisuus SETA ry
Sexual Equality Association
Oikokatu 3, SF-00170
Helsinki, Finland

Germany

Deutsche Gesellschaft für
Sexualforschung
(Based at the Universities of
Hamburg and Frankfurt/Main.)
Martinistr. 52, 20251
Hamburg, Germany

Gesellschaft für Sexualwissenschaft
(Leipzig)
Bernhard-Goering-Str.
152, 04277 Leipzig, Germany

Gesellschaft für Praktische
Sexualmedizin (Kiel)
Hospitalstr. 17-19
24105 Kiel, Germany

Deutsche Gesellschaft für
Geschlechtserziehung (Bonn/Landau)
Westring 10A
76829 Landau, Germany

Deutsche Gesellschaft für
Sozialwissenschaftliche
Sexualforschung (Düsseldorf)
Gerresheimer Str. 20
40211 Düsseldorf, Germany
Telephone: 49-211/35-45-91

Aerztliche Gesellschaft zur
Gesundheitsfoerderung der
Frau e.V. Frauenarztin
Am Bonneshof 30
D-40474 Dusseldorf, Germany
Telephone: 49-211/43-45-91
Fax: 49-211/43-45-03

Greece

Greek Society for Andrology
and Sexology
Chalcocondili 50
Athens, Greece
Telephone: 30-1/5245861

University of Athens
Department of Psychiatry
Director: C. Stefanis
74 Vas. Sophias Avenue
Athens, Greece

Athens School of Public Health
Department of Sociology
Director: Demosthenis Agrafiotis
196 Alexandras Avenue
Athens, Greece

Athens School of Public Health
Department of Epidemiology
Director: G. Papaevangelou
196 Alexandras Avenue
Athens, Greece

A Syngros Hospital
Director: G. Stratigos
6 Dragoumi
Athens, Greece

Family Planning Association (F.P.A)
121 Solonos
Athens, Greece

Hellenic Society of Paediatric and
Adolescent Gyaecology (HSPAG)
Director: C. Kreatsas
9 Kanarie str.
Athens, Greece

India

Sex Education, Counseling,
Research Training Centre (SECRT)
Family Planning Association
of India (FPAI)
Fifth Floor, Cecil Court, Mahakavi
Bhushan Marg,
Bombay 400 039, India
Telephone: 91-22/287-4689

Indian Association of Sex Educators,
Counselors and Therapists (IASECT)
203 Sukhsagar, N.S.Patkar Marg.
Bombay 400007, India
Telephone: 91-22/361-2027
Fax: 9 I -22/204-8488

Parivar Seva Sanstha
28 Defence Colony Market
New Delhi 110-024, India
Telephone: 91-1/461-7712
Fax: 91-1/462-0785

National Institute for Research in Sex
Education, Counseling and Therapy
(NIRSECT)
Saiprasad- C5/11/02, Sector-4, C.B.D.
New Bombay, 4990615, India

Indonesia

The Study Group on Human
Reproduction
Udayana University Medical School
Jl.Panglima Sudirman
Denpasar, Bali, Indonesia

The Indonesian Society of Andrology
c/o Laboratory of Pathology
Udayana University Medical School
Jl.Panglima Sudirman
Denpasar, Bali, Indonesia

Ireland

Ireland Region of the British
Association of Sexual and
Marital Therapists
67 Pembroke Road
Dublin 4, Ireland

Israel

Institute for Sex Therapy
Sheba Medical Center
Tel Hashomer, Israel
Telephone: 972-3/530-3749
Fax: 972-3/535-2888

Israel Family Planning Association
9, Rambam Street
Tel-Aviv, 65601 Israel
Telephone: 972-3/510-1511
Fax: 972-3/510-2589

Ministry of Education and Culture
Psychological and Counseling Services
2 Devorah Hanevia Street
Jerusalem, Israel
Telephone: 972-02/293-249
Fax: 972-02/293-256

Japan

Japanese Association for Sex
Education (JASE)
Miyata Bldg, 1-3 Kanada Jinbo-cho
Chiyoda-Ku, Tokyo 101 Japan
Telephone: 81-3/3291-7726
Fax: 81-3/3291-6238

Japanese Association of Sex Educators
Counselors and Therapists (JASECT)
JASE Clinic, 3F Shin-Aoyama Bldg (West)
1-1 Minarni-Aoyama
l-chome Minato-ku
Tokyo 107 Japan

Nikon Information Center for
Sexology (NICS)
N.I.C.S., Hobunkan Building, 6F
3-11-4. Kanda-Jinbo-cho. Chiyoda-Ku
Tokyo 101 Japan
Telephone: 81-3/3288-5900
Fax: 81-3/3288-5387

Japan Family Planning
Association, Inc. (JFPA)
Hokenkaikan Bekkann, 1-2
Ichigaya Sadohara-cho
Shinjuku-ku
Tokyo 162 Japan
Telephone: 81-3/3269-4041
Fax: 81-3/3267-2658

Japan Federation of Sexology (JFS)
c/o Nikon Information Center
for Sexology (NICS)
Hobunkan Building, 6F
3-11-4. Kanda-Jinbo-cho
Chiyoda-Ku
Tokyo 101 Japan
Telephone: 81-3/3288-5200
Fax: 81-3/3288-5387

Japan Society of Adolescentology (JSA)
c/o Japan Family Planning Association
Hokenkaikan Bekkann
1-2. Ichigaya Sadohara-cho
Shinjuku-ku
Tokyo 162 Japan
Telephone: 81-3/3269-4738

The Japanese Society for Impotence
Research (JSIR)
c/o First Department of Urology
Toho University School of Medicine
6-11-1. Omori-nishi, Ota-ku
Tokyo 143 Japan
Telephone: 81-3/3762-4151,
extension 3605 or 3600
Fax: 81-3/3768-8817

Japanese Society of Sexual Science
(JSSS)
c/o Hase Clinic
Shin-Aoyama Building. Nishikan
3F, 1-1-1, Minami-Aoyama Minota-ku
Tokyo 107 Japan
Telephone: 81-3/3475-1789
Fax: 81-3/3475-1789

Japan Institute for Research in
Education
4-3-6-702 Kozimachi Chiyodaku
Tokyo 7102 Japan
Telephone: 81-3/5295-0856
Fax: 81-3/5295-0856

Japanese Organization for International
Cooperation in Family Planning, Inc.
(JOICFP)
1-1, Ichigaya Sadohara-cho
Shinjuku-ku
Tokyo 162 Japan
Telephone: 81-3/3268-5875
Fax: 81-3/3235-7090

Kenya

Center for African Studies
P. O. Box 60054
Nairobi, Kenya
Telephone: 254-2/448618-20

International Planned Parenthood
Federation (IPPF) Africa Region
P. O. Box 30234
Nairobi, Kenya
Telephone: 254-2/720280
Fax: 254-2/726596

Family Planning Private
Sector Programme
Fifth Floor, Longonot Place
Kijabe Street
P. O. Box 46042
Nairobi, Kenya
Telephone: 254-2/224646
Fax: 254-2/230392

Mexico

Asociacion Mexicana de
Educacion Sexual A.C.
Michoacan 77
Mexico DF 11 Mexico

Asociacion Mexicana para la
Salud Sexual
Tezoquipa 26
Col. La Joya, Deleg Tlalpan
Mexico DF 14000 Mexico
Telephone: 52-5/573-3460
Fax: 52-5/513-1065

MEXFAM
Calle Juarez #208
Tlapan
Mexico 14000 DF Mexico

Asociacion Mexiccana de
Sexologia A.C. (AMSAC)
Apartado Postal 21-205
Mexico DF 21 Mexico

The Netherlands

Dutch Centre for Healm Promotion
and Health Education
P. O. Box 5104
3502 JC Utrecht
The Netherlands
Telephone: 31-70/35-56847
Fax: 31-70/35-59901

Netherlands Institute of Social
Sexological Research (NISSO)
P. O. Box 5018
3502 JA Utrecht
The Netherlands

Rutgers Stitching
Postbus 17430
Groot Hertoginnelaan 201
2502 CKs Gravenhage
The Netherlands
Telephone: 31-70/363-1750
Fax: 31-70/356-1049

A. de Graaf Foundation
Westermarkt 4
1016 DK Amsterdam
The Netherlands

Interfacultaire Werkgroep Homostudies
(Department of Gay and Lesbian Studies)
Utrecht University
Heidelberglaan 1
3584 CS Utrecht
The Netherlands

Jhr A. Schorer Foundation
Nieuwendijk 17
1017 LZ Amsterdam, The Netherlands

NVIO (Dutch Society for
Impotence Research)
Department of Psychology
University of Amsterdam
Weesperplein 8
1018 XA Amsterdam
The Netherlands

NVVS (Dutch Society for Sexology)
Zijdeweg 17
2811 PC Reeuwijk
The Netherlands

Rutgers Foundation
Groothertoginnelaan 201
2517 ES Den Haag
The Netherlands

Stimezo (National organization
for induced abortion)
Pieterstraat 11
3512 JT, Utrecht
The Netherlands

Dutch Centre for Health Promotion &
Health Education
P. O. Box 5104
3502 JC Utrecht
The Netherlands
Telephone: 31-70/35-56847
Fax: 31-70/35-59901

Netherlands Institute of Social
Sexological Research (NISSO)
P. O. Box 5018
3502 JA Utrecht
The Netherlands

Poland

The Polish Medical Association
Medical Center of Postgraduate
Education
Department of Sexology and
Pathology of Human Relations
Director: Kazimierz Imielinski, M.D.,
Ph.D.
ul. Fieldorfa 40
004-158 Warsaw
Poland

Medical School of N. Copernicus
Department of Sexology
Director: Julian Godlewski, M.D., Ph.D.
ul. Sarego 16
31-047 Kracow
Poland

The Academy of Physical Education
Sexual Division of Rehabilitation
Faculty
Director: Zbigniew Lew-Starowicz, M.D.,
Ph.D.
ul. Marymoncka 34
01-813 Warsaw
Poland

Polish Sexological Society
Sex Research Department
Director: Anna Sierzpowska-Ketner,
M.D., Ph.D.
ul. Marymoncka 34
01-813 Warsaw, Poland
(*Correspondence:*
ul. Londynska 12m 31
03-921 Warsaw
Poland)

Puerto Rico

Instituto Puertorriqueno de
Salud Sexual Integral
Center Building, Oficina 406
Avenida de Diego 312, Santurce
Puerto Rico 00909 USA
Telephone: 809/721-3578

Russia

An Effective Shield of Protection
(AESOP)
P. O. Box 27
Moscow 121552 Russia
Telephone and Fax: 7-095/141-8315

Center for Formation of
Sexual Culture
ul. Pionerskaya, 19
Mediko-Pedagogicheskaya Shkola
Yoroslavl 150044 Russia
Telephone: 7-085/255-6691
Fax: 7-085/225-5894

Russian Family Planning Association
18/20 Vadkovsky Per.
101479 Moscow Russia
Telephone: 7-095/973-1559
Fax: 7-095/973-1917

Russian Sexological Association
Krylatskiye Kholmy, 30-2
207, Moscow, Russia
Telephone: 7-095/288-4010
Fax: 7-095/919-2525

South Africa

Planned Parenthood Association of
South Africa
Third Floor, Marlborough House
60 Eloff Street
Johannesburg, 2001
South Africa
Telephone: 27-11/331-2695

Spain

Federacion Espanola de
Sociedades de Sexologia
c/ Valencians, 6-Principal
Valencia, 46002 Spain
Telephone: 34-96/332-1372

Societat Catalan de Sexologia
Tren de Baix, 51 2o, 2o
08223 Teraessa
Barcelona Spain
Telephone: 34-3/788-0277

Sociedad Sexologica de Madrid
C/Barbieri, 3.3 dcha
Madrid 28004 Spain
Telephone: 34-1/522-25-10
Fax: 34-1/532-96-19

Sweden

Swedish Association for Sex Education
(RFSU)
Drottningholmsvagen 37
P. O. Box 12128
S-102 24 Stockholm
Sweden
Telephone: 46-8/692-0797
Fax: 46-8/653-0823

Swedish Association for Sexology
Bygglovsgr 10
Lund, 222 47
Sweden
Telephone: 46-46/17-4120
Fax: 46-46/17-4833

Swedish Institute for Sexual Research
Lastmakargatan 14-16 S 111
Stockholm,44, Sweden
Telephone: 46-8/488-3511

Swedish Sexological Association
c/o Lars-Gösta Dahlström
Gothenburg University
Department of Psychology
P. O. Box 14158
S-400 20 Gothenburg
Sweden

Riksförbundet för Sexuell Upplysning
(RFSU)
Rosenlundsgatan 13
S-104 62 Stockholm, Sweden
(*Or:* P. O. Box 17006
S-104 62 Stockholm, Sweden)

Riksförbundet för Sexuelit
Likaberäattigande (RFSL)
Stockholms Gay-hus. Sveavägen 57
S-104 30 Stockholm, Sweden
(*Or:* P. O. Box 350
S-101 24 Stockholm, Sweden)

Thailand

Sexology Society of Thailand
Institute of Health Research
Chulalongkorn University
Bangkok. Thailand

United Nations Family Planning
Association (UNFPA)
East and Southeast Asia Region Office
Population Education Clearing House
United Nations Building
Rajdammnern Avenue
Bangkok 10200 Thailand
Telephone: 66-2/391-0577
Fax: 66-2/391-0866

Ukraine

Ukrainian Society of Sexologists
9 a In. Kotsubinskiy vul.
Kyiv 252053, Ukraine
Telephone: 380-44/216-5054
Fax: 380-44/244-6862

The Institute of Reproductive Medicine
Professor Phedir Dachno, director
2b Herojiv Kosmosu vul.
Kyiv 252148, Ukraine
Telephone: 380-44/478-3068
Fax: 380-44/478-3068

European-Asian Association
of Sexologists (EAAS)
P. O. Box 274
Kiev, 252034, Ukraine
Telephone: 380-44/446-1346
Fax: 380-44/228-0103

United Kingdom

Association of Sexual and
Marital Therapists
82 Harley Street
GB-London WIN 1AE
United Kingdom

Family Planning Association (FPA)
27/35 Mortimer Street
London Wl N 7RJ
United Kingdom
Telephone: 44-171/636-7866
Fax: 44-171/436-3288

Sex Education Forum
National Childrens Bureau
8 Wakely Street
London EC1V 7QE
United Kingdom
Telephone: 44-171/843-6000
Fax: 44-171/278-9512

International Planned Parenthood
Federation (IPPF)
Regents College, Inner Circle
Regents Park
London NW1 4NS
United Kingdom
Telephone: 171/486-0741
Fax: 171/487-7950

United Sates of America

The Society for the Scientific
Study of Sexuality (SSSS)
P. O. Box 208
Mt. Vernon, Iowa 52314 USA
Telephone: 319/895-8407
Fax: 319/895-6203

The American Association of
Sex Educators, Counselors, and
Therapists (ASSECT)
P. O. Box 208
Mt. Vernon, Iowa 52314 USA
Telephone: 319/895-8407
Fax: 319/895-6203

The Sexuality Information and
Education Council of the
United States (SIECUS)
130 West 42nd Street. Suite 350
New York, New York 10036 USA
Telephone: 212/819-9770
Fax: 212/819-9776
E-mail: siecus@siecus.org

The Society for Sex Therapy
and Research (SSTAR)
c/o Candyce Risen
The Center for Sexual Health
2320 Chagrin Blvd.
3 Commerce Park
Beachwood, Ohio 44122 USA

International Gay and Lesbian
Human Rights Commission
1360 Mission Street, Suite 200
San Francisco, CA 94103 USA
Telephone: 415/255-8680
Fax: 415/255-8662

United Nations Population
Fund FUND (UNFPA)
Education, Communication and
Youth Branch
220 Eeast 42nd Street
New York, New York 10017 USA
Telephone: 212/297-5236
Fax: 212/297-4915

World Association of Sexology (WAS)
Eli Coleman, Secretary General
University of Minnesota Medical School
Program in Human Sexuality
1300 South Second Street, Suite 180
Minneapolis, Minnesota 55454 USA
Telephone: 612/625-1500
Fax: 612/626-8311

Margaret Sanger Center International
Margaret Sanger Square
26 Bleeker Street
New York, New York 10012 USA
Telephone: 212/274-7272
Fax: 212/274-7299

Advocates for Youth
International Center on
Adolescent Fertility
1025 Vermont Avenue N.W.
Washington DC 20005 USA
Telephone: 202/347-5700
Fax: 202/347-2263

YWCA of the USA
624 9th Street N.W. 3rd Floor
Washington, DC 20001 USA
Telephone: 202/628-3636
Fax: 202/783-7123

Office of Minority Health
Resource Center
P. O. Box 37337
Washington, DC 20013-7337 USA
Telephone: 800/444-6472
Fax: 301/589-0884

Instituto Puertorriqueno de
Salud Sexual Integral
Center Building, Oficina 406
Avenida de Diego 312, Santurce
Puerto Rico 00909 USA
Telephone: 809/721-3578

BEBASHI
(Blacks Educating Blacks About
Sexual Health Issues)
1233 Locust Street Suite 401
Philadelphia, PA 19107 USA
Telephone: 215/546-4140
Fax: 215/546-6107

National Asian Women's
Health Organization
250 Montgomery Street, Suite 410
San Francisco, CA 94104 USA
Telephone: 415/989-9747
Fax: 415/989-9758

National Youth Advocacy Coalition—
Bridges Project
1711 ConnecticutAvenue N.W., Suite 206
Washington, DC 20009 USA
Fax: 202/319-7365

National Latina/o Lesbian and
Gay Organization
1612 K Street N.W. Suite 500
Washington, DC 20036 USA
Telephone: 202/466-8240
Fax: 202/466-8530

National Coalition of Hispanic Health
and Human Services Organizations
(COSSMHO)
1030 15th Street N.W Suite 1053
Washington, DC 20005 USA
Telephone: 202/387-5000
Fax: 202/797-4353

National Minority AIDS Council
1931 13th Street N.W.
Washington, DC 20009 USA
Telephone: 202/483-6622
Fax: 202/483-1135

Child Welfare League of America
440 First Street N.W. Suite 310
Washington,DC 20001 USA
Telephone: 202/638-2952
Fax: 202/638-4004

National Native American
AIDS Prevention Center
2100 Lake Shore Avenue Suite A
Oakland, California 94606 USA
Telephone: 510/444-2051
Fax: 510/444-1593

Planned Parenthood
Federation of America
810 Seventh Avenue
New York New York 10019 USA
Telephone: 212/541-7800
Fax: 212/247-6269

Feminists for Free Expression
(FFE)
2525 Times Square Station
New York, NY 10108-2525 USA
Telephone: 212/702-6292

Bay Area Surrogates Association
(BASA)
c/o Stephanie Wadell
P. O. Box 60971
Palo Alto, CA 94306 USA

International Professional
Surrogates Association (IPSA)
P. O. Box 4282
Torrance, CA 90510-4282 USA
Telephone: 213/469-4720
(answering machine)

A Comparison-Facilitating Index

T his "Comparison-Facilitating Index" is designed to help the reader quickly locate parallel discussions of specific topics in the thirty-two countries contained in the first three volumes of this *International Encyclopedia of Sexuality*. This Index enables the reader to compare an issue, such as the "sexuality education" or "contraception," in various countries within a region, or around the world. This index also provides a more conventional guide to issues and topics which are peculiar to certain cultures or countries. Sexual harassment, for instance, is a major issue in the Europe and North America, but hardly or not at all recognized in some South American, African, Eastern European, and Asian countries. Similarly, female circumcision, woman-woman, and levirate marriages are issues in a few countries, but not in others. Although this Index is a handy guide to all major issues, it is not comprehensive due to space limitations.

This Index can be used in conjunction with the outline of the main topics provided on the first page of all chapters with page references. A familiarity with the detailed content outline given in the section "Using This Encyclopedia," on pages 15 and 16 of Volume 1, will also help the reader pursue specific information, since all chapters are structured on this detailed outline.